A DIGEST

OF THE

REPORTED CASES

CONTAINED IN THE

MICHIGAN REPORTS.

EMBRACING

HARRINGTON'S CHANCERY REPORTS, - -	1	VOL.
WALKER'S " " - -	1	"
DOUGLASS'S MICHIGAN " - -	2	"
MICHIGAN REPORTS, BY MANNING, - - -	1	"
" " " GIBBS, - - - -	3	"
" " " COOLEY, - - - -	8	"
" " " MEDDAUGH, - -	1	"

PUBLISHED BY THE COMPILER.

1866.

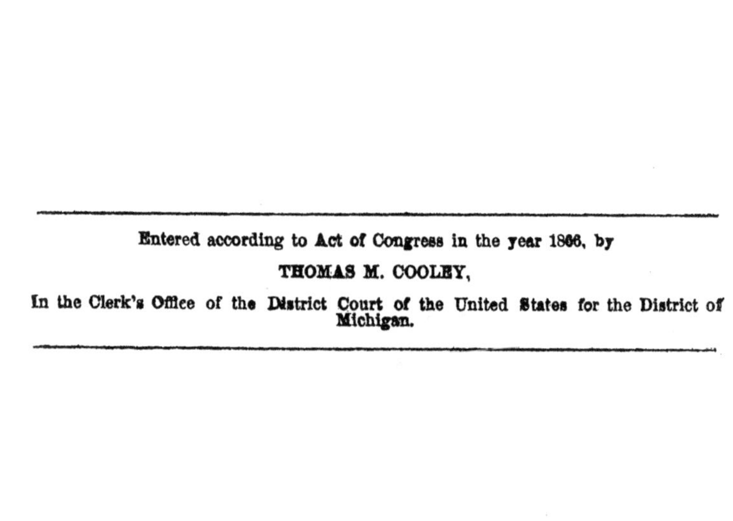

Dr. Chase's Steam Printing House, Ann Arbor, Mich.

PREFACE.

In preparing the following Digest, brevity and convenience of use have been kept in view, rather than perfection of arrangement as a mere work of art; and the object of the compiler will be fully attained if he has succeeded in placing before the Profession of the State a convenient Index to the books of Reports.

PLAN OF THE WORK.

In the arrangement of a Digest of Decisions, it is always found that many things can be properly classed under several heads; and no work of the kind is complete that does not enable the person consulting it to find at least a reference to them under any one of such heads. This is usually accomplished, either, *First*, by repetition; or, *Second*, by references under each head to the page or chapter where, under any other head, kindred matter is to be found. The *first* method would have made this work too voluminous and expensive to warrant its publication at the present time; and the second is usually found inconvenient and unsatisfactory. In the present publication *repetition* has generally been avoided; and instead of the references usually found at the conclusion of each subject, a very full TABLE OF CONTENTS is given, which, it is believed, will accomplish the purpose more completely, and prove a saving of time and labor.

For convenience of reference, the sections of the work are numbered consecutively from commencement to conclusion, and a complete table of cases is appended, which will enable the rulings in each to be traced in these pages.

THE REPORTS.

Seventeen volumes of Reports are embraced in this Digest; all of them official and authoritative, being prepared by Reporters appointed by the Courts under authority of law.

HARRINGTON'S CHANCERY REPORTS embraces the decisions of CHANCELLOR FARNSWORTH prior to 1842. The decisions for the most part are brief, and many of them, being based upon statutes now repealed, have ceased to be important. Others are still valuable, and are accepted and followed as authority.

WALKER'S CHANCERY REPORTS contains the decisions of CHANCELLOR MANNING from 1842 to 1845. The decisions are clear and concise, and were prepared for the press with a care and pains by the Reporter which have made the volume in many respects a model.

The foregoing are the only volumes of Chancery Reports ever published in the State. The Court of Chancery, as a distinct organization, ceased to exist in March, 1847, and the decisions of Chancellor Manning after March, 1845, and of Chancellor Farnsworth for the short period when he held the office in 1846–7, have never been collected or published.

DOUGLASS'S MICHIGAN REPORTS, in two volumes, embrace the decisions of the Supreme Court from January 1843 to January 1847. These reports, like Walker's, were prepared with great care and skill, and the Reporter's abstracts can always be relied on with confidence.

MANNING'S REPORTS, in one volume, includes the decisions from January, 1847, to October, 1850. The head notes are concise and reliable.

GIBBS'S REPORTS, three volumes, cover the period from January, 1851, to October, 1857.

COOLEY'S REPORTS, eight volumes, extend from January, 1858, to October, 1864.

MEDDAUGH'S REPORTS, one volume, follows Cooley's.

The series of "MICHIGAN REPORTS" begins with Manning, and now embraces thirteen volumes. The fourteenth is in press, and a number of cases to appear in it will be found digested here.

THE COURTS.

The Court of Chancery during the period covered by Harrington's and Walker's Reports, was held by a single Judge, whose decisions were subject to review by the Supreme Court, on appeal from his final decree or order. When that Court was abolished, its jurisdiction was transferred to the various Circuit Courts, and is now exercised by them by the same process and through the same forms which were in use in the former Court. No attempt, however, has been made to publish the decisions of the Circuit Judges, and they have not in any manner been preserved to the profession except incidentally as they have passed under review by the Supreme Court. As appeals can only be taken to that Court from final decrees or orders, many matters of Chancery practice are now finally disposed of in the various circuits, and it is quite probable that the practice in different parts of the State is not in all respects uniform.

The jurisdiction of the Supreme Court has always been almost exclusively appellate; but prior to January, 1858, the Judges of that Court were also Circuit Judges; meeting in banc to review the decisions made by themselves severally at the circuits. Now, the Justices of the Supreme Court, except in the few cases where they may sit as magistrates, exercise judicial functions only when sitting together in that Court. The State is divided into thirteen circuits, in each of which a Circuit Judge is elected by the people, and the Circuit Courts possess general jurisdiction of all cases, at law and in equity, civil and criminal, except where the statute has specially conferred jurisdiction upon Courts of Probate, Justices of the Peace, and municipal Courts in cities. Their decisions are reviewed by the Supreme Court as follows:

1. *Chancery Cases*, on the law and the facts, by appeal.

2. *Criminal Cases*, on the law, either on exceptions before sentence, or on writ of error after sentence,

3. *Civil Cases at Law*, on the law and the facts, or on either alone, upon case made; or on the law alone upon writ of error.

4. *Special Proceedings*, not after the course of the common law, in the Circuit Court, or in any inferior jurisdiction, are reviewed on common law certiorari.

5. *Probate Cases, and Cases before Justices of the Peace*, may be brought to the Supreme Court, in some one of the foregoing modes, after having been passed upon by the proper Circuit Court.

With these explanations—important only to practitioners outside our own State—the work is submitted to the consideration of a generous and indulgent profession.

TABLE OF SUBJECTS.

[The references are to the *Sections* of the work.]

DIGEST

OF THE

MICHIGAN REPORTS.

ACKNOWLEDGMENT OF DEEDS.

1. No part of the deed. The acknowledgment of an assignment of a mortgage is no part of the assignment itself. *Livingston v. Jones*, Har. Ch., 165. See *Dougherty & Randall*, 3 Mich., 581.

2. Clerical error in. The certificate of acknowledgment attached to a deed recited that the grantors came before the officer, and acknowledged that they had executed "the foregoing mortgage." Held to be evidently a clerical error, which did not vitiate. *Ives v. Kimball*, 1 Mich., 308.

3. By agents. Where the execution by one of the parties to an arbitration agreement under the statute was by agent, the certificate of the officer taking the acknowledgment of the agreement, that such party appeared before him by such agent, for that purpose duly appointed, and acknowledged the same, is sufficient evidence of the execution of the agreement, and of the authority of the agent, to authorize the arbitrators to act, and the Circuit Court to render judgment upon their award. *Mayor, &c., of Detroit v. Jackson*, 1 Doug., 106.

4. By married woman. The acknowledgment of the deed of a married woman is an essential part of the conveyance, without which it would be of no force. And to give the deed validity, the acknowledgment must be in compliance with the statute. *Dewey v. Campau*, 4 Mich., 565. [The deed in question was executed prior to the statute of 1855, *Comp. L.*, *p.* 966.]

5. The act of 1840 (*S. L.*, *p.* 167) provided that rights of dower should not be conveyed, unless by deed executed by the wife, and acknowledged by her "on a private examination, separate and apart from her husband, that she executed the deed without fear or compulsion *from any one.*" It was held that a certificate in accordance with the prior law, that the wife acknowledged the execution without any fear of compulsion *of her husband*, was insufficient to bar dower under this act. *Barstow v. Smith*, Wal. Ch., 394.

6. A certificate in accordance with this act, except that it did not state the acknowledgment to have been on a private examination, was held void. *Sibley v. Johnson*, 1 Mich., 380.

7. Where the statute required the certificate to show that the wife "acknowledged that she had executed the deed separately and apart from her husband," it was held that a certificate that she "*stated*" she had executed, &c., was insufficient. *Dewey v. Campau*, 4 Mich., 565.

8. The certificate is also void unless it show that the acknowledgment was taken "separately" as well as "apart" from the husband. *Ibid.*

9. Under the act of 1855, (*Comp. L.*, *p.* 966) a wife can make a mortgage of her own estate in the same manner and with the like effect as if unmarried. And an acknowledgment apart from the husband is not now requisite where a married woman conveys or incumbers her own estate. *Watson v. Thurber*, 11 Mich., 457.

10. A married woman gave a mortgage of her own lands to secure a debt of her husband. The testimony showed that it was given with reluctance, and after a good deal of persuasion by her husband, and at first she declined to acknowledge it; but the officer testified that she finally made an acknowledgment in the usual form, and she afterwards freely admitted its validity to one who had purchased it. On bill filed to foreclose it, she defended on the ground that it was obtained by undue influence or coercion. *Held*, that the defense was not made out by the evidence. *Ibid.*

11. Through interpreter. There being no statute authorizing the acknowledgment of a conveyance through a sworn interpreter, where the officer is unacquainted with the grantor's language, it cannot be thus taken. *Dewey v. Campau*, 4 Mich., 565.

12. Out of the State. Where a deed was acknowledged before a commissioner of deeds of this State, appointed for another State, and the certificate of acknowledgment has his signature and seal to it, it is sufficient, notwithstanding the certificate does not state that it was given under his hand and seal. *Harrington v. Fish*, 10 Mich., 415.

13. A deed was executed and acknowledged in another State, conveying land in this State. The certificate of the proper clerk was made and attached several years afterwards, certifying that the deed was executed and acknowledged according to the "existing" law of the State. Held a sufficient certificate to entitle the deed to record. *Ibid.* See also DEEDS.

14. Before interested officer. An officer cannot take the acknowledgment of a deed to himself. But as under the statute parol trusts in land are void, and there is no resulting trust in favor of one who furnishes the consideration money for a conveyance, it is not a valid objection to an acknowledgment that the officer who took it was the real purchaser, but had the deed made to another person for his use. *Groesbeck v. Seeley*, 13 Mich., 329.

ACTION.

1. ON THE CASE.

15. Against school officer. Where the moderator of a school district refused to sign a warrant to a rate bill for teacher's wages, and a judgment was afterwards recovered by the teacher against the district for the amount due him, which was paid by a tax on the district, it was held that a tax-payer who was assessed and had paid his part of the tax, could not maintain an action against the moderator to recover what he had paid. *Wall v. Eastman*, 1 Mich., 268.

16. Against witness. It is no answer to an action for damages, occasioned by defendant's non-attendance as a witness, in obedience to a subpœna, that the Court from which the subpœna issued refused, on motion, to impose a fine upon the defendant for contempt in disobeying the subpœna, but accepted his excuse. *Prentiss v. Webster*, 2 Doug., 5.

17. Inspectors of election act judicially in determining whether a person offering to vote has the requisite qualifications as to color or descent to entitle him to vote as a "white male citizen," under the constitution; and they are not liable to an action for improperly refusing a vote because the person offering it was partly of African descent. *Gordon v. Farrar*, 2 Doug., 411.

18. Flowing lands. See the question discussed whether, where one erects a dam on his own land, which causes the land of another to be flowed, and then conveys the land on which the dam is situated, a suit can be brought against his grantee for the nuisance before he has been served with notice of it, and requested to remove it. *Caldwell v. Gale*, 11 Mich., 77.

19. If such notice be necessary, and has once been given by the owner of the land flowed, it will enure for the benefit of his grantee, or of any one claiming title through or under him. *Ibid.*

20. Where the declaration alleged that the plaintiff was lawfully seized in fee and possessed of the land flowed, it was held that the whole averment was material, and must be proved as laid. Held also, that proof of plaintiff's possession under a claim of title, founded upon a deed not emanating from the source of title, or traced back to a person so claiming, did not raise a legal presumption of seizen in fee in the plaintiff; and, further, that if such possession was evidence of seizen, it was at most but a bare presumption, liable to be overcome by other proof, as of title in a third person. *Lull v. Davis*, 1 Mich., 77.

21. Suit for flowing land, the declaration alleging seizen and possession in plaintiff. On the trial, the only evidence of title was possession for about one year previous to bringing the action. It further appeared in evidence, that previous to and at the time plaintiff took possession a part of the tract was flowed by defendant. *Held*, that by reason of defendant's prior possession, by flowing, of that part of the tract covered by water, at the time plaintiff took possession, the latter could not sustain his action without showing title in himself to the land flowed, or that he entered and took possession of the tract by color of a paper title. *Millerd v. Reeves*, 1 Mich., 107.

22. Obstructing navigable waters. An action for obstructing a navigable stream, though local at the common law, is transitory by statute. *Comp. L.*, § 4344. *Barnard v. Hinckley*, 10 Mich., 458.

23. A county is not liable for the acts of its board of supervisors, in causing a bridge to be erected over navigable waters, through a defect in which an injury occurs to an individual using the stream. The board, in such a case, is acting in the exercise of its legislative power, and the same rule controls that would control in the case of a bridge erected by authority of the legislature. *Larkin v. Saginaw County*, 11 Mich., 88.

24. For waste the proper remedy under our statute is an action on the case. And the action may be maintained by a landlord against the assignee of the lessee. *Lee v. Payne*, 4 Mich., 106.

25. A purchaser of lands at a mortgage sale, after his title is perfected by failure of the mortgagor to redeem, may maintain an action on the case, for an injury done to the estate, maliciously, and with knowledge of his rights, by the cutting and carrying away growing timber, after the purchase and before the time for redemption expired. *Stout v. Keyes*, 2 Doug., 184.

26. Injury to bridge. A joint action cannot be brought by the overseers of two adjoining road districts, for an injury caused to a bridge which is partly in each district. *Highway Commissioners v. Stockman*, 5 Mich., 528.

27. Nor can the commissioners of highways of the township, on the refusal of the respective overseers to prosecute, sue under the statute, and recover in one action for the damages sustained by both districts. *Ibid.*

2. TROVER.

28. Trover may be brought by one having the possession of personal property, and a mere stranger cannot question his right. *Cullen v. O'Hara*, 4 Mich., 132.

29. In cases where property is wrongfully sold, the owner has his election, to bring replevin, or to recover its value in trover. *Eggleston v. Mundy*, 4 Mich., 295.

30. Conversion. If one tenant in common disposes of property to his own use, this is a conversion which makes him liable to the other. *Webb v. Mann*, 3 Mich., 139. See *Fiquet v. Allison*, 12 Mich., 328.

31. B., who was entitled to the possession of a certain chattel, replevied it of H. On the trial he was nonsuited, and H. took judgment for the value of the property, under the statute. B., still retaining the property he had so replevied, brought trover against H., and recovered the full value of the property, instead of damages for its temporary detention. H. paid the judgment, and, claiming the property by virtue of such payment, brought replevin for it against B. *Held*, that if H.'s taking judgment against B. in the original replevin suit, for the value of the property, amounted to a conversion, in paying the judgment in the trover suit, he had only paid for the property he had converted; and if, on the other hand, the Court erred in giving B. damages for the full value of the property, instead of damages for its temporary detention, such error could not transfer the title of the property to H.; and in neither case could he recover. *Hoag v. Breman*, 3 Mich., 160.

32. Right of property. In trover the right of property is in issue; and to sustain the action, the plaintiff must prove property in himself, either general or special. *Stephenson v. Little*, 10 Mich., 433.

33. Possession is evidence of property, but it does not preclude the defendant from showing property in a third person. And this may be done under the general issue. *Ibid.*

3. TRESPASS.

34. Whether trespass can be brought to recover the damages which one has sustained by the unlawful detention of his property, after he has recovered the property in replevin, *quere*. *Delevan v. Bates*, 1 Mich., 97.

35. Trespass is the proper action to be brought for an injury to plaintiff's cow, caused by defendant setting his dog upon her. *Wood v. LaRue*, 9 Mich., 158.

36. False imprisonment. If one is arrested on a void execution, and gives bond for the jail limits, the bond is void; and he cannot, in an action for the imprisonment, recover damages for remaining in the county, according to the terms of the bond. *Fuller v. Bowker*, 11 Mich., 204.

4. On Contract: General Rules.

37. A debt not due when an attachment is sued out, cannot be declared upon in the suit. *Galloway v. Holmes*, 1 Doug., 330. See also, *Hinchman v. Town*, 10 Mich., 508; *Hale v. Chandler*, 3 Mich., 531.

38. If goods were sold upon credit, the vendor cannot, before the credit has expired, maintain assumpsit therefor, even though he can prove that the vendee induced him to sell by fraudulent representations. If he affirms the sale, he must be bound by it in all respects. *Galloway v. Holmes*, 1 Doug., 330.

39. The parties to an action upon contract, must be those between whom the contract was made. *Litchfield v. Garratt*, 10 Mich., 426. See *Township of LaGrange v. Chapman*, 11 Mich., 499; *Gilbert v. Hanford*, 13 Mich., 40.

40. Suit for use of another. Where suit is brought upon a contract in the name of the promisee, for the use and benefit of another person named, the promisee is the legal plaintiff, and it is not necessary to show on the trial that the contract has been assigned to the person for whose use the suit is brought. *Farwell v. Dewey*, 12 Mich., 436.

41. Suit was brought in the name of parties to a written contract, for the benefit of assignees of such contract, and was sought to be supported by proof of labor done by the assignees in pursuance of an arrangement between them and the contracting party, modifying the terms of the contract, which arrangement was not shown to have been authorized or assented to by the assignors. Held that the action could not be maintained, as the modified contract was not between the parties to the record. *Litchfield v. Garratt*, 10 Mich., 426.

42. Survivorship. A debt due to two or more jointly, after the death of one must be sued in the name of the survivor. *Teller v. Wetherell*, 9 Mich., 464; *Cote v. Dequindre*, Wal. Ch., 64.

43. A joint and several demand cannot be treated as the joint obligation of less than all the debtors. *Winslow v. Herrick*, 9 Mich., 380.

44. Where, therefore, an action was brought on a replevin bond against all the obligors, two of whom were defaulted, and the plaintiff, instead of proceeding to trial as to the others, discontinued as to them, and took judgment against the two who were defaulted, the judgment was held erroneous. *Ibid.*

5. Assumpsit.

45. The general nature of this action considered. *Ward v. Warner*, 8 Mich., 508.

46. Waiving a tort. The owner of land on which a canal was dug, and who appeared to have incurred the major part of the expense of making it, gave notice to other individuals who had contributed to its repair, that they must compensate him for its use at a rate which he specified in his notice; and on their refusal, and continuing its use under a claim of right to do so, he brought action in assumpsit to recover compensation for the use. It was held,

That the law would not imply a promise to make compensation for the use of the canal before the notice was given, and while it was permitted by the plaintiff without objection, and without demand of compensation.

Nor would the law imply such a promise after the notice, since any implication of a promise was precluded by the denial by defendants of all right to compensation, and the assertion of an adverse right in themselves. The adverse entry, if the claim of right was unfounded, was a naked trespass, upon which no duty to compensate would arise which could be converted into a contract. *Ibid.*

47. A plaintiff may recover on a declaration for pasturing cows, on proof showing that his land was used by defendant for that purpose. If the use was without the plaintiff's assent, defendant was a trespasser, and plaintiff might either sue him in trespass, or waive the trespass and sue in assumpsit. (Manning, J.) *Welch v. Bagg*, 12 Mich., 41.

48. One tenant in common of crops harvested them, but the other drew them off, threshed them, placed them in his granary, and refused to recognize any rights of his co-tenant therein, or to deliver his share. Held, that this amounted to a conversion, but that the excluded tenant might waive the tort and sue in assumpsit. *Fiquet v. Allison*, 12 Mich., 328.

49. Quantum meruit. Where a party fails to comply substantially with an agreement, he cannot sue or recover upon the agreement at all, unless it is apportionable. But where any thing has been done under such agreement, from which the other party has received substantial benefit, and which he has appropriated, a recovery based upon that benefit may be had on a *quantum meruit.* The basis of that recovery is not the original contract, but a new implied agreement deducible from the delivery and acceptance of some valuable service or thing. *Allen v. McKibbin*, 5 Mich., 449.

50. Where action is brought on a quantum meruit for labor done under a special contract, which has not been substantially performed by the plaintiff on his part, the plaintiff can in no case recover more than the contract price; and cannot recover that if his work is not reasonably worth it, or if, by paying it, the rest of the work will cost the defendant more than if the whole had been completed under the contract. *Ibid.*

51. The party in default in such case can never gain by his default, and the other party can never be permitted to lose by it. *Ibid.*

52. Where in such case the Court excluded evidence offered by defendant to prove that the work was not worth the contract price, and charged the jury that if there had been a partial performance from which defendant had derived benefit, plaintiff was entitled to recover the contract price, deducting any damages which defendant had sustained by reason of non-performance, it was held that both the exclusion of evidence and the charge were erroneous. *Ibid.*

53. If in such case there are damages growing out of the non-performance of the special contract, which do not enter into the contract price, defendant may recoup them when sued upon a quantum meruit. *Ibid.*

54. Money had and received. An action will lie where defendant has in his possession money which in equity and good conscience belongs to the plaintiff; and it is not essential that there should be an express promise to pay, or any privity between the parties. *Beardslee v. Horton*, 3 Mich., 560.

55. If the facts are such as in a court of equity to entitle the plaintiff to a decree for the money, when that is the specific relief sought, the same state of facts will entitle him to recover at law in an action for money had and received. *Moore v. Mandlebaum*, 8 Mich., 433.

56. Accordingly where an agent to sell lands purchased them of his principal, concealing important facts, so that the transaction amounted to a fraud upon the principal, and afterwards sold the land at a higher price, it was held that the principal might recover from him in this action the difference between the price paid by the agent and the price at which the land was sold by him. *Ibid.*

57. And where an agent collected money for his principal, and the latter afterwards assigned it to the plaintiff, it was held that the plaintiff might recover it in this action after demand. *Beardslee v. Horton*, 3 Mich., 560.

58. Where plaintiffs, as agents, received a draft and forwarded it for collection, not disclosing the agency, and on its being paid at maturity, paid over the amount to defendant, and the draft proved to be a forgery, and plaintiffs were compelled to refund the amount to the drawee, it was held that they were entitled to recover from the defendant. *Little v. Derby*, 7 Mich., 325.

59. And it does not vary the case that plaintiffs, on receiving the draft, advanced to the holder a part of the amount, and gave him a certificate agreeing to account for the proceeds, and that defendant bought this certificate, having first called upon plaintiffs for information respecting the draft, and been informed that if he bought it the amount would be paid to him if collected, as it probably would be, and that plaintiffs would not have advanced money upon it, if they had not believed it was all right. *Ibid.*

60. The true ground of recovery in this and all other cases of money paid by mistake is, that the money has been paid without any consideration. *Ibid.*

61. Money collected. A justice of the peace who receives from a constable and applies upon a judgment before him depreciated bank bills, is liable to the judgment creditor for so much money in an action for money had and received. The creditor is not confined to his remedy upon the bond of the justice. *Welch v. Frost*, 1 Mich., 30.

62. And he is equally liable though the bills were current when received, and become depreciated in the hands of the justice, after he has tendered them to the creditor. *Heald v. Bennett*, 1 Doug., 513.

63. Where a note is made payable to one man in trust for another, and the payee receives the money upon it, he is liable to the party in interest for the amount, in an action for money had and received. And parol evidence is admissible to show the trust where it does not appear on the face of the note. *Catlin v. Birchard*, 13 Mich., 110. See supra, 57.

64. Subscriptions to corporate stock. Defendant having signed the articles and subscribed for a portion of the capital stock of an association formed under the plank road act of 1851, the 32d section of which provides that the directors may require payment of the sums subscribed to the capital stock, &c., it was held that such signing imported a promise to pay the amount subscribed. *Dexter and Mason Plank Road Co. v. Millerd*, 3 Mich. 91.

65. The notice which the directors give under said 32d section, that payments are required, must specify the *place* where the payment should be made. *Ibid.*

66. One who, by signing the articles of association, becomes a stockholder in a company organized under the act to authorize the formation of corporations for mining and manufacturing purposes, approved Feb. 5, 1853, and neglects to pay an assessment for the stock subscribed, for sixty days after the same is payable by the call, and due notice thereof, whereupon the stock is sold by the company in pursuance of said act, but an amount less than the assessment realized therefor, is liable to the company for the deficiency. *Carson v. Arctic Mining Co.*, 5 Mich., 288.

67. A railroad company was formed under the General Railroad Law, and commissioners appointed to open books for subscriptions to the capital stock. The commissioners, however, never opened any books, but a subscription paper was circulated by an agent appointed by the directors, on which defendant subscribed a sum which he subsequently on several occasions promised to pay. Held that the subscription was not binding. *Shurtz v. Schoolcraft and Three Rivers R. R. Co.*, 9 Mich., 269.

68. The commissioners act as a statutory board, and are alone authorized to receive subscriptions. They are not required to recognize or protect any subscriptions not under their own auspices, and such subscriptions cannot prevent other persons taking the entire amount of stock not subscribed by the articles of association, whenever the commissioners shall open books. There is, therefore, no consideration for any other subscriptions. *Ibid.*

69. For use and occupation an action will lie at the common law. *Dwight v. Cutler*, 3 Mich., 566.

70. Where the occupancy of premises by a tenant at will has been beneficial to him, that is a sufficient ground to imply a promise to pay a reasonable sum as a compensation for such occupancy, unless there is something in the circumstances inconsistent with the notion of such a promise, or of an obligation to pay. *Ibid.*

71. Defendant took possession of premises by permission, after having made an oral agreement to purchase the same, which the owner failed to carry into effect. It was held that defendant was not liable for use and occupation while the negotiations were pending. *Ibid.*

72. But held further, that if he remained in possession after all negotiation had ceased, and after being notified that he must pay rent if he did so, he would be liable. *Ibid.*

73. Action by manufacturer—order countermanded. Where an article was ordered of a manufacturer at a specified price, and work was done and materials used towards its construction, but before it was completed the order was countermanded, and the materials remained in the manufacturer's hands, it was held that the manufacturer could not recover on the common counts the value of such labor and materials, but should sue on the special contract for being prevented from performing it. *Hosmer v. Wilson*, 7 Mich., 294.

74. The manufacturer, in such case, is not compelled after the countermand to go on and complete the article ordered before he can recover for what he has done, but he may treat the countermand as a prevention of performance on his part, and sue upon the contract upon that ground. *Ibid.*

75. Account stated. It is not necessary, in support of an account stated, to show the nature of the original transaction or indebtedness, or to give the items constituting the account. It is sufficient to prove some existing antecedent debt or demand between the parties, respecting which a balance was struck. *Stevens v. Tuller*, 4 Mich., 387.

76. But where there is no acknowledgment of indebtedness, or promise to pay proven, such a count is not sustained. *Ibid.*

6. Joinder of Actions.

77. An action founded upon a statute cannot be joined with one common law. *People v. Judges of Washtenaw Circuit Court*, 1 Doug., 434.

ADMIRALTY COURTS AND JURISDICTION.

78. Process. In the absence of a treaty with Great Britain authorizing it, the process of the District Courts of the United States sitting in admiralty cannot be executed in Canadian waters. *Tyler v. People*, 8 Mich., 320.

79. Crime on high seas. Upon the high seas, every vessel, public or private, is, for jurisdictional purposes, a part of the territory of the nation where it belongs; and an offense committed on board of it is an offense committed against the sovereignty of that nation. *People v. Tyler*, 7 Mich., 161.

80. On foreign waters. But when a private ship enters a foreign jurisdiction, it becomes, with all on board, in the absence of treaty stipulations to the contrary, subject to the municipal laws and control of the country it visits. *Ibid.*

81. Crimes act of Congress of 1857. It does not necessarily follow, because this act provides for the punishment of offenses upon bays, creeks, havens and rivers, not within States nor forming a part of the high seas, that the existence of such within the admiralty jurisdiction must be assumed. *Ibid.*

82. Said act being amendatory and supplementary to prior acts of identical extent, it is not to be supposed that it was intended to use these terms in different senses at the different periods. And as there were, at the date of the first act, navigable waters open from the ocean, not admitted to have been within the exclusive jurisdiction of any particular State, and as upon the Pacific coast there are still some waters of this description, there is no necessity to go beyond our own territory to satisfy the terms of the act. The claim of jurisdiction should not be extended into foreign parts unless such an intention is clearly expressed in the act. *Ibid.*

83. The jurisdiction of the States lying upon the lakes and their connecting waters extends to the national boundary; and said Crimes Act, if it extends at all to these waters, can only take effect without the United States, and within British waters. But, as a general rule, the criminal laws of a nation cannot operate beyond its territorial limits; and the exceptions to this rule are never understood to be included in the general provisions of criminal statutes, but require to be specifically mentioned and defined. *Ibid.*

84. The treaty between the United States and Great Britain of 1842, which concedes to the vessels, &c., of both nations a right of passage through the lakes and their connecting waters divided and appropriated by the treaty, does not deprive either of that complete and exclusive jurisdiction over that part of the waters on its side the line which any nation may exercise upon land within its limits. *Ibid.*

85. Said Crimes Act was not understood or intended by Congress to extend to any waters not essentially maritime. Nor was it intended to go beyond the class of assaults made manslaughter under the former statutes to which it was amendatory and supplementary; or to do more than provide for the case of death on land resulting from assaults which were already made punishable when death resulted at the place where the fatal blow was given. *Ibid.*

86. And therefore manslaughter, committed by a mortal blow given on the River St. Clair, beyond the boundary line between the United States and Canada, and within a county of that Province, from which blow death ensued on land, is not within the intent and meaning of said act, though the blow was given on an American vessel. *Ibid.* (See the general subject of admiralty jurisdiction over the lakes and navigable waters connecting them considered, per CHRISTIANCY and MANNING, JJ.)

ADVERSE POSSESSION.

87. At common law where there is an adverse possession, the legal title cannot pass by a conveyance from a person out of possession. *Godfroy v. Disbrow*, Wal. Ch., 260.

88. But such conveyance is not invalid between the grantor and grantee; and though the latter cannot enforce his rights under it in his own name, he may do so in the name of his grantor; the latter being estopped from questioning the validity of his own deed. *Stockton v. Williams*, 1 Doug. 546.

89. A mortgage, where the land is possessed adversely to the mortgagor, is also void at the common law. *Hubbard v. Smith*, 2 Mich., 207.

90. But by statute it is now provided that "No grant or conveyance of lands, or of any interest therein, shall be void for the reason that at the time of the execution thereof such lands shall be in the actual possession of another claiming adversely." *Comp. L.* § 2726.

AFFIDAVIT.

91. Is a nullity if sworn to before a person not authorized to administer oaths. *Greenvault v. Farmers and Mechanics' Bank*, 2 Doug., 498.

92. Under the Revised Statutes of 1838, the clerks of the Circuit Courts had no power to administer oaths in vacation. *Ibid.* But the power is now conferred upon them. *Comp. L.*, § 4337. And since 1850 is possessed by their deputies. *Comp.*, § 404; *Dorr v. Clark*, 7 Mich., 310.

93. Not correctly entitled in a cause, cannot be used therein. As where in error it was entitled in the name of two as plaintiffs in error, after one of them, on motion, had been allowed to proceed severally. *Whipple v. Williams*, 1 Mich., 115. Where there are several parties it should be entitled in the names of all. *Arnold v. Nye*, 11 Mich., 456.

94. The jurat must show that the affidavit was sworn to before the officer signing it. Where it stated that it was "sworn and subscribed," without adding "before me," it was held to be a nullity. *Smart v. Howe*, 3 Mich., 590.

95. But when a complaint showed, in the body of it, that it was sworn to before the proper officer, the words "before me" in the jurat were held unnecessary. *Cross v. People*, 10 Mich., 24.

AGENT OF STATE PRISON.

96. The Statute of 1842 (*S. L.*, *p.* 130) required the agent of the state prison to give notice in a newspaper for sealed proposals for letting the convicts. The agent, without giving such notice, hired convicts to defendant for a term of years. The contract was held to be void; the mode of letting prescribed by the statute being a limitation on the power itself, and not merely directory to the agent of the prison. *Agent of the State Prison v. Lathrop*, 1 Mich., 438.

ALIMONY.

97. A Court of Chancery has no jurisdiction of a bill filed for alimony alone. *Peltier v. Peltier*, Har. Ch., 19. (For alimony in divorce cases, see DIVORCE.)

AMENDMENTS.

98. Of judgment. Ejectment. Plaintiff claimed the premises under an execution sale. To prove a judgment on which execution was issued, plaintiff gave in evidence the following journal entry, entitled in the cause: "On hearing counsel in this cause, ordered, on motion of plaintiffs' attorney, judgment for plaintiffs on demurrer, and that it be referred to the clerk to compute the amount due on the bond mentioned in plaintiffs' declaration; and the clerk having computed the amount due by the condition of said bond at $800, the penalty thereof, to be discharged on the payment of $624.11, with costs to be taxed." He also offered in evidence the execution issued for the $800 debt, with indorsement directing the collection of $624.11 and costs; also the files in the case, showing a declaration on a money bond in the penalty of $800, plea thereto, demurrer to the plea, and joinder. Also writ of error brought by defendant in the same case, the return thereto, giving a transcript of what purported to be a formal judgment record, and the proceedings in the Supreme Court thereon, where the judgment was affirmed. The Circuit Court rejected this evidence. Held erroneous. *Emory v. Whitwell*, 6 Mich., 474.

99. See the general subject of amendments considered in this case; the conclusions being substantially the following:

That where the files and records in the case clearly show that the Court intended to render a certain judgment, to which the party was entitled, but the entry actually made was defective, the Court may amend the record to what it should have been at any time thereafter.

That notice of the application to amend the record is not necessary in such case, because the effect of the record is not changed by it, and no one's rights are affected.

But that no actual amendment need be made. The whole record should be read, when brought up collaterally, precisely as if the amendments due as a matter of right had been actually made.

And *it seems* that, as under our practice, no formal judgment record need be made up except when required by one of the parties, but the judgment is to be evidenced by the files and journal entries, the transcript sent up in this case in return to the writ of error, showing a formal judgment record, is evidence of the judgment of the Circuit Court. *Ibid.*

See further on this subject, under the various titles of COURTS AND PRACTICE.

APPEAL FROM CHANCERY.

100. The right of appeal is a statutory right; and where the party has failed to comply with the provisions of the statute within the time prescribed, the Court will not allow a re-entry of the decree in order to enable him to appeal. *Weed v. Lyon*, Wal. Ch., 77.

101. Restrictions. Whether there be any, and if so what, restrictions upon the right to appeal, where default was made in the Court below, *quere*. *Stevens v. Townsend*, 1 Doug., 77.

102. If there are, the Supreme Court will not dismiss an appeal, on motion of the appellees, on the ground that the appellant, having made default in the Court below, has no right of appeal, unless the decree recites all those facts which, by the rules and practice of the Court of Chancery, entitle a party to default his adversary. *Ibid.*

103. The decree of the Court of Chancery recited that the "cause having been heretofore brought on to be heard and decided, upon the agreement and stipulation of the said Townsend and the complainants, and the answer of said Townsend, and upon exhibits read by stipulation and consent, and the said bill having been taken as confessed against [the co-defendants of Townsend], and upon hearing of counsel for the complainants, and no person appearing to argue the said cause on the part of the defendants," &c. Held that it did not show such a default of Townsend, and abandonment of his cause in the Court below, as would deprive him of the right of appeal. *Ibid.*

104. Hearing. The statute (R. S. of 1838, p. 380, § 127) was not *mandatory*, but merely *authorized* the Chancellor to sit with the Justices of the Supreme Court, and inform them of the reasons of his decree or order, on the hearing of an appeal therefrom to the Supreme Court. *Ibid.* (For a similar provision—never acted upon—see Comp. L., §3602.)

105. What is a final decree or order. An order in a foreclosure suit confirming the report of the appraisal, set off and conveyance of the mortgaged premises, under the appraisal law of 1842, was held to be a *final order*, from which an appeal would lie to the Supreme Court. *Benedict v. Thompson*, 2 Doug., 299.

106. The decree directing such appraisal might also have been appealed from; it being a *final decree* within the statute. *Ibid.*

107. An order denying a writ of assistance to the purchaser in a foreclosure suit may be appealed from. *Baker v. Pierson*, 5 Mich., 456.

108. An order striking a bill from the files is also a *final order* from which an appeal lies. *Webster v. Hitchcock*, 11 Mich., 56.

109. A decree granting a divorce from the bonds of matrimony may be appealed from, notwithstanding by the same decree a reference is ordered on the question of temporary alimony. *Shaw v. Shaw*, 9 Mich., 164.

110. An appeal will lie from an order setting aside a sale in a foreclosure suit after confirmation of the report of sale; it being *final* as to the purchaser. *Bullard v. Green*, 9 Mich., 222.

111. It will lie also from an order adjudging a party guilty of a contempt in violating an injunction, and awarding a sum of money to the opposite party to indemnify him for the violation. *People v. Simonson*, 9 Mich., 492.

112. An order refusing to set aside a decree for irregularity is a final order, and may be appealed from. *Michigan Insurance Co. v. Whittemore*, 12 Mich., 311.

113. What is not a final decree or order. An order setting aside a final decree, taken *pro confesso* in a foreclosure suit, and permitting a defendant to defend, unless the complainant should elect to assign to him the decree for a sum named in the order, is not a *decree*, or *final order*, which can be appealed from. *Prentis v. Rice*, 2 Doug., 296.

114. An order denying a motion for the dissolution of a preliminary injunction, heard on answer to a part and demurrer to the residue of the bill, before the time for filing replication had expired, is interlocutory merely, and cannot be appealed from. *Wing v. Warner*, 2 Doug., 288.

115. An order denying a motion to stay a sale under a decree of foreclosure, and vacating a temporary order staying the sale until the motion could be heard and disposed of, cannot be appealed from. *Romeyn v. Hale*, 1 Mich., 93.

116. Nor can a decree be appealed from which directs a reference to a master or other officer to do what the Court, but for its power to make such reference, would itself have to do before it could decide the case. *Caswell v. Comstock*, 6 Mich., 391.

117. Nor a decree which consists in part of a reference to a commissioner to take an account between the parties. *Enos v. Sutherland*, 9 Mich., 148.

118. Nor a decretral order allowing a general demurrer to a bill in Chancery, but not in terms dismissing the bill or awarding costs. *Blackwood v. Van Vleet*, 10 Mich., 398.

119. Nor an order overruling a demurrer. *Bennett v. Nichols*, 12 Mich., 22.

120. Nor an order opening for review a decree for permanent alimony in a divorce case, and ordering a reference to a circuit court commissioner to take proofs, &c., and to report thereon. *Perkins v. Perkins*, 10 Mich., 425.

121. A written claim of appeal is not necessary to be filed. *Warner v. Whittaker*, 5 Mich., 241.

122. Appeal bond. The officer who fixes the penalty of the appeal bond, does not acquire exclusive jurisdiction to approve the sureties; but they may be approved by any officer empowered by law to act in the premises. *Emerson v. Atwater*, 5 Mich., 34.

123. It is no objection that the bond is approved and filed before the claim of appeal. *Ibid.*

124. It is not necessary that the bond should be executed by all the appellants. It is sufficient if it appear to be executed on behalf of all. *Warner v. Whittaker*, 5 Mich., 241.

125. An indorsement upon the bond, signed by the proper officer, in the following words: "I approve of this bond, both in form and substance;" will be held an approval both of the sureties and of the penal sum; and is sufficient. *Maynard v. Hoskins*, 8 Mich., 260.

126. Where a party against whom costs are awarded in Chancery, appeals to the Supreme Court, the appeal bond covers those costs, as well as the costs of the Supreme Court, in case the decree appealed from is affirmed. *Daily v. Litchfield*, 11 Mich., 497.

127. The bond only obligates the appellant to the performance of the decree of the Supreme Court in those particulars in which he was individually bound in the decree appealed from. Accordingly, where, after decree for the complainant in a foreclosure suit, one of the defendants, not personally liable on the decree, appealed therefrom, and the decree was affirmed by the Supreme Court, it was held that the appellant was not liable for the amount of deficiency after sale had been made on the decree. *Kephart v. Farmers and Mechanics' Bank*, 4 Mich., 602.

128. The Supreme Court has no power to require the appellant to give a new or further appeal bond, in addition to the one approved by the circuit court commissioner, and which is alleged to be insufficient. *Moore v. Olin*, 6 Mich., 328.

129. The bond should have at least two sureties; but if defective in this or any other respect, the Supreme Court, if motion to dismiss is made for this cause, may allow a new bond to be filed. (Comp. L., §4543.) *Beebee v. Young*, 13 Mich., 221.

130. When appeal to be taken. Where the last of the forty days in which an appeal is allowed to be taken is Sunday, the appeal cannot be taken on the following Monday. *Drake v. Andrews*, 2 Mich., 203.

131. If taken within forty days from the time the decree is drawn up, and left with the register to be entered, it is in time, though more than forty days from the time when the judge announced orally what the decree would be. *Sellers v. Botsford*, 9 Mich., 490.

132. Motions to dismiss must be made at the earliest opportunity. *Warner v. Whittaker*, 5 Mich., 241.

133. On motion to dismiss for want of a sufficient bond, affidavits will not be received to enlarge or restrict the officer's certificate of approval. *Maynard v. Hoskins*, 8 Mich., 260.

134. The Court will not dismiss an appeal for a failure of the register to make a full return; but a further return will be ordered. *Maynard v. Hoskins*, 8 Mich., 81.

135. Nor will it dismiss for a failure of the register to cause return to be made within the time provided by the statute, if it is actually filed before the motion to dismiss is made. *Garratt v. Litchfield*, 10 Mich., 451.

136. Nor because the return has been made to the wrong clerk's office; the statute requiring return to be made to the nearest office being directory merely. *Beebee v. Young*, 13 Mich., 221.

137. Nor for a failure of the appellant to serve notice of the appeal on co-defendants, as required by Supreme Court rule 14, if the failure is sufficiently excused. *Garratt v. Litchfild*, 10 Mich., 451.

138. The appeal will not be dismissed on the ground that the order appealed from was a matter of discretion in the Court below. *Michigan Insurance Co. v. Whittemore*, 12 Mich., 311.

139. Amendment of record. The Supreme Court has no power to allow the appellant to supply, by a sworn copy, a paper discovered, after the appeal, to have been lost from the files of the Court below. But *it seems* that the Court below would have power, even after the appeal, to supply the paper, in order to give effect to the appeal. *Sears v. Schwarz*, 1 Doug., 504. On the subject of amending records after the cause is removed to a Court of review, see *O'Flynn v. Holmes*, 7 Mich., 454; *O'Flynn v. Eagle*, 8 Mich., 136.

140. The record returned on appeals should include full copies of all the proceedings in the case; so that the transcript shall present everything which appeared in the Court below. *Wright v. Dudley*, 8 Mich., 115.

141. What to be reviewed. Where appeal is taken from a final *decree* all previous orders connected with the decree, and affecting the merits, are open to review. *Benedict v. Thompson*, 2 Doug., 299. And see *Morris v. Morris*, 5 Mich., 171.

142. As where a demurrer was overruled, and the defendant then answered and the case was heard on pleadings and proofs, and decree entered for complainant, it was held that an appeal therefrom opened for review the decision on the demurrer. *Bennett v. Nichols*, 12 Mich., 22.

143. But where the appeal is from a final *order*, (as an order confirming an appraisal and set off under a decree in a mortgage case,) the Court is restricted to a review of so much of the proceedings as are connected with the final order. *Benedict v. Thompson*, 2 Doug., 299.

144. The Court is confined to an examination of the errors found in the transcript, and cannot assume, as a part of the case, facts not appearing by the transcript, though assumed by the counsel on the argument, and though, in virtue of a parol admission, they were treated as part of the case in the Court below. *Bailey v. DeGraff*, 2 Doug., 169.

145. On the hearing it was claimed that certain evidence returned as a part of the record should be excluded, on the allegation that it was not actually filed in the Court below, and was not considered by that Court in its decision. The evidence consisted of the proof of documents set out in the bill, and appeared to have been regularly taken on proper notice. There being no ground for supposing that the party objecting had been taken by surprise, and the transcript on appeal having been on file for two years, without motion to correct it, it was held that the evidence should not be disregarded. *Michigan Insurance Co. v. Brown*, 11 Mich., 265.

146. Error without injury. An appellant cannot ask a reversal of the decree for an error in no way affecting his rights. *Martin v. McReynolds*, 6 Mich., 70; *Warner v. Whittaker*, 6 Mich., 133; *Griggs v. Detroit and Milwaukee Railway Co.*, 10 Mich., 117; *Michigan Insurance Co. v. Whittemore*, 12 Mich., 427.

147. A decree made without notice of hearing to a defendant who has appeared in the cause, may be reversed for that reason. *Jenny v. O'Flynn*, 5 Mich., 215.

148. But it will not be reversed for a mere irregularity not affecting injuriously the interests of the appellants. The proper course for a party conceiving himself aggrieved by such irregularity is to apply to the Court of Chancery for relief upon showing that he has or will sustain injury therefrom; and if that application is denied, to appeal to the Supreme Court thereafter. *Kellogg v. Putnam*, 11 Mich., 344.

149. Defective pleadings. If the allegations in a bill do not entitle complainant to any relief, the bill, on appeal, should be dismissed for that cause, notwithstanding a plea to the bill, on which issue was taken, is found not to be true. *Hurlbut v. Britain*, 2 Doug., 191. But if the pleadings are good in substance, all matters of mere form are to be disregarded on the appeal. *Dye v. Mann*, 10 Mich., 291.

150. Jurisdictional defects. A decree may be reversed on appeal for jurisdictional defects, notwithstanding they are not pointed out on the argument. *Smith v. Smith*, 13 Mich., 258.

151. Errors affecting infants. Where errors were committed affecting injuriously the rights of infants, the decree should be reversed, even though no objection be taken for such errors. *Ibid.*

152. As where an order was made against infants based on their admissions, and costs awarded against them improperly. *Ibid.*

153. Appeal where witnesses were examined in open court. Where an appeal is taken in such a case, the proper course for the party desiring the testimony to be certified to the Supreme Court, under the statute, is to make a case setting it forth, present it to the Circuit Judge, and procure his order, fixing the time and place when and where it shall be settled, and for notice to the opposite party that he may attend and propose amendments; or instead thereof, take other equivalent proceedings. *Wright v. Dudley*, 8 Mich., 74.

154. Where no proceedings are taken for the settling of such a case, but the party appellant, without notice to the opposite party, procures and files with the appeal papers a certified copy of the Judge's minutes of the evidence taken on the trial, such copy cannot be treated as a case made under the statute, or considered in the Supreme Court on the hearing. *Ibid.*

155. Either of the parties has the right to procure such a case to be settled; and if the appeal is regularly taken, and neither party take steps to have a case made and settled, the cause will stand for hearing without the testimony, and it will then devolve upon the appellant to show that the decree is not warranted by the pleadings; the presumption being that there was evidence below to authorize it. *Ibid.*

156. The statute allowing three months after trial for the making of such a case, will be construed to allow three months from the time the decree is made. *Ibid.*

APPEAL FROM JUSTICES' COURTS.

157. A Judgment of nonsuit, for failure to appear, could not be appealed from under the statute of 1841, (*S. L., p.* 107, § 94) which authorized an appeal from any *final* judgment. *Bowne v. Johnson*, 1 Doug., 185.

158. A judgment for costs, of less than $4, against the plaintiff, might be appealed under the statute of 1845, (*S. L., p.* 98.) *Wilson v. Davis*, 1 Mich., 156.

159. A party who has stayed execution on a judgment against him, cannot afterwards appeal. *People v. Judges of Macomb Circuit Court*, 1 Mich., 134.

160. Garnishee cases being made appealable by the statute, the Circuit Court has jurisdiction to hear and determine the appeal. *Newell v. Blair*, 7 Mich., 103.

161. After a transcript of the judgment has been legally filed in the Circuit Court under the statute, it is not in the power of that Court to allow an appeal to be taken, under § 3842 of Comp. Laws. *Davison v. Elliott*, 9 Mich., 252.

162. The affidavit for appeal, being required by the statute on the ground of public policy, cannot be waived or dispensed with by the appellee. *Smart v. Howe*, 3 Mich., 590.

163. Where a plaintiff appealed, under the statute of 1845, (*S. L., p.* 98) from a judgment of costs against him, no affidavit was necessary. *Wilson v. Davis*, 1 Mich., 156.

164. Where defendant appealed, under said statute, and the affidavit was made by his attorney, and stated that the plaintiff recovered five dollars more than was justly and honestly due him, as the deponent believed from the facts and evidence in the cause, which were fully communicated to him, it was held sufficient. *Austin v. Strong*, 1 Mich., 259.

165. Where a cause has been tried in Justices' Court on an issue of fact, and an appeal is taken on an affidavit which is general, and relates only to the judgment on the merits, such appeal brings up only this issue of fact for trial; and the appellate court can take no note of errors in the process, or erroneous decisions of the justice, in proceedings preliminary to such issue. If the appellant desire the Circuit Court to review the decisions of the justice, on his objections to process, pleadings or proceedings anterior to the trial, he must set forth such objections specifically in his affidavit for appeal. *Chappee v. Thomas*, 5 Mich., 53.

166. Recognizance. Under the statute of 1845, which provided that "if any party shall appeal," "such party, his agent or attorney shall enter into a recognizance," it was held that the appeal might be taken, and the recognizance entered into by the party for whose use the suit was brought. *Wilson v. Davis*, 1 Mich., 156.

167. Under said statute the recognizance could only be entered into before the justice by whom the cause was tried. *Austin v. Strong*, 1 Mich., 259.

168. Objections to the jurisdiction over the person are not waived by taking an appeal. *Shaw v. Moser*, 3 Mich., 71.

169. But where one only of two defendants appealed from a judgment rendered against them by default, and afterwards both pleaded to the merits and went to trial in the appellate Court, it was held that the objection that the appeal was taken by one only, if otherwise valid, was thereby waived. *Ibid.* See also, *Tower v. Lamb*, 6 Mich., 362.

170. So where in an action for tort damages were claimed beyond the jurisdiction of the justice, and the defendant went to trial upon the merits, and after judgment against him, appealed to the Circuit Court, where trial was also had on the merits, and judgment given against him, it was held that he could not raise the jurisdictional question for the first time in the Supreme Court. *Wells v. Scott*, 4 Mich., 347; *Tower v. Lamb*, 6 Mich., 362.

171. The return to the appeal, in which the name of the justice only appears in the caption, is sufficiently signed; and the Court can as well take notice that the name there is written by the justice himself, as if it appeared at the end of the return. *Smart v. Howe*, 3 Mich., 590.

172. Facts coming to the knowledge of the justice after the trial, cannot properly constitute a part of his return, and must be rejected by the appellate Court. *Savier v. Chipman*, 1 Mich., 116.

173. Notice of trial, under the Revised Statutes of 1846, where the party to be served was not a resident of the county, and appeared in the Court below by agent or attorney, should be served on such agent or attorney. And where there was no agent or attorney in the case, notice must be sent to the party himself by mail, if his residence could be ascertained. *Chamberlain v. O'Keefe*, 2 Mich., 357.

174. Under the statutes in force in 1851, either party might notice an appeal for trial, and proceed to judgment in the same manner as in causes originally commenced in the Circuit Court. *Hoyt v. Mapes*, 3 Mich., 522.

175. Entrance fee. An appeal may be dismissed by the Circuit Court, on *ex parte* motion, for want of payment of the entrance fee; but the better practice is to make an order *nisi* in the first instance. *Chaffee v. Soldan*, 5 Mich., 242.

176. A surety for costs in the Court below is liable for the costs in the appellate Court. *Dunn v. Sutliffe*, 1 Mich., 24.

177. Judgment against surety. The statute—Comp. L., §3866—authorizing the Court on rendering judgment against the appellant, to render it against the surety also, is not unconstitutional. *Chappee v. Thomas*, 5 Mich., 53.

APPEAL IN PROBATE CASES.

178. The appeal bond, where one appeals from commissioners, under § 2936 of Compiled Laws, cannot be given by a stranger. *Appeal of Dickinson*, 2 Mich., 337.

179. Although the Judge of Probate, in allowing an appeal and passing upon the sufficiency of the sureties, acts judicially, yet until such bond is filed as the statute requires, no foundation is laid for the exercise of judicial discretion, and his acts are void. *Ibid.*

180. The bond on appeal remains filed with the Judge of Probate, but on an authenticated copy the Circuit Court may be moved to dismiss the appeal, and has authority to do so. *Ibid.*

181. Declaration in Circuit Court. Where, on appeal from the decision of commissioners disallowing a claim against the estate of a deceased person, declaration is filed in the Circuit Court on such claim, but containing, also, a count on an account stated with the administrators as such, such count may be treated as surplusage, and judgment against the claimant will not be reversed because the jury failed to pass upon the issue made on such count. *Fish v. Morse*, 8 Mich., 34.

182. Where commissioners have been appointed to examine and adjust claims against the estate of a deceased person, the estate is not bound by an account stated with the administrators. And therefore, in a suit against the estate, a count on such an account stated is bad. *Ibid.*

183. Judgment in the Circuit Court should not be rendered in the common law form, but the Court should simply allow or disallow the claim. *LaRoe v. Freeland*, 8 Mich., 531.

APPRAISAL LAW.

184. The provision of the act of 1841, (*S. L.* 1841, *p.* 45, §§ 1, 2,) prohibiting the sale of property on execution, unless it would bring two-thirds of its value, as appraised by three disinterested freeholders, so far as it applied to the remedy to enforce pre-existing contracts, was unconstitutional and void. *Willard v. Longstreet*, 2 Doug., 172.

185. But where an appraisal and sale of real estate was made under the provisions of this act, by virtue of an execution on a judgment upon contract rendered before the act took effect, and the plaintiff in the execution participated in the appraisal, and purchased the premises on the sale, at a sum exceeding two-thirds their appraised value: *Held*, that the plaintiff's rights not being affected by the appraisal, the sale was valid, and conveyed a good title. *Ibid.*

186. The "Act to provide for the transfer of real estate on execution, and for other purposes," approved February 17, 1842, (*S. L.* 1842, *p.* 135,) did not authorize an appraisal and set off of mortgaged premises in satisfaction of the mortgage, without previous proceedings to foreclose, either in equity or by advertisement. *Buck v. Sherman*, 2 Doug., 176.

ARBITRATION AND AWARD.

187. One partner cannot submit partnership matters to arbitration without a special authority for that purpose from his co-partners. *Buchoz v. Grandjean*, 1 Mich., 367.

188. A submission being thus entered into without special authority, and an award made in pursuance of it in favor of the partnership, it was held that the other party might defeat a suit on the award by objecting such want of authority. *Ibid.*

189. A submission of the subject matter of a suit to arbitration is a discontinuance of the suit. *Dunn v. Sutliffe*, 1 Mich., 24; *Vanderhoof v. Dean*, 1 Mich., 463. And it is a waiver of all irregularities in the suit prior to the submission. 1 Mich., 463.

190. A submission under the statutes of 1838, was not required to be under seal. *Mayor, &c., of Detroit v. Jackson*, 1 Doug., 106.

191. A submission bond with condition that judgment may be rendered on the award in a court of record, is valid as a common law bond, where it is evident from the conduct of the parties that they did not intend to make it a statutory arbitration, and they did not pursue the forms requisite for that purpose. *Clement v. Comstock*, 2 Mich., 359.

192. The award of arbitrators, under the statute, is an official act, and is itself the evidence and authority, upon which the court may render judgment. *Mayor of Detroit v. Jackson*, 1 Doug., 106.

193. A judgment, rendered upon an award, pursuant to the statute, (*R. S. of* 1838, 532,) will not be reversed on error, on the ground that it does not appear that an agent, who executed the agreement for submission on behalf of one of the parties, had authority to do so, where the award recites that such party was duly notified of the hearing before the arbitrators, and appeared, and was heard, with his witnesses and counsel, and where, being deemed in Court by the statute, (*R. S.* 532, §10,) he allowed the judgment to be entered on the award, without objection on the ground of such agent's want of authority; but the Court will infer from these facts a recognition and adoption, by the party, of the act of his agent, in executing the submission, even where such party is a corporation. *Ibid.*

194. A judgment rendered in favor of A. and B. against C., upon the award of arbitrators, on filing the same pursuant to the statute, (*R. S. of* 1838, 532, § 9,) will not be reversed on error, on the ground that B. had no claim against C.; he having joined with A. in executing the submission to arbitration of all matters arising out of a contract between A. and C., for the faithful performance of which contract by A., he was recited, in the submission, to be bound to A. by a separate instrument, and the award having been made in favor of both A. and B. *Ibid.*

195. Certainty in award. Where the award was that C. and H. should re-deliver to B. all the personal property which they had taken by virtue of two chattel mortgages, (describing said mortgages,) and also by a certain writ of replevin, (specifying it,); held, that as the presumption was, that the mortgages and replevin writ showed what the property was, the award in that respect was sufficiently certain. *Clement v. Comstock*, 2 Mich., 359.

196. An award directing the return of property, but not expressly determining the title to it, or directing releases to be executed, is sufficiently certain. *Ibid.*

197. An award in the alternative, (both alternatives being certain,) is not void for uncertainty. Where one of the alternatives is certain, and the other uncertain or impossible to be performed, the award has been held good, for the party could perform its requirements by performing that which was certain. *Ibid.*

198. Where a submission is general as to all controversies between the parties, the Court will intend, until the contrary appears, that the arbitrators decided all matters in difference. *Ibid.*

199. Delivery of award. An award is in time, although not made and ready for delivery until a late hour in the evening of the day limited for its completion. *Ibid.*

200. Arbitrators may retain the award in their hands until paid for their services. *Ibid.*

201. Excess of authority. Where the arbitrators, without the power being given in the submission, award as to costs, that does not vitiate the entire award, but renders it void for the excess. *Ibid.*

202. Costs. A clause in the submission bond, submitting all controversies between the parties, and "all matters relating thereto," would seem to import authority in the arbitrators to award concerning the costs of the arbitration. *Ibid.*

203. Arbitrators must all be present at the execution of the award. *Daniels v. Ripley*, 10 Mich., 237.

204. Where two of three arbitrators signed an award when the third was not present, and the third signed it afterwards when but one of the other two was present, it was held not a valid award. *Ibid.*

205. Mistake in award. Where arbitrators actually pass their judgment upon the subject matter submitted to them, strictly in accordance with the intention of the parties, but the award as written fails to express that judgment, the mistake will be held of a clerical nature; and a court of equity has the power to correct the same, and decree a specific performance. *Buys v. Eberhardt*, 3 Mich., 524.

206. It was submitted to arbitrators to determine the value of certain real estate of one of the parties, at which valuation the other party was at his option to purchase the same. The arbitrators, by omitting to take into consideration the value of a water power connected with the property, appraised it at much less than its actual value. For this mistake, the award was set aside. *Ibid.*

ARREST.

207. A constable did not acquire authority to execute writs directed to the sheriff, in consequence of being in attendance upon a session of the Circuit Court, in the discharge of his duties under R. S. 1838, p. 66, § 51. *People v. Moore*, 2 Doug., 1.

208. A sheriff having no power to constitute a deputy for a particular act, except by warrant in writing, the arrest on a bench warrant of a person indicted and under recognizance to appear, by one having only verbal authority from the sheriff, is illegal and does not discharge the recognizance. *Ibid.*

209. For felony, may be without warrant. *Drennan v. People*, 10 Mich., 169.

ASSIGNMENT.

1. In General.

210. As security—control of assignee. Where a contract is assigned for the sole purpose of enabling the assignees to collect and apply certain moneys coming due to the assignors thereon, and then to be re-assigned, the assignees are not authorized without the consent of the assignors to assume the performance of the contract, or to change its terms by agreement with the contracting party. *Litchfield v. Garratt*, 10 Mich., 426.

211. Check not an assignment. Where one *in extremis* drew his check upon a bank, with directions to the payee to defray the funeral expenses of the drawer from the amount, and pay the balance to his heirs, and the check was not accepted by the bank at the death of the drawer, it was held that it did not operate as an assignment of the fund so as to make the bank liable to the payee. *Second National Bank of Detroit v. Williams*, 13 Mich., 282.

For further decisions, see Action; Mortgages of Lands; Specific Performance.

2. For the Benefit of Creditors.

212. One partner cannot make a general assignment of the partnership effects to a trustee for the benefit of the creditors of the firm, without the knowledge or consent of his co-partner when he is on the spot, and may be consulted. *Kirby v. Ingersoll*, Har. Ch., 172. Affirmed in 1 Doug., 477.

213. An assignment void in part is altogether void. It cannot be sustained in part because of one good trust in it. *Kirby v Ingersoll*, Har. Ch., 172. See also, *Pierson v. Manning*, 2 Mich., 445.

214. Accordingly, where one partner, without the consent of the other, who was on the spot and might have been consulted, made an assignment of the partnership effects to one of the creditors, for the benefit of the creditors generally, preferring the debt of the assignee, it was held that the assignment was void *in toto*, and could not be sustained to the extent of securing the debt of the assignee. *Kirby v. Ingersoll*, Har. Ch., 172; 1 Doug., 477.

215. By a bank. The directors of a bank, with the assent of a majority of the stockholders, made a general assignment of the corporate property for the benefit of creditors, and it was held that such an assignment was valid at the common law. *Town v. Bank of River Raisin*, 2 Doug., 530; *Bank Commissioners v. Bank of Brest*, Har. Ch., 106. But it seems that without the consent of the stockholders it could not be made. Har. Ch., 106.

216. Must be of all the property. A voluntary assignment for the benefit of creditors, purporting to be general, is void if it does not fairly and in good faith assign all of the assignor's property which is liable for the payment of his debts. *Smith v. Mitchell*, 12 Mich., 180.

217. Selection of assignee. The utmost good faith is required in the selection of the assignee; and it must be made with reference to the interest of the creditors, rather than that of the debtor. When the assignment is assailed as fraudulent, evidence of a general reputation that the assignee is insolvent is admissible, as well as of any deficiency in age, health, business capacity, or standing. *Angell v. Rosenbury*, 12 Mich., 241.

218. Preferences of one creditor or class of creditors over others, may be made by a debtor in assigning. *How v. Camp*, Wal. Ch., 427; *Town v. Bank of River Raisin*, 2 Doug., 530.

219. A bona fide purchaser is not affected by a secret, fraudulent intent on the part of the assignor. *Hollister v. Loud*, 2 Mich., 309. And an assignee for the benefit of creditors is such a bona fide purchaser if the assignment contain covenants on his part, and stipulations by him beneficial to the creditors. *Ibid.* But see *Pierson v. Manning*, 2 Mich., 445; *Flanigan v. Lampman*, 12 Mich., 58.

220. One who has bought the property of the assignee, and verbally agreed to give his notes therefor on time, but has not yet made any payment or given any notes, when the property is attached, is not entitled as against the attaching creditor to be considered a bona fide purchaser. *Dixon v. Hill*, 5 Mich., 404.

221. Acceptance of the assignment by the assignee dedicates the assigned property to the purposes of the trust, notwithstanding it has been made without the knowledge of the creditors: it cannot afterwards be revoked without the express assent of the creditors. *Suydam v Dequindre*, Har. Ch., 347.

222. But if an attachment is levied upon the property assigned before the acceptance of the trust, the property will be subject to the attachment. *Pierson v. Manniny*, 2 Mich., 445.

223. Delaying creditors. That it hinders, delays or obstructs creditors does not render an assignment void for fraud. To render it so, it must have been made with that intent. *Hollister v. Loud*, 2 Mich., 309.

224. But if it be so drawn that it must, in its execution, tend to hinder or delay creditors unprovided for by it, in the collection of their demands, the legal presumption is that it was drawn with that intent. *Pierson v. Manning*, 2 Mich., 445.

225. Actual fraud in the making of an assignment is to be established by proof, like any other fact. And it must be clearly and distinctly made out, and cannot be inferred from circumstances of an equivocal tendency. *Hollister v. Loud*, 2 Mich., 309; *Baldwin v. Buckland*, 11 Mich., 389.

226. But the most liberal rules should prevail in the admission of evidence which may tend to prove fraud; as that the assignor still claims and seeks to derive a benefit from the property assigned, to the prejudice of creditors. *Flanigan v. Lampman*, 12 Mich., 58; *Smith v. Mitchell*, 12 Mich., 180.

227. Where it appeared that the assignee, a short time before the assignment, as an inducement to a third person to loan the assignor money, stated that the latter was perfectly good and not owing much, it was held that the setting up by him of a large preferred claim under the assignment, as having been owing to him before such statements were made, was strong evidence of fraud in making the assignment. *Angell v. Rosenbury*, 12 Mich., 241.

228. Facts that do not establish fraud. The assignor suffering a bill in equity which charges fraud to be taken as confessed, does not establish the fraud as against the assignee, who denies all knowledge of the assignor's fraudulent intent. *Hollister v. Loud*, 2 Mich., 309.

229. It is no objection to the validity of an assignment that it was made in anticipation, by both parties, of the immediate issuing of attachments against the property of the assignor. *Ibid.*

230. Nor that the property exempt from sale on execution was not assigned. *Ibid.* Even though the exempt property was not specified. *Smith v. Mitchell*, 12 Mich., 180.

231. Nor that the assignors were allowed by the assignees to occupy premises conveyed by the assignment during a period when such property was not usually rented, the assignees in the meantime taking the crops, and expressing their intention to charge the assignors a fair rent. *Hollister v. Loud*, 2 Mich., 309. See *Booth v. McNair*, 14 Mich.

232. If the assignor believes himself solvent, and being pressed by creditors, avows his intention to assign for the purpose of getting time, these are strong evidences of fraud, but subject to explanation. *Baldwin v. Buckland*, 11 Mich., 389; *Angell v. Rosenbury*, 12 Mich., 241. See *Booth v. McNair*, 14 Mich.

233. That the assignment was made by an embarrassed debtor to prevent a sacrifice of his property, does not necessarily render it void. *Angell v. Rosenbury*, 12 Mich., 241.

234. That the assignee is a relative of the assignor, and resides in another town, and that he employs the assignor as his agent in managing the business under the assignment, are not conclusive evidence of fraud in making the assignment. *Baldwin v. Buckland*, 11 Mich., 389 See as to selecting assignee, *Angell v. Rosenbury*, 12 Mich., 241.

235. The subsequent acts and declarations of the parties may be resorted to for the purpose of showing its fraudulent character. *Ibid; Flanigan v. Lampman*, 12 Mich., 58; *Smith v. Mitchell*, 12 Mich., 180. But the subsequent fraudulent acts of the assignor, unknown to the assignee, cannot change the character of the assignee's title, or make that fraudulent which was originally honest. *Baldwin v. Buckland*, 11 Mich., 389.

236. The acts and declarations of the assignor, made after the assignment was signed and delivered, but before the schedules were made out and attached, and while he was engaged in preparing them, are competent evidence to show fraud. *Wyckoff v. Carr*, 8 Mich., 44.

237. Rules of construction. Where an honest intent can as fairly be inferred from the terms of the assignment as a fraudulent one, the Courts are not at liberty to infer the latter. *Nye v. Van Husan*, 6 Mich., 329.

238. But if it contains illegal provisions it is absolutely void; and the statute which makes fraud a question of fact has no application to the case. *Pierson v. Manning*, 2 Mich., 445.

239. When void on its face. A clause authorizing the assignee to sell the assigned property on credit, renders the assignment void. *Sutton v. Hanford*, 11 Mich., 513.

240. So does a clause which provides that the real estate shall not be sold by the assignees until all the personal property and assets shall be exhausted, unless with the consent of the assignor. *Pierson v. Manning*, 2 Mich., 445.

241. An assignment to be valid must definitely fix the rights of the parties beneficially interested, leaving nothing subject to the future direction or control of the assignor. If it provides for a part only of the creditors, and contains no provision for the application of the surplus, if any, the assignment is void as to the creditors not provided for, since at law such surplus would revert to the assignor; and the assignment consequently contains a resulting trust for his benefit before all the creditors are paid. *Ibid.*

242. When not void on its face. It is no objection to an assignment that no time is limited for closing the trust. *Hollister v. Loud*, 2 Mich., 309.

243. Nor does a clause that assignees shall proceed to sell the property and to pay the debts within such time as to them shall seem meet, render it void. The trust in such a case is under the control of chancery. *Ibid.* But see on this point, *Sutton v. Hanford*, 11 Mich., 513.

244. Nor does a clause reserving to the assignors power to perfect the schedules attached to the assignment impair or restrict the instrument itself. *Nye v. Van Husan*, 6 Mich., 329.

245. Nor is a clause objectionable which authorizes the assignees to sell and dispose of the assigned property, "either at public or private sale, as they in their judgment may deem best, and upon such terms and conditions as they may deem most advisable, and for the best interests of the creditors, converting the same into money." It will not be considered as conferring a power to sell upon credit. *Ibid.* See a similar decision in *Booth v. McNair*, 14 Mich.

246. Nor does the preference of individual debts in a copartnership assignment, of itself, independent of an actual intent to defraud, render the assignment void. *Nye v. Van Husan*, 6 Mich., 329; *Hollister v. Loud*, 2 Mich., 445.

247. A clause in the assignment, by which the assignors nominate and appoint the assignees, "their executors, administrators, or assigns, their or each of their true and lawful attorneys, irrevocable, with full power and authority to do and perform all acts, matters or things which can or may be necessary in the premises, as fully and completely as the said assignor might or could do were these presents not executed; and attorney one or more under them to make, nominate and appoint, as they may deem necessary, with full power of substitution and revocation," &c., does not confer upon the assignees the power to delegate their trust; and is proper and unobjectionable. *Nye v. Van Husan*, 6 Mich., 329.

248. A schedule detailing at large the property conveyed, is not necessary to the validity of an assignment. *Hollister v. Loud*, 2 Mich., 309; *Nye v. Van Husan*, 6 Mich., 329.

249. The necessity or effect of a schedule, if one is referred to in an assignment, is to be determined by the intent of the parties as gathered from the whole instrument, and which, when ascertained, is to govern in the construction of assignments as in the case of other written instruments. *Nye v. Van Husan*, 6 Mich., 329.

250. An assignment which clearly manifests an intention on the part of the assignors to transfer all their property to the assignees, and that it shall have immediate operation, will have that effect, though to the general terms describing the property are added the words "as the same is more particularly described in a schedule proposed to be hereafter annexed," and which schedule is not annexed. *Ibid.*.

251. Compelling execution of the trust. Where by an assignment which was executed by the assignee, a time was limited for closing up the trust, and the assignee allowed the time nearly to expire before taking any proceedings for that purpose, it was held that creditors need not wait for the expiration of the time before filing a bill to enforce the execution of the trust. *Suydam v. Dequindre*, Har. Ch., 347.

252. The fee in lands of the debtor which are covered by the assignment will be conveyed by it without the use of words of inheritance. *Angell v. Rosenbury*, 12 Mich., 241.

ATTACHMENT.

253. The demand must be due upon which an attachment issues, at the time the writ is sued out. The plaintiff cannot declare for a cause of action which accrued afterwards. *Galloway v. Holmes*, 1 Doug., 330; *Hale v. Chandler*, 3 Mich., 531. See also, *Hinchman v. Town*, 10 Mich., 508.

254. The affidavit required by the statute is essential to confer upon the Court jurisdiction of the proceeding. *Greenvault v. Farmers and Mechanics' Bank*, 2 Doug., 498.

255. Where the affidavit was sworn to before a person not authorized to administer oaths, it was held that the whole proceedings were void for want of jurisdiction, and that a purchase of lands under them by one who was a party to the proceeding could not be sustained. *Ibid.*

256. And where the affidavit was sworn to on a day previous to the issuing of the writ, the proceeding was held to be void; the statute requiring the affidavit to show that the facts sworn to existed at the time of making application for the writ. *Drew v. Dequindre*, 2 Doug., 93; *Wilson v. Arnold*, 5 Mich., 98; *Fessenden v. Hill*, 6 Mich., 242. And it makes no difference in this respect that the party or his agent making the affidavit resided at a distance from the office of the clerk issuing the writ, and that the affidavit was transmitted to the clerk as soon as practicable by the usual course of mail. *Wilson v. Arnold*, 5 Mich., 98.

257. So where the writ was issued ten days before the affidavit was made, the proceedings were held void. *Buckley v. Lowry*, 2 Mich., 418.

258. The affidavit must state positively, and not on information and belief only, that the defendant is indebted to the plaintiff, and the amount of such indebtedness as near as may be, over and above all legal set offs; and also that the debt is on contract express or implied, or on judgment. Comp. L., § 4743. If defective in these particulars, the Court does not get jurisdiction. *Wilson v. Arnold*, 5 Mich., 98. And see *Hale v. Chandler*, 3 Mich., 531.

259. The affidavit is sufficient which states the indebtedness to be upon express contract, without stating more particularly the nature of the contract. *Drew v. Dequindre*, 2 Doug., 93.

260. The remedy by attachment is not limited to the case of liquidated damages. A demand arising *ex contractu*, the amount of which is capable of ascertainment by some standard referable to the contract itself, sufficiently certain to enable the plaintiff by his affidavit to aver it, in the words of the statute, "as near as may be," or a jury to find it, may be the foundation of this proceeding. *Roelofson v. Hatch*, 3 Mich., 277.

261. An affidavit stating that the two defendants "are not residents of the State of Michigan, and have not resided therein for three months immediately preceding the time of making this affidavit, and that [they] reside in the State of New York," sufficiently shows that neither of the defendants has resided in Michigan within three months. *Dorr v. Clark*, 7 Mich., 310.

262. The bond required to be executed by a non-resident plaintiff, his agent or attorney, by S. L. 1842, p. 118, § 3, might, when executed by such agent or attorney, be, in form, his personal obligation, and be executed by him in his own name, describing himself as such agent, and not in the name, or on behalf of, his principal. *Walbridge v. Spalding*, 1 Doug., 451.

263. Such bond is not vitiated by the omission, in the body of it, of the christian name of the principal obligor, he having executed the same by his full name. *Ibid.*

264. Where the bond is not in the name of the plaintiff in the attachment, but is the personal obligation of his agent, no power under seal need be shown, authorizing its execution by the agent. *Ibid.*

265. The proceeding is a special one, in which the Court exercises an extraordinary jurisdiction under a special statute prescribing its course, and not under its general powers. It can therefore act only according to the forms of procedure which the statute prescribes.

Buckley v. Lowry, 2 Mich., 418; *Greenvault v. Farmers and Mechanics' Bank*, 2 Doug., 498; *Roelofson v. Hatch*, 3 Mich., 277.

266. Amendments of the proceedings might be had under the general statute of amendments in R. S. 1838. *Drew v. Dequindre*, 2 Doug., 93.

267. Accordingly where the journal entries of the calling and default of the defendant failed to show the special character in which the plaintiff sued, it was held that, when motion was made by the defendant to set aside the proceedings for this cause, the omission might be supplied by amendment if in fact the defendant was properly called. *Ibid.*

268. But the making of a new affidavit, when none was made at the issuing of the writ, it is not an amendment which the Court can allow. And though the statute of 1839 (S. L., p. 228) declared that no writ should be quashed "on account of any defect in the affidavit on which the same issued, provided the plaintiff, his agent or attorney, shall, whenever objection shall be made, file such affidavit as shall be required by law," it was held that where the original affidavit was void, because sworn to before a person not authorized to administer oaths, this act did not authorize the filing of a new affidavit after judgment and sale of the attached lands. *Greenvault v. Farmers and Mechanics' Bank*, 2 Doug., 498.

269. And even if such new affidavit could be allowed, it could not make valid the title of the purchaser of the land under the attachment proceeding against one to whom they had been mortgaged by the defendant while the proceeding was pending. *Ibid.*

270. The sheriff's return of sale may be amended by leave of the Court. *People v. Judges of Calhoun Circuit Court*, 1 Doug., 417. The Supreme Court cannot grant leave to make the amendment when application is made for a mandamus to compel the Circuit Court to set aside the sale for irregularity; but if, by opposing affidavits, facts are shown which would authorize the amendment by the Circuit Court, the mandamus will be refused. *Ibid.*

271. Notice of suit. Where the notice of pendency of suit, in addition to what was required by statute, (R. S. 1838, p. 506,) erroneously stated that the writ was returnable in November *next*, instead of November *instant*, it was held that the mistake did not vitiate the proceedings. *Drew v. Dequindre*, 2 Doug., 93.

272. Appearance of defendant. Where property is seized, and the writ returned not personally served, the publication of notice as required by the statute is intended as a substitute for personal service. The defendant has the same time in which to serve notice of retainer, and to plead, after the filing of affidavit of publication, as he would have had after a return of the writ personally served. *Thompson v. Thomas*, 11 Mich., 274.

273. In such case the defendant may appear and plead as a matter of right; and the Court cannot impose terms on his doing so, in cases where terms could not have been imposed if the writ had been personally served. *Ibid.*

274. Irregularities. The defendant can only move the Court to set aside the proceedings where some defect or irregularity is apparent in the writ or affidavit. If he claims that the case is not one authorizing an attachment, he must take proceedings before a circuit court commissioner for its dissolution. *Roelofson .v Hatch*, 3 Mich., 277.

275. A motion to set aside the proceedings for irregularity, made after defendant has caused his appearance to be entered, is unseasonable. *Ibid.* And where the defendant goes to trial on the merits, he waives all prior irregularities. *Crane v. Hardy*, 1 Mich., 56.

276. A judgment in attachment suit will not be set aside for irregularity, on the motion of a person to whom the property attached had been conveyed by the defendant, after service of the attachment, but who is a stranger to the record. *People v. Judges of Calhoun Circuit Court*, 1 Doug., 417.

277. Other creditors filing claims. The discontinuance of a suit in attachment by the original plaintiff, did not impair the right of a creditor who, under R. S. of 1838, had previously filed his declaration in the cause, to proceed to judgment, nor affect his lien upon the property attached. *Ibid.*

278. Where one creditor only obtained judgment in a suit commenced by writ of attachment, it was not necessary that the order of sale of the property attached, authorized by the statutes of 1838, p. 511, § 17, should require the money arising from the sale to be paid into Court; but if it required the same to be paid to the plaintiff, this would not vitiate either the order or the proceedings under it. *Ibid.* [By the present statutes no provision is made for other creditors filing claims under the attachment.]

279. Recovery not limited to amount sworn to. The plaintiff is not limited in his recovery by the amount sworn to be due in the affidavit on which the attachment was issued, if, by the proof, a greater amount is shown to be due. *Pew v. Yoare*, 12 Mich., 16.

280. Setting aside a regular judgment. Where the defendant is a non-resident, and had no notice of the proceeding in season to make his defense, and has been guilty of no laches, the Circuit Court may, in the exercise of a sound discretion, set aside the judgment and permit him to plead, even though a term has elapsed. *Hurlburt v. Reed*, 5 Mich., 30.

281. And where the defendant on learning of the proceedings had engaged an attorney to defend, but the attorney neglected to do so, and the defendant himself was guilty of no laches; on affidavit showing these facts, and merits, it was held that the judgment and subsequent proceedings thereon should be set aside, and the party let in to defend. *Loree v. Reeves*, 2 Mich., 133.

282. Subsequent attaching creditors cannot contest the attachment proceedings in the name of the debtor; but they may, by bill in chancery, contest the lien on the ground of fraud. *Hale v. Chandler*, 3 Mich., 531.

283. Where an attachment creditor took judgment for two demands, one of which was not due when the writ was issued, it was held that the judgment was a fraud upon a subsequent attaching creditor, of whose claim plaintiff was aware, and that the lien of the judgment, so far as it was founded on the demand not due, should be postponed to the lien of the subsequent attaching creditor. *Ibid.*

284. A. sued out of the Circuit Court an attachment, which was levied upon the property of his debtor. At the time of suing it out only eleven dollars of his demand was due, but he subsequently recovered judgment for the whole amount on the debtor's admission. B. also sued out an attachment against the debtor, which was levied on the same property after that of A., but he recovered judgment first, and caused execution to be levied on the property. B. then filed a bill in chancery to have his lien decreed to have priority over that of A. It was held:

That complainant by his attachment acquired a lien on the property, subject only to any lien which A. could lawfully hold under the statute, and that this lien of complainant could not be affected by a subsequent recovery of a judgment to which he was not a party.

That he had a right to show, notwithstanding A.'s judgment, that the demand for which it was rendered was not due when the attachment was levied.

That less than a hundred dollars being due A. when his attachment was levied, the Circuit Court had no jurisdiction, and the whole amount of A.'s judgment was postponed to B.'s lien. *Hinchman v. Town*, 10 Mich., 508.

285. B. included in his judgment a demand which he believed to be due, but which was not so. It was held that he did not, by so including it, debar himself from the right to have his priority protected in equity as to the amount included which actually was due. *Ibid.*

286. Held further, that the question of priority between A.'s judgment and that portion of B.'s which was not due when his attachment was levied, must be determined by the levy of execution; and B.'s being first levied, gave him the first lien. *Ibid.*

287. The order for sale of the property attached, under the Revised Statutes of 1838, must have been directed to the sheriff in office, and not to his predecessor who served the writ. *Crane v. Hardy*, 1 Mich., 56.

288. Attachment of lands. To an attachment under R. S. 1838, the sheriff returned that he had seized certain lands, describing them, in which the defendant had an interest as one of the heirs of A., but did not state the extent of the interest; and it appeared that the lands were appraised without reference to it. Held sufficient. *Drew v. Dequindre*, 2 Doug., 93.

289. Trust estates in lands are not liable to execution or attachment. *Trask v. Green*, 9 Mich., 358; *Maynard v. Hoskins*, 9 Mich., 485; *Gorham v. Wing*, 10 Mich., 486. And this is so notwithstanding the trust is a resulting one in favor of creditors under the statute—Comp. L., §§ 2637, 2638—the land having been bought by the debtor in the name of another. 9 Mich., 358 and 485.

290. The interest of a mortgagee in lands is not subject to attachment. *Columbia Bank v. Jacobs*, 10 Mich., 349.

291. Where lands are conveyed by deed absolute on its face, for the purpose of securing a debt, and a written defeasance is given back by the grantee, and the deed is recorded but the defeasance is not, such defeasance is not made void by the statute—Comp. L., § 2751—except as to purchasers for a valuable consideration without actual notice of its existence. An attaching creditor is not such a purchaser, until the property attached has been sold in pursuance of law and purchased in by him. *Ibid.*

292. The provision in the attachment law—Comp. L., § 4751—that "Real estate shall be bound, and the attachment shall be a lien thereon, from the time when it was attached, if a certified copy of the attachment, with a description of such real estate, shall be deposited in the office of the register of deeds" "within three days after such real estate was attached," only gives the creditor a lien on the debtor's attachable interest in the lands, and in no way interferes with the previously acquired rights of third persons. *Ibid.*

293. The Mayor's Court of Detroit had no jurisdiction of attachments, under R. S. of 1838. *Welles v. City of Detroit*, 2 Doug., 77.

294. Dissolution of attachments. A circuit court commissioner has power to dissolve an attachment which was levied only on lands. *Edgarton v. Hinchman*, 7 Mich., 352.

295. The only mode by which a defendant in attachment can contest the truth of the facts stated in the affidavit upon which the attachment was issued, is by an application under the statute—Comp. L., p. 1275—for a dissolution of the attachment. He cannot, by plea in abatement, put the facts stated in the affidavit in issue. *Bower v. Town*, 12 Mich., 230.

296. Where the defendant has procured a release of the property attached, by executing a bond to the sheriff under the statute, he cannot afterwards apply for a dissolution of the attachment. *Paddock v. Matthews*, 3 Mich., 18.

297. But appearing and pleading in the case does not preclude him from making such application. *Hyde v. Nelson*, 11 Mich., 353.

298. Where the debtor has assigned the property attached, he cannot take proceedings for the dissolution of the attachment, as he has no claim to have the property restored to him. *Chandler v. Nash*, 5 Mich., 409.

299. The application for the dissolution of attachment must state the reasons therefor. *Osborne v. Robbins*, 10 Mich., 277.

300. It should show that the defendant's property was attached, and describe the property; the first because the jurisdiction of the officer is dependent upon it; the second because no order respecting the property can be made unless the property be known; and because without these there would not be sufficient certainty as to the defendant's property and right. *Ibid.*

301. A statement in an application in such a case, that "on said attachment writ some of the goods and chattels of this applicant have been seized," is insufficient. *Ibid.*

302. The application must be verified by oath. *Ibid.*

303. An application which does not describe the property, and only states that, by virtue of the writ, "property to the value of more than $3,000 was attached, and is now in possession of the sheriff," does not confer jurisdiction upon the circuit court commissioner, and he should dismiss it. *Nelson v. Hyde*, 10 Mich., 521.

304. Evidence on. An attachment having been issued on an affidavit that defendant was about to remove his property from the State with intent to defraud his creditors, defendant took proceedings before a circuit court commissioner for its dissolution. On the hearing, defendant testified that when the writ was served he did not know that he was owing any one. This evidence was given with a disclaimer of any intent to raise the question of an indebtedness to the plaintiff in this proceeding. It was held that the evidence was proper, as bearing on the question of fraudulent intent. *Hyde v. Nelson*, 11 Mich., 353.

305. On motion for the dissolution of an attachment, evidence that the defendant a short time previous made an arrangement with a person to take his property under a pretended sale, in order to cover the same from defendant's creditors, and that the person took possession of it under this arrangement, is material and should be admitted. *Parker v. Luce*, 14 Mich.

306. Suit on bond. It is no defense to a suit on an attachment bond, on which property has been delivered by the sheriff to the obligors, that the property did not belong to the defendant in the attachment, or that it was incumbered. Parties bonding property under the statute, must take it on the statutory conditions. *Dorr v. Clark*, 7 Mich., 310.

307. An assignment of the bond by the sheriff to the plaintiff, is a thing which the plaintiff may require as a matter of right, and is valid if signed by the sheriff, though not in his name of office. *Ibid.*

ATTORNEYS AND COUNSELORS.

308. Liability for officer's fees. The attorney of record cannot be made personally liable to the clerk of the Court for his fees, for services rendered on behalf of the client in the progress of the cause, unless upon proof of his express promise to pay them, or of some practice or course of dealing between him and the clerk, from which such promise can be implied. *Preston v. Preston*, 1 Doug., 292.

309. The Court may remove or suspend an attorney for other causes than those mentioned in the statute, which is not to be construed as restrictive of the general powers of the Court over its officers. *Matter of Mills*, 1 Mich., 393.

310. A charge made against an attorney for the purpose of removing him, that he is of notoriously bad character, not to be believed under oath, and unworthy to practice as an attorney, is too general. Specific acts should be charged, so as to give the respondent an opportunity of answering them.

311. But a charge that the reputation of an attorney for truth and veracity is so notoriously bad that he is not to be believed under oath, contains good cause for removal and is not too general. *Ibid.*

312. Compensation. A county was not liable under the Revised Statutes of 1846 to an attorney who, at the request of the Court, defended one charged with crime who was poor and unable to employ counsel. *Bacon v. County of Wayne*, 1 Mich., 461. Provision was made for compensation afterwards. See Comp. L., p. 1492.

313. An agreement made between attorney and client, that the former should prosecute an ejectment suit for an interest which the latter claimed in the property—the client to advance the expenses of the suit, and the attorney, in case of failure, to have nothing for his services, but, on recovery, a part of the property or its value in money —is void for champerty. *Backus v. Byron*, 4 Mich., 535.

314. Remedy of client against. A client whose attorney has neglected his case and suffered judgment to pass against him, but who has himself been guilty of no laches, is not confined to his remedy against the attorney, but the Court in the exercise of its discretion may set aside the judgment and allow him to defend. *Loree v. Reeves*, 2 Mich., 133.

315. Dealings of attorney and client. It is the policy of the law to scrutinize gifts, conveyances and securities by a client to his attorney pending the relation, especially when connected with the subject matter of litigation; and it will not permit the relation and the confidence it implies to be turned to the profit of the attorney at the expense of the client. *Gray v. Emmons*, 7 Mich., 533.

316. Where the attorneys of complainants who were assignees of a portion of a chattel mortgage on a stock of goods, with priority of payment, took possession of the mortgaged property, and without authority from complainants, sold more than was sufficient to satisfy their portion of the mortgage, and were sued by the owner of the balance, and recovery had against them:—*Held*, that the attorneys had no equity against complainants to require to be indemnified for their act in selling the excess. *Ibid.*

317. Nor does it make any difference in this respect, that the attorneys appear to have acted in making such sales on a supposed authority from the owner of the balance of the mortgage; as the law in such case, complainants not being in fault, will leave the misfortune to rest where it has fallen. *Ibid.*

318. Accordingly where, in such case, after suit brought against the attorneys for the value of the goods sold beyond what was sufficient to pay complainant's debt, they obtained from their clients a bond of indemnity against the suit—the clients supposing the suit to be brought for the whole value of the goods sold under the mortgage;—*Held*, that the bond was wrongfully obtained, and should be given up to be cancelled. *Ibid.*

319. Nor is the right of complainants to this relief affected by their employing counsel to defend the suit against the attorneys; they having already given the bond, and there being no evidence that they knew at the time what their rights were. *Ibid.*

320. Such bond of indemnity, where the only liability of the attorneys was for making sale of the excess after satisfying the claim of their clients, is without consideration. *Ibid.*

321. Privileged communications. A communication made to an attorney, under the impression that the attorney had consented to act as such for the party making it, is privileged; but it must be made to the attorney as the legal adviser of the party, and for the purpose of obtaining his legal opinion upon some legal right or obligation. *Alderman v. People*, 4 Mich., 414.

BAIL IN CIVIL CASES.

322. Exoneration. A Circuit Judge has no jurisdiction of proceedings for the commitment of a defendant, in exoneration of special bail, unless copies of the bail piece are presented to him, as the basis of his action, as required by the statute. It is not sufficient that copies of the recognizance of special bail are presented, instead of the bail piece. *Elliott v. Dudley*, 8 Mich., 62.

BAILMENT.

323. Whether bailment or sale. A warehouseman gave a receipt for wheat delivered in store, stating that the wheat was subject to the order of the person storing it, and deliverable upon the return of the receipt properly indorsed, and payment of charges. The receipt also stated that loss or damage by fire, acts of Providence and heating were at the owner's risk. It was held that the transaction was not a *sale* of the wheat to the warehouseman, but a bailment; notwithstanding a usage, well known to both parties, that the grain so received is to be mixed with other grain of like kind and quality, and that delivery of the same identical grain is not made or expected, but only an equal amount of the same kind and quality. *Erwin v. Clark*, 13 Mich., 10.

324. The proprietary interest of the owner in the wheat will remain, notwithstanding it be thus mixed; being converted, however, into a tenancy in common instead of an ownership in severalty. *Ibid.*

325. The warehouseman is liable in trover for the value of the wheat if he refuses, on demand, to deliver the requisite quantity. *Ibid.*

326. Proof of usage cannot be allowed to change a contract, which, by its terms, is plainly one of bailment, into a contract of sale. *Ibid.* And see *Harvey v. Cady*, 3 Mich., 431. For further decisions, see CARRIERS OF GOODS; MARITIME LAW.

327. Title to wheat consigned. Where wheat is sent forward by railroad, mingled in a common mass with other wheat, and made by the receipt deliverable to a consignee named, the legal title to it is in the consignee; and a sale by the consignor to a third person cannot pass the title without the co-operation of the consignee. *Perkins v. Dacon*, 13 Mich., 81.

328. The consignor having made a contract of sale, and given to the vendee an order on the consignee for the delivery of the wheat, the order was held to be an undertaking on his part that the consignee should complete the sale by making delivery; and the vendee having made an ineffectual attempt to find the consignee and obtain delivery, and the wheat in the meantime being destroyed by the accidental burning of the warehouse, the consignor was held liable on this undertaking. *Ibid.*

BANKRUPTCY.

329. A discharge in bankruptcy is conclusive on a creditor who unsuccessfully opposed its being granted; and he cannot afterwards, in a suit brought to recover his debt, show that it was fraudulently obtained. *Wales v. Lyon*, 2 Mich., 276.

330. Wher. the defendant, pending a suit against him, applied for and obtained his discharge, but neglected to avail himself of it in the suit, the Court, the neglect being satisfactorily explained, granted a perpetual stay of execution on the judgment rendered in the suit against him. *Bostwick v. Dodge*, 2 Doug., 331. See also *Parks v. Goodwin*, 1 Mich., 35.

331. After a joint plea to the merits by two defendants, one was held to be entitled to plead severally, *puis darrien*, his discharge in bankruptcy subsequently obtained. Such plea is an abandonment by him of the joint plea, which afterwards stands as the several plea of the other defendant. *Wheelock v. Rice*, 1 Doug., 267.

BANKS AND BANKING.

1. General Principles.

332. Powers of officers. It is fairly within the scope of the powers of the officers of a bank to receive for collection from an indorser of a note due to the bank securities which the maker has turned out to him, and to agree to apply the moneys on the note when collected. And if they fail to make the application, equity will compel it. *Wales v. Bank of Michigan*, Har. Ch., 308.

333. A bill of exchange directed to "J. A. W., Cashier Farmers and Mechanics' Bank of Michigan," and accepted across the face thereof, "Accepted, J. A. W., Cashier," is drawn upon and accepted by the bank, and not by W. in his individual capacity. *Farmers and Mechanics' Bank v. Troy City Bank*, 1 Doug., 457.

334. The extent of the general powers of the cashier of a bank, is a question of law and not of fact; and a charge is erroneous which refers it to the jury to determine whether a cashier, as such, had power to accept certain bills for the bank. *Ibid.*

335. The cashier of a bank has no power to accept bills of exchange, on behalf of the bank, for the accommodation, merely, of the drawers; and the holder, with notice, of bills so accepted, cannot recover against the bank. *Ibid.*

336. The general powers of the cashier of a bank being defined and limited by law, persons dealing with the bank are presumed to know their extent. *Ibid.*

337. A transfer, by way of security, of a portion of the effects of a bank, for the purpose of enabling it to continue business, is within the power of the directors. *Bank Commissioners v. Bank of Brest*, Har. Ch., 106.

338. The cashier, in the absence of proof to the contrary, will be presumed to have authority to turn out the notes and assets of the bank in payment of its indebtedness. *Kimball v. Cleveland*, 4 Mich., 606.

339. Restriction on power to hold lands. Where a bank has power, under its charter, to take and hold lands for the convenient transaction of its business, and to secure debts, but for no other purpose, it has no right to purchase lands for the purpose of selling them again; and the Court of Chancery will not assist it in enforcing a contract made with that intent. *Bank of Michigan v. Niles*, Wal. Ch., 99.

340. Restriction as to interest. A bank may take a mortgage for a debt due to it, with seven per cent. interest, notwithstanding it is prohibited by its charter, from taking more than six per cent. in advance on its loans and discounts. *Bailey v. Murphy*, Wal. Ch., 424.

341. Unauthorized agencies. The establishment by a bank of an agency for the transaction of banking business at another place than that specified in the charter, is a violation of the charter. *Attorney General v. Oakland County Bank*, Wal. Ch., 90; *People v. Oakland County Bank*, 1 Doug., 282.

342. Banking powers, what are. The issue of paper, designed to circulate, in the form and similitude of bank bills, is an act of banking. *People v. River Raisin and Lake Erie R. R. Co.*, 12 Mich., 389.

343. Discounting Paper. The buying of exchange by a bank is, in effect, discounting paper. *People v. Oakland County Bank*, 1 Doug., 282.

2. The General Banking Law of 1837.

344. The statute prescribed the mode in which the affairs of associations formed under this law should be wound up in case of insolvency; and this being designed as a part of the security to the public, was one of the conditions upon which they took their corporate powers. *Bank Commissioners v. Bank of Brest*, Har. Ch., 106.

345. So much of the law as authorized the organization of corporations under it, declared unconstitutional, as opposed to that clause of the constitution which provides that "The legislature shall pass no act of incorporation unless with the assent of at least two-thirds of each house." *Green v. Graves*, 1 Doug., 351.

346. By the General Banking Law the directors of a bank were to be individually liable for the payment of the debts in case of its insolvency. By a prior act banking was made unlawful unless authorized by law, and penalties were imposed for engaging in it. In an action brought against the directors of an association formed under the General Banking Law, to charge them with the payment of one of its debts, it was held that the law against illegal banking was not repealed by the General Banking Law, except in favor of *incorporated banks* organized under it; and as by the constitution corporations could not be created under this law, and the banks so organized were illegal, the action against the directors could not be sustained. *Brooks v. Hill*, 1 Mich., 118.

347. The directors and stockholders could neither be held liable for the bills and other indebtedness of the bank, as stockholders and directors of the association, nor as partners. *State v. How*, 1 Mich., 512.

3. Proceedings Against Banks for Insolvency, &c.

348. Insolvency. For a case where the facts were held to establish a case of insolvency within the meaning of the statute, and for the appointment of a receiver to wind up its affairs, see *Bank Commissioners v. Bank of Brest*, Har. Ch., 106.

349. Assignment to avoid the statute. Where the directors of a bank made an assignment of its assets for the benefit of creditors, with a view to evade the provisions of statute providing how insolvent banks should be wound up, it was held that such assignment was against the policy of the law, and void; and the Court of Chancery appointed a receiver. *Bank Commissioners v. Bank of Brest*, Har. Ch., 106.

350. Jurisdiction of Chancery. The jurisdiction of Chancery over corporations for the purpose of restraining their operations, or of winding up their concerns, is based upon and controlled by the statutes of the State; and it will not interfere except when a case is fairly brought within the statute. *Attorney General v. Bank of Michigan*, Har. Ch., 315. See also *Attorney General v. Oakland County Bank*, Wal. Ch., 90.

351. Suspension of payments. The fact that a bank, not authorized to do so by statute, has stopped payment, is not of itself conclusive evidence of its inability to pay its debts; but it is prima facie evidence of inability or insolvency, except where the bank is authorized to suspend by statute. *Attorney General v. Bank of Michigan*, Har. Ch., 315. See also *Barnum v. Bank of Pontiac*, Har. Ch., 116.

352. Injunction will not be granted in the first instance on an allegation alone that the bank has stopped payment; but a rule to show cause. If not explained or excused, the Court will be authorized to grant an injunction and appoint a receiver. *Ibid.*

353. See for a construction of the suspension act of 1841, *Attorney General v. Bank of Michigan*, Har. Ch., 315.

354. See the case of *Attorney General v. Oakland County Bank*, Wal. Ch., 90, for a statement of the general principles governing the Court in granting and refusing to dissolve injunctions against such corporations, on bill filed for their dissolution and for the forfeiture of charter.

355. Where the proceeding is against the bank as a failing corporation, its primary object is not for the purpose of dissolving the corporation, but to protect the assets for the benefit of creditors. The dissolution of the corportion is merely incidental. *Fay v. Erie and Kalamazoo R. R. Bank*, Har. Ch., 194.

356. The Court may, in such a case, dissolve the injunction, discharge the receiver, and permit the party to dismiss his bill, when it is satisfied that the interest of all concerned will be best subserved by permitting the corporation to manage its own affairs. *Ibid.*

357. It is the duty of the Court to look into the condition of the corporation before discharging the receiver, and to make such order, either absolute or conditional, as the case may require. *Ibid.*

358. Application for an injunction against the Bank of Pontiac. The bill alleged merely a demand and refusal on the part of the bank to pay its notes. Injunction refused. *Barnum v. Bank of Pontiac*, Har. Ch., 116.

359. In the act incorporating the Bank of Pontiac, the act of April 23, 1833, is referred to and in effect made a part of the charter. That act gives the bank sixty days in which to redeem its notes; and the further provision that the act shall not *prevent* the issuing of an injunction, does not change the law in relation to granting injunctions. *Ibid.*

360. An injunction against a bank goes to prevent all action whatever, and is rather in the nature of a final injunction which is granted at the termination of a cause, than the usual preliminary injunction. Such a case should be made out as would authorize the Court to wind up the concerns of the bank. *Ibid.*

361. Forfeiture on quo warranto. Where a bank became insolvent and suspended operations in 1840, and did not resume again until 1864, it was held that the State had not, by laches, lost its right to insist upon a forfeiture of the corporate rights under the statute—Comp. L., § 4854—for continued insolvency "for one whole year." The State shows sufficient diligence—if any is required—if it institutes proceedings and claims the forfeiture within a reasonable length of time after the resumption of business, or an attempt to resume, on the part of the corporation. *People v. Bank of Pontiac*, 12 Mich., 527.

362. Only fourteen months of the chartered existence of the bank remaining unexpired, when it resumes business after a suspension of twenty-four years, the Court, if it has a discretion so to do under the statute, will not impose a fine instead of adjudging a forfeiture of the charter. *Ibid.*

4. PROCEEDINGS TO CAUSE SECURITIES TO BE SOLD FOR THE REDEMPTION OF BILLS.

363. Evading redemption. Upon the presentation of the circulating notes of a bank for redemption, the mode adopted by the officers was to take up and separate from the rest one at a time, examine it, step back to the table, pick up the requisite amount of coin, and pay over to the bill holder; and so proceed, redeeming the notes one by one, until the close of banking hours, and then refuse to redeem further for the day. The officers also tendered to the bill holders bags of coin at the sums marked thereon, but on the condition that there should be no recourse to the bank for the correction of errors, if any, but only to those from whom the bank received the coin. The bank also refused to employ more than one person to redeem its notes; and large amounts presented failed of redemption, upon the claim that the bank was unable to make further redemption during banking hours. Held, that the course of the bank officers was evasive, and tantamount to a refusal to redeem. *People v. State Treasurer*, 4 Mich., 27.

364. Action by State Treasurer. The provision in the charter of the Government Stock Bank, that upon filing affidavit of refusal to redeem, &c., with the State Treasurer, he shall thereupon give notice that the notes of said bank will be redeemed at his office, made it the duty of the Treasurer to act at once. He had no right to wait for counter affidavits from the bank, and his doing so might be treated as a refusal on his part to act. *Ibid.*

365. On application for a peremptory mandamus, commanding the State Treasurer to pay the relator such sum as he was entitled to, as holder of some of the circulating notes of the Government Stock Bank, out of the avails of the stocks deposited with the State Treasurer, it was not necessary that the affidavits should show that the notes were countersigned as required by law. The averment that they were *issued* by the bank, necessarily implied this. *People v. State Treasurer*, 3 Mich., 544.

366. Under the charter of said bank, after the stocks deposited with the State Treasurer for securing its circulating notes had been sold for their redemption, it was his duty forthwith to apply the proceeds for that purpose. *Ibid.*

367. It did not vary the case that the bank had been declared insolvent, and a receiver appointed, and a notice published for creditors to present and prove their claims. Circulating notes were to be first paid, and did not require proof. *Ibid.*

BASTARDY.

368. Complaint. In a proceeding to compel the support of a bastard child by its father, no complaint, distinct from the "accusation and examination" of the mother in writing, under oath, is required. And where such accusation and examination appears, preceded by a formal complaint made by another person, the latter may be treated as surplusage. *Cross v. People*, 10 Mich., 25.

369. Issue. There is no necessity for a formal issue, but if the defendant does not admit the charge, it is to be left to the jury. *Ibid.*

370. Order on conviction. An order which, after adjudging defendant to be the father of a bastard child, directs him to pay towards the support of the child a specified sum, "*with the assistance of the mother*," is bad for uncertainty. It should definitely fix the liability of the defendant. *Ibid.*

371. Costs. A defendant who was found guilty and adjudged to be the father of a bastard child, under the Revised Statues of 1846, was held not liable for the costs of the proceeding; the statute being silent on the subject of costs in such a case. *Booth v. McQueen*, 1 Doug., 41.

372. Reviewing proceedings. Proceedings in the Circuit Court under the Bastardy Act cannot be removed into the Supreme Court by writ of error. *Cross v. People*, 8 Mich., 113. But may be, by common law certiorari. *Cross v. People*, 10 Mich., 25.

BILLS OF EXCHANGE AND PROMISSORY NOTES.

373. What is a bill of exchange. An instrument signed officially by the president and secretary of a corporation, requesting its treasurer to pay to K. or bearer a certain sum of money, is a bill of exchange drawn by the corporation upon itself. *Hasey v. White Pigeon Beet Sugar Company*, 1 Doug., 193.

374. Acceptance of such a bill is not necessary, the act of drawing being deemed an acceptance. *Ibid.* See post 380, 382.

375. Its legal effect is the same as that of a promissory note; it imports a promise to pay on demand, and an action may be maintained upon it without proof of a demand of payment upon the treasurer. *Ibid.*

376. What is a promissory note. An instrument unconditionally promising to pay a specified sum at a certain time, to the payee or bearer, is a promissory note, notwithstanding the consideration upon which it was given is stated in the instrument. *Beardslee v. Horton*, 3 Mich., 560.

377. An instrument by which the makers promise to pay to the order of the payees, at a time and place named, a specific sum of money, *with current exchange on New York*, is a promissory note, and the indorsee may bring suit upon it in his own name. *Smith v. Kendall*, 9 Mich., 241.

378. What is not. An instrument by which the maker promises to pay to the payee or bearer a certain sum by a time named, but which recites that the payee agrees to receive certain a less sum in satisfaction, if paid on an earlier day named, is not a promissory note. *Fralick v. Norton*, 2 Mich., 130.

379. Authority to draw. A letter of credit was given, in the following words: " To enable you to make advances on grain, or other produce, to be consigned to us, or for us, at Oswego, during the ensuing fall, you are at liberty to make drafts on us, in amounts necessary for such operations, on such terms as you can make advantageously for us. Your drafts may be made payable here, or in New York at the Corn Exchange Bank." Held to be an unconditional authority to make drafts. *Bissell v. Lewis*, 4 Mich., 450.

380. By the law of New York, whence the letter was sent, and where the drafts were made payable, such a letter is an unconditional acceptance, and should be so construed here. *Ibid.*

381. It is not necessary for the payee in such a draft, who has received it on the credit of the written authority, to show that the funds raised by it were used for making advances on grain, or other produce, to be consigned to the persons giving the authority. *Ibid.*

382. A parol acceptance of a bill is made void by statute. *Comp. L.*, §1266. A parol agreement by a tax collector, to receive in payment of taxes a draft drawn by his creditor upon himself, is within this statute. *Elliott v. Miller*, 8 Mich., 132.

383. When subject to equities. A person to whom a promissory note has been indorsed in payment of a pre-existing debt, is a holder for a valuable consideration, and is not affected by any equities between the antecedent parties, where he has received the note before it came due, without notice of such equities. *Bostwick v. Dodge*, 1, Doug., 413; *Outhwite v. Porter*, 13 Mich. 533; overruling in this particular, *Ingerson v. Starkweather*, Wal. Ch., 347. See *Baker v. Pierson*, 5 Mich., 459.

384. Whenever the consideration of negotiable paper is illegal between the original parties, especially if in violation of a positive prohibition of statute, proof of such illegality throws upon the holder the burden of proving that he got it bona fide, and gave value for it. *Paton v. Coit*, 5 Mich., 505.

385. Where, therefore, action was brought by the assignee upon negotiable paper, and defendant showed that the same was given for intoxicating drinks sold in violation of the Prohibitory Liquor Law of 1855, which makes such paper " utterly null and void against all persons, in all cases, excepting only as against the holders" " who may have paid therefor a fair price, and received the same upon a valuable and fair consideration, without notice or knowledge of such illegal consideration"—such showing by defendant was held to make out a prima facie defense, and that the burden of proof was thereby cast upon the plaintiff, to show those facts which would bring him within this exception of the statute. *Ibid.*

386. The English rule, that a negotiable note payable on demand does not become over due by mere lapse of time, has been modified in this country, so that a promissory note thus payable, unless indorsed in a reasonable time, is considered over due and dishonored. *Carll v. Brown*, 2 Mich., 401.

387. What is such reasonable time is to be determined by the Court on the facts of each particular case. *Ibid.*

388. A negotiable note, bearing date May 25th, was sued by the bearer on the 19th of June following. Held that the note could not be considered over due—no prior demand being shown—before it came to the hands of the bearer. *Ibid.*

389. A note payable to order and without contingency, on a day certain, is not the less negotiable because purporting to be according to the condition of a mortgage, when the terms of the mortgage correspond with those expressed in the note. *Littlefield v. Hodge*, 6 Mich., 326. See *Dutton v. Ives*, 5 Mich., 515.

390. Who is holder for value. A tax collector's agent received from a creditor of the collector a draft on the collector in payment for taxes, and the collector refused to accept and allow it. The agent thereupon paid over the amount of the tax himself. It was held that he was holder of the draft for value, and entitled to collect it from the parties. *Elliott v. Miller*, 8 Mich., 132.

391. Received as collateral or conditional payment. Where a party receives negotiable paper from his debtor, with the debtor's indorsement, as collateral security for his demand, and not as agent merely, it is his duty to present the same for payment when due, and take the proper steps to charge the debtor as indorser; and failing to do this, he makes the paper his own. *Jennison v. Parker*, 7 Mich., 355.

392. Where a draft is received as conditional payment, the right of action upon the debt is suspended until the draft is properly presented for payment, and payment refused. *Phœnix Insurance Co. v. Allen*, 11 Mich., 501.

393. By accepting a draft as conditional payment, the creditor accepts the duty of doing everything with respect thereto, which is necessary to fix the liability of the parties. And the *onus* is upon him to show that he has performed the duty, when he seeks to recover upon the original cause of action. *Ibid.*

394. Where one transfers notes to another for property purchased, on an agreement that if the notes are not collected the purchaser is to make up the deficiency, the purchaser only takes the notes as conditional payment; and if not paid at maturity, he is under no obligation to bring suit upon them, but may immediately sue the purchaser for the amount. [Christiancy, J.] *Dodge v. Stanton*, 12 Mich., 408.

395. The effect of thus receiving notes as conditional payment, is simply to postpone payment of the demand on which they are received until the securities fall due. *Ibid.*

396. When indorser a maker. Where two persons indorsed a note at its making, and before its delivery to the payee, to enable the maker to purchase with it certain property of the payee, it was held they were to be considered joint original promissors with the maker. *Wetherwax v. Paine*, 2 Mich., 555. See also, *Higgins v. Watson*, 1 Mich., 428. But see, *Tinker v. McCauley*, 3 Mich., 188, disapproving the last mentioned case.

397. Indorser's contract. The indorser of a note for whose benefit it was discounted does not, in consequence of that fact, incur any other liability than that of his indorsement; and proof of that fact is, therefore, irrelevant in a suit against him. *Newberry v. Trowbridge*, 13 Mich., 263.

398. Proof is also irrelevant that a note in renewal of which the one in suit was given, was purchased of the maker thereof by the indorser for less than its face; as no such evidence could change the nature of the indorser's contract, or excuse a failure to take the necessary steps to charge him upon it. *Ibid.*

399. Demand of payment. As against the maker of a promissory note, payable at a particular place, the plaintiff is not required to prove presentment or demand of payment at the place specified. *Reeve v. Pack*, 6 Mich., 240.

400. A witness called to prove the dishonor of a note, who only testifies that he went to find the maker's last place of residence, and that the note was not paid, and that he then protested it, but does not testify concerning his knowledge of the residence, nor whether, if no personal demand was made, there was any valid reason for the omission, does not sufficiently show the dishonor. *Nevius v. Bank of Lansingburg*, 10 Mich., 547.

401. A draft payable at sight should be presented for payment within a reasonable time; and a court can not, as a matter of law, say that any delay is reasonable beyond that which is required in the ordinary course of business, without special inconvenience to the holder; or by the special circumstances of the particular case. *Phœnix Insurance Co. v. Allen*, 11 Mich., 501.

402. A draft drawn at Cincinnati, May 2, 1861, on persons in Chicago, payable at sight, was received in Detroit, May 4th, but not transmitted for presentment until the 25th of that month. There was a daily mail between Detroit and Chicago, occupying from twelve to fourteen hours in its passage. No evidence was given to explain or excuse the delay in presentment; and it was held that, without any evidence bearing upon the point, it was error to submit to the jury the question whether the draft was presented for payment in a reasonable time. *Ibid.*

403. It was held further that counsel should not be permitted to read to the jury and comment upon cases found in the books of reports, upon the question, submitted to them as one of fact, whether the draft was presented for payment in a reasonable time. *Ibid.*

404. On a subsequent trial of the same case, evidence was given showing that the delay in making presentment was for the purpose of enabling the creditor to correspond with the debtor as to the funds that should be received in payment. But, as neither party could change the character of the bill, which was collectable according to its terms, it was held that the reason assigned was no excuse. *Phœnix Insurance Co. v. Gray*, 13 Mich., 191.

405. A notice of dishonor must contain words directly, or by necessary construction, showing that the note has been presented for payment and payment refused. And its sufficiency is to be determined by the Court as a matter of law. *Platt v. Drake*, 1 Doug., 296.

406. A notice to an indorser that a promissory note "has been protested for non-payment," and that the holders look to him for payment of the same, was held not sufficient, because the statement that the note had been *protested* referred rather to the making, by the notary, of the instrument called a *protest*, than to the acts which might authorize the protest to be made; and no *protest* of a promissory note was necessary. *Ibid.* Affirmed in *Newberry v. Trowbridge*, 4 Mich., 391.

407. But a similar notice to the indorser of a foreign bill was held sufficient. *Spies v. Newberry*, 2 Doug., 425.

408. And where the note was payable in another State, under whose statutes notaries public were authorized to demand payment of promissory notes and to protest them for non-payment, it was held that a similar notice was sufficient. *Snow v. Perkins*, 2 Mich., 238.

409. The two cases of Platt v. Drake, and Newberry v. Trowbridge, supra, doubted, and said to be founded on a misapprehension which led the Court to overlook both commercial usage and statutes which sanctioned protests of notes and inland bills. *Burkham v. Trowbridge*, 9 Mich., 209. See *Newberry v. Trowbridge*, 13 Mich., 263.

410. In a notice of dishonor no technical phrases are necessary; but it is only required that the terms used be such as fairly and naturally lead a mind of ordinary intelligence to the idea that the paper has been presented at maturity and dishonored, and that the party notified is looked to for payment. *Ibid.*

411. A notice to a party, dated on the day of the maturity of an inland bill, and stating that the bill was on that day, by the notary public who signed the notice, protested for non-payment, after due demand and refusal, and that the holder looked to the party notified for payment, is sufficient. *Ibid.*

412. A mistake in describing a promissory note in a notice of protest—as where the note was for $200, but was described in the notice as for $175—does not necessarily vitiate the notice; the question in such case being whether the indorser was misled by the notice. *Snow v. Perkins*, 2 Mich, 238.

413. The object of the notice is to inform the indorser of the non-payment of the note by the maker, and that the indorser is liable for the payment of it; and a notice which accomplishes this object is sufficient, although it misdescribe the note in some particulars. *Ibid.*

414. Notice of dishonor deposited in the post-office where the person to whom it is directed receives his letters is sufficient, if such person does not reside within the place. *Nevius v. Bank of Lansingburg*, 10 Mich., 547, overruling in this particular, *Newberry v. Trowbridge*, 4 Mich., 391.

415. But if the person to be notified resides in the place, the notice must be personal, or left at his place of abode or business. And where it was deposited in the post-office, proof that the person received it the second day after the dishonor, is not sufficient to charge him. *Nevius v. Bank of Lansingburgh*, 10 Mich., 547.

416. It is not necessary that a copy of the protest of commercial paper should accompany the notice. *Atwater v. Streets*, 1 Doug., 455.

417. Proof to charge indorser. Proof of any one or more of the legal conditions necessary to charge an indorser, has no tendency whatever to prove a compliance with the rest. *Cicotte v. Morse*, 8 Mich., 424.

418. Proof of notice. Where there is no direct evidence of notice to the indorser, a subsequent recognition of liability by him is presumptive evidence, in the nature of an implied admission, that notice has been given. But where the plaintiff attempts to prove due notice, and only succeeds in proving one which is defective in form or mode of service, this excludes the presumption of a proper and sufficient notice; and a part payment by the indorser afterwards will not operate as an unqualified acknowledgment of liability, unless it be shown that he knew at the time that the notice was defective. *Newberry v. Trowbridge*, 13 Mich., 263.

419. Waiver of notice. An offer by the indorser of a note to pay the sum due thereon in depreciated bank bills, without explanation can be regarded only as an offer to compromise; and cannot operate as a waiver of notice, or as an unqualified acknowledgment of his liability on the note. *Ibid.*

420. And the mere fact of part payment of the note by the indorser in depreciated bank bills, will not amount to an unconditional acknowledgment of his liability to pay the whole. *Ibid.*

421. Suit against remote indorser. Where the holder of a note, striking out intermediate indorsements, declares against a remote indorser as on a contract made directly to himself, he recovers on the contract of the defendant with his immediate indorsee. *Kinzie v. Farmers and Mechanics' Bank*, 2 Doug., 105.

422. An agent may sue in his own name a note which he holds for collection, and which is payable to bearer or indorsed in blank. *Brigham v. Gurney*, 1 Mich., 349.

423. Admission of execution by not denying. Under the statute, in justices' courts when any written instrument purporting to be executed by one of the parties is declared upon or set off, it may be used in evidence on the trial against such party without proving its execution, unless its execution be denied by oath at the time of declaring, pleading, or giving notice of set off, if such instrument shall be produced and filed with the justice. *Comp. L.*, §3767. And its execution shall not be denied except under oath as so provided. *Comp. L.*, §3714.

424. Under this statute, where plaintiff declares against two or more defendants as makers of a promissory note which is signed with a collective name, and which is produced and filed with the justice, the defendants appearing to the action and pleading without oath are to be taken to admit, not only the execution of the note in the abstract, but that it was executed by the parties declared against. *Pegg v. Bidleman*, 5 Mich., 26.

425. Where a party had failed to deny the execution of a note at the proper time, and moved for leave to amend on a subsequent day, so as to allow him to make the denial, and the justice denied the motion, and refused to allow him to show on the trial that he did not sign the note, and rendered judgment against him, the judgment was affirmed. *Fish v. Hale*, 4 Mich., 506.

426. Under rule 79 of the Circuit Courts, a promissory note a copy of which was attached to and served with the declaration, may be read in evidence under the common counts, without proof of the signature, where its execution is not denied on oath. *Hoard v. Little*, 7 Mich., 468.

427. "Current funds." A note payable in "current funds," in the absence of all evidence showing that anything else is current at the place of payment, must be regarded as payable only in such funds as are current by law. *Phœnix Insurance Co. v. Allen*, 11 Mich., 501.

428. Renewal note, when a payment. A note which two parties had indorsed for a third being over due, the holder wrote the indorsers requesting a new note in renewal. They sent one accordingly, made and indorsed by the same parties, and requested the return of the old note. No notice was taken of this request, nor were any steps taken to fix the liability of the indorsers on the new note; but after it fell due suit was brought on the old note, and the new note tendered to the indorsers on the trial, who refused to receive it. Held, that the plaintiff, by retaining the new note under the circumstances had made it his own. *Sage v. Walker*, 12 Mich., 325.

BOARD OF SUPERVISORS.

430. Record of: Quorum. It is not essential to the record of proceedings of a board of supervisors that it be signed by the clerk or chairman, or show what members composed the board, or that a quorum was present. The presence of a quorum at the transaction of business will be presumed. *Lacey v. Davis*, 4 Mich., 140.

431. Appeals from. The constitution having provided that the action of the board, in adjusting county demands, should be subject to no appeal, the Supreme Court cannot revise their action by mandamus, and compel them to allow a demand which they have rejected on the ground that the services charged for were not performed. *People v. Auditors of Wayne*, 10 Mich., 307.

432. But where a demand is by law made a charge against the county, which it is the duty of the supervisors unconditionally to allow, they may be compelled to perform this duty by mandamus. *People v. Supervisors of Macomb*, 3 Mich., 375; *People v. Auditors of Wayne*, 13 Mich., 233.

433. New county. Where a new county is created by setting off for that purpose organized townships from existing counties, the supervisors of these townships are thenceforth supervisors of the new county; their powers being conferred and duties imposed by the general laws of the State, instead of by the act creating the new county. *Carleton, People v.* 10 Mich., 250.

BOAT AND VESSEL LAW.

434. To what cases it applied. Chapter 122 of the Revised Statutes of 1846—Ch. 149 of Comp. Laws—applied to contracts made and injuries received within the State only, and not to such as had arisen out of the State. *Bidwell v. Whittaker*, 1 Mich., 469; *Turner v. Lewis*, 2 Mich., 350.

435. But no distinction was made by the law between citizens of this State and those of other States having claims. *Ibid.*

436. If the contract was made in another State, though to be performed in this State, no lien attached under the law. *Turner v. Lewis*, 2 Mich., 350.

437. A specific lien was given by the law on the boat or vessel, for all such demands as were mentioned in the first section. *Bidwell v. Whittaker*, 1 Mich., 469.

438. For means or supplies furnished, or money advanced, in the building, fitting and furnishing a vessel, the law gave no lien. The lien was restricted to work done and *materials* furnished. *Lawson v. Higgins*, 1 Mich., 225.

439. Under the act of 1839, for the collection of demands against boats and vessels, (*S. L., p.* 70) a portion of which was incorporated into said Chapter 122, it was held that no specific lien was given upon the vessel until an actual levy of attachment, and that the remedy by the act was general, and not restricted to causes of action arising within the State. *Moses v. Steamboat Missouri*, 1 Mich., 507.

440. The complaint under the act of 1839, should contain every substantial averment which would be necessary in a declaration at common law for the same cause of action, and it was governed by the rules which apply to declarations, in respect to joinder and misjoinder of counts. *Owners of Ship Milwaukee v. Hale*, 1 Doug., 306.

441. In this case the complaint contained four counts; two of which were, in substance, that plaintiff shipped on board the vessel, which was employed by the owners as common carriers, a certain quantity of wheat, and, in consideration that the plaintiff promised to pay a certain price for the transportation, the owners of the vessel received the wheat on board, and agreed to proceed directly from the place of shipment to the port of destination, and deliver the same in good order, but, on the contrary, the vessel was so carelessly managed, &c., that the wheat was lost, and not delivered. The other two counts set forth a like shipment and undertaking to deliver, &c., pursuing the ordinary route, without unnecessary deviation, &c., and alleged a deviation, during which the ship was assailed by a great storm and wrecked, &c., and the wheat was wet, damaged and spoiled, and wholly lost, &c., and not delivered. Held that all these counts were in assumpsit, and properly joined. *Ibid.*

442. In a complaint under said Chapter 122, (149) before an officer authorized to perform the duties of a Judge of the Supreme Court at chambers, it was not necessary to aver that at the time of the application the vessel was within the county where the application was made. But it was otherwise where the application was made to a Judge of a court of record. *Ward v. Willson*, 3 Mich., 1.

443. It was not necessary in order to confer jurisdiction, to set forth that the services, &c., for which the claim was made, were rendered in this State. *Ibid.*

444. A description of the vessel as "a vessel navigating the waters of this State," is equivalent to the averment that such vessel is *used* in navigating, &c. *Ibid.*

445. Lien of other creditors. Where, under the provisions of said Chapter 122, a vessel was attached at the instance of a creditor, and the notice to creditors to produce their claims was published three months, and at the end of the three months, and before any order of sale, the owner of the vessel procured her discharge by giving the bond required by said chapter; it was held that creditors who had failed to file their demands with the proper officer within the three months, lost the benefit of the lien given them by section one of said chapter. *Watkins v. Atkinson*, 2 Mich., 151.

446. Suit on bond. In declaring on a bond executed under § 13 of said chapter, it was not necessary to aver that the plaintiff made the application in writing in manner and form required by §§ 2 and 3. *Truesdale v. Hazard*, 2 Mich., 344.

447. Nor was it necessary to aver that the vessel released upon the execution of the bond was, at the time of its seizure, within the jurisdiction of the Court issuing the warrant. *Ibid.*

448. It was only necessary for the plaintiff to prove the execution of the bond, and his claim or demand as set out in the declaration, to entitle him *prima facie* to a recovery. *Ibid.*

449. The law unconstitutional. Said chapter 122 is unconstitutional. It conflicts with the provision that no person shall be deprived of property without due process of law. *Parsons v. Russell*, 11 Mich., 113. [For enactments adopted since this decision, see Laws of 1864, p. 107; Laws of 1865, p. 672.]

BONA FIDE PURCHASER.

450. Notice by possession. Where the first purchaser of lands is in possession, and the second purchaser is aware of that fact when he purchases, that is sufficient notice to him of the rights of the prior purchaser, and he takes the land subject to all equities existing between his grantor and the first purchaser. *Godfroy v. Disbrow*, Wal. Ch., 260. For further decisions on this point, see POSSESSION OF LAND.

451. Grantee of. Although a party may not himself be a bona fide purchaser without notice, yet if his grantor was such a purchaser, the former is entitled to all his rights, and to the protection which the law would give him. *Ibid.*

452. But the defense of a bona fide purchaser can only be made by the purchaser himself, or by some one claiming through his purchase. *Blanchard v. Tyler*, 12 Mich., 339.

453. Under recording laws. A subsequent purchaser whose deed is first recorded, is presumed to be a bona fide purchaser without notice, until the contrary is made to appear. *Godfroy v. Disbrow*, Wal. Ch., 260.

454. Under the recording law of 1819 it was necessary for a party who would avoid the effect of a subsequent conveyance first recorded, to show that the grantee in such conveyance had notice of the prior conveyance when he took his deed, or that he had not paid a valuable consideration. *Ibid.*

455. A person who, at the time of receiving a deed from another, knows him to have no title, or has notice of his want of title, cannot be a bona fide purchaser under the recording laws, whether the real owner of the title is known to him or not. *Fitzhugh v. Barnard*, 12 Mich., 104.

456. Constructive notice. A grantee is chargable with notice of whatever appears in the chain of title through which he claims, as well as with the reasonable inferences therefrom; as that a mortgage given twenty-four years before has probably been foreclosed. *Ibid.*

457. But in purchasing from one tenant in common, he has a right to suppose the usual relations exist, and is not bound by partnership equities between the tenants affecting the land in their hands. *Adams v. Bradley*, 12 Mich., 346.

458. Payment after notice. To constitute a bona fide purchaser, there must be a want of notice both at the time of the purchase, and at the payment of the purchase money. *Thomas v. Stone*, Wal. Ch., 117; *Dixon v. Hill*, 5 Mich., 404; *Warner v. Whittaker*, 6 Mich., 133; *Blanchard v. Tyler*, 12 Mich., 339.

459. Where a debtor had made an assignment of his property, which was void on its face as to creditors, and plaintiff had bought the property of the assignee and verbally agreed to pay for it, at certain rates, in his notes on time, but before making any payments or giving any notes, the property was taken on attachment against the fraudulent assignor; it was held, that the verbal promise to pay was not sufficient to protect the title of the purchaser against the attachment. *Dixon v. Hill*, 5 Mich., 404. See also, *Blanchard v. Tyler*, 12 Mich., 339.

460. Where land is purchased on which there is an unrecorded mortgage, of which the purchaser had no notice, but of which he is notified before a mortgage given by him for purchase money is paid; any payment made by him on his own mortgage after such notice, is made in his own wrong, and he is not protected, as to such payment, against the unrecorded mortgage. *Warner v. Whittaker*, 6 Mich., 133.

461. Notice to agent. Where a debtor, owning lands incumbered by mortgages, gave his creditor a deed of the lands, on a parol understanding that the creditor was to dispose of them for the payment of the mortgages, and of his debt, and account to the debtor for the balance, and the creditor, instead of paying off the mortgages, bought them as agent for, and in the name of, a third person, who claimed not to be aware of this understanding; held, that the latter was chargeable with notice of the facts of which his agent was cognizant, and took the land subject to the debtor's equities. *Emerson v. Atwater*, 7 Mich., 12.

462. Extinguishing equities by foreclosure. Such purchaser of the mortgages could not cut off the debtor's equities by selling the land mortgaged, under the power of sale, and bidding it in himself. *Ibid.*

463. An attachment creditor is not a bona fide purchaser within the meaning of the recording laws until the property attached has been sold in pursuance of law, and purchased in by him. *Columbia Bank v. Jacobs*, 10 Mich., 349.

464. Fraudulent mortgage. One who has given a mortgage to be sold for a fraudulent purpose, cannot set up the fraud as a defense to the mortgage in the hands of a bona fide purchaser. *Bloomer v. Henderson*, 8 Mich., 395.

465. Judicial sale: want of jurisdiction. Where a want of jurisdiction appears on the record of a Court of general jurisdiction, the record is a nullity, and no rights can be acquired by purchasers under it. *Wilson v. Arnold*, 5 Mich., 98.

466. Personal property: conditional sale. One in possession of personal property, of which he has made a conditional purchase, cannot, before the condition has been complied with, sell the property so as to vest the title in a bona fide purchaser. *Couse v. Tregent*, 11 Mich., 65.

BOND.

468. Alteration. Where the penalty of an official bond was reduced $5,000 by the board having power to fix it, after a part of the sureties had signed it, it was held that it was thereby made void as to the sureties who had signed it, but that it was valid as to those who signed it afterwards. *People v. Brown*, 2 Doug., 9.

469. When joint and several. A bond in these words: " Know all men by these presents, that I, A. B., principal, and C. D., E. F., and G. H., sureties, *are* held," &c., " for the payment of which sum well and truly to be made, we bind ourselves, our heirs, executors and administrators, *severally*, firmly by these presents," is a joint, as well as several bond. *Supervisors of St. Joseph v. Coffinbury*, 1 Mich., 355.

470. When good at common law. A bond given by the treasurer of a county for the faithful performance of his official duties, to the board of supervisors of the same county, is a good and valid bond, notwithstanding there may be no statute requiring such bond to be given. *Ibid.*

471. In suit on lost note. The bond to be executed by plaintiff to defendants, under R. S. of 1846, Ch., 102, §89—*Comp. L.*, §4326—upon bringing an action upon a lost promissory note, should run to all of the defendants, even though some of them have not been served with process. *Higgins v. Watson*, 1 Mich., 428.

472. Indemnity: right of officer to. A sheriff before levying a writ of attachment upon property of the title to which there is reasonable doubt, has a right to require a bond of indemnity, and to refuse to execute the writ by seizure of such property until the bond is given. *Smith v. Cicotte*, 11 Mich., 383.

473. If the sheriff seizes the property on promise of bond of indemnity by the creditor, which the latter afterwards fails to give, and the property is then taken away by the adverse claimant, the sheriff may make return to the writ setting forth these facts, and he will be protected. *Ibid.*

BOUNTY.

474. Vested right in. Where a bounty offered under a law of the State is actually earned, the reduction of the bounty by a subsequent amendment of the law, does not deprive the party who has earned it of the full bounty given by the original act. *People v. State Auditors*, 9 Mich., 327.

475. To volunteers: discrimination. Under the act of March 6, 1863, (S. L.. p. 60), authorizing the payment of a State bounty to volunteers in the military service of the United States, when the State authorities had offered a bounty they had no right to discriminate between the various classes of volunteers who came within the terms of the offer. A man drafted for nine months, and then allowed to volunteer for three years, was entitled to the bounty. *People v. Quartermaster-General*, 12 Mich., 191.

476. But the State authorities had the right to discriminate in making the offer. And as the "State Guard," so called, did not come within the terms of the offer actually made, they were not entitled to the bounty. *People v. Quartermaster-General*, 14 Mich.

477. Act No. 23 of 1864 (S. L., p. 53) authorizing the payment of bounties to volunteers from this State in the military service of the United States, was designed to distinguish between volunteers under the President's call of October 17, 1863, and those enlisting under the call of February 1, 1864, and to provide a bounty for the latter only *People v. Quartermaster-General*, 13 Mich., 247.

478. And where one enlisted March 12, 1864, and was credited to a town whose quota under the call of October 17 was not full, he was held not entitled to the bounty under said act. *Ibid.*

479. Township action legalized. The act of March 7th, 1863, "to legalize the action of townships, &c., in raising bounties for volunteers," (S. L., p. 92) extended to and made valid a tax voted at a meeting of the electors of a township held for the purpose of raising bounties, although such meeting was not convened in the manner required by the statutes relative to special township meetings. *Crittenden v. Robertson*, 13 Mich., 58.

480. The act of 1865 to legalize the action of the several townships, &c., in the county of Jackson in paying bounties to volunteers, and to refund money to pay bounties, (S. L., p. 477), cannot properly be extended to cover any advances of money made by individuals on their own account, and not on the credit or by the authority of the municipalities. *Miller v. Granby*, 13 Mich., 540.

481. Where, by special act, the question is allowed to be submitted to the voters of a township whether a certain class of payments and advances for bounties, &c., shall be refunded, the vote taken is void if it is so broad as to include other advances and claims not embraced by the special act. *People v. Township Board of Woodhull*, 14 Mich.

BREACH OF PROMISE TO MARRY.

482. Capacity to contract presumed. In an action for breach of promise to marry, it is not necessary for the plaintiff to prove that defendant was of full age when the contract was made. *Simmons v. Simmons*, 8 Mich., 318.

483. Aggravating circumstances. In such action it is not error to allow proof that defendant borrowed money of plaintiff, and renewed his notes therefor immediately before marrying another; as it is important for the jury to understand as fully as possible the mutual conduct of the parties during the existence of the contract, as well as the causes and circumstances attending the breaking off of the engagement. *Ibid.*

484. Excuse for breach. Proof of the frequent intermarriage of the ancestors of the parties—who are cousins—and of the evil tendency of the marriage of relations in producing deformed or sickly and imbecile children, is incompetent where the contract was not broken on any such ground. *Ibid.*

CARRIERS OF GOODS.

485. Inland navigation: exemption from liability by act of Congress. The navigation of the great American lakes and their connecting waters, is not "inland navigation" within the meaning of the act of Congress entitled "An act to limit the liability of ship-owners, and for other purposes," approved March 3, 1851. And therefore, where goods were intrusted to a common carrier, to be transported from New York to Detroit, by way of Lake Erie and the Detroit River, and while upon the steamboat of the carrier, in the harbor of Buffalo, in the course of transit, were destroyed by fire, without any negligence or fault on the part of the carrier or his agents, the carrier was held not liable to the owner for the loss. *American Transportation Co. v. Moore*, 5 Mich., 368. Affirmed by Supreme Court of United States. See 24 *How.*, 1.

486. Limitation of common law liability. Although it

devolves upon a common carrier to show affirmatively the terms of any contract which lessens his common law liability, yet the fact is to be proved like any other, by any pertinent evidence. If in writing, the writing must be shown; but if by parol, there is no rule which requires any different proof from that which would establish any other contract. The jury must be satisfied from the evidence that a certain contract exists; and if satisfied, that is sufficient. *Ibid.*

487. A common carrier cannot limit his common law liability by a mere notice indorsed upon the receipt given the consignor, or otherwise brought to the consignor's notice. The assent of the latter to the limitation is necessary, and must be proved by evidence *aliúnde:* it cannot be presumed from the terms of the receipt alone, or be implied from the posting of notices or the delivery thereof to the consignor. *Michigan Central R. R. Co. v. Hale*, 6 Mich., 243.

488. A common carrier has no power to *restrict*, in any way, his common law liability, but is bound to transport the property intrusted to him under this liability, if it be not waived or changed by contract. But he may make any contract with an individual relative to the transportation of his property which the latter may deem conducive to his interest, and enter into upon a consideration satisfactory to himself, though a diminution of the carrier's common law liability results therefrom. *Ibid.*

489. A corporation which is made a common carrier by its charter, and required to "transport merchandise and property without showing partiality or favor," has the same power to contract for a limitation of its liability as any other carrier, and no consideration of public policy is contravened by the exercise of such power. *Ibid.* This case overrules *Michigan Central R. R. Co. v. Ward*, 2 Mich., 538.

490. Carriers seeking to modify their contracts by regulations and customs of their own, must show that both parties acted in reference to them. *Moore v. Michigan Central R. R. Co.*, 3 Mich., 23.

491. Usage defining terms. Where the question between the owner of marble slabs and the carrier is whether they are to be classed as "wrought" or "unwrought" marble, the owner may show what meaning is given to those terms by custom and usage. The custom, in order to bind the carrier, need not be universal, settled or uniform among carriers or dealers, but the generally prevailing usage among them will govern. *Bancroft v. Peters*, 4 Mich., 619.

492. Liability for goods in warehouse. A railroad company are not liable as common carriers for property deposited in their warehouse, to await orders from the owner for its transportation. *Michigan Southern and Northern Indiana R. R. Co. v. Shurtz.*, 7 Mich., 515.

493. And where the company are prohibited by their charter from charging as warehousemen for storage, they are liable for property so deposited as gratuitous bailees only. *Ibid.*

494. The Michigan Central Railroad Company, under their charter, are liable only as warehousemen, and not as common carriers, for goods transported by the company, and which have arrived at their place of consignment and been deposited in the company's warehouse according to the usual course of business. *Michigan Central R. R. Co. v. Hale*, 6 Mich., 243, overruling *Michigan Central R. R. Co. v. Ward*, 2 Mich., 538, which held the company liable as carriers until the consignee had been notified of the receipt of the property, and had had a reasonable time to remove it.

495. What necessary to give lien for freight. A common carrier is bound to receive and carry goods only when offered for carriage by their owner or authorized agent; and then only upon payment of freight in advance, if required. If he obtains possession of goods wrongfully, or without the consent of the owner, express or implied, and, on demand, refuses to deliver them to the owner, such owner may bring replevin for the goods, or trover for their value. *Fitch v. Newberry*, 1 Doug., 1.

496. To justify a lien upon goods for their freight, the relation of debtor and creditor must exist between their owner and the carrier, so that an action at law might be maintained for the payment of the debt for which the lien is claimed. *Ibid.*

497. Accordingly where plaintiff had shipped goods by carriers under a special contract, and during their transit they came into the possession of other carriers without his assent, and were delivered to the defendants, who were warehousemen, and who advanced charges thereon in ignorance of the manner in which the last mentioned carriers had come to possession, it was held that the defendants had no lien on the goods for their advances and charges, and plaintiff was entitled to the possession of the goods without payment thereof. *Ibid.*

498. Construction of dray ticket. The agent of the O. & P. Railroad Co., on receipt of goods to be forwarded, gave a dray ticket, signed by himself, in the following form: "Pittsburgh, Nov. 1, 1864. To O. & P. R. R. Rec'd of F. Bros, in good order, [certain goods described] for M. I. M. & Co., Detroit. To Mansfield." A shipping bill was also given at the same time, specifying Mansfield as the place for delivery of the goods. Held, that this dray ticket, standing by itself, was not evidence of an obligation on the part of the railroad company to convey the goods to Detroit, but, under the circumstances, evidenced only an obligation to keep the goods safely, and re-deliver them or account for their value. *Fleming v. Mills*, 5 Mich., 420.

499. Departure from contract. Where a transportation company undertook to forward goods from New York to Detroit, "by sail on the lake," all dangers of the lake, &c., to be at the risk of the owner, it was held that the contract was restrictive as to the *mode* of transportation; and the company having departed from it, by shipping the goods by steam instead of by sail, and the goods having been lost on the lake, the company were liable to the owners for their value. *Merrick v. Webster*, 3 Mich., 268.

500. Recoupment of damages from freight. Where suit is brought for the recovery of freight, the defendant may recoup by showing damage to the property while being carried. But if he does so, and his damages exceed the amount of the freight, he cannot have judgment against the plaintiff for the balance. *Ward v. Fellers*, 3 Mich., 281.

501. Where one replevied his goods from a carrier who claimed the right to retain them until the freight was paid, it was held competent for plaintiff to prove damages to them in their transit, and thus reduce the amount of freight actually due, or to show that nothing was due. *Bancroft v. Peters*, 4 Mich., 619.

CARRIERS OF PERSONS.

502. Suit against: Payment of fare. In declaring against a common carrier of passengers for a refusal to carry, it is necessary to aver that the plaintiff offered, or was ready and willing, to pay the fare. *Day v. Owen*, 5 Mich., 520.

503. Carriers' rules as to accommodation. The right *to be carried* by a common carrier of passengers, is a right superior to the rules and regulations of the conveyance, and it cannot be affected by them; but the *accommodation of passengers*, while being transported, is subject to such rules and regulations as the carrier may think proper to make, provided they be reasonable. *Ibid.*

504. Such rules and regulations must have for their object the accommodation of passengers generally; and they must be of a permanent nature, and not made for a particular occasion or emergency. *Ibid.*

505. It is sufficient in pleading to state the rule or regulation; that plaintiff comes within it, and aver its reasonableness. The facts upon which the party relies to establish its reasonableness, need not be spread upon the record. *Ibid.*

506. Action against a common carrier of passengers by steamboat for refusing plaintiff a cabin passage Notice of defense that, by the regulations and established course of business of the boat, persons of plaintiff's race are not allowed the use of the cabin as passengers; which regulation and course of business are averred to be reasonable. Demurrer to the notice. Held, that the reasonableness of such a regulation was a mixed question of law and fact, to be found by the jury on the trial, under the instructions of the Court; and could not be determined on demurrer. *Ibid.*

507. Suit for lost baggage. The plaintiff, intending to take passage on the steamboat of defendants, deposited his trunk on board in the usual place for baggage, but without putting it in charge of any person, or notifying any one employed on the boat of such deposit, or of his intention to take passage; and while temporarily absent from the boat, she started on her trip, and he was left. The trunk could not afterwards be found. Held, that there was not a constructive delivery and acceptance of the trunk as the baggage of a passenger, by which the defendants could be held chargeable for its loss. *Wright v. Caldwell*, 3 Mich., 51.

508. The declaration against the carrier must aver a consideration paid, or agreed to be paid, for the transportation of the trunk and its contents; and the averment must be supported by proof. *Ibid.*

CERTIORARI.

1. At the Common Law.

509. When it lies. Proceedings were had in the County Court under the Bastardy Act, which were removed to the Supreme Court by writ of certiorari. On motion being made to dismiss the writ, on the ground that, by the statute, the judgments of the County Court might be removed to the Circuit Court by certiorari, it was held that the statute did not apply to this special proceeding; and there being no other remedy, a certiorari from the Supreme Court would lie at the common law. *Perkins v. Superintendents of the Poor of Lapeer County*, 1 Mich., 504. See also *Warner v. Porter*, 2 Doug., 358; *Cross v. People*, 10 Mich., 25.

510. Where proceedings under the statutes of 1838 were had before a justice, to determine whether a mill pond was unhealthy, &c., and the proceeding was only preliminary in its character, to lay the foundation of an action, and the justice did not act judicially in it, it was held that it could not be reviewed on common law certiorari. *Root v. Barnes*, 1 Mich., 37.

511. Where in an attachment case the Circuit Court allowed a new affidavit to be made and filed in the place of the original one, which was void, and the defendant moved in the Supreme Court for a mandamus to correct this action, it was held that he had mistaken his remedy, and that it should be by certiorari. *People v. Judges of Branch Circuit Court*, 1 Doug., 319.

511*a*. Certiorari will lie to review an order of the Circuit Court directing execution to issue on a transcript of a justice's judgment. *Jerome v. Williams*, 13 Mich., 521.

512. Not till after judgment given. Sixty days having expired after the making of an order by the Probate Court, without appeal being taken therefrom, the Circuit Court granted a party leave to appeal with the same effect as if it had been done seasonably. Certiorari was sued out to remove to the Supreme Court the order of the Circuit Court allowing this appeal. Held, that until after the adjudication upon the appeal by the Circuit Court, the proceedings could not be reviewed by the Supreme Court; and the writ was dismissed. *Palms v. Campau*, 11 Mich., 109.

513. The writ is not of right, but rests in the sound discretion of the Court, to be allowed or not, as may best promote the ends of justice. And the statutory provisions requiring the writ to be issued within two years, and providing for its allowance out of Court, do not take away the discretionary power of the Court. *Matter of Lantis*, 9 Mich., 324; *Farrell v. Taylor*, 12 Mich., 113.

514. Where an appeal can be had, by which jurisdictional questions can be brought up, the writ should not be allowed unless circumstances exist which show that a failure of justice will result from denying it. *Farrell v. Taylor*, 12 Mich., 113.

515. Laches in suing out. Where proceedings were had for the draining of swamps, &c., under the act of 1857, and the report of the commissioners was confirmed by the Circuit Court, and eleven months thereafter parties who had appeared in the Circuit Court and opposed the confirmation, sued out a certiorari to remove the proceedings to the Supreme Court, the writ was quashed for the laches of the parties in not suing it out sooner. *Matter of Lantis*, 9 Mich., 324.

516. Laches in moving to dismiss. An order of the Probate Court requiring an administrator to account, having been brought into the Circuit Court by appeal, and there reversed, and the proceedings in the Circuit Court—where no issue of fact was joined—being then moved to the Supreme Court by certiorari, that Court refused to consider an objection that this was not a proper case for certiorari, made for the first time in a brief submitted by defendant in error after the hearing on the merits. *Matter of Robinson estate*, 6 Mich., 137.

517. Evidence to be returned on. The return to a common law certiorari should set out the evidence upon which the conviction or other judicial act complained of was founded. *Jackson v. People*, 9 Mich., 111.

518. But not to be weighed. The office of a certiorari is not to review questions of fact, but questions of law. And in examining into the evidence, the appellate Court does so, not to determine whether the probabilities preponderate one way or the other, but simply to determine whether the evidence is such that it will justify the finding as a legitimate inference from the facts proved, whether that inference would or would not have been drawn by the appellate Court. *Ibid.* See also *Higley v. Lant*, 3 Mich., 612; *Hyde v. Nelson*, 11 Mich., 353; *Cicotte v. Morse*, 8 Mich., 424; *Berry v. Lowe*, 10 Mich., 9.

519. But the appellate Court will review the rulings of law upon the admission or exclusion of evidence, or other rulings in the proceedings having a bearing upon the result. *Ibid.*

520 Who to return the evidence. On certiorari to the Recorder's Court of Detroit, to remove the proceedings on conviction for a violation of a city ordinance, it was held that the evidence was properly returned by the clerk of the Court. *Jackson v. People*, 9 Mich., 111.

521. Fees for return. On a certiorari to a township board in a highway case, the township clerk, under Comp. L., § 5643, is entitled to fees, and cannot be compelled to make return until the fees are paid. *People v. Township Board of Springwells*, 13 Mich., 246.

522. Misdirection. Where commissioners of highways laid out and established a road, and an appeal was taken from their decision, which affirmed what the commissioners had done, a certiorari sued out for the purpose of reviewing the decision of the township board, directed to the *commissioners*, instead of to the township board, was dismissed for the misdirection. *Goodrich v. Commissioners of Highways of Lima*, 1 Mich., 385. And see *French v. Highway Commissioners of Springwells*, 12 Mich., 267.

2. To County Courts by Statute.

523. Where a cause was removed from the County Court to the Circuit Court by certiorari, it was held that neither the Circuit Court, nor the Supreme Court on writ of error, could review the case on conflicting testimony, but for errors of law only. *Higley v. Lant*, 3 Mich., 612. See *Herring v. Hock*, 1 Mich., 501, and the criticism thereon in *Berry v. Lowe*, 10 Mich., 9.

524. Where the return did not show that the whole of the testimony was returned, it was held that it was to be presumed that there was evidence in the Court below to sustain the finding. *Snow v. Perkins*, 2 Mich., 238.

525. The case having been brought into the County Court by certiorari to a justice, and afterwards removed by certiorari to the Supreme Court, it was held that the plaintiff in error could not assign in the Supreme Court errors not pointed out in the Court below, and which might perhaps have been there obviated. *Lee v. Hardgrave*, 3 Mich., 77.

526. A judgment in the County Court rendered upon proofs and a submission of the cause, was a final judgment, though the judge speak of it in his return to the certiorari as a nonsuit. *Ibid.*

527. An order dismissing an appeal was such a judgment as might be reviewed by the Circuit Court on certiorari, under the act of 1849. *People v. Judge of Wayne County Court*, 1 Mich., 359.

528. Under said act of 1849 the Circuit Court, in its discretion, on reversing a judgment of the County Court, might award a new trial. *Herring v. Hock*, 1 Mich., 501.

3. To Justices Courts by Statute.

529. In special proceedings. The general statute allowing this writ does not apply to the case of a judgment rendered by a justice in a summary proceeding by complaint, under village by-laws, for neglect to perform highway labor. *Warner v. Porter*, 2 Doug., 358.

530. Where appeal is given. Nor to a case under the Prohibitory Liquor Law, where an appeal is the remedy given. *People v. Farwell*, 4 Mich., 556.

531. Papers to be filed before writ issues. Before the writ issues the affidavit to procure the allowance thereof, and the allowance of the same indorsed thereon, must be filed with the clerk of the Circuit Court; and if the writ is issued before such affidavit and allowance are filed, the cause will be dismissed for want of jurisdiction. *People v. Judges of Cass Circuit Court*, 2 Doug., 116. See *Comp. L.*, §3874.

532. Service of the writ on Sunday is void under the statute prohibiting labor, &c., on that day. Comp. L., Ch. 44. *Anderson v. Birce*, 3 Mich., 280.

533. Assignments of error. In an affidavit for a certiorari, errors were alleged: 1st, That the justice erred in refusing to dismiss the cause for defective service of process. 2d, That the Court erred in rendering judgment in favor of plaintiff against defendant. 3d, That the judgment should have been rendered in favor of defendant. Held, that the second and third allegations of error were not sufficiently specific to raise any question on the merits, and must be understood as referring only to the decision of the justice on the motion to dismiss. *Fowler v. Detroit and Milwaukee Railway Co.*, 7 Mich., 79.

534. An assignment of error, that there was no evidence to sustain the verdict and judgment, is too general to be noticed. [MANNING, J.] *Welch v. Bagg*, 12 Mich., 41.

535. Presumption in favor of judgment. It will be presumed that there was evidence to sustain the finding though none appears, unless the return expressly shows that the whole of the testimony in the case is returned. *Gaines v. Betts*, 2 Doug., 98. And see *Snow v. Perkins*, 2 Mich., 238.

536. Where the justice certified as follows: "I do certify the following to have been the evidence before me in the above entitled cause:" and the objection taken before him was that certain necessary facts had not been proved, it was held that it must be presumed that the whole evidence was returned. *Cicotte v. Morse*, 8 Mich., 424.

537. Facts not to be reviewed. On certiorari, if the error alleged is a total want of evidence to prove some fact necessary to sustain the judgment, the Circuit Court should look into the testimony to see whether there was such evidence or not. If there was, it should not weight it, or inquire into its sufficiency; but affirm the judgment. If the return shows no such evidence, and it appears that all the testimony before the justice has been returned, the judgment should be reversed on the ground that the justice erred, in law, in rendering the judgment he did without such evidence. *Berry v. Lowe*, 10 Mich., 9. See also *Gaines v. Betts*, 2 Doug., 98; *Higley v. Lant*, 3 Mich., 612; *Cicotte v. Morse*, 8 Mich., 424; *Hyde v. Nelson*, 11 Mich., 353; *Welch v. Bagg*, 12 Mich., 41. The dictum to the contrary in *Elliott v. Whitmore*, 5 Mich., 532, corrected, 10 Mich., 13.

538. Costs. Replevin in Justice's Court. The Court found a part of the property to be in the plaintiff, and gave him judgment therefor, with costs, and awarded a return of the remainder. On certiorari, the Circuit Court reversed the judgment as to a part of the articles awarded to the plaintiff, and gave judgment therefor to the defendant, and also rendered judgment in favor of the defendant (plaintiff in error) for his costs before the justice. Held that this judgment for costs, not being an affirmance or reversal of the justice's judgment or any part thereof, was beyond the power of the Circuit Court. *Berry v. Lowe*, 10 Mich., 9.

539. Further return in Supreme Court. Where a writ of error brings before the Supreme Court the record of the Circuit Court, in a case brought before that Court by certiorari to a justice, the Supreme Court has no power to require a further return of the justice to the certiorari. *Wight v. Warner*, 1 Doug., 384.

CIRCUIT COURT COMMISSIONERS.

540. Power to take bail. Circuit Judges have power, independent of statutory provisions, to take bail in criminal cases at chambers; and the Legislature, under §16 of art. vi. of the constitution, may confer the same power upon circuit court commissioners, even if the power to take bail was a judicial power within the meaning of §1 of the same article, conferring the judicial power of the State upon certain specified Courts. *Daniels v. People*, 6 Mich., 381. But the power is not a judicial power within the meaning of that clause. *Ibid.*

541.—to try tax titles. The provision in the tax law of 1858, which attempts to confer upon circuit court commissioners the power to adjudicate upon tax titles, is unconstitutional and void. *Waldby v. Callendar*, 8 Mich., 430.

542.—to try forcible entries, &c. The statute—*Comp. L.*, Ch. 150—empowering circuit court commissioners to entertain summary proceedings to recover possession of lands, is not unconstitutional. *Streeter v. Paton*, 7 Mich., 341.

543.—to dissolve attachments. The act conferring upon circuit court commissioners the authority to dissolve attachments—*Comp. L., p.* 1275—does not give powers beyond those which may be properly exercised by a Circuit Judge at chambers, and therefore is not unconstitutional. *Edgarton v. Hinchman*, 7 Mich., 352.

CIRCUIT JUDGES.

544. In new circuits. The terms of the Circuit Judges and Regents of the University, elected in the ninth and tenth judicial circuits, under the act of January 29, 1858 (S. L., p. 14), commenced as soon as they had been duly declared elected. *People v. Garlock*, 5 Mich., 284.

COLLISION OF VESSELS.

545. In cases of collision, the burden of proof is on the plaintiff, not only to show negligence on the part of defendant, but ordinary care on his own part. *Drew v Steamboat Chesapeake*, 2 Doug., 33.

546. A general custom of navigation, like that for vessels to pass each other to the left, may be proved by the testimony of persons skilled in navigation. *Ibid.*

547. Such custom is a part of the law of the land; and a departure from it occasioning collision will render the party liable, unless the other party, by reasonable effort, might have prevented it; and each party should act upon the presumption that the other will adhere to the custom. *Ibid.*

COMITY BETWEEN STATES.

548. A party to a suit in another state cannot be committed in this State, for refusing to give his evidence under commission. The statute—*Comp. L.*, §4295—applies to general witnesses only. *Matter of Adams*, 7 Mich., 452. [The decision was before parties were made witnesses generally in this State].

549. A foreign corporation will not have the aid of our Courts in enforcing a contract entered into in violation of its charter. *Orr v. Lacey*, 2 Doug., 230.

550. A suit in a court of a sister state, or in one of the Federal Courts, previously commenced, will not be enjoined by the Court of Chancery. *Carroll v. Farmers and Mechanics' Bank*, Har., Ch. 197.

COMMISSIONERS OF INTERNAL IMPROVEMENT.

551. Control of streets. The Commissioners of Internal Improvement had no right, under the general powers conferred upon them, to appropriate a portion of a street in the city of Detroit for the purpose of the erection of offices and other buildings thereon. *Cooper v. Alden*, Har. Ch., 72.

COMMON LAW.

552. In force. The common law is in force in Michigan, except so far as it is repugnant to, or inconsistent with, our constitution and statutes. *Stout v. Keyes*, 2 Doug., 184.

553. Questions of right not clearly excepted from it must be determined by the common law, modified only by such circumstances as make it inapplicable to our local affairs. *Lorman v. Benson*, 8 Mich., 18.

COMPROMISE OF CLAIMS.

554. When valid. A bona fide claim, with a color of right, although there be in fact no right, so long as the party asserting it does not know he has no right, and acts in good faith, is sufficient to sustain a compromise. *Gates v. Shutts*, 7 Mich., 127.

555. Defendant charged complainant with intentionally burning his own mill, and claimed payment for wheat belonging to defendant which was destroyed with the mill, and complainant gave his note and mortgage for the value of the wheat. On bill filed by complainant to set aside these securities as obtained through threats, fear and duress, it is not necessary for the Court either to find that complainant burned his mill or to grant the relief asked; for the settlement must stand if there was no fraud or undue advantage taken to bring it about, and defendant had reason to believe the charge, and did not manufacture it to frighten complainant into a settlement. *Ibid.*

556. Disaffirmance for fraud. Where a creditor is induced, by the fraudulent representations of his debtor, to compromise, and receives part of his demand, he cannot, on discovery of the fraud, retain the sum paid, and sue in assumpsit for the balance; but he may retain the payment, and maintain an action on the case for damages sustained by the fraud. *Jewett v. Petit*, 4 Mich., 508.

557. Sale of compromise note. Where a party received a note from his debtor, with collateral security, agreeing that, if paid when due, the original debt should be discharged, otherwise of force; and after the compromise note became over due, sold and transferred it, with the collaterals and the original debt, it was held, that he thereby affirmed the compromise, and that the purchaser could not claim the amount of the original debt on the ground of forfeiture of the compromise agreement before he purchased. *Hale v. Holmes*, 8 Mich., 37.

558. And the collateral security being the note of the purchaser, which became due before the compromise note did, and was relied upon by the debtor to pay the compromise note; it was held that the purchase must be regarded as a payment of the compromise note by the note of the purchaser; and that the purchaser had no claim, at law or in equity, upon the original debt. *Ibid.*

559. Unaccepted offers by way of compromise, whether liberal or not, cannot affect the legal rights of parties. *Chandler v. Allison*, 10 Mich., 460.

CONDITIONS.

560. Extension. Where time has been extended for the performance of conditions, a party seeking to avail himself of the extension must aver a readiness to perform within the time as extended, and notice thereof. *Trowbridge v. Harleston*, Wal. Ch., 185.

561. Condition subsequent. A bank being indebted to the State, conveyed to the State in satisfaction of such indebtedness certain real and personal property. In the agreement for the conveyance of the property between the bank and the commissioners appointed by the State to settle with the bank, it was declared that the assignment of the property was made upon, and subject to, the express condition, that the State should indemnify and save harmless the bank from and against certain claims and liabilities therein mentioned. This was a conveyance upon condition subsequent, and the property would revert to the bank upon failure of the State to perform the condition. *Michigan State Bank v. Hastings*, 1 Doug., 225, overruling on this point, *Hammond v. Michigan State Bank*, Wal. Ch., 214.

562. There could be no breach of the condition until the bank was actually damnified, and an allegation that the State had not paid a bond and mortgage of the bank, which was one of the liabilities mentioned in the condition, but had permitted the same to be foreclosed, and the mortgaged premises to be sold at a great sacrifice, and that it had refused to pay off and satisfy the balance still due on said bond, for which the bank had been threatened with a suit, would not show such damnification. *Ibid.*

563. Treating the condition as a covenant to indemnify, the bank would not, upon an allegation of these facts as a breach of the covenant, be entitled to an equitable lien upon the property for the payment of the liabilities mentioned in the covenant. *Ibid.*

564. A Court of equity would not enforce specific performance of the covenant before the bank had been actually damnified; nor even afterwards, as this could only be done in a proceeding directly against the State, which could not be made defendant to a suit. *Ibid.*

565. Quere, whether such a condition could be treated as a covenant to indemnify. *Ibid.*

566. Acceptance of conditions. After the execution of the agreement between the bank and the commissioners, the State took possession of the property conveyed, and exercised acts of ownership over it. The Legislature subsequently passed an act, constituting certain State officers trustees on behalf of the State, to take charge of the property, empowering them to dispose of it, requiring the proceeds to be paid into the State treasury and used for the redemption of State script, and expressly sanctioning the agreement, except so much thereof as purported to bind the State to indemnify the bank, or to pay or advance money to discharge incumbrances or for any other purposes, which portions were thereby expressly rejected. *Held*, that the State had not the power to hold the property conveyed, and at the same time reject the condition upon which the conveyance was made; and that so much of the act as purported to do so was void. *Ibid.*

567. The declaration in the act that the State rejected the condition did not, in itself, constitute a breach. *Ibid.*

568. By acting upon the agreement between the bank and the commissioners, by exercising acts of ownership over the property conveyed, and also by said legislative act, the State had recognized and affirmed the act of the commissioners in making the agreement, whether the commissioners originally had power to agree to the condition therein contained or not. *Ibid.*

CONFLICT OF LAWS.

569. Foreign law presumed like ours. Where suit is brought upon a foreign contract, and no proof is made in regard to the foreign law, the Court will test the validity of the contract by the laws of this State. *Jones v. Palmer*, 1 Doug., 379. And see *High, Appellant*, 2 Doug., 515; *Crane v. Hardy*, 1 Mich., 56.

570. Interest. But the rates of interest being established by statute in this State, it is not a presumption of law that the rate in a foreign country is the same. No presumption can arise that foreign countries have adopted our local statutes. *Kermott v. Ayer*, 11 Mich., 181. See *People v. Lambert*, 5 Mich., 349.

571. Lex loci of contracts. The law of the place where a note is made payable determines the time and mode of presentment, and of proceedings on non payment; but the notice to the indorser must be according to the law of the place where the indorsement was made. *Snow v. Perkins*, 2 Mich., 238. See *Orr v. Lacey*, 2 Doug., 230; *Collins Iron Co. v. Burkham*, 10 Mich., 283.

572. Where authority was given in New York for drawing in Illinois bills of exchange payable in New York, it was held that the law of New York controlled the obligations of the persons giving such authority. *Bissell v. Lewis*, 4 Mich., 450.

573. Remedies. A law of New York, which would enable a vendor, of whom goods had been purchased fraudulently on credit, to maintain assumpsit for the price of the goods before the credit had expired, would be a law affecting the remedy only, and would not apply so as to enable the vendor to maintain a similar action in this State for the price of goods sold in New York. *Galloway v. Holmes*, 1 Doug., 330. See further as to foreign remedies, *Collins Iron Co. v. Burkham*, 10 Mich., 283.

574. Recording laws. Laws for recording chattel mortgages can have no force beyond the jurisdiction of the sovereignty enacting them. The record of a chattel mortgage in Canada is therefore no notice to the creditors of the mortgagor who shall find the property in his possession in Michigan. *Montgomery v. Wight*, 8 Mich., 143. Where, therefore, a chattel mortgage given by a resident of Canada, was properly put upon record as required by the Canadian law, but the mortgagor was left in possession of the mortgaged property and brought the same into this State, where it was taken and sold on execution against the mortgagor, it was held, that the title under the execution sale must prevail over that under the mortgage. *Ibid.*

575. The statute providing that every mortgage of goods and chattels shall be absolutely void as against the creditors of the mortgagor, unless the mortgage shall be filed in the office of the township clerk where the mortgagor resides, is void so far as relates to mortgages on enrolled vessels, because in conflict with the law of Congress relating to mortgages on such vessels. *Robinson v Rice*, 3 Mich., 235.

576. Boat and vessel laws. Proceedings under the boat and vessel law of another State, which allows non-resident creditors no opportunity of appearing and asserting their claims, can have no extra territorial force, and will not displace a prior lien existing upon a vessel under the laws of this State. *Wight v. Maxwell*, 4 Mich., 45.

CONFUSION OF GOODS.

577. Whether a party guilty of a fraudulent admixture of saw logs owned by himself with those owned by another, so that it is impossible any longer to identify his own, thereby loses all interest in them, and becomes remediless if such other person appropriates the whole mass to his own use, *quere*. *Stephenson v. Little*, 10 Mich., 433.

CONSIDERATION.

578. A seal imports a consideration; and it is not necessary either to aver or prove it where the agreement is under seal. *Dye v. Mann*, 11 Mich., 291.

579. Forbearance of suit. An agreement with defendant to forbear suit against a third person, who was plaintiff's debtor, is a good consideration for defendant's promise to pay the debt. *Rood v. Jones*, 1 Doug., 188.

580. But the creditor's agreement to forbear seizing certain property on attachment against his debtor, will not support a promise by a third person to pay the debt, if at the time the debtor had no interest in the property. *Ibid.*

581. In a suit on a note given in consideration of such forbearance, the *onus* is upon defendant to show that the debtor had, at the time, no interest in the property. *Ibid.*

582. Compromise. The compromise and settlement of an asserted claim, involved in legal controversy, be it never so doubtful, constitutes a sufficient consideration for the settlement, and for any obligations given by one party to the other in consummation of it. *Van*

Dyke v. Davis, 2 Mich., 144. And see *Weed v. Terry*, Wal. Ch., 501; *same case*, 2 Doug., 344; *Gates v. Shutts*, 7 Mich., 127; *Hale v. Holmes*, 8 Mich., 37.

583. But where a timid and ignorant man was induced, by threats of a prosecution for slander, to assign a mortgage to another, the assignment was held to be without consideration, and a reassignment was decreed. *Tate v. Whitney*, Har. Ch., 145.

584. Lost goods found by two jointly. While plaintiff's tug boat was towing defendant's raft in St. Clair river, the tow-line caught and raised from the river an anchor and chain, which were secured by defendant and brought upon the raft. Held, that the parties were joint finders of the property, and that the interest of the plaintiff was a sufficient consideration for the agreement of the defendant to sell it and divide the proceeds. *Cummings v. Stone*, 13 Mich., 70.

585. Stock in educational institutions. An incoporated educational institution, upon the strength of subscriptions to its fund, erected buildings and expended a large sum in furtherance of the objects of its contributors; after which a subscriber gave his note for his subscription, and received therefor a certificate, entitling him, his heirs and assigns, to an equal amount of "stock" in the institution, and also to the free tuition forever of one student therein. *Held*, that there was a sufficient consideration for the note. *Wesleyan Seminary v. Fisher*, 4 Mich., 515. See as to subscriptions to such institutions generally, *Underwood v. Waldron*, 12 Mich., 73.

586. Several considerations. If one of several considerations, which are the ground of a promise, is only frivolous and insufficient, but not illegal, and the others are good and sufficient, the former shall be disregarded, and the latter will sustain the promise. *Wesleyan Seminary v. Fisher*, 4 Mich., 515.

587. Insufficient consideration. An agreement to pay the assignor's funeral expenses, was held insufficient to support a transfer of property to the amount of over $1,000, as against one to whom the assignor owed a debt payable out of such property as he might die the owner of. *Cicotte v. Gagnier*, 2 Mich., 381.

588. Guaranty. It is not essential to the validity of a guaranty that the consideration should be expressed therein; but the actual consideration being averred in the declaration, it may be proved by parol, notwithstanding the guaranty is expressed to be "for value received." *Jones v. Palmer*, 1 Doug., 379.

CONSTITUTIONAL LAW.

1. Questions Under Constitution of the United States.

589. Legal Tender Act. The act making treasury notes a legal tender in payment of private debts, was within the legitimate powers of Congress, and is valid. *Van Husan v. Kanouse*, 13 Mich., 303.

590. Said act was not designed to confer a personal privilege upon debtors, but was based upon reasons of State policy, which, in the opinion of the law-making power, imperatively demanded that treasury notes should be made equal in legal value to coin; and parties have no right to stipulate that their agreements shall not be governed by it. And therefore, upon a note for the payment of a certain number of dollars in gold, judgment cannot be rendered for a greater sum than the amount specified and interest thereon, notwithstanding it is shown that gold commands a premium in treasury notes. *Buchegger v. Shultz*, 13 Mich., 420.

591. Commerce. The power of Congress to legislate on the liability of common carriers within the State, discussed. *American Transportation Co. v. Moore*, 5 Mich., 368.

592. Insolvent laws. Defendant, a citizen of New York, made a note in June, 1858, payable to the order of other citizens at a bank in that State, four months after date. Before maturity the note was indorsed, for a valuable consideration, to the plaintiffs, a Massachusetts corporation. In 1859, the defendant, still residing in New York, was discharged under the insolvent laws of that State. Whether this discharge is a bar to a suit brought on the note in Michigan by the indorsees, *quere*. *Brighton Market Bank v. Merrick*, 11 Mich., 405.

593. Stamp act: curing defective stamping. Where a statute makes a contract void for want of compliance with the requirements of the stamp law, the right to avoid it for this defect is not *property* which is protected by constitutional provisions; and Congress has full power by a subsequent act to waive the penal consequences, and make the contract valid on the proper stamp being affixed. *Gibson v. Hibbard*, 13 Mich., 214.

594. Retrospective Laws. There is nothing in the National Constitution forbidding Congress from passing retrospective statutes, except when they are of the class technically known as *ex post facto;* and Congress may therefore pass them, even though private rights are affected thereby, unless they are invalid for some other reason than their retrospective character. *Ibid.*

595. Obligation of Contracts. The charter of a banking corporation is a contract; and if it contain no reservation of a power to repeal, its repeal is a violation of the constitution of the United States. *Michigan State Bank v. Hastings*, 1 Doug., 225.

596. The statute requiring a new promise to be in writing, in order to revive a debt barred by the statute of limitations, does not violate the obligation of contracts. *Joy v. Thompson*, 1 Doug., 373.

597. The provision in the act of 1841, prohibiting the sale of property on execution, unless it would bring two-thirds its value as appraised, was unconstitutional and void as to pre-existing contracts. *Willard v. Longstreet*, 2 Doug., 172.

598. A law increasing exemptions from execution, affects the remedy only, and is not unconstitutional as applied to pre-existing debts. *Rockwell v. Hubbell's Adm'rs*, 2 Doug., 197.

599. A judgment is not a contract in the constitutional sense. *Crane v. Hardy*, 1 Mich., 56.

600. The act of 1843—Comp. L., § 4614—inhibiting actions of ejectment by mortgagees before foreclosure, is unconstitutional and void as to mortgages previously executed. It does not affect the remedy merely, but takes away the right to the rents and profits, which constitute a part of the mortgage security. *Mundy v. Monroe*, 1 Mich., 68. And see *Stevens v. Brown*, Wal. Ch., 41; *Blackwood v. Van Vleet*, 11 Mich., 252.

601. The law allowing a certain time for redemption after foreclosure of a mortgage under the power of sale, is a part of the contract; and a legislative act shortening the time, is unconstitutional as to mortgages in existence at the time the act is passed. *Cargill v. Power*, 1 Mich., 369.

602. A law passed in pursuance of the police power of the State, is not unconstitutional because operating to prevent the performance of a contract previously made. *People v. Hawley*, 3 Mich., 330.

603. An act subsequent to the charter of a corporation, and not assented to by it, which subjects the corporation to a total forfeiture for that which under the charter was cause for partial forfeiture only, is unconstitutional. *Per two of the Judges, People v. Jackson and Michigan Plank Road Co.*, 9 Mich., 285.

604. So also if it import a new and additional term into the charter, and impose a forfeiture of the franchise for a violation thereof. *Ibid.*

2. Questions Under the Constitution of the State.

605. General principle. To authorize a Court to declare a statute unconstitutional, it should be able to point out the discrepancy between the statute and the constitution, and the infraction should be clear and free from reasonable doubt. *Tyler v. People*, 8 Mich., 320; *Scott v. Smart's Executors*, 1 Mich., 295; *People v. Gallagher*, 4 Mich., 244;

Sears v. Cottrell, 5 Mich., 251; *People v. Blodgett*, 13 Mich., 127; *People v. Mahaney*, 13 Mich., 481.

606. A statute cannot be declared void on the ground of its violating fundamental principles of republican government, when it does not come in conflict with constitutional provisions. *People v. Mahaney*, 13 Mich., 481; *People v. Gallagher*, 4 Mich., 244. But there is no such violation in the case of the Detroit Metropolitan Police Law. *People v. Mahaney*, 13 Mich., 481.

607. In a case of doubt, every possible presumption, not clearly inconsistent with the language and the subject matter, is to be made in favor of the constitutionality of State legislation. *Sears v. Cottrell*, 5 Mich., 251.

608. Delegating legislative power. The power of enacting general laws cannot be delegated by the legislature, even to the people. *People v. Collins*, 3 Mich., 343.

609. The Prohibitory Liquor Law of 1853 provided for its submission to a vote of the electors of the State, to be taken in June of that year. If approved by a majority, the law was to take effect on the first of December following; but if not, it was to become a law from and after the first day of March, 1870. A majority of the vote cast was in favor of its adoption. Whether this submission of the question to the people was to be regarded as a delegation of legislative power, and the law inoperative in consequence, *quere. Ibid.*

610. Rules of construction. A provision of the constitution contravening the common law is to be strictly construed. This principle applied to the statutes relative to the rights of married women in property. *Brown v. Fifield*, 4 Mich., 322.

611. That a law unconstitutional in some of its provisions may be valid as to the remainder, see *Smith v. Village of Adrian*, 1 Mich., 495; *Ames v. Port Huron Log Driving and Booming Co.*, 6 Mich., 266, and 11 Mich., 139; *People v. Mahaney*, 13 Mich., 481.

612. Grand Jury. Keeping a house of ill-fame was a criminal offense within the meaning of the clause in the State constitution of 1835, which declared that "No person should be held to answer for a criminal offense, unless on presentment of a grand jury, except," &c. *Slaughter v People*, 2 Doug., 334.

613. Jury trial. A person charged in the Recorder's Court of Detroit with an offense against the general laws of the State, cannot waive his right to a trial by jury. *People v. Smith*, 9 Mich., 193.

614. Confronting witnesses. A certificate of marriage, signed only by the minister or officiating officer, or the record thereof, cannot avail as evidence of the marriage in criminal proceedings, where the defendant is entitled to be confronted with the witnesses against him. *People v. Lambert*, 5 Mich., 349.

615. Religious belief of witnesses. Under the constitution and statutes of the State, a party has no right to question a witness with respect to the belief of the latter in a Supreme Being, or to former statements in reference to such belief. And if such questions are put and answered, the witness cannot be impeached by proof of former inconsistent statements which he denies having made. *People v. Jenness*, 5 Mich., 305.

616. Due process of law. A statute which merely gives a new remedy, where none existed before, is not objectionable as depriving a party of vested rights. *Whipple v. Farrar*, 3 Mich., 436.

617. The "search and seizure clause" in the Prohibitory Liquor Law of 1855, gave no opportunity to the party accused to defend his property; required no notice to him, and provided no means by which he was to be informed when, where and before whom the search warrant was to be returned. It was therefore unconstitutional. *Hibbard v. People*, 4 Mich., 125.

618. The joint debtor act, authorizing judgment in form to be entered against all, though only one has been served with process, is not unconstitutional. *Brooks v. McIntyre*, 4 Mich., 316.

619. Nor is the provision in the Justices Act of 1855—Comp. L. § 3866—authorizing the Circuit Court, on rendering judgment against an appellant, to render it against the surety in the appeal also. *Chappee v. Thomas*, 5 Mich., 53.

620. The provision in the tax law of 1853, that "In case any person shall refuse or neglect to pay the tax imposed on him, the treasurer shall levy the same by distress and sale of the goods and chattels of said person, or of any goods and chattels in his possession," "and no claim of property to be made thereto by any other person shall be available to prevent a sale," but giving the owner of any property which might be thus seized and sold to pay the tax of another, a remedy against the person taxed—held not unconstitutional. *Sears v. Cottrell*, 5 Mich., 251.

621. The words "due process of law," as used in § 32, Art. vi. of the constitution, mean *the law of the land;* by which is to be understood laws which are general in their operation, and not special acts of legislation passed to affect the rights of particular individuals against their will, and in a way in which the same rights of other persons are not affected by existing laws. *Ibid.* See this case commented on in 8 Mich., 297, 333, and also in the two cases next referred to.

622. The provision in the constitution that "No person shall be deprived of life, liberty or property without due process of law," as applied to proceedings of a judicial character, was intended to secure to the citizen the right to a trial, according to the forms of law, of the questions of his liability and responsibility before his person or his property shall be condemned. *Parsons v. Russell*, 11 Mich., 113; *Ames v. Port Huron Log Driving and Booming Co.*, 11 Mich., 139.

623. The trial must be by an impartial tribunal, and judgment must precede the deprivation of property. *Ibid.*

624. Under the Boat and Vessel Law—Comp. L., ch. 149—a vessel might be seized and sold upon the mere assertion of a debt or demand, without any proof to substantiate the claim being made before a judicial tribunal, and without any judgment or decree of any such tribunal allowing the sale. It is threfore in conflict with the provision of the constitution above quoted, and void. *Parsons v. Russell*, 11 Mich., 113.

625. The statute of 1855 for the forming of rafting companies—Comp. L., Ch. 66—in so far as it undertakes to authorize the companies formed under it, without any necessity arising from the obstruction of their own business, to assume the control and management of the logs of unconsenting parties which are being floated on public waters, and to enforce compensation against the logs for thus controlling and managing them, is unconstitutional.

(*a.*) It allows persons thus organizing to assume a police power over the waters used, and thus to exercise a public office without either an election or any appointment.

(*b.*) And it deprives persons of their property without due process of law, since under the statute the corporation and its agents must of necessity determine when the emergency has arisen which justifies assuming control, and they must also assess their own charges, and sell the property to pay them. *Ames v. Port Huron Log Driving and Booming Co.*, 11 Mich., 139.

626. Tax deeds evidence of title. It is competent for the Legislature to make a tax deed prima facie evidence of the regularity of the proceedings, and of title in the purchaser. *Groesbeck v. Seeley*, 13 Mich. 329.

627. The provision in the tax law of 1858, that a tax deed two years recorded shall be conclusive, fell with the clause which authorized proceedings before a circuit court commissioner to test the validity of tax titles. (*Waldby v. Callendar*, 8 Mich., 430.) *Quinlon v. Rogers*, 12 Mich., 168. See post 637, 638.

628. Uniform taxation. Sec. 11, Art xiv. of the Constitution, requiring the legislature to provide an uniform system of taxation, was not operative until some new rule in conformity with such requirement was provided by the legislature: and it did not therefore affect assessments made before the establishment of the new rule contemplated thereby. *Williams v. Mayor, &c., of Detroit*, 2 Mich., 560.

629. The provisions in the Detroit city charter, authorizing the common council to provide funds for defraying the expenses of paving streets, by assessment upon the owners and occupants of adjoining lots, held constitutional. *Ibid.*

630. The amended charter provides that the common council may cause the streets to be graded and paved, and assess the whole expense of such grading and paving in front of any particular lot, to the center of the street, upon such lot, and makes such assessment a lien upon the premises until paid, and also a personal charge against the owner, and authorizes a warrant for distress and sale of his goods for the same. Whether this provision is constitutional and valid, *quere. Woodbridge v. City of Detroit*, 8 Mich., 274.

631. Taxation of cities by state agencies. There is nothing in the maximum that "taxation and representation go together," which can preclude the State legislature from establishing in a city a metropolitan police board, with power to estimate the police expenses, and compelling the city authorities to raise by taxation the amount so estimated. Every city is represented in the State legislature ; and it is for that body to determine how much power shall be conferred by the municipal charters which it grants. *People v. Mahaney*, 13 Mich., 481.

632. Restrictions upon municipal taxation. A law authorizing municipal taxation for police expenses, to the extent only of the actual estimated expenses, imposes *restriction* upon taxation within the meaning of §13, art. xv. of the constitution. *Ibid.*

633. Stating object of tax. An act which provides for levying a tax to meet the expense of the police system of a city, as estimated by the police board, sufficiently states the tax and the object to which it is to be applied, within §14 of art. xiv. of the constitution. *Ibid.*

634. Remitting taxes. The act of Feb. 12, 1853, authorizing the commissioners for the construction of the St. Mary's Falls Ship Canal, to stipulate on behalf of the State, in the contract for such construction, that any taxes to be assessed on the lands donated for that purpose should be remitted to the contractors for a period of five years, except as to any portion of such lands sooner sold, and the contracts made by the commissioners in pursuance of such act, are constitutional. *People v. Auditor-General*, 7 Mich., 84.

635. Limitation laws. The legislature has general power to pass limitation laws, prescribing the time within which parties shall assert their rights by suit; but this power is not so unlimited as to enable it, under the form of a limitation law, to take away all remedy. *Price v. Hopkin*, 13 Mich., 318.

636. A legislative act retrospective in its operation, and cutting off all remedy for the lapse of time occurring before it became a law, would violate the constitutional provision against depriving a person of property without due process of law; and would therefore be void. *Ibid.*

637. The statute of 1858 (S. L., p. 192, §135), which undertakes to make deeds given by the Auditor-General of lands bid off by the State and remaining undisposed of for five years, conclusive evidence of an absolute title in fee simple in the grantee, even against the original owner who has remained in undisturbed possession of the lands, is not valid as an act of limitation. *Groesbeck v. Seeley*, 13 Mich., 329.

638. One who is in the actual or constructive possession of property cannot be compelled to take measures against an opposing claimant; and a statute depriving him of his rights for a failure to do so is in no sense a limitation law, but an unlawful confiscation. *Ibid.*

639. Elections: presence of voters at their places of residence. The provision in the State constitution (Art. vii., §1.), that "No citizen or inhabitant shall be an elector, or entitled to vote at any election, unless he has resided in the township or ward in which he offers to vote ten days next preceding such election," was designed and has the effect to require that each elector shall cast his ballot in the township or ward of his residence. And the Military Suffrage Bill of February 5, 1864 (S. L., p. 40), which authorized polls to be opened and ballots cast out of the State, was unconstitutional, as in conflict with this provision. *People v. Blodgett*, 13 Mich., 127.

640. Election of members of legislature. Each house is the sole judge of the election and qualification of its members (Art iv. §9); and an act cannot be declared invalid on the ground that a portion of the majority voting in its favor in one house were erroneously decided by that house to be elected, and that excluding their votes the act was not adopted by the proper majority. *People v. Mahaney*, 13 Mich., 481.

641. Title of legislative act. The Detroit Metropolitan Police Act (S. L., 1865, p. 99) has for its single object the establishment of a police government for that city; and this object is fairly indicated by its title; and it is not, therefore, in conflict with §20 of Art. iv. of the constitution. *Ibid.*

642. Amendatory statutes. A statute having amendatory effect by implication, and repealing inconsistent acts, is not in conflict with §25 art. 4 of the Constitution, because not re.enacting and publishing at length the acts so altered and amended by implication. *Ibid.*

643. Appropriations for educational purposes. The act of 1857 setting apart seventy-five per cent. of the proceeds of swamp lands for the primary school fund, does not constitute such an appropriation of the *lands* to educational purposes as to place them, under

§2 Art. xiii. of the constitution, beyond legislative control. *People v. Auditor-General*, 12 Mich., 171.

644. The subsequent acts, reducing the proportion thus set apart, and appropriating lands to the construction of roads, were therefore not invalid. *Ibid.*

645. Adjusting claims against counties. The provision of the Constitution (Art. x. §10) that "The board of supervisors, or, in the county of Wayne, the board of county auditors, shall have the exclusive power to prescribe and fix the compensation for all services rendered for, and to adjust all claims against, their respective counties, and the sum so fixed or defined shall be subject to no appeal," does not embrace those cases where charges are laid upon counties by law simply as a fair way of apportioning the public expenses, and where no benefit accrues to them in their corporate capacity. *People v. Auditors of Wayne*, 13 Mich., 233.

646. Where the statute has, in such cases, pointed out any other mode of adjusting or regulating compensation, than by the county boards, the latter have no power of review, but must allow and pay the demands as thus adjusted or regulated. *Ibid.*

647. It is competent for the legislature to provide, as they have done (Laws of 1863, p. 332), that the salary of the clerk of the Police Court of Detroit shall be prescribed by the common council of Detroit, notwithstanding it is payable by the county of Wayne; and the board of county auditors of Wayne have no power to reduce the salary after the common council has fixed it. *Ibid.* See supra, 431, 432.

648. Laying out roads. Sec. 2, Art xviii. of the Constitution provides that when private property is taken for the use and benefit of the public, the necessity of using such property, &c., and the just compensation to be made therefor, except, &c., shall be ascertained by a jury. As the laws then in force relative to laying out roads were inconsistent with this provision, it was held that, until new laws were passed there was no authority for laying out roads. *People v. Kimball*, 4 Mich., 95.

649. Divorce. The legislature being prohibited from granting divorces—Const. Art. iv., §26—it was held that a legislative enactment authorizing a court to grant a divorce for a cause not sufficient by the general laws, was void, as conflicting with this provision. *Teft v. Teft*, 3 Mich., 67.

650. Legislative authority to sell lands. A special law, authorizing a plank road company to mortgage its road, is not in conflict with the constitutional provision inhibiting the legislature from authorizing the sale of any real estate of any person by private or special law. *Joy v. Jackson and Michigan Plank Road Co.*, 11 Mich., 155.

651. Judicial officer removing from district. Sec. 22, Art. vi. of the constitution providing that whenever by a change in the boundaries of a township a justice of the peace shall be placed without the same, he shall be deemed to have vacated his office, it was held that it was not competent for the legislature to provide, in organizing a city from portions of two townships, that the justices of the peace previously elected in the townships, but residing within the limits of the new city, should remain in office until the expiration of the term for which they were elected. *People v. Geddes*, 3 Mich., 70.

652. Prohibiting sale of liquors. In the exercise of its police powers, a State may prohibit, under penalties, the exercise of any trade or employment which is found to be hazardous or injurious to its citizens, without providing compensation to those upon whom the prohibition operates. *People v. Hawley*, 3 Mich., 330 ; *People v. Gallagher*, 4 Mich., 244.

653. License to sell liquors. Act No. 178 of 1851, which prohibited, under a penalty, the sale or giving away of spirituous liquors by any person, until he should have given the bond therein provided for, and upon which a right of action was given to any person injured by any such sale, &c., or by or in consequence of the intoxication of any person occasioned by the liquor so sold, &c., was not void as in effect authorizing the grant of a license to sell, and thus conflicting with § 47, Art. iv. of the constitution. *Langley v. Ergensinger*, 3 Mich., 341.

654. See the question discussed, whether the authority to sell under the Prohibitory Liquor Law of 1853 was to be regarded as a license to sell. *People v. Collins*, 3 Mich., 343.

655. The permission to sell for certain purposes under the Prohibitory Liquor Law of 1855 is not in conflict with said § 47 of Art. iv *People v. Gallagher*, 4 Mich., 244.

656. Suits against municipal corporations. Under § 18, Art. vi. of the constitution, the legislature may lawfully exempt municipal corporations from the jurisdiction of justices of the peace. *Root v. Mayor, &c., of Ann Arbor*, 3 Mich., 433.

657. Process. Sec. 35 of Art. vi., which provides that "The style of all process shall be 'in the name of the people of the State of Michigan,'" applies only to process issued by Courts or judicial officers, and would not include the supervisor's warrant appended to the tax roll. *Tweed v Metcalf*, 4 Mich., 579 ; *Wisner v. Davenport*, 5 Mich., 501.

658. General banking law. So much of the General Banking Law of 1837 as purported to confer corporate rights upon the associations organized under it, was in violation of § 2, Art, xii. of the constitution of 1835, which declared that " The legislature shall pass no act of incorporation unless with the assent of at least two-thirds of each house." *Green v. Graves*, 1 Doug., 351.

659. Two-thirds majority. The word "house" in said section meant the members present, doing business—there being a quorum —and not a majority of all the members elected. *Southworth v. Palmyra and Jacksonburgh Railroad Co.*, 2 Mich., 287.

660. Pay of speaker of the House. Under §§15 and 17 of Art. iv. the Speaker of the House of Representatives cannot, as speaker, receive any compensation or mileage beyond what he receives as a representative. *People v. Whittemore*, 2 Mich., 306.

661. Imprisonment for debt. Sec. 3633 of Comp. Laws, authorizing the issuing of a warrant in an action on contract, on the ground *solely* of the non-residence of defendant, is in violation of §33 of Art. vi., forbidding imprisonment for debt, except, &c. *Chappee v. Thomas*, 5 Mich., 53.

662. Imprisonment on an execution in replevin would not fall within the prohibition. *Fuller v. Bowker*, 11 Mich., 204.

663. Judicial power. The constitution having vested the whole judicial power of the State in certain specified Courts and officers, and provided for the election of all judicial officers by the people, the legislature cannot confer any portion of such judicial power upon any officer not elective, and not so specified. And therefore the act of Feb. 14, 1853, "to provide for the discharge of certain duties required to be performed by circuit court commissioners," in so far as it undertakes to confer judicial powers upon notaries public in certain cases, is unconstitutional. *Chandler v. Nash*, 5 Mich., 409. See, also, CIRCUIT COURT COMMISSIONERS.

CONTRACTS.

664. Construction. The intention of the parties, as expressed in their contracts, is to govern in the construction of them. *Bronson v. Green*, Wal. Ch., 56. And the object of interpretation is to ascerta this intention. *Norris v. Showerman*, 2 Doug., 16.

665. The intention is to be regarded, rather than the language employed to express it. *Bird v. Hamilton*, Wal. Ch., 361.

666. Several contracts, executed by the parties at the same time, and relating to the same matter, are to be construed together. *Bronson v. Green*, Wal. Ch., 56 ; *Norris v. Hill*, 1 Mich., 202.

667. Where one writing refers to another, the intention of the parties is to be gathered from the two, construed together. *Bronson v. Green*, Wal. Ch., 56.

668. Where one contract grows out of another, to which it refers, and both are in writing, the first may be looked into to ascertain the intention of the parties in the latter, if it is not clearly expressed therein. *Ibid.*

669. The whole instrument is to be construed together; and a construction of a detached part without reference to the rest, is erroneous. *Norris v. Showerman*, Wal. Ch., 206, and 2 Doug., 16. *Bird v. Hamilton*, Wal. Ch., 361; *Paddack v. Pardee*, 1 Mich., 421.

670. An agreement by the lessee in a memorandum signed by him at the foot of the lease, constitutes a part of the lease. *Norris v. Showerman*, Wal. Ch., 206.

671. Particular words and phrases unguardedly used, when the intention of the parties is apparent from the whole instrument, and is not repugnant to any rule of law, will be controlled by it, though such words and phrases seem to indicate a different intention. *Bird v. Hamilton*, Wal. Ch., 361.

672. The situation of the parties, and the subject matter of the transaction, may be taken into consideration in construing their contract. *Paddack v. Pardee*, 1 Mich., 421; *Norris v. Showerman*, 2 Doug., 16. See *Facey v. Otis*, 11 Mich., 213.

673. Parol agreements merged. It is a general rule that a contract cannot rest partly in writing and partly in parol. When a contract is reduced to writing, all previous parol agreements relating to the same matter are merged in the written contract. *Street v. Dow*, Har. Ch., 427.

674. When parties have deliberately and understandingly executed an instrument in writing, they cannot afterwards be permitted to insist that it does not express their real intentions, but that a different thing was designed. It is conclusively presumed that their whole engagement, and the extent and manner of their undertaking, were reduced to writing; and no evidence is permitted tending to vary or contradict the terms of the contract, or to substitute a new and different contract for it. *Adair v. Adair*, 5 Mich., 204. See, also, *Schwarz v. Wendell*, Wal. Ch., 267; *Jones v. Phelps*, 5 Mich., 218.

675. And this is so, even though the parties may have mistaken the legal intent of the contract. *Holmes v. Hall*, 8 Mich., 66.

676. But where there was a want of certainty in a written instrument, and it was not clear from its terms whether the undertaking of defendants was to the plaintiffs or to third persons named, parol evidence of the circumstances attending the making of it was held admissible, not to contradict the written instrument, but to aid the Court in giving a true construction to it. *Facey v. Otis*, 11 Mich., 213. See *Rowe v. Wright*, 12 Mich., 289.

677. Assent necessary. Where defendant gave plaintiff his check for $300 for a watch worth $15, but the whole transaction was in mere frolic and banter, the one party not expecting to buy the watch nor the other to sell it, it was held that no recovery could be had upon the check, notwithstanding defendant had retained the watch, and did not offer to return it until the trial. *Keller v. Holderman*, 11 Mich., 248.

678. Ambiguous time. A promissory note, dated July 20, was by its terms payable "One year, August 15th, after date." *Held* that it was payable one year from the 15th day of August after its date. *Washington County Bank v. Jerome*, 8 Mich., 490.

679. Unnecessary seal. Where agents executing an instrument on behalf of a corporation sign their own names and affix their own seals, such seals are merely nugatory, and the instrument is to be regarded as the simple contract of the corporation. *Regents of the University v. Detroit Young Men's Society*, 12 Mich., 138. See, also, *Sweetzer v. Mead*, 5 Mich., 107.

680. Sunday contracts. A note given for the difference in the value of horses exchanged on Sunday, held void under the statutes of 1838, which prohibited "any manner of labor, business or work" on that day, except only works of necessity and charity. *Adams v. Hamell*, 2 Doug., 73.

681. A sale made on Sunday is void under the statute—Comp. L., §1574—and the vendor may, on a subsequent day, tender back the purchase price, and recover his property by replevin if it is not restored on demand. *Tucker v. Mowrey*, 12 Mich., 378.

682. Against public policy. A contract by which a tenant is induced to desert his landlord, is corrupt and void; and the person to whom the tenant has attorned cannot maintain an action upon it. *Byrne v. Beeson*, 1 Doug., 179.

683. Against positive law. A bank having authority under its charter to hold such real estate only as was required for its accomodation in relation to the convenient transaction of its business, or such as might have been bona fide mortgaged to it by way of security, or conveyed to it in satisfaction of its debts previously contracted in the course of its dealings, or purchased at sales upon judgments which might have been obtained for such debts, was held to have no right to purchase lands for the purpose of selling them again; and the Courts would not aid either party to enforce a contract for that purpose against the other. *Bank of Michigan v. Niles*, 1 Doug., 401, and Wal. Ch., 99. See, also, *Smith v. Barstow*, 2 Doug., 155; *Hurlbut v. Britain*, 2 Doug., 191; *Orr v. Lacey*, 2 Doug., 230.

684. A subsequent contract, unconnected with the illegality, and for a new consideration, is valid and will be enforced, although it may have grown out of the illegal transaction, and the party to whom the promise was made may have had a knowledge of it. *Smith v. Barstow*, 2 Doug., 155.

685. Where a contract in violation of law has been carried into effect, the law will not aid either party to undo what has been done, and to divest a title that has passed. *Bagg v. Jerome*, 7 Mich., 145.

686. A judgment in favor of a bank organized under the unconstitutional General Banking Law, cannot support a promissory note given by the defendants, in part payment of the judgment, to one who had been appointed receiver of the bank. The illegality in the original transaction affects the new note. *Comstock v. Draper*, 1 Mich., 481.

687. Conditional. A promise upon a condition to be performed by the other party, is a valid contract when the condition is performed. It is then clothed with a valid consideration which relates back to the promise, and it then becomes valid as an express promise. *People v. Taylor*, 2 Mich., 250.

688. Express and implied. Where there is an express contract none can be implied. If, therefore, a party defrauded by an express contract rescinds it, he cannot set up an implied contract and sue the other party thereon. *Galloway v. Holmes*, 1 Doug., 330.

689. As, where goods are purchased on credit by fraud, the vendor cannot, before the credit has expired, bring suit in assumpsit for goods sold. *Ibid.*

690. Fraud does not render a contract void, but only voidable at the option of the defrauded party. If he elects to affirm it, he is bound by it in all respects. If a vendor having a right to rescind the contract of sale for fraud, brings indebtitatus assumpsit for the price of the goods, he thereby affirms the contract. *Ibid.* See, also, *Jewett v. Petit*, 4 Mich., 508.

691. If the party defrauded disaffirm the contract, he must do so altogether, and as soon as the fraud is discovered. He cannot adopt the part which is for his own interest, and disaffirm as to the residue. *Jewett v. Petit*, 4 Mich., 508.

692. Rescinding for defects. Manufacturers who had agreed to make and forward to a customer fifty sets of castings, according to a pattern and size ordered, to be forwarded from time to time as finished, sent forward fifteen sets, which the purchaser alleged were defective and refused to retain. On being notified, the manufacturers offered to make good the defects without expense to the purchaser, but to this offer the purchaser made no answer, and when the balance of the castings came, without examining whether they were defective, returned the whole to the manufacturers. It was *held* that the manufacturers were entitled to a reasonable time to fulfill the contract after being notified of the defects ; and that they might recover, according to the contract price, for such of the castings forwarded as were not defective. *Davis v. Downs*, 4 Mich., 530.

693. Hiring by the day. Under an ordinary hiring by the day, the party cannot be required to prolong his service in order to complete any particular piece of work upon which he may happen to be employed. *Wyngert v. Norton*, 4 Mich., 286.

694. Agreement not to sue. Where a creditor agrees with his debtor that he will never, or not for a specified time, pursue against him any or all of the remedies which the law gives for the enforcement of a particular demand, the agreement is not collateral to the original contract of indebtment, giving merely a claim for damages in case of its breach, but it operates directly upon the original contract, and may be pleaded in bar of suit. *Robinson v. Godfrey*, 2 Mich., 408 ; *Morgan v. Butterfield*, 3 Mich., 615. For construction of a special agreement not to sue, see *Kent v. May*, 13 Mich., 38.

695. Part delivery. Although a contract for the sale and delivery of goods be entire, and the vendor deliver a part only, yet if the vendee retain such part, the vendor may recover its value in an action for goods sold and delivered. *Clark v. Moore*, 3 Mich., 55.

696. Land purchase—delivery of deed. A purchaser gave his bond and mortgage for the purchase price, and received from attorneys who were acting for both parties a receipt therefor, stating that the attorneys were to hold the same without attempting their enforcement until conveyances of the property purchased were made. It was held that the vendors had performed on their part when they had executed the conveyances, and left them with the attorneys. *VanDyke v. Davis*, 2 Mich., 144.

697. Land clearing. In a contract for clearing land, one party was to chop all the timber suitable for rail cuts into rails, and all the other timber and brush, except some trees to be left for shade, he was to cut and burn. He cut a portion of this last timber into fire wood, and sold it—no objection thereto appearing to have been made by the other party. *Held*, that the law would not imply a promise to pay for the wood so cut and sold. *Daniels v. Mosher*, 2 Mich., 183.

698. Payment in board. By the terms of a hotel lease, the rent was made payable in monthly instalments, and the lessor agreed to take one half the same " in board as the same falls due." *Held*, that it was not optional with the lessee to pay in money or board, but that he was under the same obligation to pay the board, if demanded, as the lessor to receive it. *Evans v. Norris*, 6 Mich., 369.

699. The lessee was under no obligation to call upon the lessor, and demand that boarders be sent, but the lessor was bound to call for the board within the term, and substantially as the same fell due. *Ibid.*

700. Title to property which is being manufactured. Plaintiff had a contract with a firm engaged in sawing lumber, by which they were to receive certain saw logs belonging to him, manufacture the same into lumber, ship the lumber to parties to whom the same had been contracted, receive payment therefor, and pay over a certain proportion, retaining the balance for their services ; and the contract provided that the logs and lumber were at all times to be the property of the plaintiff until he had received the amount so to be paid him. *Held*, that the logs were not subject to levy on execution against the firm. *Bassett v. Hathaway*, 6 Mich., 397.

701. Independent agreements. For a contract in which the agreements by a purchaser to take up two incumbrances were held not to be so connected that the necessity of paying a larger sum than was anticipated for one would excuse taking up the other, see *Kibbee v. Thompson*, 6 Mich., 410.

702. Transporting goods. Persons who were not common carriers made a contract to take the staves of defendant at a certain point, and deliver and pile them at a certain other point, at prices fixed upon. There was nothing in the contract to show that they were to be compensated for any risks in transporting them, and as they did not expressly assume all risks, it was held, that they were only bound to ordinary care and diligence, and could not be held to have agreed to deliver the whole quantity of staves at all events, and to be paid nothing if the staves were lost without their fault. *Shaw v. Davis*, 7 Mich., 318.

703. Alternative contract. Plaintiff made a parol contract with L. to make certain improvements on the land of the latter, for which he was to be paid in case L. returned from California, where he was going, but if L. did not return plaintiff was to have the land. L. died in California, and it was held that plaintiff had no claim against the estate, but must look to the land as his pay. *LaRoe v. Roeser*, 8 Mich., 537.

704. Contract to find property to levy on. A contract by which plaintiff undertakes to find property upon which defendant can levy to satisfy a judgment held by him, in consideration of one-third the amount collected on the judgment, is not a transfer to the plaintiff of any present interest in the judgment, and does not give him the control of its collection. *Hickey v. Baird*, 9 Mich., 32.

705. Plaintiff pointed out property to be levied upon, and the same was levied upon accordingly. Subsequently defendant discharged the judgment on receiving a conveyance of lands which proved of no value.

Plaintiff then sued, claiming to recover one-third the amount of the judgment, but it was held that he was entitled to recover only one-third what the property levied upon was worth. *Ibid.*

706. Duplicates. Where a contract is executed in duplicate, each of the duplicates is to be treated as an original. *Crane v. Partland*, 9 Mich., 493.

707. Where parties intend to make a contract in duplicate, so that each shall have in his possession the evidence of his rights and of the obligations of the other, the contract is not complete and duly executed until duplicates at least *substantially* alike are executed and delivered. *Ibid.*

708. Where one without written authority from the owner drew contracts for the sale of a parcel of land, both of which were signed by the purchaser, and one of them delivered to him, but they differed in the following particulars: that in the one delivered to the purchaser both the agent and the owner were named as parties of the first part, but it was signed by the agent alone in his own name; and in the one retained by the agent the owner alone was named as the party of the first part, and his name was signed thereto by the agent; it was held that the contract was not complete so that the purchaser could be sued on the one retained by the agent for the purchase money. *Ibid.*

709. The acceptance by the owner of the instrument retained by the agent, and the signing his own name thereto, without the assent or knowledge of the purchaser, will not make it binding upon the latter. To make an act amount to a ratification in such a case, the two instruments must be capable of ratification by the same act. *Ibid.*

710. Indemnity or payment. One member of a firm covenanted with the other to pay the debts of the firm, and save the other harmless therefrom. Such a covenant is not one of indemnity merely, but an omission to pay the creditors as their demands fell due would constitute a breach of it. *Dye v. Mann*, 10 Mich., 291. See also *Wheelock v. Rice*, 1 Doug., 267, and *Smith v. Barstow*, 2 Doug., 155.

711. An agreement given by principals to their sureties, by which, reciting that in order to save harmless their sureties, they agree to pay the demand secured within thirty days after it comes due, is not one of indemnity merely, and the sureties have a right of action upon it on the failure of their principals to make the payment. *Hall v. Nash*, 10 Mich., 303.

712. In such action the sureties may recover the amount of the demand whether they have paid it or not. *Ibid.*

713. Where such an agreement is secured by mortgage, and suit is brought to foreclose the same before payment by the sureties, *quere* whether the Court will in any case see to the application of the money by the sureties. There is no occasion to do so where it appears that subsequent to the commencement of the suit the complainants have paid the demand secured. *Ibid.*

714. One member of a co-partnership sold his interest to his co-partner and a third party, who verbally agreed "to see that all the debts of the old firm were paid, and that he, the retiring partner, should not be called upon for any of those debts." *Held* to be a mere contract of indemnity, upon which the party's remedy was at law. *Held also*, that the agreement was not within the statute of frauds, and the actual surrender of the party's interest in the firm was a sufficient consideration to support it. *Bonebright v. Pease*, 3 Mich., 318.

715. Subscriptions for public purposes. Where a subscription is made to raise a fund for educational purposes, and something is done, or some liability or duty assumed in reliance thereon, in order to carry out the object, the promise by the subscription is binding, and may be enforced, though no pecuniary advantage is to result to the promisors. *Underwood v. Waldron*, 12 Mich., 73. See also *Wesleyan Seminary v Fisher*, 4 Mich., 515.

716. But where, by its charter, a college was located at Spring Arbor, and a subscription was entered into for the purpose of erecting a college building therefor at Hillsdale, and it did not appear that it was designed as an inducement to the college to endeavor to obtain legislative authority to remove to Hillsdale, and it could not be lawfully removed without such authority, it was held that the subscription was invalid. *Underwood v. Waldron*, 12 Mich., 73.

717. Locality of contract. A bargain was made in New York for liquors which had been sent to Michigan, the purchaser to pay freight and be allowed "outage." The purchaser examined the liquors in Michigan, and took them; and it was held that the contract was to be regarded as made in, and subject to the laws of Michigan. *Myers v. Carr*, 12 Mich., 73.

718. Terminating by notice. A contract by which parties undertake to pay for the care and board of a lunatic so long as he shall remain in the asylum, and to remove him therefrom whenever his room shall be required for preferred patients, is not terminated by a notice that the parties will no longer be responsible for his care and board. To relieve themselves from liability, they must remove him from the asylum. *Wetmore v. Aldrich*, 10 Mich., 515.

CORPORATIONS.

719. Their powers. Corporations have such powers and capacities as are given to them, and none other; and every abuse of such powers is a violation of the law of their being, and a forfeiture of their franchise. *Attorney General v .Oakland County Bank,* Wal. Ch., 90; *People v. Oakland County Bank*, 1 Doug., 282. And see *Orr v. Lacey*, 2 Doug., 230; *People v. River Raisin and Lake Erie R. R. Co.*, 12 Mich., 389.

720. Location. Accordingly where a bank was located by its charter at Pontiac, and it established an agency at Detroit, where the cashier resided, and deposits were received, drafts bought and sold, bills discounted, and the bills of the bank put in circulation at such agency, it was held that the establishment of such agency was a violation of the charter. *Attorney General v. Oakland County Bank*, Wal. Ch., 90; *People v. Oakland County Bank*, 1 Doug., 282. See also *Underwood v. Waldron*, 12 Mich., 73. But it seems that a bank may lawfully have an agency to redeem its bills at a place other than that at which it is located by its charter. 1 Doug., 282.

721. Contracts in violation of the charter are void. *Orr v. Lacey*, 2 Doug., 230; *Bank of Michigan v. Niles*, 1 Doug., 401; *Hurlbut v. Britain*, 2 Doug., 191; *Smith v. Barstow*, 2 Doug., 155. Held, therefore, that where a bank on discounting a bill of exchange corruptly received greater interest than it was authorized by its charter to receive, the bill was void. *Orr v. Lacey*, 2 Doug., 230.

722. Where by its charter a corporation is confined to one kind of business, it cannot lawfully engage in enterprises foreign to that business. A railroad company whose purposes are strictly confined to the completion and maintaining of a railroad, cannot lawfully engage in banking. *People v. River Raisin and Lake Erie R. R. Co.*, 12 Mich., 389.

723. Power to purchase lands. A corporation having power to purchase and hold real estate for the purpose of their incorporation, entered into an executory contract of purchase, by which they were to make payment at any time within one hundred years, paying taxes and interest in the meantime; and no right to possession was given until payment was made. The Courts must infer, until the contrary is alleged and proved, that the purchase is for the legitimate use of the corporation. *Regents of University v. Detroit Young Men's Society*, 12 Mich., 138.

724. The seal of a corporation affixed to a written instrument, is prima facie evidence that it was affixed by proper authority; and the contrary must be shown by the objecting party. *Benedict v. Denton*, Wal. Ch., 336.

725. Appointment of agent. A corporation may appoint an agent by parol. The authority of an agent may be inferred from the adoption or recognition of his acts by the corporation, and the acts so recognized or adopted will bind the corporation. *City of Detroit v. Jackson*, 1 Doug., 106.

726. Acts of officers. A corporation is bound by the acts of its officers de facto; and it need not be shown that they were regularly elected in order to render their acts binding. *Cahill v. Kalamazoo Mutual Insurance Co.*, 2 Doug., 124.

727. Power to make by-laws. Where the charter empowers the president and directors to make by-laws, the president and a majority of the directors may make them. And an allegation that they were made by the president and directors, is supported by proof that they were made by the president and such majority. *Ibid.*

728. A by-law making the whole amount of the premium note to a mutual insurance company collectable on default in paying an assessment thereon within thirty days—the money to be paid into the treasury of the company to meet past and future losses—held a lawful by-law. *Ibid.*

729. Proof of corporation. On plea of the general issue to an action by a corporation, the corporation must prove its corporate existence as though *nul tiel corporation* were pleaded. *Farmers and Mechanics' Bank v. Troy City Bank*, 1 Doug., 457. But it is now provided by statute, that it shall not be necessary for any corporation plaintiff, created by or under any statute of this State, to prove on the trial its corporate existence, unless the defendant shall have pleaded in abatement, or given notice under his plea to the action, that plaintiff is not a corporation; and shall thereto have annexed an affidavit of the truth of the plea or notice. *Comp. L.*, § 4838; *Smith v. Village of Adrian*, 1 Mich., 495.

730. Production of the charter, and proof of acts of user under it, were sufficient to establish the corporate existence, where the charter conferred powers in presenti and unconditionally. It was not necessary to make proof of the organization under the charter. *Cahill v. Kalamazoo Mutual Insurance Co.*, 2 Doug., 124. See also *Way v. Billings*, 2 Mich., 397.

731. Written applications to an incorporated insurance company for policies, the policies issued thereon, and the official bonds of the officers of the company are admissible to prove user. And it would seem that one who effects an insurance with an incorporated company, by the terms of whose charter he, by so doing, becomes a member of the corporate body, and on receiving his policy gives a premium note in consideration therefor, payable to the company by its corporate name, is estopped from denying the corporate existence of the company in an action on the note. *Ibid.*

732. The transactions and acts of a corporation may be provéd by entries in its books. *People v. Oakland County Bank*, 1 Doug., 282.

733. Mortgage of franchises. The power of corporations, independent of statutory provisions, to mortgage their franchises considered. *Joy v. Jackson and Michigan Plank Road Co.*, 11 Mich., 155.

734. Certificate of stock promising payment. - A certificate of stock issued by a corporation in the ordinary form, except that it contained a promise on the part of the corporation to pay interest thereon until the happening of a specified event, constitutes the person to whom it is issued a stockholder and member in the company. *McLaughlin v. Detroit and Milwaukee Railway Co.*, 8 Mich., 100.

735. Power of corporation over members. The corporation cannot, by a vote of the stockholders, without the individual assent of the holder, oblige him to receive their bond instead of money for interest upon such certificate. *Ibid.*

736. Ratification of acts of officers. Such a certificate issued by the officers of the corporation is ratified by a resolution of the stockholders at a regular meeting, for the payment of interest thereon in their bonds. *Ibid.*

737. Misnomer in repealing statute. An act repealing the charter of the "Bank of Oakland County," cannot be construed to be a repeal of the charter of "The President, Directors and Company of the Oakland County Bank." It is not necessary that a repealing act should correspond exactly, in naming the corporation, with the act of incorporation which it is meant to repeal; but there must be such a correspondence as will leave no doubt of the intention of the legislature. *Prople v. Oakland County Bank*, 1 Doug., 282.

738. Forfeiture. If a corporation has forfeited its rights by misfeasance, such forfeiture must be shown by the pleadings; it is not to be presumed; the legal presumption is against it. *Attorney General v. Bank of Michigan*, Har. Ch., 315.

739. A cause of forfeiture cannot be taken advantage of collaterally, but only by a direct proceeding for that purpose. *Cahill v. Kalamazoo Mutual Insurance Co.*, 2 Doug., 124; *People v. Bank of Pontiac*, 12 Mich., 527.

740. Waiver of forfeiture. Unreasonable delay to take advantage of a forfeiture may waive it. And where in a bank charter it was provided that the same should be void unless a certain sum of money was paid in as capital stock within two years from its passage, it was held, after a delay of five years from that period, that it was too late to institute proceedings for a forfeiture for omission to comply with such provision. *People v. Oakland County Bank*, 1 Doug., 282. But see the next case.

741. Where a corporation has been guilty of such a breach of the condition of its existence or continuance as to authorize a forfeiture of its charter, it cannot legally atone for such misconduct, and avoid the forfeiture by subsequent good behavior. *People v. Bank of Pontiac*, 12 Mich., 527.

742. A bank became insolvent and suspended operations in 1840, and did not resume again until 1864. Held that the State had not, by laches, lost the right to insist upon the forfeiture. The State shows sufficient diligence, if any is required, if it institutes proceedings and claims the forfeiture within a reasonable time after a resumption of business, or an attempt to resume, by the bank. *Ibid.*

743. Forfeiture for insolvency. The statute—Comp. L., § 4854—making a year's insolvency a forfeiture, is applicable to corporations chartered before its passage. *Ibid.*

744. A failure to elect directors annually under the charter, does not, it seems, dissolve the corporation ; but the old directors continue in office until new ones are elected in their stead. *Cahill v. Kalamazoo Mutual Insurance Co.*, 2 Doug., 124.

745. Assignment by corporation. Where the directors of an insolvent bank, with the assent of a majority, though without the knowledge of some of the stockholders, assigned all the property to trustees for the payment of the corporate debts, preferring particular creditors, it was held that the assignment was valid at common law. *Town v. Bank of River Raisin*, 2 Doug., 530.

746. It seems that such an assignment does not operate, *per se*, as a dissolution of the corporation, or a surrender of its franchises ; and that the power to make it, though not conferred by charter, is incident to the general powers conferred upon banking corporations. *Ibid.*

747. Dissolution in equity. The acts providing for proceedings in chancery against corporations, and for the voluntary dissolution of corporations—Laws 1837, p. 306 ; Laws 1839, p. 94 ; Comp. Laws, Ch., 145 and 146—are not in the nature of statutes of bankruptcy applicable to corporations. *Ibid.* And see, *Attorney-General v. Bank of Michigan*, Har. Ch., 315 ; *Attorney-General v. Oakland County Bank*, Wal. Ch., 90.

748. The primary object of proceedings in chancery against failing corporations, was held not to be for the purpose of dissolving the corporation, but to protect the assets for the benefit of creditors. The dissolution of the corporation is merely incidental. *Fay v. Erie and Kalamazoo Railroad Bank*, Har. Ch., 194.

749. The jurisdiction of chancery over corporate bodies for the purpose of restraining their operations, or of winding up their concerns, is based upon and controlled by the statutes. The Court has no such jurisdiction under its general equity powers; and it will not interfere except where the case is fairly brought within the scope and object of the statute conferring this special jurisdiction. *Attorney-General v. Bank of Michigan*, Har. Ch., 315.

COSTS.

750. Depend upon the statute. Costs are not awarded by the common law, but depend entirely upon statutory provisions. Where no authority is given by statute, there can be no taxation. *Booth v. McQueen*, 1 Doug., 41.

751. When plaintiff to pay. A plaintiff who, by his declaration in the Circuit Court, claims an amount sufficient to confer jurisdiction, but only recovers a sum within the exclusive jurisdiction of a justice of the peace, must pay costs to defendant.[1] *Strong v. Daniels*, 3 Mich., 466.

752. Against body acting judicially. Application in due form having been made to highway commissioners for laying out a road, and they having made an order for laying out a part of it only, which order, on appeal, was affirmed by the township board, the Supreme Court, on quashing these orders, refused to award costs, as the township board was acting judicially on an application giving the commissioners jurisdiction. *People v. Township Board of Springwells*, 12 Mich., 434.

COUNTIES.

753. Organization of. Fractional townships as surveyed by the United States, are *townships* within the meaning of the clause in the State constitution which provides that organized counties shall not be reduced to "less than sixteen townships, as surveyed by the United States, unless the act providing therefor be submitted to and ratified by the people of the counties. *Rice v. Ruddiman*, 10 Mich., 125.

754. Officers of. A county may be created and have existence as such, notwithstanding it has no county officers. [MARTIN, CH. J.] *Carleton v. People*, 10 Mich., 250.

755. Where a new county is created by setting off for that purpose organized townships from existing counties, the supervisors of these townships are thenceforth supervisors of the new county; their powers being conferred and duties imposed by the general laws of the State, instead of by the act creating the new county. [MARTIN & MANNING, JJ.] *Ibid.*

756. It is not absolutely necessary to the existence of a county board of supervisors that there be a county clerk. If there be none, the board may appoint a person to act as its clerk. [MARTIN, CH., J.] *Ibid.*

757. Whether those persons can be *de facto* county officers who are chosen at an election not authorized by law, *quere. Ibid.*

758. Bay county. Construction of the statute authorizing its formation. *People v. Burns*, 5 Mich., 114. The question of its organization having been submitted to a vote of the people, the question whether it was ratified by the proper vote is one of fact. *Craig v. Grant*, 6 Mich., 447.

759. Liability of. A county is not liable for the acts of its board of supervisors in the exercise of their legislative power. *Larkin v. County of Saginaw*, 11 Mich., 88.

760. The action of the board in voting money and providing for the erection of a bridge at the expense of the county is legislative in its character; and though the bridge is erected under a contract with the board, and under the personal supervision of a committee of its members, the county is not liable for damages resulting to an individual by reason of defects in the plan. *Ibid.*

761. Removal of county seat. The law which provides for submitting to the electors of a county, at the township meetings, the question of the removal of the county seat — Comp. L., §§351, 352, 353—if it can be held applicable to cities at all, is incomplete in not providing for a vote of the electors of such cities as hold charter elections at a different time from the township meetings. *Attorney-General v. Supervisors of St. Clair*, 11 Mich., 63. [The statute has since been amended. Laws of 1863, p. 30].

COUNTY CLERK.

762. The deputy of the county clerk need not sign writs in the name of the clerk. Where a writ was signed " W. M., deputy clerk, in the absence of the clerk ;" it was held sufficient. *Calendar v. Olcott*, 1 Mich., 344.

COUNTY COURTS.

763. The County Courts, as they existed in 1848, had jurisdiction of actions of ejectment. *Wattles v. Warren*, 8 Mich., 77.

764. See the case of *Stewart v. Hill*, 1 Mich., 265, for a decision on various points of statutory practice in said Court. Held in the same case, that a defendant who, after arrest, applied for and obtained an adjournment, was too late to object to irregularities in the preliminary proceedings on the adjourned day.

COUNTY TREASURER.

765. Buying at tax sales. If a county treasurer having charge of sales of land for taxes, becomes a purchaser himself, the sale is a nullity; and he cannot be allowed, under the statute, for improvements made by him on the lands purchased. *Clute v. Barron*, 2 Mich., 192.

766. Oath by deputy. The oath required to be taken by the collector of taxes on returning delinquent lands, might, under the Statutes of 1838, have been administered by the deputy county treasurer in the absence of the treasurer. *Malony v. Mahar*, 1 Mich., 26; 2 Doug., 432, same case. See also, Comp. L. §379.

767. Order for specific taxes. A county clerk drew an order on the State Treasurer, payable to the order of the county treasurer, for specific tax moneys due the county. This order was indorsed over by the county treasurer to an attorney appointed by the board of supervisors to receive the money, and the attorney presented it to the Auditor-General and applied for his warrant on the State Treasurer for the amount. Held, that the order was sufficient. *People v. Auditor-General*, 9 Mich., 141.

COURTS OF THE UNITED STATES.

768. Process from. The Federal Government has authority to regulate and control the execution of process issuing from its own Courts, irrespective of the process acts of the States. *Chamberlain v. Lyell*, 3 Mich., 448.

769. The Process Act of Congress of May 19, 1828, having been made applicable to the States subsequently admitted by the act of August 1, 1842, is to be construed as adopting such laws of said States on the subject as were in force at the last mentioned date. *Gorham v. Wing*, 10 Mich., 486.

770. When territorial courts ceased. The District and Circuit Courts of the territory of Michigan remained unaffected by the organization of the State government until the offices of the Judges were abolished by Congress by the legislation to take effect on the admission of Michigan into the Union. *Scott v. Detroit Young Men's Society's Lessee*, 1 Doug., 119.

771. Transferring suits to. A citizen of another State being sued in the State Court, caused the case to be transferred to the United States Court. Plaintiff then discontinued, and brought a new suit in the State Court, joining a citizen of the State as co-defendant. Issue was joined, and the case went to trial, and the plaintiff was then allowed to discontinue as to the citizen of the State thus joined, and to proceed and take judgment as to the other. Held, that as the proceedings were a manifest fraud, with a view to deprive the defendant of his right to remove the case to the United States Court, the order allowing the discontinuance was erroneous; and the judgment was reversed. *Yawkey v. Richardson*, 9 Mich., 529.

COVENANT.

772. In replevin bond. It is competent in giving a statutory replevin bond, to add to the condition a covenant of the same tenor, and to bring action upon it in case of a breach. In such an action damages should be recovered instead of the penalty of the bond. *Prentiss v. Spalding*, 2 Doug., 84.

773. Severable covenants. When the covenants or conditions in a deed are severable, the deed may be good in part and void as to the residue. *Kirby v. Ingersoll*, Har. Ch., 172.

CRIMINAL LAW.

1. Offenses Against the Person.

774. Homicide: self-defense. The degree of force, or the means to be employed, in protecting one's person or personal liberty, must depend on circumstances. To justify a person in taking the life of another, it must appear that his safety required him to do so. *People v. Doe*, 1 Mich., 451.

775. The necessity for taking human life need not be one arising out of actual and imminent danger, in order to excuse the slayer; but he may act upon a belief, arising from appearances which give him reasonable cause for it, that the danger is actual and imminent, although he may turn out to be mistaken. His guilt must depend upon the circumstances as they appeared to him. *Pond v. People*, 8 Mich., 150.

776. Homicide in resisting an assault not made with felonious intent, is excusable where the danger to be resisted is to life, or of serious bodily harm of a permanent character, and unavoidable by other means in the power of the slayer so far as he is able to judge at the time. But he is bound, if possible, to get out of his adversary's way, and has no right to stand up and resist if he can safely retreat or escape. *Ibid.*

777.—defense of dwelling. A man assaulted in his dwelling is not obliged to retreat, but may use such means as are absolutely necessary to repel the assailant from his house, or prevent his forcible entry even to the taking of life. *Ibid.* But a mere trespass will not justify a homicide. *People v. Horton,* 4 Mich., 67.

778.—defense of servant. The same circumstances which excuse or justify homicide in defense of one's self, will excuse or justify it in defense of his servant. *Pond v. People,* 8 Mich., 150.

779.—resisting forcible felony. When a forcible felony is attempted against person or property, the person resisting the attempt is not obliged to retreat, but may pursue his adversary, if necessary, till he finds himself out of danger. But he may not properly take life if the evil may be prevented by other means then within his power. It is immaterial to the justification whether the act was a felony at the common law, or made such by statute. *Ibid.*

780.—preventing riot. Private persons may forcibly interfere to suppress a riot or resist rioters; and they may justify homicide in so doing, if they cannot otherwise suppress them, or defend themselves, their families or property. *Ibid.*

781.—mortal blow beyond State boundary. Manslaughter, committed by a mortal blow given on the River St. Clair, beyond the boundary line between the United States and the Province of Canada, and within a county in said Province, from which death ensued within the State, may be constitutionally punished (§ 5944 *of Comp. L.,*) by the Courts of this State, but is not within the jurisdiction of the United States Courts. *Tyler v. People,* 8 Mich., 320. See ADMIRALTY AND MARITIME JURISDICTION.

782.—resisting violent arrest. Where an officer, attempting to make an arrest on reasonable suspicion of felony, is asked for his authority, and says he has a warrant, but refuses to produce it, and makes no explanation whatever, but makes the arrest with circumstances of violence, and the person arrested resists and kills the officer, he is not guilty of murder in so doing. *Drennan v. People,* 10 Mich., 169.

783.—intent to murder. In a prosecution for assault with intent to murder, the actual intent to kill must be found, and that under circumstances which would make the killing murder. *Maher v. People,* 10 Mich., 212.

784.—malice. Malice aforethought is as essential an ingredient of the offense of murder as the act of killing; and the presumption of innocence applies equally to both ingredients. Hence the burden of proof as to each rests upon the prosecution. *Ibid.*

785. Where deceased had been absent from the neighborhood of the prisoner some eight or ten months preceding the alleged offense, it was held competent for the prosecution to show the state of feeling between the prisoner and deceased immediately preceding such absence. *Dillin v. People*, 8 Mich., 357.

786. Defendant being charged with the murder of his wife, evidence that before the alleged murder he had been arrested on charge of a crime committed upon her, is competent as tending to show hostile relations existing between them, which would bear upon the question of motive, and tend to prove malice. *Washburn v. People*, 10 Mich., 372.

787.—provocation. If a homicide be committed under the influence of passion, or in heat of blood, produced by an adequate or reasonable provocation, and before a reasonable time has elapsed for the blood to cool and reason to resume its habitual control, and is the result of the temporary excitement by which the control of reason was disturbed, rather than any wickedness of heart or cruelty or recklessness of disposition, the offense is manslaughter only, and not murder. *Maher v. People*, 10 Mich., 212.

788. To reduce the offense to this grade, the reason must, at the time of the act, be disturbed or obscured by passion to an extent which might render an ordinary man, of fair average disposition, liable to act rashly, or without due deliberation or reflection, and from passion rather than judgment. *Ibid.*

789. Whether the provocation was adequate or reasonable, and whether a reasonable time had elapsed for the passion to cool and reason to resume its control, are questions of fact for the jury. *Ibid.*

790. Evidence that the prisoner saw the person attacked with the prisoner's wife, under such circumstances as to induce the belief that adultery had been committed; that he followed them in hot pursuit, and on the way was informed that they had committed adultery the day before; that he followed the person into a saloon in a state of excitement, and there attacked him, is proper evidence, as tending to show that the act was committed in consequence of the passion excited by the provocation, and in a state of mind which would have given to the homicide, had death ensued, the character of manslaughter only. *Ibid.*

791. It is proper evidence, also, because the facts stated constitute a part of the *res gestae*. *Ibid.* See as to *res gestae* also, *People v. Potter*, 5 Mich., 1.

792. One who is the mere agent of the husband for the purpose of detecting his wife's adultery, cannot justify or excuse the killing of the suspected adulterer by proof of his previous adultery with the employer's wife. *People v. Horton*, 4 Mich., 67.

793.—degrees of murder. The statute does not change the common law definition of murder, but divides the offense into degrees; and where it is sought to have the jury convict of murder in the first degree, the burden of proof is upon the prosecution to show such facts, in addition to the act of killing, as will make the act murder in the first degree. *People v. Potter*, 5 Mich., 1; *People v. Scott*, 6 Mich., 287.

794. A verdict of guilty of murder generally, without specifying whether of the first or second degree, is erroneous. *Tully v. People*, 6 Mich., 273.

795. On an indictment for assault with intent to murder, it is immaterial whether the murder intended would, if consummated, have been murder of the first or second degree. *People v. Scott*, 6 Mich., 287.

796. Rape. Carnal knowledge of the person of a female over ten years of age, unaccompanied with any circumstance of force or fraud, does not constitute the crime of rape, either at common law or by statute. *Crosswell v. People*, 13 Mich., 427.

797. Where therefore a man had carnal connection with a woman over ten years of age, who was a willing participant in the act, it was held not to be a rape, notwithstanding the testimony showed that she had not at the time an intelligent understanding. *Ibid.*

798.—of child. The carnal knowledge and abuse of a female child under the age of ten years, is rape, both at common law and by statute. *People v. McDonald*, 9 Mich., 150; [*Crosswell v. People*, 13 Mich., 427.]

799. An indictment charging assault with intent to carnally know and abuse a female child under the age of ten years, charges an assault with intent to commit rape; and under it the defendant may be found guilty of a simple assault. *Ibid.*

800.—consent. A child under ten years of age has no legal capacity to give consent to carnal knowledge, and her consent does not waive the assault. *Ibid.*

801. Mingling poison with food: intent. The intent to commit an injury as a means to the accomplishment of another ultimate and main unlawful object, is not, by the existence of such ultimate design, taken out of the operation of the statute. *People v. Carmichael*, 5 Mich., 10; *People v. Adwards*, 5 Mich., 22.

802. A person who engages in the prosecution of an unlawful design against another, and uses poison to accomplish such design, which, by its natural action, produces a greater injury than he anticipated, is not, by his ignorance of the probable extent of such injury, relieved from criminal responsibility for the act. *Ibid.*

803.—injury. Wherever there is a positive physical effect produced, and the poison administered operates to derange the healthy organization of the system, temporarily or permanently, there is an injury which, whenever it is reasonably appreciable, may be regarded as within the statute. *Ibid.*

804. Exposing child: allegation of relationship, &c. An indictment under § 5741 of Comp. Laws, which provides that "If the father or mother of any child, or any other person to whom any such child shall have been confided, shall expose such child," &c., must allege either that the defendant was the father or mother of the child, or that it has been confided to him; and this allegation must be sustained by the proof. *Shannon v. People*, 5 Mich., 71.

805.—proof of custody. To sustain an allegation that the child was confided to the defendant, it is not necessary to show that it was delivered into his immediate and manual custody; if it were delivered to some other person employed by him to receive it, and upon the faith of representations made by him to the mother, inducing the belief on her part that it would be under his control and direction, it would be sufficient. *Ibid.*

806.—intent. The intent to abandon the child, on the part of the person exposing it, has no reference to the probability or improbability of relief to the child from other hands, and it is wholly independent of any intent to injure. But the exposure and the intent to abandon must both concur to complete the offense, and the exposure must be such as may subject the child to the hazard of personal injury. *Ibid.*

807.—exposure. If the child be left at such time, in such place, and under such circumstances, as would render a parent or other person of ordinary prudence and humanity *reasonably apprehensive* of personal injury to it, then the hazard may be said to exist, and it is an exposure within the statute, and if accompanied with the intent wholly to abandon, the crime is complete. But if there be no reasonable ground to fear or apprehend such injury, then the exposure does not exist. *Ibid.*

808.—who may commit the offense. Any one receiving the care and custody of the child from a parent, guardian or master, even for a temporary purpose, would come within the statute as a party to whom the child was confided. *Ibid.*

809. But one not sustaining such a relation to the child, cannot be convicted of the principal offense under said section 5741 on proof of facts showing only that he counselled, aided or abetted the commission of the offense by others. *Ibid.*

2. Offenses Against Property.

810. Larceny: out of the State. Whether the State can lawfully provide for the punishment in Michigan of persons who, having committed a larceny in a foreign country, bring the stolen property into this State, *quere*. *Morrissey v. People*, 11 Mich. 327.

811. If the statute for that purpose—Comp. L., § 5797—is valid, whether an information under it is sufficient which charges the defendant in the ordinary form with a larceny committed in this State, *quere. Ibid.*

812.—description of property. In an indictment under the statute of 1840, (p. 42, § 1), which provided for the punishment "of larceny, by stealing, of the property of another, any bank note, bank bill," &c., it was held that a description of the property stolen as bank notes or bank bills merely, was sufficient. *People v. Kent*, 1 Doug., 42. See also, *Comp. L.*, §6059.

813. The word *chattels* in such an indictment denotes property and ownership; and an allegation that bank bills were the goods and chattels of a person named, is a sufficient averment that they were his property. *Ibid.*

814.—is a felony. The statute—Comp. L., § 5954—which defines the word felony, as used in statutes, to mean an offense for which the offender on conviction shall be liable to be punished by death, or by imprisonment in the State prison, is only a legislative definition of the term as used in those provisions of the statute where neither the particular offense, nor its grade, is otherwise indicated than by the use of this term, and where, therefore, the definition became necessary, as it was not intended to be used in the common law sense. Those acts which were felonies at the common law remain such, notwithstanding this section, though the punishment may be less than here mentioned. And therefore larceny, though of property to the value of less than $25, being a felony at common law, is still a felony in this State. *Drennan v. People*, 10 Mich., 169.

815. Receiving stolen goods: aiding. The statute—Comp. L., § 5764—has enlarged the common law offense of receiving stolen property, knowing the same to be stolen, by making persons who shall aid the principal felon in the concealment of the property, equally guilty with him who receives such property. *People v. Reynolds*, 2 Mich., 422.

816. An indictment under said section, for aiding in the concealment, &c., is supported by proof of acts of the aider, which will assist the principal felon in converting it to the use of the thief, or which will aid him in preventing its recovery by the owner; and it is not necessary to prove that the property was actually hidden or secreted anywhere. *Ibid.*

817—res gestae. Where one was charged with having received goods knowing them to be stolen, and a witness testified that he was present at an interview between the prisoner and the alleged thief a few days prior to her arrest; it was held that what was said by the alleged thief at that interview about sending the goods to the house of the prisoner, where they were afterwards found, was proper evidence to show the circumstances under which she received them. *Durant v. People*, 13 Mich., 351.

818—possession not proof of guilt. Where one is charged with receiving stolen goods knowing them to be stolen, the mere possession of the goods by him, without evidence tending to show guilty knowledge, can have no tendency to establish his guilt, but must be presumed to have been innocent. *Ibid.*

819. Embezzlement by State Treasurer: description. In an information against the State Treasurer under §5771 of Comp. L., it is not necessary to set forth the particular kind of funds embezzled, or to identify them by specifying the source whence received. *People v. McKinney*, 10 Mich., 54.

820.—bill of particulars. It is not erroneous for the Court to refuse to order the prosecution to furnish a bill of particulars under the general charge contained in such an information, where it appears that a preliminary examination has been had, and the prosecuting officer states that he shall confine himself to the same charges as on such examination. *Ibid.*

821. But such order ought never to be refused where the Court can see any reason to believe the particulars necessary to inform the defendant of the particular transactions intended to be proved against him, so as to enable him to meet them. *Ibid.*

822.—evidence of receipts. The account books kept in the office of defendant during his official term, and purporting to show all his receipts and disbursements as State Treasurer, are admissible to show that the sums alleged to have been embezzled have not been credited to the State; and this notwithstanding no part of the book is in his handwriting. *Ibid.*

823. So also are his annual reports as Treasurer, printed by the State printer under his direction. *Ibid.*

824.—treasurer indictable. Said section 5771, which provides for the punishment of "any officer, clerk, or any other person employed in the treasury of this State," who shall commit any fraud or embezzlement therein, includes within the terms used the State Treasurer. *Ibid.*

825—what is the treasury. The word "treasury" as used in said section, is not to be understood in the sense of locality, as descriptive of the particular building within which the Treasurer keeps his principal office or place of official business; but moneys are to be considered as in the State treasury whenever or wherever they are in the official custody of the Treasurer, or subject to his direction and control. *Ibid.*

826. It is sufficient to allege in the information that the money charged to have been embezzled was at the time the property of the State, and in the treasury, or in the official custody or control of the Treasurer, without showing how it got there. *Ibid.*

827.—evidence of embezzlement. The omission by the Treasurer to charge himself with the receipt of moneys in the county where his office is required to be kept, or a denial of its receipt there, would be evidence to go to the jury of embezzlement in that county. *Ibid.*

828. Any act by the Treasurer, by which money should be abstracted from the treasury, or diverted from the use of the State, with intent to apply or appropriate it to his own use or benefit, would constitute embezzlement. *Ibid.*

829.—venue. As such an act might be done by the Treasurer without at any time being personally present where the money happened to be, it was held not error for the Court to charge the jury that it was not necessary that the money should have been in the county where the Treasurer's office is required to be kept, to warrant their finding that he embezzled it in that county. *Ibid.*

830.—what is a payment to the State. Where the Treasurer received from a railway company several drafts for a tax due the State, which drafts were payable at different times, it was held that the payment of each of these drafts was a payment of so much into the treasury; and it was not necessary that all should be paid before any part could be regarded as in the treasury. *Ibid.*

831. Burglary : curtilage. A barn standing eighty feet from a dwelling-house, in a yard or lane with which there was a communication from the house by a pair of bars, was held to be within the curtilage. *People v. Taylor*, 2 Mich. 250.

832.—description. Under the statute—Comp. L., § 5756—which punishes " every person who shall break and enter, in the night time, any office, shop, railroad depot or warehouse, not adjoining to or occupied with a dwelling-house, " with intent to commit a felony, an information which fails to describe the building entered as " not adjoining to or occupied with a dwelling-house," is fatally defective. *Koster v. People*, 8 Mich., 431.

833. Conspiracy, to cheat of real estate, is indictable, as well as one to cheat of personal property. *People v. Richards*, 1 Mich., 216.

834. The offense consists in the unlawful agreement, and not in the acts which follow it. *Ibid.* And see, *People v. Clark*, 10 Mich., 310 ; *Alderman v. People*, 4 Mich. 414. It is not necessary either to allege or prove any overt act was done in pursuance of the agreement. *Ibid.*.

835.—merged in felony. A conspiracy to commit a felony,

when executed, is merged in the felony; but a conspiracy to commit a misdemeanor is not merged in the misdemeanor. *People v. Richards*, 1 Mich., 216.

836.—indictment. In the indictment the agreement or combination must be set out, but the means to be used in executing the conspiracy need not be set forth unless they are a component part of the offense; as where the combination and the object to bé attained are not in themselves unlawful, but the means to be used, to effect the object, are unlawful. Where the conspiracy is to cheat an individual of his lands and goods, the indictment need not state the means by which it was to be accomplished. *Ibid.*

837. If a conspiracy be to commit an offense known as such at the common law, so that by describing it by the term by which it is generally known, the nature of the offense is clearly indicated, then it will only be necessary to use such term in describing the object of the conspiracy. *Alderman v. People*, 4 Mich., 414.

838. If there be a combination to do an act not in itself unlawful, but which it is agreed to accomplish by criminal or unlawful means, those means must be particularly set forth, and be such as constitute an offense, either at common law or by statute. *Ibid.* But if it be to do an unlawful act, the indictment must set forth the unlawful thing agreed upon, but need not specify the means to be resorted to for the purpose. *People v. Clark*, 10 Mich., 310.

839.—the pretences. Cheating and defrauding are punishable only when effected by false tokens and pretences, and the words of themselves do not import an offense. An indictment for conspiracy to cheat and defraud, must therefore set out the false tokens to be used in effecting tbe contemplated fraud. *Alderman v. People*, 4 Mich., 414.

840. But an allegation that the parties conspired "by divers false pretences, subtle means and devices, to obtain and acquire to themselves, of and from one W. a sum of money, to wit, ten dollars of the moneys of said W., and to cheat and defraud him the said W. thereof," is sufficient. *People v. Clark*, 10 Mich., 310.

841. It is not essential to the offense that the cheat designed be by means of a token, writing, or similar device, or even that the means should be of any specific character. The crime may be complete notwithstanding the conspirators leave the particular means by which the fraud is to be accomplished to be determined by circumstances. *Ibid.*

842. It is not essential that the pretences by which a fraud is accomplished be expressed in words. Falsehood when deliberately acted is the same as spoken falsehood. *Ibid.*

843. False pretences: intent. The act of procuring, by falsehood, the indorsement of a promissory note, is not, in itself, a false pretence within the statute, unless done with intent to defraud. The prosecution must therefore show something more than the falsehood and procuring the indorsement thereby, before a conviction can be had. *People v. Getchell*, 6 Mich., 496.

844. Where an intent is made the gist of an offense, that intent should be shown by such evidence as, uncontradicted, will fairly authorize it to be presumed beyond a reasonable doubt. *Ibid.*

845. Defendant was put on trial for false pretences in procuring the indorsement of the prosecutor to a promissory note, by the falsehood that a former note for the same amount, indorsed in like manner, was destroyed. Held, that evidence offered by the defendant that he was a partner of the prosecutor ; that the latter was bound by agreement to indorse for him to an amount considerably larger than the two notes, but had refused to perform the agreement, and that the money obtained on the notes was used in their business for their joint benefit, was admissible, as tending to disprove the presumption of intent to defraud. *Ibid.*

846. Attorney, neglecting to pay over. An indictment against an attorney, for collecting and receiving, in the capacity of an attorney at law, moneys belonging to the prosecutor, and neglecting to pay the same to him when demanded, &c., but not distinctly averring that the relation of attorney and client existed between the defendant and the prosecutor, is insufficient. *People v. Tryon*, 4 Mich., 665.

3. Offenses Against Public Justice.

847. Perjury : materiality. The indictment must aver that the false allegation was material to the matter in question, or it must clearly appear by the indictment to have been so from the statement alleged to be false. *People v. Collier*, 1 Mich., 137.

848. Where the indictment stated that " it became and was material to ascertain the truth of the matters hereinafter alleged to have been sworn to"—stating what the defendant swore to—the averment was held insufficient. *Ibid.*

849. But a general allegation of the materiality of the testimony is sufficient ; and it is not necessary to set forth so much of the proceedings as will show it to be material. *Hoch v. People*, 3 Mich., 552.

850. Defendant was indicted for having falsely made oath that one S. " did feloniously steal, take and carry away a rifle, of the value of fifteen dollars, of the property" of defendant. It was objected to the indictment that the matters set forth were not facts, but conclusions of law ; but the objection was held not well taken. *Ibid.*

4. Offenses Against Chastity, Morality and Decency.

851. Seduction. An act of carnal intercourse with an unmarried woman, to which her assent was obtained by a promise of marriage made at the time, and to which, without such promise, she would not have yielded, constitutes the offense of seduction under the statute. *People v. Millspaugh*, 11 Mich., 278.

852. Where a woman was seduced on a promise of marriage, and the intercourse was afterwards broken off, but was renewed again on the promise of marriage being renewed, and only in consequence of such promise, it was held that a prosecution might be commenced for the seduction at any time within one year from such last intercourse. *Ibid.*

853. Incest: indictment. An information for incest, which charges the crime to have been committed with one H; "she, the said H., being then and there the daughter" of the accused, is sufficient without also averring, in the words of the statute, that the parties were "within the degrees of consanguinity within which marriages are prohibited," &c. *People v. Hicks*, 10 Mich., 395.

854.—proof of relationship. The defendant's admission that he is the brother of the girl's mother, and his treatment as such by the family, are competent evidence. *People v. Jenness*, 5 Mich., 305.

855. Incest does not depend upon the legitimacy of the parties, or upon whether they are relatives of the whole or of the half blood. *Ibid.*

856.—proof of former acts. In case of a crime consisting of illicit sexual intercourse, which can only be committed by the concurrent acts of two persons of opposite sexes, evidence of previous familiarities and acts of intercourse is admissible, as tending to show concert, and a common design of both parties to commit the act charged, and habitually to indulge the criminal desire as opportunity might offer. *Ibid.*

857. Bigamy: proof of marriage. Where the first marriage is alleged to have taken place in another State, proof of a valid marriage according to the laws of that State must be given. And there being evidence that the law of that State on the subject is in statute form, it cannot be presumed, against the innocence of defendant, that the statute is like our own. *People v. Lambert*, 5 Mich., 349.

858. Cohabitation as man and wife, and the acknowledgment of the parties, are not sufficient evidence of the marriage in such case. *Ibid.*

859. Nor is a certificate of marriage, or the record thereof, competent in a criminal case, where the defendant is entitled to be confronted with the witnesses against him. *Ibid.*

860. Bawdy houses. Keeping a house of ill-fame was a "criminal offense" within the meaning of the constitution of 1835, which declared that "no person should be held to answer for a criminal offense unless on presentment of a grand jury, except," &c. *Slaughter v. People*, 2 Doug., 334.

861. Indictment is the appropriate remedy for this offense, both at the common law and under the statute. *Welch v. Stowell*, 2 Doug., 332.

862.—abating. The common council of Detroit, under the power given by the charter to prevent and suppress houses of ill-fame, are not authorized, by ordinance and resolution, to require the city marshal to demolish a house occupied as a house of ill-fame, and adjudged by the council to be a common nuisance. *Ibid.*

863. Neither have individuals the right to abate the nuisance by destroying the building. A nuisance is to be abated by the removal of that in which the nuisance consists; which in this case is the use to which the building is put, and not the building itself. *Ibid.*

864. Obscene publications: indictment. In an indictment for publishing a bawdy and obscene paper, it is not necessary to set forth the obscene matter on which the people rely for a conviction. *People v. Girardin*, 1 Mich., 90.

865. Lewd and lascivious cohabitation is a joint offense, of which both parties must be guilty or neither. *Delany v. People*, 10 Mich., 241.

866. And both must be joined as defendants in the same information or indictment, unless one of the parties be unknown, or since dead. *Ibid.*

867. But though both must be jointly charged, the trials may be separate; and one may be convicted and sentenced before the other is tried. *Ibid.*

4. Forgery and Counterfeiting.

868. Counterfeiting coin: indictment. An indictment for knowingly having in possession instruments adapted and designed for making counterfeit coin, to wit, Mexican dollars, with intent to use the same, need not allege that the defendant was not employed in the mint of the United States. *Harlan v. People*, 1 Doug., 207.

869.—States may punish. The power vested in Congress by the Federal Constitution to provide for the punishment of counterfeiting the current coin of the United States, is not exclusive, but may be exercised by the several States concurrently with Congress. *Ibid.*

870. An indictment for violating the statute of the State against such counterfeiting, properly charges the offense as committed against the sovereignty of the people of the State. *Ibid.*

871. Forgery, &c.: uttering. The presentation of a forged draft or order for money, to the person to whom it purports to be directed, for payment thereof, is an uttering and publishing, notwithstanding payment is refused, and the draft returned to the presenter. *People v. Brigham*, 2 Mich., 550.

872.—money order. A draft made payable to the bearer—no payee being mentioned therein—is nevertheless an order for money, within the meaning of the statute. *Ibid.*

873.—possession of bills with intent, &c. Section 5809 of Comp. L., which provides that every person who shall have in his possession a counterfeit bill, with intent to utter or pass the same, or to render the same current as true, knowing the same to be counterfeit, shall be punished, &c., embraces two distinct offenses; one, which consists in having in possession a counterfeit bill with intent to utter or pass the same as true; the other, in having it in possession, with intent to sell or otherwise dispose of it as a counterfeit bill, to be rendered current, or uttered or passed as true. *People v. Stewart*, 5 Mich., 243.

874. On the trial of an indictment for the second of those offenses, evidence of the possession by defendant of counterfeit bills on other banks is inadmissible. *Ibid.*

875. The words "as true," as used in said statute in defining the first of said offenses, refer both to "the intent to pass" and to "render the same current;" and an indictment charging the possession of such bills, "with intent to utter and pass the same," omitting the words "as true," is insufficient. *People v. Stewart*, 4 Mich., 655.

876.—indictment: setting forth instrument. The act of 1855 relating to indictments—Comp. L., § 6048—obviates the necessity of setting forth in the indictment a copy of the alleged forged paper or counterfeit bill. *Ibid.*

877.—description of genuine bills. It is not essential in an indictment for counterfeiting bank bills, to describe the genuine bills of the bank to which the forged bills are assimulated. *Ibid.*

878.—foreign bank. Under the statute—§ 5811 of Comp. L.—which provides that "the lawful existence of any bank out of this State shall be presumed upon evidence that such bank is actually engaged in the business of a bank," evidence of general reputation in the community of the existence of a bank in another State, and that its bills pass current in the business transactions of the day, is admissible as tending to show that there was *de facto* a bank "engaged in the business of a bank." *Jennings v. People*, 8 Mich., 81.

879. Being admissible, its weight is for the jury, who may be satisfied with it. *Ibid.*

880. An averment in the indictment, that the bank whose bills are counterfeited is an incorporated company, in a place and State mentioned, is equivalent to an averment that it is *established* in such State. *People v. Stewart*, 4 Mich., 655.

5. Offenses Against the Public Health.

881. Nuisance: what is. A person is not punishable criminally for maintaining a dam whereby no greater nuisance is created, and of no different character, than would have existed without it. *Beach v. People*, 11 Mich., 106.

882. On the trial of an indictment for causing a nuisance by a mill dam, the question whether the stream as dammed is as healthy to the neighborhood as it would be if the mill pond was drawn down, the river channel ditched, the water drained from the low lands, and the whole converted into a beautiful meadow, is not admissible as a test of nuisance. *Ibid.*

883.—evidence of former acquittal. On trial for nuisance by keeping up a mill dam, it is competent for defendant to show that the former owners of the mill were indicted for keeping up the same dam, tried and acquitted; and that the question litigated on the former trial was whether the dam was a nuisance or not. The acqnittal would be evidence that the dam was not a nuisance at that time, though not that it has not since become such. *Crippen v. People*, 8 Mich., 117.

884.—judgment; errors in. Verdict of guilty being rendered in such case, a judgment or order thereupon entered, that the dam be removed, and that a writ issue to the sheriff for its removal, is such a final judgment or determination as error will lie upon. *Ibid.*

885. The order of removal cannot precede, but must be exercised at the time of imposing punishment by fine or imprisonment, and form part of the same judgment; and no such punishment having been imposed, the order to remove the nuisance was erroneous. *Ibid.*

886. But the errors assigned in the case being all based on decisions of the Court preceding the judgment, the Supreme Court will look into the errors assigned, and if any of them are sustained, will reverse the judgment on that account, and order a new trial, instead of ordering an absolute reversal for the error in the judgment itself. *Ibid.*

6. Offenses Against Public Policy.

887. Illegal banking. The mere paying out of a draft in the similitude of a bank bill, without being in any way connected with, responsible for or interested in it, except as might be inferred from the single fact of paying it out, is not sufficient to establish the offense of illegal banking under § 5899 of Comp. L. *People v. Wells*, 8 Mich., 104.

888. Selling liquors. Indictment for selling whisky without license, alleging it to be spirituous liquor, sustained under R. S. 1838, p. 203, § 1. *People v. Webster*, 2 Doug., 92.

889. The penalty for selling without license, might, under the Statutes of 1846, be recovered by indictment; the penalty being $100. *People v. Hart*, 1 Mich., 467.

890.—election of penalties. Where suit was brought for the penalty, and the plaintiff declared in the form given by the statute, it was held that he could not, on the trial, be compelled to elect the penalty or penalties he would seek to recover. *Smith v. Village of Adrian*, 1 Mich., 495.

891.—sale by a partner. Where two persons as partners were keeping a recess where liquors were sold without license, it was held that the sale by one was the act of both, and might be given in evidence against the other in an action against him alone for the penalty. *Ibid.*

892.—under Statutes of 1846. To recover the penalty given by R. S. of 1846, ch. 41, § 1, it was not necessary to show that defendant assumed to act as tavern keeper or common victualler. *Ibid.*

893. In an action for such penalty, it was not necessary for the prosecution to prove that defendant had no license, or that the question of license or no license was submitted to the people in pursuance of said chapter. *Ibid.*

7. Offenses Against Election Laws.

894. Inspectors refusing to receive vote. Since the act of 1859 requiring the registration of voters, an information against inspectors of an election for refusing to administer to a person offering to vote one of the oaths prescribed by Comp. L., § 49, is fatally defective if it fails to allege that the name of the person offering to vote was duly registered. *Wattles v. People*, 13 Mich., 446.

8. Miscellaneous Matters.

895. Foreign offenses. Whether the fraudulent acts of a debtor, occurring without the State, can be made the basis of proceedings against him in this State, under the Fraudulent Debtor's Act, *quere*. *Bromley v. People*, 7 Mich., 472. See also, *ante* 781, 810, 811.

896. As a general principle the criminal laws of no nation can operate beyond its territorial limits; and to give any government the right to punish any act or transaction as a crime, it must have occurred within those limits. *People v. Tyler*, 7 Mich., 161.

897. Non-performance of official duty. Indictment for non-performance of an official act, must set forth such a state of facts as under the law imposed upon defendant the duty to perform the act. *Wattles v. People*, 13 Mich., 446.

898. Arrest for felony. A constable who has knowledge that a warrant has been issued for the arrest of a person for felony, may himself lawfully make the arrest, without having the warrant in his possession. But he should inform the person arrested of the facts, or at least of the offense for which he is arrested. *Drennan v. People*, 10 Mich., 169. See *ante* 782.

899. Commitment for trial. A warrant for commitment, charging that L. "did, on the 20th day of April, instant, enter the possession of C., and wrongfully and feloniously take and drive away from the possession of said C. forty-five sheep and twenty lambs, of the value of $180," shows no criminal offense. *Matter of Leddy*, 11 Mich., 197.

900. A commitment for trial is invalid, if the magistrate fails to fix the amount of bail. *Ibid.*

901. Examination preliminary to information. The defendant may waive his right to have a preliminary examination before an information is filed against him, as well when called upon to plead to the information as when brought before the examining magistrate. And if at the time of pleading he make no objection on the ground that such examination has not been had or waived, he must be understood to admit that it has been had, or that he has waived, or then intends to waive it. *Washburn v. People*, 10 Mich. 372; *Hicks v. People*, 10 Mich., 395.

902. It is not necessary that the information should show on its face that a preliminary examination had been had or waived. If the defendant intends to insist upon the want of such examination, he should take the objection by plea in abatement, or by motion to quash based upon affidavit. *Ibid.*

903. But where an examination has been had before a magistrate on a criminal charge, and the accused is discharged, an information cannot afterwards be lawfully filed against him for the same offense. *Morrisey v. People*, 11 Mich., 327

904. And if an information is filed after such examination and discharge, the defendant may prove those facts in bar of the prosecution, under the plea of not guilty. *Ibid.*

905. The examination is designed to accomplish, to some extent, the purpose of a presentment by a grand jury; but not that the complaint or warrant shall stand in the place of a formal presentment, nor that in the Circuit Court the prosecuting officer should be limited by it in the mode of charging the offense. So long as he does not undertake to proceed against a person for a different transaction than that to which the examination relates, it is competent for him to put his information in such form as, in his opinion, will enable him to try the offense upon the merits in the way most effectually to advance the ends of justice. *Annis v. People*, 13 Mich., 511.

906. Where two or more are jointly complained of and bound over, separate informations may be filed against them in the Circuit Court, and they may be used as witnesses against each other. *Ibid.*

907. Verification of information. The verification by the oath of the prosecuting attorney, that he "knows the contents of the foregoing information, and that he has good reason to believe and does believe the same to be true as therein set forth," is sufficient. *Washburn v. People*, 10 Mich., 372.

908. Grand jurors: challenges. Grand jurors drawn and appearing upon summons, are presumed to be legally qualified and properly returned; and the Court will not interfere to set aside the panel, or any part of it, unless upon cause shown by a person having a right to question its legality. *Thayer v. People*, 2 Doug., 417.

909. A challenge either to the array or to the poll can only be made by a person who shows that he is under prosecution, and his case about to be brought before the jury. *Ibid.*

910. Resummoning grand jury. Where a grand jury have finished their business, and been dismissed before the adjournment of the Court without day, they may be resummoned at any time during the term, to inquire into an offense committed subsequent to their discharge; and grand jurors who were originally summoned, but did not appear, may be resummoned, and on appearing and being sworn and impaneled, may act with their fellows. *Findley v. People*, 1 Mich., 234.

911. Juror subsequently appearing. A grand juror who appears after the jury have been sworn and received the charge of the Court, may or may not be sworn, in the discretion of the Court, where there are enough grand jurors without him. *Ibid.*

912. Indictment. An inuendo in an indictment is bad when there is nothing previous to which it can refer. *People v. Collier*, 1 Mich., 137.

913. Where a statute enumerates several elements as combining to create a crime, the crime cannot properly be described without including all those elements. *Koster v. People*, 8 Mich., 431.

914.—one bad count. Where an indictment contains two counts, each for the same offense, one of which is bad, the other, being good, is sufficient to warrant a general verdict of guilty, and judgment thereon. *Shannon v. People*, 5 Mich., 71; *People v. McKinney*, 10 Mich., 54.

915.—amendment. A prosecuting attorney, having discovered an error in an indictment, corrected it without leave of the Court, and the case went to trial on the indictment as corrected. Attention being called to the alteration on the trial, the Judge decided that the alteration in a material point would vitiate the indictment. Held, that this ruling was erroneous. *People v. Cook*, 10 Mich., 164.

916. The defendant might object to allowing such amendment to stand, and the effect of his objection would be that the indictment must stand in its original shape. But the prosecuting attorney could not treat it as a nullity; and if the cause was tried and defendant acquitted on the indictment as amended, the acquittal would be a bar to a subsequent prosecution for the same offense, provided the indictment, as it stood at the time of the trial, was sufficient. *Ibid.*

917.—omission of matter of form. Under the statute of 1855 relative to indictments, if an indictment or information contains direct and unequivocal averments of such facts—not being mere evidence—as lead immediately and of necessity to a single and inevitable conclusion, the omission to draw that conclusion will not vitiate the plèading. *Evans v. People*, 12 Mich., 27.

918. An information for murder was in the full common law form of indictments, except that in the conclusion, where it was averred that the respondent "did kill and murder," the name of the person killed was omitted. The respondent was convicted of manslaughter; and it was held that, under this statute, the information was sufficient to sustain the conviction. *Ibid.*

919. Election of offenses. On trial of an information for incest, the prosecutor may, before the evidence is introduced, select any one act of criminal intercourse which occurred within the jurisdiction of the Court, and within the period of the statute of limitations applicable to the offense, as the one upon which a conviction will be sought. But when evidence has been introduced tending directly to the proof of one act, and for the purpose of procuring a conviction upon it, the prosecutor is deemed to have made his election, and that act must thereafter be considered the one charged against the defendant, and for which alone he can be found guilty. *People v. Jenness*, 5 Mich., 305.

920. Charging accessories as principals. By § 6065 of Comp. L., it is provided that the distinction between an accessory before the fact and a principal, and between principals in the first and second degree, in cases of felony, is abrogated; and all persons concerned in the commission of a felony, whether they directly commit the act constituting the offense, or aid and abet in its commission, though not present, may be indicted, tried and punished as principals, as in case of misdemeanor. *Held*, that in all cases where only persons of a certain class, or standing in a certain relation, are competent to commit the offense, the indictment against aiders and abettors, not belonging to such class, or standing in such relation, must set out the aiding and abetting, in which alone the crime consists, and which, *in* *such case*, is the only principal offense within the meaning of this statute. *Shannon v. People*, 5 Mich., 71.

921. Plea in abatement. A plea in abatement to an indictment, that states several distinct facts having no relation to or dependence upon each other, is bad for duplicity. It should be certain to every intent, and conclude by praying judgment of the indictment, and that it may be quashed; and it must be verified by affidavit. *Findley v. People*, 1 Mich., 234.

922. Jury. It is not error for the Court, after the jury have retired to consult of their verdict, to permit them to have the statutes defining the offense in their room, although the same is objected to by defendant's counsel. *Findley v. People*, 1 Mich., 234.

923.—distinctions between challenges. The distinction between challenges for favor and challenges for cause is practically abolished by the statute, (Comp. L., § 4400), all challenges being now for cause, and to be tried in the same manner; and when there is no dispute about the facts upon which a challenge is based, the question arising upon it is purely one of law, and open to review upon exceptions. *Holt v. People*, 13 Mich., 224.

924.—doubt of juror's indifference. In a criminal case if the examination of a juror upon challenge leaves a reasonable doubt of his impartiality, the prisoner should have the benefit of the doubt, and the juror be excluded. *Ibid.*

925.—burden of showing partiality. A person called as a juror is presumed to be qualified and impartial; and the party challenging assumes the burden of proving the contrary. He does not relieve himself of that burden until he has made out a prima facie case, or, in criminal cases, such a case as leaves the partiality of the juror in reasonable doubt. *Ibid.*

926.—opinion as cause of challenge. The law does not require a juror to be entirely unimpressed with any opinion as to the guilt or innocence of the person on trial, but simply that he shall not have an opinion of such a fixed and definite character as to leave a bias on his mind which will preclude his giving due weight to the presumption of innocence. *Ibid.*

927. The statement of one called as a juror that he has formed a partial opinion as to the guilt or innocence of the prisoner, from rumors heard in the streets, but not a positive opinion, does not establish his incompetency. *Ibid.*

928. Accomplices as witnesses. The credibility of an accomplice, like that of any other witness, is exclusively a question for the jury, who *may* convict on such testimony alone, without confirmation. *People v. Jenness*, 5 Mich., 305.

929. An accomplice who consents to become a witness for the people on the trial of his associates, must disclose all that his associates may have said or done in relation to the offense, and cannot be excused from testifying to statements made by him to his attorney on the ground of their being privileged communications. *Alderman v. People*, 4 Mich., 414.

930. Wife of co-defendant a witness. Under act No. 125 of 1861, the wife of a defendant in a criminal prosecution, may be examined as a witness on behalf of a co-defendant of her husband. *Morrissey v. People*, 11 Mich., 327. For the former rule see *Pullen v. People*, 1 Doug., 48.

931. Defendant's statement. The defendant in a criminal case is not entitled, under the act of 1861 (S. L., p. 168) to be sworn as a witness on his own behalf, but only to make a statement to the Court or jury without oath. *People v. Thomas*, 9 Mich., 314.

932. The purpose of said act was to give every person placed on trial on a charge of crime an opportunity to make full explanation to the jury in respect to the circumstances given in evidence which are supposed to have a bearing against him, and to make such further statements as he may deem material. *Annis v. People*, 13 Mich., 511.

933. Such statement is for the consideration of the jury, who may give it such credit, in whole or in part, as under all the circumstances they think it entitled to. *Maher v. People*, 10 Mich., 212; *Durant v. People*, 13 Mich., 351. And it is error for the Court to instruct the jury that where it conflicts with the testimony of an unimpeached witness they must believe the latter in preference. *Durant v. People*, 13 Mich., 351.

934. Defendant being on trial for the larceny of a mare, made his statement in reference to material points in the case, but said nothing on the subject of the mare alleged to have been stolen. His counsel thereupon, without defendant's knowledge, submitted to the Court for approval in writing a suggestion as follows: "I call your attention to the subject of the stolen mare, so that you may make a statement in reference to it or not." The Judge refused to permit the suggestion to be made. Held, that defendant was entitled to this assistance from his counsel, and that the suggestion in the manner proposed should have been allowed. *Annis v. People*, 13 Mich., 511.

935. The error in refusing it was not cured by the defendant being afterwards allowed to go upon the stand to make a further statement, in which he said only, "I know nothing about the stealing, and had nothing to do with it;" as the defendant evidently needed the aid which counsel proposed to give as much at this time as he had needed it before. *Ibid.*

936. Exceptions before sentence. A bill of exceptions in a criminal case, being signed by the Judge and filed with the clerk, becomes, when the case is brought into the Supreme Court by writ of error, a part of the record for review in that Court. *Shannon v. People*, 5 Mich., 36.

937. Convictions in the Recorder's Court of Detroit, for offenses against city ordinances, cannot be brought before the Supreme Court for review on exceptions before sentence, under Ch. 197 of Comp. L. *People, v. Jackson*, 8 Mich. 110.

938. Where the case comes up on exceptions before sentence, under Chap. 197, Comp. Laws, the sufficiency of the information in matters of substance is involved, to the extent, at least, of determining whether it charges a criminal offense. *People v. Wattles* (reported as Wattles v. People), 13 Mich., 446.

939. Bail after exceptions. Where exceptions in a criminal case are transmitted to the Supreme Court for review before sentence, that Court has no power to admit the defendant to bail. *People v. McKinney*, 9 Mich., 444.

940. Sentence. Under the statute which requires Courts sentencing offenders to the Reform School, to certify to the keeper thereof the age of the person sentenced as nearly as can be ascertained by testimony, a Court which has certified the age of a convict to be under six teen years, must be conclusively presumed, in all collateral inquiries, to have performed its duty correctly. *Matter of Mason*, 8 Mich., 70.

941. Such Court cannot afterwards, on the ground of mistake in the convict's age, treat the sentence as void, and proceed to give a new one. *Ibid.*

942. Imprisonment in Detroit House of Correction. Under the act establishing the Detroit House of Correction (S. L., 1861, p. 268), where a Court sentences an offender to imprisonment in the House of Correction instead of the county jail, the sentence cannot be for a longer term than would have been lawful in the jail. *Elliott v. People*, 13 Mich., 365.

943. Sentence in excess of authority. Where the only error in a criminal case is in the judgment rendered, there can neither be a new trial nor a new judgment rendered. Where therefore a prisoner is sentenced to imprisonment for a longer period than is allowed by law, the Supreme Court on error can only reverse the judgment and discharge the prisoner. *Elliott v. People*, 13 Mich., 365. See *Crippen v. People*, 8 Mich., 117.

944. Illegal commitment. A fine was imposed by a justice of the peace, with imprisonment for ten days in default of payment. Payment not being made, the justice issued his warrant, directing that defendant be imprisoned until the fine was paid, or until he was discharged by due course of law. Held, that as the warrant did not follow the judgment, it was clearly in excess of jurisdiction, and void. *LaRoe v. Roeser*, 8 Mich., 537.

CURTESY.

945. The legislature has the power to cut off the right of curtesy initiate before it becomes vested. *Hathorn v. Lyon*, 2 Mich., 93. [See Comp. L., §§ 2803, 3291, and the subsequent law of 1855 §§ 3292, et seq.]

DAMAGES.

946. General rule in actions on contract. In actions on contract, the party complaining can recover such damages only as are shown to be the natural and proximate consequence of the breach complained of, and not such as arise from circumstances so far out of the ordinary course of nature, or human affairs, that they could not fairly be presumed to have been anticipated by the parties at the time of making the contract. *Clark v. Moore*, 3 Mich., 55. See *Burrill v. N. Y. and Saginaw Solar Salt Co.*, 14 Mich.

947. Entire sale of goods: only a part delivered. Plaintiff made a contract for delivery of certain goods as an entirety. He delivered a part only; but the defendant retaining them, plaintiff brought suit for the value. There being no evidence of their value except the contract of sale, it was held no ground for reversing the judgment that the Court instructed the jury that plaintiff was entitled to recover the contract price for the quantity delivered. *Clark v. Moore*, 3 Mich., 55.

948. Purchase for special purpose. By the contract of purchase the vendors were to furnish the cordage "necesssary to rig a vessel" the vendee was then building. It was held that this designation of the use to which the cordage was to be put, being merely to designate the quantity to be furnished, and not an undertaking that the vendee should have it for that purpose, the vendee could only be allowed as damages for non-delivery the difference between the contract price and the market value. *Ibid.*

949. Vendor refusing to complete sale. Plaintiffs bought hogs of defendant, paying ten dollars down, and were to pay the balance on delivery. Defendant refused to deliver, and plaintiffs sued. The market value of the hogs at the time of the refusal was no more than plaintiffs were to pay. Plaintiffs on the trial claimed to recover a loss which they had sustained by reason of not having the hogs to ship with others then on hand, upon cars hired by them for the purpose after the purchase was made; but it was held that, as the contract of sale was not made with reference to any such extraordinary liability, the plaintiffs could only recover the ten dollars paid and interest thereon. *Cuddy v. Major*, 12 Mich., 368.

950. To create such extraordinary liability, there must, in every case, be something in the terms of the contract, read in the light of surrounding circumstances, which shows an intention on the part of the vendor to assume an enlarged engagement, a wider responsibility than is assumed by the vendor in ordinary contracts for the sale and delivery of merchandise. *Ibid.*

951. Interest as damages. In an action for the non-delivery by defendant, at the time agreed upon, of an article purchased and paid for by plaintiff, the jury may, without proof of special damage, award interest on the price of the article from the time when it should have been, until it actually was, delivered. *Edwards v. Sanborn*, 6 Mich., 348.

952. Order to manufacturer countermanded. An order for an article from a manufacturer being countermanded after work had been done and materials used towards its construction, the value of the labor upon the materials is not the proper criterion for his damages, since this labor may have increased the value of the materials, in which case the manufacturer, still owning them, is compensated to the extent of such enhanced value; or it may have diminished such value, and then payment for the labor will not be adequate compensation. The question whether the labor has enhanced or diminished the value of the materials is necessarily one for the jury in estimating the damages. *Hosmer v Wilson*, 7 Mich., 294.

953. Shipment delayed. By a contract between plaintiffs and defendants, the latter bound themselves to convey, from Saginaw to Chicago, six vessel loads of lumber, at a specified price, as follows: One in August, two in September, two in October, and one in November. Defendants carried but five, as follows: One in August, one in September, one in October and two in November. Freights rose slightly in October, and largely in November. In an action for neglect to carry the sixth cargo, there being no evidence of any agreement by the parties, or election by defendants, to apply the extra cargo carried in November to the default in September or October, it was held that they had a right to have it stand as a substituted performance for the cargo which they failed to carry in October: and that plaintiffs would be entitled to such damages only as they had sustained by the failure of defendants to carry one of the cargoes which they were bound to carry in September. *Lord v. Strong*, 6 Mich., 61.

954. Liquidated damages. The principle at which the law aims in awarding damages is that of just compensation for the injury sustained; and the parties will not be permitted by express stipulations to set this principle aside. *Jaquith v. Hudson*, 5 Mich., 123.

955. In determining whether a sum named in a contract to be paid on a breach is to be regarded as a penalty, or as liquidated damages, the question is not what the parties *intended*, but whether the sum fixed is in fact in the nature of a penalty; and this is to be determined by the magnitude of the sum, in connection with the subject matter; and not by the words or understanding of the parties. *Ibid.*

956. Where from the nature of the contract, and the subject matter of the stipulation for the breach of which the sum is provided, it is apparent to the Court that the actual damages for a breach are uncertain in their nature, difficult to be ascertained, or impossible to be estimated with certainty; and where the parties themselves are more intimately acquainted with all the peculiar circumstances, and therefore better able to compute the actual or probable damages than Courts or juries from any evidence which can be brought before them;—the law in such cases permits the parties to ascertain for themselves, and provide in the contract, the amount of damages which shall be paid on a breach, and adopts their estimate as the best and most certain mode of ascertaining the actual damage, or what sum will amount to a just compensation. *Ibid.*

957. In the cases where the law allows the parties to determine the damages for themselves, their intention as expressed in the contract is the governing consideration. And the reason for allowing them to fix the amount of damages in the one class of cases, and denying it in the other, is the same, namely: the law adopts the most practicable mode of ascertaining the actual damage or just compensation. *Ibid.*

958. An agreement in selling out an interest in an existing business, not to engage in a rival business in the same place for three years, is one in which the parties can agree upon the damages which shall be recovered on a breach; and a stipulation therein for a "forfeiture of the sum of $1,000, to be recovered by the said [purchaser] as his damages," is an agreement for liquidated damages which will be enforced by the Courts. *Ibid.*

959. But where one party agreed to draw for another a quantity of timber at one dollar fifty cents per thousand feet; one dollar per thousand of which was to be advanced, and the remainder to be "settled, fixed and liquidated damages," in case the contract was not completed; it was held that the sum so fixed was to be regarded as a penalty; since otherwise the nearer the contract was completed the greater the damages to be recovered ; while if the party should fail to draw any of the timber there could be no recovery. *Davis v. Freeman*, 10 Mich., 188.

960. Where by the terms of a contract a sum is mentioned as liquidated damages for the non-performance of several distinct stipulations of very different degrees of importance, and this sum is to be payable equally on a failure to perform the least as of that to perform the most important, or the whole of them together, it is in legal effect a penalty, and not stipulated damages. *Daily v. Litchfield* 10 Mich. 29.

961. General rule in torts. Except in those actions where punitory or exemplary damages may be given, and those whose principal object is the establishment of a right, and where nominal damages may be proper, the only just theory of an action for damages, and its primary object, are, that the damages recovered shall compensate for the injury sustained. *Allison v. Chandler*, 11 Mich., 542.

962. Latitude of inquiry. Where from the nature of the case the amount of the damages in an action of tort cannot be ascertained with certainty, or only a part of them can be so estimated, all the facts and circumstances of the case, having any tendency to show damages, or their probable amount, may be placed before the jury, so as to enable them to make the most intelligible and probable estimate which the nature of the case will permit. *Ibid.*

963. The distinction between the rule in actions on contract, and those of actual, aggressive tort, pointed out. *Ibid.*

964. When market value not a test. Where by reason of defendant's trespass the plaintiff is deprived, for the remainder of his term, of premises leased by him, he is not limited in his recovery of damages to such sum as the term might be worth to others, or the difference between the rent he was paying and the fair rental of the premises, if they were of much greater and peculiar value to him on account of the business he had established, and the resort of customers to that particular place, or the good will of the place in his trade or business. *Ibid.*

965. And where, in consequence of the trespass, the plaintiff was obliged to remove to another place of business, he is entitled to show, in an action for the trespass, that his business fell off in consequence, and how much. *Ibid.*

966. Profits lost. As a general thing, in an action purely of tort, where the amount of profits lost by the injury can be shown with reasonable certainty, they are not only admissible in evidence, but they constitute, thus far, a safe measure of damages. *Ibid.*

967. Evidence of past profits in the same business at that place may be given, and allowed such weight by the jury, in determining the actual loss, as they think it entitled to. *Ibid.*

968. Good faith of defendant. If trespass was committed while the defendant was acting in good faith, and under an honest belief that he had a legal right to do the act complained of, the plaintiff is entitled to recover only the actual damages sustained by him, and not damages of a punitory or exemplary character. *Ibid.*

969. But it is immaterial whether he actually contemplate the damages which result or not. He must be held to contemplate all the damages which legitimately follow from his illegal act. *Ibid.*

970. Landlord destroying demised premises. Trespass for destroying a store leased by plaintiff from defendant, whereby the former was deprived of its use, and prevented from carrying on his business. The declaration was silent on the subject of the tenancy. Held, that it was not competent for plaintiff to prove and recover as damages the amount and value of repairs made by him upon the store prior to the trespass, but that he might recover for those made to counteract an attempt upon the property by defendant before its final demolition. *Chandler v. Allison*, 10 Mich., 460.

971. It was competent for plaintiff to show that, before the trespass, he had underlet portions of the premises, and at what rates; as such evidence went to show whether the portion he retained and occupied was held by him at an advantageous rate, and whether, therefore, his rights were worth anything. *Ibid.*

972. It was also competent for him to show that after the trespass he procured another store for his business, which was the best he could obtain for the purpose, but less advantageous than the one destroyed. *Ibid.*

973. And where the declaration alleged that plaintiff's store was rendered uninhabitable, and that plaintiff was, up to the commencement of the suit, hindered and prevented from carrying on his business, it was held competent to give evidence, under this declaration, of a partial deprivation of business, which would have been total had no other building been attainable. *Ibid.*

974. Treble damages in trespass. Section 4717 of Compiled Laws authorizes one who is ejected in a forcible or unlawful manner from lands or tenements, to recover of the wrong doer three times the amount of damages. The plaintiff averred that being in possession of certain premises, the defendant entered upon, took possession of, and ejected him therefrom, &c.; and also, that at the same time he took possession of and converted to his own use certain personal property described. Plea, the general issue. General verdict for plaintiff. Held, that the averment as to the personal property was not mere matter of aggravation of the eviction, but of a distinct cause of action; and that the verdict being general, the plaintiff was not entitled to have it trebled as he would have been had he declared for the entry and eviction only. *Thayer v. Sherlock*, 4 Mich., 173.

975. The statute giving treble damages against one who intentionally cuts down or carries off the timber, &c., from the land of another, was not framed to protect mere possessory rights, but to give the owner of the fee the right to sue, under the form of trespass, for injuries to his inheritance. It is, therefore, not a defense to the action that defendant had disseized the plaintiff, though it may prevent treble damages. *Achey v. Hull*, 7 Mich., 423.

976. Where such action is brought for cutting down timber, the plaintiff is entitled to recover the amount by which the value of the estate is diminished by its destruction, and not merely the value of the trees. *Ibid.*

977. Action by one joint owner. Where the proof given in such action without objection only shows plaintiff to own an undivided half of the premises, but no plea in abatement has been interposed, the non-joinder of the other as plaintiff only goes to apportion the damages. And on error, where it is not objected that entire damages were assessed, the Court must presume they were apportioned. *Ibid.*

978. Trover: sale by defendant as evidence of value. Where the defendant was sued in trover for logs which he had cut without authority on plaintiff's land, and sold, it was held that, in the absence of evidence that the sale was for more than the real value, it was proper to award as damages the price for which the logs were sold, and interest thereon. *Symes v. Oliver*, 13 Mich., 9.

979.—auction sale as evidence of value. Evidence of what the property brought at an auction sale made shortly after the alleged conversion, is competent as having some tendency to prove value. *Smith v. Mitchell*, 12 Mich., 180.

980.—deducting prior liens. Trover by assignee for conversion of property levied upon by defendant, by virtue of executions against the assignor. Evidence on behalf of defendant, that property levied upon was held and sold under a prior levy, is admissible, to show that defendant had not damnified the plaintiff, and had not converted the goods. *Ibid.*

981. So also is evidence admissible to show that goods levied on were held and sold for railroad charges which were a prior lien. *Ibid.*

982.—adding former judgment. One whose property had been wrongfully taken from him replevied it, but being non-suited in the replevin suit, defendant had judgment against him for the value of the property. Plaintiff then sued in trespass for the taking of the property, and it was held that he was entitled to recover in this suit not only damages for the detention of the property while defendant held it, but also its value as assessed in favor of defendant in the replevin suit. *Haviland v. Parker*, 11 Mich., 103.

983. Trover for note. Where defendant has converted a promissory note belonging to plaintiff, and the Court is satisfied that the note was available at its nominal amount to the plaintiff, he may recover that amount, notwithstanding the maker is proved not to have property from which collection might be enforced by execution. *Rose v. Lewis*, 10 Mich., 483.

984. Refusing to obey subpœna. In an action for damages occasioned by defendant's non-attendance as a witness in obedience to a subpœna, plaintiff is entitled to recover any damages immediately consequential upon such non-attendance; like that occasioned by the postponement of the trial in consequence of the failure to attend. *Prentiss v. Webster*, 2 Doug., 5.

985. Evidence in mitigation. In an action of tort, everything that may properly be considered by the jury in mitigation of damages, may be given in evidence under the general issue. *Delevan v. Bates*, 1 Mich., 97.

986. Province of the Court and jury. In an action for false imprisonment the jury may find such damages as they think appropriate for the arrest and detention, as well as any special damages which are lawfully proved to their satisfaction; and it is error in the Court to confine them to damages for mere loss of time. *Page v. Mitchell*, 13 Mich., 63.

987. This is so even though there is evidence that the confinement was only nominal, and to a considerable extent under the plaintiff's own control. The jury are to judge of all the facts; and if they find that he was his own jailor in a voluntary martyrdom, he has no substantial grievance to complain of. *Ibid.*

988. Allegation of special damage. Action for false imprisonment, by one who had been arrested on a void execution. The declaration alleged that plaintiff was greatly hindered and prevented from performing and transacting his necessary affairs and business, and from engaging and embarking in business which he might and would otherwise have embarked in. Plaintiff proved that his business was collecting and securing claims. He had given bonds for the jail limits on being arrested, and he was allowed to show that his business occasionally called him out of the county, and that he was applied to twice to go out of the county after he had given bond. Held that the averments in the declaration did not warrant this evidence of special damages. *Fuller v. Bowker*, 11 Mich., 204.

989. But the arrest in such case being void, and the bond void, plaintiff cannot recover damages for remaining on the jail limits according to the terms of the bond. *Ibid.*

DEDICATION.

990. If the laying down of alleys, by the Governor and Judges, on the plan of Detroit, can be treated as a dedication for any other public purpose than that of ways for passage or travel, an acceptance or adoption of that dedication is just as essential to give them a public character, for any other purpose, as to give them that character as ways. *Tillman v. People*, 12 Mich., 401.

See further the titles TOWN PLATS, AND WAYS.

DEED.

991. Without witnesses. A deed without subscribing witnesses is good in equity, as a contract for the sale of the land, and may be enforced as such. *Godfroy v. Disbrow*, Wal. Ch., 260.

992. It is good as a conveyance of the land, as between the parties thereto; witnesses being required only for the purpose of registry. *Dougherty v. Randall*, 3 Mich., 581.

993. Parties. A deed to "A., administrator of the estate of B.," and to his successors and assignees for ever, where no express trust appears in the deed, and the estate is coupled with no conditions, conveys the legal interest in the land to A., who can convey the same without any license of the Probate Court for the purpose. *Little v. Lesia*, 5 Mich., 119.

994. Execution by attorney. To make a valid deed under a power of attorney, it is essential that there should be an intention on the part of the attorney to execute the deed under and by virtue of the power; or at least that the contrary intention should not appear. *Davenport v. Parsons*, 10 Mich., 42.

995. Where a deed purported to be made by attorneys under a power from the two grantors, and there was some testimony that a joint power had existed, but it was not given in evidence, and only a separate power from one of the grantors was proved, it was held that the execution of this deed could not be referred to the separate power, and the deed sustained as the deed of the grantor who had executed that. *Ibid.*

996. Delivery in escrow. A deed cannot be delivered to the grantee in escrow. If delivered to him, whatever be the form of words accompanying the delivery, it is absolute, and the deed takes effect at once. *Dawson v. Hall*, 2 Mich., 390.

997. Delivery—presumption as to time. Where a deed is acknowledged on a day subsequent to its date, and there is no proof of delivery prior to the acknowledgment, it must be presumed to have been delivered afterwards ; such being the usual course and practice in reference to the delivery of deeds and other instruments intended for record. *Blanchard v. Tyler*, 12 Mich., 339.

998. Possession of the deed is prima facie evidence of its delivery. *Dawson v. Hall*, 2 Mich., 390.

999. Description. A deed describing the lands as "supposed to be thirty-eight acres of land off from the east side of the southeast fractional quarter of section thirty-two, township four south of range sixteen west ; being the same number of acres off from said east side of said southeast fractional quarter as there is in the west part of the southeast fractional quarter of section four in township five south of range sixteen west, heretofore occupied and owned by [the grantee], and in exchange for which this conveyance is made ;"—is a good deed ; the description being made sufficient by reference to the other tract, and thus capable of being identified by survey. *Daily v. Litchfield*, 10 Mich., 29.

1000. Abbreviations. A deed is not invalid because of the description of the lands being in figures, and well understood abbreviations. *Harrington v. Fish*, 10 Mich., 415.

1001. Uncertainty in exception. Where the covenant against incumbrances in a deed contained an exception of a "certain mortgage," without giving the date or amount of the mortgage, or the name of the mortgagee, but the proof disclosed only one mortgage upon the property, it was *held* that such exception was not void for uncertainty, but would be understood as referring to the only mortgage proven in the case. *Cooper v. Bigley*, 13 Mich., 463.

1002. Mistaken description. Land was described as the east half of the northwest quarter of section twenty-one, in the township of Logan, being township twenty-six south of range three. There was no township twenty-six south in Logan, and there were two sections twenty-one—one in township six south, and the other in township seven south. It was held that parol evidence might be received to show on which of these two sections land was intended to be conveyed by the deed. *Ives v. Kimball*, 1 Mich., 308.

1003. Where one part of the description in a deed is false and impossible, but, by rejecting that, a perfect description remains, such false and impossible part should be rejected, and the deed held good. *Anderson v. Baughman*, 7 Mich., 69. See *Johnstone v. Scott*, 11 Mich., 232.

1004. A deed or other written instrument is to be construed so as to render it valid and effectual, rather than void. *Anderson v. Baughman*, 7 Mich., 69.

1005. And where an error in a deed appears by construction, the record of the deed is notice to subsequent purchasers of the real land intended. *Ibid.* See also *Cooper v. Bigley*, 13 Mich., 463.

1006. Construction. In giving a construction to a deed, the whole of it must be examined, and every part of it be taken into consideration; and the situation of the parties, and the subject matter of the transaction may also be taken into consideration. *Paddack v. Pardee*, 1 Mich., 421.

1007. If the construction is doubtful, it is to be construed most strongly against the grantor. *Cicotte v. Gagnier*, 2 Mich., 381.

1008. A plat referred to in a deed may be referred to for the purpose of giving a construction to it. *Paddack v. Pardee*, 1 Mich., 421.

1009. Monuments to control. In the construction of grants both course and distance must give way to natural or artificial monuments or objects; and courses must be varied, and distances lengthened or shortened, so as to conform to the natural or ascertained objects or bounds called for in the grant; but where there is nothing in a conveyance to control the call for course or distance, the land must be run according to the course and distance given in the description. *Bruckner's Lessee v. Lawrence*, 1 Doug., 19.

That a "quarter post" fixed in the original survey is binding upon patentees from the government, notwithstanding errors in the survey, see *Britton v. Ferry*, 14 Mich.

1010. Grant of water. A grant of fifty square inches of water, "to be applied five feet from the surface of the Clinton river, opposite the place of taking the water from the race," does not authorize the grantee to draw the water through an orifice of fifty square inches into a flume or reservoir upon his own premises, and then apply it by a larger discharge than fifty square inches; thereby enabling him, a portion of every twenty-four hours, to drive machinery requiring more than fifty square inches to propel it. *Paddack v. Pardee*, 1 Mich., 421.

1011. Owners in common of land upon which a mill had been situate (then burned down), the power to operate which was obtained by a dam below the premises, upon a stream running through them, of which power they were also tenants in common, made partition of their rights, and the mill site was conveyed to one exclusively. *Held*, that he thereby became entitled to the water power exclusively, unless a contrary intention clearly appeared from the conveyances. *Mandeville v. Comstock*, 9 Mich., 536.

1012. Town lots: plat not recorded. Deeds of town lots are valid, notwithstanding the failure of the proprietors to acknowledge and record the town plat. And though the deeds refer to the plat as of record when it is not, they are still good, and the statement that it is recorded is to be rejected as *falsa demonstratio*. *Johnstone v. Scott*, 11 Mich., 232.

1013. Grant limited to the operative words. Where the operative terms of a grant are confined to one parcel of land, and the Court is asked to extend it to another, the intention of the grantor to convey that other should so clearly appear on the face of the deed as to leave no reasonable doubt in regard to it; and no principle of law should be violated in carrying it out. *Ryan v. Wilson*, 9 Mich., 262.

1014. A deed by which the grantor conveyed to his son the one-half of his farm, "consisting of forty acres more or less, namely: The N. E. quarter of the N. E. quarter of section 12, town 7 N. of range 10 E.; the said party of the first part reserving to himself the other part of said farm, namely: the N. W. quarter of the N. E. quarter of section 12, for and during his natural life, and after his decease the said N. W. quarter of the N. E. quarter to revert to the said party of the second part and his heirs forever," does not convey to the grantee any interest in the last described parcel. *Ibid.*

1015. Boundary on stream. A grant of land bounded on a stream, carries with it the bed of the stream to the center, unless a contrary intention clearly appears from the conveyance itself. *Norris v. Hill*, 1 Mich., 202.

1016. This principle is applicable to the Detroit River. *Lorman v. Benson*, 8 Mich., 18. It is also applicable to Lake Muskegon; and the ownership of land bordering on the lake carries with it the ownership of the land under the shallow water so far out as it is susceptible of beneficial private use, but subordinate to the paramount public right of navigation, and the other public rights incident thereto. *Rice v. Ruddiman*, 10 Mich., 125.

1017. General description not conveying streets. A deed by the trustee of a village company conveying "all lands of said company not designated and numbered by lots on the plat of the company's purchase," will not convey a street on the plat which by non-user had reverted to the company. *Wanzer v. Blanchard*, 3 Mich., 11.

1018. Execution out of State. Under the act of April 12, 1827—Code 1827, p. 258; Code 1833, p. 281 — the record of a deed acknowledged in the State of New York, in conformity with the laws of that State, with the acknowledgment certified by the officer taking it, in his official capacity, is evidence, without proof of the official character of the person taking the acknowledgment, or the genuineness of his signature. *Ives v. Kimball*, 1 Mich., 308; *Galpin v. Abbott*, 6 Mich., 17.

1019. But the execution and witnessing of the deed was required to be the same as if done within the territory. Two witnesses were, therefore, essential. *Galpin v. Abbott*, 6 Mich., 17.

1020. A deed was executed and acknowledged in another State, conveying lands in this State. The certificate of the proper clerk was made and attached several years afterwards, certifying that the deed was executed and acknowledged according to the "existing" law of that State. Held sufficient under the statutes now in force. *Harrington v. Fish*, 10 Mich., 415.

1021. By assignee in bankruptcy. The deed of an assignee in bankruptcy, containing a copy of the decree declaring the bankruptcy, which decree recites the appointment of the assignee, is sufficient under the law of Congress which prescribes what the deed shall contain. *Ibid.*

1022. Restricting use of premises. One conveying an easement in water may restrict the use thereof to such purposes as he may specify in the grant. *Mandeville v. Comstock*, 9 Mich., 536.

1023. Restraint upon alienation. A covenant in an indenture conveying a fee, that the grantee will not alien without the grantor's consent, is void. *Campau v. Chene*, 1 Mich., 400.

1024. The healing act of 1861. In order to bring a deed, executed in another State not in compliance with our laws, within the saving of the confirming act of 1861—Laws of 1861, p. 16—it is necessary to show that, although not valid under the laws of Michigan as a conveyance for all purposes, it was executed according to the laws of the State where the execution took place, as well as regularly acknowledged. And these facts cannot be presumed without evidence. *Brown v. Cady*, 11 Mich., 535.

1025. In the absence of a statute authorizing it, the record of a deed is not primary evidence of the existence and genuineness of the original. And under said statute the record of a deed defectively executed is not made evidence of a valid sale without the production of the deed itself. The law makes such a record "hereafter operate as legal notice of all the rights secured by such instrument;" but does not render it of any validity except for notice. *Ibid.*

1026. Deeds presumed to show the actual title. A partnership of three persons owned lands, which, however, had been conveyed to the three without any reference in the deed to the partnership. It was held that a mortgage given by one of the three, on an undivided third, to one who had no notice that it was partnership property, was not affected by the partnership equities. Such mortgagee had a right to presume that the common possession of the three was under and in accordance with the record title, and not under some other and parol arrangement. *Adams v. Bradley*, 12 Mich., 346.

DETROIT CITY.

1027. Conveyances by the Land Board. The power of the Governor and Judges to convey lots in the town of Detroit, was not confined to a conveyance of lots in such forms and dimensions as they should delineate upon their plan. The claims to be adjusted by them were such as any person might have, legal and equitable; and when satisfactory proof had been made, they had no right to deprive a claimant of any portion of the land actually belonging to him under the acts of Congress, whether it interfered with any projected plan or not. And the Courts cannot go behind their conveyances while they acted within their jurisdiction. *People v. Jones*, 6 Mich., 176. [See the two cases of *Tregent v. Whiting*, and *Ready v. Kearsley*, 14 Mich., as to conveyances by the Land Board, and especially as to the "Trust Deeds," so called.]

1028. The plan of the city, when made, was liable to modification by interfering claims and reserves, and the Land Board had power to adapt it to contingencies when necessary. *Ibid.*

1029. Vacating public grounds. Where the common council proceeds to vacate public grounds, under the charter of 1857, it is not necessary that they should specify in the resolution any subsequent use to which they may contemplate putting the grounds. *Hinchman v. City of Detroit*, 9 Mich., 103.

1030. Nor is it necessary that the jury impanelled to assess the damages and benefits to individuals by reason of the improvement in vacating such grounds, should pass upon the necessity of the contemplated improvement. *Ibid.*

1031. Licenses. The ordinance of the common council, which provides that no person shall keep a ferry or boat for transporting persons and property across to the Canada shore without a license therefor from the mayor, and imposes a penalty for its violation, is a valid ordinance. *Chilvers v. People*, 11 Mich., 43.

1032. The city may lawfully charge a license fee with a view to revenue for the keeping of such a ferry. The license fee is a price paid for the franchise, and not a *tax*, within the meaning of that term as used in the constitution of the State and the charter of the city. *Ibid.*

1033. The ordinance prohibiting the keeping of stalls for the sale of fresh meats outside of the public markets, without license from the mayor, and requiring payment of a license fee of five dollars, is valid. The fee is not a tax, but a reasonable compensation which the city demands from those who will not sell in the public markets, for the additional labor of its officers and expense thereby imposed. *Ash v. People*, 11 Mich., 347.

1034. Fire limits. The common council has power to establish fire limits, and forbid the rebuilding or repair of wood buildings within the limits. *Brady v. Northwestern Insurance Co.*, 11 Mich., 425.

1035. Control of streets. Where a plank road company is authorized by its charter to take possession of a street in the city and construct a plank road thereon, and is required to keep the road in repair, and the road is constructed, a toll gate erected and tolls exacted of travelers, the city is thereby divested only of so much of its power over the street as would conflict with the rights of the company; and if the city authorities proceed to tear up the plank and cause the street to be paved, the company alone can complain. A bill by one who is assessed for the paving, to restrain the assessment, cannot be sustained. *Bagg v. City of Detroit*, 5 Mich., 336.

1036. Contracts by the city. Where labor was performed under a contract with the city before the revised charter took effect, and the common council, after the new charter, passed a resolution for the settlement of the contractor's claim, it was held that the resolution did not require the approval of the mayor. *Chaffee v. Granger*, 6 Mich., 51.

1037. Under the revised charter, claims for the construction of a sewer are to be paid only from a fund specially voted and raised for the purpose. While a claim against a sewer fund, which the city disputes, is pending and unadjusted, the rights of the claimant cannot be affected by a transfer to the sinking fund of the balance standing to the credit of such sewer fund. *Ibid.*

1038. Held, that a Court of equity should not, on the application of a tax-payer, interfere with the settlement of a claim against the city by the common council, where the council appear to have acted in good faith, and there could be no serious doubt of the legality of the larger portion of the demand, and the question as to the remainder was at most one of doubtful construction of the contract under which the claim accrued. *Ibid.*

1039. Under the charter of 1857, the city has no power to make itself responsible for any public work; and such work can only be paid for by funds actually in the hands of the city treasurer, provided for the specific purpose. *Goodrich v. City of Detroit*, 12 Mich., 279.

1040. Collector of taxes. Under the ordinances of the city the collector for 1855–6 was not entitled to collect from the city a percentage for his fees on that portion of the taxes returned uncollected. *Kelsey v. City of Detroit*, 7 Mich., 315.

1041. The act of 1853, p. 145, § 62—which required that upon the neglect of any township treasurer to pay over or account for the taxes required by his warrant to be collected, the county treasurer should issue his warrant to the sheriff, requiring him to collect the money of the township treasurer and his sureties—did not authorize the issuing of such a warrant against a defaulting ward collector of Detroit. *James v. Howard*, 4 Mich., 446.

1042. City marshal: term of office. The term of office of city marshal under the amended charter (S. L. 1861, p. 181–2), is two years; and the common council has no authority to limit it to one year in making the appointment. *Stadler v. City of Detroit*, 13 Mich., 346.

1043. Constables. Notwithstanding the repeal of the provision in the city charter which defined the powers and duties of constables, these officers within the city possess the same general powers belonging to the office in the towns. *People v. Smith*, 9 Mich., 193.

1044. Water commissioners. The board of water commissioners do not exceed their powers in contracting to themselves furnish and put in water pipe on private property, in a case which they regard, in good faith, as a proper one for the exercise of their discretion in using means to prevent waste and insure security. *Hale v. Houghton*, 8 Mich., 458.

1045. So far as third persons are concerned, the superintendent and engineer is the proper medium of negotiation with the board. And if he make a contract which exceeds his authority, and which the board refuse to sanction, he may sue and recover upon it in his own name. *Ibid.*

1046. Notice of council proceedings. Electors of a city are presumed to have notice of the proceedings of the common council, which are published in the official paper of the corporation. They are therefore presumed to have notice of a vacancy which has been declared by the council. *People v. Hartwell*, 12 Mich., 508. See *Williams v. Mayor, &c., of Detroit*, 2 Mich., 560.

DIVORCE.

1047. Wife's property. Under the Statutes of 1838, on a divorce for any cause except the adultery of the wife, she was entitled to the immediate possession of her real estate in the same manner as if the husband were dead. *Johnson v. Johnson*, Wal. Ch., 309. And see *Comp. L.*, § 3239.

1048. Non-resident defendant. The Statutes of 1838 required a different order for the appearance of a non-resident defendant in divorce cases from that in other suits in chancery; and an order in the form required in other cases gave the Court no jurisdiction to decree a divorce. *Freeman v. Freeman*, 1 Mich., 480.

1049. Reference. On a bill being taken as confessed, and a reference to a master to take proof of the material facts stated in the bill, he must report his opinion on them, with the testimony taken. The object is to guard against collusion by the parties; and the master in addition to the questions asked by the complainant, should examine the witnesses himself, that he may give his opinion understandingly. *Emmons v. Emmons*, Wal. Ch., 532.

1050. Withdrawal of answer. Where, in a divorce suit, an answer is filed and subsequently withdrawn, no divorce should be granted without some satisfactory evidence showing that the withdrawal was voluntary, and at the same time not collusive. *Leavitt v. Leavitt*, 13 Mich., 452.

1051. Admissions of parties. Divorce will not be granted upon the admissions of a party unsupported by evidence; but the amount of evidence required varies with the danger of collusion. *Sawyer v. Sawyer*, Wal. Ch., 48.

1052. Alimony. In a suit by or against a wife for a divorce, if she have no separate property of her own, the Court, when necessary, on petition, will grant her temporary alimony pending the suit, and require her husband to advance money to enable her to prosecute her suit, or make her defense. *Story v. Story*, Wal. Ch., 421.

1053. The affidavit of the husband, denying the ground on which the wife asks a divorce, is no answer to an application for alimony during the suit, but may be read to aid the Court in the exercise of its discretion as to the amount to be allowed. *Ibid.*

1054. Alimony on appeal. On an appeal from chancery in a divorce case, the Supreme Court has power to allow the wife temporary alimony, and to compel the husband to furnish her with pecuniary means to prosecute or defend the appeal. *Goldsmith v. Goldsmith*, 6 Mich., 285.

1055. That the decree of the Court below was adverse to the wife, is not sufficient ground for denying such temporary alimony on appeal, where it appears that the appeal is taken in good faith. *Ibid.*

1056. An order for such alimony was vacated on its being made to appear by affidavits that the appellant had been guilty of repeated acts of adultery pending the appeal. *Ibid.*

1057. Modifying decree for alimony. The statute—Comp. L., § 3249—which provides that, after a decree for alimony, the

Court may, from time to time, on the petition of either of the parties, revise and alter such decree, &c., must be construed as only authorizing the change on new facts thereafter transpiring, which are of such a character as to make the change necessary to suit such new state of facts. *Perkins v. Perkins*, 12 Mich., 456.

1058. Annulling marriage for fraud. Those frauds which will invalidate a marriage are usually, at least, such as negative any consent to be married, without reference to previous inducement. The common cases are duress, surprise or stratagem in procuring the marriage to be carried out; and the fraud must usually be nearly, if not absolutely, co-incident in time with the marriage, and operate to destroy that intelligent consent which is required for the marriage itself, rather than the preliminary engagement. *Leavitt v. Leavitt*, 13 Mich., 452.

1059. A bill was brought by a husband, some twenty years after marriage, to procure a decree of nullity, on the ground of fraud in the marriage contract, and the bill alleged that the defendant was guilty of ante-nuptial inchastity, that her chastity was made the subject of frequent and diligent inquiry by him before marriage, and that the defendant made specific and open assertion to him on the subject, upon the falsehood of which, and his own inability to ascertain anything on the subject, he based his sole claim to relief. Several children had been born to the parties, and no complaint was made of defendant's conduct during the coverture. Bill dismissed as unprecedented and shameful. *Ibid.*

DOMICIL.

1060. See definitions of, and how and from what circumstances it may be inferred. *High, appellant*, 2 Doug. 515.

DONATIO CAUSA MORTIS.

1061. What sufficient. No mere contract, liability or obligation of the party himself, can be the subject of a gift *causa mortis* by him; and therefore an unaccepted bank check, which, if not paid, merely creates a liability against the drawer, cannot be valid as a gift by him *causa mortis*. *Second National Bank of Detroit v. Williams*, 13 Mich., 282.

1062. The check of a third person which is given *causa mortis*, though invalid at the time for want of a sufficient stamp, if subsequently stamped according to act of Congress of June 30, 1864, is thereby made valid from its inception so as to support the gift. *Gibson v. Hibbard*, 13 Mich., 214.

DOWER.

1063. In wild lands. In this state a widow is entitled to dower in wild lands. *Campbell, appellant*, 2 Doug., 141.

1064. Under Ordinance of 1787, a widow was entitled to dower, as at common law, in all the lands of which her husband was seized during coverture. *May v. Rumney*, 1 Mich., 1.

1065. Non-residents. The widow of a non-resident of the State has dower in those lands only of which her husband died seized. Comp. L., § 2792. *Pratt v. Tefft*, 14 Mich.

1066. Statutes of limitations, however broad and comprehensive, do not apply to dower, unless they expressly name, or by necessary implication include it. Dower was not within the limitation act of November 5, 1829, Code 1833, p. 408. *May v. Rumney*, 1 Mich., 1.

1067. The husband's grantee is estopped from disputing the widow's right to dower, though the husband had no legal title, if the grantee obtains the legal title afterwards on a claim based on the husband's warranty deed. *May v. Tillman*, 1 Mich., 262. See also, *May v. Specht*, 1 Mich., 187.

1068. Husband cannot sell. The wife cannot be compelled to release her dower in lands which her husband has contracted to sell; and she is not a proper party to a bill by the purchaser for specific performance. *Richmond v. Robinson*, 12 Mich., 193. See *Weed v. Terry*, 2 Doug. 344.

1069. Conveyance in fraud of. A deed given by a man to his sons shortly before his marriage, and kept secret until after the marriage, is fraudulent as to the wife's right of dower, and does not bar it. *Cranson v. Cranson*, 4 Mich., 230.

1070. In mortgaged lands. Where the holder of a mortgage given by the husband and wife became owner of the husband's equity of redemption, and subsequently conveyed the lands with warranty, and the widow of the mortgagor afterwards claimed dower, it was held that the amount of the mortgage must be deducted from the whole value of the premises, and dower only assigned in the balance. *Snyder v. Snyder*, 6 Mich., 470.

1071. The conveyance of the equity of redemption to the assignee of the mortgage is, in such circumstances, such a merger as authorizes him to stand in the position of an assignee of the mortgage satisfying it, under § 2777 Comp. Laws. *Ibid.*

1072. The deduction may be made when the proceeding for the recovery of the dower is by ejectment. *Ibid.*

1073. Assignment in Probate Court. Under R. S. 1838, notice to the administrator of proceedings in the Probate Court for the assignment of dower, was not necessary. The proceeding was one entirely between the widow and the heirs. *Campbell, appellant*, 2 Doug., 141.

DRAFT FOR MILITARY DUTY.

1074. One Spangler was returned by the proper officer as liable to military duty. For the purposes of a draft the names of those thus returned were written upon ballots and placed in a box to be drawn from. By mistake in writing Spangler's name, the final letter was omitted, but it was held that this error did not invalidate the draft. *Matter of Spangler*, 11 Mich., 298.

DRAINAGE LAWS.

1075. Drainage laws of 1857 and 1859. Proceedings being taken under the act of 1857 "to provide for the draining of swamps, marshes and other low lands," as amended in 1859, a venire was issued by the chairman of the drain commissioners, without any application being made to the commissioners by resident freeholders. As the amendatory act plainly requires this, the proceedings were held void. *Palmer v. Rich*, 12 Mich., 414.

1076. Saving clause in act of 1859. The saving of "any engagement or undertaking heretofore entered into by the commissioners," in the act of 1859, does not keep alive any proceedings commenced under the old law, in any incipient stage, where no vested rights have accrued. *Ibid.*

DURESS.

1077. Imprisonment. A mortgage given to a county as the condition of a pardon, is upon sufficient consideration, and the lawful imprisonment when it was given, is not such duress as can avoid it *Rood v. Winslow*, 2 Doug., 68, and Wal. Ch., 340.

1078. Threats. Where a timid and ignorant man was induced by threats of a prosecution for slander to assign a mortgage to another, the transfer was held without consideration, and a re-assignment decreed. *Tate v. Whitney*, Har. Ch., 145.

DWELLING HOUSE.

1079. What is. A building thirty-six feet distant from a man's dwelling house, used for preserving the nets employed in the owner's ordinary occupation of a fisherman, and also as a permanent dormitory for his servants, is in law a part of his dwelling, though not enclosed with the house by a fence. A fence is not necessary to include buildings within the curtilage, if within a space no larger than that usually occupied for the purposes of the dwelling and customary outbuildings. *Pond v. People*, 8 Mich., 150.

EJECTMENT.

1080. Who to be defendant. The person in actual possession of the premises, if they were occupied by any one, was to be made defendant under the Statutes of 1838. *Lockwood v. Drake*, 1 Mich., 14. The present statute is to the same effect. Comp. Laws, § 4557.

1081. By mortgagee, is now forbidden until after foreclosure, by the statute of 1843—Comp. L., § 4614. But this statute does not apply to mortgages previously given. *Mundy v. Monroe*, 1 Mich., 68; *Stevens v. Brown*, Wal. Ch., 41; *Blackwood v. Van Vleet*, 11 Mich., 252.

1082. Venue. The Circuit Courts have power to order a change of venue for cause. *Campau v. Dewey*, 9 Mich., 381.

1083. Recovering for improvements. Where a claim is filed under the statute—Comp. L., § 4603—for the value of improvements made by defendant on the premises in controversey, the case may be tried by the Court without a jury, if no jury be demanded. *Rawson v. Parsons*, 6 Mich., 401.

1084. Where such a claim is filed, and the plaintiff files none for an estimation of the value of the land had no improvements been made, the jury must estimate the increased value under defendant's claim, and if the verdict be for the plaintiff, he will be entitled to judgment for the recovery of the premises, but will be deemed, under the statute, to have abandoned all claims thereto, unless he pays the estimate for improvements within a year. If the plaintiff would have the jury estimate the value of the land without the improvements, he must file a claim for that purpose. *Ibid.*

1085. Such claim of the plaintiff when filed is an essential part of the record, and must appear therein. It is not sufficient that there be a recital in the entry of judgment that such a claim has been filed. *Ibid.*

1086. If the trial is had before the Judge without a jury, his finding of facts is in the nature and stands in the place of a special verdict, and must be filed in writing before any judgment can be entered. *Ibid.*

1087. The plaintiff has his election to take judgment for the possession of the premises subject to the obligation to pay for the improvements, or for the value independent of the improvements. But he is bound by his election once made. *Ibid.*

ELECTIONS.

1088. Canvassers' statement only prima facie evidence. The statement required by law to be made out by the canvassers, showing the votes given for the respective offices, is prima facie evidence only of the facts stated in it. The county canvass may be corrected by the township canvasses, and these by the ballots them selves. *People v. Van Cleve*, 1 Mich., 362.

1089. The determination by the board of county canvassers as to' the persons elected, is only prima facie evidence of their election. The duties of the board of canvassers are wholly ministerial. *Ibid.*

1090. The evidence contained in the ballots is the foundation of the statements to be prepared both by the inspectors and by the county canvassers; and also of the certificates of election issued by the latter. A party may go behind the canvass and certificate to the ballots, to show the number of votes cast for him. *People v. Tisdale*, 1 Doug., 59; *People v. Van Cleve*, 1 Mich., 362; *People v. Higgins*, 3 Mich., 233.

1091. The intention of the voter must be ascertained from the ballot; and if that fails to express the intention, evidence cannot be allowed to explain it. A ballot for *J. A. Dyer* cannot by extrinsic proof be shown to have been meant for *James A. Dyer*. *People v. Tisdale*, 1 Doug., 59; *People v. Higgins*, 3 Mich., 233.

1092. Abbreviations. Where the designation of an individual upon a ballot is by an abbreviation, sanctioned by common usage, and universally understood—as Jas. for James—the ballot may be counted for the person for whom it was evidently designed. *People v. Tisdale*, 1 Doug., 59.

1093. An error in spelling the name does not prevent the ballot being counted for the person for whom it was designed—the rule of *idem sonans* applying. *People v. Mayworm*, 5 Mich., 146; *People v. Tisdale*, 1 Doug., 59.

1094. Mistake in depositing ballots. An elector is not to be deprived of his vote, either by the mistake or fraud of the inspector in depositing it in the wrong box, if the intention of the voter can be ascertained with reasonable certainty. *People v. Bates*, 11 Mich., 362.

1095. Nor should ballots be rejected because of being put in the wrong box by the honest mistake of the voters themselves. *Ibid.*

1096. Where, therefore, a city and State election were both held at the same time, under the charge of the same inspectors, and seven ballots for city officers were found at the closing of the poll in the State box, and the circumstances of the case made it reasonably certain that these ballots were in good faith put in by electors who did not put in other ballots for city officers at the same election, it was held that they were properly counted by the inspectors. *Ibid.*

1097. Only one officer voted for when two to be chosen. Under a law authorizing the election of two circuit court commissioners an election was held, but it was conducted in all respects as if one only was to be chosen: two persons were opposing candidates, and each elector voted for one of the two, but in no instance did a ballot contain more than one name for this office. It was *held* that only the one receiving the highest number of votes was chosen, and as to the other there was a failure to elect. *People v. Canvassers of Kent Co.*, 11 Mich., 111.

1098. Preserving ballots. The failure of the inspectors to keep the ballots in the manner pointed out by the statute, will not affect the rights of persons for whom they are cast. *People v. Higgins*, 3 Mich., 233.

1099. Neglect to give notice of election. Where a city charter required a vacancy in a city office to be filled at the next general election, and directed the city clerk to give notice of the election, and of the offices to be filled, and the notice actually given by him took no notice of the vacancy, it was held that this default of the clerk did not invalidate the election for the vacancy; that the statute requiring the notice to be given was directory merely. *People v. Hartwell*, 12 Mich., 508.

1100. Elections in Pontiac. A legislative act authorizing the annual meetings of the township of Pontiac to be held within the city of Pontiac, would not authorize the polls for said township, for a general election, to be held in the city. *People v. Knight*, 13 Mich., 424.

EMINENT DOMAIN.

1101. Taking lands for railroads. The territorial legislature had power to incorporate railroad companies, and to authorize the appropriation of private property for their purposes, without the consent of the owner; and an act to that effect was not repugnant either to the Constitution of the United States or the Ordinance of 1787. *Swan v. Williams*, 2 Mich., 427; *Mercer v. Williams*, Wal. Ch., 85.

1102. Property of individuals taken by railroad corporations for the purpose of constructing their roads, is, in legal contemplation, taken not for *private* but for *public* use. The tenure of the corporations in the land is in the nature of a trust for public use, subject to the supervision of government. *Swan v. Williams*, 2 Mich., 427.

1103. Making compensation. Land may be taken for the public use without stipulation between the owners and the legislature, or the intervention of a jury, or of commissioners mutually chosen. It is only requisite that an impartial tribunal be provided for assessing the compensation; and such tribunal may be constituted without the intervention of the owner of the land. *People v. Michigan Southern R. R. Co.*, 3 Mich., 496.

1104. See the statutes providing for the construction of the State railroads, and constituting a board to which claims might be presented for lands taken, considered. *Ibid.*

1105. Lands taken by the State for its railroads passed by the sale of the roads to the purchasers, notwithstanding the owners of the lands had failed to present their claims and obtain compensation. *Ibid*; *Smith v. McAdam*, 3 Mich., 506.

1106. Notice to owner. The charter of a railroad corporation is not unconstitutional because not expressly requiring notice to the owners of proceedings to assess the compensation for property taken—the charter evidently contemplating notice, so that it is the duty of the tribunal in which the proceeding is taken to see that it is given. *Swan v. Williams*, 2 Mich., 427.

1107. Enjoining appropriation. Where a railroad corporation had, in good faith, obtained an assessment of damages for land needed for their road long before they wanted the use of it, and afterwards, when any delay would have been injurious to them, and while the confirmation of the inquisition was pending in the Supreme Court, to which it had been reserved, had tendered the damages assessed and proceeded to use the land, an injunction to restrain the use was refused notwithstanding the inquisition was not valid until confirmed; inasmuch as the corporation could only be delayed, and could not be prevented from finally obtaining the land. *Mercer v. Williams*, Wal. Ch., 85.

EQUITY: GENERAL PRINCIPLES.

1. Where there is a Remedy at Law.

1108. The Court of Chancery will not take jurisdiction of a case where there is a plain and adequate remedy at law. *Barrows v. Doty*, Har. Ch., 1; *Bennett v. Nichols*, 12 Mich., 22. See the principle discussed in *Wales v. Newbould*, 9 Mich., 45.

1109. Complainant's intestate had leased premises for the purpose of erecting a steam saw-mill thereon, had placed upon them a frame for the building, ready for erection, and had contracted and partly paid for an engine for the same. After his death the land was sold by the lessor, and the purchaser, together with the contractor for the engine, put up the frame, and completed and commenced operating the mill. Complainant, as administrator, filed his bill against them to compel payment of the value of the mill frame, and of the moneys paid towards the engine, and to have the amount declared a lien on the premises. Held, that his claims were not of equitable jurisdiction, and his remedy was at law. *Bennett v. Nichols*, 12 Mich., 22.

1110. Remedy at law doubtful. If the remedy at law is doubtful, a Court of equity may relieve. A bill was filed to set aside a contract, and compel the delivery up of certain notes obtained from complainant by fraud. As under the circumstances shown by the bill it was doubtful if the defense to the notes would be good at law, and complainant was liable to be harrassed with a series of suits thereon, the Court overruled a demurrer for want of equity, and required the defendant to answer. *Ankrim v. Woodworth*, Har. Ch., 355. See *Wheeler v. Clinton Canal Bank*, Har. Ch., 449.

1111. If relief is prayed which cannot be had at law, that is sufficient to confer jurisdiction. *Rowland v. Doty*, Har. Ch., 3; *Wales v. Newbould*, 9 Mich., 45.

1112. How the defense made. The objection that there is a remedy at law should be taken by demurrer. If the object of the suit is embraced under any of the appropriate heads of equitable jurisdiction, the Court will take cognizance of it, notwithstanding there may be a remedy at law, or other circumstances exist which would induce the Court to refuse to entertain jurisdiction of the particular case, unless the defendant takes the objection by demurrer, or claims the benefit of it by his answer. *Williams v. Mayor, &c., of Detroit*, 2 Mich., 560.

1113. But where the subject is not one of equitable cognizance, relief cannot be given in equity, notwithstanding the defendant has answered, and gone to a hearing on the merits. *Bennett v. Nichols*, 12 Mich., 22.

1114. Where parties were trying their rights to land at law, and the claim of defendants was a legal and not an equitable one, with nothing to prevent their establishing it as fully at law as in equity, it was held that equity would not interfere on their application, but leave them to establish their defense at law. But bill being filed, and the defendant, instead of demurring, having submitted to answer, and not in his answer insisting on the objection, it was further held that he was too late to raise the objection at the final hearing on pleadings and proofs. *Stockton v. Williams*, Wal. Ch., 120. See *Moran v. Palmer*, 13 Mich., 367.

1115. Election of remedies. A party defrauded in a contract of sale must make his election on the discovery of the fraud, or within a reasonable time thereafter, whether he will rescind the contract, or resort to an action on the case for damages. If the condition of the property has been so changed that the parties cannot substantially be placed back where they were before the sale, the party defrauded must resort to his action. *Carroll v. Rice*, Wal. Ch., 373.

1116. Complainant having filed his bill for relief against a judgment at law, and having subsequently sued out a writ of error upon the judgment, he was required to make election in which Court he would proceed. *Webb v. Williams*, Wal. Ch., 452.

1117. Concurrent jurisdiction. Equity has concurrent jurisdiction with the Courts of law in cases of fraud. And where the remedy at law is difficult or doubtful, equity will entertain jurisdiction. *Wheeler v. Clinton Canal Bank*, Har. Ch., 449.

1118. Jurisdiction for one purpose retained for another. Where equity has acquired jurisdiction for the purpose of granting an injunction, it may retain the suit for the purpose of awarding damages to complainant. *Brown v. Gardner*, Har. Ch., 291.

1119. So where a bill was filed to rescind a contract for fraud, and the Court under the circumstances refused this relief, yet, the fraud being established, the bill was retained for the purpose of giving damages to complainant. *Carroll v. Rice*, Wal. Ch., 373.

1120. And where the Court had determined that the equitable title was in complainant, it decreed a surrender of the possession to him, instead of leaving him to his remedy by ejectment. *Whipple v. Farrar*, 3 Mich., 436.

1121. Relief against judgment. If a party has a defense at law which he neglects to make, he cannot, after judgment against him, have relief in equity. *Wright v. King*, Har. Ch., 12.

1122. Where one is induced to become indorser of a note by the statements of the payee that it is mere matter of form, and he will not be troubled about it, and afterwards suit is brought upon the note, and he makes no defense, and judgment is obtained, he is thereafter precluded from claiming that the judgment is not binding upon him. *Roberts v. Miles*, 12 Mich., 297.

1123. But where, after the judgment, statements to a similar effect were made, under such circumstances as to justify the indorser in believing and acting upon them, and in supposing he was not liable, and he was thereby induced to abstain from securing himself when he might easily have done so, until the maker became insolvent, and an execution was then levied upon his property, it was held that he was entitled to a perpetual injunction. *Ibid.*

1124. Ignorance of defense. Where a defendant was

ignorant of the facts which constituted his defense at law pending the suit, or the defense was not available at law, the case forms an exception to the general rule that equity will not interfere to relieve against a judgment at law. *Wales v. Bank of Michigan*, Har. Ch., 308.

1125. Fraud of plaintiff, &c. So does the case of a party who, without any neglect or default on his part, was prevented by fraud or accident, or the act of the opposing party, from making his defense. *Mack v. Doty*, Har. Ch., 366; *Burpee v. Smith*, Wal. Ch., 327.

1126. Where complainants were prevented from making their defense at law by the act of the plaintiff, until the only witness by whom the defense could be proved was dead, it was held that they were entitled to relief in equity, and that it was not necessary to entitle them to this relief that they should appeal from the judgment at law. *Mack v. Doty*, Har. Ch., 366.

1127. Complainants were sureties for another party, for whom defendant had from time to time extended the payment, without their consent, until the principal had become insolvent. Suits being brought against complainants, they appeared and pleaded, and the suits were discontinued; but the witness by whom the defense could be made out dying, suits were again brought and judgments recovered. It was held that complainants were entitled to relief against the judgments. *Ibid.*

1128. Negligence of defendant. If a party's ignorance of his defense at law is connected with negligence, and might have been avoided by the use of ordinary means to obtain the necessary information, equity will not relieve. *Wixom v. Davis*, Wal. Ch., 15.

1129. Setting aside execution sale. Irregularities in a sale under an execution must be corrected by applying to the Court out of which the writ issued, to set the sale aside. There must be fraud to give equity jurisdiction; it is not sufficient there is irregularity. *Cavenaugh v. Jakeway*, Wal. Ch., 344.

1130. In restraining proceedings at law, equity does not assume jurisdiction over the Courts in which they are had, but restrains the proceedings by controlling the parties thereto by injunction. *Burpee v. Smith*, Wal. Ch., 327.

2. Discovery.

1131. Equity will compel a discovery in aid of a defense at law, and stay proceedings at law until an answer to a bill for discovery can be obtained. *Wright v. King*, Har. Ch., 12.

1132. Where a bill is filed for relief, the discovery is ancillary; and a demurrer which is good to the relief is good to the discovery. And where a complainant is entitled to discovery only, and goes on by his bill to pray relief, the whole bill is demurrable. *Welles v. River Raisin and Grand River Railroad Co.*, Wal. Ch., 35.

1133. Parties in pari delicto. Where a party is sued at law on account of an illegal transaction equity will not aid him by discovery. *Ibid.*

3. INJUNCTION.

1134. Against public officers. Equity may restrain public officers by injunction, where they are proceeding illegally and improperly, under a claim of right, to do any act to the prejudice of individual rights. *Cooper v. Alden*, Har. Ch., 72; *Brown v. Gardner*, Har. Ch., 291.

1135. The interference in such cases is to prevent great and irreparable injury. Where an injunction was awarded to restrain the opening of a road, but before it was served or defendants had knowledge of it, the road was opened, and the equity of the case was doubtful and the injury slight, the Court refused to retain the suit and close up the road, and also refused to award an issue *quantum damnificatus*. *Brown v. Gardner*, Har. Ch., 291.

1136. The common council of Detroit having authority by law to make an assessment for paving streets, an injunction will not be granted to restrain the collection of such assessment by warrant against the goods and chattels of complainant; but he will be left to his remedy at law. *Williams v. Mayor, &c., of Detroit*, 2 Mich., 560.

1137. An individual has no right as a tax payer, either in his own name or on behalf of himself and the other tax payers, to file a bill to enjoin proceedings in advance of the actual levy of a tax. He cannot seek redress until his own tax can be ascertained, and he cannot then proceed in equity except to protect his individual interests from injuries not remediable otherwise. *Miller v. Grandy*, 13 Mich., 540.

1138. Private persons cannot assume to themselves the right to institute proceedings in chancery to redress grievances on behalf of the public. They can only proceed where the individual grievances are distinct from those of the public at large, and such as give them a private right to redress. *Ibid.*

1139. The only cases where individuals can sue on behalf of themselves and others are where the interests, though numerous, are all separate, individual, and not joint or public interests identical in character and origin, but all private and independent rights growing out of the same transaction or frauds. *Ibid.*

1140. Nuisances may be stayed or prevented by injunction, and the complainant will not be first required to establish his right at law, unless doubtful and in dispute. *White v. Forbes*, Wal. Ch., 112.

1141. Where the aid of the Court is sought to protect the enjoyment of property, it will not be governed by the mere value of property, but will interfere if the injury will materially lessen the enjoyment of it by the owner. *Ibid.*

1142. A perpetual injunction was granted to prevent the erection of a dam which would have flooded the lands of complainant, on the grounds of injury to the property, and the probability that disease would be generated by the overflowing of the water. *Ibid.*

1143. The provision in the statute—Comp. L., § 4722—as to the jurisdiction of chancery in cases of nuisance, was not intended to extend or enlarge their jurisdiction. *Norris v. Hill*, 1 Mich., 202.

1144. Personal property. The ground upon which injunctions are granted against third persons in possession of personal property, and ostensibly its rightful owners, upon an ex-parte application, is for the protection of the fund or property when shown to be in danger without its interposition. *Thayer v. Swift*, Har. Ch., 430.

1145. And where it is not alleged that such persons are insolvent, or transient, or that the fund is in a hazardous condition, an injunction will not be granted, as they will be equally responsible to those whose rights to the property or fund should be established though the property should be converted into money, and the money paid away pending the suit. *Ibid.*

1146. Possession of lands is not to be obtained by injunction. The Court cannot, by ex-parte order or process, turn even a wrongdoer out of possession. *People v. Simonson*, 10 Mich., 335.

1147. Complainant, claiming to be in the actual possession of certain premises, obtained a preliminary injunction enjoining respondents from trespass of a nature likely to injure the buildings, and the writ also enjoined them from in any way interfering or meddling with the possession, and from entering into the premises; and it appearing that respondents were actually in possession at the time the injunction was issued, it was held that they could not be punished as for contempt in maintaining this possession by force. *Ibid.*

1148. Tenants in common of water. Where complainants owned the water power on the east side of a river, and one half the water power on the west side—the defendant owning the other half—and defendant had occasionally used more than his half the water on the west side, but no suit had been brought against him for so doing, and complainants had no machinery on that side of the river to be propelled by water, an injunction restraining defendant in the use of the water was refused. *Norris v. Hill*, 1 Mich., 202.

4. Fraud, Mistake, &c.

1149. A contract by which lands were exchanged for goods, set aside for fraud in representations in regard to the land. *Jones v. Wing*, Har. Ch., 301. And so where lands were exchanged for lands with similar representations. *Rood v. Chapin*, Wal. Ch., 79. See supra, 1115 to 1117.

1150. So where one had purchased lands at a tax sale, but on application by the owner had agreed to assign to him the tax certificate, and the owner was induced not to redeem the land from the sale in consequence of this promise, but after the time for redemption expired the tax purchaser obtained a deed from the Auditor-General to himself, he was decreed to convey to the owner on being paid the tax bid and interest. *Laing v. McKee*, 13 Mich., 124.

1151. Party must act promptly. A party entitled to rescind a contract must not sleep on his rights, or take time to speculate on the course of events. If he goes on, with a full knowledge of his rights, recognizing the contract as still in force, and by his acts and conduct tacitly gives his assent to its execution in a manner different from the original understanding of the parties, he is not entitled to have the contract rescinded, or to any relief inconsistent with what may fairly and reasonably be presumed, from his own acts, to have been assented to by him. *De Armand v. Phillips*, Wal. Ch., 186.

1152. An assignee of a contract cannot insist upon fraud used in making the contract, on the party under whom he claims. *Carroll v. Potter*, Wal. Ch., 355.

1153. Mistake. Where a lot which had been surveyed, located and platted on a diagram, was sold by an erroneous description, but the purchaser and all succeeding purchasers occupied it as marked out by the survey, a decree was made to correct the mistake, and releases were ordered to be made between the parties, whose lands were affected by the erroneous description, to make their lots conform to the location. *Norris v. Hurd*, Wal. Ch., 102.

1154. Defense of failure of consideration. A mistake in description occurred in a deed given on behalf of the United States, of a lot in Detroit, in exchange for other lands. The city was afterwards, by act of Congress, made the donee of the undisposed of lands on the city plan. To a bill filed against the city to correct the mistake, it is not a valid defense that the title to the land given to the United States in exchange subsequently failed. *Farmers and Mechanics' Bank v. City of Detroit*, 12 Mich., 445.

1155. Defense of bona fide purchase. Neither the city, as donee of the United States, nor persons taking conveyance from the city with notice, can claim protection, as bona fide purchasers, against such correction. *Ibid.*

1156. Laches. The deed was given in 1816. The grantee took possession of the land intended to be conveyed, and he and his grantees retained it until 1848, when the city went into possession. A bill was filed in 1861 to correct the mistake. Held that the remedy was not lost by laches. *Ibid.*

1157. Mistake in voluntary deed. Bills by purchasers for a valuable consideration from the grantee, against the heirs and administrator of the grantor, to reform a deed by correcting the description of the lands, which, by reason of the omission of four out of fourteen courses and distances, embraced but a small portion of the lands intended to be conveyed. Defense—which was fully proved—that the deed was made without consideration, and for the purpose of defrauding the creditors of the grantor. There was no proof of debts existing against the estate of the grantor at the time the bills were filed, but the administrator was taking proceedings in the Probate Court for the sale of the lands—for what purpose did not appear. The deeds to complainants described the respective parcels purchased by them correctly. Both parties to the fraudulent conveyance were dead before the mistake was discovered. A full consideration was described in this deed; the grantee assumed possession and control of the premises under it, and the grantor, who died before complainants purchased, had always after giving the deed represented, and twice made oath, that the land belonged to the grantee. Whether equity can reform the deed in such case, *quere*, the Court being equally divided. *Quirk v. Thomas*, 6 Mich., 76.

1158. Refusing relief because of mistake. A mistake in a deed or other written instrument is a good ground for refusing relief to which complainant would otherwise be entitled. *Garlinghouse v. Dixon*, Wal. Ch., 440.

1159. Reforming contract. Equity will not reform a contract by the addition of new provisions which, it is claimed, were embraced in the understanding of the parties when the contract was made, where there is no allegation of fraud or mistake in drafting the contract. *White v. Port Huron and Milwaukee Railway Company*, 13 Mich., 356.

5. Trusts.

1160. Where one procured an allowance to himself of a claim due to a third party under a treaty, and received the money upon it, he was held the trustee of the rightful claimant. *Edwards v. Hulbert*, Wal. Ch., 54.

1161. That a fraudulent grantee shall hold in trust for the person equitably entitled, see *Adams v. Bradley*, 12 Mich.,346.

1162. Where in a voluntary assignment for the benefit of creditors it is provided that the assignees shall proceed to sell the property and pay the debts within such time as to them shall seem meet, this puts the execution of the trust under the control of the Court of Chancery, which will compel the assignee to use reasonable diligence. *Hollister v. Loud*, 2 Mich., 309. But see what is said on this subject in *Sutton v. Hanford*, 11 Mich., 373.

6. Bills of Peace and to Quiet Title.

1163. Bills of peace are only allowed where the complainant has established his right at law, or where the persons who controvert the right are so numerous as to render an issue under the direction of Chancery indispensable to embrace all the parties concerned, and save a multiplicity of suits. *County Commissioners of Lapeer v. Hart*, Har. Ch., 157.

1164. An injunction staying proceedings in sixty seven suits at law on county orders, was dissolved, on the ground that the defense was at law. *Ibid.*

1165. Settling titles to land. The Court of Chancery is not the appropriate tribunal to try conflicting titles to land generally. *Devaux v. Mayor, &c., of Detroit*, Har. Ch., 98; *Blackwood v. Van Vleet*, 11 Mich., 252.

1166. Annulling patent. After confirmation of a claim to land by the Board of Land Commissioners under the act of Congress of May 11, 1820, and after patent issued, if it be competent for a Court of equity to go behind the patent to settle conflicting claims, it should only be done upon the clearest and most irrefragible proof. *Bernard v. Heirs of Bougard*, Har. Ch., 130.

1167. Quieting title. Where the complainant is in possession of land, the Court of Chancery is expressly authorized by statute—Code 1833, p. 358; Comp. L., § 3490—to adjudicate upon conflicting claims. *Rowland v. Doty*, Har. Ch., 3.

1168. The complainant must show a complete title in himself, or a right to such title, before he can call upon a defendant to release. *Stockton v. Williams*, Wal. Ch., 120.

1169. He must show: 1, Possession; 2, A legal or equitable title; 3, A claim set up by the defendant; 4, His own claim must be substantiated. He cannot rely upon the weakness of his adversary's title. *Same case*, 1 Doug., 546.

1170. A Court of equity will not restrain a person from asserting a title to real estate in the course of judicial proceedings, or decree a release by one to another, unless in a case entirely free from doubt. *Ibid.*

1171. A bill to quiet title will be entertained on behalf of the legal owner when he is not in a position to force the adverse claimant into a Court of law to test its validity ; but when each party claims the legal title, and a Court of law is already possessed of the case, and it is not alleged that either fraud, accident or mistake has intervened to prevent the possessor establishing his title at law, equity will not interfere on his behalf. *Moran v. Palmer*, 13 Mich., 367.

1172. Bill against one in possession of lands claiming them under tax titles, to have these titles declared void, and complainant's right to the lands quieted, and for an injunction to restrain the commission of waste by defendant. Complainant had not established his right at law, and had brought no suit for the purpose. Held that the bill could not be sustained. *Blackwood v. Van Vleet*, 11 Mich., 252.

1173. The fact that there may be two new trials in an action of ejectment, is no reason for the interposition of equity to try titles to land. *Ibid.*

1174. Persons cannot be joined as defendants to a bill for this purpose whose claims to the land are in no way connected. *Hunton v. Platt*, 11 Mich., 264.

1175. A bill was filed to quiet complainant's title to land bounded on a river, of the whole of which he was in possession, except a small portion, being a boom, embracing the bed of the stream and a footpath along the bank. His title to the whole was the same, and was undoubted. A decree quieting his title to the whole was affirmed. *Fitzhugh v. Barnard*, 12 Mich., 104.

1176. But the Court cannot go further, and take an account of the rents and profits of the boom while occupied by defendants as wrong doers. *Ibid.*

1177. Possession by complainant, ostensibly of the whole land, and rightfully at least for an undivided half, is sufficient to enable him to maintain a bill under the statute to quiet his title against a third person claiming it. *Blanchard v. Tyler*, 12 Mich., 339.

1178. Cloud upon title. Where an illegal tax is assessed upon lands, and by statute the deed given on a sale of the land therefor would be prima facie evidence of regular proceedings in the assessment and subsequent steps to a sale, such sale would operate to create a cloud upon complainant's title, notwithstanding the illegality must appear on the face of the proceedings ; and the owner may therefore maintain a bill in equity to stay the tax sale. *Palmer v. Rich*, 12 Mich., 414. See as to injunctions to restrain public officers in the performance of their duties, *supra*, 1134 to 1139.

1179. Parol evidence to divest title. To warrant a Court of equity in divesting a title to land, on parol evidence that an unrecorded deed given therefor was subsequently, by agreement between the parties, surrendered by the grantee to be cancelled, the preponderance of evidence should be clear, and the proof so convincing as to leave no reasonable doubt upon the mind. *Hunter v. Hopkins*, 12 Mich., 227.

7. Partition.

1180. Courts of equity have jurisdiction and will entertain proceedings for partition of lands. *Thayer v. Lane*, Har. Ch., 247. And now by statute full jurisdiction is given. See *Comp. L., Ch.* 135.

1181. On bill filed by tenants in common, an administrator who was proceeding to sell under a probate license a larger interest in the lands than the estate had, was enjoined from making the sale until the interest was ascertained and settled. *Thayer v. Lane*, Har. Ch., 247.

1182. Not permitted in violation of agreement. Where the owner of lands conveyed an undivided moiety to another, for a sum of money which was less than its value, to be paid from the proceeds of sales to be made of the lands, and which was secured by mortgage on the lands, and a part of the consideration consisted in the services of the purchaser in taking charge of and selling the joint property under a contract between them, and a principal part of the seller's security for the purchase price, and for the efficiency and fidelity of the purchaser in the management and sale of the property, consisted in the control he would have over the sales of the purchaser's interest, it was held, that so long as the seller was not guilty of refusal to perform his part of the contract, or of any default which would relieve the purchaser from the obligation to perform, or prevent his performance, the latter was not entitled to partition. *Avery v. Payne*, 12 Mich., 540.

1183. Mortgages executed by the seller on his own undivided half, not alleged or shown to have interfered with sales, or otherwise to have operated to the prejudice of the purchaser, will constitute no reason for partition. *Ibid.*

8. Conditions and Penalties.

1184. Relief against conditions. Relief may be given against the breach of a condition precedent in the nature of a penalty; and there is no good reason why it should not be given in the case of a condition precedent, when it would be against a condition subsequent. The substantial question is, not whether the condition is precedent or subsequent, but whether compensation can or can not be made. *Chipman v. Thompson*, Wal. Ch., 405.

1185. The Court is not bound, in all cases where compensation can be made, to give relief; for the party seeking relief may have so conducted himself as to have lost all claim to its interposition; but where this is not the case, and it is equitable under the circumstances that relief should be given, it is competent for the Court to give it. *Ibid.*

1186. Relief given where the condition—which was to support the grantor—had not been strictly performed by the guardian of a minor. *Ibid.*

1187. Enforcing penalties. Equity will not lend its aid to enforce a penalty or forfeiture. *Crane v. Dwyer*, 9 Mich., 350; *White v. Port Huron and Milwaukee Railway Co.*, 13 Mich., 356; *Wing v. Railey*, 14 Mich.

1188. Under a contract for the purchase of lands the vendee took possession and erected a dwelling. The vendor subsequently declared the contract forfeited for non-payment of an instalment of purchase money. Pending proceedings to recover possession, he applied for an injunction to restrain the vendee from removing the house. Injunction refused, on the ground that to grant it would be aiding to enforce a forfeiture. *Crane v. Dwyer*, 9 Mich., 350.

9. Creditor's Bills.

1189. In what cases. There are two classes of cases in which a creditor may come into chancery for relief. *First*, In aid of his execution at law. *Second*, To have his judgment satisfied out of choses in action, or other property of the debtor not liable to execution. *Williams v. Hubbard*, Wal. Ch., 28.

1190. In the first class of cases the complainant must show that an execution has been sued out, but it is not necessary to show that it has been returned. *Ibid.* And see *Beach v. White*, Wal. Ch., 495.

1191. In the second class there should appear an execution issued, and returned unsatisfied in whole or in part; and this should be shown by the officer's return. *Williams v. Hubbard*, Wal. Ch., 28; *Steward v. Stevens*, Har. Ch., 169; *Thayer v. Swift*, Har. Ch., 430; *Stafford v. Hulbert*, Har. Ch., 435; *Smith v. Thompson*, Wal. Ch., 1; *Beach v. White*, Wal. Ch., 495.

1192. Return of execution. The officer's return of an execution, to be sufficient for the purpose of a creditor's bill, must be such as, if untrue, will render him liable for a false return. *Williams v. Hubbard*, Wal. Ch., 28.

1193. A return of the execution unsatisfied by order of the party suing it out, is not sufficient. *Ibid.*

1194. The execution cannot be legally returned unsatisfied until the return day. *Smith v. Thompson*, Wal. Ch., 1; *Beach v. White*, Wal. Ch., 495. But a return on the return day is good. *Williams v. Hubbard*, 1 Mich., 446.

1195. A return of an execution against two defendants, that they have no goods or chattels, lands or tenements, without in terms negativing the fact that either of them had, is sufficient. *Williams v. Hubbard*, 1 Mich., 446.

1196. Return conclusive. The return of the execution is conclusive between the parties to the suit, when it is good on its face, and has not been made by collusion between the creditor and the officer, or by direction of the creditor. *Albany City Bank v. Dorr*, Wal. Ch., 317.

1197. Delay after return. The execution must be returned a reasonable time before the bill is filed. Nine years is not a reasonable time; and where a bill was filed on an execution returned nearly nine years before, a motion for a receiver was denied. *Gould v. Tryon*, Wal. Ch., 353.

1198. New execution. The issuing of a new execution does not take away the right to file a creditor's bill which has once accrued by the return of an execution unsatisfied. *Clark v. Davis*, Har. Ch., 227.

1199. A strict and rigid compliance with all the rules of law must be shown by a judgment creditor, before the Court will administer the harsh remedy of depriving the debtor of all control of his property. *Thayer v. Swift*, Har. Ch., 430. See *Smith v. Thompson*, Wal. Ch., 1.

1200. But where a lien has been acquired by the levy of an execution, and a fraudulent obstruction is interposed by the debtor, a bill may be filed to remove such obstruction. *Thayer v. Swift*, Har. Ch., 430. But it cannot be filed to set aside a fraudulent conveyance until levy is made. *McKibben v. Barton*, 1 Mich., 213, overruling on this point, *Beach v. White*, Wal. Ch., 495.

1201. Void levy. An attachment was served on an equitable interest not subject to levy. The defendant was not served with process, and did not appear in the suit. It was held that the attachment creditor could not, by virtue of any judgment and execution in that suit, acquire any lien on the land which equity could enforce in his favor. *Trask v. Green*, 9 Mich., 358.

1202. Death of defendant. The filing of a bill to reach equitable assets, without answer or the appointment of a receiver, creates no lien upon the debtor's property; and complainant, upon defendant's decease in such case, loses his right to prosecute the suit. *Jones v. Smith*, Wal. Ch., 115.

1203. Defense to suit. The regularity of the judgment and execution cannot be inquired into on a judgment creditor's bill. *Williams v. Hubbard*, 1 Mich., 446.

1204. It is a good plea to the bill that while the execution was out the defendant offered to turn out real estate for the officer to levy on, which the officer, under instructions from the plaintiff's attorney, refused to accept. *Wharton v. Fitch*, Wal. Ch., 143.

1205. But the creditor is not bound to point out property to be levied upon; he has done all that the law requires of him when he has placed his execution in the hands of the sheriff, whose duty it is to make the money. *Albany City Bank v. Dorr*, Wal. Ch., 317.

1206. Non-joinder. Where one of several judgment debtors is wholly irresponsible and destitute of property, he need not be joined as defendant. *Williams v. Hubbard*, 1 Mich., 446.

1207. Bill against stockholders in corporations. Independent of statutory provisions, chancery may, on behalf of the creditors of corporations, compel stockholders to pay in any amount that may be unpaid on their stock. *Pettibone v. McGraw*, 6 Mich., 441.

1208. Parties. To a creditor's bill against stockholders in a corporation, after execution against the corporation returned unsatisfied, it was held not necessary to make all the stockholders defendants. *Ibid.*

1209. Fraudulent corporators. Bill sustained to enforce a demand against parties charged with having assumed to organize under the general banking law, and fraudulently contracted debts. It is immaterial that in another suit by a different creditor they have been treated as a corporation and a receiver appointed. *Wheeler v. Clinton Canal Bank*, Har. Ch., 449. See *Cook v. Wheeler*, Har. Ch., 443.

1210. The rules applicable to ordinary creditors bill do not apply to such a case. *Ibid.*

10. Limitation, Laches and Lapse of Time.

1211. A party seeking to set aside a conveyance on the ground of fraud, must be prompt in communicating the fraud when discovered, and consistent in his notice to the opposite party of the use he intends to make ot it. *Disbrow v. Jones*, Har. Ch., 102; *Street v. Dow*, Har. Ch., 427. And see *Supra*, 1151; *McLean v. Barton*, Har. Ch., 279.

1212. Where complainant had rested several months after he had knowledge of the fraud complained of, and until the condition of the property had changed, before he took any steps to rescind the contract, the Court refused to interfere, and left him to his remedy at law. *Disbrow v. Jones*, Har. Ch., 102.

1213. The defense of the statute of limitations and lapse of time may be made by demurrer. *Campau v. Chene*, 1 Mich., 400 ; *McLean v. Barton*, Har. Ch., 279. And if there be any ground of exception within the statute to prevent the bar, or ground to rebut the presumption arising from lapse of time, it should be stated in the bill. *Campau v. Chene*, 1 Mich., 400.

1214. Delay of twenty years after the right accrued not being in any way excused, a demurrer to a bill to compel a conveyance of lands was sustained. *McLean v. Barton*, Har. Ch., 279.

1215. What delay not unreasonable. Where a bill, asking, among other things, relief against a note, was filed within three years and a half after it was given, and within six months after it fell due, the delay was held no ground for refusing relief. *Schwarz v. Wendell*, Wal. Ch., 267.

1216. Disabilities. In the case of presumptive bar from lapse of time, the rule as to subsequent disabilities is different from that of the statute of limitations. Under the statute the party must bring himself within the exceptions of the statute, whereas in cases of presumptive bar he may show any circumstance that outweighs the presumption. *Abbott v. Godfroy's heirs*, 1 Mich., 178.

1217. Equity asserted against an equity. The rule of limitation will be applied where a bare equity is sought to be enforced against an equity ; and will not be confined to cases where it is sought to enforce an equity against the legal estate. *Campau v. Chene*, 1 Mich., 400.

11. Set Off.

1218. A party seeking to make a set off in equity beyond that given by the statute, must show affirmatively the existence of all the facts necessary to raise the equity. *Lockwood v. Beckwith*, 6 Mich., 168.

1219. Equity will not allow a set off where the law would not, unless there be special equities, growing out of the transaction itself, requiring it. *Ibid.*

1220. Insolvency. Where a partnership became insolvent, and made a general assignment for the benefit of creditors, including therein a note past due, and the maker of the note held the acceptance of the partnership not then due, it was held that the insolvency of the acceptors was not, of itself, sufficient to authorize a set off in equity of the acceptance against the note in the hands of the assignee, in the absence of evidence that the acceptance was based upon the note, or that the maker of the note trusted to it at the time, as a means of discharging his obligation. *Ibid.*

1221. The insolvency of one party, in the case of mutual credits, is not of itself sufficient to authorize an equitable set off. *Hale v. Holmes*, 8 Mich., 37.

1222. Mutuality. Equity cannot compel a vendor to receive his own paper on the contract of sale, when he has not agreed to do so, and the purchaser has not bound himself to take and pay for the property. It is not a case for set off, inasmuch as there is no contract on the part of the purchaser against which to allow the paper. *Ibid.*

1223. The bill cannot be sustained unless the party seeking to obtain the set off is the real owner and has the control of the counter claim, so that the creditor who sues him is his debtor as to the claim offered in reduction. *McGraw v. Pettibone*, 10 Mich., 530.

1224. So held where stockholders in an insolvent plank road company, against whom decree had been rendered for debts of the company, sought to set off against the decree demands in favor of the company. *Ibid.*

1225. Former suit as a bar. A set off against a judgment cannot be made in equity of demands which might have been proved in reduction of plaintiff's claim in the former suit. *Ibid.*

1226. But where in the foreclosure of a mortgage given for the purchase price of land, the defendant sought to set off certain incumbrances which were a lien on the land when he bought, and the relief was denied because he had not paid off the incumbrances, and he paid them off after decree, it was held that he might then file a bill to have the set off allowed. *Detroit and Milwaukee R. R. Co. v. Griggs*, 12 Mich., 45.

12. Miscellaneous Matters.

1227. Lost note. To give equity jurisdiction where recovery is sought of the amount of a lost note, it is not necessary that it should be lost before due. *Green v. Stone*, Wal. Ch., 109. See Comp. L., §§ 4324, 4325, 4326 and 4428, for provisions as to the remedy at law upon lost notes.

1228. Contribution. Where complainants, who were the owners of three-fourths of a water power, were compelled to purchase a piece of land to secure to the proprietors of the power the right to flow it, equity will not compel the owner of the other fourth to contribute to the purchase. *Norris v. Hill*, 1 Mich., 202.

1229. Failure of consideration. Where defendant received a grant of the right to use certain water power, and dig a race on complainant's land, in consideration of erecting a mill at a certain place where their lands joined, and then built his mill at another place, and diverted the water from complainant's land, it was held that the consideration had failed, and that complainant was entitled to a reconveyance; and defendant was enjoined from setting up his deed in defense of any action for a previous diversion of the water. *Jacox v. Clark*, Wal. Ch., 508.

1230. Creating lien. Equity cannot create a lien on real estate to secure a debt not contracted on its credit, and not charged upon it by agreement. *Bennett v. Nichols*, 12 Mich., 22.

1231. Equal equities. Where the equities of the parties are equal, and neither has the legal title, the prior equity will prevail. *Wing v. McDowell*, Wal. Ch., 175; *Norris v. Showerman*, Wal. Ch., 206.

1232. Subsequently obtaining the legal title in right of another and not in one's own right, or with notice of the prior equity, will not aid the holder of the postponed equity. *Ibid.*

1233. Equitable estoppel. Equity will not interfere to relieve a party on the ground that assessments are irregular and unauthorized by the strict provisions of law, where they are substantially authorized and made in reliance upon his own express agreement. *Jackson v. City of Detroit*, 10 Mich., 248.

1234. Where complainants had verbally promised to allow defendants to draw water for running a mill from a certain lake, the outlet of which flowed through complainant's lands, and had suffered them to go on and construct a mill and race at an expense of $3,000 before informing them that they did not intend to abide by the promise, an injunction which had been granted to restrain the taking of the water of the lake for the mill, was dissolved. *Payne v. Paddock*, Wal. Ch., 487.

1235. New trial at law. Chancery will not award a new trial in a suit at law, on the ground of newly discovered evidence, when the proposed evidence only goes to contradict the evidence given on the former trial in an immaterial point. *Morris v. Hadley*, 9 Mich., 278.

1236. Nor on the ground of newly discovered evidence will it decree a new trial to enable a defendant to make a wholly different defense from that which he made and failed in on the first trial. *Ibid.*

EQUITY PLEADINGS.

1. The Bill.

1237. Averments to be positive. Facts essential to the complainant's title to maintain his bill and obtain the relief, must be alleged positively, and cannot be inferred from other facts stated. *Manning v. Drake*, 1 Mich., 34.

1238. A bill to reach land alleged to have been fraudulently conveyed by a judgment debtor, is bad on general demurrer if it contain no direct averment that at the time of the alleged fraudulent conveyance the debtor had, or pretended to have, an interest in the lands. *Ibid.*

1239. Averment of administration. An averment that A. and B. were appointed and acted as administrators, without alleging that they accepted the trust, is sufficient. *Ibid.*

1240. But a bill to foreclose a mortgage in which complainants describe themselves as executors of the last will and testament of the mortgagee, but without setting out his death, and in no way alluding to the probate of the will, shows no right of action in complainants. *Middlesworth v. Nixon*, 2 Mich., 425.

1241. Certainty. An allegation that W. was declared a bankrupt, and that "by virtue thereof all the property, effects and rights of property of W. became divested out of him and vested in H., the official or general assignee in bankruptcy, appointed and designated under the act of Congress by the said District Court," is a sufficient allegation that H. was the assignee in bankruptcy of W. *Williams v. Hubbard*, 1 Mich., 446.

1242. No relief can be given on evidence establishing a case not stated in the bill. *Thayer v. Lane*, Wal. Ch., 200; *Jerome v. Hopkins*, 2 Mich., 96; *Cicotte v. Gagnier*, 2 Mich., 381; *Warner v. Whittaker*, 6 Mich., 133; *Bloomer v. Henderson*, 8 Mich., 395; *Bomier v. Caldwell*, 8 Mich., 463; *Barrows v. Baughman*, 9 Mich., 213; *Wurcherer v. Hewett*, 10 Mich., 453; *Peckham v. Buffum*, 11 Mich., 529; *Dunn v. Dunn*, 11 Mich., 284; *Perkins v. Perkins*, 12 Mich., 456; *Moran v. Palmer*, 13 Mich., 367.

1243. The bona fide assignee of a mortgage, not charged in the bill with knowledge of the complainant's equities against the assignor in respect to the mortgage, will not be held affected with those equities. *Cicotte v. Gagnier*, 2 Mich., 381.

1244. Where a bill contains a general charge against a defendant, of co-operation with other defendants to procure a deed to the latter, but makes no specific charge against him predicated upon or sustained by any statement of facts, which could be met and denied, admitted or explained by the answer, neither his acts nor omissions are put in issue. *Dawson v. Hall*, 2 Mich., 390.

1245. Estoppels, where they form the foundation of the relief asked, and are relied on to defeat a legal title, cannot be proved unless alleged in the bill. *Cicotte v. Gagnier*, 2 Mich., 381; *Moran v. Palmer*, 13 Mich., 367.

1246. Reference to deed. By referring in the bill to a deed or other written insrument, as follows: "as in and by the said indenture, reference being thereunto had, when produced will more fully and at large appear"—the whole document referred to is made a part of the record, although not fully and accurately described in the bill; and the complainant may, at the hearing, avail himself of the portions not recited, as well as of those inaccurately set forth. *Swetland v. Swetland*, 3 Mich., 482.

1247. Abbreviated names: allegation of identity. A bill to foreclose a mortgage given by Alexander Eaton, junior, to O. P. Ramsdell, was filed by Orrin P. Ramsdell against Alexander Eaton. The bill was in the usual form, but contained no direct averment that the parties to the suit were identical with the parties to the mortgage. Held sufficient on pro confesso. The question of identity would have been open to proof if disputed. *Ramsdell v Eaton*, 12 Mich., 117.

1248. Legal effect. It is sufficient to allege the undertaking in a written instrument according to its legal effect. *Jerome v. Hopkins*, 2 Mich., 96.

1249. Charge of fraud. Where an act alleged in the bill to have been done does not of itself import a fraud—a fraudulent intent must be charged; but no such averment is requisite where from the statement of facts fraud is plainly to be inferred. *Hale v. Chandler*, 3 Mich., 531.

1250. Averment of notice. Bill to enforce a builder's lien upon real estate, and to have it declared a prior lien to a certain mortgage taken with notice. But the bill did not allege such notice, and it was held that it was not in issue. *Barrows v. Baughman*, 9 Mich., 213. And see *Bloomer v. Henderson*, 8 Mich., 395.

1251. Exception in statute. Where a bill is filed under a statute, and there is an exception in the enacting clause, it must negative the exception; but where there is no exception to the enacting clause, but an exemption in a proviso thereto, or a subsequent section of the act, it is matter of defense, and must be shown by defendant. *Attorney General v. Oakland County Bank*, Wal. Ch., 90. See *Myers v. Carr*, 12 Mich., 63.

1252. Offer to refund. Bill to set aside a tax title fraudulently obtained by defendant. It is not necessary to offer in the bill to refund the money paid by defendant therefor. *Taylor v. Snyder*, Wal. Ch., 490.

1253. Amount in controversy. Where, in a suit respecting property, (not a foreclosure suit, or between partners), the bill shows the amount in controversy to be less than one hundred dollars, the Court must dismiss the bill whether the objection of want of jurisdiction is taken by the defendant or not. *Gamber v. Holben*, 5 Mich., 331.

1254. But a bill to restrain the collection of a tax, which states its amount as about one hundred and fifty dollars, sufficiently shows it to be over one hundred. *Palmer v. Rich*, 12 Mich., 414. As to case of nuisance, see supra 1141.

1255. Parties. Only those whose interests would be affected by the decree need be made parties. To a bill to correct a mistake in a deed, one whose land is bounded on the land in controversy is not a necessary party where it is not sought to change the location. *Norris v. Hurd*, Wal. Ch., 102. See also *Suydam v. Dequindre*, Har. Ch., 347.

1256. Complainants with differing interests. The executors and devisees of a deceased tenant in common, not asking partition among themselves, may jointly file a bill to have their interests set off from that of the co-tenant. *Page v. Webster*, 8 Mich., 263.

1257. Interest incorrectly stated. Defendants were described in the bill as heirs of their father, when in fact they claimed as heirs of their mother. It was held that they were properly made parties as claiming an interest in the property in controversy; it was too late to take the objection for the first time at the hearing that their interest was not properly made to appear by the bill; proofs having been taken, and the proper parties being before the Court. *Chipman v. Thompson*, Wal. Ch., 405.

1258. Assignor need not be a party. The assignor of a judgment, or chose in action on which a judgment has been obtained in the name of the assignor, is not a necessary party to a judgment creditor's bill filed by the assignee. *Morey v. Forsyth*, Wal. Ch., 465.

1259. But where there is a controversy between the assignor and assignee, touching the assignment, the Court will direct the assignor to be made a party for the protection of all. *Ibid.* And he may be made a party in any case. *Beach v. White*, Wal. Ch., 495.

1260. Where the judgment creditor has assigned the demand upon which the judgment was rendered, to secure a debt of equal amount, the assignee alone, or those succeeding to his rights, can bring suit in equity to enforce the judgment. *Andrews v. Kibbee*, 12 Mich., 94.

1261. The fact that, in such a case, one of the defendants has become the assignee, will not enable the complainant to sustain his bill, which avers the ownership to be in himself; since the testimony showing the assignment would also show that complainant had no right of action such as he set out in his bill. *Ibid.*

1262. Cestui que trust. Where the object of the bill is merely to collect money, or reduce it to possession, it is not necessary for the holder of a chose in action to make his cestuis que trust parties, though the rule is otherwise where the existence or enjoyment of trust property is to be affected by the prayer of the bill. *Cook v. Wheeler*, Har. Ch., 443; *Wheeler v. Clinton Canal Bank*, Har. Ch., 449; *Sill v. Ketcham*, Har.

Ch., 423; *Martin v. McReynolds*, 6 Mich., 70; *Adams v. Bradley*, 12 Mich., 346.

1263. The holder of the legal title is a necessary party where the holder of the equitable title files a bill to foreclose a mortgage. *Martin v. McReynolds*, 6 Mich., 70.

1264. The grantee of one who has conveyed lands with warranty, need not be made a party to a bill filed by the grantor to set aside a fraudulent tax purchase which might affect his covenants. *Taylor v. Snyder*, Wal. Ch., 490.

1265. Identity of interest among defendants. A bill may be sustained against different persons, relative to matters of the same nature, in which all of the defendants were more or less concerned, though not jointly in each act. *Wheeler v. Clinton Canal Bank*, Har. Ch., 449.

1266. Where the matter in litigation is entire in itself, it is not necessary that each defendant should have an interest in the suit coextensive with the claim set up by the bill; he may have an interest in a part of the matter in litigation, instead of the whole. *Ingersoll v. Kirby*, Wal. Ch., 65.

1267. But where two persons claim different parcels of land by different titles, they cannot be joined as defendants in a bill to quiet the title by one who claims both. *Hunton v. Platt*, 11 Mich., 264.

1268. A joint maker of a note need not be made a party to a bill by another joint maker to restrain proceedings on a judgment recovered on the note against the latter alone. *Burpee v. Smith*, Wal. Ch., 327.

1269. Officers not interested. A magistrate before whom a judgment was rendered, is not a proper party to a bill to restrain proceedings upon it. But an officer having an execution in his hands still in force, is. *Ibid.*

1270. The Auditor General is a necessary party to a bill filed against the county treasurer, to restrain a sale of lands for taxes assessed under the drainage law of 1859; the county treasurer being merely his agent in the sale. *Palmer v. Rich*, 12 Mich., 414.

1271. But contractors for making the drains are not necessary parties. *Ibid.*

1272. Complainant's interest. It is a good ground of demurrer to the whole bill that one of the complainants has no interest in the suit; there is no such rule as to defendants. *Barstow v. Smith*, Wal. Ch., 394.

1273. Parties to foreclosure. The survivor of two assignees of a mortgage may foreclose it, and it is not necessary for him to join the personal representative of the deceased assignee. *Martin v. McReynolds*, 6 Mich., 70.

1274. Defendants. The fraudulent grantee of a title which is equitably subject to the mortgage, is a proper party defendant. *Adams v. Bradley*, 12 Mich., 346.

1275. The mortgage covered two parcels of land. A defendant answered, claiming one of them by paramount title, and disclaiming as to the other; and as to the last a decree was taken. It was held that the bill should have been dismissed as to this defendant with costs; as he was under the necessity of appearing and answering to protect his interest in the parcel claimed by him. *Gregory v. Stanton*, 12 Mich., 61.

1276. The description of premises in the mortgage was erroneous in one particular. To a bill to foreclose it and correct the error, a person is not a proper party who owns lands which would be affected by the erroneous description, but who has never been owner or incumbrancer of any portion of the mortgaged premises as identified by the proofs. *Ramsdell v. Eaton*, 12 Mich., 117.

1277. Parties not connected with the title. Bill was filed to foreclose a mortgage, which made persons other than the mortgagor parties, charging that one of them had given a prior mortgage on the same premises, which had been since paid, but caused to be assigned to one of the other defendants for the purpose of keeping it alive against complainant's mortgage; and asking that it be decreed to be satisfied; but the bill did not show any privity of title to the land between the parties to the first and the parties to the second mortgage, or what was the state of the title at any time, or any obligation on the part of the first mortgagor which would entitle the second mortgagor or his assigns to require him to pay or remove such first mortgage. Held, that the bill showed no title to relief as against the parties to the first mortgage. *Wright v. Dudley*, 8 Mich., 115.

1278. Personal representatives of a deceased mortgagor are not necessary parties to a suit to foreclose the mortgage against the heirs, unless the personal estate is sought to be charged with any deficiency. *Abbott v. Godfroy's Heirs*, 1 Mich., 178.

1279. Adverse claimants cannot be made parties to a foreclosure suit for the purpose of litigating their titles. The only proper parties are the mortgagor and mortgagee, and those who have acquired rights and interests under them subsequent to the mortgage. *Chamberlain v. Lyell*, 3 Mich., 448; *Horton v. Ingersoll*, 13 Mich., 409.

1280. But where one claims an interest in the equity of redemption, it is proper to make him a party for the purpose of foreclosing such interest, notwithstanding he also claims the land by tax title. *Horton v. Ingersoll*, 13 Mich., 409.

1281. Prior owners. Where the title of complainant was acquired without warranty, the grantee in a conveyance through which he claims is not a necessary party to a bill to correct a mistake in such conveyance. *Farmers and Mechanics' Bank v. City of Detroit*, 12 Mich., 445.

1282. Sureties who have undertaken, not for the payment of the mortgage debt, but that the mortgagor shall provide a sinking fund in certain specific securities for its payment, cannot be joined as defendants in a suit to foreclose the mortgage under § 3567 of Compiled Laws. *Joy v. Jackson and Michigan Plank Road Co.*, 11 Mich., 155.

1283. Oath to bill. A bill need not be under oath, when no preliminary order is required, notwithstanding an answer on oath is not waived. *Atwater v. Kinman*, Har. Ch., 243.

1284. Bills of discovery. Where a bill seeks discovery in aid of proceedings at law, complainant must charge in his bill that the facts are known to defendant, and ought to be disclosed to him, and that the complainant is unable to prove them by other evidence; and it must be affirmatively stated in the bill that the facts sought to be discovered are material. *Carroll v. Farmers and Mechanics' Bank*, Har. Ch., 197.

1285. Injunction bills. An injunction bill, strictly speaking, is one seeking no other relief. When the bill prays other relief, the injunction is regarded as ancillary to such relief, and falls with it. *Blackwood v. Van Vleet*,, 11 Mich., 252.

1286. Staying proceedings at law. Where an injunction is asked to stay proceedings at law, it is incumbent on the plaintiff to show in his bill the state of the pleadings, and the Court in which the suit is pending, that the officer may judge of the propriety of the allowance, and prescribe the terms on which it shall be issued. *Carroll v. Farmers and Mechanics' Bank*, Har. Ch., 197.

1287. Foreclosure suits: Allegation of assignment. An allegation that an assignment of the mortgage was duly acknowledged before a commissioner of deeds, according to the laws of New York, where the same was executed, is sufficient on demurrer. *Livingston v. Jones*, Har. Ch., 165.

1288.—averment that debt is due. The allegation that the mortgage debt is due, is material in a foreclosure suit; and when the answer does not admit it, any proof is receivable to disprove it which would be receivable under the general issue at the common law. *Morris v. Morris*, 5 Mich., 171.

1289. An allegation that no part of the mortgage debt has been collected or paid, when the bill sets out fully the mortgage, and shows the amount of the several instalments, and when they became due, sufficiently shows the amount due. *Martin v. McReynolds*, 6 Mich., 70.

1290.—where judgment has been had at law. Where

bill was filed to foreclose a mortgage given to secure the payment of three notes, and the bill stated that a judgment had been recovered on the first note, which had been nearly paid, but did not show that an execution had been issued on the judgment and returned unsatisfied in whole or in part, nor distinctly claim a decree for the amount of the other two notes only, nor waive the right to the mortgage security as to the judgment, it was held that the bill could not be maintained; the statute—Comp. L., § 3569—forbidding a foreclosure suit after judgment at law, unless an execution has been returned unsatisfied in whole or in part. *Cooper v. Bresler*, 9 Mich., 534. See *Dennis v. Hemingway*, Wal. Ch., 387.

1291. To prevent proceedings on a foreclosure bill, it is not necessary that judgment shall have been rendered on the bond or note accompanying the mortgage, but for the money for which the mortgage was given. *Dennis v. Hemingway* Wal. Ch., 387.

1292.—subsequent purchasers. The allegation under Chancery Rule 91, that a defendant claims an interest in the mortgaged premises "as subsequent purchaser, incumbrancer or otherwise," will not entitle the complainant to show that a deed to such defendant, subsequent to the mortgage but recorded first, is fraudulent. If he claims the deed to be fraudulent, he must set forth in the bill the facts which show the fraud. *Wurcherer v. Hewett*, 10 Mich., 453.

1293.—indemnity mortgage. Bill by persons who had guaranteed the performance of a covenant to pay certain debts, to foreclose an indemnity mortgage. They averred that they had paid on the debts $1,000, "as they were obliged to do by the terms and legal effect" of the covenant, "on account of the default" of the covenantor. It was held that this was a sufficient statement that they had paid after their liability accrued, and that it was not necessary to set forth in the bill the particular sums paid. *Dye v. Mann*, 10 Mich., 291.

1294. It is immaterial in such case that the payment of the debts was by part of the defendants only, and not by all jointly. *Ibid.*

1295. Creditors' bills. Rule 109 [of 1839] required the bill to state, either positively or on belief, the true sum due on the judgment; that defendant had equitable interests, &c., to the value of $100 or more, which complainant had been unable to reach; and that the bill was not exhibited by collusion, &c. The bill was bad if it failed to set forth these facts; and they must be sworn to. *Clark v. Davis*, Har. Ch., 227.

1296.—to avoid fraudulent conveyance. Where a creditor seeks in chancery to reach property alleged to have been purchased with the money of his debtor, and conveyed to the debtor's wife to keep the same beyond the reach of creditors, he must show either that his debt existed at the time, or that the debtor was indebted to others, and that the purchase money was paid by him and the deed taken to his wife with actual intent to defraud existing creditors; or that the purchase money was paid by the debtor and the conveyance taken to the wife for the purpose of defrauding future creditors. *Hopson v. Payne*, 7 Mich., 334.

1297. Where the bill was inconsistent; averring in one part that the purchase price was paid by the wife, and in another that the husband paid the money, or furnished the money wherewith it was purchased by the wife; it was held that, as the law presumes honesty rather than fraud, it was to be inferred that the wife paid for the land with her own money rather than the contrary. *Ibid.*

1298. Partition: statement of interests. Bill by executors and devisees set forth that the undivided interest was devised to the latter in common, with the power, nevertheless, in the executor to sell and dispose of the same. Held a sufficient statement of the respective interests of complainants; they asking no partition as between themselves. *Page v. Webster*, 8 Mich., 263.

1299. Partition will be decreed according to the equitable rights of parties. But to enable the Court to make such decree, their equitable rights should appear from the pleadings. *Thayer v. Lane*, Wal. Ch., 200.

1300. Redemption: who may file. Equity will not lend its aid to enable a volunteer to pay off a mortgage on the lands of another, or to subrogate him to the rights of a mortgagee in a mortgage so paid. *Smith v. Austin*, 9 Mich., 465.

1301. Where any other person than the mortgagor files a bill to redeem, the bill must show that complainant has some title or interest in the land derived through the mortgagor, or in some way springing out of his general equity of redemption. And it must show the nature or derivation of the title or interest so claimed. *Ibid.*

1302. Where such a bill only stated that complainant, after the giving of the mortgage, became interested in the land by contract, but without setting out the contract, or stating the parties, or its terms, or the interest contracted, it was held insufficient. *Ibid.*

1303. Recitals in exhibits attached to the bill, and which the bill prays may be made a part of the bill with all their averments, which recitals speak of complainant as having "become the purchaser" of the mortgaged premises, cannot aid the bill in this particular; the recitals not showing from whom the purchase was made, nor the interest purchased, nor whether it was subject to the mortgage or not. *Ibid.*

1304. One whose sole interest in lands is under a trust deed, by virtue of which he is to be entitled to the lands after payment of the mortgages upon it and certain other specified demands, is not entitled, if he repudiates the trust, to file a bill to redeem from the mortgages. *Smith v. Austin*, 11 Mich., 34.

1305.—excusing laches. Bill to redeem from a conveyance claimed to be a mortgage. The bill was not filed until thirty-four years after the maturity of the mortgage, which the bill alleges to have remained unpaid, and twenty-four years after the grantee had sold and conveyed the land. A party seeking to redeem after such a lapse of time, is bound to show affirmatively in his bill such facts as will establish the instrument as continuing in force and subject to redemption. *Reynolds v. Green*, 10 Mich., 355.

1306. The bill showed that the grantee in the mortgage conveyance, and those claiming under him, had claimed and disposed of the premises as absolute owners for more than twenty years, and that possession had been had under them. It averred that the possession had not been continuous and adverse for twenty years, but did not show that it was *taken* within that time. No excuse was shown for the delay in applying to redeem, and it was held, that the averments in the bill were too uncertain to found a right to redeem upon. *Ibid.*

1307. Vendor's lien. A bill to establish and enforce a vendor's lien upon lands, should set forth the contract of purchase, both as to the consideration and terms of payment; and the allegations with respect thereto should be clearly proved, in order that the Court may compel the execution of the agreement of the parties, and not one of its own creation. *Mowrey v. Vandling*, 9 Mich., 39.

1308. A bill which alleges a sale at a certain price, but does not state the mode of payment agreed upon, is not supported by evidence that the unpaid purchase price was to be paid in work. *Ibid.*

1309. Multifariousness. See a discussion of the general question of multifariousness in *Wales v. Newbould*, 9 Mich., 45. And see *Wheeler v. Clinton Canal Bank*, Har. Ch., 449; *Ingersoll v. Kirby*, Wal. Ch., 65; *Page v. Webster*, 8 Mich., 263; *Hunton v. Platt*, 11 Mich., 264.

1310. Several different things, having no connection with each other, and requiring different decrees, cannot be demanded of several defendants by one bill. *Ingersoll v. Kirby*, Wal. Ch., 65; *Hart v. McKeen*, Wal. Ch., 417.

1311. But different causes of complaint of the same nature, and between the same parties, may be united in one suit where the same relief is asked. *Hart v. McKeen*, Wal. Ch., 417.

1312.—how determined. To determine whether a bill is multifarious, we must look to the stating part rather than to the prayer; for if the complainant asks for several things, to some of which his case would entitle him and others not, he may have at the hearing that relief which is consistent with the case stated. *Hammond v. Michigan State Bank*, Wal. Ch., 214.

1313.—objection at the hearing. The objection made for the first time at the hearing will not be allowed where the Court can make a decree which will do entire justice between the parties. *Reed v. Wessel*, 7 Mich., 139.

1314. One of two complainants sought to have certain judgments against him decreed satisfied, and the other to have sales made under the judgments declared fraudulent and void, and the relief sought by each depended upon the same state of facts, and the decree, if relief was due to either, would dispose of the whole equities without confusion. Objection to the misjoinder not being taken until the hearing, the bill was sustained. *Ibid.*

1315. Bill must be consistent. A bill with a double aspect must be consistent with itself. It should not set up different and distinct causes of complaint that destroy each other. *Hart v. McKeen*, Wal. Ch., 417.

1316. Cross bill : when necessary. A cross bill is necessary where the defendant is entitled to some positive relief, beyond what the complainant's bill would afford him. On a bill to redeem, a decree cannot be entered that a sale of the premises be had in case they should not be redeemed, unless a cross bill has been filed for that purpose. *Schwarz v. Sears*, Wal. Ch., 170.

1317. It is designed for the purpose of enabling a defendant to avail himself of some defense which can only be made complete by granting him some relief against complainant, or against some other defendant. *Andrews v. Kibbee*, 12 Mich., 94.

1318. Bill to foreclose a mortgage. A subsequent incumbrancer may take the objection by answer that the mortgage is of a homestead, and invalid for want of the wife's signature. A cross bill is not necessary for the purpose. *Dye v. Mann*, 10 Mich., 291.

1319. The defendant conveyed certain premises without his wife's signature. A judgment creditor of the defendant levied upon the premises, and filed a bill in aid of his execution. It was contended by defendant that, as his wife did not join in his conveyance, it was void under the Homestead Law of 1848, and that she was entitled to be protected in the enjoyment of forty acres under that law. Held, that the claim could not be adjudicated in that suit, but she must bring it before the Court by cross bill. *Wisner v. Farnham*, 2 Mich., 472.

1320. A portion of the land covered by a mortgage having been conveyed subject to the payment of the entire mortgage by the grantee, the purchaser of another parcel is not obliged to file a cross bill in the foreclosure suit to protect his rights, but may set out the facts in his answer, and the Court, where it can be done without prejudice to the complainant, should make decree protecting his priority. *Caruthers v. Hall*, 10 Mich., 40.

1321.—what to embrace. It must be strictly confined to the matters involved in the original cause. Where a bill introduces other distinct matters, it is an original bill, and the suits are separate and distinct. *Andrews v. Kibbee*, 12 Mich., 94.

1322. Creditor's bill, to enforce the payment of a judgment, making one a defendant who was alleged to be indebted to, and also the fraudulent grantee of, the judgment debtor. This defendant afterwards filed his bill against the complainant, claiming to have become the owner of the debt for which the judgment was rendered, and of a collateral mortgage given to secure it, and praying to have his title to these securities established. The judgment debtor—who was the mortgagor in the collateral mortgage—and the holder of a prior mortgage, were also made parties, and the bill prayed leave to redeem from the prior mortgage, and the foreclosure of the other. Held that this was an original, and not a cross bill. *Ibid.*

2. Pleas.

1323. A plea must rest the defense upon a single point. If it contains two distinct points, it is bad. *Albany City Bank v. Dorr*, Wal. Ch., 317 ; *Carroll v. Potter*, Wal. Ch., 355.

1324. Of former suit pending. A plea of a former suit pending in another Court for the same cause of action, must set forth the general character and objects of the former suit, and the relief asked. *Bank of Michigan v. Williams*, Har. Ch., 219.

1325. Of account stated. A plea of an account stated must aver that the settlement was of all dealings between the parties ; that the accounts were just, fair and due ; and these averments must be supported by an answer to the same effect. *Schwarz v. Wendell*, Har. Ch., 395.

1326. Of release. A plea of a release, unsupported by an answer, is insufficient. *Ibid.*

1327. Of bona fide purchase. A plea of a bona fide purchase without notice must aver not only a want of notice at the time of the purchase, but also at the time of its completion, and the payment of the money. The money must have been actually paid, or the defendant become so bound therefor that the Court could not relieve him from the payment of it. *Thomas v. Stone*, Wal. Ch., 117.

1328. A plea that one is the bona fide purchaser and owner of an absolute title to lands, is not sustained by evidence that he is owner of a mortgage interest only. *Emerson v. Atwater*, 7 Mich., 12.

1329. Of fraud. Where fraud is alleged in defense of a bill, and it consists of a variety of circumstances, it should be taken advantage of by answer, and not by plea. *Carroll v. Potter*, Wal. Ch., 355.

1330. How facts to be stated. A plea must be positive, and not on belief, when it states a fact within defendant's knowledge, or touching his own acts; but when it relates to the acts of third persons, and not to defendant's own acts, it may be on information and belief. *Parker v. Parker*, Wal. Ch., 457.

1331. In a plea that one of the defendants is a married woman, and her husband not a party to the suit, it was held not necessary to show by the plea that she could not sue and be sued as an unmarried woman under the statute, where the bill did not make out a case bringing her within the statute. *Ibid.*

1332. To part of bill. A defendant may plead to one part of a bill and answer to another; but the defenses must clearly refer to separate and distinct parts. If both are to the same part, the answer overrules the plea. *Clark v. Saginaw City Bank*, Har. Ch., 240.

1333. Complainant's interest assigned. A plea that complainant has parted with his interest in the suit, presents a good defense. *Wallace v. Dunning*, Wal. Ch., 416. See *Webster v. Hitchcock*, 11 Mich., 56.

1334. Issue upon. Where replication to a plea is filed, the truth of the plea is the only question to be tried; and if established, it is a bar to so much of the bill as it professes to cover. *Hurlbut v. Britain*, Wal. Ch., 454.

1335. But if found not to be true, complainant will be entitled only to the same decree as if the bill had been taken as confessed; and if the allegations of the bill do not entitle him to any relief whatever, the bill will be dismissed. *Hurlbut v. Britain*, 2 Doug., 191.

3. Answer.

1336. Certainty in. Where an allegation is made in the bill with divers circumstances, the defendant should not in his answer deny the allegation literally, as laid in the bill, but should answer the point of substance positively and with certainty. *Jones v. Wing*, Har. Ch., 301.

1337. Where the answer admitted a deed referred to in the bill, and stated no fact which invalidated it, but denied its validity generally, it was held to be insufficient, because not stating the facts which made the deed invalid. As a question of law a party is estopped by his deed; and if he attempts to impeach it in equity, he must show in what his equity consists. *Payne v. Atterbury*, Har. Ch., 414.

1338. Must be full. If a defendant submits to answer the whole bill, he must answer fully, notwithstanding he might by demurrer or plea to the whole bill have protected himself against a particular discovery. *Gilkey v. Paige*, Wal. Ch., 520.

1339. Where irrelevancy is made a ground for refusing to answer a part, it must appear that an answer to such part would, in no aspect of complainant's case as made by the bill, be of service to him. *Ibid.*

1340. Must be signed. An answer must be signed, notwithstanding complainant has, by his bill, waived an answer under oath. *Kimball v. Ward*, Wal. Ch., 439.

1341. Must state facts. An answer should show facts, and not conclusions of law. *Attorney-General v. Oakland County Bank*, Wal. Ch., 90.

1342. Denials not conclusive on Court. The denial of fraud in an answer under oath, is not conclusive on the Court, if the facts and circumstances of the case are such as irresistably to lead the mind to a different conclusion. *How v. Camp*, Wal. Ch., 427.

1343. How far evidence. When an answer is called for on oath, whatever is responsive to the bill is evidence for as well as against defendant. *Schwarz v. Wendell*, Wal. Ch., 267. But new matter brought into the case by the answer is not evidence for defendant. *Ibid*; *Attorney-General v. Oakland County Bank*, Wal. Ch., 90; *Van Dyke v. Davis*, 2 Mich., 144; *Hunt v. Thorn*, 2 Mich., 213.

1344. If a fact stated in the bill, and answered by defendant, is material to complainant's case, or is a circumstance from which a material fact may be inferred, the answer, in such case, is responsive to the bill, and is evidence in the cause. *Schwarz v. Wendell*, Wal. Ch., 267.

1345. An answer may sometimes be evidence of a fact not stated in the bill; as where the bill sets forth part of complainant's case only, instead of the whole, and the part omitted, and stated in the answer, shows a different case from that stated in the bill, and is not in avoidance merely. *Ibid.*

1346. Where complainant alleged in his bill a right to certain shares of partnership property, and defendant denied the right, and set up an independent contract to show himself entitled to one half the shares, the answer was held not to come within the rule of being directly responsive to the allegations of the bill, and the new contract was required to be proved. *Millard v. Ramsdell*, Har. Ch., 373.

1347. Where the answer is called for on oath, and the defendant of his own knowledge fully and fairly negatives any allegation of the bill, complainant can have no relief depending upon that allegation, unless the answer is overcome by more than the equally full testimony of one witness. *Roberts v. Miles*, 12 Mich., 297.

1348. But this rule amounts simply to this: that there can be no decree in favor of complainant unless the evidence preponderates in his favor; and that where answer and opposing witness are equally fair and explicit, there can be no such preponderance. *Ibid.*

1349. Defendant orally examined. If defendant, after having thus answered, is called upon the stand as a witness under the statute—Laws of 1861, p. 168—and furnishes the means of destroying his own answer, and corroborating complainant's case, his testimony on the oral examination and cross-examination is preferable to his answer. *Ibid.*

1350. Since said statute the defendant's answer on oath, responsive to the bill, is to be regarded as of the same force only which it would have were it the defendant's deposition as a witness. *Ibid.*

1351. Answer conclusive on defendant. By his answer defendant had alleged the consideration of a certain deed (decreed by the Court to be a mortgage) to have been a debt to a certain amount. The answer estops him from showing that a larger sum was due. *Emerson v. Atwater*, 12 Mich., 314.

1352. If the amount of the indebtedness was incorrectly stated in the answer by mistake, defendant should have applied to the Court, showing how it occurred, and asking leave to amend the answer in that particular. *Ibid.*

1353. Conclusive on privies. Bill to redeem. The present holder of the mortgage security was undefended in the case except by the answer of the mortgagee from whom he derived his right. Held that he was entitled to the benefits of that answer, but was also concluded by its statements. *Ibid.*

1354. Answer not on oath. Where answer on oath is waived, complainant may use the answer as an admission by defendant of any facts stated in it necessary to establish his case. But he cannot use one part and exclude other parts relating to the same subject that would be responsive to the bill had the answer been under oath. *Durfee v. McClurg*, 6 Mich., 223.

1355. The answer without oath is a mere pleading, and of no effect as evidence. So far as it admits the case made by the bill, it relieves the complainant from proof. So far as it controverts that case, it puts the complainant to his proof. But so far as it alleges any new matter of avoidance, or any matter the burden of proving which would naturally rest upon the defendant, it is of no effect without proof. *Morris v. Hoyt*, 11 Mich., 9.

1356. As to what is responsive to the bill, see *Mandeville v. Comstock*, 9 Mich., 536. That nothing is to be regarded as admitted by it unless expressly admitted, see *Morris v. Morris*, 5 Mich., 171.

1357. Multiplicity of issues. Three persons who had held land in partnership sold it, and gave separate conveyances to the purchaser, who, in pursuance of an arrangement to that effect, gave back a mortgage for the purchase price to one of them. The purchaser afterwards bought up a mortgage given by one of them, on an undivided one third of the land, and sought to make a set off of this in a suit to foreclose his own mortgage. But the set off was refused, the Court holding that claims under that mortgage could be better litigated in a separate suit; and the decree was so framed as to leave that mortgage untouched. *Adams v. Bradley*, 12 Mich., 346.

4. Demurrers.

1358. A general demurrer for want of equity cannot be sustained unless the Court is satisfied that no discovery or proof properly called for by, or founded upon, the allegations in the bill can make the subject matter of the bill a proper case for equitable cognizance. *Clark v. Davis*, Har. Ch., 227. See *Thayer v. Lane*, Har. Ch., 247.

1359. It must be good to the whole bill, or it will be overruled. *Williams v. Hubbard*, Wal. Ch., 28.

1360. If a defendant who should have demurred to discovery only, demurs to both discovery and relief, the demurrer will be overruled. *Edwards v. Hulbert*, Wal. Ch., 54; *Burpee v. Smith*, Wal. Ch., 327.

1361. Where the discovery sought by a bill can only be assistant to the relief prayed, a ground of demurrer to the relief will also extend to the discovery; but if the discovery have a further purpose, the complainant may be entitled to it though he has no title to the relief. *Manning v. Drake*, 1 Mich., 34.

1362. Ore tenus. Where a new cause of demurrer is assigned *ore tenus*, the cause must be co-extensive with the demurrer. *Clark v. Davis*, Har. Ch., 227.

1363. By one defendant. Where one of several defendants demurs to discovery, on the ground that it would subject him to a criminal prosecution, his demurrer should be confined to such parts of the bill as tend to implicate him in the supposed crime. *Burpee v. Smith*, Wal. Ch., 327.

1364. A joint demurrer may be good as to one defendant and bad as to other defendants. *Barstow v. Smith*, Wal. Ch., 394.

1365. It is a good ground of demurrer to the whole bill that one of the complainants has no interest in the suit, and has improperly joined with others in filing the bill; but there is no such rule in regard to defendants. *Ibid.*

EQUITY PRACTICE.

1. The Bill.

1366. A married woman filed in her own name, without the appointment of *prochien ami*, a bill against her husband for alimony. Held irregular. *Peltier v. Peltier*, Har. Ch., 19.

1367. The appointment of next friend is sufficient, if made in writing by the complainant, accompanied by the written consent of the next friend, and the appointment and consent annexed to the bill. *Markham v. Markham*, 4 Mich., 305.

1368. But in respect to her separate property, she may sue in her own name. And by statute—Comp. L., §§ 3290, 3294—she may sue in respect to her own property, at law as well as in equity, without next friend. *Ibid.* And see Husband and Wife.

1369. Oath to bill. Where a creditor's bill is verified under rule 110 of 1839 (103 of 1858) by complainant's agent, who is not also his solicitor, the jurat should state the person to be the complainant's agent; but where it is verified by the oath of the solicitor, the Court will take notice of that fact from the records and proceedings in the cause. *Bergh v. Poupard*, Wal. Ch., 5.

1370. Amendments. It is not a matter of course to allow the filing of an amended bill after replication and testimony. A special application should be made to the Court, with a full statement of the facts intended to be incorporated in the amended bill, so that the Court can judge of their materiality. *Hammond v. Place*, Har. Ch., 438.

1371. Facts which have transpired subsequent to the filing of the bill cannot be set forth by way of amendment. *Ibid.*

1372. Leave was granted to amend an injunction bill so as to waive answer under oath ; an answer not having been filed. *Bronson v. Green*, Wal. Ch., 486.

1373.—when to be applied for. A complainant wishing to amend his bill must take the first opportunity, after being made acquainted with the defects in it, to ask leave to do so. *Bank of Michigan v. Niles*, Wal. Ch., 398.

1374.—after demurrer. It is usual on allowing a demurrer for any cause which the Court sees may be obviated by amendment, to give leave to amend on paying costs of the demurrer. But where the Court cannot see on the argument from the facts before it, how the objection on which the demurrer was sustained could be removed, it is necessary for the complainant to apply for leave to amend, by petition setting forth the additional facts sought to be incorporated in the bill. *Ibid.*

1375.—at the hearing. Where the complainant has stated his case defectively, and no demurrer has been interposed, but defendant has only claimed the benefit of a demurrer by his answer, and the case is brought to a hearing on pleadings and proofs, it may be proper to allow the defect in the bill to be corrected at the hearing, if the proofs show complainant entitled to relief. *Gorham v. Wing*, 10 Mich., 486.

1376.—after appeal. The Supreme Court has no original equity jurisdiction, and cannot act upon any facts which do not constitute a part of the case appealed from; and leave to amend can only be granted by the Court where the cause orginated. *Bank of Michigan v. Niles*, Wal. Ch., 398. See *Sears v. Schwarz*, 1 Doug., 504; *Palmer v. Rich*, 12 Mich., 414.

1377. Where petition was presented for leave to amend, by inserting additional facts, after a decree sustaining a demurrer to the bill had been affirmed by the Supreme Court on the same reasons which had governed in chancery, leave was refused. *Bank of Michigan v. Niles*, Wal. Ch., 398.

1378. An administrator having filed a bill to compel the specific performance of a contract for the conveyance of land to his intestate, without making the heirs parties, with prayer that a conveyance be decreed to himself, the Court would not allow the bill to be amended at the hearing on appeal, by substituting the heirs as complainants. *House v. Dexter*, 9 Mich., 246.

1379. An objection for the want of a necessary party in chancery was not made until the hearing. The bill made out a case on all other points, and the Court granted decree for complainant, as prayed. On appeal, the Supreme Court, in reversing the decree for want of parties, granted leave to amend, and allowed an injunction, which had been decreed below, to stand until the further order of the Court below to which the cause was remitted. *Palmer v. Rich*, 12 Mich., 414.

1380. Where complainant had stated a case not entitling him to relief, but on cross bill an issue had been made which allowed the whole equities of the parties to be shown, and it appeared from the evidence that the complainant should have relief, the Supreme Court on appeal, instead of dismissing the bill, ordered the case remanded, with leave to complainant to amend without prejudice to the proofs taken. *Moran v. Palmer*, 13 Mich., 367.

2. Supplemental Bill.

1381. Is necessary to bring before the Court facts which have transpired subsequent to the filing of the original bill. *Hammond v. Place*, Har. Ch., 438; *Graves v. Niles*, Har. Ch., 332.

1382. If material facts have occurred subsequent to the commencement of the suit, the Court will give leave to file a supplemental bill; and in doing so, will permit other matters to be introduced which might have been incorporated into the original bill by way of amendment. This is especially proper where the matter which occurred prior, is necessary to the proper elucidation of that which occurred subsequent to the filing of the original bill. *Graves v. Niles*, Har. Ch., 332.

1383. Change of title. The purchaser of land at a foreclosure sale may file a bill to compel the foreclosure of a prior mortgage upon that and other property, and to have the other property first sold; and if, pending the suit, the prior mortgagee purchases the interest of the complainant, he may file an original bill, in the nature of a supplemental bill, setting up the change of title, and is entitled to the same relief that could have been had under the original bill. *Cooper v. Bigley*, 13 Mich., 463.

1384. Where the parties in interest to a decree remain unchanged, and no new rights have arisen, a defendant interested in having the decree executed should proceed by petition. But where a third person has acquired an interest in the decree, a bill is necessary to bring him before the Court. *Griggs v Detroit and Milwaukee Railway Co.*, 10 Mich., 117.

1385. A defendant in a foreclosure decree who had a residuary interest in the mortgage foreclosed, after complainant's demand should be satisfied, filed a bill the object of which was to have the benefit of that decree, and also to foreclose the mortgage against the defendants who were not, but should have been, parties to the first suit. Such a bill is not objectionable. It is an original bill as to those who were not parties to the first bill, and a supplemental bill as to those who were. *Ibid.*

1386. Revivor. Where a complainant in chancery dies, the suit is revived by an order substituting his representative as complainant, without amendment of the bill. *Webster v. Hitchcock*, 11 Mich., 56.

1387. Where the subject matter of a suit in chancery is assigned by the complainant, the suit can no longer be prosecuted in his name after the assignment is brought to the notice of the Court; and the only mode in which the assignee can revive, or get the benefit of the original suit, is by filing an original bill in the nature of a bill of revivor and supplement. A bill may be filed by the assignee for this purpose, without the previous leave of the Court, and in the name of a new solicitor. *Ibid.*

3. Subpoena.

1388. A subpœna is the first process. It is irregular to have injunction and ne exeat issued and served before the issue of subpœna. *Peltier v. Peltier*, Har. Ch., 19.

1389. Service. The service of a subpœna out of the State is irregular. *Pratt v. Bank of Windsor*, Har. Ch., 254.

1390. Where defendant was confined in State prison, service upon the keeper of the prison was held sufficient. *Johnson v. Johnson*, Wal. Ch., 309.

1391. Error in copy. Where the copy served differed from the original, in being tested October 31, 1840, instead of 1843, the service was set aside as irregular. *Gould v. Tyron*, Wal. Ch., 339.

4. Answer.

1392. Amending. Where leave is given to amend an answer, a new answer, with the amendments added, must be filed and served, or the original answer withdrawn by leave of the Court, and the amendments added ; or the amendments must refer to the portions of the answer on file intended to be amended, and specify their nature and application. *Mason v. Detroit City Bank*, Har. Ch., 222.

1393. Amendments in the form of affidavits, not referring to the answer, are irregular. *Ibid.*

1394. Leave to amend. Leave to file a supplemental or amended answer is seldom granted, and never without the utmost caution, and when a just and necessary case is clearly made out ; and it is then generally confined to a clear case of mistake as to matter of fact, and as to that only. *Graves v. Niles*, Har. Ch., 332. See *Emerson v. Atwater*, 12 Mich., 314. Effect of laches upon the application. *Graves v. Niles*, Har. Ch., 332.

1395. Leave should not be granted to change entirely the character of the defense by supplemental or amended answer, not upon the ground of any actual mistake in matter of fact, or upon any discovery of new facts, but upon the ground that the defendant did not mean to be understood as he had stated in his answer. *Ibid.*

1396. But where the answer was obscure, and there was a possibility of great injustice to defendant, the Court, with reluctance, permitted a supplemental answer to be filed explaining the ambiguity. But defendant having incorporated other matters of defense in his supplemental answer, without leave, it was ordered to be taken off the files. *Ibid.*

1397. Defense of one protecting another. Bill to remove a cloud upon complainants' title. As under the statute, in order to obtain the decree they sought, the complainants were required to substantiate their own title, it was held that the defense of one enured for the benefit of all. *Stockton v. Williams*, Wal. Ch., 120.

1398. Bill against the grantee named in a deed of lands, and purchasers under him, to set aside the deed for fraud. The grantee answered fully, denying the fraud ; and as to the others the bill was taken as confessed. It was held that the defense of the grantee enured to the benefit of the others ; and the bill being dismissed as to him was dismissed as to all. *Buchoz v. Lecour*, 9 Mich., 234. See also *Emerson v. Atwater*, 12 Mich., 314.

1399. Exception to. Where defendant both answers and demurs to different parts of the bill, and the demurrer is overruled, complainant, to obtain a further answer, must except. *Bragg v. Whitcomb*, Wal. Ch., 307.

5. Plea.

1400. When superseded. A plea is superseded by amending the bill; and the defendant should plead, answer or demur to the amended bill as if no plea had been interposed before. *Peck v. Burgess*, Wal. Ch., 485.

1401. Amending. Amendments proposed to a plea should be stated in the application for leave; and a defendant will not usually be permitted to set up a fact or state of facts inconsistent with the original defense. *Freeman v. Michigan State Bank*, Har. Ch., 311.

1402. Motion for leave to amend, based upon an affidavit stating an additional fact which was unknown to defendant at the time of filing the original plea, and consistent with the facts pleaded. Leave was granted, but fixing a short time for making the amendments in. *Ibid.*

6. Demurrer.

1403. Signed by wrong solicitor. Where a solicitor has appeared in a cause, and a demurrer is filed by other solicitors, it may be treated as a nullity. But where it appeared that the signature of the wrong solicitor was put to the demurrer by mistake, and that injustice would be done if the defendant should not be allowed to answer, a default for want of answer was set aside on terms. *Graham v. Elmore*, Har. Ch., 265.

7. Injunction.

1404. To stay suit in equity. Application by a party or privy to stay a proceeding in chancery, must be made to the Court itself, by petition in that proceeding. An officer out of Court has no authority to allow an injunction for that purpose. But where the case was such that an order would have been granted, and the objection was not taken on the argument, the injunction was allowed to stand for such order. *Mason v. Payne*, Wal. Ch., 459.

1405. Prayer for. Where the bill prays an injunction, but it is omitted in the prayer for process, it is good ground for refusing the injunction, but not for dissolving it when it has been allowed. *Taylor v. Snyder*, Wal. Ch., 490.

1406. Motion for. On the motion for an injunction, the statements in the bill must be taken as true, and the relief sought must be consistent with the case made by the bill. *Michigan State Bank v. Hastings*, Wal. Ch., 9.

1407. Bond. The Court cannot dispense with the filing of a bond as preliminary to the injunction, when it is required by the statute.

Carroll v. Farmers and Mechanics' Bank, Har. Ch., 197. See further, INJUNCTION BOND.

1408. Dissolution of. See supra 1405. An injunction will be dissolved on motion, where the equity of the bill is fully denied by plea. *Eldred v. Camp*, Har. Ch., 162. Or by answer, if the answer is full and satisfactory. *Attorney-General v. Oakland County Bank*, Wal. Ch., 90. And without answer or plea, the defendant may move to dissolve for want of equity in the bill. *Cooper v. Alden*, Har. Ch., 72.

1409. On motion to dissolve, an affidavit is admissible which goes to show that the injunction was irregularly issued, or that the officer granting it was misled, or induced to grant it contrary to law. *Carroll v. Farmers and Mechanics' Bank*, Har. Ch., 197.

1410. If complainant fails to appear on motion to dissolve, after due notice, the motion will be granted. *Kellogg v. Barnes*, Har. Ch., 258.

1411. If the motion is made before answer, the allegations of the bill are to be taken as true. *Schwarz v. Sears*, Har. Ch., 440.

1412. The granting and continuance of injunctions rest in the discretion of the Court; and they will not always be dissolved when the equity of the bill is fully denied. If by a dissolution the complainant is likely to be deprived of all benefits he might otherwise derive by succeeding in the suit, it will not be dissolved as a matter of course, on the coming in of answer denying the equity of the bill. *Attorney-General v. Oakland County Bank*, Wal. Ch., 90.

1413. It will not be dissolved on an answer admitting the equity of the bill, and setting up new matter as a defense. *Ibid.*

1414. Affidavits will not, as a general rule, be allowed to be substituted for an answer for the purposes of this motion. Exceptions in case of waste or irreparable mischief and partnership. *Sacket v. Hill*, 2 Mich., 182.

8. MOTIONS, PETITIONS, ORDERS, &c.

1415. Consent rule. A rule entered by consent, without fraud or misrepresentation, will not be vacated. *Hammond v. Place*, Har. Ch., 438.

1416. Agreements between counsel must be in writing, or reduced to the form of an order by consent, or the Court will not notice them. [Rule 84.] *Brooks v. Mead*, Wal. Ch., 389; *Suydam v. Dequindre*, Wal. Ch., 23.

1417. Signing petition. A petition was not signed by the petitioner, but was verified by an affidavit signed by her, which stated that she had read it, and knew its contents, and that it was true. Held sufficient. *Johnson v. Johnson*, Wal. Ch., 309.

1418. Notices. A defendant who has appeared in the cause, is entitled by statute—Comp. L., § 3500—to notice of all subsequent proceedings. And where the rules fix the period of notice, such notice should in all cases be given. *Jenny v. O'Flynn*, 5 Mich., 215.

1419. Decree being made without notice of hearing to a defendant who had appeared, it was reversed on appeal. *Ibid.*

1420. Where, in a foreclosure case, the bill is taken as confessed by a part of the defendants, the evidence taken on the issue as to the others is evidence as to those who are defaulted, and a reference to take separate proofs as to them, covering the same ground, is not necessary. If such reference is had, notice of it to the defendants who have appeared is not requisite. *Michigan Insurance Co. v. Whittemore*, 12 Mich., 427.

1421. And notice is not necessary of a reference to compute the amount due on a basis already fixed by the Court, by interlocutory decree. *Kellogg v. Putnam*, 11 Mich., 344.

1422. Deposit in Court. Where a party comes to have a foreclosure set aside, and for leave to redeem, he must bring into Court the amount admitted to be due. The deposit will only be dispensed with where there is uncertainty as to the amount. *Schwarz v. Sears*, Har. Ch., 440.

1423. Receiver: of moneyed corporation. After injunction and the appointment of a receiver in a suit against a moneyed corporation, and the receiver has taken upon himself the trust, and other creditors have filed their claims, it is not a matter of right for the complainant, on being paid his claim, to dismiss the suit and discharge the receiver. *Fay v. Erie and Kalamazoo R. R. Bank*, Har. Ch., 194.

1424. The Court has power to permit it, when satisfied that the interest of all concerned will be best subserved by permitting the corporation to manage its own concerns. But the Court should look into the condition of the corporation, before discharging the receiver, and make such order, absolute or conditional, as the case may require. *Ibid.*

1425.—in mortgage cases. Before appointing a receiver in a foreclosure suit, the Court must be satisfied, *first*, that the premises are insufficient to pay the debt, and second, that the party personally liable is insolvent, so that an execution for any deficiency on a sale would be unavailing. And the application therefor must be made in a reasonable time after the suit is commenced. *Brown v. Chase*, Wal. Ch., 43.

1426.—against vendee in possession. Where a vendee is in possession, holding over against his own deed, and is irresponsible, and there are large outstanding incumbrances which he is not keeping down the interest upon, a receiver will be appointed. And although answer is filed putting material parts of the bill in issue, yet if there still remains a strong presumption against the defendant from the answer itself, a receiver will be appointed. *Payne v. Atterbury*, Har. Ch., 414.

1427.—in creditors's suit. Notice of motion for a receiver having been given, and the defendant failing to appear, the fact that a demurrer has been interposed will not be regarded a sufficient reason for denying the motion. *Howard v. Palmer*, Wal. Ch., 391.

1428.—motion for. Affidavits are not admissible to contradict the answer, on motion for a receiver. *Connor v. Allen*, Har. Ch., 371.

1429. Renewal of motions. After a motion has been denied on its merits, it should not be renewed, without leave of the Court, on the same facts, or on any new facts which might have been included in the first motion. The party must present all of his case at once, whether he have several grounds or not. *Johnson v. Johnson*, Wal. Ch., 309.

1430. Service of papers on motions. On making a motion based upon the fact that a writ of error has been sued out of the Supreme Court, it is not necessary to serve a copy of the proceedings in that Court. *Webb v. Williams*, Wal. Ch., 452.

1431. Irregularity: laches. A motion to set aside proceedings for irregularity should be made at the first opportunity. *Johnson v. Johnson*, Wal. Ch., 309. And a defendant who has failed to appear is entitled to no more indulgence than one who has. *Ibid.*

1432.—waiver. Where complainant had failed to serve his replication on a defendant, but the latter attended and cross examined witnesses, this was held to be a waiver. *Brooks v. Mead*, Wal. Ch., 389.

1433. So where complainant had failed to serve a copy of the bill, but defendant had answered, and made a motion to dissolve an injunction, he was held to have waived the default. *Higgins v. Carpenter*, Har. Ch., 256.

1434.—a defendant in contempt cannot move to set aside proceedings; but where he has simply failed to comply with the requirements of an interlocutory order, he may move to discharge the order for irregularity. *Peltier v. Peltier*, Har. Ch., 19.

1435. Order in part erroneous not void, so far as relates to matters properly contained in it. *Howard v. Palmer*, Wal. Ch., 391.

1436. Setting aside default. A regular order to take the bill as confessed will not be set aside on a simple affidavit of merits, notwithstanding an excuse is shown for the default. The defendant must either produce the sworn answer he proposes to put in, or must in his petition or affidavit, show the nature of the defense, and his belief in the truth of the matters constituting it. *Stockton v. Williams*, Har. Ch., 241.

1437. The general rule is, that when the answer shows a defense, and an excuse is given for the delay, the Court will open the default, and allow the answer to be filed, on terms. *Smith v. Saginaw City Bank*, Har. Ch., 426.

1438. Extending time to take testimony. Where a party applies for leave to take testimony after the time allowed by the rules has expired, he must state in his application what he expects to be able to prove by the witnesses he seeks leave to examine. *Thayer v. Swift*, Wal. Ch., 384.

1439. A complainant seeking to set aside the rules of the Court, will be required to make as strong a case as a defendant to set aside a default. *Ibid.*

1440. Where complainant had allowed the time given by the rules for taking testimony to expire, without showing any excuse for neglect, except that his counsel were occupied with other business, the motion was denied. *Ibid.*

1441. Affidavit of merits must state what the merits are. *Ibid.* And must be made by the party himself, or a reason shown why it is not. *Bank of Michigan v. Williams*, Har. Ch., 219.

9. The Master ; Proceedings before him, and his Report.

1442. Solicitor. It is improper for a master to perform any official act as master in a cause in which he is solicitor, or partner of the solicitor. *Brown v. Byrne*, Wal. Ch., 453.

1443. Summons. The time fixed for service of the summons should be stated in the summons itself, or form a part of the underwriting, where the latter is necessary to inform the party of the object of the hearing ; and the underwriting, as well as the summons, should be signed by the master. *Whipple v. Stewart*, Wal. Ch., 357.

1444. Appearing before the master to object that no time was fixed for the service, is not a waiver of the irregularity. *Ibid.*

1445. It is not necessary to serve with the summons a copy of the order under which the reference is had. *Ibid.*

1446. Service of a copy of the summons, without showing the original, is void. *Howard v. Palmer*, Wal. Ch., 391.

1447. The return of a master charged with the execution of an order of the Court, showing the failure of a person to appear and submit to an examination as required by the order, is sufficient foundation for a rule to show cause why an attachment should not issue against him for contempt. *Whipple v. Brown*, Har. Ch., 436.

1448. The return on the summons, or the affidavit of service, should show how it was served. *Ibid.*

1449. Where the notice was to appear before one Master, and the return was by another that defendant did not appear, it was held irregular. *Ibid.*

1450. Proceedings on reference. Where on a reference to a master to ascertain the amount due on a mortgage, the mortgagor appeared, and at the first refused to take part in the proceedings, but after remaining an hour or more, and before the opposite party had left, offered to prove certain payments on the mortgage, and the master refused to hear the testimony on the ground that it was too late, the decision was held erroneous. *Schwarz v. Sears*, Wal. Ch., 19.

1451. The proper mode to correct the error is by motion to the Court for an order requiring the master to receive the testimony; and this should be made immediately, and without waiting for the master to make his report. *Ibid.* See also *Ward v. Jewett*, Wal. Ch., 45.

1452. The master, in such case, should make out and deliver to the party requiring it a certificate briefly stating the facts, and the reasons for his action; that the Court may review his decisions with as little delay as possible. *Schwarz v. Sears*, Wal. Ch., 19.

1453. If he errs in not calling parties before him, to produce books, papers, &c., the proper remedy of the party deeming himself aggrieved, is to apply to the court for an order requiring him to do so. *Emerson v. Atwater*, 12 Mich., 314.

1454. If the proceedings before the master have been irregular, his report may be set aside on motion. In such a case an order should be obtained enlarging the time to except until the motion can be heard and decided. *Suydam v. Dequindre*, Wal. Ch., 23.

1455. Exceptions to report. If the master decides against allowing a claim, the proper mode of bringing the question before the Court is by exceptions to his report. *Ibid.*

1456. Exceptions are only proper when the master has come to an erroneous conclusion, of law or fact, on the whole or some part of the evidence before him, touching the matter referred. *Schwarz v. Sears*, Wal. Ch., 19; *Emerson v. Atwater*, 12 Mich., 314.

1457. An exception that he "has credited to complainant the sum of $9,210 37, for amount defendant has received on sales of lots, and interest thereon to May 5, 1860, whereas he should have credited a less sum," is too indefinite and uncertain to admit the raising under it of an objection that the commissioner did not allow to defendant a sum paid to a third person to perfect the title to the mortgaged lands. *Emerson v. Atwater*, 12 Mich., 314.

1458. Confirming report. A special motion to confirm a report is not necessary; but an order *nisi* should be entered under the rule (82 of old rules, 79 of new). *Suydam v. Dequindre*, Wal. Ch., 23.

1459. Examination in creditor's suit. The examination of the defendant under the rule (111 of old rules, 105 of new), is not confined to defendant's property or effects, but extends to any matter which he would be required to disclose by answer; and authorizes the examination of witnesses on any matter charged in the bill, and not admitted by the defendant on his examination. *Howard v. Palmer*, Wal. Ch., 391.

1460. Irregularity in the appointment of a receiver is no ground for the defendant objecting to submit to an examination. *Ibid.*

1461. Transferring reference. Where one master has commenced proceedings under an order of reference, he should complete them; and the party obtaining the order cannot transfer the proceedings to another master to be completed. *Bishop v. Williams*, Wal. Ch., 423.

1462. Examination of witnesses. Where an agent of complainant—defendant not appearing—examined witnesses and wrote their depositions, and the master was absent from the room several times during the examination, the proceedings were held irregular, and the depositions suppressed. *Burtch v. Hogge*, Har. Ch., 31.

1463. Impeachment. The practice on impeachment of witnesses is the same in chancery as at law. *Sawyer v. Sawyer*, Wal. Ch., 48. See post, 1686 to 1698.

1464. Re-examination. A witness once examined is not to be re-examined to the same facts without an order of the Court; but he may be as to other facts, or new matter arising out of the testimony of other witnesses. *Sawyer v. Sawyer*, Wal. Ch., 48.

1465. Irregular depositions. Where an order to take proofs was duly entered, but notice was not given within the thirty days required by rule (50 of the old rules; 47 of the new), and the examination of a witness was objected to before the master on that ground, the deposition was suppressed. *Bachelor v. Nelson*, Wal. Ch., 449.

1466. Notice being given of the examination of witnesses, and the opposite party having appeared at the time and place appointed, and waited an hour and a half, during which the party giving the notice did not appear, and then left, it was held irregular for the latter to appear and take depositions afterwards. *Stockton v Williams*, Wal. Ch.. 120.

1467. Disregarding master's report. Foreclosure suit. Answer being filed denying anything due, the case was referred to a commissioner, who reported that nothing was due to complainant when the suit was commenced. This report was not excepted to, and it was held that defendant had a right to rely upon it, and the Court could not inspect the documents which were before the commissioner, or take evidence, to test the correctness of the commissioner's conclusion. *Thorne v. Hilliker*, 12 Mich., 215.

10. Proof of the Issue.

1468. Answer. A complainant in chancery must be prepared to support his own case, and to meet any evidence fairly controverting it. Nothing will be regarded as admitted by the answer unless expressly admitted. *Morris v. Morris*, 5 Mich., 171.

1469. But where complainant averred that a mortgage had been assigned to him, and the answer was silent on the point, and based the defense solely on the ground of infancy, and there was no evidence of assignment except what was contained in the record of a prior cause, which was put in evidence by consent, wherein the former owner of the mortgage had testified that the mortgage was assigned to complainant; and the objection that the assignment was not proved was taken on appeal from a decree in favor of complainant, it was held that complainant was entitled to the most liberal construction of the evidence as to the assignment, and its competency not having been objected to, it was sufficient. *Young v. McKee*, 13 Mich., 552.

1470. The defendant can only defend on the grounds set up in his answer. *Smith v. Brown*, 2 Mich., 161; *Van Dyke v. Davis*, 2 Mich., 144.

1471. He cannot, by his answer, vary the terms of a written contract. *Schwarz v. Wendell*, Wal. Ch., 267. See further, supra, 1343 to 1356.

1472. Admission by default. If the defendant suffers the bill to be taken as confessed against him, this is an admission of all its material allegations, and he cannot give evidence before the master to disprove them. *Ward v. Jewett*, Wal. Ch., 45.

1473. Admisssons as to infants. No decree can be taken against an infant on a bill taken as confessed, or on the answer of his guardian ad litem admitting the facts as stated in the bill. The answer in such case is regarded as a pleading merely, and the complainant must prove his case. *Thayer v. Lane*, Wal. Ch., 200. See *Chandler v. McKinney*, 6 Mich., 217; *Smith v. Smith*, 13 Mich., 258.

1474. Facts proved, but not put in issue by the pleadings, cannot be regarded at the hearing. *Cicotte v. Gagnier*, 2 Mich., 381; *Warner v. Whittaker*, 6 Mich., 133; *Bloomer v. Henderson*, 8 Mich., 395; *Barrows v. Baughman*, 9 Mich., 213; *Peckham v. Buffum*, 11 Mich., 529; *Dunn v. Dunn*, 11 Mich., 284; *Wurcherer v. Hewett*, 10 Mich., 453.

1475. Court refusing to receive evidence. The cause having gone to trial in open Court on an issue of fact, the Judge refused to receive evidence, and dismissed the bill for want of equity. Held that the dismissal was erroneous. The complainant was entitled of right to put in his evidence, since in no other way could he render his statutory right of appeal effectual. *Hewlett v. Shaw*, 9 Mich., 346.

11. Feigned Issue.

1476. The verdict of a jury on an issue out of chancery is of no binding force, and a new trial will be ordered on much slighter grounds than in an ordinary action at law. [Campbell, J.] *Dunn v. Dunn*, 11 Mich., 284.

1477. The Court may entirely disregard the verdict, and render a decree against it, notwithstanding it satisfies the Judge who tried the cause. *Ibid.*

1478. An issue awarded at the hearing in chancery, to be tried by jury, must be confined not only to facts put in issue by the pleadings, but to facts concerning which some testimony has already been introduced and read at the hearing. [CAMPBELL, J.] *Ibid.*

1479. Where therefore the pleadings put in issue adultery committed by one of the parties in April, May and June, 1858, but no testimony was taken tending to show its commission in April, and at the hearing issues were framed for trial by jury covering the months named, and also December and January preceding, such issues, so far as they related to the months of December, January and April, were irregular, and a general verdict of guilty rendered thereon must be disregarded. [CAMPBELL, J.] *Ibid.*

1480. But if no evidence was given on the trial of transactions outside the pleadings, the verdict should not be set aside because the issue was too broad. [CHRISTIANCY, J.] *Ibid.*

1481. Where several issues are framed for trial by a jury, the jury should pass upon each separately. [CAMPBELL, J.] *Ibid.*

1482. A deposition taken in the cause cannot be read on the trial of issues by a jury, where the witness is personally present at the trial. *Ibid.*

12. EXHIBITS AT THE HEARING.

1483. It is not a matter of course to allow a deed to be proved at the hearing; but a satisfactory excuse must be given for the failure to prove it before the master. *Batchelor v. Nelson*, Wal. Ch., 449.

1484. The documentary evidence referred to in the fifty-sixth rule, has reference to documents which prove themselves. But to entitle a party to use such documentary evidence, there must have been an order entered for taking proofs, to give the opposite party an opportunity of exhibiting witnesses relative thereto, or of introducing countervailing proofs. *Ibid.*

1485. Where the assignee of a mortgage files his bill to foreclose, setting forth the mortgage and assignment, he may, upon the notice required by the rule, (62 of old rules, 61 of new) have an order to prove the assignment as an exhibit at the hearing under rule 56. *Jerome v. Seymour*, Har. Ch., 255.

13. DECREE.

1486. Under general prayer: creditor's suit. A bill may be filed by a judgment creditor for the double purpose of setting aside a fraudulent conveyance and of reaching choses in action; and if there is no special prayer to have the fraudulent conveyance set aside, the complainant is entitled to have it set aside under the general prayer for other and further relief. *Williams v. Hubbard*, Wal. Ch., 28.

1487. When pronounced. A final decree, or an interlocutory order upon the merits of the case, will not be pronounced until all the parties in interest are before the Court, and the case in readiness for hearing as to all. *Graham v. Elmore*, Har. Ch., 265.

1488. If the cause is not in readiness as to one defendant, but is as to another, the latter cannot notice it for hearing, but if complainant does not proceed with the case, he may move to dismiss it for want of prosecution. *Ibid.*

1489. What is final. An application to dismiss a bill, is an application for a final decree. *Higgins v. Carpenter*, Har. Ch., 256. Supra 105 to 120.

1490. The practice of making decrees final in form, which consist in part of a reference to a commissioner to take an account between the parties, is objectionable. *Enos v. Sutherland*, 9 Mich., 148.

1491. Between defendants. A decree may be made between co-defendants grounded upon the pleadings and proofs between complainant and defendants. *Thurston v. Prentiss*, 1 Mich., 193.

1492. Complainant dismissing bill. The complainant may at any time before there has been an interlocutory or final decree in a cause, dismiss his bill, of course, on payment of costs. *Seymour v. Jerome*, Wal. Ch., 356.

1493. Where an interlocutory order had been entered by consent of parties, operating as an adjudication to some extent upon the rights of the parties, the Court refused to allow complainant to dismiss. *Ibid.*

1494. If complainant has leave to dismiss conditionally, the defendant, until the condition is complied with, may consider the case as in Court or out of Court, at his discretion; he may either proceed in it, or consider it dismissed, and apply to the Court to enforce payment of his costs. *Jerome v. Seymour*, Wal. Ch., 359.

1495. Form of decree. One of the defendants in a foreclosure decree, who had a residuary interest in the mortgage foreclosed after complainant's demand should be satisfied, filed a bill, the object of which was to have the benefit of that decree, and also to foreclose the mortgage against parties who were not but should have been parties to the first suit. A decree was made in the case, in the ordinary form of foreclosure decrees, and it was held not objectionable—it appearing that since the original decree payments had come due as well on the mortgage as on complainant's debt secured by it. *Griggs v. Detroit and Milwaukee Railway Co.*, 10 Mich., 117.

1496. Where, on bill to redeem, a deed absolute in form is adjudged to be a mortgage, and the mortgagee had, before the bill was filed, conveyed to one of the other defendants, the decree should direct the amount due to be paid to such grantee instead of the mortgagee. *Emerson v. Atwater*, 12 Mich., 314.

1497. It is proper, in such a case, to direct a sale of the premises to satisfy the amount due, in default of payment by the time fixed, instead of decreeing a strict foreclosure. *Ibid.*

1498. Foreclosure case: filing mortgage. Before decree is granted in a foreclosure case, the mortgage and accompanying securities, if any, should be filed in Court, as evidence of complainant's present right to control them. *Young v. McKee*, 13 Mich., 552; *Bailey v. Gould*, Wal. Ch, 428; *Bassett v. Hathaway*, 9 Mich., 28. But where a case was contested on the sole ground that the mortgage and notes were of no original validity, and they were not put on file, the Supreme Court declined to reverse the decree for complainant on that ground, but required them to be produced and filed, or their absence accounted for by affidavit, before affirming it. *Young v. McKee*, 13 Mich., 552.

1499. Correcting decree. The Court may correct a mistake in a decree after it has been entered, either upon motion or petition. *Bates v. Garrison*, Har. Ch., 221; *Jerome v. Seymour*, Wal. Ch., 359.

1500. Setting aside decree. On motion to set aside a decree for irregularity, the affidavits should show that the party is injured by the irregularity. *Michigan Insurance Co. v. Whittemore*, 12 Mich., 427.

1501. When the facts upon which the motion is made appear by the record, it is not necessary to present them by petition. *Graham v. Elmore*, Har. Ch., 265.

1502. Opening decree. Each application to open a decree regularly obtained by default, must depend upon its own circumstances, and the sound discretion of the Court. *Russell v. Waite*, Wal. Ch., 31; *Hart v. Linsday*, Wal. Ch., 72.

1503. The decree should only be opened under special circumstances, and to promote justice. *Ibid.*

1504. A stronger case must be made to open a decree than to set aside a default. *Hart v. Linsday*, Wal. Ch., 72,

14. Costs.

1505. Mortgage cases. Where complainant has a sale adjourned, he should pay the expense of adjournment himself. *Hart v. Linsday*, Wal. Ch., 72. Rule for costs and commissions laid down. *Ibid.*

1506. Taking depositions. Each party must pay for taking down the cross examination of his adversary's witness, as well as the direct examination of his own. *Sawyer v. Sawyer*, Wal. Ch., 48.

1507. A defendant unnecessarily made a party, should have the bill dismissed as to him with costs. *Gregory v. Stanton*, 12 Mich., 61; *Ramsdell v. Eaton*, 12 Mich., 117.

1508. Partnership cases. Where complainant was compelled by the improper conduct of defendant, and without fault of his own, to come into Court for a settlement of partnership accounts, he was held entitled to costs. *Ward v. Jewett*, Wal. Ch., 45.

1509. Against infants costs should not be awarded when they are respondents in the litigation, and could not by any act of theirs have dispensed with it. *Smith v. Smith*, 13 Mich., 258.

1510. Against administrator. Where a bill is dismissed at the hearing, the costs are in the discretion of the Court, except where special provision is made by statute; even though the complainant be administratrix, and the bill be filed in her representative character. *Daniels v. Eisenlord*, 10 Mich., 454.

1511. Discretionary. Bill and cross bill. Decree for complainant in the original bill. Appeal to the Supreme Court, where the decree was reversed, and both bills dismissed. Under the circumstances of the case, costs of the Court below were awarded to neither party. *Avery v. Payne*, 12 Mich., 540.

1512. When due. It is the determination of the suit which entitles a party to costs, and the law then in existence is the rule by which they are to be ascertained. *Sawyer v. Studley*, Wal. Ch., 153.

1513. Retaxation. Where a party applies for a retaxation of costs, he must bring the question before the Court by petition or motion, specifying the items objected to as erroneously allowed. Or, if he complains of irregularity, he must make a motion to have the taxation set aside on that account. *Reeves v Scully*, Wal. Ch., 346. Retaxation will be refused where there has been gross negligence. *Hart v. Linsday*, Wal. Ch., 72.

15. Rehearing.

1514. A rehearing will not be granted where a party by lapse of time has lost his right to appeal. *Benedict v. Thompson*, Wal. Ch., 446.

16. Supplemental Order of Sale.

1515. How obtained. Where after decree in a foreclosure suit another instalment falls due on the mortgage, and a petition is presented for a further order of sale, the petition should set forth briefly all the facts necessary to enable the mortgagor, as well as the Court, to understand its object. *Albany City Bank v. Steevens*, Wal. Ch., 6.

1516. A copy of the petition, with notice of the time of presentation to the Court, must also be served on the mortgagor, or, if it cannot be served personally by reason of his absence from the State, it should be served on his solicitor. *Ibid.*

1517. A copy of the petition need not be served on defendants made parties as subsequent incumbrancers. *Ibid.*

17. Setting Aside Sales.

1518. A much stronger case must be made to set aside the sale after confirmation of report of sale than before. *Bullard v. Green*, 10 Mich., 268.

1519. What can be inquired into. On application to set aside a sale, the Court cannot inquire into the regularity of the proceedings resulting in the decree, nor whether the decree was for a greater or less sum than it should have been. *Ibid.*

1520. Surprise. The sale will not be set aside on the ground of surprise, when the surprise springs from the negligence and inattention of the party himself who complains of it. *Ibid.*

1521. Inadequacy of consideration. A sale at $350 will not be set aside on the ground of inadequacy of consideration, when the petition states the premises to be worth $700, and the evidence is that they have since been sold by the purchaser at that price on long time, but that for cash they would not sell for over $400. *Ibid.*

1522. Laches. Nor, if the inadequacy of price was sufficient, would it be set aside on a petition presented six months after the sale, and which does not sufficiently excuse this delay. *Ibid.*

1523. Where the delay had continued until an execution had been issued for a deficiency, and a sale made under which third persons had acquired vested interests, and the purchaser had made payments to redeem from former sales, the Court refused to set aside the sale on the ground of surprise and inadequate consideration. *Leonard v. Taylor*, 12 Mich., 398.

1524. Complainant not appearing to have been guilty of any oppression, or unwilling at any time to receive the amount due him, it was held a fatal objection to the petition that it neither offered to pay the decree, or to increase the bid if a resale was ordered. *Ibid.*

18. Writ of Assistance.

1525. A writ of assistance will be granted to put the purchaser of mortgaged premises in possession, if the defendant, on being shown the master's deed, and a certified copy of the order confirming the sale under the seal of the Court, refuse to deliver possession. *Hart v. Linsday*, Wal. Ch., 144.

1526. But it will not be granted against a person not a party to the suit, who has come into possession since the suit was commenced, unless notice of the motion, with a copy of the affidavit on which it is founded, is served upon him. *Benhard v. Darrow*, Wal. Ch., 519.

1527. Where a subsequent mortgagee, who was not a party to the suit, obtained possession of the mortgaged premises after decree, by some arrangement with the owner of the equity of redemption, who was a party—having at the time notice of the foreclosure proceedings—it was held that his right to possession thus acquired was terminated by a sale under the decree, and the purchaser was entitled to this writ against him. *Baker v. Pierson*, 5 Mich., 456.

19. Non-Resident Defendants.

1528. Appearing after default. Two things only are required by the statute of non-resident defendants to entitle them to appear and defend in mortgage cases: appearance before the premises are sold under a decree, and payment of such costs as the Court shall direct. The costs only are discretionary with the Court. *Bailey v. Murphy*, Wal. Ch., 305.

1529. The statute as to non-resident defendants, makes no distinction between mortgagors and subsequent incumbrancers. *Ibid.*

1530. Effect of appearing. The only effect of non-resident defendants appearing and answering after decree, is to vacate the decree as to them, leaving it to stand as against other defendants. *Griggs v. Detroit and Milwaukee Railway Co.*, 10 Mich., 117.

1531. If they appear and answer after decree, and after supplemental bill filed to execute the same, and no further proceedings are taken in the original suit, they must answer the supplemental bill if they would protect the rights acquired by so appearing and answering the original bill. *Ibid.*

1532. Decree for deficiency. If the bill is filed to foreclose a mortgage against a non-resident mortgagor, who does not appear, a personal decree cannot be made against him for any deficiency that may remain after sale. *Lawrence v. Fellows*, Wal. Ch., 468.

1533. In partition cases. The jurisdiction of Courts of Chancery over proceedings in partition as to non-residents, is special and limited, and dependent entirely upon the statute. All the necessary facts to confer jurisdiction must therefore affirmatively appear upon the record. *Platt v. Stewart*, 10 Mich., 260.

1534. An affidavit of non-residence is an essential pre-requisite to an order for the appearance of non-resident defendants in such cases; and without such affidavit the order is void, and the Court acquires no jurisdiction of the non-residents by its publication. *Ibid.*

1535. The recital of an affidavit in the order is not evidence that such an affidavit was made. *Ibid.*

1536. Personal decree against, is void. Where a non-resident defendant has not appeared, a decree for the payment of a sum of money by him is void. And where another defendant in the case appealed, and the decree against him was reversed, the void decree against the non-resident defendant was also set aside. *Outhwite v. Porter*, 13 Mich., 533.

20. SURPLUS MONEYS AFTER FORECLOSURE.

1537. Petition for: notice. All the parties to a foreclosure suit are entitled to notice of an application for surplus moneys after foreclosure and sale, that they may appear and contest the right of the applicant, and assert their own; and an order for the payment of the moneys to the petitioner without such notice, or the appearance of the parties, is erroneous. *Smith v. Smith*, 13 Mich., 258.

1538. If the owner of the equity of redemption dies after sale, the surplus moneys are personal estate; and his personal representatives should be made parties to a petition to obtain them. *Ibid.*

ERROR.

1539. Matters of discretion. Error cannot be assigned on the decision of the Court below of a motion, founded upon affidavits, to vacate a judgment; such motion being addressed merely to the sound discretion of the Court. *City of Detroit v. Jackson*, 1 Doug., 106; *Van Rensselaer v. Whiting*, 12 Mich., 449.

1540. Nor, for the same reason, upon its decision in granting or refusing a motion for a new trial. *Dibble v. Rogers*, 2 Mich., 404; *Bourke v. James*, 4 Mich., 336; *Crippen v. People*, 8 Mich., 117; *Cuddy v. Major*, 12 Mich., 368.

1541. Nor on its order dismissing an appeal case for want of payment of the entrance fee. *Chaffee v. Soldan*, 5 Mich., 242. Or refusing to open a cause which has been submitted, and allow further proofs. *Lee v. Hardgrave*, 3 Mich., 77.

1542. If the Circuit Court, on appeal from an order of the Probate Court refusing a will to probate, can allow part of the proponents to renounce and be discharged, the power to do so is discretionary, and a refusal cannot be reviewed on error. *Beaubien v. Cicotte*, 12 Mich., 459.

1543. But it is not a matter of discretion in a Court to allow a discontinuance at the trial as to a defendant who is manifestly made a party for the sole purpose of depriving the other defendant, who is a citizen of another State, of his right to remove the case to the United States Court. *Yawkey v. Richardson*, 9 Mich., 529.

1544. Error without injury. On a writ of error, the Supreme Court corrects only such errors as have been committed adversely to the interest of the party suing out the writ. *Berry v. Lowe*, 10 Mich., 9. And see *People v. Scott*, 6 Mich., 287.

1545. Judgment will not be reversed because counsel for one party, in the argument to the jury, is permitted to take an erroneous view of the law, if the Judge in his charge corrects the error, and truly states the law on the point. *People v. Jenness*, 5 Mich., 305.

1546. A charge in favor of the party excepting will not be reviewed on error, whether right or wrong. *Brigham v. Gurney*, 1 Mich., 349. See *Berry v. Lowe*, 10 Mich., 9.

1547. An erroneous charge which could not affect the verdict, is no ground of error. *Clark v. Moore*, 3 Mich., 55; *Cummings v. Stone*, 13 Mich., 70.

1548. Where exception is taken to a charge which is not strictly correct, but the Court can clearly see that the jury could not have been misled by it, to the injury of the party excepting, a new trial will not be ordered for that error. *People v. Scott*, 6 Mich., 287.

1549. A plaintiff in replevin cannot complain that the Court awarded nominal damages to him when the jury gave none; the error, if any, being in his favor. *Sleight v. Henning*, 12 Mich., 371.

1550. A judgment will not be reversed for a failure to award nominal damages to a plaintiff entitled to them, when a judgment therefor would not have carried costs. *Hickey v. Baird*, 9 Mich., 32.

1551. The admission of evidence from which no injury could result to the plaintiff in error, is no ground for reversing a judgment. *Minnesota Mining Co. v. National Mining Co.*, 11 Mich., 186. See *Rose v. Lewis*, 10 Mich., 483; *Lyell v. Sanbourn*, 2 Mich., 109.

1552. A judgment will not be reversed because inconsistent instructions were given to the jury, if those adverse to the plaintiff in error were all correct. *Niagara Fire Insurance Co. v. DeGraff*, 12 Mich., 124.

1553. Unfair suggestions. A defendant having claimed and been allowed his exemption from testifying, on the ground that his answers might tend to criminate him, counsel was permitted to comment on that fact to the jury; the Court remarking in the presence of the jury, that "the refusal of the defendant to answer the question propounded to him on the ground stated, was not evidence against him in the cause, yet it was impossible to prevent the jury from having the whole case, and knowing what was done in open Court in the course of the trial before them, or to prevent counsel commenting upon it." Held, that this suggestion by the Court, the effect of which might be to deprive the defendant of the benefit of his exemption, was erroneous. *Carne v. Litchfield*, 2 Mich., 340.

1554. Charge without evidence to warrant it. A charge to the jury as to the conclusive nature of a written contract between the parties, if they shall find such contract established by the evidence, when there is no evidence in the case showing or tending to show a written contract of the kind mentioned, is improper, as tending to mislead the jury. *American Transportation Co. v. Moore*, 5 Mich., 368.

1555. Request how construed. On error the Supreme Court must construe a request for instructions to the jury as it must have been understood by the Court and jury had it been given. It must therefore be construed in reference to the evidence upon the subject to which it relates. *Angell v. Rosenbury*, 12 Mich., 241. See *People v. Scott*, 6 Mich., 287.

1556. Verdict against evidence. The question whether the jury did not find against evidence or perversely, cannot be considered on writ of error. *Niagara Fire Insurance Co. v. DeGraff*, 12 Mich., 124.

1557. Curing error. Where a question put by a party to his own witness is erroneously overruled, the error is not cured by his being allowed afterwards to put the same question to the witness of the other party on cross examination. *Flanigan v. Lampman*, 12 Mich., 58.

1558. Where an objection to a question is improperly overruled, and the witness in reply to it says "I can't say," the answer renders the question immaterial, and an exception to the ruling cannot be sustained on error. *Peck v. Snyder*, 13 Mich., 21.

1559. Action on promissory note. Defense, set off and payment. The defendant offered evidence of a payment of five dollars, which was excluded by the Court on the ground that the item was not mentioned in the bill of particulars of set off. Plaintiff having recovered judgment was allowed by the Court to remit five dollars of the amount, with a view to curing the error. Held, that the error was not cured, as by rejecting evidence of this payment, the Court in effect denied the defendant the right to prove any item of payment without giving notice; and it cannot be seen, therefore, that other payments were not excluded. *Olcott v. Hanson*, 12 Mich., 452. See supra 935.

1560. Waiving error. Action in the County Court by plaintiffs as co-partners. On the trial a contract signed by defendant, in which a partnership (which plaintiffs claimed to be themselves) was mentioned, was produced and proved, under objections by defendant. The case being removed to the Circuit Court by certiorari, the nature of the objections did not appear, nor did any direct evidence of plaintiffs' partnership appear. Held, that as affirmative proof of plaintiffs' partnership was necessary to a recovery, they could not claim that it was made out by the contract, unless they showed affirmatively that the objections made by the defendant were such as to amount to an admission of the partnership, or to a waiver of proof of it. *Lee v. Hardgrave*, 3 Mich., 77.

1561. Where application to make the opposite party a witness upon a ground provided by the statute (of 1846) was denied in the Court below, the party applying cannot, upon error, allege other facts making such party a competent witness, which, though appearing in the proceedings, were not suggested in the Court below. *McBride v. Cicotte*, 4 Mich., 478.

1562. Error will not be presumed, but must be made to appear affirmatively. *Comstock v. Hollon*, 2 Mich., 355; *Burnham v. People*, 3 Mich., 195; *Rash v. Whitney*, 4 Mich., 495; *Sweetzer v. Mead*, 5 Mich., 33; *Achey v. Hull*, 7 Mich., 423; *Maynard v. Penniman*, 10 Mich., 153; *Kermott v. Ayer*, 11 Mich., 181; *Morrissey v. People*, 11 Mich., 327; *Dann v. Cudney*, 13 Mich., 239.

1563. It will not be presumed that facts were given in evidence not admissible under the pleadings. *Comstock v. Hollon*, 2 Mich., 355.

1564. In support of a judgment the evidence will be presumed to have been sufficient. *Farmers and Mechanics' Bank v. Troy City Bank*, 1 Doug., 457.

1565. Where a cause is tried in the Circuit Court without a jury, and no exceptions are taken to the legal rulings, upon which the Court arrives at its application of the facts and the evidence, and no case, made under the statute, is brought before the Supreme Court, that Court is not at liberty, on writ of error, to examine into the propriety of anything in the decision of the Court below, based upon its finding of facts; but must take its conclusions as founded upon the law and the evidence. *Sweetzer v. Mead*, 5 Mich., 107.

1566. But where a cause was tried by the Circuit Judge without a jury, and improper evidence was admitted to establish a material point, and the nature of the case was such that it could not be presumed other evidence was given on that point; it was held that the judgment should be reversed, notwithstanding the bill of exceptions did not state that all the evidence was set forth. *Bliss v. Paine*, 11 Mich., 92.

1567. A writ of error did not lie from the Supreme Court to the County Court; a remedy by certiorari being given. *Hiney v. Cade*, 1 Mich., 163.

1568. To authorize the writ there must be a final judgment or determination in the inferior Court; it will not lie to bring up interlocutory proceedings merely, or discretionary orders made pending the litigation. *Holbrook v. Cook*, 5 Mich., 225.

1569. Nor will it lie where the proceedings are not after the course of the common law; it is not enough that they are had in a Court which ordinarily and primarily exercises common law jurisdiction. *Ibid.* And see *Parker v. Copland*, 4 Mich., 528.

1570. Held, therefore, that an order of the Circuit Court reversing an order of the Probate Court for the removal of an administrator, and remanding the case to that Court for action upon the administrator's account filed therein, could not be removed to the Supreme Court by writ of error. *Holbrook v. Cook*, 5 Mich., 225.

1571. But when a proceeding to recover possession of lands, under the statute "of forcible entries and detainers," is appealed to the Circuit Court, it becomes, in that Court, a proceeding according to the course of the common law; and error is the only mode of reviewing, in the Supreme Court, the judgment of the Circuit Court. *Parker v. Copland*, 4 Mich., 528.

1572. Error will not lie on a conviction in the Recorder's Court of Detroit for an offense against a city ordinance. *Jackson v. People*, 8 Mich., 262.

1573. Where an appeal has been taken to the Circuit Court from the decree of the Probate Court allowing or disallowing a will, and a trial is had, error lies to remove to the Supreme Court the adjudication of the Circuit Court upon the appeal. *American Missionary Union v. Peck*, 9 Mich., 445.

1574. It makes no difference that a formal issue was not made up in the Circuit Court, since the substance of the issue is the same, whether made up in form or not. *Ibid.*

1575. Who may bring error. Where one party appeals from the decision of the Judge of Probate to the Circuit Court, and in that Court the decision appealed from is affirmed, the party appealing is the only one who can bring error: since he alone can be said to be *aggrieved* by the judgment of the Circuit Court. *Jackson v. Hosmer*, 14 Mich.

1576. Errors of fact. The Supreme Court has jurisdiction of errors of fact, as well as errors of law. *Teller v. Wetherell*, 6 Mich., 46.

1577. If necessary a venire may be issued for a jury to try in that Court the issue joined on assignment of error of fact; or it may be sent to the proper circuit for trial. *Ibid.*

1578. Errors of fact may be assigned in the Supreme Court on the common writ of error. *Ibid.*

1579. Circuit Courts have no power in any case to issue writs of error. *Ibid.*

1580. Writ barred by lapse of time. A motion to dismiss is the proper form of objection to a writ of error supposed to be barred by lapse of time. *Teller v. Willis*, 12 Mich., 268.

1581. The statute limiting the time for bringing writ of error, commences running from the rendition of the judgment, and is not affected by the settlement of exceptions afterwards. *Teller v. Willis*, 12 Mich., 384.

1582. Settlement of exceptions after error brought. A party is not obliged to wait until his exceptions are settled before suing out his writ of error. The exceptions, if sealed and filed after error brought, may be brought up like any other omitted portion of the record. *Ibid.*

1583. The Supreme Court will always give a plaintiff in error the benefit of his exceptions—unless by his fault or laches he has occasioned the delay himself—by extending the time for return, or for the assignment of errors, or by allowing a new assignment, as the case may require. *Ibid.*

1584. What reviewed. On error, the case can be reviewed on errors of law only; not on conflicting testimony. *Higley v. Lant*, 3 Mich., 612; *Miller v. Chaffee*, 1 Mich., 257; *Bromley v. People*, 7 Mich., 472.

1585. Where there was a finding of facts by the Circuit Judge, the evidence can be examined on error only so far as to see whether it *tends* to support the finding; and the finding can be reviewed only so far as to see whether the legal conclusions and judgment are warranted by the facts found. *Tillman v. Fuller*, 13 Mich., 113. See *Sweetzer v. Mead*, 5 Mich., 107.

1586. Where the plaintiff sued on a parol agreement as a demise, and the Judge in his finding did not directly find that there was a demise, and did not find such facts as would warrant the conclusion as one of law, it was held that plaintiff could not recover. *Ibid.*

1587. On exceptions every part of the charge of the Court must be presumed to be correct, and to be warranted by the evidence, so far as the bill does not show the contrary. *People v. McKinney*, 10 Mich., 54. To enable the Court to judge of the propriety of instructions to the jury, which instructions assume the existence of certain facts, the bill of exceptions must either contain the evidence of those facts, or a statement that there was such evidence. *Tyler v. People*, 8 Mich., 320.

1588. Affidavits on which a motion for a new trial was based, though sent up with the record, form no part of it, and cannot be looked into for the purpose of determining whether the Court erred in denying the motion. *Crippen v. People*, 8 Mich., 117.

1589. Where an objection was taken on the trial to the recovery of certain damages on the ground solely that they were not allowed by the statute, and the objection correctly overruled, it was held that the Court would not, on error, reverse the judgment on the ground that the declaration was too general to include such damages. *Achey v. Hull*, 7 Mich., 423.

ESTATES OF DECEASED PERSONS.

1590. Title to personalty. Until administration and distribution, no title to the personal property of an intestate passes to the next of kin, and they can maintain no action in respect to it unless it be founded upon their own actual possession, and against a mere wrong doer. *Cullen v. O'Hara*, 4 Mich., 132.

1591. Insolvent estate. Where, under R. S. of 1838, an estate had been represented insolvent by an administrator de bonis non, a motion was granted staying proceedings on executions for balances due on mortgage foreclosures which had been levied before such representation of insolvency. *Quackenboss v. Campbell*, Wal. Ch., 525.

1592. Administrator's control of lands. Before the Statutes of 1846 an administrator had no interest in or authority over real estate, unless the personal property of the intestate was insufficient to pay his debts; and then he could only dispose of it as empowered by the Probate Court. *Thayer v. Lane*, Wal. Ch., 200.

1593. The Statutes of 1846—Comp. L., § 2904 — empowering executors and administrators to take possession of the lands, does not exclude the possessory right of heirs or devisees, but merely permits the executors or administrators to claim and have possession, if they see fit to demand it. *Streeter v. Paton*, 7 Mich., 341 ; *Marvin v. Schilling*, 12 Mich., 356. The heir or devisee, therefore, when possession has not been demanded by the personal representative, may maintain ejectment against third persons. *Ibid.*

1594. The interest of the executor or administrator under this statute is not a chattel, and cannot be sold by him. It is only given to enable him to receive the rents and profits of the land while the estate is being settled. *Kline v. Moulton*, 11 Mich., 370.

1595. On the death or removal of the administrator, his possessory right, and the rents and profits connected with it, pass to his successor, who may maintain ejectment to recover possession from one claiming under the first administrator. And this notwithstanding the first administrator was one of several heirs, and had made a contract in his own name to sell the lands to the person in possession. *Ibid.*

1596. Waiving land contract. An administrator, as such, has no authority to waive or release a contract made by his intestate for the purchase of lands, unless the personal property is insufficient to pay the debts; and then only by order of the Probate Court, duly obtained. *Hunt v. Thorn*, 2 Mich., 213.

1597. Selling land contract. An administrator cannot sell the interest of the estate in an executory contract for the purchase of lands, except as real estate and after license. *Baxter v. Robinson*, 11 Mich., 520.

1598. Neglecting payments on. Where payments fell due on such a contract, which the administrator had no funds in his hands to pay, but money for that purpose was promised by creditors of the estate, which he neglected to obtain, and the contract became forfeited ; it was held that these facts did not render the administrator liable to the heirs for the value of their interest in the land thus forfeited. *Ibid.*

1599. Sale by administrator : credit. Whether, under the Code of 1833, an administrator was authorized, in any case, to give credit upon a sale of real estate of the intestate for the payment of his debts, under a license of the Probate Court, and whether, if he did so, he was not chargeable with the price as money in his hands, *quere. Palmer, et al appellants*, 1 Doug., 422.

1600. Administrator purchasing. An administrator cannot become the purchaser of the estate or effects of his intestate. And where two administrators made sale of lands of the intestate to one of the two, and executed a deed therefor, the deed was held void, notwithstanding the sale and conveyance were under the order of the Probate Court. The question of intent or fairness cannot be considered in such a case. *Dwight v. Blackmar*, 2 Mich., 330.

1601. And a sale was set aside in chancery where an administrator procured another person to bid in the premises in his own name, and then deed them over to the administrator. *Beaubien v. Poupard*, Har. Ch., 206.

1602. A Judge of Probate cannot become interested in a sale made under his order. *Walton v Torrey*, Har. Ch., 259.

1603. Adjournment of sale. Where the day appointed for an administrator's sale is rainy and inclement, and but few persons appear and bid, and the bids do not exceed half the value of the property, it is the duty of the administrator to adjourn the sale. *Beaubien v. Poupard*, Har. Ch., 206.

1604. Right to sell terminated. Where license to sell real estate was granted by the County Court, and after license but before sale the law giving that Court jurisdiction was repealed, it was held that the repeal of the law was a revocation of the license, and a sale subsequently made was void. *Campau v. Gillett*, 1 Mich., 416.

1605. A sale under a license granted under the territorial statute of July 27, 1818, was held void where it was made more than four years after the license was granted ; — the statute of limitations then in force barring all claims against the estate after four years. *Ibid.*

1606. See also *Matter of Godfrey Estate*, where it was held that if the creditors have lost their remedy against the executor or administrator by lapse of time, the Courts will not license a sale of the real estate for the payment of claims thus barred. 4 Mich., 308.

1607. Held also, where the administrator, seventeen years after the estate was reported insolvent, petitioned for license to sell lands to pay debts, that the license should be refused whether the action of creditors against the administrator was barred by the statute or not. *Ibid.*

1608. Under the Statutes of 1838 the license to sell lands was in force for a year. Held, that if the sale was made within the year, the deed might be executed and delivered afterwards. *Howard v. Moore*, 2 Mich., 226.

1609. Defects in proceedings. Irregularities in the proceedings by an administrator for the sale of the real estate of the decedent, will not affect the title of the purchaser, where there has been a compliance with so much as the statute makes essential to the validity of the sale, and the good faith of the purchaser is not questioned. *Coon v. Fry*, 6 Mich., 506; *Howard v. Moore*, 2 Mich, 226; *Palmer v. Oakley*, 2 Doug. 433.

1610. Accordingly where, in such case, the application of the administrator for license to sell was not verified by oath; guardians were not appointed for the infant heirs; and the administrator's report of the sale to the Probate Court omitted to show the price at which the land was sold, it was held that none of the omissions affected the title of the purchaser. *Coon v. Fry*, 6 Mich., 506.

1611. Commissioners to audit claims. Where commisioners have been appointed to examine and adjust claims against the estate of a deceased person, the estate is not bound by an account stated with the administrators. *Fish v. Morse*, 8 Mich., 34.

1612. Appeal. Where an appeal is taken to the Circuit Court from the action of the commissioners upon a claim, the Circuit Court should not render judgment in the common law form, but simply allow or disallow the claim. *LaRoe v. Freeland*, 8 Mich., 531.

1613. Costs. Where an executor resisted a claim against the testator in the Circuit Court, and after decision by the Court allowing it, removed the case to the Supreme Court, and that Court was of opinion that there was no reasonable ground for resisting the claim, costs of the Supreme Court were awarded to the claimant. *Dodge v. Stanton* 12 Mich., 408.

1614. Suits against administrator. A bill filed by a creditor against the administrators of his deceased debtor, and others, to set aside a conveyance made by the deceased as fraudulent, and subject the land to the payment of debts, is not within the Statutes of 1838, p. 288 § 10, prohibiting the commencement of suits against administrators within one year after their appointment, &c. *Manning v. Drake*, 1 Mich., 34.

1615. A foreign administrator has no interest in the real or personal property of his intestate in this State. *Thayer v. Lane*, Wal. Ch., 200.

1616. When next of kin to act. Suit in equity to compel the execution of the trust in an assignment for the benefit of creditors. On a reference to ascertain the amount of the debts, it was held that the assignor was not entitled to appear on behalf of an estate of which he was administrator, to prove a claim against himself in favor of such estate; but that the next of kin of the deceased, or other persons entitled to the moneys from him as administrator, might do so. *Suydam v. Dequindre*, Wal. Ch., 23.

ESTOPPEL.

1617. A tenant is estopped from disputing the title of his landlord. *Byrne v. Beeson*, 1 Doug., 179; *Falkner v. Beers*, 2 Doug., 117; *Lee v. Payne*, 4 Mich., 106. And see *Blanchard v. Tyler*, 12 Mich., 339. But after eviction by one having paramount title, he is excused from paying rent. *Marsh v. Butterworth*, 4 Mich., 575.

1618. A lessee of a mortgagor is not estopped, in an action of ejectment brought against him by the mortgagor, from showing, to protect his possession, that he has become assignee of the mortgagee. *Niles v. Ransford*, 1 Mich., 338.

1619. A promise void under the statute of frauds, cannot be enforced as an estoppel where the party has not been misled as to the facts. Accordingly where an administratrix promised one that if the latter would attend a sale of real estate to be made by her, and bid a certain amount, her right of dower in the land should pass by the sale, it was held that she was not thereby estopped from claiming it. *Wright v. DeGroff*, 14 Mich.

1620. By deed. One who gives a deed of lands which are in the adverse possession of another, is estopped from disputing the deed; and the grantee may enforce his rights under it, against the person in possession, in the name of the grantor. *Stockton v. Williams*, 1 Doug., 546.

1621. A lease which one executes as agent of the lessor, would estop him from setting up any claim to the land inconsistent with the lease. *Blanchard v. Tyler*, 12 Mich., 339.

1622. The deed of an administratrix, containing a covenant to warrant the title against any one claiming under the grantor, does not estop her from claiming dower in the premises as widow of the deceased. *Wright v. DeGroff*, 14 Mich.

1623. Privies. Where R. made claim to a lot in Detroit under a warranty deed from M., and the Governor and Judges deeded the lot to R. in pursuance of such claim, it was held that, in proceedings by the widow of M. to recover dower in the lot, those claiming under R.

were estopped from denying the seizin of M. *May v. Tillman*, 1 Mich., 262.

1624. The purchaser of an equity of redemption, who has gone into possession under his purchase, is estopped, when proceedings are taken to foreclose the mortgage, from denying the title of the mortgagor. *Wanzer v. Blanchard*, 3 Mich., 11.

1625. Invalid contract. A paper signed by a judgment debtor and delivered to the attorney of his creditors, agreeing to compromise the judgment in a certain way, or in default thereof to deliver certain property levied upon in payment, cannot estop him from claiming the levy to be invalid, where it appears that the attorney had no authority to enter into such an agreement, or to compromise the judgment in any manner. *Hickey v. Hinsdale*, 12 Mich., 99.

1626. Estoppel by non-claim. Where a creditor was advised by his debtor and a third party, that the two were in treaty for a transfer to such third party of the debtor's property, but was not informed that by such transfer the debtor was to deprive himself of the means of paying his debts; and he was called upon by them to declare whether he had any claim against the debtor, or the property in question, and declined to answer; it was held that he was not, by his silence, estopped from seeking relief against the transfer as a voluntary one. *Cicotte v. Gagnier*, 2 Mich., 381.

1627. Where one standing in position of mortgagor of a mortgage, was present at and assented to a subsequent assignment of the mortgage by his assignee, to secure a debt of the latter less than the amount that it was first assigned to secure; it was held that he was not thereby estopped from asserting his right to redeem, since he must be understood as assenting only to an assignment of such interest as his assignee had in the mortgage. *Graydon v. Church*, 7 Mich., 36.

1628. Nor would statements made by him at the time, that if the debt he was owing was paid from the mortgage he would be satisfied, estop him from redeeming. *Ibid.*

1629. And where a receiver in chancery, to whom such a mortgagor of the mortgage had assigned, was called upon by a subsequent assignee to redeem his interest in the mortgage, and was told that unless such redemption was made, such assignee was about to transfer the mortgage to another; and the receiver declined to redeem, and told the assignee he might sell to whom he pleased, whereupon the assignee did sell, but to one who was aware of the conditional nature of the assignments; it was held that the receiver was not thereby estopped from asserting his right to redeem. *Ibid.*

1630. After an irregular foreclosure of a mortgage, one of two subsequent joint mortgagees was inquired of by one who contemplated a purchase of the land, whether he had any claim upon it, and was told that he had not. The inquirer then purchased the land from the first mortgagee. It was held that such subsequent mortgagees were estopped from setting up any claim under their mortgage against such purchaser. *Cook v. Finkler*, 9 Mich., 131.

1631. Where the husband of a woman sold a horse belonging to her, without her authority, and she was informed of the sale before payment had been made, and had ample opportunity afterwards to inform the purchaser of her rights, but neglected to do so until he had made payment to the husband, it was held that she was thereafter estopped from asserting title to the horse against the purchaser or those claiming under him. *Dann v. Cudney*, 13 Mich., 239.

1632. By recognizing right. A corporation which, with full knowledge of the facts, has issued to the finder of a certificate of shares therein, a new certificate in its place, is estopped, as against a purchaser of such new certificate, from setting up the doubt as to the title as a reason for refusing to allow a transfer of the certificate on its books. *Mandlebaum v. North American Mining Co.*,, 4 Mich., 465.

1633. By destroying deed. Where land has been sold and paid for, and a deed executed and delivered, the subsequent refunding of the consideration to the purchaser, and the destruction of the deed by agreement of the parties to it, will not revest the title to the land in the grantor. But if the grantee or those claiming under him afterwards set up title to the land, they are estopped from showing by parol the contents of the destroyed deed. *Gugins v. Van Gorder*, 10 Mich., 523.

ESTRAYS.

1634. No one but a resident freeholder of the township being authorized by statute—Comp. L., § 1605—to take up stray beasts, the act by any one else is a trespass which cannot afterwards be assumed and made lawful by a freeholder. Accordingly, where the minor son of a resident freeholder, took up a stray beast without authority, and the father subsequently adopted the act, but stated that he should not himself have taken up the beast, it was held that the proceedings were unauthorized, and the subsequent sale of the estray under the statute void. *Newsom v. Hart*, 14 Mich.

EVIDENCE.

1. General Purpose.

1635. In all testimony the object of the law is, to enable the jury to know all that the witness knows which is pertinent to the issue; and every rule of evidence is designed to secure this end. *Beaubien v. Cicotte*, 12 Mich., 459.

1636. In general the rules of evidence are the same at law as in equity, and the principles which govern the means of obtaining proof are substantially the same in the one Court as in the other; and the rules of property and interpretation are or should be the same in both. *Dougherty v. Randall*, 3 Mich., 581.

2. Competency of Parties.

1637. Action against carriers for the value of a trunk containing wearing apparel, alleged to have been lost by their negligence. The declaration was on the contract of affreightment, and did not aver that the clothing was the ordinary wearing apparel of a person who had taken passage on defendants' boat, or that it was received as such. Held, that plaintiff could not be allowed to prove by his own evidence the contents of the trunk. *Clark v. Moore*, 3 Mich., 55.

1638. Proving accounts. Section 85 of chap. 93 of R. S. of 1846, authorized parties to be witnesses to prove their own accounts, after making oath that there was no disinterested witness whose attendance could be procured, by whom the same could be proved. Plaintiff sued for the balance of a book account, and the defendant admitted the debts charged to him on the plaintiff's books; and it was held that the plaintiff could not then be sworn to prove his account under this section. *Morse v. Congdon*, 3 Mich., 549.

1639. This statute did not make a party a competent witness to prove that on a settlement of accounts he gave the other party credit by mistake for a sum which had not been paid. *Ibid.*

1640. Under R. S. 1846, ch. 102, sec. 100. This section —Comp. L., § 4340—provided that whenever either party should file an affidavit, setting forth that any facts material to the issue or question to be tried were within the knowledge of any other party, and that there was no competent witness whose testimony he could procure by whom such facts could be proved, the parties to the suit or proceeding, or any other person interested, might be examined on oath in relation to such facts. It was held that a party would not be permitted to call upon his opponent to testify under this section, where it was apparent from the affidavit made, or the prior proceedings in the cause, that there were other witnesses attainable by whom the same facts could be shown. *McBride v. Cicotte*, 4 Mich., 478.

1641. The "other party" referred to in said section, was the *opposite* party. *Ibid.*

1642. Plaintiff in an action upon a premium note, having given the defendant notice to produce the policy upon which the note was given, which he refused to do, made the affidavit required by this section, setting forth the facts within the knowledge of the defendant to be, the issuing of the policy, its number, its receipt by defendant, its contents, and the policy. Held that under this affidavit plaintiff was entitled to examine the defendant as to the existence of the policy, its receipt by him, its contents, and to its production in Court if in his possession or under his control. *Way v Billings*, 2 Mich., 397.

1643. Where a party sworn as a witness under this section gave an answer clearly evasive, and uncandid, it was held that the Court should permit the broadest latitude of inquiry necessary to elicit the truth and effectuate the object of the law. *Ibid.*

1644. The office of the affidavit under this section was, to point out the fact to be proved, and not the evidence of the fact. Within the range of the affidavit the party was to be examined like any other witness ; and it was as competent for him to prove a fact by the admissible declarations of others, as it was for any other witness. *Hogan v. Sherman*, 5 Mich., 60.

1645. Under R. S. 1846, Ch. 102, § 102. This section—Comp. L., § 4342—which authorized the examination of the parties as witnesses in certain cases, was only applicable to actions *ex contractu. Carne v. Litchfield*, 2 Mich., 340.

1646. Under Circuit Court rule 48. Where the Circuit Court made an order that the parties be examined as witnesses, and they were examined accordingly, it was held not error to refuse to permit one of them to be sworn on his own behalf on a second trial — the other not being present. *Lester v. Sutton*, 7 Mich., 329. [The rule authorized the Circuit Courts, " at any time, in accordance with and for the furtherance of justice," to call upon all or any of the parties to be sworn].

1648. Parties in chancery. Where one defendant answered, and the other interposed a plea which was put in issue, and the defendant answering was examined as a witness for his co-defendant, it was held that his testimony must be restricted to matters, in support of the plea, in which he was not himself interested. *Emerson v. Atwater*, 7 Mich., 12.

1649. It was the interest of the party in the subject matter to which he was examined, and not the effect his evidence might have in the final determination of the issue, that rendered him incompetent. *Ibid.*

1650. In a contest between two mortgagees as to the priority of their respective liens, the mortgagor, being personally liable for both the mortgage debts, was disinterested, and might be made a witness under chancery rule 55. *Wilcox v. Hill*, 11 Mich., 256.

1651. Where a bill was filed to restrain the foreclosure of a mortgage which was alleged to have been discharged, the defendant claiming to own the mortgage could not be called as a witness by the other defendants, since there was no part of the case in which he was not personally interested. *Bassett v. Hathaway*, 9 Mich., 28.

1652. Nor could a defendant be called as a witness to sustain the mortgage when the effect of sustaining it would be to charge the land with the payment of his personal obligation. *Ibid.*

1653. Complainant could not examine as a witness a defendant against whom he sought relief; if the answer was insufficient, he should except; and if his testimony was sought to facts not stated in the bill, it should be amended. *Thomas v. Stone*, Wal. Ch., 117. The deposition of such a party suppressed, and the taking of it by complainant held not to amount to a release to him. *Norris v. Hurd*, Wal. Ch., 102.

1654. By statute since all the foregoing decisions were made, parties to suits, and all other persons interested, are made competent witnesses generally. *Laws of* 1861, *p.* 168.

3. Competency of Other Persons.

1655. A witness is presumed competent until the contrary appears. *Norris v. Hurd*, Wal. Ch., 102.

1656. A person is not incompetent to testify on behalf of the plaintiffs, in a suit brought by the highway commissioners of a township in their name of office, by reason of having himself been one of the commissioners when the suit was brought. *Highway Commissioners v. Stockman*, 5 Mich., 528.

1657. Stockholders in a corporation, who were personally liable for its debts, were competent witnesses for the plaintiff in a suit against the corporation. *Hasey v. White Pigeon Beet Sugar Co.*, 1 Doug., 193.

1658. A legatee, it seems, was a competent witness to a will; the Statutes (of 1838) making the legacy void. *High, appellant*, 2 Doug., 515.

1659. He would be a competent witness in support of the will under Comp. L., § 4339; although interested. *Lawyer v. Smith*, 8 Mich., 411.

1660. The acceptor of a bill for whose accommodation it was drawn and indorsed, and who first negotiated it to the plaintiff, was held a competent witness in a suit between the first indorsee and the indorser, to prove facts which would render the bill void. *Orr v. Lacey*, 2 Doug., 230.

1661. A joint defendant in an action ex contractu, not served with process, and not appearing, was held not a competent witness for his co-defendant under said §4339, although released by him; as he still remained a party to the record. *Brooks v. McIntyre*, 4 Mich., 316.

1662. Interest balanced. A person equally liable to both parties was a competent witness for either. *Woodbury v. Lewis*, Wal. Ch. 256.

1663. A surety in an appeal bond might be a witness for the appellant under said § 4339. He is not a party to the appeal, nor is it prosecuted " in his immediate and individual behalf." *White v. Bailey*, 10 Mich., 155.

1664. Husband and wife. Where two persons were jointly charged in the same complaint with the commission of the same offense, and neither of them had been either acquitted or convicted, the husband of one was held not a competent witness for the other, who, by leave of the Court, was tried separately. *Pullen v. People*, 1 Doug., 48. But it is otherwise under the Statute of 1861 (p. 168). *Morrissey v. People*, 11 Mich., 327.

1665. It seems that in a trial between other parties, the husband cannot, save in a few exceptional cases, be permitted to testify to facts which would subject his wife to imprisonment. *People v. Horton*, 4 Mich., 67.

1666. A child seven years of age is competent to testify; the question of his credibility is for the jury. *Washburn v. People*, 10 Mich., 372.

4. Examination of Witnesses.

1667. Leading questions. An objection to a question that it is leading must be taken before the question is answered. [Manning, J.] *Morrissey v. People*, 11 Mich., 327.

1668. Trial for larceny. The question " Will you state whether or not in your judgment the samples (of cloth) now shown to you are off the pieces that were stolen," is not objectionable as being leading. [Manning, J.] *Ibid.*

1669. Objection to be stated. Where a question put to a witness is objected to, the reason for the objection should be stated, and must appear by the bill of exceptions, or it cannot be presumed on error that it was erroneously overruled. [Manning, J.] *Ibid.*

1670. The party objecting should state the true ground of the objection; and if that stated is untenable, the judgment should not be reversed on a new objection for the first time taken in a Court of review if it is one that might have been obviated on the trial. [Manning, J.] *Young v. Stephens*, 9 Mich., 500.

1671. An objection to papers as incompetent and irrelevant, does not assail their genuineness, but impliedly admits it. *Ibid.*

1672. The defendant in an action of trespass, gave a notice with his plea, setting up a certain judgment, and stating with great particularity certain facts preliminary to the issuing of execution thereon; and on the trial he offered to read the docket entry of the judgment; to which the plaintiff objected, because all the preliminary facts set forth in the notice had not been proved. Held, that the objection should have specified the particular facts not proved; and was properly overruled as being too general. *Rash v. Whitney*, 4 Mich., 495.

1673. An objection by defendant to plaintiff being sworn under the statute, on the ground of incompetency to prove the facts to which he offered to testify, was held a sufficient objection to the plaintiff's testimony after being sworn. *Morse v. Congdon*, 3 Mich., 549.

1674. Witness giving reasons for recollection. A witness may be allowed to state any reason or circumstance which induced him to give particular attention to the facts observed by him, and to which he has testified. *Angell v. Rosenbury*, 12 Mich., 241.

1675. But in giving the reasons for his recollection of a transaction, he cannot be permitted to state facts inadmissible by the rules of evidence, nor to relate his own conversation with other persons, containing reflections on the motives of another witness. *McBride v. Cicotte*, 4 Mich., 478.

1676. Refreshing recollection. In order to refresh the recollection of a witness, his attention may be called to his evidence on a former trial, and counsel's minutes of the former testimony read for the purpose. *Beaubien v. Cicotte*, 12 Mich., 459.

1677. Cross examination. A party has no right to cross examine witnesses upon facts and circumstances not connnected with the matters stated in his examination in chief. *People v. Horton*, 4 Mich., 67; *Campau v. Dewey*, 9 Mich., 381. See *Dann v. Cudney*, 13 Mich., 239.

1678. The object of cross examination is to elicit the whole truth concerning transactions which may be supposed to have been only partially explained, and where the whole truth would present them in a different light. *Chandler v. Allison*, 10 Mich., 460. See *Thompson v. Richards*, 14 Mich.

1679. Whenever an entire transaction is in issue, evidence which conceals any part of it is defective; and any question which fills up the omissions of the witness is legitimate and proper on cross examination. A party cannot glean out certain parts which alone would make out a false account, and save his own witness from the sifting process without which these omissions cannot be detected. *Chandler v. Allison*, 10 Mich., 460.

1680. Nor can one be compelled to make his adversary's witness his own to explain or fill up a transaction which the witness has partially explained already. *Ibid.*

1681. A party having testified on her direct examination that she never sold or authorized the sale of certain property, may be properly asked on cross examination questions with a view to show that she is estopped by her conduct from setting up any claim to the property in opposition to a sale made of it by another person. *Dann v. Cudney*, 13 Mich., 239.

1682. Adultery by a party being in issue, and evidence having been given to establish it, the alleged *particeps criminis* was called to disprove it, and denied its commission. He was asked on cross examination, if he had not stated, the year before the alleged offense, that he had had illicit intercourse with the party charged. Held that the inquiry was outside the issue, and it was error to allow it to be put. *Dunn v. Dunn*, 11 Mich., 284. See *Fisher v. Hood*, 14 Mich.

1683. Where evidence is ruled out as not proper on cross examination, the correctness of the ruling will not be inquired into on error, where it appears that the witness is afterwards called by the party offering the evidence, and examined fully on the subject. *Dillin v. People*, 8 Mich., 357.

1684. Re-examination. A witness on the probate of a will testified on his cross examination that, some years before, he had a conversation with the deceased; but he gave no part of the conversation, and it did not appear to have had any bearing on the case. Held not competent for the other party, on re-examination, to inquire what was said by the deceased on that occasion. *Beaubien v. Cicotte*, 12 Mich., 459.

1685. Recalling witness. It is discretionary with the Court to allow the plaintiff, after his rebutting evidence is closed, to recall one of his own witnesses to give evidence which would have been proper when the witness was on the stand before. *White v. Bailey*, 10 Mich., 155.

5. Impeachment of Witnesses.

1686. General reputation. A witness who has testified that he does not know the reputation of a prior witness for truth and veracity, cannot be asked the further question whether he had heard people acquainted with him speak of his character. *Webber v. Hanke*, 4 Mich., 198.

1687. The same witness testified that he knew the prior witness "in the old country," and that he had resided in this country about five years. Held not competent to ask him if he knew the reputation of the prior witness, for truth and veracity, in the old country. *Ibid.*

1688. Where a witness called for the purpose of impeaching another, testifies to his bad reputation for truth, and upon cross examination gives the name of a person he has heard speak against him, he may then be required to state what was said by such person. *Annis v. People*, 13 Mich., 511.

1689. Nothing short of a cross examination which compels the impeaching witness to state the sources of the reports, and their nature, will enable the party either to test the correctness of the impeaching evidence, or to protect the witness who is assailed, if assailed unjustly. *Ibid.*

1690. Contradictory statements. The testimony of a witness as to the nature of a certain message being somewhat contradictory, it was held proper, on cross examination, to call his attention to his testimony on a former trial, and to ask him if he did not then state that a particular message was brought. *Beaubien v. Cicotte*, 12 Mich., 459.

1691. And where a witness had testified to the due execution of a will by a competent testator, it was held competent by way of impeachment to give evidence of his statement at another time that the will was not worth the snap of his fingers. *Ibid.*

1692. Before the credit of a witness can be impeached by proof of inconsistency in his statements, a foundation must be laid by questioning him as to his former statements, that he may have an opportunity for explanation. The practice is the same in chancery as at law. *Sawyer v. Sawyer*, Wal. Ch., 48.

1693. He must not only be inquired of as to the statements, but the time, place and person involved in the supposed contradiction. *Smith v. People*, 2 Mich., 415.

1694. If on being properly questioned the witness neither admits nor denies having made the conflicting statement, and says he does not recollect having done so, he may still be impeached by showing that he did make it. *Ibid.*

1695. So also, where he says he does not recollect making the statement, but if he did it was false. *Ibid.*

1696. A witness questioned about immaterial matters cannot be impeached by proof of contradictory statements in regard to them. *Dunn v. Dunn*, 11 Mich., 284. See *Fisher v. Hood*, 14 Mich.

1697. Uncandid statements. A question to a witness, whether he did not, on a former trial, testify that he said yes and no, and played good Lord and good devil, because he did not know into whose hands he might fall, is admissible, as going directly to his fairness and candor. *Beaubien v. Cicotte*, 12 Mich., 459.

1698. Party making the witness his own. Where defendant, after plaintiff has closed his case, recalls one of plaintiff's witnesses and proves by him facts material to the defense, he has thereby made the witness his own, and he cannot afterwards be allowed to impeach him, unless he was a witness he was compelled to call—like the subscribing witness to an instrument—or he was surprised, or induced to call the witness by statements previously made by him differing from the testimony given. *Craig v. Grant*, 6 Mich., 447.

6. Admissions and Declarations.

1699. Construction of. Where a defendant admitted the receipt by himself of one of two certain amounts, from the plaintiff's intestate, but omitted on the trial to show which, it was held proper to charge him with the larger sum. *Bigelow v. Paton*, 4 Mich., 170.

1700. When made for the purposes of a trial, they will be construed as the parties must have understood them at the time. As an admission on the trial of an ejectment suit that defendant is in possession, will be held to refer to the time the suit was brought, instead of the time of trial. *Wright v. Dunham*, 13 Mich., 414.

1701. Contracts. The admission of a policy of insurance in a premium note, is sufficient evidence of the policy in a suit on the note. *Way v. Billings*, 2 Mich., 397.

1702. An invalid agreement may be used as a parol admission of the facts recited in it, and open to explanation and contradiction as such. *Hickey v. Hinsdale*, 12 Mich., 99.

1703. A written contract is not to be varied by the parol admission of the party. *Hunt v. Thorn*, 2 Mich., 213.

1704. Where by a written contract defendant promised plaintiff to pay a third person a sum therein recited to be due to him from the plaintiff, it was held not necessary, in a suit on the contract, to give other proof that plaintiff was so indebted. *Tefft v. McNoah*, 9 Mich., 201.

1705. Conclusions of law. Admissions of parties as to conclusions of law cannot bind the Court. *Rice v. Ruddiman*, 10 Mich., 125.

1706. Admission by claim. If both parties in ejectment claim through deeds which refer to a plat as recorded, the claim must be regarded as an admission of the plat, and of its being recorded, if a record is necessary. *Johnstone v. Scott*, 11 Mich., 232.

1707. Where the defendant in ejectment undertakes to establish title in himself derived from the same person through whom the plaintiff claims, and sets up no other right in himself, it seems that he must be regarded as admitting the title of the person through whom he thus claims. *Ibid.* And see *Salisbury v. Miller*, 14 Mich.

1708. By nominal plaintiff. Action on promissory note in the name of the payee. Held competent to prove the admission of the plaintiff that he did not own the note, and did not know who did; that it was given for money won at cards by a third person, and made payable to him without his knowledge or consent. *Hogan v. Sherman*, 5 Mich. 60.

1709. Where one party has voluntarily made his trustee or agent the ostensible principal, and the only one capable of legal action, he will be bound by the admissions of such trustee or agent. *Ibid.*

1710. Where action is brought in the name of one person for the benefit, as is claimed, of a bona fide assignee, the question whether there has been a bona fide assignment is not for the Court, but the jury; and the admissions of the nominal plaintiff cannot therefore be excluded on the assumption that such assignment has been established by the evidence. *Ibid.*

1711. Under Prohibitory Liquor Law. Plaintiff presented to defendant an account, for what purported to be foreign wines and ales, opposite each item of which were added the words "imported and sold in the original packages;" and defendant admitted the correctness of the account. Held that this was not such "positive proof" that they were "imported under the laws of the United States, and in accordance therewith, and contained in the original packages in which they were imported, and in quantities not less than the laws of the United States prescribe," as is required by the Prohibitory Liquor Law to entitle the seller to recover therefor. *Niles v. Rhodes*, 7 Mich., 374.

1712. By former holder to show amount due on note. In a suit upon a promissory note which the plaintiff in interest had purchased at a receiver's sale, evidence on the part of defendant to show what was stated at the time of the sale to be due on the note, is not admissible when not offered in connection with proof of some payment made to the receiver, and for the purpose of showing such payment. *Newberry v. Trowbridge*, 13 Mich., 263.

1713. To disprove warranty. The vendee of a steam engine which proved of little or no value, defended a suit for the purchase price, claiming that he bought with warranty, and relying upon statements of the vendor at the time of the sale to establish the warranty. But it appeared that after the engine had been thoroughly tested and proved a failure, he had written letters to the vendor from time to time, apologizing for not having paid for the engine as he had agreed, and asking more time; in none of which was any allusion made to a warranty, or claim set up to damages. Held that these letters satisfactorily negatived any idea that the statements of the vendor at the sale were regarded as a warranty. *Deuel v. Higgins*, 9 Mich., 223.

1714. By one of several parties. The admissions of one of several parties on the same side are admissible against him, but not evidence to affect the others, unless there is some joint interest or privity of design between them. *Dawson v. Hall*, 2 Mich., 390. And where the interest is joint, if the effect of the admission is to create an obligation—as, for example, where it is an admission that a condition precedent has been performed—it is evidence only against the party making it. *Thompson v. Richards*, 14 Mich.

1715. Husband and wife. The declarations of husband and wife are subject to the same rules of exclusion which govern their testimony as witnesses. *Dawson v. Hall*, 2 Mich., 390.

1716. The wife cannot be bound by the admissions of the husband as to her own property. *Ibid; Glover v. Alcott*, 11 Mich., 470.

1717. Where defendants are sued in trespass by the husband for the taking of personal property which is proved to belong to the wife, defendants are entitled to prove her request to them to remove the property from plaintiff's possession. *Starkweather v. Smith*, 6 Mich., 377.

1718. By agent. The declaration of an agent, made at the time of doing an act within the scope of his authority, and relating to the subject matter of the act, are evidence, as a part of the *res gestæ*; but statements subsequently made by him stand on the same footing with the declarations of other persons. *Benedict v. Denton*, Wal. Ch., 336. See also, *Horner v. Fellows*, 1 Doug., 51; *Converse v. Blumrick*, 14 Mich.

1719. The acts and declarations of one who assumes to be acting as the agent of another are not evidence against the supposed principal until the fact of agency is established by other evidence. *Hatch v. Squier*, 11 Mich., 185.

1720. By partner. The acts and declarations of a partner actually engaged in a venture in his own name, cannot be proved for the purpose of fixing a liability upon the partnership in respect to such venture. *Lockwood v. Beckwith*, 6 Mich., 168.

1721. By party since deceased. The declarations of a person since deceased cannot be made evidence on behalf of his representatives, any more than on his own behalf while living. *Wilson v. Wilson*, 6 Mich., 9; *Jones v. Tyler*, 6 Mich, 364. But a bill filed and sworn to by a person who is deceased, is evidence against his heirs to prove what might be proved by his declarations. *Chipman v. Thompson*, Wal. Ch., 405.

1722. To identify property. Replevin for certain barrels of apples. Defendant claimed a part of them. It became a question whether these could be distinguished from the rest; and the question of title was also material. On the trial, the defendant being a witness, it was held competent for him to testify that when the apples were replevied his agent pointed out certain barrels, and stated that they were the ones purchased by defendant. The evidence was competent, not to establish title, but as tending to show whether there was such a confusion of goods that the officer was justifiable in taking possession of more apples than belonged to the plaintiffs. *Sleight v. Henning*, 12 Mich., 371.

1723. Admissions by pleadings. The admissions in a bill or answer in chancery, to be conclusive on the party making them, must be full and unequivocal. They must not be inferred from other admissions, unless the express admissions are so closely connected with the one to be inferred that to disprove the latter would disprove the former. *Schwarz v. Sears*, Wal. Ch., 19.

7. Experts and Opinions.

1724. When opinions incompetent. Quere, whether witnesses can be allowed to state their views as to the materiality of facts withheld from insurers at the time of the execution of the policy. *Hill v. Lafayette Insurance Co.*, 2 Mich., 476.

1725. A medical witness having testified to seeing the decedent some two or three months before the making of a will in controversy, was asked, "From what you saw, what was his mental capacity?" As this question must be understood as referring to the mental capacity to make a will, it is incompetent, because presenting a question of law, and not of medical science. [Manning, J.] *White v. Bailey*, 10 Mich., 155.

1726. Only experts can be allowed to testify to their opinions, based upon the testimony they may have heard in a cause, and then only upon a matter of skill. *Daniels v. Mosher*, 2 Mich., 183.

1727. Opinions by others than experts. Where a witness proved to have been acquainted with pieces of cloth which had been stolen, was shown samples, and asked if in his judgment they were off the stolen pieces, the question was held not to be objectionable on the ground of the witness not being shown to be an expert. *Morrissey v. People*, 11 Mich., 327.

1728. The cases considered in which the opinions of witnesses, other than experts, may be given in evidence. *Evans v. People*, 12 Mich., 27; *Beaubien v. Cicotte*, 12 Mich., 459.

1729. Whether any sickness exists in a particular locality is not a question requiring the testimony of experts. *Evans v. People*, 12 Mich., 27.

1730. There is nothing in the nature of inquiries concerning mental capacity which requires juries to be informed, of necessity, by other than ordinary witnesses. *Beaubien v. Cicotte*, 12 Mich., 459.

1731. Therefore in an inquiry concerning mental capacity to perform a certain act, witnesses who are not experts may testify to their opinions upon the question in controversy, based upon their own observations. *Ibid.*

1732. It is proper to put the question to the witness in such a way as to call for his opinion upon capacity with reference, as near as may be, to the very act in dispute. *Ibid.*

1733. Accordingly on a question of capacity to execute a will, it was held proper to ask a witness who had seen and conversed with the decedent near the time of executing the instrument, whether, from the conversation then had, or from what the witness then saw, the decedent was capable of comprehending or understanding a document of any considerable length, if it had been read to him. *Ibid.*

1734. Also what capacity the decedent had at the time to understand business matters, and whether he was then capable of holding a conversation like one testified to by another witness. *Ibid.*

1735. Opinions must be based on facts. Neither medical experts nor other witnesses can be allowed in any case to give an opinion upon mental capacity or condition, without first showing the circumstances and facts upon which the opinion is based. *White v. Bailey*, 10 Mich., 155.

8. Hearsay and Reputation.

1736. General hearsay and public reputation are inadmissible to prove which of two persons claiming by the same name a particular grant or reservation by a treaty was the person intended. But what was said at the time of the treaty, by the parties to it, indicating for whose benefit the grant was intended to be made, is admissible as a part of the *res gestæ*. *Stockton v. Williams*, 1 Doug., 546, modifying decision in same case, Wal. Ch., 120. See to the same point, *Campau v. Dewey*, 9 Mich., 381.

1737. An Indian child six years of age at the date of a treaty claimed land under it. A witness was called to prove that for seven years after the treaty he heard no claim made by the band to which the child belonged that any reservations were made for Indians of full blood. Held that the evidence was not competent, since neither the neglect of others to make the claim, nor of the child herself at that age, could affect her claim. *Campau v. Dewey*, 9 Mich., 381.

1738. Executors cannot prove their office by general reputation in an action brought by them. *Middlesworth v. Nixon*, 2 Mich., 425.

1739. What a witness has heard *post litem motam*—by which is meant since the dispute has arisen, and not merely the commencement of suit —is not evidence. *Stockton v. Williams*, Wal. Ch., 120.

9. Res Gestæ and Relevancy Generally.

1740. Circumstances attending contract. Where there was a want of certainty in a written instrument, and it was not clear from its terms whether the undertaking of defendants contained in it was to the plaintiffs or to third persons named, parol evidence of the circumstances attending it was held admissible, not to contradict the writing, but to aid the Court in giving a true construction to it. *Facey v. Otis*, 11 Mich., 213. See also *Norris v. Showerman*, 2 Doug., 16; *Ives v. Kimball*, 1 Mich., 308.

1741. Circumstances attending a will. Where a will is contested on the ground of fraud or undue influence, a very broad inquiry is permitted into the whole chain of circumstances attending its preparation; and the transaction must be deemed to embrace all the immediate preliminaries. *Beaubien v. Cicotte*, 12 Mich., 450.

1742. Undue influence being charged against the wife, statements of the decedent that he regretted the marriage; that he was not master at home; that he was afraid of his wife, and was compelled to submit to her demands, or otherwise there would be trouble in the house, were held admissible in evidence. *Ibid.*

1743. The will disinheriting the decedent's relatives in favor of the wife and her relatives, it was held competent to prove the wife's abuse of the husband's relatives, and her quarrel with him about a former will by which he had made provision for them. A wide range of inquiry into the family relations, and the terms upon which they lived, is allowable in these cases. *Ibid.*

1744. Evidence that the decedent made no complaint of any importunities on the part of his relatives is also admissible, where it appears that the wife made charges to him of their rapacity. *Ibid.*

1745. Evidence of former wills, and of other pecuniary arrangements for the wife, is also admissible, as having a bearing upon the question whether the decedent has understandingly, and of his own free will, changed his settled views. *Ibid.*

1746. Declarations made by a party subsequent to a transaction, as to his motives or intentions at the time, are not receivable in evidence to affect the rights of others. It is only the intention declared at the time which, as a part of the *res gestæ*, can bind or affect others. *Dawson v. Hall*, 2 Mich., 390. See supra 1736.

1747. The exception to the rule is where the statements are made to the party to be affected, under circumstances from which his acquiescence in their truth can fairly be inferred; and then the degree of consideration to which they are entitled depends on the circumstances under which they are made. *Ibid.*

1748. Trial for murder. Evidence was given by the prosecution which indicated strong mental agitation and excitement on the part of the prisoner, with an attempt to conceal it, near the supposed time of the murder. Held competent for the prisoner to prove the conversation had by him at the time, as bearing upon the question of his mental agitation and excitement, and tending to disprove the excitement, or to show its nature and extent. *Dillin v. People*, 8 Mich., 357.

1749. Corroborating facts. Wherever a witness has testified to a fact or transaction which, standing alone and entirely unconnected with anything which led to or brought it about, would appear in any degree unnatural or improbable in itself, the previous facts which led to it are admissible, since without them it would be impossible for the jury properly to appreciate the testimony in reference to such principal transaction. *People v. Jenness*, 5 Mich., 305.

1750. This rule is especially applicable where the principal transaction in question is unlawful intercourse between the sexes. *Ibid.*

1751. Letter referred to by another. Where a letter is put in evidence, the letter to which that is an answer, and which is referred to in it, is proper evidence. *Lester v. Sutton*, 7 Mich., 329.

1752. The relevancy of evidence depends on the issue to be tried. A will disinheriting the testator's children being contested for fraud, it is competent for the propounder to put in evidence all those facts which might have contributed to alienate the testator's feelings from his children, as such a state of mind would furnish a motive for giving his property to another, and tend to repel the suspicion of undue influence. *White v. Bailey*, 10 Mich., 155.

1753. Plaintiffs claimed property under a chattel mortgage, and defendants claimed to hold it under attachments against the mortgagors. The evidence tended to show that there was no manual delivery of the mortgage to plaintiffs—who lived in another State—but that the mortgagors were indebted to the plaintiffs in more than its amount. Held competent for the plaintiffs to put in evidence a letter from the mortgagors, written some time before the levy of attachments, informing them of the execution of the mortgage. The letter would tend in some degree to prove that the true intent of the mortgage was to secure an actual indebtedness, and not to make a mere cover of the transaction. *Sweetzer v. Mead*, 5 Mich., 107.

1754. To the statements of a witness which were not properly admissible in the cause, contradictory evidence was given by the opposite side; evidence corroborative of the statements of such first witness is equally inadmissible, though offered as rebutting merely to such contradictory evidence. *McBride v. Cicotte*, 4 Mich., 478.

1755. Where two plaintiffs sue upon contract, a letter from defendants to one of them, which is claimed to relate to such contract, is relevant if followed up by evidence showing it does relate to such contract. *Shaw v. Davis*, 7 Mich., 318.

1756. A builder's contract is irrelevant to a suit brought by him for extra work which in no way depends upon the contract; and the incidental mention of the contract by one of his witnesses does not make it necessary to produce it. *Webber v. Hanke*, 4 Mich., 198.

1757. A witness for the prisoner was examined as to the prisoner being present and transacting business near the scene of the alleged murder, and near the time when it was claimed to have been committed; and it was held not improper to permit the prosecution to show, on his cross examination, any facts having a tendency to show from which direction the prisoner came to that place; as that the witness went out and found tracks which, at the time, he believed and stated were the prisoner's, coming towards the place; and the like. *Dillin v. People*, 8 Mich., 357.

1758. It is competent for a Court to admit evidence which will not be relevant unless brought home to the prisoner by further proof. But if such further proof is not given, it is error in the Court to refuse to strike out the evidence. *Ibid.*

1759. Showing relevancy. To make a question, in itself apparently irrelevant, proper to be put as a link in a chain of evidence, it must be accompanied by a proposition to follow it up at the proper time by proof of other facts which, if true, would make the question put legitimately operative. *Wyngert v. Norton*, 4 Mich., 286.

1760. Res inter alios. Ejectment for land reserved by the treaty of Saginaw of 1819, by the force of which the title itself passed and required no patent. Proof of a subsequent act of Congress and proceedings taken under the same to identify the reservee, held incompetent, as by the treaty itself the title was placed beyond the control of federal legislation. *Campau v. Dewey*, 9 Mich., 381.

10. Parol Evidence to Affect Writings or Records.

1761. General rule. Parol evidence will not be received to add to or vary the terms of a written instrument. It may be introduced in chancery for the purpose of showing fraud, or a mistake in drawing the instrument, when the fraud or mistake is set forth in the bill, and the relief asked is based upon it; but not otherwise. *Sutherland v. Crane*, Wal. Ch., 523.

1762. Where a chattel mortgage is given by one member of a partnership in his own name, and there is nothing on its face to indicate that it was intended to secure a partnership debt on partnership property, parol evidence is inadmissible to show that it was the partnership mortgage and not that of the person executing it. *Jones v. Phelps*, 5 Mich., 218.

1763. And in equity a mortgage of lands purporting to secure a sum of money, cannot be shown by parol to have been given to secure not the payment of money, but the performance of a parol agreement for the payment of certain debts of the mortgagee, and to aid in his support. *Adair v. Adair*, 5 Mich., 204.

1764. Bill of Sale. A simple bill of sale does not embody the preliminaries nor the essential terms of a contract, in such a way as to exclude parol evidence. It is designed merely to show the transfer of title. *Picard v. McCormick*, 11 Mich., 68.

1765. And it may be shown by parol, notwithstanding a receipted bill of parcels, that the property mentioned therein was not to be delivered until paid for in the manner verbally agreed upon at the time of the sale. *Rowe v. Wright*, 12 Mich., 289.

1766. A bill of sale of personal property, though absolute on its face, may at law be shown to have been given as a mortgage. *Fuller v. Parish*, 3 Mich., 211. And in equity a deed of lands, absolute in form, may be shown to be a mortgage. *Wadsworth v. Loranger*, Har. Ch., 113; *Emerson v. Atwater*, 7 Mich., 12.

1767. Impeaching patent. A patent of lands from the United States cannot be impeached in an action at law, on the ground of fraud or mistake in any of the proceedings required as prerequisites to its issuing, by one claiming under a subsequent grant. *Bruckner's Lessee v. Lawrence*, 1 Doug., 19.

1768. But where a patent was issued to one as the person to whom lands were reserved in a treaty with a tribe of Indians, it is competent for another claimant to show that the patentee is not the person intended, and that such claimant is. *Stockton v. Williams*, Wal. Ch., 120, and 1 Doug., 546; *Campau v. Dewey*, 9 Mich., 381.

1769. Identifying lands. In ejectment for lands described as "a certain lot according to the plat of the village of Portsmouth," the identity of the lands may be proved by persons acquainted with it, without the production of the recorded plat. *Johnstone v. Scott*, 11 Mich., 232.

1770. If the plat be actually, though not legally, recorded, it may be used for the purpose of identifying lands described in deeds referring to it. *Ibid.*

1771. Parol evidence of the circumstances surrounding the giving of a deed, and collateral facts, may be received to show which of two sections coming within the terms of a grant was intended by the grantor. *Ives v. Kimball*, 1 Mich., 308. See supra 1740.

1772. Where the boundary of the land was described by course and distance terminating at a post, and neither any mark indicating such boundary, nor any post indicating its termination can be found on the land, and no evidence was introduced showing where the post was originally placed; parol evidence that a line found marked upon trees variant from the call in the patent, and not indicated by the monuments called for in the patent, was the actual line surveyed, run and marked as such boundary, by the government surveyor, is inadmissible. *Bruckner's Lessee v. Lawrence*, 1 Doug., 19. And see *Moore v. People*, 2 Doug., 420.

1773. Disproving delivery. A member of a bankrupt partnership having executed a written acknowledgment to one of the creditors, of a debt discharged by the bankruptcy, it was held competent to show, when suit was brought for the demand, that the acknowledgment was avowedly obtained by the plaintiff and executed to him to facilitate proof of the demand against the estate in bankruptcy; and not with a view to revive the demand. Such evidence would show that the paper was never delivered to have effect as a contract. *Atwood v. Gillett*, 2 Doug., 206.

1774. Official character may be proved by parol. *Scott v. Detroit Young Men's Society's Lessee*, 1 Doug., 119. See also *Cahill v. Kalamazoo Mutual Insurance Co.*,, 2 Doug., 124.

1775. But a conveyance by the Governor and Judges of Michigan Territory can neither be proved by parol, nor by resolution passed by them. *Scott v. Detroit Young Men's Society's Lessee*, 1 Doug., 119. And where one has agreed to execute and deliver a deed of certain lands as a condition precedent to the performance of a contract by the other party, he cannot prove the execution and delivery by the admission of such other party, without first calling upon him to produce the deed. *Thompson v. Richards*, 14 Mich.

1776. Proof of custom. Where parties entered into a special contract for digging a ditch, the terms of which were clear and explicit, it was held that no rule adopted by surveyors or civil engineers, and no custom of the country in relation to digging ditches from point to point over low and uneven land, could be introduced in proof to vary the terms of the contract. *Harvey v. Cady*, 3 Mich., 431. See also, *Erwin v. Clark*, 13 Mich., 10.

1777. But proof of custom is allowable to establish the meaning in a contract of a word of doubtful signification. *Bancroft v. Peters*, 4 Mich., 619.

1778. Contradicting record. When a Court of record has jurisdiction, no proof can be given in opposition to the record. And *it seems* that this rule applies to the docket of a justice. *Clark v. Holmes*, 1 Doug., 390.

1779. But the record of an inferior Court may be contradicted for the purpose of showing a want of jurisdiction of the person or of the subject matter. *Ibid.*

1780. The record of a judgment rendered in a Court of record of another State, cannot be impeached when sued upon here, by showing, in opposition to its recitals, that process was not served upon defendant. *Wilcox v. Kassick*, 2 Mich., 165.

1781. Parol evidence of the existence of certain marked trees and monuments not called for in the survey of a road, is inadmissible to establish, by those marks and monuments, a line of the road variant from that called for by the courses and distances, by which alone such line is designated in the survey. *Moore v. People*, 2 Doug., 420. See to the same effect, *Bruckner's Lessee v. Lawrence*, 1 Doug., 19.

1782. Where a justice in pursuance of the statute (Comp. L., § 3893) certifies a transcript of a judgment from the docket of a former justice, which he certifies is in his control, full credit will be given to such certificate, and it will be presumed that the docket is legally in his possession. In a suit upon the judgment, the docket entry of the justice, that the defendant appeared and pleaded in such action, cannot be disproved. *Facey v. Fuller*, 13 Mich., 527.

11. Proof of Records.

1783. To be proved as a whole. The survey of a road from its commencement to its termination, is an entire thing; and a part of the record of such survey, giving the course and distance across a particular section only, cannot be read in evidence without permitting the whole record of the survey to go to the jury. *Moore v. People*, 2 Doug., 420.

1784. In a suit involving the title to lands which are claimed by one party under proceedings in chancery, it is incumbent on the party setting up those proceedings to give in evidence the whole enrolled record, or at least all those parts of it which have a bearing on the question whether the proceedings as a whole divested the title of the former owners. *Platt v. Stewart*, 10 Mich., 260.

1785. The deposition of a register of deeds as to the contents of deeds recorded in his office, without giving copies thereof, is inadmissible. And where the purpose for which the evidence is offered is collateral to the issue, the rule is still the same. *Angell v. Rosenbury*, 12 Mich., 241.

1786. Record not required by law. A book of township plats, found in the office of the register of deeds, is not evidence, where there is no law requiring it to be kept or declaring it to be evidence. *Smith v. Lawrence*, 12 Mich., 431.

1787. Supplying omissions. Where the entry on a justice's docket does not show the time summons was served, and the files are lost, the time of service may be proved by the justice—the statute not requiring the time to be entered on the docket. *Van Vleet v. Eggleston*, 7 Mich., 511.

1788. Tax sales book. A book kept by a county treasurer, containing his entries of tax sales, though not distinctly required by any statute to be kept, yet being necessary to the adequate discharge of his duties, is an official book, and admissible in evidence to prove the facts therein stated. *Groesbeck v. Seeley*, 13 Mich., 329.

1789. Lost patent. A government patent of land being lost, a copy of the record thereof from the General Land Office, properly certified by the Commissioner, is evidence. The laws of the United States govern the case, and not the State statute. *Lacey v. Davis*, 4 Mich., 140.

1790. Parol evidence cannot be given to prove a public document, on the ground simply that the document belongs in a public office and cannot be removed. *People v. Lambert*, 5 Mich., 349.

1791. Judgment how proved. A judgment of the Circuit Court is to be proved by the files and journal entries, which, under the statute, are a substitute for a judgment record. *Norvell v. McHenry*, 1 Mich., 227; *Crane v. Hardy*, 1 Mich., 56; *Prentiss v. Holbrook*, 2 Mich., 372.

1792. If the files have been lost, the calendar entries may be given in evidence to show the steps taken in the cause before judgment. *Norvell v. McHenry*, 1 Mich., 227.

1793. A warrant of attorney and plea of the defendant are evidence in the same Court of the appearance of defendant in the suit in which they are filed. *Crane v. Hardy*, 1 Mich., 56.

1794. The Court will take judicial notice of its own officers, but not of those of another Court. *Norvell v. McHenry*, 1 Mich., 227.

1795. Lost indictment. Action on a recognizance. The indictment, which the recognizance bound the principal to answer to, was lost or destroyed, and it was held that parol evidence was admissible of its contents. *People v. Dennis*, 4 Mich., 609.

1796. Printed reports of the State officers, printed by the State printer under their direction, are evidence against such officers. *People v. McKinney*, 10 Mich., 54.

1797. Decree in chancery. Journal entries and interlocutory orders and decrees in chancery are to be considered as originals; and are admissible in evidence without producing the enrollment. *Lothrop v. Southworth*, 5 Mich. 436.

1798. Judgment not entered. After judgment is pronounced by a justice of the peace, and before the proceedings are entered on his docket, it is competent to prove the judgment by the oath of the justice who produces for that purpose his minutes of the trial, which are as full as the docket entries are required to be. *Hickey v. Hinsdale*, 8 Mich., 267.

1799. Foreign laws. The statute laws of other States and countries must be proved by copies, authenticated in some mode recognized by law. *People v. Lambert*, 5 Mich., 349. Laws regulating the rates of interest are no exception to this rule. *Kermott v. Ayer*, 11 Mich., 181.

1800. One who had been a peace officer in another State, and who did not swear to any general knowledge of the laws of that State, but said he had, on account of a difficulty with his wife, looked into those laws, was held incompetent to testify what the written laws of that State were on the subject of marriage. *People v. Lambert*, 5 Mich., 349.

12. Presumptions and Judicial Notice.

1801. Foreign law. The Court will presume the law of a sister State to be the same as our own, unless the contrary is shown. *Crane v. Hardy*, 1 Mich., 56.

1802. The common law, as in force in this State, will be presumed to prevail in a foreign country in the absence of proof to the contrary. *High, appellant*, 2 Doug., 515.

1803. But our local statutes cannot be presumed to have been adopted elsewhere. And Courts cannot, therefore, presume that the rate of interest of a foreign country is the same as that established by statute in Michigan. *Kermott v. Ayer*, 11 Mich., 181. See also, *People v. Lambert*, 5 Mich., 349.

1804. A security presumed sufficient until the contrary is shown. *Brown v. Chase*, Wal. Ch., 43.

1805. Due execution of lost deed. The fact that a mortgage for purchase money, given at the time the conveyance was made, was executed with all proper formality, raises the presumption that the deed (which was unrecorded and lost) was likewise properly executed. *Godfroy v. Disbrow*, Wal. Ch., 260.

1806. Identity of cause. A cause having been removed to the Supreme Court by certiorari, an order made by the Supreme Court dismissing a case of the same title, must be presumed to relate to the same case. *Howard v. Rockwell*, 1 Doug., 315.

1807. Time of execution of guaranty. On the back of a promissory note made by R., was indorsed "I guaranty;" which was signed by W., but not dated. Held, that it must be presumed to have been contemporaneous with the making of the note. *Higgins v. Watson*, 1 Mich., 428.

1808. Quorum of public body. Where the record of the proceedings of a board of supervisors was offered in evidence, it was held that a quorum of the body must be presumed to have been present, though the record did not show the fact. *Lacey v. Davis*, 4 Mich., 140.

1809. Settlement of accounts. A settlement of accounts

between parties is prima facie a settlement of *all* accounts; but the contrary may be shown. *Bourke v. James*, 4 Mich., 336.

1810. Violation of law. Sale of liquors in a tavern will not be presumed, where by law there might be a license to keep tavern without authority to sell liquors. *Savier v. Chipman*, 1 Mich., 116.

1811. Time when debt accrued. When there is no evidence as to the time when an indebtedness accrued upon which a judgment was rendered, it must be regarded as having accrued at the date of the judgment. *Glover v. Alcott*, 11 Mich., 470.

1812. Judicial notice. A Court will take judicial notice of its own officers, but not of the officers of another Court. *Norvell v. McHenry*, 1 Mich., 227.

1813. Chancery may take judicial notice of the terms of a Court of law out of which an execution has issued, for the purpose of seeing whether a levy was made during its lifetime. *Williams v. Hubbard*, 1 Mich., 446.

1814. Judicial notice will be taken of an act organizing a township. *Ives v. Kimball*, 1 Mich., 308. And of the political divisions of the State generally. *Wright v. Dunham*, 13 Mich., 414.

1815. The Courts will take judicial notice that a part of St. Clair river is beyond the State boundary. *Cummings v. Stone*, 13 Mich., 70.

1816. A township treasurer gave bond to "The People of the State of Michigan," instead of to the township as required by law. It was held that an action could not be brought on this bond in the name of the township, notwithstanding an averment in the declaration that the defendants "acknowledged themselves held and firmly bound unto the plaintiff, by the name and description of the people of the State of Michigan." The Court must take notice that the State and township are separate political organizations, and the averment is therefore inconsistent with the bond, which parol evidence cannot be received to contradict. *Township of La Grange v. Chapman*, 11 Mich., 499.

1817. The Courts must take judicial notice of public statutes, and disregard all allegations in pleadings which are inconsistent with them. *People v. River Raisin and Lake Erie R. R. Co.*, 12 Mich., 389. See *Hurlbut v. Britain*, 2 Doug., 191.

1818. Courts are bound judicially to take notice what the law is; and to enable them to determine whether all the constitutional requisites to the validity of a statute have been complied with, they can take notice of the journals of the legislature. But they have no such power as respects the facts attending the election of the several members of the legislature, even after those facts have been spread upon the legislative journals. *People v. Mahaney*, 13 Mich., 481.

13. Miscellaneous Matters.

1819. Plaintiff's evidence in reply. That which in a replication would not be a departure in pleading, may be given in evidence in reply to a defense under the general issue. *Caldwell v. Gale*, 11 Mich., 77.

1820. A collector's receipt for taxes is an official paper which the law requires him to give, and it is therefore evidence of the payment of the taxes in suits between third persons. *Johnstone v. Scott*, 11 Mich., 232.

1821. A deed the record of which is admissible in evidence, is also itself admissible without preliminary proof. *Comp. L.*, § 2750; *Lacey v. Davis*, 4 Mich., 140.

1822. But a deed is no evidence of title in the grantor, where he is not otherwise connected with the title, or shown to have ever had possession. *Smith v. Lawrence*, 12 Mich., 431.

1823. The recital of the consideration in a deed is not evidence of the real consideration in a suit by the vendor to enforce in equity his lien for the purchase price. *Mowrey v. Vandling*, 9 Mich., 39.

1824. The seal of a corporation is itself prima facie evidence that it was affixed by the proper authority. *Benedict v. Denton*, Wal. Ch., 336.

1825. Sale fixing value. An indorser having assigned a mortgage as collateral security to his debt, and the creditor having foreclosed the mortgage and bid in the land for the amount of the debt, on an agreement with such indorser that he should do so, and if the debt was not paid within a period fixed, that the land should then be sold to satisfy it; and a public sale having been made under this agreement, and the land bid in by the creditor for a small sum, it was held that, in a suit brought by him for the balance, the debtor could not show in bar, that the lands at the time of the sale were worth the amount of the note. *Weed v. Snow*, 1 Mich., 128. See *Smith v. Mitchell*, 12 Mich., 180.

1826. Statutory foreclosure. A sheriff's deed by itself is no evidence of a regular and legal foreclosure of mortgage by advertisement under the statute. *Barman v. Carhartt*, 10 Mich., 338.

1827. Recital in writing. An instrument purporting to be an assignment of a certificate of purchase therein recited, although duly proved, does not establish the existence of the certificate of purchase as against persons not parties to it. *Lee v. Payne*, 4 Mich., 106.

1828. Books of account. A party's own entries in his books of account cannot be admitted as evidence in his behalf, unless a foundation be first laid by proving that he had no clerk; that some of the articles charged have been delivered; that the books produced are the account books of the party containing original entries ;—and by further proof by those who have dealt and settled accounts with him, that he keeps fair and honest accounts. *Jackson v. Evans*, 8 Mich., 476.

1829. The servant of a man dealing in brick, who keeps a tally-book or slate upon which he keeps memoranda of sales during the day, reporting them to his employer at night, who enters them upon his regular account books, is not a *clerk* within the meaning of this rule ; and such regular account books are to be considered the books of original entries. *Ibid.*

1830. Where in charging the brick there was entered opposite each charge of a load the name of the teamster who hauled it, these teamsters should all be called to verify the charges, or their absence accounted for before the books are received in evidence. *Ibid.*

1831. It is not competent, in order to dispense with the necessity of calling the teamsters, to prove by others that if called it would not be possible for them to testify from recollection to the quantity hauled. The main fact to be established is that the articles have been delivered; and it is only on failure to prove the delivery, or the quantity, by the teamsters when called, that the books are received as the next best evidence. The books are receivable on the presumption that no other proof exists which has not been adduced. *Ibid.*

1832. The witnesses to prove that the party keeps honest books should be able to identify the books, and to testify to settlements made from the entries on such books. It is not sufficient that they testify to having made settlements from bills presented, which they found honest without being able to testify whether such bills were from the account books or not. *Ibid.*

1833. Secondary evidence : loss of note. In a suit on a note alleged to have been lost, a witness stated that he had the entire care of the notes belonging to the plaintiff ; that the pocket book containing the note disappeared; and that diligent search was made for it without success. He also stated that an individual was prosecuted criminally for stealing the note, and confessed his guilt, and stated what he had done with the note. Held, that the loss of the note was sufficiently proved to allow parol evidence of its contents. *Higgins v. Watson*, 1 Mich., 428.

1834.—subscribing witness disqualified. Where a party brings suit before a justice of the peace, and in order to make out his case it becomes necessary to prove the execution of a written instrument to which the justice is the only subscribing witness, the disability of the justice to be sworn is not a sufficient reason for admitting other proof of the execution of the instrument. *Jones v. Phelps*, 5 Mich., 218.

1835.—copy not objected to. Where a copy of a map is put in evidence without objection, any right to insist upon the production of the original is thereby waived. *Johnstone v. Scott*, 11 Mich., 232.

1836.—trover for note. Where trover is brought for the conversion of a promissory note, plaintiff is entitled to prove its existence and contents, without giving defendant notice to produce it. *Rose v. Lewis*, 10 Mich., 483.

1837.—a notice to quit may also be proved by parol, without calling upon the defendant, upon whom it was served, to produce the original. *Falkner v. Beers*, 2 Doug., 117.

1838. Burden of proof: testamentary capacity. The burden of proof is upon the propounder of a will to show that at the time of its execution the decedent was of sound mind. *Beaubien v. Cicotte*, 8 Mich., 9.

1839.—breach of bond. Where a bond other than for the payment of money is sued upon, and the plaintiff assigns a breach as the statute requires, the burden of proving the breach rests upon him, notwithstanding it may involve the proving of a negative. But the same clear proof is not necessary in such case as where proof of an affirmative is required. *Young v. Stephens*, 9 Mich., 500.

1840. Suit was brought upon a statutory bond conditioned that one of the obligors should within thirty days apply for an assignment of his property and a discharge as an insolvent, and diligently prosecute the same until he procured his discharge. The plaintiff gave in evidence a petition for such discharge, dated on the thirtieth day, but so defective as not to confer jurisdiction upon the officer to proceed upon it; also an order made by the officer upon the petition, requiring creditors to appear. Held that this petition and order raised a presumption that no proper application was made within the prescribed time. *Ibid.*

1841. Contempts by witnesses. A witness committed until he shall submit to answer, is entitled to be discharged when the proceeding in which he was called as a witness is discontinued. [MANNING, J.] *Matter of Hall*, 10 Mich., 210.

1842. A magistrate having jurisdiction, under Ch., 194 of Comp. L., to examine and commit for trial persons charged with crimes, has no power to commit a witness for refusing to testify on such examination. He has no powers except such as are expressly conferred by said chapter. *Matter of Farnham*, 8 Mich., 89.

FENCES.

1843. When required. The act of 1847—Comp. L., § 628—providing that "no person shall recover for damages done upon lands by beasts, unless in cases where, by the by laws of the township, beasts are prohibited from running at large, except where such lands are enclosed by a fence" four and a half feet high and in proper repair, or something equivalent thereto, did not require individuals to fence their lands, but only precluded recovery for damages done by beasts thereon if not fenced. *Williams v. Michigan C. R. R. Co.*, 2 Mich, 259; *Wood v. La Rue*, 9 Mich., 158. See amendment to this statute, Laws of 1861, p. 294.

1844. The cattle of other persons going upon such lands are wrongfully there, and the owner of the land may drive them off by any of the ordinary means to which a prudent man would ordinarily resort. *Wood v. La Rue*, 9 Mich., 158.

1845. Where a cow, under such circumstances, was injured by being driven off by a dog set on by the owner of the land, it was held the owner was not liable for the injury, unless there was something in the size, character or habits of the dog, or in the mode of setting him on or pursuing, which would negative the idea of ordinary care and prudence. *Ibid.*

1846. Said act of 1847 has no reference to the land occupied by a railroad company for its track. *Williams v. Michigan C. R. R. Co.*, 2 Mich., 259.

1847. Said act has reference only to exterior fences. Where, therefore, one of two owners of adjoining lands put cattle upon his own lands from which they entered upon the land of the other—there being no partition fence — it was held that he was liable to an action therefor. *Johnson v. Wing*, 3 Mich., 163. Under the amendatory act of 1861 he would only seem to be liable in such case if it was his own duty to build the fence. *Laws of* 1861, *p.* 294.

1848. Railroad companies are not bound to fence their road for the protection of the domestic animals of other persons. And as the act of running the cars over the road is a lawful act, they cannot be held liable for accidental injuries occasioned thereby, unless the running was without proper care, or in an unreasonable manner. *Williams v. Michigan C. R. R. Co.*, 2 Mich., 259.

1849. The vote of a township authorizing cattle to run at large, does not affect this rule. Railroads are not to be regarded as ordinary highways, and the vote of the township cannot confer the right upon individuals to graze their cattle upon them. *Ibid.* For the liability of railroad corporations while constructing their roads, see RAILROAD CORPORATIONS.

FIXTURES.

1850. One who puts a steam engine and its appurtenances in a mill on the land of another, on the agreement that they shall remain his until the owner of the land shall secure him the payment of the price thereof by chattel mortgage, and who receives the mortgage accordingly, is entitled to claim and hold them under such mortgage as against one who held a prior mortgage upon the land. *Crippen v. Morrison*, 13 Mich, 23.

1851. There is no inflexible rule of law which will make chattels that have been attached to the soil a part of the realty, where they are capable of being severed without injury to the freehold. The general rule respecting such annexations is always open to variation by agreement of parties. *Ibid.*

1852. Under our statutes—Comp. L., § 4614—the mortgagor being rightfully entitled to the possession of mortgaged land until foreclosure, he may make such arrangements for the use of the property, and for attaching and severing fixtures, as any other person might during his term. *Ibid.*

FOREIGN RECEIVERS.

1853. Where a receiver has been appointed in a creditor's suit in another State, and the debtor has made an assignment to him, such receiver is authorized to bring suits in this State in respect to the assigned property. He sues, in such case, not strictly in his official character as receiver, under his foreign appointment, but as holding the legal interest in the property under the assignment. *Graydon v. Church*, 7 Mich., 36.

1854. To establish his right to sue, in such case, it is not necessary to go behind the recitals in the assignment and prove proceedings resulting in his appointment. The Courts of this State will recognize and act upon them as true for the purpose of enabling him to make property in this State available, but it is for the Court which has appointed him to hold him to his accountability as trustee. *Ibid.*

FORMER SUIT.

1855. To render a former judgment a bar to a subsequent action, it must have been rendered upon the merits, upon the same subject matter, and between the same parties. *Tucker v. Rohrback*, 13 Mich., 73.

1856. To bar a set off introduced in a suit between A. and B., the plaintiff put in evidence a former suit brought by B. and his wife against A., in which a recovery was sought upon the same claim now sought to be set off. It was shown that judgment was rendered in that case, but it did not appear whether it was upon the merits or not. Held no bar. *Ibid.*

1857. Plaintiff brought an action against a sheriff for taking certain personal property, which, on final hearing was determined against the plaintiff. After the sheriff had sold the property, plaintiff brought his action to recover the same against the purchaser at the sheriff's sale, but it was held that the suit against the sheriff was a bar to the action against the purchaser. *Prentiss v. Holbrook*, 2 Mich., 372. See *Delevan v. Bates*, 1 Mich., 97.

1858. An insurance agent gave bond to his principals, conditioned to account for and pay over the moneys received by him as such. Judgment having been recovered by them on this bond for money not accounted for and paid over, a scire facias was issued, assigning as a breach that the obligor had, before the judgment, received a further sum for which he failed to account, and the receipt of which he fraudulently concealed. On demurrer, it was held that the fraudulent concealment was a sufficient reason for not including this sum in the original pleadings and judgment; and the demurrer was overruled. *Johnson v. Provincial Insurance Co.*, 12 Mich., 216.

FRAUD AND FRAUDULENT CONVEYANCES.

1859. Fraud defined. By the term fraud, is meant in law the legal effect and intent of the acts complained of. *Kirby v. Ingersoll*, Har. Ch., 172.

1860. The law has a standard for measuring the legal intent of parties, and declares an illegal act, prejudicial to the rights of others, a fraud upon such rights, although the party denies all intention to commit a fraud. *Ibid.*

1861. Parties to. A grantee who voluntarily becomes a party to a deed which is fraudulent in part, forfeits his right to claim benefit from another part which would have been good. *Ibid.*

1862. Fraudulent contract voidable. Fraud does not render a contract void, but only voidable at the option of the defrauded party; and a suit by him on the contract will affirm it. *Galloway v. Holmes*, 1 Doug., 330; *Jewett v. Petit*, 4 Mich., 508.

1863. Where a creditor is induced, by the fraudulent representations of his debtor, to compromise, and receives a part of his demand, he cannot, on discovery of the fraud, retain the sum paid and sue in assumpsit for the balance. But without returning the amount paid, he may sue in case for damages sustained by the fraud. *Jewett v. Petit*, 4 Mich., 508.

1864. Proof of fraud. Fraud will not be presumed on slight circumstances. The proof should be so clear and conclusive as to leave no rational doubt on the mind as to its existence. *Buck v. Sherman*, 2

Doug., 176. See also, *Baldwin v. Buckland*, 11 Mich., 389; *Hubbard v. Taylor*, 5 Mich., 155; *Orr v. Lacey*, 2 Doug., 230.

1865. Fraud upon creditors. Proof that a party was indebted in the sum of $300 at the time of making a voluntary conveyance, is not sufficient evidence of fraud to avoid the conveyance in favor of a subsequent creditor. *Page v. Kendrick*, 10 Mich., 303.

1866. The alleged fraudulent conveyance being by a man to his intended wife, whom he soon after married, it was held that the continued occupation of the land by him after the marriage, the neglect for some years to record the deed, and the mortgaging of the land by husband and wife for the husband's benefit, did not raise a presumption of fraudulent intent in making the conveyance. *Ibid.*

1867. One of two co-partners sold out his interest in the partnership to the other, who agreed to pay the debts, but instead of doing so, caused them to be bought up by a confederate, and the lands of the other partner to be sold on judgments obtained thereon. Held that these sales might be avoided as fraudulent by one to whom the other partner had conveyed, and that it was not necessary for the complainant to aver or prove that he bought for value. *Reed v. Wessel*, 7 Mich., 139.

1868. A debtor mortgaged his lands in consideration of the negotiable notes of the mortgagee of equal amount, payable on time. Actual fraudulent intention was denied, and it did not appear whether the notes had been negotiated. It was held that fraud was not sufficiently established by the facts to authorize the Court to decree a release of the mortgage. *Buck v. Sherman*, 2 Doug., 176.

1869. Fraud in fact, or an express intent to commit fraud, is not necessary in order to render a conveyance fraudulent as against creditors. It is sufficient if the effect of the conveyance is to delay or hinder creditors in the collection of their debts. *Ibid.* And see *Pierson v. Manning*, 2 Mich., 445. *Hollister v. Loud*, 2 Mich., 309, *contra.*

1870. Every voluntary conveyance by a parent to a child is not fraudulent against creditors; but, when made in good faith, by way of advancement, and abundant property is retained by the parent to pay all his debts, it is good against existing as well as subsequent creditors. *Cutter v. Griswold*, Wal. Ch., 437.

1871. A parol ante-nuptial promise by a husband, to hold money belonging to his wife at the time of marriage as her trustee, and invest it in real estate in her name and for her separate use, cannot sustain a post-nuptial settlement upon the wife, as against creditors. *Wood v. Savage*, 2 Doug., 316.

1872. Such settlement would be void as to existing creditors, and prima facie void as to subsequent creditors; but the presumption of fraud as to them may be rebutted. *Ibid.*

1873. A conveyance voidable by creditors can only be avoided by a judgment creditor, or one claiming under him, who has taken out execution and levied on the property fraudulently conveyed. *Fox v. Willis*, 1 Mich., 321, overruling same case sub. nom. *Fox v. Clark*, Wal. Ch., 535.

1874. A mortgagee of the debtor, though he be a judgment creditor, cannot call in question the validity of a prior conveyance by the mortgagor. *Fox v. Willis*, 1 Mich., 321.

1875. A conveyance was made to enable the grantee to purchase goods for the joint benefit of both parties, who were to become partners. The goods were not purchased, and a creditor of the grantor who had sued his claim before the conveyance was made, levied upon the premises. It was held that the conveyance was fraudulent and void as to such creditor. *Wisner v. Farnham*, 2 Mich., 472.

1876. Intent. Where one makes false statements by means of which another is induced to enter into a contract, the right of the latter to have the contract rescinded does not depend upon whether the person knew the statements to be false when he made them or not. The law has regard rather to the effect of the false statements upon the party to whom they are made, than to the actual intent to deceive by the other. *Converse v. Blumrick*, 14 Mich.

1877. Fraudulent grantee becoming bankrupt. Where the debtor makes a voluntary conveyance in fraud of his creditors, and his grantee becomes bankrupt, the creditors are entitled to the property in preference to the assignee in bankruptcy. *Manning v. Drake*, 1 Mich., 34.

1878. Accounting by fraudulent grantee. The conveyance being actually and not only constructively fraudulent, it was held, on bill filed by the creditors to set it aside, that the grantee should be credited with taxes paid and improvements made by him, but not for advances made to the fraudulent grantor, unless the money was used by the latter before complainants filed their bill, to pay debts due at the time of the conveyance. *How v. Camp*, Wal. Ch., 427.

1879. Avoiding by subsequent creditors. As a general rule a conveyance which is void as to existing creditors, is void as to subsequent creditors also. *Herschfeldt v. George*, 6 Mich., 456.

1880. Conveyance by a husband to his wife, which was fraudulent as to existing creditors, set aside as to subsequent creditors also; the husband having represented himself the owner of the land at the time of contracting the subsequent debts. *Ibid.* See also, *Beach v. White*, Wal. Ch., 495.

1881. A small and inadequate consideration having been received from the wife for the conveyance, it will be sustained in equity only so far as to secure to her the repayment of that sum. *Herschfeldt v. George*, 6 Mich., 456.

1882. Fraud a question of fact. The question of fraud arising from a want of delivery and of a continued change of possession of goods sold or assigned by way of security is a question of fact. *Jackson v. Dean*, 1 Doug., 519. See *Oliver v. Eaton*, 7 Mich., 108; *Bagg v. Jerome*, 7 Mich., 145; *Gay v. Bidwell*, 7 Mich., 519; *Snook v. Davis*, 6 Mich., 156.

1883. The burden of proving good faith and an absence of intention to defraud, was held, under the Statutes of 1838, to be on the party claiming under the assignment. *Jackson v. Dean*, 1 Doug., 519.

1884. Conveyance fraudulent on its face. Where an instrument contains illegal provisions, or such as are not reconcilable, on any possible hypothesis, with an honest or legal intent, the law declares it void on its face, because no evidence can change its character. But in all other cases where property is transferred with the alleged intent to hinder, delay or defraud creditors, the question of fraudulent intent is one of fact for the jury, and the law cannot determine for them that the showing, in a specified case, conclusively establishes such fraudulent intent. *Oliver v. Eaton*, 7 Mich., 108; *Bagg v. Jerome*, 7 Mich., 145; *Gay v. Bidwell*, 7 Mich., 519; *Nye v. Van Husan*, 6 Mich., 329; *Orr v. Lacey*, 2 Doug., 230.

1885. This principle applied to the case of general assignments for the benefit of creditors. *Pierson v. Manning*, 2 Mich., 445; *Sutton v. Hanford*, 11 Mich., 513; *Booth v. McNair*, 14 Mich.

1886. A chattel mortgage of a stock of goods which leaves the mortgagor in possession, and by inference allows him to make sales in the usual course of business, is good between the parties and not necessarily void as to creditors. *Gay v. Bidwell*, 7 Mich., 519. See *Oliver v. Eaton*, 7 Mich., 108.

1887. A creditor is not in position to attack such a mortgage, unless he was a creditor at the time it was given. *Gay v. Bidwell*, 7 Mich., 519.

1888. A contract by which A. is to work for B. in the sale of merchandise, in the store formerly occupied by A., taking charge of the business, being accountable for all bad debts; to have all the profits over and above ten per cent., and to give up the store and goods whenever required, is not necessarily fraudulent on its face as against creditors, but the question of fraud is for the jury, and would depend on the evidence outside the instrument itself. *Snook v. Davis*, 6 Mich., 156.

1889. That a chattel mortgage is given to a trustee to secure demands in favor of several creditors, instead of being given to the creditors themselves, and that it contains a provision that the trustee shall be liable in the premises for his own neglect or default only, are matters to be taken into account in determining the question of fraud, but they do not render the instrument fraudulent in law. *Bagg v. Jerome*, 7 Mich., 145.

1890. Change of possession. The appointment of the clerk of the mortgagor as agent of the mortgagee, for the purpose of taking care of and selling the goods, where there is no announcement of change in business, no change of books, and no other apparent change of ownership or possession, is not a change of possession within the meaning of the statute—Comp. L., § 3191. *Doyle v. Stevens*, 4 Mich., 87.

1891. Creditor must have judgment. Trover by mortgagee against the sheriff who had taken possession of the mortgaged property. The sheriff, defending under an execution in favor of a creditor of the mortgagor, must allege in his pleading and prove a judgment, before he can question the good faith of the mortgage. *Comstock v. Hollon*, 2 Mich., 355.

1892. Administrator's right to avoid. The right which the statute confers upon an administrator, in case of a deficiency of assets, to institute proceedings to avoid fraudulent dispositions of property by the intestate, can not be assigned by him. And, therefore, one who takes from an administrator a note and mortgage given to the intestate, upon which the latter had made an indorsement with a view to discharging to that extent the debt, cannot attack such indorsement as fraudulent against creditors, though he himself be a creditor and the estate insolvent. *Morris v. Morris*, 5 Mich., 171.

1893. A conveyance valid when made cannot be invalidated by subsequent acts of the grantor, nor by the creation of subsequent debts. *Page v. Kendrick*, 10 Mich., 300.

1894. For cases where certain facts were held not to prove fraud, see *Hubbard v. Taylor*, 5 Mich., 155 (upon creditors), and *Titus v. Minnesota Mining Co.*, 8 Mich., 183. For case of fraud by husband upon wife in procuring a conveyance of her land, see *Stiles v. Stiles*, 14 Mich.

FRAUDULENT REPRESENTATIONS.

1895. Scienter. Representations made by a vendor at the time of a sale, as to the quality of the article sold, are merged in an express warranty. And an action of fraud cannot be based upon such representations unless the vendor knew them to be false when made. *Horner v. Fellows*, 1 Doug., 51.

1896. Representations as to value. A mere assertion of value, made by the seller, where no warranty is intended, is no ground of relief to a purchaser, because the assertion is a matter of opinion which does not imply knowledge, and in which men differ. Every person reposes at his peril in the opinions of others where he has equal opportunity to form and exercise his own judgment. *Picard v. McCormick*, 11 Mich., 68.

1897. But it cannot be laid down as a rule of law that value is never a material fact. And when the purchaser expressly relies upon the knowledge of the seller as to quality or value, the seller is bound to act honorably and deal fairly with the purchaser. *Ibid.*

1898. A jeweller knowing the purchaser's ignorance, deliberately and designedly availed himself of it to defraud him by false statements of the value of articles in his trade which none but an expert could reasonably be expected to understand. It was held that an action would lie for the fraud. *Ibid.*

FRAUDS, STATUTE OF.

1899. Agreement to pay debt of another. A debtor transferred to his creditor the note of a third person in part payment, and guaranteed its payment. Such guaranty is an original undertaking, and not within the statute of frauds. *Jones v. Palmer*, 1 Doug., 379. Its consideration may be shown by parol. *Ibid.* See *Wellington v. Huntington*, 12 Mich., 10.

1900. Where the guaranty of another's debt is merely incidental to a principal contract made by the guarantor himself, on his own account, it is regarded as in effect a promise to pay his own debt; and it need not therefore be in writing. *Huntington v. Wellington*, 12 Mich., 10.

1901. A verbal agreement by which partners buy out the interest of a co-partner, and agree to indemnify him against the partnership debts, is not within the statute. *Bonebright v. Pease*, 3 Mich., 318.

1902. Defendant verbally promised a debtor of plaintiff to pay the debt on condition that the debtor would deliver defendant a certain cow. But the plaintiff not having discharged the debtor, the promise, not being upon any consideration moving from plaintiff, was void by the statute. *Brown v. Hazen*, 11 Mich., 219.

1903. A contractor having abandoned the building he was erecting, resumed work and did certain extra labor on the promise of defendant—a third person—to pay him. But the evidence showed that he still looked to the original debtor for payment, and to defendant only as guarantor; and the promise of defendant was held within the statute. *Bresler v. Pendell*, 12 Mich., 224. See *Farwell v. Dewey*, 12 Mich., 436.

1904. Suit on a guaranty, not in writing, that certain notes sold by defendant to plaintiffs were good and collectable, and the makers responsible; that the maker of a certain mortgage sold at the same time was responsible; that the land mortgaged was ample security and the title perfect and unincumbered. The guaranty was held not within the statute. *Huntington v. Wellington*, 12 Mich., 10.

1905. Representations as to credit. Such guaranty is not within the provision which exempts persons from being charged upon parol representations concerning the credit and ability of others; as that is confined to cases where the representations form no part of the contract. *Ibid.*

1906. Interest in lands. The guaranty of the mortgage does not in any way affect the title to lands, or raise or affect any trust, power or authority in or over the land mortgaged. It is simply an undertaking that certain facts exist. *Ibid.*

1907. A party who, by promising to assign a tax-purchase certificate to the owner of the land, has induced the latter not to exercise his legal right to redeem, cannot, after the time for redemption has expired, shield himself behind the statute to avoid performance. *Laing v. McKee*, 13 Mich., 124.

1908. Sale of chattels. The delivery required by the statute where no payment is made or earnest given, is not dispensed with by agreement at the time that the vendee should take the property where it then was, and the vendor not be troubled to make any delivery. *Alderton v. Buchoz*, 3 Mich., 322. Inquiry about the property by the vendee afterwards not an exercise of ownership over it. *Ibid.*

1909. Acceptance of draft. A parol agreement by a tax collector to receive a draft by his creditor on himself in payment of taxes, is void—the statute, Comp. L., § 1266, requiring an acceptance of a draft to be in writing. *Elliott v. Miller*, 8 Mich., 132.

1910. Contract for a lease. A contract for a lease is performed by the making of the lease; and therefore a verbal contract made in April for a lease for one year from the first of May following, is not within the provisions of the statute. Section § 3179 of Comp. L. governs such a contract; while a lease is governed by § 3177. *Tillman v. Fuller*, 13 Mich., 113.

1911. Writing must be complete. A promise in writing to pay the debt of another must show the whole terms of the contract; no resort can be had to parol evidence to add to them. *Hall v. Soule*, 11 Mich., 494.

1912. Void contract not a consideration. A verbal promise to pay the debt of another, being void under the statute of frauds, is not a valid consideration for a subsequent promise in writing *Ibid.*

1913. Ratification. A void contract by two to purchase goods of the value of more than fifty dollars, is not ratified as to both by a subsequent acceptance of the goods by one without the knowledge or assent of the other. *Chamberlain v. Dow*, 10 Mich., 319.

1914. Party setting up statute must show his case to fall within in. Goods being found by two jointly in the St. Clair river, it was agreed that defendant should sell the same and divide the proceeds. Suit being brought upon this agreement, defendant claimed that under the statute relative to lost goods no sale could lawfully have been made within a year, and the agreement, which was not in writing, was therefore void. Held that to render the statute applicable, he should have shown that the finding was in that part of the river which lies within the State. *Cummings v. Stone*, 13 Mich., 70.

GARNISHEE PROCEEDINGS.

1915. Act for, to be strictly construed. The act to authorise proceedings against garnishees being in derogation of the common law, must be strictly construed. *Maynards v. Cornwell*, 3 Mich., 309.

1916. Affidavit for. The affidavit, when made by an agent or attorney, need not state affirmatively that the affiant is such agent or attorney. The statement by way of recital is sufficient. *Wetherwax v. Paine*, 2 Mich., 555.

1917. Against one joint debtor. A judgment rendered in garnishee proceedings against one of several joint debtors is void, and no bar to a subsequent suit against all. *Ibid.*

1918. Jurisdiction of justice. The jurisdiction of a justice of the peace does not depend on the amount due from the garnishee to the principal debtor, but upon the sum claimed to be due from the latter to plaintiff. *Ibid.*

1919. Trial: admissions by garnishee. Upon a trial of a suit against a garnishee, proof of the admissions or declarations of the garnishee, as to his indebtedness to or possession of property of the principal debtor, is inadmissible. *Maynards v. Cornwell*, 3 Mich., 309.

1920. Garnishee's evidence conclusive. The plaintiff is not at liberty to controvert the statements of the garnishee on his examination, either in the Justice's Court, or in the Circuit Court on appeal; but he may examine the garnishee anew in the Circuit Court for the purpose of a more full discovery. *Newell v. Blair*, 7 Mich., 103; *Thomas v. Sprague*, 12 Mich., 120.

1921. The examination before the justice, taken in writing and signed by the garnishee, is evidence against him on appeal. *Ibid.*

1922. But he may be permitted to correct, under oath in the Circuit Court, a mistake made by him on his examination before the justice. *Ibid.*

1923. Where the garnishee, on his examination before the justice, admitted that he had in his hands moneys collected for defendant, but stated that he had been informed that these moneys had been assigned before service of the garnishee process, he was held entitled, on appeal, to introduce evidence to prove the assignment. *Ibid.*

1924. Negotiable paper not overdue is not liable to be reached by garnishee process against the maker. *Littlefield v. Hodge*, 6 Mich., 326.

GIFT.

1925. What is not. Plaintiff's intestate, a few days before his decease, put into the hands of defendant a sum of money, with instructions to pay certain bills with a portion of it, and to dispose of the balance to suit himself. Defendant paid out a small sum before the intestate's death, and it was held that there was no absolute disposition of the money by the intestate to prevent its becoming assets of his estate. *Bigelow v. Paton*, 4 Mich., 170.

1926. Proof of. Bill by the widow and heir at law of A., against the widow, heirs at law and administrator of B. (who was the father of A.), to compel the conveyance to complainants of certain premises alleged to have been given by B. to A. in consideration of natural affection, but not conveyed. Held, that in such a case conveyance would only be decreed on the most conclusive proof of the gift, and of some satisfactory reason why it was not consummated by a conveyance. *Jones v. Tyler*, 6 Mich., 364.

1927. Possession of the premises by A. subsequent to the alleged gift would be sufficiently explained by the relationship between the parties, and could not avail complainants. *Ibid.*

1928. A mortgagee of B. subsequent to the alleged gift, but not charged with notice of it, could not in any event be affected thereby. *Ibid.*

GOVERNOR AND JUDGES OF MICHIGAN TERRITORY.

1929. When their offices ceased. Notwithstanding the previous organization of the State government, the Governor and Judges of the territory of Michigan remained in office and competent to execute the powers conferred upon them by the act of Congress, entitled "An act to provide for the adjustment of titles of land in the town of Detroit and territory of Michigan, and for other purposes," approved April 21, 1806, until after July 1, 1836. *Scott v. Detroit Young Men's Society's Lessee*, 1 Doug., 119.

1930. Over the territory west of lake Michigan, their powers continued until the organization of the territory of Wisconsin. *Ibid.*

1931. The jurisdiction and powers of the Judges of the territory of Michigan, as a District and Circuit Court of the United States, remained unaffected by the organization of the State government, and were retained by them until their offices were abolished by express legislation of Congress, to take effect on the admission of Michigan into the Union. *Ibid.*

1932. A stranger not to dispute their grants. Congress having authorized the Governor and Judges of the territory of Michigan, for the time being, to convey certain lands, the fee of which was in the United States, and having, by acts of legislation, recognized the persons who assumed to convey such lands, by virtue of such authority, as incumbents of those offices, and the offices as being in existence, at and subsequent to the time when such conveyances were made, a mere stranger will not be permitted to controvert the title under such a conveyance, on the ground that the grantors were not, at the time of the grant, such Governor and Judges, and that there were then no such offices. *Ibid.*

1933. Organization of the Land Board. The Land Board constituted by said act of Congress of April 21, 1806, did not consist of two integral parts, the Governor and the Judges; but of four persons designated by their names of office, any three of whom were authorized to execute any of the powers conferred by the act. A deed of bargain and sale executed by the Judges only is therefore valid. *Ibid.*

1934. They will all be presumed to have been present, and to have deliberated upon an act done by the majority, unless the contrary expressly appears. *Ibid.*

1935. Proof of grant by. A resolution of the Governor and Judges that a certain lot be assigned to a person named, their parol declarations that it had been conveyed, and parol proof that their records had been inaccurately kept, and many grants had been made and deeds given which did not appear thereon, were all held incompetent evidence in opposition to a subsequent conveyance by them. *Ibid.* And see *Ready v. Kearsley*, 14 Mich.

1936. Laying out Detroit. The power to lay out the town of Detroit, given to the Governor and Judges by said act of Congress of April 21, 1806, was fully executed by them on 27th April, 1807. *People v. Carpenter*, 1 Mich., 273.

1937. Power over streets in Detroit. They had no power to grant the exclusive use of any of the streets or alleys in Detroit to individuals. *Ibid.* For further decisions as to the dedication of streets and alleys to the public by the plan of Detroit, see WAYS.

1938. Ratification of deed by. Where the Governor and Judges deeded a lot in Detroit, in 1816, in exchange by the grantee of another lot to the United States, and the United States took possession of the last mentioned lot, and occupied it for fourteen years and more, it was held that this ratified and made valid the deed by the Governor and Judges even if originally invalid. *Farmers and Mechanics' Bank v. City of Detroit*, 12 Mich., 145.

GRANTS.

1939. Public grants are to be construed strictly; nothing passes under them by implication. *La Plaisance Bay Harbor Company v. Monroe City*, Wal. Ch., 155.

1940. Reservations. Where, by a treaty with the Chippewa Indians, lands were reserved for certain individuals specified, to be afterwards located in such manner as the President might direct, it was held that this reservation was equivalent to an absolute grant; and the title was conferred by the treaty, though not perfect until the location was made, which was necessary to give the grant identity. *Dewey v. Campau*, 4 Mich., 565; *Stockton v. Williams*, Wal. Ch., 120, and 1 Doug., 546. See this last case, and *Campau v. Dewey*, 9 Mich., 381, as to the evidence admissible on the question of the identity of the reservee.

1941. A patent was not necessary to perfect the title. Lands may be granted by act of Congress, or by treaty, as well as by patent. *Stockton v. Williams*, 1 Doug., 546.

1942. A patent issued by the President to one who claimed to be, but was not, one of the reservees, was void, and could not affect the title of the real reservee. *Ibid.* Even though issued under a special act of Congress. *Campau v. Dewey*, 9 Mich., 381.

1943. A certified copy of a map from the General Land Office, on which a certain section was designated as the tract of one of the reservees, was held evidence of the due location of such section, according to the conditions of the treaty. *Dewey v. Campau*, 4 Mich., 565.

1944. Impeaching government grant. A patent of land from the United States, cannot be impeached in an action at law, on the ground either of fraud or mistake, in any of the proceedings required as pre-requisites to its issuing, by one claiming under a subsequent grant. *Bruckner's Lessee v. Lawrence*, 1 Doug., 19. See supra, 1166.

GUARANTY.

1945. Continuing. A bond was executed by defendant to plaintiff, reciting: That, whereas, P. C. & Co. were then, or might thereafter become indebted to plaintiffs in divers sums of money, and might become liable from time to time to pay plaintiffs divers sums of money, to the amount of $3,000, by means of notes, discounts and overdrafts made and indorsed by said P. C. & Co., and for their benefit, and conditioned that if said P. C. & Co. should pay or cause to be paid to plaintiffs all and singular the notes, &c., made by said P. C. & Co., and for their benefit, to the amount of $3,000, and should pay or cause to be paid to plaintiffs all said liability assumed by the said P. C. & Co. to the amount of $3,000, then said obligation to be void, otherwise to remain in full force and effect for three years from January 1, 1837, unless notice to the contrary should sooner be given to the plaintiffs. Held that the bond was a continuing guaranty, and intended to cover successive notes, discounts and overdrafts, made by P. C. & Co. at any time within the three years, as often and whenever the antecedent transactions were discharged. *Farmers and Mechanics' Bank v. Kercheval*, 2 Mich., 504.

1946. The following was held not to be a continuing guaranty, but to be limited to a single purchase or transaction: "St. Joseph, Sept. 18, 1858. Joseph Gard: Dear Sir—If you will let the bearer have what leather he wants, and charge the same to himself, I will see that you have your pay in a reasonable length of time. J. E. Stevens." *Gard v. Stevens*, 12 Mich., 292.

1947. Application of payments. The first moneys received by the creditor on the debtor's general account, after a purchase under this guaranty, should be applied upon such purchase. *Ibid.*

1948. Demand and notice. In the case supra, 1945, demand of the principal, and notice to the guarantor, at the close of the period covered by the guaranty, was not necessary. *Farmers and Mechanics' Bank v. Kercheval*, 2 Mich., 504.

1949. No general rule can be laid down in respect to demand and notice in case of guaranties; but where from the terms of a guaranty, or the facts disclosed in a given case, demand and notice are required, the omission cannot be available as a defense unless the defendant can show that he has been damnified thereby. *Ibid.*

1950. Notice of acceptance of a guaranty by the creditor, is not required to be given to the guarantor. *Ibid.*

1951. Discharge by extension of time. If the creditor gives time to the principal, without the consent of the guarantor, the latter is discharged. *Ibid.*

1952. So if one of several principals gives his own obligation for the original debt, and time is given him without the guarantor's assent. *Ibid.*

1953. Guaranty of collection. The assignor of a note and mortgage covenanted with the assignee that in case the latter should fully prosecute the note to judgment, and foreclose the mortgage, and should not collect a specified sum, with costs; and if upon execution or foreclosure the mortgaged lands should be taken for sale or set off, then the assignor would pay said sum. The mortgage was foreclosed in chancery; and it was held, in a suit upon the covenant, that the assignor could not set up, in defense, a mere irregularity in the foreclosure. *Barnes v. Baker*, 2 Mich., 377.

1954. Decree having been taken for the sum due, and execution awarded for any deficiency after sale of the mortgaged premises, this was held a sufficient compliance with the condition of the covenant, that the note should be prosecuted to judgment. *Ibid.*

1955. Before the assignee could sue upon the covenant, he must exhaust his remedy against the mortgagor, by issuing execution to the county of his residence. *Ibid.*

1956. Where the amount of a note guaranteed is such that suit may be brought upon it either in Justice's Court or the Circuit Court, the condition of a guaranty of collection is complied with by obtaining judgment in a Justice's Court, and making due endeavor to collect it by execution. *Thomas v. Dodge*, 8 Mich., 51.

1957. And it is not necessary that a transcript of such judgment should be filed in the Circuit Court, and execution issued against lands thereon, where it clearly appears that the judgment debtor has no real estate liable to execution. *Ibid.*

1958. Where one guarantees the collection of a note which is secured by a collateral mortgage, and at the same time assigns the mortgage with the note, he is not liable upon his guaranty until resort has been had to the mortgage, as well as to the note, for collection of the moneys secured. *Barman v. Carhartt*, 10 Mich., 338.

1959. Naming promissee. The guaranty of a promissory note need not name the promissee. *Thomas v. Dodge*, 8 Mich., 51; *Nevius v. Bank of Lansingburgh*, 10 Mich., 547.

1960. Such a guaranty becomes fixed whenever any one takes it upon the guarantor's credit. And where suit is brought upon it, the presumption that the plaintiff is the promissee will prevail in his favor, at least until rebutted by showing that the guaranty had previously been operative in other hands. *Nevius v. Bank of Lansingburgh*, 10 Mich., 547.

1961. Guarantor of note not a maker. One who indorses upon a negotiable promissory note a guaranty of payment contemporaneously with its execution, cannot be treated as a joint maker of the note. His undertaking is distinct and separate from that of the maker. *Tinker v. McCauley*, 3 Mich., 188; overruling *Higgins v. Watson*, 1 Mich., 420.

1962. Guaranty not negotiable. A guaranty of payment is not negotiable, though indorsed upon a negotiable promissory note. *Ibid.*

GUARDIAN AND WARD.

1963. Power of guardian over property. A guardian has the right to collect and receive money due to his ward, on a bond and mortgage, or to sell and assign the bond and mortgage, in the exercise of his discretion as guardian. *Livingston v. Jones*, Har. Ch., 165.

1964. But he cannot accept a deed of lands in lieu of money paid into the Court of Chancery under a decree for his infant ward, and if he does so, the infant is not bound thereby. *Westbrook v. Comstock*, Wal. Ch., 314.

1965. The Court of Chancery has a general supervisory power over the persons and estates of infants; and when any part of an infant's estate is in litigation there, it is under the immediate guardianship and protection of the Court; and neither the general guardian, nor the guardian ad litem has any right to receive it. *Ibid.*

1966. Before the Court of Chancery will order money to be paid to a guardian, it must be satisfied that he has given sufficient security for the performance of his trust, and that he has not abused it. *Ibid.*

1967. Guardian's bond. It was not necessary that the guardianship bond, required by Code of 1827, (p. 59, § 5) should be executed by the guardian; it was sufficient if *a* bond, with sufficient sureties, was given. *Palmer v. Oakley*, 2 Doug., 433.

1968. If the guardian was a married woman, and united with sureties in executing the bond, it seems that the bond was good, notwithstanding her incompetency. *Ibid.*

1969. The bond was not a condition precedent to the execution of the trust of guardian. *Ibid.*

1970. Married woman guardian. Both at the common law and under the Code of 1827, a married woman was competent to be a guardian, with the assent of her husband, but not without such assent. *Ibid.*

1971. Letters granted to her without his assent would be voidable merely, not void. And his assent might be presumed from his joining with her in the bond which the statute required the guardian to give before making sale of the ward's real estate. *Ibid.*

1972. Jurisdiction to appoint guardians. Said Code of 1827, (p. 57, § 1) defined and limited to the cases therein specified the jurisdiction of the Probate Court over the appointment of guardians for minors conferred in general terms by same Code, p. 55, § 1. *Ibid.*

1973. The Probate Court had no power to appoint a guardian for a minor over fourteen, and within the territory, without first citing him to appear and choose his own guardian. And an ex-parte application, representing the minor to be over fourteen, conferred no jurisdiction to appoint without citation, if, in fact, the minor was over that age. *Ibid.*

1974. A decree of the Probate Court, appointing a guardian, appeared upon its face to have been made upon an application representing the minor to be under fourteen, and did not show any citation to the minor. Held to be valid on its face, though showing no formal finding of the fact that the minor was under fourteen; but held, further, that it might be impeached, in a collateral action, by showing that the minor was, at the time, over fourteen. *Ibid.*

1975. Sale of lands by guardian: petition. A petition by the guardian of a minor, to the Probate Court, for license to sell the lands of his ward, stating that a part only of the land was under improvement, and the rest unproductive; and that it was necessary a portion of the lands should be used to pay certain debts incurred in behalf of the ward, and that, in the opinion of the petitioner, it would be for the interest of the minor to have the land sold, and the proceeds, after paying the debts, put out at interest, is sufficient. *Nichols v. Lee*, 10 Mich., 526.

1976. In a petition under the act of February 28, 1840, it was necessary to set forth fully all the facts and circumstances rendering a sale or other disposition of the minor's property necessary, that the Court might judge of the propriety of the proposed sale. *Dorr, petitioner*, Wal. Ch., 145.

1977. The guardian should not make an absolute sale of the real estate of the ward, and then apply to the Court to authorize him to do what he has already bound himself to do; and the Court will not ratify such agreements. The proper course is to obtain leave of the Court in the first instance. *Ibid.*

1978. One claiming adversely to the title of the ward, cannot contest the validity of a sale of lands made by the guardian on the ground that the petition for license to sell was defective (Comp. L., § 3092). *Marvin v. Schilling*, 12 Mich., 356.

1979. Nor can he contest it on the ground that the sale was a fraud upon the ward. The ward, or any one claiming under him, has a right to inquire into anything wrong in the proceedings: but a third person cannot drag the ward's rights into Court in a litigation between himself and the purchaser. *Ibid.*

1980. A married woman who is a guardian can convey the real estate of the ward without her husband joining in the deed. *Palmer v. Oakley*, 2 Doug., 433. For further decisions applicable to sales made by guardians, see ESTATES OF DECEASED PERSONS.

1981. Redemption by guardian. A guardian has a right to redeem the lands of his ward from a mortgage sale. *Marvin v. Schilling*, 12 Mich., 356.

HABEAS CORPUS.

1982. Federal jurisdiction. Where one is imprisoned under the authority and in right of the Federal Government, the State judiciary has no jurisdiction to inquire into the legality of the imprisonment on habeas corpus. *Matter of Spangler*, 11 Mich., 298.

1983. The Recorder of Detroit has no authority to issue a writ of habeas corpus to take a prisoner from the Reform School, who has been lawfully sentenced there, unless to testify as a witness. He cannot bring the prisoner up for a new sentence, on the ground of a mistake as to his age when the former sentence was imposed. *Matter of Mason*, 8 Mich., 70.

1984. Inquiry into jurisdiction. Where the petitioner is held by virtue of a commitment fair on its face, charging him with contempt of Court in refusing to give evidence, it is competent for him to go behind the commitment, and show that the Court committing him had no jurisdiction of the proceeding in which he was called as a witness. *Matter of Morton*, 10 Mich., 208; *Matter of Hall*, 10 Mich., 210.

1985. Remanding petitioner to proper custody. Where it appeared that the petitioner was held by an officer who had no legal authority for that purpose, but that there was authority in the keeper of the State Reform School to detain him, under a legal commitment from which he had not been properly discharged, the Court would not order him released, but remanded him to the custody of the keeper of the Reform School. *Matter of Mason*, 8 Mich., 70.

HOMESTEAD.

1986. Selection of. The mere ownership and occupancy of premises was not sufficient to constitute the same a homestead, under the act of March 25, 1848—Comp. L., § 4495—unless there was an actual selection and choice of the premises as such, by the owner and occupant. *People v. Plumsted*, 2 Mich., 465.

1987. And it was accordingly held, that a conveyance of premises so owned and occupied, but which had not been previously selected as a homestead, was valid without the signature of the owner's wife. *Ibid.*

1988. The constitution of 1850 is repugnant to said act of 1848, as respects the value of the homestead to be exempted, and to that extent repeals it. If a place occupied as a homestead is within the constitutional quantity, but exceeds the value of $1,500, it may be reduced in quantity so as to bring it within the required value, provided it can be so reduced by division as to leave a homestead, within the specific value, without cutting off any of that which, in fact, goes to constitute it a homestead; in other words, so as to leave a dwelling house, with the out-buildings and appurtenances necessary to its ordinary use as such. *Beecher v. Baldy*, 7 Mich., 488.

1989. But if, when reduced so far as it is divisible, the homestead still exceeds the value of $1,500, it is not such a homestead as is exempted by the constitution. *Ibid.*

1990. Selection is, under the constitution, only required where the tract out of which a homestead is claimed consists of a greater quantity, or is of greater value than that instrument exempts. If the tract claimed by the debtor as exempt is all that he claims and occupies as a homestead, and is of the limited quantity and value, the whole is exempt without any other selection than is evinced by its ownership and occupation as a homestead. *Ibid.* See also *Thomas v. Dodge*, 8 Mich., 51; *Dyson v. Sheeley*, 11 Mich., 527.

1991. As neither the constitution nor any legislation has [1859] provided any mode of determining the value of premises claimed as a homestead, when the value is disputed, either party, after a levy has been made, may file a bill in equity asking that a selection may be made by the householder, should the property be found divisible, and that the value may be ascertained, whether divisible or not. The value may then be ascertained either by directing an issue to a jury, or by reference to a commissioner to take proofs and report; and in this manner the rights of both parties may be secured according to the nature of the case. *Beecher v. Baldy*, 7 Mich., 488. For subsequent legislation, providing for selection, and for a jury to appraise the premises when it is claimed that they exceed $1,500 in value, and if they do, for the payment of the excess by the debtor, or for a sale and the payment to him of $1,500 from the proceeds, see *Laws of* 1861, *p.* 540.

1992. The notification to the officer, of a homestead claim, was not required to be in writing under the law of 1848. It might be in any form which indicated to the officer, with reasonable certainty, the land claimed as a homestead, and might be made within a reasonable time after the debtor had notice of the levy. *Beecher v. Baldy*, 7 Mich., 488.

1993. Under said act of 1848, the homestead exemption was to be claimed after a levy and before a sale. And when the land consisted of a town lot, the value was to be estimated at that time. *Herschfeldt v. George*, 6 Mich., 456.

1994. Ownership and occupancy essential. To entitle a party to claim land exempt as a homestead, under the law of 1848, he must both own and occupy it. *Wisner v. Farnham*, 2 Mich., 472. And see *Beecher v. Baldy*, 7 Mich., 488; *Dyson v. Sheeley*, 11 Mich., 527.

1995. A lot cannot be claimed as exempt under the law, which the debtor has caused to be conveyed to his wife, on the pretence that such conveyance was made for the purpose of vesting the title in her as a homestead. *Herschfeldt v. George*, 6 Mich., 456.

1996. The premises must have been set apart as a home for the purposes of the owner and his family. Where the owner of a city lot built a double house upon it, in such a way as to show that he designed it for the use of two families, and not for one, and leased one part of it, occupying the other part himself, it was held that he could not claim the whole as exempt from execution as a homestead. *Dyson v. Sheeley*, 11 Mich., 527.

1997. The fact that the yard of the part leased was used by the owner in common with the tenant, would not vary the case. *Ibid.*

1998. Waiver of the right. Held, that the constitutional and statutory provisions for a homestead exemption, conferred upon the householder a right which he might waive at his option; and that where both husband and wife joined in the execution of a mortgage of their homestead, it was a renunciation of this privilege, and on foreclosure, the purchaser would succeed to all their rights, precisely as if no exemption had ever existed. *Chamberlain v. Lyell*, 3 Mich., 448.

1999. Where a waiver is claimed, it lies upon the party asserting it to show it by affirmative proof. But where the debtor is a married man, he cannot, by any waiver, consent to a sale on execution, so as to render the sale valid, without the consent of the wife, any more than he could convey it by deed without the wife's signature. Such deed would be void, even as to the husband, by the express words of the constitution. The object of the exemption was quite as much to protect the wife and family, as the husband. *Beecher v. Baldy*, 7 Mich., 488.

2000. Under the constitution, the homestead exemption is not a personal privilege, to be claimed by the debtor, but an absolute right, necessary to the welfare of the household, of which he cannot be deprived, if an unmarried man, without some act of his relinquishing it, or, if a married man, without the joint conveyance of himself and wife. *Dye v. Mann*, 10 Mich., 291.

2001. Who may take advantage of invalid convey-

ance. A subsequent mortgagee, whose mortgage is executed by both husband and wife, may take advantage of the invalidity of a mortgage given by a married man upon his homestead without his wife's signature. Such mortgage by the husband alone is void for all purposes, and not merely as to the homestead interest. *Ibid.*

2002. And where bill is filed to foreclose the invalid mortgage, and the subsequent mortgagee is made a party defendant, he may take advantage of the invalidity of the first mortgage by answer, without filing a cross bill. *Ibid.*

2003. Where a defendant conveyed premises, after 1848, and before the new constitution, and the wife did not unite in the deed, and a judgment creditor levied upon them, and then filed bill in equity in aid of the execution, it was contended that, as the wife did not join in the conveyance, the deed was void, and she was entitled to be protected in the enjoyment of forty acres as a homestead. It was held, that if she had any equitable interest in a homestead to be selected from the premises, it could not be adjudicated in that suit, but she must join her husband in a cross bill for the purpose. *Wisner v. Farnham*, 2 Mich., 472.

2004. Conveyance valid in part. Where a married man gives a mortgage covering his homestead, without his wife's signature, and the premises are of more than $1,500 value, the mortgage, though void as to a homestead of that value, is good as to the residue. On bill filed to foreclose such a mortgage, the Court ordered a reference to a commissioner to set off as a homestead so much of the premises, with the improvements, as was worth $1,500 at the date of the mortgage, including the dwelling house, and, as far as practicable, such of the outbuildings and other improvements as might be found most essential to the enjoyment of the homestead; to the end that, on the coming in and confirmation of the report, the mortgage might be declared void as to the homestead thus set off, and good as to the residue. *Dye v. Mann*, 10 Mich., 291.

2006. Homestead in land contracted for. A homestead may be claimed in land of which a party is in possession, under a contract to purchase. And the vendee, in such case, if a married man, cannot alienate his interest in the land under the contract without his wife joining with him. *McKee v. Wilcox*, 11 Mich., 358.

2007. If the husband neglects or refuses to perform such a contract, his wife may perform it for him. *Ibid.*

2008. Accordingly, where a married man, who was in possession of land not exceeding in quantity and value what is exempt from execution as a homestead, under a contract to purchase the same, surrendered and cancelled his contract of purchase without the assent of the wife, it was held that such surrender was invalid, and that the wife might file a bill in equity in her own name, and have a specific performance of the contract. *Ibid.*

2009. The decree in such a case should be that the land be conveyed to the husband, but subject to a lien in favor of the wife for the amount she pays in fulfilling the contract. *Ibid.*

HUSBAND AND WIFE.

2010. Deed by wife. Before the statutes were passed giving to a married woman full control of her property, a deed executed by her without her husband joining in it, was void. *Goff v. Thompson*, Har. Ch., 60.

2011. But in case of a conveyance by her since the statute of 1855—Comp. L., § 3292—it is not essential that the husband join in or assent to the deed, notwithstanding she was owner of the land at the time the statute was passed. *Farr v. Sherman*, 11 Mich., 33. And see *Watson v. Thurber*, 11 Mich., 457.

2012. Conveyance by husband to wife. Under the present statutes a deed of lands may be made by a husband directly to his wife without the intervention of any third person. *Amperse v. Bordeno*, 14 Mich.

2013. Husband's right in wife's property. A legacy left to a married woman was held, before the statutes of 1844 and 1855—Comp. L., §§ 3289 and 3292—to be liable to an attachment issued against her husband; but the attaching creditor must take it subject to her equity, which is to have the whole, or so much as the Court of Chancery may see fit, set apart to her for her support. *Westbrook v. Comstock*, Wal. Ch., 314.

2014. The wife is not entitled to compensation from the husband's estate for personal property which she brought to him upon marriage, unless there was an ante-nuptial contract respecting it, securing it to her after marriage. *Cranson v. Cranson*, 4 Mich., 230.

2015. Wife's control of her property. Held, that although by § 5 of article 16 of the constitution, the real and personal estate of every female acquired before marriage, and all property to which she may afterwards become entitled, by gift, &c., shall remain the estate, &c., of such female, and not be liable for her husband's debts, yet that she was not empowered by said section to sell and dispose of the same without her husband's consent. *Brown v. Fifield*, 4 Mich., 322.

2016. But since said statute of 1855, she has the same power, in all respects, over her property that she would have if unmarried. *Stark-*

weather v. Smith, 6 Mich., 377; *Watson v. Thurber*, 11 Mich., 457; *People v. Horton*, 4 Mich., 67; *Durfee v. McClurg*, 6 Mich., 223. And persons obeying her directions in removing her personal property from the possession of her husband, are not liable to an action by the husband for so doing. *Starkweather v. Smith*, 6 Mich., 377.

2017. She may make a gift of her property to her husband; but when he claims that a gift has been made, the burden of proof is upon him to establish it. *Penniman v. Perce*, 9 Mich., 509; *Wales v. Newbould*, 9 Mich., 45; *Durfee v. McClurg*, 6 Mich., 223. See as to such a gift, *Stiles v. Stiles*, 14 Mich.

2018. Where complainant, a married woman, made an unconditional assignment of a mortgage to defendant, and delivered it to her husband, who delivered it over to defendant, and the latter gave the husband a receipt, stating that the mortgage was received of the husband as collateral security for a debt owing by him to defendant, and there was no evidence of any negotiations between complainant and defendant, or of any understanding on her part that the transfer of the mortgage was to be upon any condition, or of any instructions by her in reference to it; it was held that the Court could not say, from these facts, that the assignment was intended by complainant as security only, and not to be absolutely passed to defendant. *Durfee v. McClurg*, 6 Mich., 223.

2019. Complainant's husband having made an arrangement of the debt secured by the assignment, and agreed with defendant that the latter should have and retain an absolute title to the mortgage; it was held that this arrangement was binding upon complainant, and that she could not require defendant to re-assign to her the mortgage. *Ibid.*

2020. The property of the wife does not become the husband's by her permitting him to have possession of and use it. He cannot acquire it except by gift or purchase, and that gift or purchase must be established by some other evidence than that of use and possession. So held in a suit between the wife's administrator and the husband. *White v. Zane*, 10 Mich., 333.

2021. Where the husband who acted as agent in making a compromise by which she was to receive certain lands, took the deed thereof in his own name, and afterwards sold the same in his wife's lifetime; in a suit between him and the wife's administrator, it was held that the deed of the lands made to him, in the absence of proof that it was so made by the wife's direction, consent or knowledge, was no evidence of a gift to him, and warranted no presumption against the right of the administrator. *Wales v. Newbould*, 9 Mich., 45.

2022. The wife may give a mortgage to secure the debt of the husband. *Watson v. Thurber*, 11 Mich., 457.

2023. If a married woman willingly allows her separate property to be so mixed and mingled with that of her husband as not to be distinguishable, or acquiesces in its being so mingled, such property, as to the husband's creditors, is to be treated as relinquished to the husband. *Glover v. Alcott*, 11 Mich., 470.

2024. Said statute of 1855 does not empower a married woman to carry on, on credit, a general trade or business—like that of the purchase of wheat and the manufacture and sale of flour—so as to make the proceeds of the business her own. *Ibid.*

2025. Accordingly, where a married woman was owner of a flouring mill, and her husband, assuming to be her agent, carried on in the mill the business of buying and manufacturing wheat, and selling flour, mill feed, &c., as well as doing custom grinding—the business amounting to from $50,000 to $100,000 a year, and being done mostly on capital borrowed on the credit of the business—it was held that the property acquired in the business was not protected by this statute from being liable to the debts and obligations of her husband. *Ibid.*

2026. Settlement on wife. Held, before said statute of 1844, that a settlement after marriage, on the wife, of property belonging to her before marriage, in pursuance of ante-nuptial parol agreement, was void as against creditors; the promise to make such settlement being founded solely upon the consideration of marriage, and therefore within the statute of frauds (Code 1833, p. 342, § 10). *Wood v. Savage*, 2 Doug., 316; *reversing same case*, Wal. Ch., 471.

2027. Post-nuptial settlements, by the husband upon the wife, are good, if made without fraud, by a party not indebted at the time, or whose debts are trifling compared with his property. *Beach v. White*, Wal. Ch., 495.

2028. If a husband who is insolvent at the time causes real estate to be conveyed to his wife, the conveyance will be void both as to existing and as to subsequent creditors. *Ibid.*

2029. Conveyance in fraud of dower. A deed given by a husband to his sons, shortly before marriage, without consideration, and kept secret until after the marriage, is fraudulent as to the wife, and does not bar her right of dower. *Cranson v. Cranson*, 4 Mich., 230.

2030. Wife's interest in husband's personalty. A wife cannot claim a distributive share in property transferred by the husband by bill of sale and actual delivery before his death. And it is immaterial whether the transfer was a gift, or a sale for a consideration. *Ibid.*

2031. Suit for wife's property. Held, in a suit brought in 1854, by the husband alone, for personal property acquired by the wife before her marriage, that the wife should have been joined; and that it was not necessary to plead the non-joinder in abatement. *Brown v. Fifield*, 4 Mich., 322.

2032. Action for injury to wife. In an action by husband and wife for an assault upon the wife, no act or words of the husband, unless the wife was privy to or participated in them, can be proven in mitigation of damages. *Everts v. Everts*, 3 Mich., 580.

2033. Wife as agent of the husband. The wife, in the absence of the husband, is his agent for the purpose of exercising the usual and ordinary control over his property, unless it be expressly shown that he has constituted some other person his agent for that purpose. She has a right to enter and remain in her husband's house, if she does so without breach of the peace. *People v. Horton*, 4 Mich., 67.

2034. Action by wife for exempt property. Under the statute —Comp. L., § 3294—which provides that in cases where the property of the husband cannot be sold, mortgaged, or otherwise incumbered without the consent of the wife, or when his property is exempted from sale on execution, the wife may bring an action in her own name, with the like effect as in cases of actions in relation to her sole property, the action brought by her cannot be defeated by showing that the property was turned out by the husband to be levied upon. *King v. Moore*, 10 Mich., 538.

IMPRISONMENT FOR DEBT.

2035. The act abolishing imprisonment for debt—Laws 1839, p. 76; Comp. L., Ch. 166—operated upon the remedy to enforce contracts made before it took effect. *Bronson v. Newberry*, 2 Doug., 38.

2036. Debt by B. against N., on a recognizance of special bail. The recognizance was entered into, in 1837, in an action upon contract, brought by B. against one C., wherein judgment was rendered against C. in 1842, upon which *ca sa.* was afterwards issued, and returned *non est inventus*. N. moved that an *exoneretur* be entered upon the recognizance. Held that the motion should be granted, for said act of 1839 operated to prohibit the arrest or imprisonment of C. upon any process issued upon the judgment against him, and thereby rendered the recognizance void. *Ibid.*

2037. Upon the hearing of the motion, it appeared that the demand for which the judgment was rendered, was moneys collected by C. for B. on a claim against the government, which he had been employed by B. to procure to be adjusted and paid; that C. was not an attorney at law; and that he refused to pay over the moneys so collected. It was held, that the action was not "for misconduct or neglect in a professional employment within the purview of the second section of said act. *Ibid.*

2038. It also appeared that C. was, and ever since the action against him had been, a non-resident of the State, without property in the State out of which the money could be made to satisfy the judgment, but that ever since the rendition of the judgment he had had property and effects elsewhere which he refused to apply to its payment. Held that these facts in no way affected the liability of N. on the recognizance. *Ibid.*

2039. The U. S. Process Act—5 Stat. at Large, 321—operates to prohibit imprisonment for debt on process from the United States Courts, except in the cases allowed by the State law. *Ward v. Cozzens*, 3 Mich., 252.

2040. The provision in the State Constitution—Art. 6, § 33—excluding cases of fraud from the prohibition of imprisonment for debt, includes as well cases where the fraud is made use of to avoid payment of the debt, as those where there was fraud in contracting the debt. [CHRISTIANCY, J.] *Bromley v. People*, 7 Mich., 472.

2041. A petition for a discharge under said statute, which only professes to set forth in the schedule such property as is not exempt from execution, and the affidavit verifying which omits the clause required by the statute to be contained therein, "that I have in no instance created or acknowledged a debt for a greater sum than I honestly owed," is so defective as to give the officer to whom it is presented no jurisdiction to proceed thereon. *Young v. Stephens*, 9 Mich., 500.

INFANT.

2042. A mortgage given by an infant feme covert, to secure the debt of her husband, is absolutely void, and not merely voidable. *Chandler v. McKinney*, 6 Mich., 217.

2043. An agreement with a minor to give him board, clothing and schooling in payment for his labor, if reasonable under all the circumstances, or not so unreasonable as to be evidence of fraud or undue advantage, cannot be repudiated by the minor after it has been executed. *Squire v. Hydliff*, 9 Mich., 274.

2044. Affirmance. Where an infant receives a conveyance of land, and gives back a mortgage for the purchase price, he affirms the mortgage if he claims to retain the land as his own after coming of age. He cannot retain the land and at the same time disaffirm the mortgage on the ground of infancy. *Young v. McKee*, 13 Mich., 552.

INJUNCTION BOND.

2045. An injunction bond is a perfect obligation as soon as filed with the register in chancery, in compliance with the statute. *Lothrop v. Southworth*, 5 Mich., 436.

2046. Where action is brought upon an injunction bond without procuring it from the files, and without obtaining an order of the Circuit Judge to take it from the files for prosecution, the want of such order is no defense to the suit. *Ibid.*

2047. The decree of the Court of Chancery, awarding damages in an injunction suit, is conclusive of the amount of damages in a subsequent action upon the injunction bond. And defendants in such action cannot be permitted to show in defense, that in fact plaintiff sustained no damages, or less than was awarded him. *Ibid.*

2048. The surety in an injunction bond, having, by his obligation, undertaken to abide the decree of the Court of Chancery, and pay such damages as may be awarded against his principal by reason of the issuing of the injunction, is bound by such decree, and can raise no question of its correctness in an action brought upon the bond. *Ibid.* As to when a judgment against one of two joint obligors is not evidence against the other, see *Thompson v. Richards*, 14 Mich.

INNKEEPER.

2049. Liability of: who is a "guest." In order to make one liable as innkeeper at the common law, for goods lost at his inn, it must appear that he was acting in the capacity of innkeeper on the occasion when the goods were received, and that the owner was his guest; in other words, that the latter visited the inn for purposes which the common law recognizes as the purposes for which inns are kept. *Carter v. Hobbs*, 12 Mich., 52.

2050. A ball was given by a fire company at the inn of defendant, the defendant furnishing dancing room, supper and dressing room, and being paid therefor by the company at the rate of one dollar for each supper ticket. The ball tickets were sold by the fire company at two dollars each, and these were taken up at the door of the dancing room by a person employed by the fire company, and supper tickets given in their stead. The plaintiff, who was a guest at another inn in the town, went to the ball, purchased a ticket therefor at the baggage room, delivered his overcoat, fur collar and gloves at the office of the hotel to the clerk, and registered his name, and remained at the ball until it broke up in the morning, when, on calling for his overcoat, collar and gloves, they could not be found. During the night the plaintiff had spent some money, for liquor and cigars, at a saloon kept by defendant in connection with the hotel. It was held that these facts did not show the relation of innkeeper and guest to exist between the defendant and the plaintiff; that the former did not receive the goods in his capacity as innkeeper, but merely as an ordinary bailee. *Ibid.*

INSURANCE AGAINST FIRE.

2051. A personal contract. Insurance is a personal contract, and does not pass with the title of the property insured. *Disbrow v. Jones*, Har. Ch., 48.

2052. Concealment of facts. Where the fact of a pending litigation, affecting premises insured, was not communicated to the insurer, at the time of executing the policy, it was held that the omission to disclose did not vitiate the policy. *Hill v. Lafayette Insurance Co.*, 2 Mich., 476.

2054. Conditions. A policy of insurance, one of the conditions of which is that, " in case of any sale, transfer or change of title in the property insured, such insurance shall be void and cease," is avoided by a conveyance which is absolute in form, though given as security for a debt merely. *Western Massachusetts Insurance Co. v. Riker*, 10 Mich., 279.

2055. And where the insurance is upon a single building, and the conveyance is of an undivided interest only, the conveyance avoids the whole policy, notwithstanding the interest of the insured remaining unconveyed is shown to exceed in value the sum insured. *Ibid.*

2056. It was provided in the policy that it should be void if the premises were used for storing or keeping therein any articles included in certain classes of hazards annexed to the policy, "except as herein specially provided, or hereafter agreed to by the insurers upon this policy." It was held that where a stock was insured under the general designation of " groceries," which included some of these hazardous articles, the insurance by this designation did specially provide for them " in writing upon the policy." *Niagara Fire Insurance Co. v. De Graff*, 12 Mich., 124.

2057. A clause in a fire policy which provided that if gunpowder, or other articles subject to legal restriction, should be kept in greater quantities or in a different manner than was provided by law, the policy should be void, was held to have reference only to articles of an intrinsically dangerous nature, as liable to cause injury accidentally or by carelessness, and not to refer to liquors, the traffic in which was made illegal by statute. *Ibid.*

2058. The policy provided that the keeping of gunpowder, " without written permission in the policy" should render it void. It was held that if the agent taking insurance on a stock of goods knew that gunpowder was kept and to be kept, the keeping it would not render the policy void, whether permission to keep it was indorsed or intended or neglected to be indorsed or not. *Peoria Marine and Fire Insurance Co. v. Hall*, 12 Mich., 202.

2059. Notice of this fact to the agent was notice to the principal; and by taking the premium and issuing the policy, the insurer must be regarded as having waived the condition which prohibited gunpowder being kept. *Ibid.*

2060. By one of the conditions attached to a fire policy it was provided that no suit should be brought upon it unless within twelve months next after the loss; and in case any suit should be commenced after the expiration of twelve months, the lapse of time should be deemed and taken as conclusive evidence against the validity of the claim. It was held that if such a condition was valid at all it was valid as a contract only; and that the limitation fixed by it must, upon the principle governing contracts, be more flexible in its nature than one fixed by statute, and liable to be defeated or extended by any act of the insurer which prevents action being brought within the prescribed period. *Ibid.*

2061. Held further, that the insured had the whole of the twelve months within which to commence suit, and that the limitation must rest upon the tacit condition, without which it could not be valid, that the insurer should be accessible to the service of process by which suit may be commenced against him, if not for the whole period, at least for a sufficient time immediately preceding its close to enable the insured to commence his suit in the ordinary legal mode. *Ibid.*

2062. And process having been issued before the expiration of the twelve months, returnable two days after their expiration, and no agent of the insurer—a foreign corporation—being found in the county upon whom to make service, and new process being issued on the return of the first, it was held that the failure to commence suit within the twelve months was sufficiently excused; and the second suit, under the circumstances, was brought in season. *Ibid.*

2063. Insurance by one part owner. If one partner insure the partnership property against loss by fire in his own name only, and it does not appear that the insurance was really intended for the benefit of the firm, the premium paid from the partnership funds, and the transaction subsequently ratified by the other partner, the policy will cover only the individual interest of the party insuring. *Ibid.*

2064. It makes no difference in this respect that the agent of the insurer knew the interest of the parties, and that it was the intention of both the insurer and insured, at the time of issuing the policy, that the insurance should cover the whole. *Ibid.*

2065. The rule may be otherwise where the partner making the insurance has made advances to the firm, which, by agreement, are to constitute a lien on the property insured. *Ibid.*

2066. Where a policy when made covers the interest of one partner only, the remaining interest cannot be brought within it by the partner insured subsequently becoming the owner of the whole. *Ibid.*

2067. Insurance of liquors. Spirituous liquors illegally kept for sale may notwithstanding be lawfully insured against destruction by fire. The risks insured against are not the consequences of illegal acts, but of accidents. *Niagara Fire Insurance Co. v. De Graff*, 12 Mich., 124.

2068. Description of insured property. Where an insurance was effected on "groceries," and there was evidence that the insurer was informed that alcohol and spirituous liquors constituted a part of the stock, it was held that whether they were included in the term "groceries" in the policy was a question of fact for the jury. *Ibid.*

2069. Renewal. Each renewal of a policy of insurance is a new contract, and is subject to the local laws in force at the time of the renewal. *Brady v. Northwestern Insurance Co.*, 11 Mich., 425.

2070. What is insured against. The policy covers all loss which necessarily follows from the occurrence of a fire, whenever the injury arises directly or immediately from the peril, or necessarily from incidental and surrounding circumstances the operation and influence of which could not be avoided. *Ibid.*

2071. Rebuilding clause. A wooden building situated within the fire limits of Detroit was injured by fire, and, by the ordinances of that city, could not be repaired without the consent of the Common Council. This consent was refused. The building was insured for $2,000, and the policy contained a clause that, in case of loss or damage to the property, it should be optional with the company to rebuild or repair the building within a reasonable time. The cost of repairing the building would be much less than the amount of the insurance, but without leave to repair, the building, which before the fire was worth $4,000, would now be worth less than $100. It was held that the insured was entitled to recover the whole insurance, and the insurers could not discharge their obligation by tendering the cost of repair. *Ibid.*

INTEREST.

2072. A township is not liable to pay interest on damages assessed for laying out a highway. *People v. Township Board of La Grange*, 2 Mich., 187.

2073. When payable. Where credit is given for a specified period, without any agreement as to interest, interest is not allowable until the term of credit has expired. And if the term of credit is for an indefinite time, interest is not allowable until after demand of payment. *Beardslee v. Horton*, 3 Mich., 560.

2074. Compound interest. The non-payment of an instalment of interest when due does not convert it into principal, nor entitle the creditor, without express agreement of the debtor, to collect interest upon it. *Van Husan v. Kanouse*, 13 Mich., 303.

JOINT DEBTORS.

2075. When judgment a merger. Plaintiff having recovered a judgment in Ohio against one of the defendants, on a promissory note signed by them in their partnership name, brought action on the same note against both in this State. The defendants set up in defense the rendition of the judgment in Ohio. Held that such judgment, although against one of the defendants only, was a merger of the note, and an extinguishment of the joint liability of the defendants ; and that either defendant might avail himself of such extinguishment in bar of a recovery in a suit on the note against both. *Candee v. Clark*, 2 Mich., 255.

2076. Where suit was brought in the State of New York against two joint debtors, one of whom was not served with process, and did not appear in the action, and judgment in form was rendered against both under the joint debtor act, it was held, that this judgment was not an extinguishment of the demand sued upon, and that an action brought subsequently in this State against the two, was properly brought on the original demand instead of upon the judgment. *Bonesteel v. Todd*, 9 Mich., 371.

2077. Garnishee proceedings against. Where one of three joint debtors was proceeded against by garnishee process, and a judgment recovered, it was held that the judgment was void, and no bar to a subsequent suit against all three on the joint demand. *Wetherwax v. Paine*, 2 Mich., 555.

2078. Joint and several note. Proof of execution by a party not sued is unnecessary, in a suit against one of the makers of a joint and several promissory note. *Chandler v. Lawrence*, 3 Mich., 261.

JUDGE OF PROBATE.

2079. Appointment to fill vacancy. A Judge of Probate was re-elected, but died before the commencement of his new term, and an appointment was made by the Governor to fill the vacancy. January 1st (when the new term would commence), the Governor, on the supposition that there was now a new vacancy, made a new appointment. It was held that the second appointment was void, and that under the Constitution the person first appointed would hold until a successor was elected and qualified. *People v. Lord*, 9 Mich., 227.

2080. Held further, that if the second appointment could be treated as an attempt at a removal of the first appointee, it would be void, as the Governor has no power to remove without cause. *Ibid.*

2081. The Governor could not, by any provision in the commission, limit the first appointment, or make its continuance depend upon his pleasure. *Ibid.*

2082. The appointment so made ceases when a successor has been elected and qualified in pursuance of an order of the Board of Supervisors. And the act of February 17, 1857—Comp. L., § 491—which provides that when a vacancy in a county office shall have been filled by appointment of the Governor, the appointee shall hold for the unexpired portion of the regular term, cannot constitutionally apply to the office of Judge of Probate. *Ibid.*

JUDGMENTS AND EXECUTIONS.

2083. Judgment in name of deceased person. A judgment rendered in favor of two plaintiffs after the death of one of them, cannot be sustained by showing that the deceased plaintiff left a son surviving him who was living when judgment was rendered. *Teller v. Wetherell*, 9 Mich., 464.

2084. Suit on stayed judgment. An action of debt lies on a judgment recovered before a justice of the peace, immediately on its rendition, notwithstanding execution upon it has been stayed pursuant to the statute. *McDonald v. Butler*, 3 Mich., 558.

2085. Title by judgment. A judgment for the plaintiff in trespass *de bonis asportatis*, and the satisfaction thereof, will vest the right of property in the goods in defendant, and his title will relate back to the time when suit was commenced; but this cannot affect third persons, so as to make them trespassers, as against defendant, for acts done by them intermediate the commencement of suit and the rendition of judgment. *Bacon v. Kimmel*, 14 Mich.

2086. Execution: mistake in. The omission in a justice's execution of the year in which the judgment was rendered, will not vitiate the execution, it being in all other respects regular. *Perkins v. Spalding*, 2 Mich., 157.

2087. Irregular execution. An *alias fi. fa.* issued on return of a previous execution levied upon real estate which remained unsold for want of bidders, is irregular merely, but not void. *Spafford v. Beach*, 2 Doug., 150.

2088. Mistake in levy. A constable levied upon wheat on the ground, on the farm of C., in the township of Dover, which farm was then occupied by the defendant in the execution; and made a correct indorsement of the levy on the execution, except that by mistake the name of the township was stated as Madison. The mistake was held not to vitiate the levy. *Perkins v. Spalding*, 2 Mich., 157.

2089. A constable's notice of sale need not state whose property it is that is advertised, nor who is the defendant in the execution. *Ibid.*

2090. A constable's sale of standing wheat, made within sight of the wheat, and of the road corners where it was advertised to take place, but 30 or 35 rods therefrom, is substantially at the place appointed. *Ibid.*

2091. It is the duty of a constable to sell property in such lots or parcels as to command the highest price; and if he wilfully sacrifices the property by disregarding his duty, he is liable to the party injured; but he has a large discretion. Where three parcels of wheat, separated only by fences, containing 25 acres in all, were sold together, and there was no reason to suppose they would have sold better separately, the sale was held valid. *Ibid.*

2092. Satisfaction by execution: judgments against joint trespassers. Where separate judgments are obtained against two or more joint trespassers, the suing out of execution on one of them is an election by the plaintiff to enforce that judgment; and no action will afterwards lie on the others. *Boardman v. Acer*, 13 Mich., 77.

2093. Satisfaction by levy. A levy on real estate is not a prima facie satisfaction of the judgment. *Spafford v. Beach*, 2 Doug., 150. But a levy on chattels is. *Farmers and Mechanics' Bank v. Kingsley*, 2 Doug., 379.

2094. What may be sold: school lands. Since the act of 1851—Comp. L., § 2451—the interest of any purchaser of primary school lands, holding by certificate of purchase, is liable to levy and sale under executions. *Kercheval v. Wood*, 3 Mich., 509.

2095. Choses in action cannot be levied upon or sold. *People v. Auditors of Wayne Co.*, 5 Mich., 223.

2096. Trust estates are not subject to levy and sale on execution in this State. *Trask v. Green*, 9 Mich., 358; *Maynard v. Hoskins*, 9 Mich., 485; *Gorham v. Wing*, 10 Mich., 486.

2097. Since the Statutes of 1846, where land is purchased by one in the name of another, no trust results to the purchaser, and the trust in favor of creditors cannot be enforced by levy and sale on execution. *Ibid.*

2098. Proceedings to a sale. A non-compliance by the sheriff with the requirements of the statute in regard to the levy, advertisement, or sale of real estate, is a mere irregularity, and must be complained of in due time, by motion, or it will be waived. *Spafford v. Beach*, 2 Doug., 150.

2099. Chattel interests in lands are to be sold on execution as personal estate. A sale of an estate for years in lands, made in accordance with the statutory provisions for the sale of real estate, is void. *Buhl v. Kenyon*, 11 Mich., 249.

2100. Fraudulent purchase. Where a purchaser at a sheriff's sale, by a fraudulent combination with the sheriff and judgment debtor to prevent competition at the sale, is enabled to purchase property at much less than its value, the sale is void as to creditors. *Aldrich v. Maitland*, 4 Mich., 205.

2101. Resale for inadequate price. And where, after such a fraudulent sale, the same property was sold by another officer, on an execution in favor of another creditor, and the latter bid it off at an inadequate price, it was held that this inadequacy would not defeat the purchase; the cloud cast upon the title by the former sale being a sufficient answer to the objection of inadequacy. *Ibid.*

2102. Deed of lands to assignee of purchaser. Under the act of 1851—Comp. L., § 3151—one who had previous to the passage of the act become equitably vested with the title which the purchasers at an execution sale acquired by the expiration of the time to redeem, is entitled in equity to a conveyance of the property from the successor of the officer who made the sale. *Whipple v. Farrar*, 3 Mich., 436.

2103. Said act is not liable to the objection that it creates any new, or divests any pre-existing rights; for although retrospective in its operation, it is only so in providing a remedy where none existed before. *Ibid.*

2104. A motion to set aside an execution, and proceedings under it, for irregularity merely, made five years after the sale of real estate by virtue of the execution, is too late. *Spafford v. Beach*, 2 Doug., 150.

2105. Evidence of purchaser's right. The title of a purchaser of real estate sold on execution, is not affected by the insufficiency of the officer's return. The certificate of sale and the deed—not the return—are the evidence of his title. *Ibid.*

2106. To pass the title to real estate sold on execution under the appraisal law of 1841, it was not necessary it should appear from the officer's return to the execution, that either of the appraisers was chosen by defendant, or that he had an opportunity to choose one. *Crane v. Hardy*, 1 Mich., 56.

2107. The settled doctrine as to sales under decrees and judgments, is, that the purchaser is not concerned with anything except the judgment, levy and sale. All other questions are between the parties to the judgment and the officer making the sale. *Ibid.*

2108. Under the Revised Statutes of 1838, a sale of lands on execution did not divest the title of the judgment debtor until consummated by deed. And a deed given before the time of redemption expired, was void. *Gorham v. Wing*, 10 Mich., 487.

2109. Redemption under Statutes of 1838. The time for redemption under said Statutes, was to be computed exclusive of the day on which the sale was made. *Ibid.*

2110. On sales made by the United States Marshal in Michigan, on demands accruing in 1842, for moneys collected by a public officer, or for misconduct or neglect in office, two years redemption was allowed. *Ibid.*

2111. Redemption by judgment creditors. Judgment creditors who were entitled, under § 3147 of Compiled Laws, to acquire the rights of a purchaser of premises sold on execution, applied to the purchaser for that purpose, and took from him an assignment of his certificate of sale, but without having presented him with the statutory proofs of their title to acquire such rights. Held, that where the application was thus made to the purchaser himself, and evidences produced which were satisfactory to him, it was sufficient; though if the application had been made to the register of deeds or sheriff, the statutory proofs must have been produced. *People v. Fralick*, 12 Mich., 234.

2112. Held, further, that the creditors, by thus taking an assignment of the certificate of sale, did not debar themselves from holding as judgment creditors under the statute; and that a subsequent creditor applying to become purchaser of the premises under the statute, must pay their judgment as well as the original bid. *Ibid.*

2113. Exemptions. It is competent for the legislature in passing a statute increasing the exemptions from execution, to make it apply to contracts entered into before its passage. *Rockwell v. Hubbell's Administrators*, 2 Doug., 197.

2114.—several kinds of business. Where a debtor claiming the exemptions allowed by Comp. L., § 4465, carries on several kinds of business, the exemption covers only such property as is requisite for carrying on that particular business in which he is principally engaged. *Morrill v. Seymour*, 3 Mich., 64.

2115. Exemption to specified amount. Where property which is exempt from execution to a specified amount or value is levied upon, the officer, if he would protect himself from the consequences of an action for taking it, must cause an inventory and appraisement of the whole of such property belonging to the debtor to be made, and the amount exempt to be set out to the debtor. *Elliott v. Whitmore*, 5 Mich., 532.

2116. The statute exempting from execution a sufficient quantity of hay, grain, feed and roots for properly keeping for six months the animals specified as exempt from execution, does not exempt any more of those articles than may be necessary for keeping such of the animals mentioned as the debtor has at the time of the levy. *King v. Moore*, 10 Mich., 538.

2117. Whether the statute exempting "provisions for the comfortable subsistence of a householder and family for six months," would exempt growing crops of corn and potatoes recently planted, and which have just become visible above ground, *quere*. *Ibid.*

2118. Order for new execution. Where lapse of time since issuing an execution renders it necessary to apply to the Court for leave, it cannot properly be granted where such delay has intervened that no action will lie on the judgment. *Jerome v. Williams*, 13 Mich., 521.

2119. One became surety for stay of execution upon a justice's judgment. Executions were issued upon the judgment, and returned unsatisfied. Some years afterwards a transcript of the judgment was filed in the office of the county clerk. More than four years after the filing of the transcript, and when more than six years had intervened since the return of the last execution on the stay, the original stay was filed in the office of the county clerk, and the Circuit Court, on the application of the judgment creditor, ordered a new execution against both the judgment debtor and the surety. The surety removed the proceedings to the Supreme Court by certiorari, and the order as to him was reversed. *Ibid.*

2120. Void judgment no consideration. Where a mortgage was given to secure the payment of judgments confessed, which were void for want of compliance with the statute, it was held that the mortgage was without consideration. *Austin v. Grant*, 1 Mich., 490.

2121. What a judgment decides. An order of the Supreme Court, dismissing a certiorari to a justice, is a decision by that Court that the cause has not been in fact removed from the justice into that Court, and that the judgment of the justice is in full force. *Howard v. Rockwell*, 1 Doug., 315.

2122. The judgment of a Court of competent jurisdiction is, as a plea, a bar, and as evidence, conclusive between the same parties and their privies. *Wales v. Lyon*, 2 Mich., 276; *Prentiss v. Holbrook*, 2 Mich., 372.

2123. Accordingly it was held, that one who had unsuccessfully opposed the discharge of his debtor as a bankrupt, was estopped afterwards, in a suit brought to recover the debt, in which the discharge was pleaded, from showing that the discharge was fraudulently obtained. *Wales v. Lyon*, 2 Mich., 276.

2124. Plaintiff sued a sheriff for taking certain personal property; and on trial, the sheriff recovered judgment. After the sheriff had sold the property, plaintiff sued the purchaser. Held, that the suit against the sheriff was a bar. *Prentiss v. Holbrook*, 2 Mich., 372.

JURISDICTION.

2125. Rule as to inferior jurisdictions. Inferior jurisdictions, not proceeding according to the course of the common law, are confined strictly to the authority conferred upon them. *Wight v. Warner*, 1 Doug., 384; *Clark v. Holmes*, 1 Doug., 390; *Chandler v. Nash*, 5 Mich., 409.

2126. The facts necessary to give them jurisdiction must appear affirmatively in their proceedings, and cannot be presumed. *Ibid.*

2127. They must have jurisdiction of the person, by means of the proper process or appearance of the party, as well as of the subject matter of the suit; and when they have not such jurisdiction, their proceedings are absolutely void, and they become trespassers by any act to enforce them. *Clark v. Holmes*, 1 Doug., 390.

2128. The want of jurisdiction, either over the person or the subject matter, may be shown by evidence, even when it tends to contradict the minutes or docket which the inferior jurisdiction is required to keep as a record of its proceedings. *Ibid.* But see *Facey v. Fuller*, 13 Mich., 527, where it was held that the recital on the docket of a justice of the peace, that parties appeared and proceeded to trial, was conclusive.

2129. When jurisdiction exists, the proceedings cannot be impeached collaterally. *Clark v. Holmes*, 1 Doug., 390.

2130. What are inferior and special jurisdictions. These rules applied to Courts of justices of the peace — *Clark v. Holmes*, 1 Doug., 390; *Wight v. Warner*, 1 Doug., 384 — to proceedings before circuit court commissioners for the dissolution of attachments — *Chandler v. Nash*, 5 Mich., 409 — to proceedings against non-resident defendants for partition in the Circuit Courts in Chancery — *Platt v. Stewart*, 10 Mich., 260.

2131. Court of general jurisdiction. Where the want of jurisdiction appears on the record of a Court of general jurisdiction, the record is a nullity. *Greenvault v. Farmers and Mechanics' Bank*, 2 Doug., 498; *Wilson v. Arnold*, 5 Mich., 98; *Farrand v. Bentley*, 6 Mich., 281.

2132. Notice essential. No man's rights can be affected by legal proceedings, without notice of them, actual or constructive. *Buck v. Sherman*, 2 Doug., 176.

2133. Waiver of jurisdictional defects. A defect of jurisdiction as to the subject matter, cannot be waived by the parties. As where a party notices a cause for hearing in the Supreme Court as on case made, and the paper filed as a case made has never been settled and signed by the Judge as such, the party who has given notice of hearing will not be precluded from moving to dismiss on that ground. *Farrand v. Bentley*, 6 Mich., 281.

2134. Where a defect of jurisdiction exists, the defendant does not, by neglecting to take advantage of it on the first opportunity, waive the right to do so, as in case of a mere irregularity; but he may question the proceedings at any time. *Turrill v. Walker*, 4 Mich., 177.

2135. A defendant moved to quash proceedings before a circuit court commissioner for want of due service of the summons. The commissioner took time for giving his decision; the complainant stipulating to submit the motion without argument, if defendant would plead to the complaint, which he did. It was held that defendant did not, by so pleading, waive his objection to the service. *Sallee v. Ireland*, 9 Mich., 154.

2136. A confession of judgment before a justice is void unless in accordance with the statute authorizing it. *Clark v. Holmes*, 1 Doug., 390; *Beach v. Botsford*, 1 Doug., 199; *Spear v. Carter*, 1 Mich., 19; *Wilson v. Davis*, 1 Mich., 156. And see *Shadbolt v. Bronson*, 1 Mich., 85.

2137. Unauthorized stay of judgment. A stay of execution having been taken by a justice for six months, where the statute only authorized it to be taken for three, it was held that an execution issued thereon against the surety, after the expiration of the six months, was void. *Shadbolt v. Bronson*, 1 Mich., 85.

2138. Transfer of jurisdiction where Court is abolished. When the State government was organized, and the Supreme Court of the Territory abolished, certain causes pending therein were not transferred to any Court. It was held competent for the legislature to pass an act afterwards transferring these causes to the Supreme Court of the State. *Scott v. Smart's Executors*, 1 Mich., 295.

2139. Judgment of another State. In an action in one State upon the judgment of a Court of general jurisdiction of another State, no plea or proof can be received in contradiction of any material fact appearing by the record, unless such plea or proof would be received in an action on the judgment in the State in which it was rendered. *Wilcox v. Kassick*, 2 Mich., 165.

2140. If the record shows a want of jurisdiction, the judgment is a nullity. *Ibid.*

2141. If the judgment does not show either that the Court had, or that it had not jurisdiction, the jurisdiction will be presumed; but in such case, facts showing a want of jurisdiction may be alleged by plea, and if established, a recovery may be defeated. *Ibid.*

2142. When the record shows that the process was not personally served, and that the defendant did not appear personally in the suit, but that an attorney appeared for him and made defense, the authority of such attorney to appear for him will be presumed. But whether the authority may be disproved, *quere. Ibid.*

JURY.

2143. Jurors judges of the law in inferior jurisdictions. It *seems*, that in inferior jurisdictions, deriving their authority from the statute, and not proceeding according to the course of the common law, the jury are the judges both of the law and the fact. *Chamberlain v. Brown*, 2 Doug., 120.

2144. Juror once rejected not to be resummoned. On an inquest of the value of property required for a railroad, after a juror had been struck from the panel by one of the parties, and the jury completed, it was held that he could not be resummoned by the officer in the place of one who had been excused. *In re Detroit and Pontiac R. R. Co.*, 2 Doug., 367.

JUSTICES' COURTS.

2145. Jurisdiction. A justice's Court, being one of inferior and limited jurisdiction, is confined strictly to the powers conferred upon it, and its proceedings must appear to be within those powers.

Wight v. Warner, 1 Doug., 384; *Clark v. Holmes*, 1 Doug., 390. Nothing can be presumed in favor of its jurisdiction. *Spear v. Carter*, 1 Mich., 19.

2146. The jurisdiction of the justice, in actions on contract to recover less than $100, is not exclusive. *Webb v. Mann*, 3 Mich., 139.

2147. These Courts have no jurisdiction of suits against municipal corporations. *Root v. Mayor, &c., of Ann Arbor*, 3 Mich., 433; *Comp. L.*, § 3700. The provision in a municipal charter, that the corporation may sue and be sued in all Courts of law and equity, &c., will not confer jurisdiction upon them. Such a provision must be understood to mean, in all Courts of law and equity having jurisdiction of the case. *Gurney v. Mayor, &c., of St. Clair*, 11 Mich., 202.

2148. Matters of form. The Court will overlook matters of form in proceedings before justices of the peace, and regard them according to the merits. *People v. Foote*, 1 Doug., 102.

2149. Where an issue formed upon a plea of not guilty in replevin, was tried by a jury, who returned a verdict as follows: "This jury find for the plaintiff;" held sufficient. *People v. Foote*, 1 Doug., 102. And the justice having refused to enter the verdict and render judgment thereon, on the ground that it was insufficient, and awarded a *venire de novo*, the Supreme Court compelled him by mandamus, to enter the verdict and render judgment. *Ibid.*

2150. The finding of a verdict in a justice's Court, is itself, in legal effect, a judgment. *Gaines v. Betts*, 2 Doug., 98; *Overall v. Pero*, 7 Mich., 315.

2151. The pleadings should be viewed with liberality, technicalities discountenanced, and substance instead of form required. The object of pleading in any Court is to apprise the opposite party of the grounds of the claim or defense, as the case may be, so that there shall be no misapprehension as to what matters are to be litigated on the trial. And defects will be waived by the defendant if he pleads issuably, and goes to trial on the merits. *Hurtford v. Holmes*, 3 Mich., 460.

2152. But a declaration must show a cause of action. Where the plaintiff exhibited a promissory note, and stated that he declared against the defendant as indorser, without making any averment or statement as to the presentation of the note for payment, and notice of non-payment to the defendant, the declaration was held bad in substance, and judgment thereon for the plaintiff—the defendant not appearing—was reversed. *Barber v. Taylor*, 1 Mich., 352. See *Cicotte v. Morse*, 8 Mich., 424.

2153. A declaration in a statutory action referred to the chapter of the statute by the wrong number, but otherwise cited it correctly, and was not demurred to. Held sufficient to support a verdict for plaintiff. *Achey v. Hull*, 7 Mich., 423.

2154. Docket. The docket entry of a justice's judgment must be as certain, in matters of substance, as the judgment of a Court of record. *Rood v. School District, &c.*, 1 Doug., 502.

2155. Under the proper entitling of a cause with the names of the parties, an award of judgment was entered as follows: "It is therefore considered that the said P. do recover of the said D. the sum," &c. Debt being brought on this judgment, it was held that the entry did not show with sufficient certainty in whose favor and against whom the judgment was rendered, and that therefore a transcript thereof offered in evidence was inadmissible. *Ibid.*

2156. Held, also, that parol evidence was not admissible to prove that the letters *P.* and *D.* in the docket entry, meant plaintiff and defendant. *Ibid.*

2157. The docket of a justice stated that a cause was called and judgment rendered "*on the return of process.*" Held to mean on the return *day* of process, and not the time of its actual return. *Aldrich v. Maitland*, 4 Mich., 205.

2158. A statement in the docket that judgment was rendered in favor of plaintiff—there being only one defendant—sufficiently shows that judgment was rendered against defendant. *Ibid.*

2159. Certificate of justice. The certificate of a justice to the transcript of a judgment from the docket of a former justice, in which he certifies that such docket is in his control, will be evidence of that fact. *Facey v. Fuller*, 13 Mich., 527.

2160. A justice entered across a judgment on his docket, that it was paid, stating the day, and signed the entry in his official capacity. Held that such entry was prima facie evidence that the judgment was satisfied, and that this evidence was not rebutted by proof, unaccompanied by any explanatory testimony, of another entry immediately below the former, on the same docket, without date, and signed by the justice in his individual capacity, stating in effect that the judgment had not been paid, according to the import of the former entry. *Beach v. Botsford*, 1 Doug., 199.

2161. Court in bar-room. The statute of 1842—S. L., p. 135—provided that no justice of the peace should hold any Court, or hear an examination, in any bar-room, grocery, or other room or place where spirituous or intoxicating liquors should be sold. On special appeal, where it was stated in the justice's return that, on the day of the trial, the cause was called in the bar-room of a tavern, and adjourned to an adjoining room in the same house, but that the justice had no knowledge that spirituous or intoxicating liquors were sold there, and that no proof of such fact was offered on the trial, the Court refused to reverse the judgment. The Court would not presume that spirituous liquors were sold in the bar-room of a tavern, when by the law as it then stood, every license to keep a tavern did not authorize the sale of spirituous liquors. *Savier v. Chipman*, 1 Mich., 116.

2162. Service of summons. The return to a summons in these words: "Served the within by reading personally"—the statute (of 1833, p. 194) requiring it to be served by reading it to defendant, and delivering to him a copy—is bad, and does not give the justice jurisdiction of the person of defendant. *Campau v. Fairbanks*, 1 Mich., 151.

2163. But under the Revised Statutes of 1846, (p. 389, § 15) which required that the summons should be served "by reading the same to defendant, and (if required by him) delivering a copy thereof," a return in these words: "Personally served true copies of the within by reading," properly dated and signed by the constable, was held sufficient. *Shaw v. Moser*, 3 Mich., 71.

2164. Failure of defendant to appear. A defendant waives nothing by a failure to appear on the return day of process; but the plaintiff must prove his case in the same manner as if he had appeared. *Gilbert v. Hanford*, 13 Mich., 40. See *Barber a. Taylor*, 1 Mich., 352.

2165. Absence of justice. On the adjourned day of a cause, the absence of the justice for a few minutes more than an hour after the time to which the cause had been adjourned, for the purpose of holding a coroner's inquest, will not operate as a discontinuance of the cause. *Stadler v. Moors*, 9 Mich., 264. See *post*, 2173.

2166. Illegal adjournment. An adjournment by a justice, on his own motion, in the absence and without the consent of the defendant, at any other time than on the return day of the writ, is a discontinuance of the cause. *Ibid.*

2167. Submission to arbitration of the subject matter of a suit, being a discontinuance of the suit, will discharge a surety for costs. *Dunn v. Sutliff*, 1 Mich., 24.

2168. Title to lands. Under the Justices Act of 1841 (S. L., p. 81, §§ 1, 39, 43), a justice had no power to try a cause in which it appeared by the pleadings that a question of title to real estate was involved, and the title was disputed; but where title was admitted—as by demurrer to a declaration alleging it—the justice had jurisdiction. *Stout v. Keyes*, 2 Doug., 184. See Comp. L., §§ 3654, and 3729 to 3737 for provisions somewhat different.

2169. Under section one of the same statute, which provided that justices should have jurisdiction of civil actions, &c., except "actions in which the title to real estate shall come in question," it was held that, under a declaration against defendant for falsely representing himself to have title to a piece of land, which plaintiff was induced to buy of him, the title to the land must necessarily come in question, and that the justice, therefore, had not jurisdiction of the case. *Brooks v. Delrymple*, 1 Mich., 145.

2170. Replevin. The forms provided by statute—Comp. L., Ch. 152—for actions of replevin, are applicable alike to Justices Courts and Courts of record. *Elliott v. Whitmore*, 5 Mich., 532.

2171. Process against corporations. The act of March 28, 1849—Comp. L., § 4846—authorizing the service of process against railroad companies upon conductors, &c., is not repealed, as respects Justices Courts, by section 49 of the Justices Act of 1855—Comp. L., § 3701. *Fowler v. Detroit and Milwaukee Railway Co.*, 7 Mich., 79.

2172. Since said Justices Act of 1855, justices of the peace have no jurisdiction to issue attachments against foreign corporations. *Brigham v. Eglinton*, 7 Mich., 291.

2173. Confession of judgment. C. and L. were duly summoned to answer to M. before a justice of the peace at his residence. They appeared there on the return day, but neither the justice nor M. appeared; and no proceedings were had in the cause. Three days afterwards, L., in the presence of C. and of a witness, but in the absence of the justice, indorsed on a joint and several note of C. and L. found in the office of the justice, his individual confession of judgment thereon, upon which the justice, on the same day, without any continuance of the cause from the return day of the summons, or any declaration filed, rendered judgment in favor of M. against C. and L. for the amount of the note. Held, that at the time of rendering judgment the justice had no jurisdiction over the person of C.; the summons having spent its force on the return day, and the parties being out of Court, and the cause discontinued. *Clark v. Holmes*, 1 Doug., 390.

2174. Under the Statutes of 1838—*R. S., p.* 389, §2—a judgment by confession was held void, where it did not appear to be "signed by the person making the same, in the presence of the justice and of one or more competent witnesses." The statute was construed to require the witnesses to subscribe their names as such. *Beach v. Botsford*, 1 Doug., 199.

2175. Under the Code of 1833—p. 193—the jurisdiction of justices was restricted to certain actions, and judgments by confession might be entered, "provided that such confession be in writing, signed by the person making the same, in presence of the justice and one or more competent witnesses." A judgment was rendered by a justice in these words, after the title of the cause, "Judgment by written confession of the above named defendants, in favor of the above named plaintiff, for eighty eight dollars and eighteen cents damages and costs of suit."

Held, that the judgment did not show, and was not prima facie evidence, that the justice had jurisdiction of either the persons of the defendants, or of the subject matter of the suit, and that it was therefore void. *Spear v. Carter*, 1 Mich., 19.

2176. Held further, that the justice could render judgment on confession only in those actions which he had jurisdiction to try. And that where jurisdiction was unqualifiedly withheld, consent, or the confession of a judgment, would not render the proceedings valid. *Ibid.*

2177. Under the same code, it was held that a judgment rendered on a confession not in writing was void; and that where such judgment had been stayed, an action could not be maintained on the undertaking of the surety, for want of consideration to support it. *Wilson v. Davis*, 1 Mich., 156.

2178. Section 3655 of Compiled Laws, authorizes judgment to be entered with consent of the creditor upon confession in writing, signed by the debtor in the presence of the justice, " that he is indebted to another upon contract in a certain specified sum." Where parties appeared before a justice, and confessed judgment in favor of another, on a demand arising upon contract, for a sum specified, and authorized judgment to be entered thereupon, it was held a substantial acknowledgment of their indebtedness, and sufficient under this statute. *Kinyon v. Fowler*, 10 Mich, 16.

2179. Where two persons thus confessed judgment, and the entry recited that " the parties appeared," it was held that this phrase purports that the creditor, as well as the debtors, was present and participated in the proceedings. *Ibid.*

2180. It is only where the parties appear without process that a written confession signed by the defendant is required by the statute. If the defendant appears after due service of process, and orally admits the cause of action for which the plaintiff declares, this is sufficient to authorize judgment to be entered against him. *Crouse v. Derbyshire*, 10 Mich., 479.

2181. Stay of execution. The undertaking of one who becomes surety for stay of execution is in the nature of a confession of judgment; and to render it obligatory upon the surety, it must be executed in the presence of the justice, and be witnessed by him. *Cox x. Crippen*, 13 Mich., 502.

2182. The approval of the stay entered by the justice in his docket, but not showing his presence when the stay was entered into, cannot be regarded as an attestation. *Ibid.* See further, supra 2137.

2183. Execution. Where, under the Revised Statutes of 1846, the docket entry showed judgment rendered and execution issued on the same day, it was held that it must be presumed that execution was awarded at the *same time* that judgment was rendered, in which case the notice required by the Statutes—Ch. 93, § 113—where execution issued before five days had elapsed, need not be given. *Rash v. Whitney*, 4 Mich., 495.

2184. The evidence in support of an application for execution before the expiration of the five days, was not required to be in writing. Nor was the justice required to set forth in his docket the facts stated in support of the application. Where the docket recited that the party "stated, under oath, that he was in danger of losing his debt unless execution issued immediately," a statement of the necessary facts was inferred. *Ibid.*

2185. It was further held, that what would be competent evidence on such an application, was a question for the justice to determine ; and if he awarded execution upon improper testimony, his action would be erroneous merely, and not an excess of jurisdiction. *Ibid.*

2186. Transcript. The Revised Statutes of 1846—Ch. 93, § 102—required the justice, upon proper demand, to give the party applying "a certified transcript of such judgment, and of the proceedings in the case, so far as they appear upon the docket ;" and upon the filing of such transcript with the clerk of the Circuit Court, the judgment became, in effect, that of the Circuit Court. Held, that this statute, providing for an entirely ex-parte proceeding, and followed by such unusual consequences, must be strictly complied with by the party seeking the benefit of its provisions ; and that where a transcript was authenticated by a certificate of the justice in this form : "I hereby certify that the above is a true transcript of the above judgment, and of the *subsequent* proceedings thereon," the certificate was insufficient to authorize the filing of the transcript, and issuing execution thereon. *Jewett v. Bennett*, 3 Mich., 198.

2187. Criminal cases. A judgment rendered by a justice in a criminal case is not valid unless the entry thereof on the docket is signed officially by the justice. *Howard v. People*, 3 Mich., 207.

2188. Where the statute has prescribed as the penalty for an offense, fine or imprisonment for a limited time, or both, a judgment that the defendant pay a fine, and *stand committed until paid*, is void, because adjudging an indefinite term of imprisonment. *Ibid.* See also, supra, 944.

JUSTICES OF THE PEACE.

2189. Fees as witness. The statute of 1840 allowing to "the Secretary of State, Auditor-General, *any clerk*," &c., one dollar a day "for attending on subpœna with bills, records, or other written evidence," was held not to apply to a justice in attendance with his docket. He is not such a *clerk* as was intended by the statute. *Prentiss v. Webster*, 2 Doug., 5.

2190. What he may receive on judgments. In the absence of special instructions, a justice of the peace can receive nothing but current money of the United States in satisfaction of a judgment on his docket. *Heald v. Bennett*, 1 Doug., 513; *Welch v. Frost*, 1 Mich., 30.

JUSTICES OF THE SUPREME COURT.

2191. Compensation as Circuit Judges. Under the constitution of 1850, and prior to the present organization of the Supreme Court, the office of Judge of the Supreme Court was not a distinct office from that of Circuit Judge, but two sets of duties were attached to one office under the latter designation. And the salary of the Circuit Judges, as fixed by the constitution, was a remuneration for all duties attached to the office, and could not be increased by the legislature. *People v. Auditor-General*, 5 Mich., 193.

LAND CONTRACT.

2192. Position of parties to. In equity a vendee, under a contract for the sale of lands, is considered as a trustee of the purchase money for the vendor, who is regarded as a trustee of the land for the former. The land is in equity the property of the vendee, who may dispose of or incumber it in like manner with land to which he has the legal title, subject to the rights of the vendor under the contract. *Wing v. McDowell*, Wal. Ch., 175.

2193. A mortgage given by the vendee conveys no legal interest, and the registry of the mortgage is notice to no one. *Ibid.*

2194. Possession by vendee: tender of deed: covenants. The defendant made proposals to plaintiff's agent for the purchase of certain lands, and a parol agreement was made that if plaintiff, who was a non-resident, accepted defendant's proposition, a deed should be executed by plaintiff to defendant, as soon as convenient. In pursuance of the agreement, and anticipating its acceptance by plaintiff, defendant, with the agent's permission, took possession of the premises. Plaintiff ratified the agreement, and executed a deed, which was tendered to defendant, who refused to receive it because it contained no covenants of warranty. After he had occupied the premises for nine months, and all negotiation between the parties had ceased, the agent notified defendant that if he remained in possession he must pay rent. He continued in possession fifteen months longer. Held, that plaintiff was entitled to recover for the last fifteen months of occupancy, but that no promise could be implied to pay for the occupation during the negotiations for the purchase, if the plaintiff refused to ratify the agreement, or, after acceptance, to perform its conditions. *Dwight v. Cutler*, 3 Mich., 566.

2195. In every contract for the sale of lands, unless the contrary intention is expressed, there is an implied undertaking on the part of the vendor, available at law as well as in equity, while the contract remains executory, to make out a good title, clear of all defects and incumbrances. *Ibid.*

2196. In this country, where titles are registered, the burden of proof is upon the vendee to show a defect of title which will justify the refusal of a proper deed when tendered. *Ibid.*

2197. The vendor, unless there is something in the contract to show a contrary intention, or unless he acts in a ministerial or fiduciary capacity, impliedly engages to convey by a deed containing the usual covenants ; and in this State lands are usually conveyed by deeds containing a general warranty. *Ibid.*

2198. The deed tendered by the plaintiff, as it did not contain a general warranty, was not such as the contract required, and the defendant was justified in refusing it. The failure to consummate the sale occurred, therefore, through the plaintiff's default, and he was not entitled to recover for the defendant's occupancy pending the negotiation. *Ibid.*

2199. Vendee a tenant at will. The estate of one in possession of lands under a contract of purchase, is that of a tenant at will. *Dwight v. Cutler*, 3 Mich., 566 ; *Crane v. O'Reiley*, 8 Mich., 312.

2200. A clause in the contract, that on default by the purchaser the seller might declare the contract void, and the purchaser should thereafter be deemed a mere tenant at will, and liable to be proceeded against as such, confers no additional rights, and is merely declaratory of the actual relation and rights of the parties. *Crane v. O'Reiley*, 8 Mich., 312.

2201. Notice to quit may be waived by the purchaser in such a contract. *Ibid.*

2202. Forfeiture. The contract will not be treated as forfeited by non-payment at the day, where the parties themselves have not treated time as essential, and it is not expressly made so by the terms of the contract. *Shafer v. Niver*, 9 Mich., 253. For further decisions on this point, see SPECIFIC PERFORMANCE.

2203. Effect of vendor terminating contract. A vendor having, on default by the vendee, elected to treat the contract as void, and having given the vendee notice to quit, must be regarded as having relinquished his right to the amount then due on the contract. He cannot treat the contract as void in respect to the rights which it secured to the vendee, and valid in respect to those which it secured to himself. *Goodspeed v. Dean*, 12 Mich., 352.

2204. Effect of release by vendee. Where the vendor in an executory contract for the purchase of lands, receives from the vendee a quit claim deed for the lands, this is a recission of the contract; and he cannot afterwards maintain an action on notes which were given for the purchase price. *Ives v. Bank of Lansingburg*, 12 Mich., 361.

LAND WARRANT.

2205. The holder of a land warrant has an absolute right to locate land with it, and to receive a patent therefor. *Merrill v. Hartwell*, 11 Mich., 200.

2206. Where plaintiff located land with a warrant which had been sold to him with a guaranty, and was afterwards notified from the land office that the entry was suspended because the Commissioner of Pensions had cancelled the warrant on the allegation that it was issued on forged papers, and plaintiff then brought suit on the guaranty; it was held that this ex-parte and extra judicial proceeding of the Commissioner could not conclude private rights, and that evidence of this action did not show plaintiff entitled to recover. *Ibid.*

LANDLORD AND TENANT.

2207. Disputing landlord's title. A tenant cannot dispute his landlord's title, nor, by his own act merely, change the tenure, so as to enable himself to hold against his landlord. He cannot, during the continuance of the lease or tenancy, make a valid attornment to a third person without his landlord's consent. *Byrne v. Beeson*, 1 Doug., 179; *Lee v. Payne*, 4 Mich., 106; *Falkner v. Beers*, 2 Doug., 117; *Blanchard v. Tyler*, 12 Mich., 339; *Niles v. Ransford*, 1 Mich., 338.

2208. A contract by which a tenant is induced to desert his landlord, is corrupt and void, and no action can be maintained upon it. If he accepts a lease from a third person, either he or his landlord may defend his possession against proceedings by such third person, by showing the prior existence of the tenancy. *Byrne v. Beeson*, 1 Doug., 179.

2209. Eviction. Where a tenant is dispossessed by one who enters under a paramount title, such entry is equivalent to an eviction by legal process, and will excuse the tenant from paying rent to the landlord. The tenant is not bound to retain possession until actually expelled by legal process; but may quietly yield possession, incurring the risk of being able to show that the entry was under a paramount title. *Marsh v. Butterworth*, 4 Mich., 575.

2210. Where a landlord, during the continuance of a lease, without the consent of the tenant, enters upon the demised premises, which have been vacated by the tenant, and the entry is followed by a continuous possession inconsistent with the possessory right assured to the tenant by the lease, such possession amounts to an eviction, and precludes the recovery of rent while it continues. *Day v. Watson*, 8 Mich., 535.

2211. And this is so whether the entry be for condition broken or not. If for condition broken, it signifies an intention to terminate the lease entirely; while, if the landlord regard the lease as still continuing, the right to rent is suspended during the occupancy. *Ibid.*

2212. Assignment and sub-letting. A covenant by a lessee not to transfer the lease without the consent of the lessor, does not inhibit a sub-letting by the lessee. *Copland v. Parker*, 4 Mich., 660.

2213. A lease by the lessee, of the three lower stories and the cellar of a four-story store, which the lessee held under a lease in which he had covenated " not to transfer this lease," was held no breach of this covenant. *Ibid.*

2214. Where the lessee assigns his interest in the whole or a part of the demised premises, for the residue of the unexpired term, the assignee is substituted in place of the original lessee as tenant, and stands in that relation to the original lessor. But where the demised premises are let for a part only of the unexpired term, the assignee is only a sub-lessee, and the relation of landlord and tenant does not exist between him and the original landlord. *Lee v. Payne*, 4 Mich., 107.

2215. Surrender. A., by deed, leased premises to B., who afterwards assigned the lease to C. A. assented to the assignment, and agreed, by parol, to accept C. as his tenant, and to look to him for the rent. Held that there had been a sufficient surrender of the lease by operation of law to satisfy the statute—Code of 1833, p. 342, § 9—which declared that " no lease, &c., shall at any time hereafter be assigned, granted or surrendered, unless it be by deed or note in writing, signed," &c., " or by operation of law;" and that A. could not afterwards maintain covenant against B. for the rent. *Logan v. Anderson*, 2 Doug., 101.

2216. Notice to quit. Where a lease is invalid by the statute of frauds, the lessee having taken possession is a tenant at will; and if the agreement was to pay rent monthly, he is entitled to a month's notice to surrender possession before the proceedings can be taken to dispossess him. And this month's notice must terminate with one of the regular monthly periods. *Huyser v. Chase*, 13 Mich., 98.

2217. Where premises are let at a fixed monthly rent, with the understanding that the tenant shall give up possession whenever the landlord may require them for his own use, the letting creates a tenancy at will which can only be terminated by a full month's notice to quit at the end of one of the regular monthly periods. *Woodrow v. Michael*, 13 Mich., 187.

2218. Where rent is payable weekly, or at other stated intervals, in advance, the tenant has the whole of the first day of each succeeding week, or other interval of time, in which to make the payment. *Sherlock v. Thayer*, 4 Mich., 355.

LIBEL.

2219. What is libelous. It is not libelous to publish of and concerning one who is a druggist, "The above druggist in the city of Detroit refusing to contribute his mite with his fellow merchants for watering Jefferson avenue, I have concluded to water said avenue in front of T.'s store, for the week ending June 27, 1846." *People v. Jerome*, 1 Mich., 142.

2220. To render a publication libelous, it must indicate the person intended by name, or connect him with some fact or circumstance, known to those to whom the publication is addressed, by which they may understand who is meant. And to enable a jury to determine upon the application, such fact or circumstance should be in proof; and that cannot be unless it is pleaded. *Lewis v. Soule*, 3 Mich., 514.

2221. In giving a construction to words declared upon as libelous, resort cannot be had to the innuendo, the office of which is to explain the context, not to add to it. *Ibid.*

2222. Action based upon the publication of the following words: "It must be and is painful to all who feel the force of conscientious impulses, and who regard the solemn responsibility of an oath, to witness at our elections the frequent violations of truth, committed by those brought forward at the polls. The recurrence of false swearing is too common to pass unpunished. No casuistry can palliate or excuse it." The inducement set forth was, that plaintiff was supervisor of the township; that there was a general election; that plaintiff was a member of the board of election; and also a candidate for re-election. Held, that the alleged libelous words were too vague and uncertain to constitute a charge of perjury; and that in connection with the extrinsic facts pleaded, the perjury was not sufficiently alleged. *Ibid.*

LIBRARY MONEYS.

2223. Under the present constitution and statutes, all moneys which are paid into the office of the county treasurer, on account of fines, penalties, forfeitures and recognizances, are to be credited to the library fund, and apportioned and paid over by the treasurer to the proper local officers, without any deduction for expenses, either attending the collection of the particular sums paid in, or embracing the general criminal expenses of the county. *People v. Treasurer of Wayne County*, 8 Mich., 392.

LIMITATION OF ACTIONS.

2224. The statute of limitations is a statute of repose, as well as of presumption. *Jewett v. Petit*, 4 Mich., 508.

2225. New promise. Where a new promise is set up, it ought to be proved in a clear and explicit manner, either expressly, or by such an unqualified acknowledgment as authorizes its implication. *Ten Eyck v. Wing*, 1 Mich., 40.

2226. The acknowledgment should contain an unqualified and direct admission of a present subsisting debt, which the party is liable and willing to pay, and be unaccompanied by circumstances or declarations which repel the presumption of a promise or intention to pay. *Ibid.*

2227. Debt on judgment recovered in 1824. Plea, statute of limitations. Replication, that in November, 1832, a *pluries* execution was taken out on the judgment; that on the 17th of the same month, defendant filed a bill in chancery and obtained an injunction restraining proceedings on the execution; that on November 17, 1835, it was stipulated between the parties to the chancery suit, that the injunction be dissolved; that the *pluries* execution be set aside; that there be a reference to a master to take testimony in the chancery suit, and to state an account between the parties; to state the amount due upon the judgment, and ascertain the amount of any and all legal and equitable set offs to the judgment; that testimony was taken under the stipulation by both parties; that the master made his report in January, 1838, and that in March, 1846, the case was heard in the Court of Chancery and the bill dismissed, with costs. On demurrer, it was held, that the replication did not show such an acknowledgment of the debt as would warrant the implication of a new promise. *Ibid.*

2228. If the acknowledgment of a debt, or a partial payment of it, is accompanied by declarations or circumstances which rebut the implication of a promise to pay, or that the debtor, by the partial pay ment, admitted his obligation to pay the residue, the demand is not revived. *Jewett v. Petit*, 4 Mich., 508.

2229. Payment. The indorsement of a partial payment upon a promissory note, written by the party to be charged thereby, is competent evidence of such payment to take the case out of the statute. *Chandler v. Lawrence*, 3 Mich., 261.

2230. Although the statute requires a new promise to be in writing, the fact of payment may be proved by the admission of the defendant, or by any other competent parol evidence. *Ibid.*

2231. Saving clauses. The case stated, *supra*, 2227, held not to come within the clauses of the statute saving the cases of arrest and reversal of judgments, of judgments upon plea in abatement and upon demurrers, &c. *Ten Eyck v. Wing*, 1 Mich., 40.

2232. Suit being commenced in justice's Court, the plaintiff employed an attorney to appear and prosecute the suit for him on the return day. The attorney was prevented from attending to the suit on that day, and requested another to appear, who did so, but his authority being required, he was not able to prove it, and the action failed. It was held that these facts did not make out a case within the clause allowing a new action within one year where "in any action duly commenced," &c., "the suit shall fail of a sufficient return, by any unavoidable accident, or by any neglect or default of the officer to whom it is committed, or if the writ shall be abated, or the action otherwise avoided or defeated, by the death of any party thereto, or for any mater of form; or if, after verdict for the plaintiff, the judgment shall be arrested, or if a judgment for the plaintiff shall be reversed on writ of error." R. S. 1838, pt. 3, tit. 6, ch. 2, § 11. *Spier v. McQueen*, 1 Mich., 252.

2233. The term "persons beyond seas," in the statute of 1820—Code of 1833, p. 569—meant *persons out of the State. Hulburt v. Merriam*, 3 Mich. 144.

2234. Said statute of 1820, limited the time for bringing ejectment, for causes of action thereafter accruing, to twenty years. An act of 1829—Code 1833, p. 408—limited the period to ten years, where the cause of action *had then accrued.* The Statutes of 1838 repealed these acts, and substituted a new limitation of twenty years, with a proviso, however, that causes of action already accrued should not be affected, but be determined by the law under which the same *accrued.* In ejectment commenced in 1840, for a cause of action which accrued in 1822, it was held, in view of the various provisions of the Statutes of 1838 relating to the same subject, that the action was barred by the act of 1829. *Lastly v. Cramer*, 2 Doug., 307. And see *Hulburt v. Merriam*, 3 Mich., 144.

2235. Defendant went into actual possession of lands, under a tax title, in August, 1842, and by the act of February 17, 1842—Laws of 1842, p. 133—the time for bringing action of ejectment in such case was limited to ten years. This act was repealed by the Revised Statutes of 1846, but it was held that § 9 of chap. 139 of those Statutes continued it in force as to all rights of action which had accrued under it, and that an action commenced more than ten years from the time defendant entered into possession, was barred. *Perry v. Hepburne*, 4 Mich., 165.

LOG DRIVING AND BOOMING COMPANIES.

2236. Constitutionality. The act for the formation of Log Driving and Booming Companies—Comp. L., ch. 66—in so far as it provided for the formation of companies, and their power to make contracts, was constitutional and valid. *Ames v. Port Huron Log Driving and Booming Co.*, 6 Mich., 266. [See supra, 622, 623, 625.]

2237. Organization. The affidavit of organization, to be made by two directors under section two of said act, is sufficient if made strictly according to the terms of said section; and it need not contain any detailed statement of the proceedings had in the formation of the company, *Ibid.*

2238. Contract with. The delivery by a person of a list of his log marks to a company formed under said act, does not operate as a contract for the receiving by the company of all logs so marked that he may have upon the stream within the limits of the company's operations. The object of the provision requiring such list was to entitle the person furnishing it to notice of sale in case, by any casualty, his logs should become so placed as to authorize the company to assume their management. *Ibid.*

2239. In the absence of any contract, such company was only authorized, by the sixth section of said act, to assume control of the logs of others, and acquire a lien for services in respect thereto, where, by reason of the logs having been put into the stream without adequate provision for running them without obstruction, some obstruction had actually been created. *Ibid.*

See a new statute for the formation of such companies, *Laws of* 1864, *p.* 23.

MANDAMUS.

2240. When will be issued. The writ of mandamus is only issued where there is a clear legal right, and the party has no other remedy. *People v. Judges of Branch Circuit Court*, 1 Doug., 319.

2241. Mandamus to compel the Circuit Court to quash an attachment, where the original affidavit was void, and a new one had been alllowed to be filed in its stead, was refused. The proper remedy is by certiorari. *Ibid.*

2242. Mandamus will not be granted to compel the Circuit Court to set aside defective proceedings, when the defects are such as may be obviated by amendment in that Court. *People v. Judges of Calhoun Circuit Court*, 1 Doug., 417.

2243. Mandamus is the proper remedy of the party seeking the reversal of a decision of the Circuit Court on a motion to strike a declaration from the files in a common law action. The motion and decision would constitute no part of a common law record, and exceptions could not be alleged to the decision. *People v. Judges of Washtenaw Circuit Court*, 1 Doug., 434.

2244. Mandamus may be granted to compel the board of auditors of Wayne county to deliver their warrant on the county treasurer to the person in whose favor an account has been allowed. And it is no answer to the application that such a warrant was made out, but before delivery, was taken on execution against the payee, and the money received thereon by the officer from the county treasurer—such a warrant not being the subject of levy on execution. *People v. Auditors of Wayne County*, 5 Mich., 223.

2245. Where after the division of a township, the township boards have met and determined the amount of indebtedness to be paid by the new township, such amount is a fixed and liquidated demand against such new township, which it is the duty of its township board to allow, and to issue an order on the township treasurer for; and if the board refuse, the remedy is by mandamus, and not by action against the township. *Marathon v. Oregon*, 8 Mich., 372.

2246. Its office. A mandamus is allowed only to set the inferior jurisdiction in motion; but not for the purpose of requiring it to come to any particular conclusion, or of retracing its steps where it has already acted; and this notwithstanding the party has no other remedy. *People v. Judge of Wayne County Court*, 1 Mich., 359; *People v. Inspectors and Agent of State Prison*, 4 Mich., 187.

2247. The writ is granted to compel the performance of a ministerial act, but not to inquire into the proper exercise of judicial discretion. *People v. Auditor General*, 3 Mich., 427.

2248. Though generally used to enforce the performance of public rights and duties, it may also be resorted to for the enforcement of private rights, when withheld by public officers. *People v. Supervisors of Macomb*, 3 Mich., 475.

2249. A private citizen cannot, in a matter where he is not directly injured, apply for a mandamus to compel the performance of an omitted duty by a public board; though cases might arise where the Court would permit it, in the absence of the Attorney General or prosecuting attorney, or his refusal without good cause to act. *People v. Regents of the University*, 4 Mich., 98. See also, *People v. Inspectors and Agent of State Prison*, 4 Mich., 187.

2250. A corporator may apply for the writ, to compel the custodian of the corporate records and documents to allow him an inspection of them. But he must show that he has made a proper demand for such inspection, at a proper time and place, and for a proper reason. The writ will not be granted to enable a corporator to gratify idle curiosity. *People v. Walker*, 9 Mich., 328.

2251. Where, therefore, a corporator demanded of the secretary of the corporation an inspection of its books, records and papers, and the demand was not shown to have been made at the office of the corporation, and no excuse was given for not making it there; and the only ground stated for the application was, that the corporator had a desire "to ascertain the rights, duties, privileges and liabilities, and for the protection" of the corporator, the writ was refused. *Ibid.*

2252. Practice. The writ will not be granted where the application is for something different from that for which the party has laid the foundation. The refusal of the Circuit Court to grant a motion for an assessment of damages in replevin, is not a proper foundation for an application to the Supreme Court for a mandamus commanding the Circuit Court to impanel a jury to assess the *value of the property* replevied. *People v. Judges of Jackson Circuit Court*, 1 Doug., 302.

2253. On a motion for a peremptory mandamus, the Court will not allow the relator to amend his order on the respondent to show cause, where it is too broad and asks more than he is entitled to, so as to include that only to which he is entitled. *People v. Township Board of La Grange*, 2 Mich., 187.

2254. An order to show cause why a peremptory mandamus should not issue, has, in the Supreme Court, been uniformly substituted for an alternative mandamus. *Ibid.*

2255. An alternative mandamus is answered by a return, which is in the nature and performs the office of a plea; while the order to show cause is answered by affidavit. *Ibid.*

2256. Costs on granting a mandamus denied, where the defendants were a public body, and it did not appear that they had acted in bad faith. *People v. Auditors of Wayne County*, 5 Mich., 223.

MARITIME LAW.

2257. General average. The steamer Missouri, being a new and seaworthy boat, and having on board passengers and a cargo of goods, on a voyage from Buffalo to Chicago, encountered a very severe gale on Lake Huron. She was in great danger of perishing from the violence of the winds and the roughness of the waves. After long struggling with the tempest, the master and crew agreed that it was necessary to lighten her, in order to save her with the freight and passengers. Accordingly a quantity of goods were, for that purpose, thrown overboard by the crew. The boat was saved, though much injured, and returned to Detroit with the residue of her cargo. Held, that these facts would constitute a proper case, under the maritime law, for general average. *Rossiter v. Chester*, 1 Doug., 154.

2258. The doctrine of general average is known only to the maritime law, and cannot be enforced in a Court of common law jurisdiction. *Ibid.*

2259. Pro rata freight. Freight *pro rata itineris* is due when the ship, by inevitable necessity, is forced into a port short of her destination, and is unable to prosecute her voyage, and the goods are there voluntarily accepted by the owner. *Ibid.*

2260. The owner of goods was deemed to have voluntarily accepted them at the intermediate port when, knowing that the voyage had been abandoned, its further prosecution having become impossible, or extremely hazardous, he there demanded his goods of the agent of the forwarders, with whom they were stored, tendering payment of their charges for storage, and brought replevin to recover possession on the refusal of such agents to deliver them. *Ibid.*

2261. Jurisdiction over the lakes. The great lakes of this country held not subject to admiralty jurisdiction, which was said to be restricted to the open sea, and to waters navigable therefrom as far as the tide ebbs and flows. *Ibid.* See supra, 78 to 86.

2262. Collision. In cases of collision the burden of proof is on the plaintiff, not only to show negligence on the part of the defendant, but ordinary care on his own part. *Drew v. Steamboat Chesapeake*, 2 Doug., 33.

2263. A general custom of navigation—as, for example, for vessels to pass each other to the left—may be proved by the testimony of persons skilled in navigation. Such custom is a part of the law of the land; and a departure from it occasioning collision, will render the party liable, unless the other party, by reasonable effort, might have prevented it; and each party should act upon the presumption that the other party will adhere to the custom. *Ibid.*

MECHANIC'S LIEN.

2264. To what it attaches. The lien (under Code of 1833, p. 406), of a mechanic or material man, for labor done or materials furnished in the construction of a building, attached only upon the interest of the person for whom it was erected ; and did not incumber any pre-existing right or title of any other person. *Scales v. Griffin*, 2 Doug., 54.

2265. If, therefore, when the lien attached, the person causing the building to be erected had no title to the premises on which it stood, but a mere right resting in contract, to a conveyance on the performance of a condition precedent, and that right was afterwards lost by his failure to perform the condition, subsequent proceedings to enforce the lien would convey no right or title to the purchaser. *Ibid.*

2266. When it will not attach. A builder's lien, under the statute—Comp. L., Ch. 154—will not exist where the agreement itself provides that the contract price shall be secured by mortgage on the premises built upon. *Barrows v. Baughman*, 9 Mich., 213.

2267. A tender, sufficient in amount, will discharge a mechanic's lien for the repair of personal property; and, if not accepted, the creditor must thereafter rely upon the personal responsibility of his employer. *Moynahan v. Moore*, 9 Mich., 9.

MICHIGAN CENTRAL RAILROAD COMPANY.

2268. It is provided by section five of the charter of the Michigan Central Railroad Company—Laws 1846, p. 43—that no railroad or railroads from the eastern or southern boundary of the State shall be built, constructed or maintained, or shall be authorized to be built, constructed or maintained, by or under any law of this State, any portion of which shall approach, westwardly of Wayne county, within five miles of the line of said railroad, as designated in said act, without the consent of said company ; and that no railroad or railroads shall be authorized or constructed, which shall commence within twenty miles of the city of Detroit, and extend to lake Michigan, or the southern boundary of the State, the line of which shall, on an average, run within twenty miles of the main line of said Michigan Central Railroad : *Provided*, that said section shall not be construed to restrict or prevent the construction of public roads, or canals, or railroads, or private ways, under, above or across the road of said company, when deemed expedient ; but so as not unnecessarily to obstruct the same. It was held, that the prohibition contained in said section did not prevent the Michigan Southern Railroad Company from completing the construction of the Tecumseh branch of their road, from its junction with their main line to Jackson on the line of the Michigan Central Railroad Company. *Michigan Central R. R. Company v. Michigan Southern R. R. Co.*, 4 Mich., 361.

2269. For construction of the 16th section of the charter, see *Michigan Central Railroad Co. v. Hale*, 6 Mich., 243, overruling *M. C. R. Co. v. Ward*, 2 Mich., 538. And see supra, 487 to 494.

MICHIGAN SOUTHERN RAILROAD COMPANY.

2270. Right to land for their route. Certain lands lying east of the village of Hillsdale, were, in the year 1838, taken and appropriated by the State for the use of the Michigan Southern Railroad, which was completed and brought into use over said lands in 1844; and in 1846 all the right, title and interest of the State, in the railroad, was transferred to the Michigan Southern Railroad Company. It was held that under the law of 1838, providing for the acquisition of lands for the purposes of railroads, and the settlement of claims for the appropriation of property for such uses, the lands in question vested in the State, whether the claim for damages for their appropriation had been adjudicated upon and satisfied or not; that the transfer of the road by the State to the company imposed upon the latter no obligation to pay said damages, and that the company took such lands, relieved of any claim or lien for such claim. *People & Michigan Southern Railroad Company* 3 Mich., 496; *Smith v. McAdam*, 3 Mich., 506.

2271. Taxation. Under the charter of said company—which subjects the company to an annual tax of three-fouths of one per cent. upon its capital stock paid in, including the $500,000 purchase money, and also upon all loans made to the company for the purpose of constructing their road, or purchasing, constructing, chartering or hiring of steamboats authorized by the charter—the company cannot claim exemption from taxation on sums of money paid out for commissions and other expenses attending the sale of its bonds and the obtaining of loans. *Michigan Southern and Northern Indiana Railroad Co. v. The Auditor-General*, 9 Mich., 448.

2272. Nor can the company claim exemption from taxation upon any sum of money borrowed by it, and afterwards loaned upon worthless securities, whereby it became lost to the company. *Ibid.*

2273. Whether a deduction from the taxable amount should be made of bonds of the company which were loaned, and for which worthless securities were subsequently taken in payment, *quere.* Held in 4 Mich. 398, that it should not. In 9 Mich. 448 the Court was equally divided on the question.

2274. Whether the amount of the bonds of the company issued for loans, is to be taken as the amount of its loans, for the purposes of taxation, or whether from this amount should be deducted the discount allowed on the sale of the bonds, *quere*. Held in 4 Mich. 398 that the discount should not be deducted. In 9 Mich. 448 the Court was equally divided on the question.

2275. No deduction should be made for the 3,000 shares of capital stock alleged by the company to have been distributed as a bonus among the original stockholders without any consideration being received therefor ;—the allegation not being sustained by the facts in the case. 4 *Mich.*, 398 ; 9 *Mich.*, 448.

2276. The act authorizing the consolidation of said company with the Northern Indiana Railroad Company provides that said corporation shall continue subject to the same rate of tax as though such consolidation should not take place ; and the amount of its capital and loans thereafter, upon which such taxation should be paid, should be such portion of its capital and loans as is actually employed in the State of Michigan. It was held, that the act of consolidation was not designed to change the principle of taxation fixed by the original charter of the Michigan company, but that all the stock and loans formerly taxable were to continue taxable without diminution by losses or unproductiveness. And that, therefore, no deduction can be made from the amount taxable for the cost of steamboats destroyed by accident, or lying idle within the limits of another State, and taxable there. The term " actually employed in the State of Michigan," in the act of consolidation, has no reference to the actual use of the property purchased by the company, but is merely designed to distinguish the Michigan investment from the Indiana investment. 9 *Mich.*, 448.

MILLERS AND MILL OWNERS.

2277. The statute regulating the duties of millers and mill owners —Comp. L., § 1333 et seq.—is meant to apply to such mills only as are in the habit of grinding for toll. *Merrill v. Cahill*, 8 Mich., 55.

2278. Under this statute, millers who hold themselves out to the community as millers grinding for the public generally, are bound to a similar impartiality to that required of common carriers, innkeepers, and those following such public avocations. And it is as clearly their duty to receive grain, when the mill is running, as to grind it when received. *Ibid.*

2279. The conversation between the person bringing grain to the mill to be ground, and the agent of the owner, who, under the owner's direction, refuses to receive the grain, is competent evidence, as part of the *res gestæ*, in a suit against the owner, under the statute, for such refusal. *Ibid.*

2280. Where two or more persons own and run such a mill, they are all liable for a refusal to receive grain brought to be ground, whether the refusal comes from one or all such owners, or from the agent in charge. *Ibid.*

MORTGAGE OF CHATTELS.

2281. Is a transfer of title. By a mortgage of chattels the legal title to the property mortgaged passes to the mortgagee upon condition; and upon breach of condition this title becomes absolute. *Tannahill v. Tuttle*, 3 Mich., 104.

2282. Right of possession. The general title being in the mortgagee, he is entitled to immediate possession, to hold until condition performed, unless the parties otherwise stipulate. *Ibid.*

2283. If the mortgagor is suffered to retain possession, such possession is, in law, the possession of the mortgagee, who may maintain trespass, trover or replevin for any intermeddling with the property by a third party; and this right of action exists where the property is taken by an officer under color of legal process against the mortgagor. *Ibid.*

2284. Levy on mortgaged property. The mortgagor's interest in the property cannot be seized and sold on execution, before condition broken, unless he is entitled to possession for some definite period, under an agreement to that effect with the mortgagee; nor then if that period has elapsed. *Ibid.* *Eggleston v. Mundy*, 4 Mich., 295; *Bacon v. Kimmell*, 14 Mich.

2285. Nor can it be seized and sold after condition broken. The statute—Comp. L., § 4461—does not authorize such levy and sale, either before or after condition broken, where no right of possession was reserved to the mortgagor. *Tannahill v. Tuttle*, 3 Mich., 104.

2286. A clause in a mortgage providing that if the mortgagor should sell, assign or dispose of the property, or attempt to do so, or to remove the same from the township, without the written assent of the mortgagee, the latter might enter upon the premises of the mortgagor, or any other place where the property might be, and take possession of, and sell and dispose of the same—is neither an express nor an implied covenant for possession by the mortgagor, so as to subject the property to levy and sale on execution against him. *Eggleston v. Mundy*, 4 Mich., 295.

2287. Where the officer levied upon the property, and offered the same for sale, but being informed of the mortgage, changed his offer to a sale of the mortgagor's *interest*, and made return that he had levied upon the property and sold *all the debtor's right therein*, which was bid off by a third party; it was held that the sale so made protected neither the officer nor the purchaser from liability to the mortgagee. *Ibid.*

2288. Consideration. As between the parties to it and their representatives, in a controversy respecting the property, the mortgage is sufficient evidence of consideration. *Webb v. Mann*, 3 Mich., 139.

2289. What is not a mortgage. A writing given by a debtor to his surety for the debt, providing that on failure of the debtor to pay the debt within thirty days, the surety may take immediate possession of the goods, &c., in possession of the debtor, in the store and premises occupied by him, and sell so much as will pay the debt, and a reasonable compensation for his services, and re-deliver the balance to the debtor—is not a mortgage, for it does not purport to change, in any way, the title to the property. It is a mere naked power, giving no right in the property itself until reduced to possession. *Holmes v. Hall*, 8 Mich., 66.

2290. What is. A debtor assigned to his creditor certain shares of railroad stock, and at the same time gave a note for the debt, reciting therein that if the said debt and interest is not paid at maturity, the railroad stock "hereby assigned to secure the payment aforesaid is to be deemed and taken as forfeit for the above payment." This constituted in legal effect a chattel mortgage of the stock, under which the holder of the note was entitled to possession of the stock certificates. *Davis v. Rider*, 5 Mich., 423.

2291. A partner may give a mortgage on the co-partnership property. It is not necessary that it be under seal, but if a seal be affixed, it is a nullity, and will not vitiate the mortgage. *Sweetzer v. Mead*, 5 Mich., 107.

2292. Description. A chattel mortgage given by a merchant of "goods in [his] store," will not be held, under these words, to include a safe kept in his store, not for sale, but for his own private use. *Curtis v. Phillips*, 5 Mich., 112.

2293. As against others than the parties to the mortgage, "one sorrel horse" is not a sufficient description under the Canada statute, which requires that a mortgage of chattels "shall contain such efficient and full description thereof that the same may be thereby readily and easily known and distinguished." *Montgomery v. Wight*, 8 Mich., 143.

2294. Notice and record of mortgage. Notice of the existence of an unpaid prior mortgage of personal property destroys the preference which a second mortgagee might otherwise be entitled to claim in consequence of the omission of the first mortgagee to refile his mortgage within a period prescribed for that purpose by statute. *Wetherell v. Spencer*, 3 Mich., 123.

2295. The second mortgagee, having notice of the existence of the prior mortgage at the time of taking his own, is not a subsequent mortgagee *in good faith*, within the meaning of the statute. *Wetherell v. Spencer*, 3 Mich., 123 ; *Doyle v. Stevens*, 4 Mich., 87.

2296. The notice must be so clear and distinct as to render it bad faith in the second mortgagee to insist upon his mortgage in preference to the former. *Doyle v. Stevens*, 4 Mich., 87.

2297. Being notified of a prior mortgage at the time of taking a conveyance of or lien upon the property, the subsequent purchaser is put upon inquiry as to the extent of the prior mortgage, and takes subject to its amount. *Ibid.*

2298. One having a chattel mortgage on file in the city clerk's office, took it away for a few days, and without his knowledge the clerk made an entry in the file book that the mortgage had been delivered to the mortgagee. It was held, that this entry was unofficial, and did not enable one who had bought the mortgaged property to hold it as against the mortgage, which had been returned to the files before his purchase had been made. *Woodruff v. Phillips*, 10 Mich., 500.

2299. A chattel mortgage properly filed is a public record, and belongs to the office ; and the clerk has no right to deliver it to the mortgagee to be taken away. If allowed to be taken from the files and afterwards returned, no second indorsement of the filing by the clerk is necessary to make it notice thereafter under the statute. *Ibid.*

2300. A chattel mortgage was given in evidence which purported to be given to secure a certain promissory note. A note of the description was not produced, but one of a different date was offered as the one designed to be secured. It was held that the filing of the mortgage was not notice of any other claim than the one described in it. *Hinchman v. Town*, 10 Mich., 508.

2301. Tender and payment. A tender of the amount due at maturity discharges the lien of the mortgage ; and if the mortgagee refuses to receive it and deliver up the property, he cannot have the amount of his debt allowed, by way of recoupment or otherwise, in an action of trover brought by the mortgagor to recover the value of the property. *Fuller v. Parish*, 3 Mich., 211. See also, *Moynahan v. Moore*, 9 Mich., 9.

2302. Where one holding property in mortgage converts it to his own use, the mortgage debt is thereby satisfied to the extent only of the value of the property. *Davis v. Rider*, 5 Mich., 423.

2303. Where a chattel mortgage was assigned by the mortgagee as collateral security for a debt, it was held that an appropriation by the assignee of sufficient of the property to satisfy the debt, would extinguish his interest in the property, and the residuum of the mortgage interest, if any, would revert to the mortgagee. *Place v. Grant*, 9 Mich., 42.

2304. Effect of suit on demand. The commencement of a suit upon a promissory note does not extinguish the lien of a chattel mortgage collateral to the note. *Thurber v. Jewett*, 3 Mich., 295. But it is a waiver of the forfeiture of the condition of the mortgage. *Ibid.*

2305. Redemption after forfeiture. A mortgagor of chattels, notwithstanding the forfeiture of the condition of the mortgage, may redeem in equity at any time before the mortgagee has foreclosed, by a reduction of the property into possession, or by a sale pursuant to the power conferred by the mortgage. *Van Brunt v. Wakelee*, 11 Mich., 177. See on the same subject, *Tannahill v. Tuttle*, 3 Mich., 104.

2306. Illegal conditions. A chattel mortgage of a stock of goods, which leaves the mortgagor in possession, and by inference authorizes him to sell in the usual course of business, is good between the parties, and not necessarily fraudulent as to creditors. *Gay v. Bidwell*, 7 Mich., 519.

2306*a*. Being good between the parties, such a mortgage could not be fraudulent on its face as against creditors, since it would not show that there are any creditors, or, if it did, it would not appear but that they had assented to it, or were themselves sufficiently secured. *Ibid.*

2306*b*. A creditor who does not show that he was such at the time of the giving of such a mortgage, is not in a position to attack it as fraudulent, on the ground that it allows the mortgagor to remain in possession and dispose of the mortgaged property. *Ibid.*

2307. Where it was shown that the mortgagee of a stock of goods left the same in the hands of the mortgagor, with power to sell and dispose of the same in the usual course of business, for cash or upon credit, and the mortgagor applied the proceeds of sales in the purchase of other goods to keep up the stock, in the support of himself, and in paying other debts than that secured by the mortgage — the mortgagee not asserting a right to the possession of the property, or the specific proceeds of the sales thereof, or preventing or prohibiting such sales—these facts do not render the mortgage absolutely void in law as against the creditors of the mortgagor; but the question of fraud is for the jury. *Oliver v. Eaton*, 7 Mich., 108.

MORTGAGE OF LANDS.

2308. A deed absolute on its face, given by a debtor to his creditor, may in equity be shown by parol to have been given to secure the payment of the debt ; and when that fact appears, it will be held to be only a mortgage. *Wadsworth v. Loranger*, Har. Ch., 113 ; *Emerson v. Atwater*, 7 Mich., 12.

2309. One who takes the land with knowledge of the purpose for which the deed was given, holds it subject to the debtor's right to redeem. *Ibid.*

2310. Mortgage or trust. A. conveyed a farm to B., his son-in-law, in consideration of $2,500. By the same instrument, B. bound himself to pay the debts of A., especially a mortgage on the farm, and to account to A. for the balance of the $2,500, after paying the debts ; and B. promised and obligated himself, besides the payment of the $2,500, to board, lodge and clothe A., in health and in sickness, during his natural life, &c., and A. reserved to himself the right to live with B.; and for the security of the payment of the $2,500, and the fulfilling the "clauses and conditions" above stated, B. was not to give, alien, exchange or sell the farm without permission of A., and the farm was to stand hypothecated until the payment in full of the $2,500, when A. was to " release the present mortgage in a legal manner." Held not to be a deed of trust, or a deed upon condition ; but an absoute deed, incorporating within it a lien in the nature of a mortgage. *Campau v. Chene*, 1 Mich., 400.

2311. Where a judgment debtor gave to the attorney of the creditor a deed of lands, authorizing him to sell and dispose of them, and apply the money in payment of the judgment, and to execute and deliver to the purchaser a deed, provided the judgment was not paid in six months from that time ; and the judgment not being paid, the attorney caused the lands to be sold at public auction, and they were struck off to the creditor, who was the highest bidder ; it was held that the deed was a mortgage, and the right of redemption could not be barred except by foreclosure, either at law or in equity. *Comstock v. Howard*, Wal. Ch., 110.

2312. Equitable mortgage. An agreement in writing, intended by the parties to give a lien on real estate for the payment of a debt, though not witnessed as required by statute to convey real estate, is good as an equitable mortgage. *Abbott v. Godfroy's heirs*, 1 Mich., 178.

2313. In form of contract of purchase. Where A., being indebted to B. in the sum of $2,000, secured on real estate, conveyed to him the same real estate, and took back a contract for the purchase of it from B. for $2,000, payable as therein specified, which contract provided that " time is now, and shall be at all times, considered and deemed a material part of this contract ;" and that on default being made by A. in any of its conditions to be performed by him, he should thereupon forfeit all rights under the same, and be thereafter a tenant at will to B. at a specified yearly rent; and it appeared that the transaction was intended merely to secure B. the $2,000 due him: Held to be a mortgage; and that A. did not forfeit his right to redeem by a failure to pay at the times specified. *Batty v. Snook*, 5 Mich., 231. And see to the same effect, *Enos v. Sutherland*, 11 Mich., 538.

2314. If the creditor, in such a case, conveys the land to a bona fide purchaser, he must account to the debtor for its value at the time of the sale, whether he received that amount or not. *Enos v. Sutherland*, 11 Mich., 538.

2315. Where a contract is thus given, which is really an instrument of defeasance, it is not essential that it be sealed. *Ibid.*

2316. In doubtful cases, Courts of equity incline to construe a deed with a condition to be a mortgage; and may do so where a deed and bond to convey are concurrent instruments, in the absence of facts showing the intention of the parties to be otherwise. *Swetland v. Swetland*, 3 Mich., 482.

2317. To render a conveyance absolute in its terms a mortgage, it must be so in its inception. It can never become a mortgage by any subsequent act; and if it once becomes an absolute deed for a moment, it must always remain so. *Ibid.*

2318. Where it appears that, by express agreement of the parties, a debt due from the grantor to the grantee was extinguished by the deed, or that the money paid was not advanced by way of loan, or that it is at the option of the grantor to refund or to keep the money, the transaction is a conditional sale and not a mortgage. But if the remedies of grantor and grantee are reciprocal—the former bound to repay the money, the latter to reconvey the premises—then the deed will be construed a mortgage. *Ibid.*

2319. Nature of a mortgage. A mortgage is no longer, in this State, what it was originally at the common law—a grant of the land to the mortgagee, defeasible upon condition subsequent, and to become absolute on failure to pay at the specified time. It is but a security for the debt. The estate in the land is still in the mortgagor: and payment at any time before a foreclosure becomes absolute, with the legal costs, if any, will discharge the mortgage, and no reconveyance is necessary. *Caruthers v. Humphrey*, 12 Mich., 270; *Van Husan v. Kanouse*, 13 Mich., 303. And see *Ladue v. Detroit and Milwaukee Railroad Co.*, 13 Mich., 380.

2320. Mortgage of a mortgage. Where the owner of a mortgage on which nothing was to become due for several years, assigned the mortgage to secure a debt of his own to an amount less than the mortgage, and the assignment was upon condition that if the assignor should pay his indebtedness to the assignee on or before the first day of May following, then the assignment was to be void, but if not, and the assignee should collect the moneys, he should, after retaining the amount of his debt, interest and charges, pay over the surplus to the assignor; held,

1. That this was a mortgage of the mortgage.

2. That the assignor, or those claiming under him, would be entitled to this surplus from the assignee or any person claiming through him, at whatever period in the future it might be collected.

3. That, the mortgage itself being executed prior to the statute abolishing ejectment by mortgagees, the assignor's right to redeem must be placed upon the same footing as that of a mortgagor of real estate.

4. That where a subsequent assignee of the mortgage took a deed of the mortgaged premises from the original mortgagor to himself, this deed had the effect to foreclose the mortgage as to the mortgagor so deeding; that the land now represented the mortgage, and the mortgagor of the mortgage, or one claiming under him, might file his bill in chancery and have decree that the amount of the mortgage, less the sum it was assigned to secure, be paid to him, and in default thereof the premises be sold to satisfy, first the sum the mortgage was assigned to secure, and next, to pay him the amount of the mortgage less such sum.

5. And such bill being filed, and it appearing that possesion had been taken under such deed, and complainant having been remiss in asserting his rights, whereby he might have induced defendants to treat the property as their own, discharged of the lien of the mortgage, he was held not entitled to an account of the rents and profits of the premises as against defendants. *Graydon v. Church*, 7 Mich., 36.

2321. Consideration. Foreclosure by assignee. The mortgagee was sworn as a witness, and testified that the mortgage was made to him, and assigned to complainant at the request of one of the mortgagors, without any consideration moving from or to him for the mortgage or assignment. Held, that this evidence cast upon complainant the burden of proof to show a consideration for the mortgage. *Bishop v. Felch*, 7 Mich., 371.

2322. A mortgage was given to secure the payment of judgments confessed by the mortgagor, but which were void for want of compliance with the statute. Bill being filed to foreclose, and no proof made of any indebtedness, the bill was dismissed. *Austin v. Grant*, 1 Mich., 490.

2323. Bill to foreclose a mortgage conditioned for the payment of a certain sum of money. Held competent to show in defense, by parol evidence, that the mortgage was given to indemnify sureties in a recognizance of bail, and that the liability of the sureties had been discharged without their being damnified. *Colman v. Post*, 10 Mich., 422.

2324. Alternative condition. J. gave a mortgage for $10,000, payable in several instalments. As further security for the first four instalments, he gave a second mortgage on other premises, conditioned to pay said four instalments as they fell due. The second mortgage also contained a stipulation that whenever J. should build on the premises covered by the first mortgage, and cause the buildings to be insured for $2,000, and assign the policy to the mortgagee, and agree to keep the same so insured during the continuance of the first mortgage, then the mortgagee should discharge the second mortgage. J. built on the premises covered by the first mortgage, and caused the buildings to be insured, but did not assign the policy. The said four instalments of the first mortgage having become due, and three of them remaining unpaid, a bill was filed to foreclose the two mortgages. J. (who had become insolvent) now tendered an assignment of the policy of insurance, together with a written agreement to keep the buildings insured, which the holder of the mortgages declined to receive, It was held, that under the second mortgage J. had his election, to pay the said four instalments as they fell due, or to perform the stipulation therein with respect to building and insuring; that his right to elect terminated when the moneys fell due, and he had no right thereafter to a discharge of the second mortgage on tendering the policy of insurance and agreement to keep insured. *Chapin v. Jacobs*, 10 Mich., 405.

2325. Conditioned for support: who may foreclose. A mortgage conditioned for the support of the mortgagee by the mortgagor, during her lifetime, cannot be foreclosed for the benefit of persons who had boarded the mortgagee at the request of the mortgagor. Such a mortgage is for the benefit of the mortgagee, and not for the benefit of those who may, at the request of the mortgagor, furnish her with support. *Daniels v. Eisenlord*, 10 Mich., 454.

2326. Ambiguous condition. Where there was some doubt whether a mortgage was, by its condition, payable in work or in money, it was held to be the duty of the Court to construe it most strongly against the mortgagor, and in such manner as to make it a valid and binding security which might be enforced against him. *Jerome v. Hopkins*, 2 Mich., 96.

2327. Indemnity. Where a mortgage is conditioned to indemnify a surety, the mortgagee cannot foreclose until he has been damnified. *Thurston v. Prentiss*, Wal. Ch., 529.

2328. But where it is conditioned to *pay* the demand, as well as to save the surety harmless, the mortgagee may foreclose on failure of the mortgagor to pay, in order to raise the money to pay the demand, and rid himself of responsibility. *Thurston v. Prentiss*, 1 Mich., 193. And see *Dye v. Mann*, 10 Mich., 291; *Butler v. Ladue*, 12 Mich., 173.

2329. A condition in a mortgage that the mortgagor "shall promptly pay and discharge all notes and papers of his upon which the mortgagees shall become indorsers or acceptors, together with all the interest, cost and charges accruing thereon, so as to save said mortgagees harmless by reason of their connection with such paper," is broken at once on a failure to pay the paper at maturity, and a right to foreclose accrues, without further action of the mortgagees. *Butler v. Ladue*, 12 Mich., 173.

2330. In a mortgage with the condition above set forth, the power of sale was limited to the case of the mortgagees being damnified by paying the debts. It was held that the power of sale need not be co-extensive with the condition of the mortgage, and that the remedy in equity was open for every breach of the condition, whether the parties had seen fit to provide for such a breach in the power of sale or not. *Ibid.*

2331. For future advances or liabilities. Where a mortgage is given to secure the mortgagee for liabilities which it is optional with him to incur or not, such mortgage is at any time a lien upon the land only to the extent of the liabilities then actually incurred; and a deed given by the mortgagor and placed upon record will take precedence of the mortgage as to liabilities subsequently incurred. *Ladue v. Detroit and Milwaukee Railroad Co.*, 13 Mich., 380.

2332. The mortgage being duly recorded is notice to a subsequent purchaser; but he is chargable with notice only to the extent of the liabilities which had been actually incurred prior to his purchase. *Ibid.*

2333. For excessive amount. Where, in a conditional pardon, the person pardoned was required to secure the payment of $1,000 to the county, and the county commissioners obtained a mortgage for $1,150, the mortgage was held good for $1,000, and void as to the residue. *Rood v. Winslow*, Wal. Ch., 340, and 2 Doug.. 68.

2334. For indefinite amount. A mortgage given to secure all existing debts of the mortgagor to the mortgagee, is valid without specifying the debts or their amounts. And a subsequent purchaser of the land, with actual or constructive notice of the mortgage, takes subject to it. *Michigan Insurance Co. v. Brown*, 11 Mich., 265.

2335. Attorney's fee in mortgage. A mortgage empowered the mortgagee in the usual manner to sell, "rendering the surplus moneys, if any there be, to the said mortgagor, after deducting the costs and charges of such vendue and sale aforesaid, and also $100 as an attorney's fee, should any proceedings be taken to foreclose this indenture." It was held that this fee was limited to the case of a foreclosure under the power of sale; and could not be recovered on foreclosure in equity. *Sage v. Riggs*, 12 Mich., 313.

2336. Once a mortgage always a mortgage, is a maxim of equity. *Thompson v. Mack*, Har. Ch., 150; *Batty v. Snook*, 5 Mich., 231; *Comstock v. Howard*, Wal. Ch., 110.

2337. A mortgagor may release to the mortgagee the equity of redemption for a valuable consideration, when it is done voluntarily, and there is no fraud, and no undue influence is brought to bear upon him for that purpose by the creditor; but this cannot be done by an executory contract, by which the equity of redemption is to be forfeited if the mortgage debt is not paid by the day stated in such contract. *Batty v. Snook*, 5 Mich., 231.

2338. Right to possession. The mortgagee at the common law is entitled to possession of the land mortgaged, and the Court of Chancery will not prevent him from taking possession, or, if he is in possession, deprive him of it, so long as there is anything due on the mortgage. *Schwarz v. Sears*, Wal. Ch., 170.

2339. The legal title to the lands mortgaged was, at the common law, in the mortgagee, who might, at any time after default, if not before, unless the mortgage should otherwise provide, put the mortgagor out by ejectment. *Stevens v. Brown*, Wal. Ch., 41; *Mundy v. Monroe*, 1 Mich., 68.

2340. But now it is provided by statute that "No action of ejectment shall hereafter be maintained by a mortgagee, or his assigns or representatives, for the recovery of the mortgaged premises, until the title thereto shall have become absolute upon a foreclosure of the mortgage." *Comp. L.*, § 4614. This statute is invalid as applied to mortgages given before its passage. *Mundy v. Monroe*, 1 Mich., 68; *Blackwood v. Van Vleet*, 11 Mich., 252.

2341. The effect of this statute is to take away, not merely the right to bring ejectment, but all right to the possession of the premises until foreclosure. *Baker v. Pierson*, 5 Mich., 456; *Caruthers v. Humphrey*, 12 Mich., 270; *Crippen v. Morrison*, 13 Mich., 23.

2342. The mortgagor now having a legal right to possession until the mortgage is foreclosed, may make any arrangement for the use and enjoyment that any other person might during his term. *Crippen v. Morrison*, 13 Mich., 23.

2343. Tacking. The English doctrine of tacking mortgages has never been adopted in this country. *Wing v. McDowell*, Wal. Ch., 175.

2344. Defeasance: record of. An agreement in the nature of a defeasance is required by statute to be recorded only when it relates to a conveyance which, on its face, purports to be absolute. *Russell v. Waite*, Wal. Ch., 31.

2345. Rights of subsequent mortgagees. Anything done by a first mortgagee to the prejudice of a second, with a knowledge of the second mortgage, should, to the extent of such injury, postpone the first to the second mortgage. *Bailey v. Gould*, Wal. Ch., 478; *James v. Brown*, 11 Mich., 25. See post, 2373, 2374.

2346. But the rule of notice, in such case, is different from the rule equity acts on to protect bona fide purchasers. Where one purchases property which was subject to an equity in the seller's hands, it is enough that he have knowledge of such facts and circumstances indicating the equity as would have led a prudent man to inquire in regard to it, and that he omitted to do so; while in the case of mortgages, the existence of the second mortgage should be clearly brought home to the knowledge of the first mortgagee, in such a way that any act injuriously affecting the interests of the subsequent mortgagee will show an intentional disregard of the interests of such subsequent mortgagee. *James v. Brown*, 11 Mich., 25. And see *Cooper v. Bigley*, 13 Mich., 463.

2347. Notice of a prior incumbrance to charge a subsequent incumbrancer or purchaser, need not come from a party in interest. *Willcox v. Hill*, 11 Mich., 256.

2348. Such notice as men usually act upon in the ordinary affairs of life, is all that can be required. If it is sufficient to direct attention to to the prior right, and to enable its nature to be ascertained by inquiry, it is enough. *Ibid.*

2349. Taxes. Taxes upon mortgaged lands are as much a lien upon the mortgaged interest as upon the equity of redemption; and where one having a second mortgage allows the land to be sold for taxes and obtains a tax deed, he cannot use it adversely to the first mortgage. *Horton v. Ingersoll*, 13 Mich., 409.

2350. Merger. Where one owning the equity of redemption of lands which are subject to two mortgages, buys in the first, and takes an assignment thereof to himself, such mortgage is not thereby merged in the fee. *Dutton v. Ives*, 5 Mich., 515.

2351. The purchase, by a mortgagee, of the equity of redemption will not merge the mortgage, where there are intermediate rights, or the interest of the mortgagee requires that the titles should be kept separate. *Cooper v. Bigley*, 13 Mich., 463.

2352. Assignment. The assignment of a debt secured by a mortgage carries with it the mortgage, as an incident to the debt, although there is no mention made of the mortgage in the assignment. So the assignment of a part of a debt, or of one of several notes, secured by a mortgage, carries with it a proportional interest in the mortgage, unless it is otherwise agreed between the parties at the time. *Cooper v. Ulmann*, Wal. Ch., 251. See also *Martin v. McReynolds*, 6 Mich., 70; *Dougherty v. Randall*, 3 Mich., 581.

2353. Where there are several notes falling due at different times, the fact that one note becomes due first will not, of itself, give it a preference over the rest, where the mortgaged premises are insufficient to pay the whole. But by agreement the assignor may, if he see fit, give it such preference. *Cooper v. Ulmann*, Wal. Ch., 251.

2354. The assignment of a mortgage, without the debt which it is given to secure, carries no beneficial interest in the mortgage to the assignee, who would hold it subject to the will and disposal of the creditor. *Bailey v. Gould*, Wal. Ch., 478.

2355. Void proceedings having been taken to foreclose a mortgage, and the holder of the mortgage having bid in the premises, he afterwards sold them and gave a warranty deed thereof. It was held, that this deed conveyed his mortgage interest in the lands. *Niles v. Ransford*, 1 Mich., 338. See post, 2363.

2356. It is no defense to a bill for foreclosure by the assignee of a mortgage, that the assignment to him was without consideration. The mortgagor has no interest in the question whether the assignment was for or without consideration, except as the want of it may enable him to make available any defense he might have had as against the mortgagee. *Adair v. Adair*, 5 Mich., 204.

2357. Assignment subject to equities. The assignee of a mortgage takes it subject to all equities existing between the parties to it at the time of the assignment. *Russell v. Waite*, Wal. Ch., 31; *Dutton v. Ives*, 5 Mich., 515; *Nichols v. Lee*, 10 Mich., 526; *Bloomer v. Henderson*, 8 Mich., 395.

2358. But if the mortgage is given to secure a negotiable promissory note, and is assigned before the note is due, the assignee is not affected by any equities between the original parties. *Dutton v. Ives*, 5 Mich., 515; *Reeves v. Scully*, Wal. Ch., 248.

2359. Nor does the assignee take the mortgage subject to any equities which any third person may have against the mortgagor. Where he has purchased the mortgage in good faith, it is not subject in his hands to any equities between the mortgagor and his grantor, growing out of the fraud of the mortgagor in procuring the title to the land. *Bloomer v. Henderson*, 8 Mich., 395.

2360. Account by mortgagee in possession. Where the mortgagee has been in possession of the mortgaged premises, and the mortgagor comes with his money to redeem, the mortgagee must account for the profits of the mortgaged premises, of which the crops he may have appropriated or destroyed will be considered a part. *Stevens v. Brown*, Wal. Ch., 41.

2361. Annual rests directed in adjusting accounts, and interest computed on each item of the account, where this course was found to be warranted by the practice of the parties. *Emerson v. Atwater*, 12 Mich., 314.

2362. Foreclosure under power of sale. If irregular, the mortgagee may waive it, and proceed anew in equity. *Atwater v. Kinman*, Har. Ch., 243 ; *Gilbert v. Cooley*, Wal. Ch., 494.

2363. If a sale takes place under irregular proceedings, though it is no bar to the equity of redemption, yet the purchaser at such sale succeeds to all the interest of the mortgagee, and a bill to foreclose the mortgage must be filed by him. *Gilbert v. Cooley*, Wal. Ch., 494. See supra, 2355.

2364. Under the Revised Statutes of 1838—p. 501, Ch. 8—it was held that where a mortgage was foreclosed under the power of sale, for default in the payment of one of several instalments, and the mortgaged premises were bid off for the amount of such instalment only, they were thereby forever disincumbered of the mortgage. *Kimmell v. Willard's Administrators*, 1 Doug., 217. But now it is provided by statute that each instalment " shall be taken and deemed to be an independent mortgage, and such mortgage for each of such instalments may be foreclosed in the same manner, and with the like effect, as if such separate mortgages were given for each of such subsequent instalments," &c. *Comp. L.*, § 5178.

2365. An assignment pending the foreclosure proceedings puts an end to them, and a sale afterwards made under an advertisement in the name of the assignor does not cut off the equity of redemption. *Niles v. Ransford*, 1 Mich., 338.

2366. Under the statute—Comp. L., § 5183, 5187—if the premises consist of several parcels not adjoining each other, the sale of the parcels must be separate, and the deed given in pursuance of the sale must show the price at which each parcel was sold. *Lee v. Mason*, 10 Mich., 403.

2367. Where the deed given on such a sale was for several parcels, for one sum named as the purchase price of all, the foreclosure was held invalid. *Ibid.*

2368. The foreclosure is not void by reason of the sheriff erroneously stating the time of redemption, in his certificate indorsed upon the deed, as one year instead of two. To avoid the foreclosure it must be shown that a tender of the redemption money was actually made within the two years. *Johnstone v. Scott*, 11 Mich., 232.

2369. An affidavit of publication of notice of sale, made between seven and eight years after the sale took place, was held not presumptive evidence of the facts therein stated, under R. S. 1838, p. 501 § 9. *Mundy v. Monroe*, 1 Mich., 68.

2370. Foreclosure in equity: marshalling securities. Upon the foreclosure of a mortgage upon premises which have been conveyed or incumbered in parcels subsequently to the mortgage, the premises should be sold in the inverse order of such conveyances or incumbrances, unless the mortgagee will be prejudiced by having the property so sold. And this rule does not depend upon the existence or non-existence of covenants of warranty. *Cooper v. Bigley*, 13 Mich., 463.

2371. An exception of the mortgage from the covenants of warranty contained in a subsequent deed of the lands, could not affect the grantee's equitable rights in reference to the order of sale of the property covered by said mortgage. *Ibid.*

2372. One who purchases a parcel of land, subject to a mortgage upon that and other property, and with full record notice of a conveyance of the other property, gets no greater rights by virtue of such purchase than his grantor had ; and in a suit for the foreclosure of the prior mortgage, and to marshal the securities, he is not in a position to attack such deed for want of consideration. *Ibid.*

2373. Where two persons have a lien on the same piece of property, which is not sufficient to satisfy both, and one of them has a lien for his debt on another piece of property, he must exhaust the latter before resorting to the common fund. *Trowbridge v. Harleston*, Wal. Ch., 185.

2374. Where A. had a mortgage upon lots one, two and three, and B. had a subsequent mortgage upon lot three, and they, having no knowledge of conveyances which had been made of lots one and two subsequently to their mortgages, conjointly released a part of lot three, it was *held* that B.'s equitable right to have lots one and two first sold was not thereby affected. *Cooper v. Bigley*, 13 Mich., 463.

2375. Effect of decree on defendant's rights. Where one is made defendant in a foreclosure suit, who is holder of both a second mortgage on the lands and a chattel mortgage of fixtures, the decree in the usual form will bar his rights under the mortgage of the lands, but will leave his chattel mortgage unaffected. *Crippen v. Morrison*, 13 Mich., 23.

2376. Surplus moneys on foreclosure. A levy of execution on the mortgaged lands, made at a time when the mortgagor (and judgment debtor) had no title to it, and not followed by any sale by virtue of it, will not entitle the judgment creditor to the surplus moneys after foreclosure, notwithstanding the mortgagor, pending the foreclosure proceedings, became vested with the title to the land subject to the mortgage. *Smith v. Smith*, 13 Mich., 258.

2377. Conveyance by mortgagor subject to mortgage. Where a part of the mortgaged premises has been aliened by the mortgagor, subsequent to the mortgage, the rule in equity, on a foreclosure and sale, is to require that part of the premises in which the mortgagor has not parted with the equity of redemption to be first sold, and then, if necessary, that which has been aliened; and, where the latter is in possession of different vendees, in the inverse order of alienation. *Mason v. Payne*, Wal. Ch., 459. See supra, 2371–2374.

2378. But where a part of mortgaged premises is conveyed by the mortgagor subject to the payment of the whole of the mortgage, that part, as between the vendor and vendee, constitutes the primary fund for its payment. *Ibid.*

2379. Where a lot of land was conveyed by complainant subject to the payment of a mortgage on certain other lands, and proceedings were had in chancery to foreclose the mortgage, and the decree became the property of one of the defendants who also purchased the lot on which payment was charged, it was held that such purchase amounted to a satisfaction of the mortgage to the value of the lot so purchased. *Ibid.*

2380. Where a portion of the land covered by a mortgage is conveyed subject to the payment of the entire mortgage by the grantee, the subsequent purchaser of another parcel has a right to insist that the parcel so before conveyed shall be first sold to satisfy the mortgage, before resort is had to the parcel so purchased by himself. And on bill filed to foreclose the mortgage, he need not file a cross bill to protect this right, but may have the proper decree made by setting out the facts in his answer. *Caruthers v. Hall*, 10 Mich., 40.

2381. The vendee of an equity of redemption stands in the place of the mortgagor, and holds the property subject to all incumbrances; and where there were two mortgages, and the mortgaged premises had been sold on foreclosure at law, on the first mortgage, it was held that the vendee of the equity of redemption could not, by paying the redemption money, and taking an assignment from the purchaser of all his interest in the land, claim the rights of such purchaser for the purpose of defeating the second mortgage. *Johnson v. Johnson*, Wal. Ch., 331.

2382. Tender discharges mortgage. Where a mortgagor, after the mortgage has become due, but before foreclosure, tenders to the holder the full amount due, which the latter refuses to receive, the lien of the mortgage is thereby discharged; and if a bill is afterwards filed by the holder to foreclose, it is not necessary for the mortgagor to bring the tender into Court, or to show that it has been kept good.

Caruthers v. Humphrey, 12 Mich., 270; *Van Husan v. Kanouse*, 13 Mich., 303.

2383. Redemption. If a mortgagor wishes to test in the Court of Chancery the validity of a statutory foreclosure, he must file a bill to redeem. He cannot file a bill to set aside the sale, and have the property resold, although the mortgagee may have abused the power to sell, and purchased the property himself. *Schwarz v. Sears*, Wal. Ch., 170.

2384. A subsequent mortgagee had a right, under the Statutes of 1838—p. 501, § 10—to redeem premises sold on the foreclosure of a prior mortgage. *Kimmell v. Willard's Administrators*, 1 Doug., 217.

2385. Where a subsequent mortgagee pays the redemption money of the mortgaged premises to the purchaser under the foreclosure of a prior mortgage, he does not succeed to the rights of such purchaser, but stands in the place of the prior mortgagee; the only additional right which he acquires being the right to be reimbursed what he has paid, with interest, on foreclosing his own mortgage. *Johnson v. Johnson*, Wal. Ch., 331.

2386. When a mortgagor redeems, it should always be construed as payment; he being personally liable for the debt. But when his vendee redeems, who is not personally liable, and there is an intervening mortgage between the one redeemed by him and his equity of redemption, the same rule should prevail as in case of redemption by a subsequent mortgagee. *Ibid; Webb v. Williams*, Wal. Ch., 544.

2387. The statute of 1840 for the foreclosure of mortgages—Laws of 1840, p. 145—required redemption moneys to be paid to the register of deeds, and to no other person; and it was his duty, upon such payment, to destroy the deed, and pay over the money to the purchaser, his heirs or assigns. *Woodbury v. Lewis*, Wal. Ch., 256.

2388. He had no right to receive in redemption anything but money. A check upon a bank, received by him, was held to be no payment. *Ibid.*

2389. The register's receipt is not conclusive evidence of the payment of the redemption money to him, as against a purchaser. *Ibid.*

2390. A., the holder of the first of five mortgages on a piece of land, took proceedings in chancery to foreclose it, making all the subsequent mortgagees parties except D., the last. Decree for the sale was obtained, and a sale made, at which B., the administrator of C., the second mortgagee, became the purchaser for a few dollars over the amount of the first mortgage. B. bought in his own name, but stated at the time that he bought to protect the interests of the C. estate. He then filed his bill against D., setting up all the facts, and praying that D. be decreed to redeem by paying the amount of both the A. and C. mortgages, and costs, or be foreclosed. D. filed a cross bill, claiming the right to redeem on paying the amount of B.'s bid, with interest. The mortgaged premises were shown to be worth at least the amount of the A. and C. mortgages. Held that D. could not be permitted to redeem without paying the amount of both. *Baker v. Pierson*, 6 Mich., 522.

2391. Payment and satisfaction. Where one holding property in mortgage converts it to his own use, the mortgage debt is thereby satisfied to the extent only of the value of the property. *Davis v. Rider*, 5 Mich., 423. And see, *Place v. Grant*, 9 Mich., 42.

2392. An agreement to discharge a mortgage in consideration of something to which the holder was legally entitled before, is void for want of consideration. *Davis v. Rider*, 5 Mich., 423.

2393. A quit claim deed from the mortgagee to the owner of the equity of redemption, who is liable to pay the mortgage debt, discharges the mortgage. *Jerome v. Seymour*, Har. Ch., 357.

2294. Where one pays a mortgage as the agent and with the funds of the mortgagor, and instead of having it discharged, causes it to be assigned as security for a debt owing by himself, the assignee cannot hold the mortgage as against the mortgagor or his heirs. *Nichols v. Lee*, 10 Mich., 526.

MUNICIPAL CORPORATIONS.

2395. Nuisance by. A municipal corporation which creates a public nuisance, is prima facie liable for its continuance. *Pennoyer v. Saginaw*, 8 Mich., 534.

2396. Injunction against. If Courts of equity have jurisdiction to interfere by injunction, to restrain the action of a municipal corporation, on a bill filed by a tax payer on behalf of himself and other tax payers, the circumstances to authorize such interference must be such as to show that the proposed action will be inequitable and injurious to the public interest. *Chaffee v. Granger*, 6 Mich., 51.

2397. Sewers. A municipal corporation is not liable for damages arising from the insufficiency or defective construction of a public sewer, where such damages result directly to the party injured from his use of it for his private convenience. *Dermont v. Mayor, &c., of Detroit*, 4 Mich., 435.

2398. The payment of a sum annually by an individual for the privilege of connecting his drain with a public sewer, is evidence of a license only, and not of an undertaking and guaranty on the part of the city to furnish ample drainage for his premises. *Ibid.*

2399. But where an excavation in a city street for a sewer is left open without being properly guarded, and an injury occurs in consequence to one passing along the street, the city is liable for the damage, notwithstanding the contract for the construction of the sewer had been let by the city to one who was bound by the contract to keep the excavation fenced in and carefully guarded. *City of Detroit v. Corey*, 9 Mich., 165.

2400. Legislative control over. The charter and by-laws of municipal corporations are subject to the general legislation of the State. *Smith v. Village of Adrian*, 1 Mich., 495. See *People v. Mahaney*, 13 Mich., 481.

2401. Suits by Romeo village. Under the act incorporating the village of Romeo (Laws, 1837–8, p. 87), a suit to recover a penalty under Chap. 41 of R. S. of 1846, should have been brought in the name of the "Village of Romeo," instead of the "President and Trustees of the Village of Romeo," which was the corporate name of the village authorities. *President, &c., of the Village of Romeo v. Chapman*, 2 Mich., 179.

2402. Justices of the peace, under the Statutes of 1846, had no jurisdiction of suits against municipal corporations. *Root v. City of Ann Arbor*, 3 Mich., 433. See also, *Comp. Laws*, § 3700; *Gurney v. City of St. Clair*, 11 Mich., 203.

NAVIGABLE WATERS.

2404. Provision relative to, in Ordinance of '87. Navigable waters are public highways at the common law; and the only object of the clause in the Ordinance of 1787 relating thereto, was, to secure to the citizens of the States such rights, in relation to such waters within the territory northwest of the Ohio, as were already possessed by the inhabitants of that territory; and to prevent any tax or duty on persons navigating them. *La Plaisance Bay Harbor Co. v. City of Monroe*, Wal. Ch., 155.

2405. There is nothing in the ordinance prohibiting the State from improving its navigable waters through a corporation empowered thereto. *Ibid.*

2406. The ordinance supersedes the common law doctrine of the necessity of usage or custom to establish a public right in the navigable waters of the territory, even if that rule would otherwise prevail there. *Moore v. Sanborne*, 2 Mich., 519.

2407. What are navigable streams. The common law rule that those rivers only are subject to the servitude of the public interests which are of public or common use, for carriage of boats or lighters, and for transportation of property, has been enlarged in this country so as to embrace rivers upon which, in their natural state, there is capacity for valuable floatage, irrespective of the fact of actual public use, or the extent of such use. The fact that a floatable stream has not been used by the public, or has only been used by persons following a particular occupation, does not prevent such stream assuming a public character. In the new States of the Union, from necessity and the nature of things, use cannot be the foundation of the public right. *Ibid.*

2408. The true test in determining the right of public use in fresh water streams, as public highways, is, whether the stream is inherently and in its nature, capable of being used for the purposes of commerce, for the floating of vessels, boats, rafts or logs. And where it is, the public easement exists, leaving to the owners of the bed of the stream all other modes of use not inconsistent with it. *Ibid.*

2409. It is not necessary that the stream should be susceptible of navigation by boats, to render it a public highway. The servitude of public interest depends rather upon the purpose for which the public requires its use, than upon any particular mode of use. *Ibid.*

2410. The public right is not affected by the fact, that the stream has not a capacity for floatage, in its natural and ordinary stage, at all seasons of the year. It is a *valuable*, and not a *continual* capacity for use, which determines the right. *Ibid.*

2411. The term "navigable waters," as used in § 5944 of Compiled Laws, has the same meaning as in the Ordinance of 1787, and it is not limited to waters where the tide ebbs and flows. *Tyler v. People*, 8 Mich., 320.

2412. Although in England, in the common law sense of the term, those streams only are navigable in which the tide ebbs and flows, yet all rivers and streams above the ebb and flow of the tide, which are of sufficient capacity for useful navigation, are public rivers, and subject to the same general rights which the public exercise in highways by land, and which they possess in navigable waters. *Lorman v. Benson*, 8 Mich., 18.

2413. Ownership of bed of stream. The common law principle, that the soil under such tideless public rivers to the thread of the stream is in the owner of the adjacent bank, prevails here, and is applicable to the Detroit river. *Ibid*; overruling *La Plaisance Bay Turnpike Co. v. City of Monroe*, Wal. Ch., 155. See the same principle of private ownership applied to lake Muskegon. *Rice v. Ruddiman*, 10 Mich., 125.

2414. Rights of owner. The owner of the bank is entitled to every beneficial use of the soil under the river which can be exercised with a due regard to the public easement, and any trespass which interferes with such use—like an obstruction which prevents the taking of ice—gives him a right of action for the damages thereby occasioned. *Lorman v. Benson*, 8 Mich., 18.

2415. Rights of the public. The right to raft logs down a stream does not involve the right of booming them upon private property, for safe keeping and storage. *Ibid.*

NEGLIGENCE.

2416. Mutual. Where an injury of which a plaintiff complains is the result of his own negligence or fault, or of the negligence or fault of both parties, without intentional wrong on the part of the defendant, no action can be maintained. *Williams v. Michigan Central Railroad Co.*, 2 Mich., 259. And see *Michigan Central Railroad Co. v. Leahey*, 10 Mich., 193.

2417. Respondeat superior. Where an employee is exercising a distinct and independent employment, and is not under the immediate control, direction or supervision of the employer, the latter is not responsible for the negligence or carelessness of the employee. *De Forest v. Wright*, 2 Mich., 368.

2418. This principle applied to the case of a licensed drayman, employed to draw merchandise from a warehouse and deliver at the store of his employer, and through whose carelessness a barrel of the merchandise rolled against and injured the plaintiff. *Ibid.*

2419. To render an employer liable for the fault or negligence of his employee, the injury complained of must arise in the course of the execution of some service lawful in itself, but negligently or unskilfully performed. *Moore v. Sanborne*, 2 Mich., 519.

2420. For the wanton violation of law by a servant, although when occupied about the business of his employer, the servant alone is liable. *Ibid.*

2421. An employer made a bargain with his employee to cut all the logs the employer had on certain land, and to deliver them to the employer, at a place named; the employer having no interest in the running of the logs, until they reached the point of delivery, nor obliged to render any assistance, pecuniary or otherwise, in the cutting or running of the logs. It was held that the relation of master and servant did not exist, and that the employee alone was liable for any injury occasioned to others by his conduct in performing his contract. *Ibid.*

2422. Liability to employee. See the principle recognized, that an employer is not liable to an employee for an injury resulting from the negligence of another employee while engaged in the same general employment. *Michigan Central Railroad Co. v. Leahey*, 10 Mich., 199.

2423. Municipal corporations: negligence of contractor. Although in ordinary transactions the relation of contractor excludes that of principal and agent, or master and servant, yet there is not necessarily such a repugnance between them that they cannot exist together. *City of Detroit v. Corey*, 9 Mich., 165.

2424. In the case of one contracting with a municipal corporation for the construction of a sewer through one of its public streets, both relations necessarily exist, from the peculiar character of the case. The contractor has no right to make the excavation for the purpose, except as agent of the corporation; and, if proceeded against by indictment for creating a public nuisance, could not justify in his own right, but only as agent of the corporation under the contract. *Ibid.*

2425. The power conferred upon the city of Detroit to construct sewers under public streets, is not a power given to the city for governmental purposes, or a public municipal duty imposed on the city—like that to keep its streets in repair, or the like—but a special legislative grant to the city for private purposes. The sewers of the city, like its works for supplying the city with water, are the private property of the city; the corporation and its corporators—the citizens—are alone interested in them: the outside public, or people of the State at large, have no interest in them, as they have in the streets of the city, which are public highways. *Ibid.*

2426. The city takes this power with the understanding that it shall be so exercised as not unnecessarily to interfere with the rights of the public, and that all needful and proper measures shall be taken, in the execution of it, to guard against accident to persons lawfully using the highways at the time. The city is bound for the performance of these obligations, and cannot rid itself of their performance by executing the power through an agent. *Ibid.*

2427. The city of Detroit let to the lowest bidder, as required by its charter, the contract for the construction of a sewer through one of its streets. The contract bound the contractor at all times to keep the excavation fenced in, and carefully guarded to prevent accidents; and provided that the contractor should be liable for all damages that might arise from accidents caused by his neglect. For want of proper guards to the excavation, an injury occurred to a person passing along the street. Held, that the city was liable therefor. *Ibid.*

NOTICE.

2428. In equity, that is notice of a right which is sufficient to put parties on inquiry. *Norris v. Showerman*, 2 Doug., 16. And see, *Rood v. Chapin*, Wal. Ch., 79; *Godfroy v. Disbrow*, Wal. Ch., 260; *Disbrow v.*

Jones, Har. Ch., 48 ; *Hubbard v. Smith*, 2 Mich., 207 ; *Bloomer v. Henderson*, 8 Mich., 395 ; *James v. Brown*, 11 Mich., 25 ; *Willcox v. Hill*, 11 Mich., 256.

2429. Through title deeds. Where a purchaser cannot make out a title but by a deed which leads him to a certain fact, he must be presumed to have knowledge of that fact. *Norris v. Hill*, 1 Mich., 202; *Fitzhugh v. Barnard*, 12 Mich., 104.

NOVATION.

2430. Evidence that a debtor offered to pay the debt to the assignee of the contract, provided the time of payment should be extended, does not make out a case of novation, which makes it necessary to sue in the name of the assignee. *Tefft v. McNoah*, 9 Mich., 201.

NUISANCE.

2431. Abatement of. The power to abate a nuisance consists in the removal of that in which the nuisance consists. *Welch v. Stowell*, 2 Doug., 332.

2432. The nuisance of a house of ill-fame consists not in the building itself, but in its being used as a resort for purposes of prostitution. And neither individuals, nor the common council of a city under the statute empowering it " to make all such by-laws and ordinances as may be deemed expedient for the purpose of preventing and suppressing houses of ill-fame within the limits of the city," have the right to abate the nuisance by demolishing the building. *Ibid.*

OFFICER.

2433. Protection by process. Where a defendant, in an action of replevin, rests his claim to the property upon a seizure as constable, by virtue of an execution, he must, before proving the execution, show a valid judgment upon which it issued ; and he will fail to establish any right to the property by virtue of the levy, if it appears that the judgment was void, or had been paid before the issuing of the execution. *Beach v. Botsford*, 2 Doug., 199.

2434. The rule that a ministerial officer is protected in the execution of process, issued by a Court or officer having jurisdiction of the subject matter, and of the process, if it be regular on its face and do not disclose a want of jurisdiction, does not apply in such a case. That rule merely protects the officer when proceeded against as a wrong doer ; it confers upon him no right of property ; and in replevin the right to property, and not whether the defendant is a trespasser, is in issue. *Ibid.*

2435. A ministerial officer executing, in good faith and without oppression, a warrant regular upon its face, and issued by an officer having jurisdiction of the subject matter, will be protected by the warrant, and is not required to look beyond it for his authority to serve it. *Ortman v. Greenman*, 4 Mich., 291.

2436. Where an officer levied upon goods, and after offering them for sale, was informed of the existence of a mortgage upon them (which mortgage did not stipulate for possession of the goods by the mortgagor), and he then changed his offer to a sale of the *defendant's interest* in the goods, and sold accordingly; it was held that a sale in this form did not protect him from liability to the mortgagee, who might either replevy the goods, or recover the value from the officer and purchaser. *Eggleston v. Mundy*, 4 Mich., 295.

2437. Where the jurisdiction of the subject matter, in the tribunal issuing process, depends upon matter of fact, the existence of which cannot be determined from the law, and which is not of public notoriety, a ministerial officer will not be held bound to ascertain it at his peril, unless the law has clearly given him the right to demand the information and to determine the fact. *People v. Rix*, 6 Mich., 144.

2438. Where, therefore, the statute conferred jurisdiction of certain proceedings only, as was claimed, upon the circuit court commissioner of the county holding the senior commission, and did not provide a period when the term of either should commence, or what should be the date of the respective commissions, but the Governor might appoint and issue commissions at any time ; and no provision was made for making public the fact of the priority of either, or by which it could be obtained in any county office, and no power given to the sheriff to demand inspection of the commissions, or to require the information from the proper State office ; it was held, that the sheriff who had obeyed process issued in such proceedings by the commissioner who in fact held the junior commission (though the sheriff was not shown to have known that fact), and delivered up, in pursuance of such process, property which he had attached, was not liable on his official bond for so doing. *Ibid.*

2439. Sale by, to himself. A public officer charged with the duty of selling property for the best price, cannot himself become the purchaser. As a county treasurer, who has charge of the sale of lands for delinquent taxes. *Clute v. Barron*, 2 Mich., 192. And see *Walton v. Torrey*, Har. Ch., 259; *Ingerson v. Starkweather*, Wal. Ch., 346 ; *People v. Township Board of Overyssel*, 11 Mich., 222.

2440. Return of, when not binding on third parties.

Where a sheriff made return to an execution that he had made levy on goods on a day named, which was prior to the giving of a mortgage thereon, it was held that the mortgagee was not precluded by this return from showing that in fact the levy was made after the mortgage was given, and that a false return of the time was made by collusion with the purchaser at the sheriff's sale. *Nall v. Granger*, 8 Mich., 450.

2441. Restricting legal term. Where the statute prescribes the duration of an official term, it is not competent for the appointing power to restrict the term to a shorter period in making the appointment. *Stadler v. City of Detroit*, 13 Mich., 346.

2442. Appointment to office when a removal of incumbent. An officer cannot be removed from his office by the body possessing power for that purpose, without an intent on their part to remove him. And where the duration of his term is fixed by statute, and the body possessing the power of removal and appointment makes a new appointment on the mistaken idea that a vacancy exists, such appointment does not have the effect to remove the incumbent. *Ibid.*

2443. Officers de facto. The actual legal right of one who is the incumbent of an office cannot be tried in a collateral action between third persons; but in any such action the mere proof of user by any one who knows the fact will be sufficient to show his official action valid. *Facey v. Fuller*, 13 Mich., 527. See supra, 757. See also, *Quo Warranto.*

ORDINANCE OF 1787.

2444. Superseded by State constitution. The ordinance of 1787, for the government of the territory northwest of the river Ohio, is no part of the fundamental law of the State, since its admission into the Union. It was then superseded by the State constitution; and such parts of it as are not to be found in the Federal or State constitution, were then annulled by mutual consent. *La Plaisance Bay Harbor Co. v. City of Monroe*, Wal. Ch., 155.

2445. The ordinance was enacted before the constitution of the United States, with a view to the existing circumstances; and was intended to operate between the Confederacy and the territory as the Articles of Confederation did between the States. In construing it, the Articles of Confederation, and not the Federal Constitution, must be looked at. *Ibid.*

2446. Navigable waters. The object of the clause in the ordinance relating to navigable waters, was to secure to citizens of the confederated States such rights, in relation to those waters within the territory as were already possessed by the inhabitants therein; and to prevent any tax or duty on persons navigating them. There is nothing in the ordinance prohibiting the State, when formed, from improving through corporations its navigable waters. *Ibid.*

2447. The declaration in the ordinance that "the navigable waters leading into the Mississippi and St. Lawrence, shall be common highways, and remain forever free," supersedes the common law doctrine of the necessity of usage or custom to establish a public right, even if that rule would otherwise prevail in the region over which the ordinance extended. *Moore v. Sanborne*, 2 Mich., 519.

2448. Right to form a State government. Article V. of the ordinance, secured, absolutely and inviolably, to the people of the territory of Michigan, as established by act of Congress of January 11, 1805, the right to form a permanent constitution and State government, whenever said territory should contain sixty thousand free inhabitants; and that right could in no way be modified or abridged, or its exercise controlled or restrained, by the general government. The formation of the constitution and government of the State of Michigan must, of necessity, have preceded her admission into the Union by Congress. *Scott v. Detroit Young Men's Society's Lessee*, 1 Doug., 119.

2449. The assent of Congress to the admission of Michigan into the Union was only necessary, because the older States possessed the physical power to refuse a compliance with the terms of the compact contained in the ordinance, and there was no third party to which the State could resort to enforce such compliance. *Ibid.* And see STATE OF MICHIGAN.

2450. When the ordinance became operative in Michigan. The territory comprising the present State of Michigan remained under the control and jurisdiction of the British Government until the year 1796; and the ordinance of 1787 was not in force while the territory was under such jurisdiction. *Abbott v. Godfroy's heirs*, 1 Mich., 178.

PARTNERSHIP.

2451. Construction of agreement for. Where the question of partnership arises, not with third persons, but between the parties themselves, the agreement out of which the supposed partnership arises is to be construed as any other instrument between the same parties. *Bird v. Hamilton*, Wal. Ch., 361.

2452. Waiver of covenants in agreement. Where a party had failed to perform the preliminary conditions, upon a compliance with which a copartnership was to be formed, and the other party to the agreement, to enable him to perform, furnished his own capital, and for a short time carried on the business in the name of the proposed firm, it was *held* that this was no waiver, and could not entitle the defaulting party to the rights of a partner. *Ibid.*

2453. Agency of partners. Where a member of a mining company, who was also one of the managers of the company, employed the plaintiff to work for the company, it was held immaterial whether his powers as manager were general, special or limited, if the plaintiff at the time had no notice of any abridgement of his powers by the articles of co-partnership. *Burgan v. Lyell*, 2 Mich., 102.

2454. Every member of a partnership, in legal contemplation, without any special powers being conferred upon him by the articles of co-partnership, is not only a principal, but a general agent for all the co-partners in the transaction of the company business. *Ibid.* See *Moran v. Palmer*, 13 Mich., 367.

2455. But one cannot bind his co-partner by any contract not within the immediate scope of the partnership, unless with such co-partner's knowledge and assent. *Barnard v. Lapeer and Port Huron Plank Road Company*, 6 Mich., 274.

2456. Such knowledge and assent must be established by evidence affirmatively showing it, or from which it may be clearly affirmed. *Ibid.*

2457. That a plank road will be of incidental benefit to a co-partnership engaged in the lumber business, will not authorize one partner, without the assent of the other, to bind the firm by a subscription to the stock of a corporation organized for constructing such road. *Ibid.*

2458. Where one partner subscribed the name of the firm to stock in a corporation, without the assent of the co-partner, it was held that the latter did not recognize his relation as stockholder in the corporation, and become liable to pay the subscription, by failing to express his dissent when demand of payment was made upon the firm. *Ibid.*

2459. A partner binds his firm only on the theory of an implied agency for the purposes of the mutual adventure; and the agency does not extend beyond what may be fairly regarded as coming within its reach. *Hotchin v. Kent*, 8 Mich., 526.

2460. The articles of a joint stock mercantile association prohibited the officers intrusted with the conduct of its business from making purchases on credit. They, notwithstanding, made a purchase on credit, first giving the seller a copy of the articles. *Held*, that the association were not liable for the purchase, unless subsequently ratified by them; and that the officers themselves were not competent to ratify their own unauthorized act. *Ibid.*

2461. The receipt of the goods by the association, or even the sale of them in the course of their business, would not alone amount to a ratification, since the members could not be supposed to know that the purchase was made in violation of their articles. *Ibid.*

2462. Execution of a specialty. As a general rule one partner cannot execute a specialty in the name of the firm, binding, as such, upon the firm. *Fox v. Norton*, 9 Mich., 207. And see *Sweetzer v. Mead*, 5 Mich., 107.

2463. A bond was declared upon as the individual bond of two defendants. The bond offered in evidence was signed by one with the name of a co-partnership composed of the two, but there was no evidence that it was executed by the one in the presence of the other, or that the other had previously assented to its execution, or subsequently recognized or ratified it as the act or obligation of the firm. It was held, that the action could not be maintained. *Fox v. Norton*, 9 Mich., 207.

2464. Presumption of authority. Where one member of a co-partnership gives a note in the co-partnership name, the presumption is that it is given for partnership purposes; and the burden of proof is upon the co-partnership to show the contrary. *Littell v. Fitch*, 11 Mich., 525.

2465. Ratification. Where a third person does an act for the benefit of a partnership, a subsequent ratification of it, during the partnership, by one of its members, is a ratification by all. *Lyell v. Sanbourn*, 2 Mich., 109. See further as to ratification, *supra*, 2458 to 2461.

2466. Where two persons who have entered into a contract for a co-partnership rescind it, one of them has no power afterwards to bind the other by ratifying a contract previously made by them, and which was void under the statute of frauds when made. *Chamberlain v. Dow*, 10 Mich., 319.

2467. Notice by retiring partner. Where a member of a mining co-partnership assigns his stock in the company to a third person, he is still liable as a co-partner for debts subsequently contracted by the company to a person who had no notice of his withdrawal. *Burgan v. Lyell*, 2 Mich., 102.

2468. Admission by partner. The acknowledgment by one partner during the continuance of the partnership, of a debt as due by the partnership, will amount to a promise binding on the firm. *Ibid.*

2469. One partner cannot, after the dissolution of the firm, create a new partnership contract by his admission, nor revive a claim against the firm which has been barred by the statute of limitations. But except as to claims so barred by the statute, and others coming within a similar reason, the admission of one partner, made after such dissolution, having reference to previous actual partnership dealings or transactions, stands upon the same ground, and is evidence against the firm in like manner, as if made before the dissolution. *Pennoyer v. David*, 8 Mich., 407.

2470. But such admission, made after dissolution, must be confined to cases where there has been *in fact* previous partnership dealings with the plaintiff, or some transaction with the firm out of which a partnership liability to the plaintiff might have originated; and the fact that there have been such dealings or such transaction, must be shown by some evidence outside of the admission itself. *Ibid.*

2471. Partnership real estate. In equity, as between partners themselves, real estate purchased by them with partnership effects is partnership property, and, on the dissolution of the firm, should be divided as such, each party taking the same share in it as in the personal property, unless at the time of the purchase it was understood not to be a partnership transaction. *Thayer v. Lane*, Wal. Ch., 200.

2472. Lands conveyed to the members of a partnership in satisfaction of a partnership debt, are to be regarded, for all purposes of arranging balances between the partners, paying debts and closing up the partnership business, as personal property. And where one of the partners afterwards exchanged a lot so received for another, giving a deed in his own name alone, and the lot so received in exchange was sold by him, and the proceeds received by the partnership, it was held that the Court must presume knowledge of the exchange by all the partners, and that the receipt by the partnership of the proceeds of the lot sold, estopped the heirs of the partners not joining in the conveyance from afterwards setting up a claim to the first mentioned lot. *Moran v. Palmer*, 13 Mich., 367.

2473. Suits by partners. Where plaintiffs bring suit as partners composing a certain firm, it is necessary for them to prove that they compose the firm before giving evidence of transactions between the firm and the defendants. *Lee v. Hardgrave*, 3 Mich., 77.

2474. Partners must sue in their individual names. A writ of replevin issued on behalf of partners in the name of their firm, is a nullity. *Smith v. Canfield*, 8 Mich., 493.

2475. An agreement for the formation of a limited partnership, executed under the laws of another State, but not recorded so as to become effectual for the purposes designed, has no tendency to prove an actual general partnership between the persons named in it, in the absence of extrinsic evidence to show that they had actually entered into business as partners. *Gray v. Gibson*, 6 Mich., 300.

2476. Where plaintiffs sue as partners, not upon any contract made or dealings had with them as such, nor upon negotiable paper, and the partnership is put in issue, the real question to be submitted to the jury is, whether the plaintiffs are partners *as between themselves*, and not whether they have, in any way, made themselves liable as partners to third persons. And it is erroneous for the Court to charge the jury, that if the evidence shows the plaintiffs have made themselves partners as to third persons, they have in fact become general partners, and as such are entitled to maintain the action. *Ibid.*

2477. Whether persons are partners *inter se* is to be determined by the understanding and intention of the parties as between themselves; and they cannot be made such without the assent of every member, and his actual intention to become a member. *Ibid.*

2478. Fraud upon the firm by a partner. If one member of a co-partnership enter into a transaction on his own behalf which is within the scope of the partnership business, his co-partners may insist that it is a fraud upon them, and claim the benefits resulting from it. But this is a right which the partners alone can assert, and is not available to third persons, for the purpose of fixing a liability upon the partnership, when such claim has not been asserted. *Lockwood v. Beckwith*, 6 Mich., 168.

2479. The acts and declarations of a partner actually engaged in an adventure in his own name, cannot be proved for the purpose of fixing a liability upon the partnership in respect to such adventure. *Ibid.*

2480. Bankruptcy of the partners dissolves the partnership. And if, after the bankruptcy, the partners continue the same kind of business, under the same partnership name, it is a new partnership. *Atwood v. Gillett*, 2 Doug., 206.

2481. Remedies of creditors: receiver. It is no objection to the appointment of a receiver to take charge of partnership effects, that one of the partners has assigned his interest therein to a third person. *Kirby v. Ingersoll*, 1 Doug. 477.

2482. Suit against survivor. The presentation to and allowance by commissioners on the estate of a deceased partner, of a partnership debt, does not make it necessary, in an action by the creditor against the surviving partners for the same debt, to show that he has exhausted his remedy against the estate of the deceased partner. *Manning v. Williams*, 2 Mich., 105.

2483. A surviving partner having the legal right to the possession of the partnership property, a Court of equity will not deprive him of that right, unless upon proof of mismanagement, or danger to the partnership effects. *Connor v. Allen*, Har. Ch., 371.

2484. Rights of representatives of a deceased partner. Where one of several partners dies, and the business is carried on by the survivors without the assent of his representatives, they have, as a general rule, the election to demand interest on the amount of the share of the deceased, or to take a share of the profits. *Millard v. Ramsdell*, Har. Ch., 373.

2485. Rights of creditors in the property. As between the creditors of a previous firm, and the separate creditors of a partner who continued the business and was the sole visible owner of the property employed in trade, and where the separate creditors had given credit, relying on the property employed in trade for payment, such creditors should be preferred to the creditors of the firm. *Topliff v. Vail*, Har. Ch., 340.

2486. The creditors of a partnership have a right to payment out of the partnership effects, in preference to the creditors of an individual partner. *Ibid.*

2487. In the absence of any agreement to the contrary, it is fair to presume that a surviving partner does not intend that the partnership property shall be used for the individual benefit of a partner who continues the business, leaving the debts of the firm unpaid; and this was held to be the presumption where the retiring partner transferred the partnership effects to a partner continuing the business, who agreed to pay the partnership debts, and gave bond to that effect. *Ibid.*

2488. Dissolution of the co-partnership puts an end to the authority of one partner to bind the other by contracts. If the firm has been discharged from its debts in bankruptcy, he cannot revive a debt afterwards by an acknowledgment of it. *Atwood v. Gillett*, 2 Doug., 206.

PAYMENT.

2489. By note. The giving of a promissory note or other security for goods sold is no payment, unless it is specially agreed to be so taken. *Gardner v. Gorham*, 1 Doug., 507. See *Sorrel v. Brewster*, 1 Mich., 373.

2490. Where goods were sold, and securities, executed by third persons, were received for the purchase price, one of which the vendor collected, and the other offered to return; it was *held*, in an action brought by the vendor for goods sold, that whether the securities were received by him in payment for the goods sold was a question for the jury, and it was erroneous for the Court to exclude evidence offered by the plaintiff from which it might be inferred that there was no such agreement. *Gardner v. Gorham*, 1 Doug., 507.

2491. The understanding and assent of the parties that securities taken shall be received in payment, may be proved by their subsequent acts and conduct, as well as by direct proof of an express agreement. *Hotchin v. Secor*, 8 Mich., 494.

2492. The note of two of several partners was taken for a partnership debt, and this note was afterwards paid in part, and notes on longer time taken for the balance. Suit being brought against the firm on the original debt, the Court was asked by defendants to charge the jury, that it was not absolutely necessary to show an express agreement on the part of the plaintiffs to receive the note in payment, but that if the jury find, from all the circumstances of the case, and the subsequent acts of the plaintiffs in regard to the note, that they had acted and treated it as their own, and as received in payment of their claim, then the jury were authorized to take such facts into consideration, and find that it was received in payment if the evidence satisfied them that such was the fact. Held, that this request presented substantially a correct view of the law, and the Court erred in declining to charge accordingly. *Ibid.*

2493. Where the vendor of lands takes the note or obligation of a third party for the purchase price, the presumption is that it is taken in payment, and not merely as security. *Sears v. Smith*, 2 Mich., 243.

2494. Payment as an admission of the debt claimed. Payment by the defendant to the plaintiff, pending an action of assumpsit, of part of the demand to secure which the action is brought, is not equivalent, in its effect as an admission of the cause of action, to a payment of money into Court. *Galloway v. Holmes*, 1 Doug., 330.

2495. Indorsements upon notes, unexplained, prove payment, and whether explained or not, prove an extinguishment and release of liability to their extent as between the parties, unless it be shown that they were not intended so to operate. *Morris v. Morris*, 5 Mich., 171.

2496. But indorsements are not of themselves evidence of payment, as against the debtor, to take the case out of the operation of the statute of limitations [Comp. L., § 5377]. *Michigan Insurance Company v. Brown*, 11 Mich., 265.

2497. Presumption of payment can never arise from lapse of time alone, short of the period of limitations fixed by law. *Adair v. Adair*, 5 Mich., 304.

2498. But on bill to foreclose a mortgage given to secure a note, it was held that the law did not raise a presumption of non-payment, but of payment, when due, unless the contrary is shown by the production of the note, or evidence accounting for it. *Bailey v. Gould*, Wal. Ch., 478. See *Young v. McKee*, 13 Mich., 552.

2499. Purchase of lien when a payment. For a case where a party, under an agreement to pay for lands by taking up incumbrances upon it, was held to have satisfied an incumbrance by buying it in, see *Michigan Insurance Co. v. Kibbee*, 6 Mich., 410.

2500. When a mortgagor redeems, it should always be construed as a payment; he being personally liable for the debt. But when his vendee redeems, who is not personally liable, and there is an intervening mortgage between the one redeemed by him and his equity of redemption, the same rule should prevail as in case of a redemption by a subsequent mortgagee. *Johnson v. Johnson*, Wal. Ch., 331.

2501. Written order as proof of. A written order directing the drawee to pay what money he has of the drawer's, without specifying any sum, is not of itself proof in the hands of the drawee of the payment of any sum, but only of *authority* to pay to the person named in the order. *Beardslee v. Horton*, 3 Mich., 560.

2502. Application of. A debtor, upon paying money to his creditor, has a right to say on which one of several demands the payment shall be applied. *Thayer v. Denton*, 4 Mich., 192.

2503. Where the application has been once made upon a joint debt, it operates to extinguish so much of the debt, and the application cannot be subsequently changed by the concurrent act of the creditor and paying debtor, and the claim thus revived, without the consent of the co-debtor. *Ibid.*

2504. Where one has given an undertaking, that if the person to whom it is addressed will let the bearer have a bill of goods, he will see the amount paid in a reasonable length of time, and the goods are delivered accordingly, the first moneys afterwards received by the creditor on the debtor's general account, must be applied on the purchase under this guaranty. *Gard v. Stevens*, 12 Mich., 292.

2505. What an officer may receive. A sheriff or constable has no power to receive anything except the legal currency of the United States on an execution in his hands for collection, and if he does so, without special instructions, it is at his own risk. *Heald v. Bennett*, 1 Doug., 513. This rule applied to justices of the peace in the same case, and also in *Welch v. Frost*, 1 Mich.,, 30.

PHYSICIANS.

2506. Proof that one practices as a physician, is prima facie evidence of his professional character. The question whether one is a practicing physician within the meaning of the exemption laws, relates rather to the business in which he is engaged, than to the degree of skill with which he exercises it; though some degree of skill is necessary. *Sutton v. Facey*, 1 Mich., 343.

PLANK ROAD COMPANIES.

2507. Taking highways by. Section four of the charter of the Detroit and Howell Plank Road Company (Laws 1848, p. 398), authorizing the company, when duly organized, to enter upon and take possession of so much of the Detroit and Grand River road, so called, as lies between the city of Detroit and Howell, was held to dispense with the necessity of a release or consent of the supervisors and commissioners of highways of the several townships, as required by section 27 of the General Plank Road Act of 1851. *Detroit and Howell Plank Road Company v. Fisher*, 4 Mich., 37.

2508. The Detroit and Erin Plank Road Co., being specially authorized by their charter to take possession of so much of the Fort Gratiot road as lies between the city of Detroit and the township of Erin, and construct and maintain a plank road thereon ; it was held that they might do so without any grant or release from the supervisor and commissioners of highways of the township through which the road would run, notwithstanding the General Plank Road Act of 1848 was also made a part of the charter, and by that act, where a plank road company might wish to use a public highway for their road, they were to obtain the right by procuring a grant for the purpose from the officers mentioned. *Attorney-General v. Detroit and Erin Plank Road Co.*, 2 Mich., 138.

2509. Right to demand tolls. Under the provisions of section 17 of the General Plank Road Act of 1848, a company may exact toll whenever the road, or five consecutive miles thereof, are completed, notwithstanding the survey of the road is not recorded as directed by section 12 of said act. *Detroit and Howell Plank Road Co. v. Fisher*, 4 Mich., 38.

2510. The company may demand toll of any person in advance of his actually travelling upon the road ; and on his refusal to state how far he proposes to travel over the road, may require payment of toll to the next gate. *Ibid.*

2511. Forcibly passing the gates. Where the traveller, without paying the legal toll, passes the gate against the express will or order of the gate keeper, but without actual force, the gate being open, and the keeper offering no resistance, such an act constitutes a forcible passing under section 17 of said act of 1848. *Ibid.*

2512. Changing location of gates. A plank road company has general power to change the location of its gates, and to erect new ones, unless specially restricted. *City of Detroit v. Detroit and Erin Plank Road Co.*, 12 Mich., 333.

2513. Exclusion of gates from city limits. A plank road company occupying for their purposes a road leading from the city of Detroit, procured an amendment to their charter, by which they were " empowered to extend their road on Gratiot street to Randolph street in the city of Detroit ; provided that no toll gate shall be erected or maintained within the limits of said city by said company." Subsequently the city limits were extended by statute so as to embrace a portion of the original road upon which a gate had before been erected. It was held that the amendatory act did not restrict the original powers of the company to erect and maintain a gate on any portion of the road then outside the city limits, but only prohibited any gate upon the extension of the road which was authorized by the amendatory act. *Ibid.*

2514. Amendment of charter. The clause in the fiftieth section of the General Plank Road Act of 1851, which provides that any subsequent alteration or amendment of the act shall not operate as an alteration or amendment of the corporate rights of companies formed under it, unless specially named in the amendatory act, was inserted solely for the protection of the companies, and does not prevent the legislature, by general amendment, from removing any restriction, or releasing or diminishing any obligation or burden imposed upon such companies by the general act. *People v. Grand Blanc and Holley Plank Road Company*, 10 Mich., 400.

2515. Therefore companies formed under said act may, as to the road subsequently constructed, claim the benefit of the act of 1859 (*Laws* 1859, *p.* 155), which permits them to adopt a grade of not exceeding one foot in ten, instead of one foot in twenty as under the general act. *Ibid.*

2516. An amendment to a charter of a plank road company, authorizing it to mortgage its corporate property to raise money for the completion of its road, is an amendment which may be accepted by a majority of the stockholders. *Joy v. Jackson and Michigan Plank Road Co.*, 11 Mich., 155.

2517. Mortgage by. Under a special statute authorizing a plank road company to " mortgage the road and other property of the company," the franchise of taking toll is to be understood as included with the road and its fixtures. *Ibid.*

2518. But the company could not, under this power, mortgage any franchise essentially corporate in its character, and which could not be enjoyed by a natural person. *Ibid.*

2519. Under an authority to mortgage the whole road, the company might give a valid mortgage on any specific portion of it, upon which separate tolls can lawfully be collected. *Ibid.*

2520. Forfeiture of franchise. Under the Plank Road Act of 1848, on the completion of five consecutive miles of plank road, the right to take tolls became vested; and whatever might be the length of the road required by the charter, the right to tolls on the part so completed could not be forfeited or affected by the failure to construct the balance of the road. *People v. Jackson and Michigan Plank Road Co.*, 9 Mich., 285.

2521. The following question discussed but not decided—the Court being divided in opinion :—Where a part of the road actually completed is constructed in a manner not allowed by the said act of 1848, is this such a misuser as will forfeit the whole grant? *Ibid.*

2522. Also, under said act of 1848, can the five consecutive miles of road first constructed be forfeited by a failure to keep any other portion of the road, when constructed, in repair? *Ibid.*

2523. Also, what certainty of pleading is required in a proceeding to have a forfeiture declared for misuser? *Ibid.*

2524. Also, what standard of perfection can be required as the standard of repairs, and when repairs must be made? *Ibid.*

2525. Liability of stockholders. Stockholders in a plank road company organized under the General Plank Road Act of 1851, are *severally* liable for demands against the company (not for labor done) to the amount of the stock held by each when the debt accrued, and not merely for the amounts which remain unpaid on their stock. *Pettibone v. McGraw*, 6 Mich., 441.

2526. It is not indispensable that a judgment creditor who, after return of execution against the company unsatisfied, files his bill to compel payment by the stockholders, should make them all defendants. *Ibid.*

2527. Nor is it necessary that all be made parties to the bill, when the demand for which the judgment was rendered was for labor done. *Ibid.*

2528. Sale of franchise on execution. The authority to sell the franchise of a plank road corporation on execution, is derived entirely from the statute; and the sale can be made in no other mode than that pointed out by the statute. That mode is a sale of the franchise to such person as will satisfy the execution, with the legal fees, and take the franchise for the shortest period of time. *James v. Pontiac and Groveland Plank Road Co.*, 8 Mich., 91.

2529. A sale of the franchise for a certain period, in part payment of the execution, is unauthorized and void. *Ibid.*

2530. The acquiescence of the stockholders in the purchaser taking possession under such a sale, their payment to him of tolls for passing over the road, and the expenditure by him of moneys in repairing the road, with their knowledge, will not confirm and render valid such a sale. *Ibid.*

PLEADINGS.

1. General Principles.

2531. The object of pleading in any Court is to apprise the opposite party of the grounds of the claim or defense (as the case may be), so that there shall be no misapprehension as to what matters are, to be litigated on the trial. *Hurtford v. Holmes*, 3 Mich., 460.

2532. Surplusage. It is not necessary for a party to allege any more, in pleading, than will constitute, prima facie, a sufficient cause of action or defense; all beyond this is surplusage. *Attorney-General v. Michigan State Bank*, 2 Doug., 359.

2. The Declaration.

2533. Statute of frauds. A declaration on a guaranty within the purview of the statute of frauds, need not aver that the guaranty was in writing. *Dayton v. Williams*, 2 Doug., 31.

2534. Nor need it aver that the undertaking guaranteed, though that also was within the purview of the statute, was made with the formalities which the statute requires. *Ibid.*

2535. Covenant on replevin bond. The declaration set forth a covenant alleged to be contained in a replevin bond, of the same tenor with the condition of such a bond as prescribed by the statute. Default for want of plea, and final judgment. On error to reverse the judgment, it was *held*,

(*a.*) That it was competent for the parties to add to the condition of a replevin bond a covenant of the same tenor; and, on breach, covenant broken might be maintained upon it.

(*b.*) That it must be presumed in this case that the bond contained such a covenant, and not that the action was founded upon the condition of the bond.

(*c.*) That it was not necessary that the declaration should set forth the penal part of the bond; it being sufficient for the plaintiff to set forth so much only of an instrument as constitutes the foundation of his action. *Prentiss v. Spalding*, 2 Doug., 84.

2536. Suit for goods sold, where securities have been taken. Where plaintiff sold goods and received securities for the purchase price, one of which he collected and the other offered to return, and he afterwards brought suit to recover the balance, it was held not necessary that he should declare specially. *Gardner v. Gorham*, 1 Doug., 507.

2537. Suit on note where there is a collateral agreement. In declaring on a promissory note absolute on its face and in the ordinary form, it is not necessary to notice a cotemporaneous agreement in writing varying the terms of the note, contained in a separate paper. Such agreement is matter of defense only. *Smalley v. Bristol*, 1 Mich., 153.

2538. Declaration on a lease. In declaring on an agreement as a demise, there are but two proper modes of stating it: first, by its legal effect; or, second, by setting it forth in such a manner that its legal character can be seen. *Tillman v. Fuller*, 13 Mich., 113.

2539. Suit to recover rents. The declaration set forth an agreement on the part of the plaintiff to lease the premises to the defendant, in consideration of which the defendant did actually rent and hire the premises. It was held that such agreement to lease could not be a consideration for an actual renting, unless it was so stated as to amount to a present demise. *Ibid.*

2540. Guaranty: goods sold. The plaintiff sold and delivered to one S. certain goods, taking from him a mortgage thereon for the purchase money. The defendant agreed with plaintiff in writing, that the goods so sold should at all times remain in the possession of the purchaser, ready to be delivered upon default of any payment—except what had been sold from day to day at regular sales—and that if, upon default in payment, there should not be sufficient goods to liquidate the sum remaining due on the mortgage, the balance should be made up by defendant. The agreement provided that in the event the plaintiff should retake said goods, the same " should be invoiced and applied;" and it was held, that an averment in the declaration, that plaintiff" did proceed to take possession of the remaining goods, and invoice the same, to wit, at," &c., was a sufficient averment of an invoice in compliance with the contract. *Mills v. Spencer*, 3 Mich., 127.

2541. A declaration upon such agreement, setting forth the amount of the purchaser's original indebtedness for said goods, held not defective by reason of its omitting to state the amount due the plaintiff after the goods so inventoried had been applied, and the non-payment of that amount; no demurrer having been interposed, and the objection being taken on error. *Ibid.*

2542. An averment that the invoice of goods amounted to a certain sum, leaving a deficiency of a certain sum, and which last sum was due to the plaintiff, was sufficient, under the statute of 1849 regulating pleadings in the County Courts. *Ibid.*

2543. The defendant under this agreement, was held liable for the whole deficiency, without regard to the manner in which the goods had been disposed of; and not merely for such portions as plaintiff could show had been diverted from the ordinary sales by the purchaser. *Ibid.*

2544. Declaring on statute. In declaring on a statute, where there is an exception in the enacting clause, the pleader must negative the exception; but where there is no exception in the enacting clause, but an exemption in a proviso to the enacting clause, or in a subsequent section of the act, it is matter of defense, and must be shown by defendant. Where, therefore, suit is brought for the price of liquors sold in Michigan, the plaintiffs cannot recover unless they bring themselves within the exemptions of the statute. [MANNING, J.] *Myers v. Carr*, 12 Mich., 63. See *Attorney-General v. Oakland County Bank*, Wal. Ch., 90.

2545. Allegations conflicting with statutes. A Court is bound to take judicial notice of a public statute, and to disregard all allegations in conflict with it. *People v. River Raisin and Lake Erie Railroad Co.*, 12 Mich., 389.

2546. Where a township treasurer gave bond to "The People of of the State of Michigan," instead of to the township as required by law, it was held that an action could not be maintained upon it in the name of the township by averring that the bond was given to the township by the name and description of the People of the State of Michigan. The Court must take judicial notice of the fact that the State and the township are distinct organizations. *Township of La Grange v. Chapman*, 11 Mich., 499.

2547. Declaration on contract with agent. Where a contract purported to be executed by agents of the respective parties, and it was set forth at length in the declaration, and alleged to be the contract of the parties, the declaration was held sufficient without showing how the agency was constituted. *Regents of the University v. Detroit Young Men's Society*, 12 Mich., 138.

2548. Action for interest: demand. Where action was brought for interest due at a fixed time without any conditions, and it was alleged to be unpaid, it was held that no special demand was necessary, and that the breach of the contract sufficiently appeared. *Ibid.*

2549. Surplusage. When a contract is set forth at length in the declaration, any allegation in respect to its description or effect, in a matter which must appear on its face as set forth, is superfluous, and should be treated as surplusage. *Ibid.*

2550. As where the contract of corporations was alleged to be "sealed with the seals of the respective parties;" but upon its face it appeared to be executed by agents who had only affixed their own seals. *Ibid.*

2551. Profert. In declaring upon a contract thus executed it is not necessary to make profert. But if it could be considered a sealed instrument, no further profert or oyer is necessary when it is thus set forth in full. *Ibid.*

2552. Statement of promise in assumpsit. A declaration in assumpsit on the common counts, which, after stating the several causes of action, omits to allege an express promise, though bad on special demurrer, is cured by judgment. *Hoard v. Little*, 7 Mich., 468.

2553. Particularity required. A pleading should contain allegations of facts, and not of evidence. Under a count for a false and fraudulent representation of the value of an article sold by defendant, plaintiff may prove false statements made by defendant at the time, as to the value of particular parts of the article, notwithstanding such statements are not detailed in the declaration. *Picard v. McCormick*, 11 Mich., 68.

2554. Separate counts. Each count of a declaration is to be regarded as a separate claim, and the declaration is not defective because one count claims damages below the jurisdiction of the Court. *Ibid.*

2555. Variance. Where a writ is alleged to have *issued*, or a written instrument to have been *made*, on a certain day, and the writ or instrument, when offered in evidence, *bears date* a different day, this is no variance. *Lothrop v. Southworth*, 5 Mich., 436.

2556. A variance between the declaration and the proof should be disregarded at the trial, when the instrument is otherwise sufficiently described in the declaration, so that defendant cannot be surprised or misled by the evidence. *Ibid.*

2557. Where the consideration for a promise is stated as consisting of two parts, each of which is material and pertinent, proof of but one is a variance fatal to plaintiff's recovery, notwithstanding either would have been sufficient by itself to sustain the promise if alleged as the sole consideration. *Tillman v. Fuller*, 13 Mich., 113.

2558. In an action on a warranty of a span of horses, the declaration stated the consideration to be a yoke of oxen and a note for twenty dollars, and on the trial it appeared the note was for ten dollars only. The variance was held to be fatal. *Harrington v. Worden*, 1 Mich., 487.

2559. An allegation that the president and directors of a certain corporation (naming all of them) made certain by-laws, is supported by evidence that they were made by the president and a majority only of the directors. *Cahill v. Kalamazoo Mutual Insurance Co.*, 2 Doug., 124.

2560. Declaration against one who had subscribed with others for the erection of a college building at Hillsdale, for the use of the Michigan Central College incorporated at Spring Arbor. The declaration averred that this college decided not to use the building when completed, and the subscribers afterwards renewed their subscriptions, and indebtedness was incurred and the building completed in reliance thereon. It was shown in evidence that the renewal of the subscriptions, and the erection of the buildings, were for the benefit of a new college to be established at Hillsdale. This fact not being averred in the declaration, which only showed a subscription for a college not located at Hillsdale, it was held that no recovery could be had thereon. *Underwood v. Waldron*, 12 Mich., 73.

2561. Variance in name: allegation of identity. A declaration on a judgment which avers that it was rendered in favor of A., the present plaintiff, by the name of B., but which does not allege that A. was ever known by the name of B., is bad on demurrer. *Gilbert v. Hanford*, 13 Mich., 40. See supra, 2546.

2562. Allegation of consideration. In declaring upon a simple contract, unless it is one which imports a consideration, the whole consideration should be set forth, so as to show distinctly in what it consists, that the Court may judge of its sufficiency to sustain the promise alleged. *Kean v. Mitchell*, 13 Mich., 207.

2563. In a declaration on a contract for the purchase of goods, an allegation that the defendant agreed to deliver the goods "for a good and valuable consideration paid by the plaintiff to the defendant," is not a sufficient statement of the consideration to support the declaration on demurrer. *Ibid.*

2564. Defect cured by verdict. But such a defect cannot be taken advantage of on the trial of an issue of fact, by objection to the admission of evidence to establish the plaintiff's case; and after verdict for the plaintiff, the allegation will be sufficient to sustain it. *Ibid.*

2565. A defective allegation of consideration will be cured by verdict when, from the issue as actually made, it can fairly be presumed that the evidence necessary to establish a case was given under it. *Ibid.*

3. Pleas in Abatement.

2566. Certainty. A plea in abatement must have the highest degree of certainty and precision. Every allegation necessary to make out the case covered by it must be distinctly, and not inferentially, set forth. *Belden v. Laing*, 8 Mich., 500. See *Findley v. People*, 1 Mich., 234.

2567. In replevin a plea in abatement was interposed, setting up the pendency of a prior suit in replevin, by virtue of the writ in which the property in controversy was taken and held by one of the defendants as sheriff. The plea did not allege that any affidavit was attached to the writ in the first suit, nor that the writ commanded the sheriff to take the property in controversy. Held that the plea was insufficient on both grounds. *Belden v. Laing*, 8 Mich., 500.

2568. Former suit pending. Plaintiff commenced two suits against the defendant on the same day, for the same cause of action; one by declaration, and the other by attachment. The Court presumed, nothing appearing on the record to the contrary, that the suit by declaration was first commenced, and held that a plea of that suit in abatement of the attachment suit was bad, because the plea did not state that it was still pending. *Wales v. Jones*, 1 Mich., 254; *Pew v. Yoare*, 12 Mich., 16.

2569. Where a plea in abatement averred that another suit was commenced at the same time, upon and for the not performing the same identical promises and undertakings, without adding, *in the said declaration in this present suit mentioned*, or other equivalent words, it was held bad on that account. *Ibid.*

2570. Non-joinder of plaintiffs. Where the husband sues alone for property of the wife, held in her own right or that of another, he will be non-suited on the trial. It is not necessary to plead the non-joinder in abatement. *Brown v. Fifield*, 4 Mich., 322.

2571. Non-joinder of defendants. In actions *ex contractu* the non-joinder of a co-contractor, unless it appear on the face of the declaration, can only be taken advantage of by plea in abatement. This rule applies to actions on recognizances. *People v. Dennis*, 4 Mich., 609.

4. Pleas in Bar.

2572. The general issue, under the Revised Statutes of 1846, (*Comp. L.*, §§ 4176, 4177) in all civil actions, traverses every material averment in the plaintiff's declaration which must be proved, whatever the nature or form of the action may be. *Kinne v. Owen*, 1 Mich., 249. See *Taff v. Hosmer*, 14 Mich.

2573. Under the general issue in covenant, the defendant may show that the deed is not his, by proving a lack of power in the agent who executed it on his behalf. *Agent of State Prison v. Lathrop*, 1 Mich., 438.

2574. In assumpsit, illegality of consideration between the original parties to a promissory note, may be shown under the general issue. If any notice of defense under the Prohibitory Liquor Law were necessary, a notice that the note was given for the purchase price of intoxicating liquors, contrary to the statute, is sufficient. [Manning, J.] *Myers v. Carr*, 12 Mich., 63.

2575. In an action of tort, everything which may properly be considered by the jury in mitigation of damages, may be given in evidence under the general issue. *Delavan v. Bates*, 1 Mich., 97.

2576. In trespsss *de bonis*, the defense that the goods were taken under attachment against a third person alleged to be the owner, is not admissible under the general issue, without notice. *Rosenbury v. Angell*, 6 Mich., 508.

2577. In trover against a sheriff, by parties claiming property levied on by him, a judgment in favor of the party for whom the sheriff levied must be specially alleged and proved, to authorize the defendant to put in evidence showing that a chattel mortgage given by the debtor, under which the plaintiff claims, is fraudulent. *Comstock v. Hollon*, 2 Mich., 355.

2578. Plea puis darrein continuance. After a joint plea to the merits by two defendants, it was held that one of them might plead severally, *puis darrein continuance*, his discharge in bankruptcy subsequently obtained. But such plea would be an abandonment by him of the former joint plea, which would thereafter stand as the several plea of the other defendant. *Wheelock v. Rice*, 1 Doug., 267.

2579. Statute of limitations. A plea of the statute of limitations, that the plaintiff's cause of action did not accrue within six years next before the filing of the plaintiff's *amended* declaration, is bad. *Wilcox v. Kassick*, 2 Mich., 165.

2580. Another suit pending for the same cause of action in another State, is not a good plea in bar. *Ibid.*

2581. Two pleas; one bad. Where to a declaration in assumpsit the defendant pleaded *non-assumpsit*, and *not guilty*, and a jury trial had been had; it was held that the plea of not guilty might be treated as a nullity, and stricken from the record. *Owners of Ship Milwaukee v. Hale*, 1 Doug., 306.

2582. Special pleas good after judgment. The statute abolishing special pleadings, does not make special pleading void, where the parties have voluntarily adopted it, joined issue, and proceeded to trial and judgment. *Wales v. Lyon*, 2 Mich., 276.

2583. Notices of defense. A notice of special matter to be given in evidence, must contain all the substantial requisites necessary to constitute a special plea which would be good on general demurrer. *Thompson v. Bowers*, 1 Doug., 321.

2584. A notice that apprises the plaintiff with reasonable certainty of the matter of defense, so that he may not be taken by surprise on the trial, is sufficient under the statute. *Rosenbury v. Angell*, 6 Mich., 508; *McHardy v. Wadsworth*, 8 Mich., 349. And see *Porter v. Kimball*, 1 Mich., 239.

2585. A notice that "three several writs of attachment were issued out of the Circuit Court for the county of L., and under the seal thereof in due form of law," giving the names of the parties, and dates and command of the writs, and the taking of the property by virtue thereof, is sufficient, without alleging the making of the affidavits which authorized the attachments; and the affidavits as well as the writs may be given in evidence. *Rosenbury v. Angell*, 6 Mich., 508.

2586. In an action on a promissory note made by two defendants, notice of defense was interposed, that the note was given for the purchase price of cows sold with warranty by plaintiff to defendants, the damages for a breach of which warranty defendants claimed to recoup from the amount of this note. The proof showed the note to have been given for the consideration stated, but the sale was made by the plaintiff to *one* of the defendants. *Held*, that the notice was sufficient, especially as the plaintiff, in his bill of particulars, evidently designed to cover the consideration for the note, had claimed to recover for cows sold by him to the defendants. *McHardy v. Wadsworth*, 8 Mich., 349.

2587. To a declaration in slander, alleging that the defendant charged the plaintiff with having sworn falsely, the defendant pleaded the general issue, and gave notice that he would prove on the trial, "that the plaintiff was guilty of the facts charged upon and imputed to him by the defendant, in the several conversations in the declaration mentioned, and that, if the words were uttered and published as charged in the declaration, the defendant had good reason for uttering and publishing, and did it from good motives and for justifiable ends." *Held*, that this notice was fatally defective; especially in omitting any averment that the plaintiff *wilfully* and *deliberately* swore falsely; and that the defendant could not, upon the trial, introduce any evidence under it. *Thompson v. Bowers*, 1 Doug., 321.

2588. What notice was insufficient under the County Court system of 1846. *Porter v. Kimball*, 1 Mich., 239.

5. Demurrer.

2589. Insufficient description. In replevin a defective description of the property, must be taken advantage of by special demurrer, as it would be held sufficient after verdict, avowry, or plea of property in defendant. *Stevens v. Osman*, 1 Mich., 92.

2590. Defective allegation of notice. That the averment in a declaration on a guaranty, of notice to the defendant of nonperformance by his principal, omits to state *when* or *where* the notice was given, is no ground for arresting judgment, but only of special demurrer. *Dayton v. Williams*, 2 Doug., 31.

6. Replication.

2591. Replication to a notice of defense was held not necessary, under the Circuit Court rules of 1853, where the matters set out in the notice were admissible in evidence under the general issue. *Craig v. Grant*, 6 Mich., 447.

POLICE COURT OF DETROIT.

2592. Appeal from. Whether an appeal lies from a conviction in the Police Court of Detroit, to the Circuit Court for the county of Wayne, *quere*—the Court being equally divided on the question. *People v. Police Justice*, 7 Mich., 456.

2593. Jurisdiction. The Police Court of Detroit has no jurisdiction of a criminal case where the maximum punishment allowed by law exceeds a fine of one hundred dollars, or three months imprisonment, or both such fine and imprisonment. *Matter of Berry*, 7 Mich., 467.

POSSESSION OF LANDS.

2594. When it is notice of title or claim. Where a party purchases land in the possession of a third person, with a knowledge of that fact, he takes it subject to all equities existing between his vendor and the person in possession. *Rood v. Chapin*, Wal. Ch., 79; *Godfroy v. Disbrow*, Wal. Ch., 260; *Disbrow v. Jones*, Har. Ch., 48; *McKee v. Wilcox*, 11 Mich., 358; *Norris v. Showerman*, 2 Doug., 16.

2595. It is the duty of the purchaser before buying to inquire of the person in possession what claim he makes to the premises. *McKee v. Wilcox*, 11 Mich., 358.

2596. But possession alone is not such *actual notice*, as, under § 25, p. 260 of Revised Statutes of 1838, would protect the title of one claiming and occupying under an unrecorded deed, against one who subsequently took a mortgage from the grantor without being aware of such possession. *Hubbard v. Smith*, 2 Mich., 207.

2597. Not affected by injunction. Where an injunction had been granted, enjoining defendant from interfering with or incumbering certain lands and premises, and defendant, at and previous to the granting of the injunction, being in possession of, and claiming title to, a mill on the land, forcibly put out two agents of complainant who came into the mill after the injunction had been served, and refused to leave when requested, it was held to be no violation of the injunction, which was not intended to dispossess the defendant. *Hemingway v. Preston*, Wal. Ch., 528. And see supra, 1146, 1147.

2598. Summary proceedings to recover: who to bring. Under the Revised Statutes of 1838, a suit against a lessee, to recover possession of the demised premises, on account of the nonpayment of rent, &c., was held properly brought by the lessor in his own name, although he had previously assigned the rents to accrue under the lease, to a third person. *Chamberlin v. Brown*, 2 Doug., 120.

2599. The summary remedy given by Laws of 1840, p. 85, § 5, where premises had been sold on mortgage foreclosure or on execution; applied only where there was *privity* between the parties; and not where the grantee of a purchaser at an execution sale sought to recover possession from a person holding adversely to the judgment debtor. *Royce v. Bradburn*, 2 Doug., 377.

2600.—previous notice. The Statutes of 1838 requiring the landlord to demand possession of the premises, in writing, from his tenant, at least twenty days before summary proceedings to recover possession, it was held, that a demand requiring the tenant to quit the premises in *ten* days, but which was served twenty days before proceedings were instituted, was sufficient. *Chamberlin v. Brown*, 2 Doug., 120. See further as to notice, *Huyser v. Chase*, 13 Mich., 98; *Woodrow v. Michael*, 13 Mich., 187.

2601.—the complaint should allege all the facts necessary to give the Court jurisdiction. *Royce v. Bradburn*, 2 Doug., 377; *Caswell v. Ward*, 2 Doug., 374; *Davis v. Ingersoll*, 2 Doug., 372; *Bush v. Dunham*, 4 Mich., 339; *Bryan v. Smith*, 10 Mich., 229.

2602. In a proceeding under the Statutes of 1838, for an unlawful and forcible entry, &c., a complaint which showed merely an *unlawful* entry and detention, but did not show that they were accompanied with *violence*, or a breach of the peace, was held insufficient. *Davis v. Ingersoll*, 2 Doug., 372.

2603. A complaint under the Statutes of 1846, which did not show that *at the time the complaint was made* the complainant was entitled to the premises, was held insufficient. *Bush v. Dunham*, 4 Mich., 339; *Bryan v. Smith*, 10 Mich., 229.

2604. A complaint was held insufficient to confer jurisdiction which only showed that complainant *became entitled* to the possession upwards of fourteen months before the proceeding was instituted. *Bryan v. Smith*, 10 Mich., 229.

2605. Form of a complaint suggested. *Bush v. Dunham*, 4 Mich., 339. And see *Bryan v. Smith*, 10 Mich., 229.

2606. The complaint stands in lieu of a declaration. *Caswell v. Ward*, 2 Doug., 374.

2607.—process under the Statutes of 1838 might have been served by a constable. *People v. Gay*, 2 Doug., 367.

2608.—continuances might have been granted under the Statutes of 1838, though the power to continue was not expressly conferred; it being incident to the jurisdiction to hear and determine. *Caswell v. Ward*, 2 Doug., 374.

2609.—jury. Where (under the Statutes of 1838) a warrant and venire were issued and served, and on the return day the parties and most of the jurors summoned appeared, and the cause was then adjourned to a future day, and the justices thereupon issued a second venire by which another jury was summoned, before whom the cause was tried; *Held*, that the justices had no power to direct the second jury to be summoned, but that they should have required the jurors who appeared in obedience to the first venire to appear on the adjourned day, and if their number was insufficient to complete the panel, the deficiency should have been supplied by summoning additional jurors by virtue of the same venire. *Latimer v. Woodward*, 2 Doug., 368.

2610. Under the Statutes of 1838, as amended in 1840, the jury were the judges of both the law and the facts. Misdirection of the Court to the jury could not, therefore, be assigned for error. But it might be assigned for error that the verdict was against law. *Chamberlin v. Brown*, 2 Doug., 120.

2611.—pleading the general issue to the complaint was held a waiver of irregularities in the summons and venire. *Falkner v. Beers*, 2 Doug., 117.

2612.—the evidence must be confined to proof of the facts alleged in the complaint. *Caswell v. Ward*, 2 Doug., 374.

2613. Where the proceeding is by the purchaser at a statutory foreclosure of a mortgage, the complainant must prove the regularity of all the proceedings on the foreclosure. *Ibid.*

2614. Evidence which shows merely an *unlawful* entry and detention, without showing that they were accompanied with violence, or a breach of the peace, will not support a complaint for forcible entry and detainer. *Davis v. Ingersoll*, 2 Doug., 372; *Harrington v. Scott*, 1 Mich., 17. And evidence which shows a forcible detention only, but not force or violence in making the entry, will not support the complaint. *Latimer v. Woodward*, 2 Doug., 368.

2615. Where A. obtained possession of premises occupied by B., by knocking a door open with a hammer in B.'s absence, and B. soon afterwards, in A.'s absence, re-entered by similar violence, it was held, that A.'s temporary occupation so acquired was not such *quiet and peaceable* possession as would entitle him to maintain forcible entry and detainer against B. *Harrington v. Scott*, 1 Mich., 17.

2616. Proof that the defendants (there being only two of them) repaired alone to the premises, and that one of them pounded upon the door and it was opened, whereupon they both entered, is not sufficient to sustain a complaint for forcible entry and detainer. *Ibid.*

2617.—appeal. Where judgment was rendered in favor of the complainant, in a case where the complaint was insufficient to confer jurisdiction, and an appeal was taken to the Circuit Court, it was held that that Court had jurisdiction, on reversing the judgment, to render judgment against the complainant for costs. *Bryan v. Smith*, 10 Mich., 229.

2618. A writ of error is the proper process to bring the judgment of the Circuit Court before the Supreme Court for review. *Parker v. Copland*, 4 Mich., 528.

POWERS.

2619. To two or more. Where several persons are empowered by law to execute a public trust or power, and in the execution thereof, all are present to deliberate, the act of a majority will be valid. *Scott v. Detroit Young Men's Society's Lessee*, 1 Doug., 119.

2620. They will all be presumed to have been present, and to have deliberated upon the act, unless the contrary expressly appears. *Ibid.*

2621. Land Board in Detroit. The powers conferred upon the Governor and Judges of Michigan Territory to grant donation lots in Detroit, are not to be construed with the technical strictness applicable to those of an ordinary attorney or donee of a power; but they were vested with a large discretion, and their acts are entitled to liberal intendments in their support. These powers cannot be held exhausted until they had fulfilled the purposes for which they were conferred, by causing the title to a lot to be vested in each person entitled. *Ready v. Kearsley*, 14 Mich.

2622. Where the Board conveyed a lot in Detroit to A., and afterwards by mistake gave a deed of the same lot to B., and A. took possession of another lot on the supposition that it was the one granted to him, and the Board afterwards, assuming that A. had lost the title to the first mentioned lot, gave him a deed of the one of which he had taken possession; it was held that the Board had not exhausted their power to grant a donation lot to A. by giving the first deed, and that the second deed to him was valid. *Ibid.*

2623. Unauthorized conditions. Where the donee of a power to be executed by conveyance to another, attaches unauthorized conditions, such conditions are void and the deed good. But only the grantee and those in privity with him are entitled to question the act. *Ibid.*

2624. And therefore a third person is not at liberty to question the validity of a clause inserted in a deed given by the Land Board, by which the grantee was to hold "in trust for the rightful owners," &c. *Ibid.*

PRACTICE IN THE CIRCUIT COURTS.

2625. Service of process can only be made in the county in which the Court is held. *Turrill v. Walker*, 4 Mich., 177.

[Exceptions to the rule are made by statute in the case of executions; Comp. L., §§ 4442, 4448 ; attachments ; Laws of 1861, p. 479 ; and process generally against joint debtors ; Laws of 1861, p. 485.]

2626. Notice of rule to plead. The omission to serve notice of rule to plead with the declaration, is an irregularity for which the proceedings will be set aside at any time. The defendant waives no rights by failing to notice the defect within any specific time, for he has no notice of the purpose for which the declaration is served. *Ibid.*

2627. Return of service of declaration. Where the suit is commenced by declaration, the certificate of service may be indorsed on the original declaration on file, or on a copy. *Larned v. Wilcox*, 4 Mich., 333.

2628. Where a notice was attached to a declaration, that a note, a copy of which was given, would be read in evidence under the declaration, and the sheriff returned that he had served on the defendant a copy of the declaration and notice, it was held that the return necessarily implied service of a copy of the note, since that constituted an essential part of the notice. *Bliss v. Paine*, 11 Mich., 92.

2629. Where the under sheriff serves the writ, he may make the return in his own name. *Callendar v. Olcott*, 1 Mich., 344.

2630. Prochien ami. The prochien ami for an infant plaintiff must be appointed by the Court. If the suit is commenced by declaration without such appointment, it will be dismissed on motion. *Haines v. Oatman*, 2 Doug., 430. The proper practice on appointing *prochien ami* indicated in this case. See statutory provisions, Comp. L., Ch. 143 ; Laws of 1858, p. 9.

2631. Rule to plead under Statutes of 1838. Rule 11 of 1843, requiring defendants, in suits commenced by declaration, to plead thereto within thirty days after service of a copy of the declaration, was a rule the Court had power to make. *Norvell v. McHenry*, 1 Mich., 227.

2632. Amendment of declaration. Where a plaintiff suffers the time to elapse within which, by the rules, he may amend of course, the right becomes extinguished. Held, therefore, that after a trial of the issue, verdict for the plaintiff, verdict set aside, a new trial granted, leave given to the parties, by special order of the Court, "to file new pleadings under the general rules," an amended declaration filed under this order, and demurrer thereto, the plaintiff had no right to file a second amended declaration without special leave granted by the Court. *People v. Judges of Washtenaw Circuit*, 1 Doug., 434.

2633. A declaration may be amended by adding new counts, so as to lay the contract or wrong in a different manner; but a new cause of action cannot be introduced by amendment. *Ibid.* Nor the cause of action changed; as from trover to assumpsit. *People v. Judge of Wayne Circuit Court*, 13 Mich., 206.

2634. Bill of particulars. The office of a bill of particulars is to inform the opposite party of the causes of action to be relied on upon the trial, which are not specially set out in the declaration. *Davis v. Freeman*, 10 Mich., 188.

2635. By a written contract defendant promised plaintiff to pay a third person $1,700, due to him from plaintiff, and also $1,300 for plaintiff's services thereafter to be performed. In an action on this contract, plaintiff, by his bill of particulars, confined his claim to the contract. This did not preclude him from showing, by parol evidence, the performance of the subsequent services. *Tefft v. McNoah*, 9 Mich., 201.

2636. Affidavit of merits. Under the act of 1844 (S. L., p. 11, § 2), which authorized the plaintiff, in actions on contract, to take an inquest or assessment unless an affidavit of merits was filed, it was held that the affiant, whether the affidavit was made by the defendant or his agent or attorney, should swear to a defense upon the merits from his own knowledge of the facts constituting such defense, and not from information and belief. *Brown v. Cowee*, 2 Doug., 432.

2637. Supplying lost files. Where a recognizance of special bail was lost from the files of the Court, and plaintiff moved to substitute a copy to stand in lieu of the original, it was held that the Court had no jurisdiction to order the substitution to be made without notice to the sureties. *Montgomery v. Henry*, 10 Mich., 19.

2638. Adjournments of the Court from day to day during the same term, are not continuances which require to be stated in the record. *Owners of Ship Milwaukee v. Hale*, 1 Doug., 306.

2639. Sale of a demand in suit does not abate the suit, but it may be prosecuted to judgment for the benefit of the purchaser. *Newberry v. Trowbridge*, 13 Mich., 263.

2640. Discontinuance as to part of defendants. Where action was brought on a replevin bond against all the obligors, two of whom were defaulted, and the plaintiff, instead of proceeding to trial as to the others, discontinued as to them, and took judgment against those who were defaulted, this action was held erroneous. *Winslow v. Herrick*, 9 Mich., 380. See supra, 771.

2641. Under § 10 of the schedule to the constitution, vesting in the Circuit Courts jurisdiction of suits commenced in the County Courts, such Circuit Courts had power, in suits brought against several defendants on joint and several demands, to allow a discontinuance as to one or more of the defendants. *Chandler v. Lawrence*, 3 Mich., 261.

2642. Demurrer. Where a demurrer is overruled and the party pleads over, the right of objection is thereby waived, and he cannot afterwards object, on error, that it was erroneously overruled. *Wales v. Lyon*, 2 Mich., 276. (Though this case has not been distinctly overruled on this point, it is believed not to be now followed.)

2643. Judgment on demurrer will be given against the party committing the first error in substance, and not in matter of form merely. *Ibid.* See *People v. River Raisin and Lake Erie R. R. Company*, 12 Mich., 389.

2644. Trial: the jury. Where the record showed that the jury were "duly elected, tried and sworn," instead of that they were "sworn well and truly to try the issue," &c., it was held that the error, if any, must be regarded as clerical, and under the Statute—R. S. of 1838, p. 461-2—might be amended after error brought. *Owners of Ship Milwaukee v. Hale*, 1 Doug., 306. See also, *Comp. L., p.* 1201-2.

2645. The record in error showed that talesmen were called and sworn on a jury, but did not show that they had the requisite qualification of jurors. It was held—no challenge appearing to have been taken on that ground—that they must be presumed to have been properly qualified. *Ibid.*

2646. Held further, that by going to trial without challenge a party waives any objection to the want of proper qualification of jurors, as well as to the sufficiency of the oath administered to the jury. *Ibid.*

2647. Where it does not appear from the record that the jury retired to consult, it will be presumed that they found their verdict without leaving their seats. *Ibid.*

2648. Where one of the jurors had sat on a former trial of the same cause, and this fact was known to the counsel of one of the parties before the verdict was rendered, and he omitted to object until afterwards, it was held that he was bound by the verdict. *Bourke v. James*, 4 Mich., 336. See to the same effect, *Sleight v. Henning*, 12 Mich., 371.

2649. Challenges. On the impannelling of a jury it is irregular for counsel to put questions to the jurors called, without interposing any challenge; and no error can be assigned to the action of the Court in allowing jurors thus questioned, but not challenged, to be sworn to try the case. *Crippen v. People*, 8 Mich., 117.

2650. A challenge to the array must be in writing. *People v. Doe*, 1 Mich., 451.

2651. Where a juror is challenged for favor, the usual mode of trying his impartiality is by triers appointed for the purpose, on the demand of the challenging party. If the challenging party, when asked by the Court how he will have the challenge tried, refuses to indicate the mode of trial, it may be tried by the Court, by administering an oath to the juror, and propounding questions to him. *Ibid.*

2652. If a party or his counsel interposes a challenge for favor, or raises any other preliminary question involving an inquiry, and then neglect or refuses to move the trial or examination thereof, he thereby waives such challenge or question. *Ibid.*

2653. A person who has formed and holds an opinion that mill dams generally in that part of the country are nuisances, and that all he is acquainted with are such, is not a competent juror for the trial of an indictment for nuisance in keeping up a mill dam, though he states that he is not much acquainted with the dam in question, and has not formed or expressed any opinion in regard to it. *Crippen v. People*, 8 Mich., 117. See as to challenges generally, supra, 923 to 927.

2654. Province of court and jury. Where a corrupt agreement is charged in an instrument fair on its face, the question of intent is for the jury. *Orr v. Lacey*, 2 Doug., 230. See also, *Oliver v. Eaton*, 7 Mich., 108; *Bagg v. Jerome*, 7 Mich., 145; *Nye v. Van Husan*, 6 Mich., 329; *Snook v. Davis*, 6 Mich., 156.

2655. Where action is brought in the name of one person, for the benefit, as is claimed, of a bona fide assignee, the question whether there has been a bona fide assignment is not for the Court, but for the jury; and the Court is not warranted in excluding the admissions of the nominal plaintiff, on the assumption that such assignment has been established by the evidence. *Hogan v. Sherman*, 5 Mich., 60.

2656. Where a contract in duplicate was left by the parties with a third person, and the evidence as to the arrangement for its subsequent delivery, and the terms upon which it was to become operative, was conflicting, it was held that the question of the terms and conditions upon which the contract was to become operative was one of fact for the jury, depending upon the intention of the parties to be gathered from the whole transaction; and that the Court was right in refusing to charge that delivery in a particular mode was essential. *Jaquith v. Hudson*, 5 Mich., 123.

2657. Whether in a particular case a merchant in New York, shipping goods to his correspondent in the interior, had authority to make a contract on behalf of the correspondent for shipment on different terms from those ordinarily adopted by common carriers, is a question of fact to be determined by the jury from the evidence; and the Court cannot, properly, be asked to make any charge that shall absolutely dispose of the fact in controversy. *American Transportation Co. v. Moore*, 5 Mich., 368.

2658. Where there is a conflict of evidence, and the jury, by weighing it, are to find facts, it is the duty of the Court, in instructing the jury, to propound the law, and direct its application to the facts as they may be found. But when the fact is admitted, or undisputed, and there is no conflict of evidence, the question is one of law, upon which direct instruction ought to be given. *Wisner v. Davenport*, 5 Mich., 501.

2659. Whether a custom of merchants sought to be established is reasonable or not, is a question of law for the Court, but user, which is the evidence of custom, is matter for the jury, which the Court will submit to them or not, as it shall find the custom legal and reasonable or otherwise. *Bourke v. James*, 4 Mich., 336.

2660. The city of Saginaw was incorporated with territory which constituted about one-fourth of school district No. one of the township of Saginaw. The officers of the district being within the city, thereafter assumed to be officers of school district No. one of the city of Saginaw, and brought suit in that name to recover moneys levied and collected for said school district No. one of the township of Saginaw, claiming an identity of corporate existence. The question of identity having been submitted to the jury as a question of fact; held, that this was erroneous. *Township of Saginaw v. School District No. One of the City of Saginaw*, 9 Mich., 541.

2661. The question of the sufficiency of an indictment cannot be referred to the jury as one of fact. *People v. Cook*, 10 Mich., 164.

2662. Whether a contracting party has, by agreement with an assignee of a contract, estopped himself from making any claim to damages for the non-fulfillment of the contract by the assignor, is a question of fact for the jury; and in an action on the contract the Court has no right, after evidence has been given of such an agreement, to assume it as established, and exclude all evidence of damages. *Litchfield v. Garratt*, 10 Mich., 426.

2663. Where plaintiffs were to run for defendant his staves "at and near T.," at a specified price, it was held, that whether a point a mile and a half from there was "near T.," within the meaning of the contract, was a question of fact for the jury, and could not be decided by the Court as a matter of law. *Shaw v. Davis*, 7 Mich., 318.

2664. Charge to the jury. The language of a Judge's charge to the jury must be construed with reference to the facts in evidence upon which it is given. *People v. Scott*, 6 Mich., 287. See *Angell v. Rosenbury*, 12 Mich., 241.

2665. If the charge contains an abstract proposition of law, having no particular reference to the evidence submitted, it will be presumed, although the language is general, that the jury properly applied it to the case before them. *People v. Reynolds*, 2 Mich., 422.

2666. The Court cannot be required to charge upon abstract propositions of law not having a bearing upon the evidence submitted. *Doyle v. Stevens*, 4 Mich., 87. See supra, 1546 to 1548, 1552 to 1555.

2667. Non-suit. The Court cannot compel a plaintiff to become non-suit. He has always a right, if he chooses, to go to the jury with his case. *Cahill v. Kalamazoo Mutual Insurance Co.*, 2 Doug., 124.

2668. Special verdict. The Court can add nothing to a special finding, or infer any facts which the jury have not inferred and set forth. The Court can only draw the legal conclusions from the facts found. *People v. Wells*, 8 Mich., 104.

2669. Where the jury find the facts specially, it is entirely beyond their province to go further, and, applying the law to such facts, determine that one of the parties is entitled to recover. And any such determination is to be disregarded by the Court, and such judgment given as the facts found will warrant. *Erwin v. Clark*, 13 Mich., 10.

2670. The jury will find a special verdict at their option; the Court cannot compel them to do so, or to give reasons for a general finding. *Peck v. Snyder*, 13 Mich., 21.

2671. What verdict covers the issues. Where there are two issues—the general issue, and an issue on a special plea—and the jury find a verdict for the plaintiff on the general issue, but render no verdict on the other issue, the judgment will not be reversed if the verdict on the general issue negatives the special plea of defendant on which the other issue was joined, and the jury could not have found for the plaintiff had defendant established the truth of his special plea. *Brooks v. Delrymple*, 1 Mich., 145.

2672. The issue was submitted to a jury whether an alleged will was the last will and testament of the decedent, and whether at the time of executing it he was of sound and disposing mind, and not under the undue influence of the devisee therein named. The jury returned a verdict that the will was the last will and testament of the decedent, and that at the time of executing it he was of sound disposing mind and memory, and capable of disposing of his property by will. Held that it covered the whole issue, and necessarily negatived all undue influence. *White v. Bailey*, 10 Mich.. 155. See supra, 181.

2673. Certainty in verdict. A verdict in ejectment that defendant is guilty of unlawfully withholding "the west three-fourths of the north-west fractional quarter" of a certain section, "excepting twenty-five acres on the west half of said section, and three acres cut off by the road from the south-west corner of said section," is so uncertain in the description it gives that no judgment can be rendered upon it. *Munger v. Grinnell*, 9 Mich., 544.

2674. Verdict for the plaintiff in ejectment for four certain parcels of land, describing them, "except so much of said last two described portions or parcels of land as is contained in the plat of the village of Royal Oak, recorded in the record of deeds for said county of Oakland," was held sufficiently certain. *Lockwood v. Drake*, 1 Mich., 14.

2675. Ejectment for dower. Verdict that "The jury find for the plaintiff, and that the plaintiff is entitled to the possession, during her lifetime, of the undivided third part of [land described] as the reasonable dower of said plaintiff in said premises." Held sufficient. *Ibid.*

2676. Shaping verdict. Juries rarely give very formal verdicts; and inquiries of the jurors in Court, and amendments for the purpose of putting in due form what the jury mean by their finding, are unobjectionable. *Sleight v. Henning*, 12 Mich., 371.

2677. Amending verdict. A jury brought in a sealed verdict, "We find for the plaintiff the full amount claimed by him on the note." It is not objectionable to permit the plaintiff's counsel to state to the jury what the amount was, and for them to return a verdict for that amount in due form. [MARTIN, CH. J.] *Olcott v. Hanson*, 12 Mich., 452.

2678. Finding by Judge. A Circuit Judge may amend his finding, and his action in so doing is not subject to review. *Sweetzer v. Mead*, 5 Mich., 33.

2679. No written request for a finding by the Circuit Judge is necessary, except where a party desires a detailed finding on the facts in the case, as well as on the law points. *People v. Littlejohn*, 11 Mich., 60.

2680. The right to except for supposed errors of decision is not affected by the absence of a written finding. *Ibid.*

2681. On trial without a jury, rulings of law which might affect the finding of facts—as upon the admission or rejection of evidence—cannot be reviewed except upon exceptions. But when the only question is whether the facts found support the judgment, the finding of facts is to be treated as a special verdict, and no exceptions are necessary. *Trudo v. Anderson*, 10 Mich., 357; *Wood v. La Rue*, 9 Mich. 158.

2682. The finding of facts must set forth the *facts found*, and not merely the evidence tending to prove them. *Ibid; Thomas v. Sprague*, 12 Mich., 120.

2683. Where, as a conclusion of law from a finding of facts, the Judge holds the plaintiff entitled to recover, the finding must contain all the facts and circumstances necessary to make out a cause of action. *Wood v. La Rue*, 9 Mich., 158.

2684. Testimony by deposition. Where a deposition was taken by stipulation before a justice, who had no power to take it except that derived from the stipulation, it was held not to be a valid objection that the justice had not attached to it such a certificate as would have been required had it been taken under the statute by an officer authorized to take depositions for the Circuit Courts. *Knight v. Emmons*, 4 Mich., 554.

2685. It is no objection to the reading of a deposition on the trial that notice of its filing was not given. If the party taking the deposition gives notice under the rule, (Rule 50 of 1853—Rule 51 of 1858), objections of form must be filed within the time limited; but if he chooses to take the risk of such objections on the trial, he can do so. *Ibid.*

2686. The deposition of a witness who does not understand the English language, may be taken under the act of 1848—*Comp. L.*, § 4270, *et seq.*—though an interpreter. *Campau v. Dewey*, 9 Mich., 381.

2687. And it may be taken down in narrative form, instead of through interrogatories. *Ibid.*

2688. The notice of taking depositions under said act, when not served by an officer, must be verified by the affidavit of the party himself, or, at least, if a suit be pending, by his attorney of record. *Ibid.*

2689. The answer of a witness under a commission is not admissible, unless it would have been admitted had he been examined in open Court on the stand. *Bliss v. Paine*, 11 Mich., 92.

2690. Where the testimony of a foreign witness was taken by commission, and the commission was returned and filed with the clerk, an objection that no instructions for the return of the commission were sent with it was held to be an objection of form, which, under rule 51, was waived if not filed in writing and served within two days after notice of the filing of the commission. *Facey v. Otis*, 11 Mich., 213.

2691. By the Statutes of 1838, an objection to the competency of a witness whose deposition was taken in the cause, was required to be made at the taking of the deposition, or it was deemed waived. *Hasey v. White Pigeon Beet Sugar Company*, 1 Doug., 193.

2692. Where the deposition was taken before a justice under the Statutes of 1838, it was held not necessary to produce proof to the justice that notice of taking it had been given to the opposite party, who was not present. The fact that notice was duly given might be proved in the Court to which the deposition was returned. *Pickard v. Polhemus*, 3 Mich., 185.

2693. Interrogatories will be presumed to have been settled in the ordinary way, under the statute and rules, where nothing appears to the contrary; and in such case the party may make objection to the competency of the evidence for the first time on the trial. (Comp. L., §§ 4257, 4248). *Angell v. Rosenbury*, 12 Mich., 241.

2694. Objection to variance between evidence and the pleading under which it is offered, must be held to be waived where the evidence is received and submitted to the consideration of the jury without the objection being taken. *McHardy v. Wadsworth*, 8 Mich., 349.

2695. Admission of instrument sued on. See supra, 426. A recognizance of special bail is not such a " written instrument" as is intended by Circuit Court rule 79, which provides that, in any action brought upon a written instrument the plaintiff shall not be put to the proof of its execution, or the hand writing of the defendant, unless its execution be denied by affidavit. *Elliott v. Green*, 10 Mich., 113.

2696. The genuineness of a recognizance of special bail may be disproved by defendants in an action brought thereon. *Ibid.*

2697. Evidence before auditor. Where a cause has been referred by the Circuit Court to an auditor, under Comp. L., § 4197, depositions which have been taken by the auditor and returned into Court with his report, but not attached to or forming a part of it, cannot be used as evidence on the trial of the cause in the Circuit Court. *Beard v. Spalding*, 12 Mich., 309.

2698. Trial before referees. The Circuit Court, after report of a referee has been filed in Court, cannot, on his application, refer the case back to enable him to review his conclusions upon the facts. The power of the Court to refer the case back is only given where exceptions have been taken, and is to be exercised upon hearing such exceptions. *Smith v. Warner*, 14 Mich.

2699. Where the report of a referee is not excepted to, it will stand as the finding or determination of the Court for the purpose of enabling the party in whose favor it is made to take judgment upon it as of course. *Amboy, Lansing and Traverse Bay R. R. Co. v. Byerly*, 13 Mich., 439.

2700. The question whether the referee's finding of facts sustains his conclusions of law, can only be raised by excepting to his report. *Ibid.*

2701. Assessment of damages by clerk. Under the Statutes of 1838—p. 450, § 4—the clerk might assess the plaintiff's damages, on default to a declaration on a covenant to pay the costs and damages which should be awarded in a certain cause, alleging a recovery in the cause, and its date and amount. *Prentiss v. Spalding*, 2 Doug., 84.

2702. The Court can only refer to the clerk, for assessment and report, those cases on default in which such a written obligation or contract as is specified in the statute is set forth in the declaration as the cause of action, or in which the action is upon a promissory note or bill of exchange, and the plaintiff has filed and served with his declaration a copy thereof. *O'Flynn v. Holmes*, 8 Mich., 95.

2703. For the reversal of a judgment rendered on default and assessment by the clerk, the following reasons were assigned:

1. That the notice of assessment of damages did not state the place where it would be made.

2. That the assessment was not made by the clerk at his office, but in the Court room—Court being in session—in the absence of defendant's attorney.

3. That the case was not a proper one for assessment by the clerk—the declaration containing counts for goods sold and delivered, as well as the common money counts. (A copy of the note upon which the assessment was made was served with the declaration).

4. Final judgment was entered on the same day on which the clerk's report was filed.

5. The Circuit Court overruled, with costs, a motion to set aside the judgment for these reasons.

It seems that none of the reasons assigned is sufficient for reversing the judgment. *Beeson v. Hollister*, 11 Mich., 193.

2704. The assessment of damages, under the Statutes of 1838, was considered as made by the Court, and should appear to have been so made in the judgment record, although the journal entry, from which such record was made up, showed that the damages were assessed by the clerk. *Prentiss v. Spalding*, 2 Doug., 84.

2705. Where it was recited in the judgment entry under the present statutes, in a case not proper for a reference to the clerk, that judgment was rendered upon the clerk's assessment of damages, but the prior order of reference to assess was to the Court, as it should have been, it was held that the Court could not make any presumption, against the recital in the judgment, based upon such prior order, that the Court actually assessed the damages; but the judgment imports absolute verity. *O'Flynn v. Holmes*, 8 Mich., 95.

2706. A judgment was taken against P. and F. on their joint covenant that P. should pay all costs and damages that should be awarded against him in a certain cause. The entry did not show that it was shown to the Court, nor did the record show it to be certified by the clerk, which of the defendants was principal, and which surety or bail. (R. S. 1838, p. 451, § 9). Held no ground for reversing the judgment. *Prentiss v. Spalding*, 2 Doug., 84.

2707. Assessment by the Court. It is competent for the Court to assess damages after interlocutory judgment, without calling a jury, if none is demanded. *O'Flynn v. Holmes*, 8 Mich., 95.

2708. Assessment by jury. Where the maker and indorser of commercial paper are sued jointly under the statute, and one is defaulted, and issue joined as to the other, it is competent for plaintiff to have damages assessed against the defaulted party, by the jury sworn to try the issue as to the other; and on their verdict and assessment to proceed to a joint judgment against both. *Storey v. Bird*, 8 Mich., 316.

2709. A motion for judgment as in case of nonsuit, is a special motion, and must be founded upon affidavit, showing the facts necessary to entitle the party to it. *Storey v. Child*, 2 Mich., 107.

2710. If any part of the ground of a motion consists of facts not apparent on the face of the proceedings, an affidavit or other competent evidence of its existence must be presented. *Ibid.*

2711. A motion to strike an amended declaration from the files, and the decision of the Circuit Court thereon, form no part of the record, and are not the subject of exception. *People v. Judges of Washtenaw Circuit Court*, 1 Doug., 434. And see *Millerd v. Reeves*, 1 Mich., 107.

2712. Laches. A motion to set aside a judgment for irregularity, made two years after it was rendered, the delay being unexplained, is too late. *People v. Judges of Calhoun Circuit*, 1 Doug., 417.

2712*a*. A motion for an assessment of damages in a replevin suit, made the next term after judgment in the case, was held too late; the parties being out of Court. *People v. Judges of Jackson Circuit Court*, 1 Doug., 302. But as to the lapse of a term affecting the power of the Court, see *Jagger v. Coon*, 5 Mich., 31; *Emory v. Whitwell*, 6 Mich., 474.

2713. Motion by stranger. A judgment in a suit commenced by attachment will not be set aside for irregularity on the motion of a person to whom the property attached had been conveyed by the defendant after service of the attachment, but who is a stranger to the record. *People v. Judges of Calhoun Circuit Court*, 1 Doug., 417.

2714. Judgment on demurrer. On overruling a demurrer, judgment goes for the plaintiff, unless leave is given the defendant to plead. To the order allowing leave the Court may attach such conditions as the circumstances of the case may require, and its action cannot be reviewed on error. *Tefft v. McNoah*, 9 Mich., 201.

2715. Judgment by confession. It is no objection to a judgment entered up by confession, that the warrant of attorney is upon the same piece of paper as the note it authorizes judgment to be taken upon. The warrant of attorney and note are still to be regarded as separate instruments, (*Comp. L.*, § 4441) notwithstanding they are thus connected. *Twombly v. Parsons*, 10 Mich., 272.

2716. The note and warrant of attorney bearing different dates, are presumed to have been executed at the times they respectively bear date, notwithstanding they are upon the same paper. *Ibid.*

2717. But it would not be a valid objection to a judgment taken by confession, that they were both executed at the same time. *Ibid.*

2718. Judgment in covenant on a replevin bond, may be for damages, instead of the penalty of the bond. *Prentiss v. Spalding*, 2 Doug., 84.

2719. Setting aside judgment. Where the Court makes an order vacating a judgment as to one of two joint debtors, the effect is to vacate it as to both. *Van Rensselaer v. Whiting*, 12 Mich., 449.

2720. Notice of judgment. The party against whom a decision is rendered by the Circuit Judge in vacation, is entitled to a written notice, either from the clerk or from the opposite party, before the ten days allowed him for making a case commence to run. *People v. Wilson*, 12 Mich., 25.

2721. But a party who, after judgment rendered against him on trial before the Judge, has acted upon the judgment, and procured orders allowing time to settle a case or bill of exceptions, cannot object that he has had no written notice of the judgment, and insist upon a right to make and serve a case, under Rule 81, until ten days after such written notice. *Richardson v. Yawkey*, 9 Mich., 139.

2722. Exceptions. A party may allege exceptions to the charge given to the jury, at any time before verdict. *Doyle v. Stevens*, 4 Mich., 87. *Comp. L.*, § 4404.

2723. A bill of exceptions signed by the Circuit Judge, showing the exceptions to have been properly taken on the trial, is to be presumed properly signed, and within the proper time, though dated several months after the trial and judgment, and though nothing appears in the bill itself, or in the record, to show affirmatively that time was allowed for its preparation and settlement. *Sweetzer v. Mead*, 5 Mich., 33.

2724. To enable the Supreme Court to judge of the propriety of instructions to the jury in the Court below, which instructions assume the existence of certain facts, the bill of exceptions must contain either the evidence of those facts, or a statement that there was such evidence. *Tyler v. People*, 8 Mich., 320.

2725. Settlement of exceptions. Where time has been allowed for preparing and settling exceptions, and it has expired without action, the Circuit Judge has power to make a further order for that purpose. *People v. Littlejohn*, 11 Mich., 60.

2726. Such further order having been made by the Circuit Judge, he cannot afterwards disregard it, and refuse to settle the exceptions because not presented for the purpose within the time first allowed. *Ibid.*

2727. Amendments. The omission of the clerk to enter defendant's appearance in a cause, is a mere matter of form, which may be amended by an order *nunc pro tunc*. *Norvell v. McHenry*, 1 Mich., 227.

2728. Where the sheriff's return of sale does not show all the steps required by law to make the sale valid, the Circuit Court may, upon application founded upon affidavit, grant an amendment of the return. *People v. Judges of Calhoun Circuit*, 1 Doug., 417. See *Calender v. Olcott*, 1 Mich., 344.

2729. After a trial without a jury, and judgment for plaintiff in the ordinary form, defendant moved for a new trial, and the Court set aside the order for judgment, and immediately entered judgment again for the same amount, embodying therein a finding of the facts and law by the Judge. Defendant brought error, contending that the Court could not wholly set aside and vacate a judgment without granting a new trial. Held, that the action of the Court amounted substantially to an amendment of the judgment, and was not erroneous. But the amendment was unnecessary, as the statute does not require the Judge's finding to be embraced in the judgment. *Lorman v. Benson*, 9 Mich., 237. And see AMENDMENT.

2730. Costs. On a trial by jury, if the plaintiff recover less than $100, the judge is to determine whether his claim as established at the trial exceeded $200, and was reduced by set off; and if so, the plaintiff should recover costs. *Davis v. Freeman*, 10 Mich., 188. And see COSTS.

2731. Revivor. The suggestion of the death of the plaintiff, cannot be the subject of an issue; and whether the defendant is entitled to any notice, is a question that can only be raised on motion to set aside the proceedings for irregularity. *Larned v. Wilcox*, 4 Mich., 333.

2732. Cases made for review by Supreme Court. The act of 1851 (S. L., p. 311) did not intend that parties to suits in Circuit Courts should be at liberty to have a case at law re-heard in the Supreme Court upon the merits, like an appeal in chancery. The Court were to judge of the case as if it were an application for a new trial, and to ascertain from an inspection of the whole case whether the Circuit Judge manifestly erred, either in his conclusions upon the facts, or in respect to the law applicable to them. *Hill v. La Fayette Insurance Company*, 2 Mich., 476. (This act was repealed in 1853, and a different practical construction has been put upon the provision adopted in its stead.)

2733. Case made after judgment by default. The proceedings in taking judgment on default and an assessment of damages by the clerk, cannot be reviewed on case made. *Beeson v. Hollister*, 11 Mich., 193.

2734. Election of case or exceptions. A party having taken exceptions on a trial in the Circuit Court, has his election to remove the case to the Supreme Court for review upon bill of exceptions or on case made. But when he has procured a bill of exceptions to be settled, and has filed the same, he has made his election, and is not entitled thereafter to make and settle a case. *Richardson v. Yawkey*, 9 Mich., 139.

2735. Case must be settled. Where one of the parties caused a case to be filed in the Supreme Court, which he claimed was a case settled after judgment, but it did not conclusively or necessarily show on its face that it was so intended; and the Circuit Judge who tried the suit and signed the document, certified to the Supreme Court that, in so signing it, he did not suppose he was settling a case under the statute, and that the one signed did not set forth the whole facts as they existed; held, that the papers should be remitted to the Circuit Court for such action as that Court should deem proper under the circumstances. *Farrand v. Bentley*, 6 Mich., 281.

2736. The case should show on its face that it is settled and signed by the Circuit Judge for the purpose of review by the Supreme Court. *Gard v. Stevens*, 12 Mich., 9.

2737. Presumption of proper settlement. Where the case is duly signed by the Judge, and purports to have been settled before him, all previous steps necessary to its settlement must, in the absence of any showing to the contrary, be presumed to have been regularly taken. *Sallee v. Ireland*, 9 Mich., 154.

2738. Certifying case to Supreme Court. When the case is settled, and filed with the clerk of the Circuit Court, either party desiring action upon it, may cause it to be certified to the Supreme Court. *Robertson v. Little*, 10 Mich., 371.

2739. But if the party who has caused the case to be made, neglects for more than two years to cause it to be certified to the Supreme Court, that Court, by analogy to the statute limiting the time for bringing writs of error to two years, will dismiss the case—at least unless the delay is sufficiently accounted for. *Van Blarcom v. The Ætna Insurance Co.*, 6 Mich., 299. But the case cannot be dismissed until actually sent up. *Robertson v. Little*, 10 Mich., 371.

2740. Presumptions from the case. A case of summary proceedings before a circuit court commissioner, to obtain possession of lands, was appealed to and tried in the Circuit Court, and after judgment for the complainant, a case was made presenting certain jurisdictional questions for review; but the case did not set forth the affidavit for appeal; and objection was taken in the Supreme Court that only the issue *upon the merits* was brought up by the appeal, unless such a special affidavit was made as was necessary for a special appeal from a justice's Court. It was held that, if such special affidavit was necessary, the Court must infer that one was made—the jurisdictional questions having been raised and passed upon in the Circuit Court without objection to the affidavit. *Sallee v. Ireland*, 9 Mich., 154.

2741. Evidence to be set forth. If the case is made for review on the whole facts, it should embody all the evidence given on the trial. *King v. Moore*, 10 Mich., 538; *Gray v. Howard*, 12 Mich., 171. But it will be presumed to contain all the evidence unless the contrary appears. *Gard v. Stevens*, 12 Mich., 292.

2742. If the case shows on its face that all the evidence is not embraced, the Court above will refuse to hear it, and remand it for correction. *Lee v. Lake*, 13 Mich., 220.

2743. What to be reviewed on case made. Only those questions are before the Supreme Court which appear to have been passed upon by the Court below. *Van Kleek v. Eggleston*, 7 Mich., 511.

2744. Though the record shows that judgment below should have been for the party against whom it was rendered, yet if the case does not show that it is brought up for review upon the facts, the Supreme Court cannot render such judgment as the Court below should have given, but can only order a new trial. *Brown v. Cady*, 11 Mich., 535.

2745. Where a cause was tried in the Circuit Court without a jury, and improper evidence received, and it was then brought to the Supreme Court for review on the whole facts on case made, it was held that that Court would not reverse the judgment for the admission of improper evidence if there was sufficient of an unexceptionable character to sustain it. *Rose v. Lewis*, 10 Mich., 483.

2746. But the Court must reverse if improper evidence was given to establish a material point, and the nature of the case is such that it cannot be presumed that other evidence was given on that point. *Bliss v. Paine*, 11 Mich., 92.

2747. Review of jury trial. If the case is made after verdict by jury and judgment thereon, the Supreme Court cannot review the facts, but only the rulings and decision of the Circuit Court. *Peck v. Snyder*, 13 Mich., 21.

2748. What questions of law may be reviewed. Under Comp. L., § 3421, other questions of law besides those arising upon the evidence, may be reviewed on case made. *Sallee v. Ireland*, 9 Mich., 154.

2749. New trial. Where a case is made for review on the facts, the Supreme Court cannot send the case back for a new trial. *Barman v. Carhartt*, 10 Mich., 338.

2750. Cases agreed upon. A case agreed upon by the parties, and submitted to the Circuit Court for its decision, under § 3421 of Compiled Laws, must be signed by the parties or their attorneys. *Farrand v. Bentley*, 6 Mich., 281.

2751. The case is not a mere stipulation concerning evidence, from which inferences of fact are to be drawn; but it is equivalent to a finding of facts by a Court, or the special verdict of a jury, in which every fact necessary to a recovery must be expressly found. *Goodrich v. Detroit*, 12 Mich., 279.

2752. Where, therefore, a contractor claimed to recover of the city of Detroit the contract price of a certain public work, on the ground of negligence on the part of the city in collecting the assessment therefor, and a case was agreed upon and submitted to the Court which only set forth the steps which the city had taken for the collection, it was held that the Court had no right, upon such a case, to find the fact of negligence from the facts agreed upon and set forth. *Ibid.*

PRACTICE IN THE SUPREME COURT.

2753. Irregular judgment. A judgment rendered by the late Supreme Court when but two of the Judges were present who had heard the argument of the case, is irregular, and will be vacated on motion, though more than a term has elapsed since its entry. *Jagger v. Coon*, 5 Mich., 31.

2754. Voluntary dismissal. A plaintiff in error will be allowed to dismiss his writ of error on motion, on payment of costs. *Birch v. Brown*, 5 Mich., 31.

2755. Laches in motions. Motion to dismiss must be made at the earliest opportunity. *Warner v. Whittaker*, 5 Mich., 241; *Steward v. Dixon*, 6 Mich., 391.

2756. Motions based upon the irregular action of the opposite party must be made at the earliest opportunity, and will not be entertained after the lapse of a term, unless some very satisfactory reason is shown for the delay. *O'Flynn v. Eagle*, 7 Mich., 306.

2757. The Court will not set aside a writ of error for want of proper return, after the lapse of several years, during the most of which time the papers have been in possession of the counsel for defendant in error, and joinder in error was filed while the counsel had the return in his hands. *Wattles v. Warren*, 7 Mich., 309.

2758. A copy of the bill of exceptions was sent up instead of the original; but three terms having elapsed since the return to the writ, and issue in error having been joined without notice of the irregularity, and no explanation being made of the delay, the Court refused to interfere to require the original to be sent up. *Evans v. Norris*, 6 Mich., 69.

2759. Certiorari in a probate case to the Circuit Court, where no issue of fact had been joined. The Supreme Court will not consider the objection that this is not a proper case for certiorari, made for the first time in a brief submitted by defendant in error, by leave of the Court, after the hearing. *Matter of Robinson Estate*, 6 Mich., 137.

2760. In a case which originated before a circuit court commissioner, and was appealed to and tried in the Circuit Court, and then removed to the Supreme Court, a motion made after four weeks in term, and after the filing of joinder in error, to amend the assignment of errors so as to take an objection to the jurisdiction of the commissioner which was not made before the commissioner or in the Circuit Court, presents no equitable claim upon the discretionary power of the Court, and will be denied. *Parsons v. Copland*, 5 Mich., 144.

2761. Where plaintiff in error failed to give notice of suing out the writ of error, but served assignment of errors, a motion to dismiss, made a year and a half afterwards, for want of notice of suing out the writ, was held too late. *Smith v. Mitchell*, 9 Mich., 261.

2762. Waiver of irregularities. A notice of hearing given by an appellee in chancery is a waiver of irregularities in taking the appeal. *Durfee v. McClurg*, 5 Mich., 532.

2763. A bill of exceptions, returned with a writ of error, appeared to have been signed after the writ was sued out. Held to be at most an irregularity, which was waived by joinder in error. *Brown v. Bissell*, 1 Doug., 273.

2764. Laches in procuring return. Where plaintiff in error has neglected to cause the return to be made in time, and applies to the Supreme Court for relief, he must explain and excuse the delay. *Lathrop v. Hicks*, 2 Doug., 223.

2765. He will not be relieved merely upon the affidavit of his attorney, that in his opinion there was good and legal cause for suing out the writ of error, and that if the case should be heard on its merits, the judgment below would be reversed. *Ibid.*

2766. It is not a sufficient excuse that the clerk below promised to make out the transcript and deliver it to the attorney within the time required by the rule; that the attorney relied upon this promise, and the neglect occurred in consequence of the clerk's failure to perform it. *Ibid.* See also, *Carne v. Hall*, 7 Mich., 159.

2767. On a motion for such relief, counter affidavits may be read, showing that it would be against good faith for the plaintiff in error to avail himself of the error complained of. *Ibid.*

2768. Reinstating cause. A case which had been dismissed for want of prosecution was reinstated on terms, on affidavit of merits, and of a verbal agreement with counsel for defendant in error giving time; and this, though the verbal agreement was denied. *Scott v. Scott*, 5 Mich., 106.

2769. When a motion is made to reinstate a cause at a term following its dismissal for want of prosecution, the party making the motion should show himself in position to proceed at once to the hearing if the motion should be granted. *Bingham v. Parsons*, 9 Mich., 144.

2770. Notice of special motions is in all cases necessary where the opposite party has appeared in the cause. *Scribner v. Doseman*, 5 Mich., 283.

2771. Counter affidavits may be read in opposition to a motion, without having been served. *Lathrop v. Hicks*, 2 Doug., 223.

2772. A motion not called up on the day for which it was noticed, cannot be taken up on any subsequent day in term, except by consent, unless it has been ordered to stand over to such subsequent day. *Ireland v. Spalding*, 11 Mich., 455.

2773. Service on agent. No agent for the service of papers can be recognized under the rules, unless residing at Detroit or Lansing. *Maynard v. Penniman*, 7 Mich., 333.

2774. When notices are served upon an agent, the distance of the attorney's residence from the place of holding the Court will determine the time for which notice must be given, and not the distance of the agent's residence from the Court. *Ibid.*

2775. Motion to amend. The entry of a special motion for leave to amend, must show in what particular an amendment is desired. And a copy of the proposed amendment, with notice of the motion, should be served on the opposite party. *Parsons v. Copland*, 5 Mich., 143.

2776. Amending records sent up. The Supreme Court has no authority to amend the records sent up from inferior tribunals. *Sweetzer v. Mead*, 5 Mich., 33; *Scribner v. Gay*, 5 Mich., 511; *Evans v. Norris*, 6 Mich., 69.

2777. But it may in a proper case compel their correction by the Court below, by mandamus. *Scribner v. Gay*, 5 Mich., 511; *Evans v. Norris*, 6 Mich., 69.

2778. It cannot strike out a bill of exceptions on proof that it was settled without notice to defendant in error. *Scribner v. Gay*, 5 Mich., 511.

2779. Though the Court may, on a proper showing, compel bills of exception to be corrected so as to conform to the facts, it will not do so until it is shown that mistakes exist which are injurious to the party applying for the correction. *Ibid.*

2780. And where the Judge who signed a bill of exceptions has since gone out of office, the bill cannot be remanded for correction. *Ibid.*

2781. Where an amendment has been made in the Court below, since the cause was removed to the Supreme Court by writ of error, but no further return has been had, the Court cannot entertain a motion based upon such amendment, on an affidavit that such an amendment has been made. *O'Flynn v. Eagle*, 7 Mich., 306.

2782. Where, six months after errors had been assigned in the Supreme Court, the defendant in error obtained, without leave from the Supreme Court, an amendment to the record in the Court below, with a view to obviate the errors assigned, and then moved the Supreme Court for an order for a further return to bring up the amendment, it was held that the application was too late. *O'Flynn v. Holmes*, 7 Mich., 454. And it would not be granted if there were no objection from laches. *O'Flynn v. Eagle*, 8 Mich., 136.

2783. The proper practice when such an amendment is desired, is to apply to the Supreme Court, on affidavit showing the reasons for the amendment, to remit the record for that purpose; and the Court can then judge whether the case is a proper one to permit an amendment with a view to affect proceedings already taken in the Supreme Court. *Ibid.*

2784. The Court will not, by consent of parties, treat that as a part of a bill of exceptions which is not actually incorporated therein by the Judge who settled the same. *Niagara Fire Insurance Co. v. De Graff*, 12 Mich., 10.

2785. But where the record shows an objection taken on the trial in the Court below to the admission of evidence, which was overuled, the Supreme Court will consider the question presented by the objection, notwithstanding the bill of exceptions does not show an exception to the ruling. The Court will presume, from the sealing of the bill of exceptions, that the ruling was duly excepted to. *McBride v. Cicotte*, 4 Mich., 478.

2786. The original files should not be altered, even by consent of parties. If an addition is desired, it should be done by stipulation, or other separate paper, without changing the original. *Farrand v. Collins Iron Co.*, 8 Mich., 136.

2787. The general power of the Court to allow amendments for the purpose of correcting mistakes, and errors of haste and inadvertence, considered. *Farrand v. Bentley*, 6 Mich., 281.

2788. Assignment of errors. Where a cause came to the Circuit Court by certiorari, errors cannot be newly assigned in the Supreme Court. *Lee v. Hardgrave*, 3 Mich., 77.

2789. Errors of fact may be assigned in the Supreme Court; and if necessary a trial of an issue upon them may be had by jury in that Court, or the issue may be sent to the proper circuit for trial. *Teller v. Wetherell*, 6 Mich., 46.

2790. Uncertainty and informality in the assignment of errors are no ground for quashing the assignment, or for dismissing the writ. *Ibid.*

2791. Under the rule (12) which requires all assignments of error to be special, the general assignment, that judgment should have been given for the plaintiff in error, cannot be noticed by the Court. *Webster v. Fisk*, 9 Mich., 250.

2792. A plaintiff in error had failed to procure a return to a writ of error in time, and made application for leave to file it and assign errors. The only special assignment was of errors occurring on the trial, and the record showed no exceptions. As the errors proposed to be assigned could not be noticed by the Court, leave was refused, though the delay was sufficiently excused. *Ibid.*

2793. Where an objection purely technical was made to an assignment of errors at the hearing, and it was evident that the defendant in error could not have been misled, the Court permitted an amendment. *Trudo v. Anderson*, 10 Mich., 357.

2794. Where error is brought in the Supreme Court upon a judgment in the Circuit, in a case brought there by certiorari to a justice of the peace, an assignment of errors that "the Circuit Judge erred in holding that the justice's judgment was erroneous in the several causes of error assigned in the affidavit for certiorari, " is a sufficient special assignment. *Berry v. Lowe*, 10 Mich., 9.

2795. Where several exceptions were taken to the charge of the Court, an assignment that the Judge " gave the several instructions to the jury asked by the defendant, and refused to give the several instructions, or any or either of them, asked for by the plaintiffs," is sufficiently special, and the words " several instructions " must be rendered distributively, and as applying to each. *Niles v. Rhodes*, 7 Mich., 374.

2796. An objection to a writ that it is not *tested* in the name of the people of the State of Michigan, is not sufficient to allow the party to make the point that the *style of the writ* is not in the name of the People, &c. And as the objection is purely technical, an amendment should not be allowed to rectify it to the overthrow of substantial justice. *Johnson v. Provincial Insurance Co.*, 12 Mich., 216.

2797. Assignments of error are not necessary on common law certiorari. *Stokes v. Jacobs*, 10 Mich., 290.

2798. Notice of hearing. What is a sufficient notice of hearing. See *Franklin v. Mansfield*, 8 Mich., 99.

2799. In computing time on notices of hearing, the day on which the notice is served is to be excluded, and the first day of term included. An intervening Sunday is not to be excluded. *Anderson v. Baughman*, 6 Mich., 298.

2800. An affidavit of the service of regular notice of hearing, and of the filing of proof thereof with the clerk, is sufficient evidence of those facts until denied by affidavit, though the proof so filed cannot now be found in the clerk's office. *Matter of Robinson Estate*, 6 Mich., 137.

2801. Printing the case. Counsel must exercise his own discretion in omitting to print the formal, and what he may deem the unimportant parts of the record in chancery appeals; and the Court will not interfere with the exercise of this discretion, unless it clearly appears to have been abused. *Wilson v. Wilson*, 6 Mich., 272. [The rule —31—has since been amended so as to require the printing of the whole record, "except the formal parts."]

2802. Calendar causes. Where cause has been shown in opposition to an application for a mandamus, and an argument is not had until a subsequent term, the case must be noticed and placed upon the docket for argument as a calendar cause, and printed briefs furnished. *People v. Township Board of Fillmore*, 11 Mich., 197.

2803. Default at hearing. Where the appellant, or plaintiff in error, makes default at the hearing, the decree or judgment of the Court below will be affirmed on motion. *Jackson Iron Co. v. Farrand*, and *Scott v. Scott*, 5 Mich., 249.

2804. Hearing. Where, on writ of error, an objection is taken which goes to the jurisdiction of the Court below, and is fatal to the judgment brought up for review, the Court will not pass upon the other questions raised by the record. *Fessenden v. Hill*, 6 Mich., 242.

2805. Where one party concedes that the judgment of the Court must be for his adversary, to the full extent of what he could claim on argument, the Court will not hear an argument for the purpose of expressing their opinion on points thus rendered unnecessary to a decision of the cause. *Sanger v. Truesdail*, 7 Mich., 9.

2806. A question as to whether a principle heretofore settled by the Court is or is not applicable to a case now pending, is a question to be discussed at the hearing, and not on motion to docket and dismiss. *Tower v. Detroit and Milwaukee Railway Co.*, 7 Mich., 10.

2807. So whether the plaintiff in error appeared and argued the cause in the Court below, or consented to the judgment then entered, is one which cannot be raised on affidavit, on motion to dismiss. *Ibid.*

2808. Where, after a case reserved for the opinion of the Supreme Court had been noticed for hearing, an addition of specific questions was made to it by the Circuit Judge without the consent of one party, it was held that such party should not be required to go to a hearing of the case upon the notice previously given. *Farrand v. Collins Iron Co.*, 8 Mich., 136.

2809. Matters appearing in the transcript filed, but which constitute no proper part of the record, cannot be considered by the Court.

As, a motion to set aside the service of a declaration, appearing in the return to a writ of error. *Millerd v. Reeves*, 1 Mich., 107. See supra, 1588.

2810. On the hearing of an application for a mandamus, the party showing cause is entitled to open and close the argument. *People v. Treasurer of Wayne Co.*, 8 Mich., 392.

2811. Judgment on exceptions. The Supreme Court cannot, on reversing a judgment on exceptions, proceed to give such judgment as the facts set forth in the bill of exceptions would warrant. The Court can only consider those facts as they bear upon the rulings of the Court below; and order a new trial if the exceptions are sustained. *Pond v. People*, 8 Mich., 150.

2812. Damages for delay. Where error was brought on a judgment taken by confession on a promissory note, and the errors assigned consisted of mere irregularities in the entering up of judgment; held, on affirming the judgment, that the case was a proper one for awarding damages for the delay and vexation consequent upon issuing the writ of error. *Waterman v. Toms*, 7 Mich., 78.

2813. See a case where damages were refused. *Storey v. Bird*, 8 Mich., 316.

2814. Costs on motions are allowed to the prevailing party as a matter of course, unless some special reason is shown why they should not be imposed. *O'Flynn v. Eagle*, 7 Mich., 306. They are also allowed to the prevailing party on the hearing. *Supreme Court Rule* 48.

2815. The judgment of the Circuit Court being reversed, with costs, and a new trial ordered, it was held that the plaintiff in error was not entitled to tax in his bill of costs those which had accrued in the Circuit Court, but that, unless otherwise specially directed, they must abide the result of the new trial. *Lester v. Sutton*, 7 Mich., 329.

2816. Where a party has given notice of a motion which he declines to call up, costs of the motion will be awarded against him. *Johnson v. Provincial Insurance Co. of Toronto*, 11 Mich., 455.

2817. Authority of attorney. The Court will not require attorneys to produce their authority to prosecute a writ of error on behalf of one of the plaintiffs, where there is no showing that they are not duly authorized, and on the contrary it appears that the attorneys were employed by the other plaintiff to take charge of the case generally, and that the one so employing them was, in fact, the party responsible in the case, and bound to protect the other from liability. *O'Flynn v. Eagle*, 7 Mich., 306.

PRINCIPAL AND AGENT.

2818. General agency, how proved. If the facts and circumstances, or the habit and course of dealing show either an original appointment, or a subsequent and continued ratification of the acts done, they will be sufficient to establish the agency. *Lyell v. Sanbourn*, 2 Mich., 109. For a discussion as to whether certain facts established a trust or an agency, see *Titus v. Minnesota Mining Co.*, 8 Mich., 183.

2819. Contract by agent. It seems that the execution of a submission to arbitration by an agent, not under seal, need not be in the name of the principal. *City of Detroit v. Jackson*, 1 Doug., 106.

2820. Where it distinctly appears in the body of a parol agreement, signed by an agent in his own name, without the addition of the name of his principal, that the principal is the contracting party, the agreement will be construed to be that of the principal and not of the agent. *Ibid.*

2821. Agent's authority. A person is not bound by his dealings with an agent whose authority the principal repudiates. *Pratt v. Campbell*, Har. Ch., 236.

2822. If the principal recognize and affirm the existence and acts of an agent, a mere stranger will not be permitted to controvert either. *Scott v. Detroit Young Men's Society*, 1 Doug., 119.

2823. A principal will be bound by the acts of one who has acted for him, to the extent to which he has held him out as his agent. *Sorrel v. Brewster*, 1 Mich., 373.

2824. As to authority generally, and the consequences of exceeding it, see *Hammond v. Michigan State Bank*, Wal. Ch., 214 ; *Michigan State Bank v. Hastings*, 1 Doug., 225 ; *Michigan State Bank v. Hammond*, 1 Doug., 527.

2825. An authority to an agent to *sell* property does not authorize him to *exchange* it for other property. *Trudo v. Anderson*, 10 Mich., 357.

2826. Where the statute required the agent of the State prison to give notice, in a newspaper, for sealed proposals for letting the convicts, and the agent, without giving such notice, hired them out for a term of years, the hiring was held void—the mode of letting prescribed by the statute being a limitation on the power itself, and not merely directory to the agent. *Agent of the State Prison v. Lathrop*, 1 Mich., 438.

2827. Agent acting for himself. A sale made by an agent to himself, is void in law. *Clute v. Barron*, 2 Mich., 192 ; *Dwight v. Blackmar*, 2 Mich., 330 ; *Beaubien v. Poupard*, Har. Ch., 206 ; *Ingerson v. Starkweather*, Wal. Ch., 346 ; *Ames v. Port Huron Log Driving and*

Booming Co., 11 Mich., 139. Public officers are agents within this rule. *People v. Township Board of Overyssel*, 11 Mich., 222.

2828. Where persons were authorized to act on behalf of certain townships in letting a contract for the improvement of a harbor, with power in regard to the plan of the work, the materials to be used, the time and mode of completion, security for performance, &c., and a portion of their number, though less than a majority, united with others in taking the contract, such contract was held void. *People v. Township Board of Overyssel*, 11 Mich., 222.

2829. One acting as agent for the owner of property has no right to make himself the agent of others for the purchase of the property, nor to take any advantage of the confidence his position inspires to obtain the title himself. *Moore v. Mandlebaum*, 8 Mich., 433.

2830. Nor can such agent make a valid purchase from his principal without fully and fairly disclosing all the propositions he has received, and all the facts and circumstances within his knowledge in any way calculated to enable the principal to judge of the propriety of the sale. *Ibid.*

2831. Ratification. Where, in plaintiff's absence, his clerk received from his debtor a draft, and accepted the same, to be applied, when paid, on the debtor's account, and after the draft fell due the plaintiff wrote the debtor respecting it, not repudiating the act of the clerk, and, on subsequently suing the debtor, offered to return the unpaid draft, it was *held* that these facts furnished evidence from which a jury might infer a ratification by plaintiff of the act of the clerk. *Jennison v. Parker*, 7 Mich., 355. See *Peninsular Bank v. Hanmer*, 14 Mich.

2832. An agent is incompetent to ratify his own unauthorized act. *Trudo v. Anderson* 10 Mich., 357. See *supra*, 709, 2460.

2833. As to admissions by agent, see supra, 1718, 1719. That a reference by a party to the business men of a place for information as to his responsibility, would not make their statements concerning him evidence against him on the ground of agency, see *Rosenbury v. Angell*, 6 Mich., 508.

PRINCIPAL AND SURETY.

2834. When surety liable. Where a debtor made a note to his creditor, and signed his own name thereto, and then, without authority, that of two co-partnerships of which he was a member, and then went with the creditor's agent to the defendants, who also, at his request, signed the note as sureties, and neither the agent nor the defendants were aware of the want of authority in the debtor to sign the co-partnership names to the note, it was *held* that the defendants were liable thereon. *Bowen v. Mead*, 1 Mich., 432.

2835. Giving time to principal. Where a guarantor obligated himself to pay all the liabilities up to a sum certain, of the principal, for advances by way of notes, &c., if the principal should fail to pay the same, such obligation "to remain in full force and virtue for the space of three years from the first day of January, 1837," and for the notes so constituting the indebtedness guaranteed, new notes were taken within the three years, falling due after the three years, it was *held*, that such credit to the principal beyond the time limited in the bond, discharged the surety. *Farmers and Mechanics' Bank v. Kercheval*, 2 Mich., 504.

2836. The guarantor is equally discharged though the renewal notes be signed by and binding upon one only of several principals constituting a partnership. *Ibid.*

2837. But a creditor may extend the time for his debtor to pay in, without discharging sureties, if he, by the same agreement, expressly reserves his remedy against them. *Bailey v. Gould*, Wal. Ch., 478.

2838. New promise after time given. A surety who, after time given by the creditor to the principal, promises to pay the debt with full knowledge of the facts, is liable without any new consideration for the promise. The action in such case is upon the original contract, and not upon the new promise. *Porter v. Hodenpuyl*, 9 Mich., 11.

2839. Discharging securities. Where the vendor in a land contract had taken notes payable to his own order for the purchase price, which notes he indorsed to a bank, and at the same time gave the bank a deed of the lands as security for the payment of the notes, and the bank afterwards took from the vendee a quit claim deed of the lands without the vendor's knowledge, it was held that such deed was a recision of the contract, and that the vendor was thereby discharged from his liability as indorser of the notes, at least to the extent of the value of the land. *Ives v. Bank of Lansingburg*, 12 Mich., 361.

2840. An agreement between the vendee and the bank, at the time of the delivery of the quit claim deed, made without the knowledge of the vendor, that such deed should not affect the liability of the vendee on his notes, would not prevent its having this effect upon the rights of the vendor as indorser. *Ibid.*

2841. When surety bound by judgment against principal. The surety in an injunction bond who has undertaken to abide the decree of the Court of Chancery, and pay such damages as may be awarded against his principal by reason of the issuing of the injunction, is bound by such decree, and can raise no question of its correctness in an action upon the bond. *Lothrop v. Southworth*, 5 Mich., 436.

2842. Payment of usury by surety. A surety who pays usurious interest to obtain time to pay the debt of his principal in, cannot collect the excessive interest so paid by him of his principal. *Thurston v. Prentiss*, 1 Mich., 193.

2843. But where judgment is given by principal and surety on a note which includes usury, and the judgment is afterwards paid by the surety, he may collect the whole amount of the principal. *Ibid.*

2844. Special case: construction. Plaintiff sold certain goods to S., taking from him a mortgage thereon for the purchase money. Defendant agreed with the plaintiff in writing that the goods so sold should at all times remain in the possession of the purchaser, ready to be re-delivered upon the default of any payment, except what had been sold from day to day at regular sales, and that if, upon default of payment, there should not be sufficient goods to liquidate the sum remaining due on the chattel mortgage, the balance should be made up by defendant. Under this agreement defendant was liable for the whole deficiency, without regard to the manner in which the goods had been disposed of, and not merely for such portions as plaintiff could show had been diverted from the ordinary sales by the purchaser. *Mills v. Spencer*, 3 Mich., 127.

PROBATE COURTS.

2845. Power to issue commission. The Court of Probate had power, under the Statutes of 1838, to issue a commission to take the deposition of a witness to a will residing out of the State. *Matter of Rue High*, 2 Doug., 515.

2846. Power to record prior decrees. A record made in October, 1847, by a Probate Court, of a decree made by the same Court in February, 1837, admitting a will to probate, was held good evidence of the probate of the will. *Ives v. Kimball*, 1 Mich., 308.

2847. Approval of a void bond. Although a Judge of Probate acts judicially in allowing an appeal from commissioners to audit claims against estates of deceased persons, and in passing upon the sufficiency of the sureties in the appeal bond, yet until such bond is filed as the statute requires, no foundation is laid for the exercise of judicial discretion, and his acts are void. *Matter of Dickinson*, 2 Mich., 337.

2848. A bond given by a stranger, conditioned that the appellant shall prosecute, &c., is not a compliance with the statute which requires that the appellant shall give a bond with sufficient sureties, &c. *Ibid.*

2849. Verification of petitions, &c. Though the Probate Judge may properly require an absolute verification of anything whereon his action is required upon the merits, yet when the party complained of is cited to appear, and has an opportunity to controvert the facts, there is no rule which renders it imperative on the Probate Court to decline receiving an unsworn petition. *Matter of Robinson*, 6 Mich., 137.

2850. And where, in such case, the respondent opposes the relief asked on the ground that the petition is not properly verified, and makes no issue of fact, there is nothing for the Court to pass upon but the sufficiency of the allegations in the petition. *Ibid.*

2851. Under our probate system, a very large portion of the old equity jurisdiction is vested in the Courts of probate; and it seems that the Court of Chancery has jurisdiction in those cases only in which an adequate remedy does not exist in the Probate Court. *People v. Wayne Circuit Court*, 11 Mich., 393.

PROCESS.

2852. Protection by. Where parties act within the scope of an order of a Court of superior jurisdiction, or of an inferior Court in a case where such Court has jurisdiction, they are protected by the same immunities that are extended to the members of the respective Courts. Accordingly, where attorneys procured an order for a capias from a Court having authority to issue process against the person of the defendant, and under which he was arrested, and they were sued in trespass therefor, it was held, that though the order for capias might be erroneous, it was not void, and the attorneys were protected by it. *Ward v. Cozzens*, 3 Mich., 252. For general rules of protection to officers in the service of process, see OFFICER.

PROHIBITION.

2853. The writ of prohibition cannot be issued to restrain any action of inferior Courts which can be reviewed by any of the ordinary methods. *People v. Wayne Circuit Court in Chancery*, 11 Mich., 393.

PROHIBITORY LIQUOR LAW OF 1853.

2854. Strong beer and ale were included within the prohibitions of this act. *People v. Hawley*, 3 Mich., 330.

2855. Jury trial. In an action before a justice of the peace to recover a penalty under the fourth section, the defendant was not entitled to a jury without paying the fees therefor. *People v. Hoffman*, 3 Mich., 248.

PROHIBITORY LIQUOR LAW OF 1855.

2856. Complaint. A complaint under section nine, which does set forth any facts or circumstances, but merely states the belief of the complainant that the person complained of has, between certain specified days, sold liquors in violation of the act, is not sufficient to confer jurisdiction upon the justice to whom it is made, to issue subpœnas and compel the attendance of witnesses to testify concerning supposed violations. *Matter of Morton*, 10 Mich., 208; *Matter of Hall*, 10 Mich., 210.

2857. Mortgage of liquors. A mortgage of liquors under which possession has been taken by the mortgagee, cannot be treated as void as between the parties, or as between the mortgagee and the creditors of the mortgagor. *Bagg v. Jerome*, 7 Mich., 145.

2858. Sales. The Statute—Comp. L., § 1662—authorizing moneys paid for liquors to be recovered back, is aimed at sales in the ordinary sense of the term, where the title passes from one owner to a new and different one; and not to releases on dissolution of a partnership. *Jacobs v. Stokes*, 12 Mich., 381.

2859. Although the law avoids all contracts the consideration of which, in whole or in part, consists of liquors sold in violation of the statute, yet if a purchase includes other articles besides liquors, and has been paid for, the statute does not authorize a recovery by the purchaser beyond the amount actually paid for the liquors. *Ibid.*

2860. Liquors may be insured against loss by fire, notwithstanding the statute. *Niagara Fire Insurance Co. v. De Graff*, 12 Mich., 124.

PROSECUTING ATTORNEY.

2861. No person who has not been admitted as an attorney at law is eligible to the office of prosecuting attorney. *People v. May*, 3 Mich., 598.

PUBLIC LANDS.

2862. Section sixteen. The act of Congress of March 1, 1847, "to establish a Land Office in the northern part of Michigan," does not authorize, by pre-emption or otherwise, the sale by the United States of any lands which, on survey, might fall within section sixteen. *Minnesota Mining Co. v. National Mining Co.*, 11 Mich., 186. Affirmed by the Supreme Court of the United States.

2863. Trespass on. The general government has all the common law rights of an individual in respect to depredations committed upon the public lands. And the Commissioner of the General Land

Office may lawfully direct the seizure and sale, by the local land officers, on behalf of the government, of timber cut by trespassers on the public lands. *Stephenson v. Little*, 10 Mich., 433.

2864. Town sites. The act of Congress "for the relief of citizens of towns upon the lands of the United States, under certain circumstances," approved May 23, 1844, was intended to apply exclusively to actual and existing towns, and not to such lands as may have been selected by non-resident claimants as the site for a prospective town. *Matter of Selby*, 6 Mich., 193.

2865. The act was intended for the protection of citizens of villages and cities that had grown up or might grow up on government lands, and to secure to them severally, at the minimum price, all lands actually occupied by them respectively for village or city purposes; and to them collectively, for the use of the village or city, such other lands as might be embraced in the government subdivisions within its limits. *Ibid.*

2866. The rules and regulations to be prescribed by State legislation under the act, are to relate to the determination of claims to possession, and the extent of possession that may fairly be considered as falling within an occupancy for town purposes, as well as to the disposition of the part of the land not actually occupied for town purposes by individuals. *Ibid.*

2867. The act of the legislature of Michigan relative to Ontonagon, approved February 29, 1853, was held void under said act of Congress: *First*, because undertaking to dispose of the whole trust to the person named therein, and his grantees, and authorizing no one else to be considered or receive any relief; and, *Second*, because not prescribing any rules and regulations for the execution of the trust. *Ibid.*

2868. A claimant under said act of Congress, whose petition shows that the land claimed had not been actually occupied at the time the State legislation designed to carry out the act was adopted, and that it was afterwards occupied only as a farm, does not come within the provisions of said act, and is entitled to no relief. *Ibid.*

2869. Where land has been entered by the County Judge under said act of Congress, and the trustee is proceeding to adjudicate upon a claim made to a portion thereof, a person who sets up a right to such portion as a pre-emptioner for agricultural purposes, and claims that the same was never occupied for town purposes, and was not legitimately entered by the trustee, has a right to appear before the trustee and be heard. *Ibid.*

2870. On the hearing by the County Judge of a claim under said act of Congress, a citizen and tax payer of the town, who objects that the claimant is not entitled to the land claimed, but that it is a part of the common fund, to be disposed of for the benefit of the town, is entitled to appear and be heard. *Ibid.*

QUESTIONS RESERVED.

2871. What may be reserved. The Circuit Court can reserve for the opinion of the Supreme Court questions of law only, and not questions of fact, or questions involving both law and fact. *People v. Adwards*, 5 Mich., 22; *Bagg v. City of Detroit*, 5 Mich., 66; *English v. Fairchild*, 5 Mich., 141; *Clark v. Dorr*, 5 Mich., 143.

2872. A motion for a new trial, on the ground that the verdict is against evidence, for the reason that the facts proved, or to prove which evidence was given, did not make out the crime, embraces both law and fact. A motion for a new trial on the ground that the verdict is against the weight of evidence, presents a question of fact alone. And neither of these questions can be reserved for the opinion of the Supreme Court. *People v. Adwards*, 5 Mich., 22.

2873. In equity. Questions of law may be reserved in equity cases. *Bagg v. City of Detroit*, 5 Mich., 66.

2874. How presented. The questions must be presented directly and definitely; and the Supreme Court cannot be requested to look at a statement of facts and objections, and infer what questions, among the many which arise on them, are the questions which were meant to be reserved. *Ibid.* They must be distinctly propounded. *English v. Fairchild*, 5 Mich., 141; *Clark v. Dorr*, 5 Mich., 143.

2875. Where trial was had by jury, and various objections were raised as to the admissibility of evidence, and to its sufficiency, and the party objecting conceded that the opposite party was entitled to judgment if the objections were not well taken, and the whole case was thereupon reserved for the opinion of the Supreme Court upon the objections so taken; it was held that the Court had no jurisdiction. *English v. Fairchild*, 5 Mich., 141; *Clark v. Dorr*, 5 Mich., 143.

2876. Must be case of doubt. The statute does not intend that questions should be reserved unless the Judge below has well founded doubts upon them, save where they are new and of public importance. *Bagg v. City of Detroit*, 5 Mich., 66.

2877. Appeal afterwards. It is no objection to the jurisdiction of the Supreme Court on questions reserved, that the same questions may afterwards come up on exceptions or appeal. *Ibid.*

2878. The Recorder of Detroit cannot reserve for the opinion of the Supreme Court, questions arising upon the trial of offenses against the city ordinances. *People v. Jackson*, 8 Mich., 78.

2879. Want of constitutional power. A plea in bar was

interposed in chancery, and the Circuit Judge, instead of passing upon it, reserved the question of its sufficiency for the opinion of the Supreme Court. Held, that the Supreme Court had no jurisdiction of the question; the constitution having conferred upon it appellate jurisdiction only, except in certain special cases, of which this was not one. *Sanger v. Truesdail*, 8 Mich., 543. [This case is regarded as having settled, for all practical purposes, that the Supreme Court has no jurisdiction of questions reserved.]

QUO WARRANTO.

2880. To try right to an office. Where a person intrudes himself into an office, in consequence of the unlawful decision of a board of canvassers, the proper remedy is by motion to the Supreme Court for leave to file an information in the nature of a quo warranto, to try the right to such office. But the Court has a discretion as to the granting of such motion. *People v. Tisdale*, 1 Doug., 59.

2881. Consent of relator to filing. The fact that an information was filed by the Attorney General as on the relation of a claimant to an office, without the knowledge or authority of such relator, will not entitle him to have the information dismissed on motion. But the Court will allow him, at his option, to withdraw from the proceeding. *People v. Knight*, 13 Mich., 230.

2882. Office terminated. An information to try the right to a public office, will not be dismissed on the ground that the office has expired since information filed. To oust the incumbent is not the sole object of the proceeding, but, under the statute, if he is found guilty of the intrusion, a fine may be imposed, and costs recovered; and if the relator claims the office, and is found entitled to it, he may recover damages. *People v. Hartwell*, 12 Mich., 508.

2883. Plea to. All that is necessary to state in a plea of title to an office, is the authority for holding the election, the holding it, and that defendant received the greatest number of votes for the office. *People v. Van Cleve*, 1 Mich., 362.

2884. But it is not enough that an officer appointed for a temporary purpose should show a legal appointment. He must show the continued existence of every qualification necessary to the enjoyment of the office. *People v. Mayworm*, 5 Mich., 146.

2885. Relator's title. Where the information, charging the defendant with usurping the office, and requiring him to show his right thereto, contains in addition an allegation that the relator, by virtue and warrant of due and regular election, is in law and in right entitled to have, hold and exercise said office, it is not necessary that the relator's title to the office be set forth. *People v. Miles*, 2 Mich., 348.

2886. Against corporations. Whether quo warranto or scire facias is the proper remedy by which to proceed against a corporation for violating its charter, *quere. People v. Oakland County Bank*, 1 Doug., 282. [The Revised Statutes of 1846—Comp. L., ch. 161—contain provisions giving this remedy against corporations.]

2887. It is not necessary to set forth the franchises and privileges alleged to be usurped, except in general terms. It is always the right of the government to call upon those who assume corporate powers, to show by what warrant they do so; and when the defendants set forth their claims by plea, the Attorney General may show by replication the special grounds he relies on. *People v. River Raisin and Lake Erie R. R. Co.*, 12 Mich., 389.

2888. Pleas.. Information calling upon the defendants to show by what right they assume to exercise certain banking powers. Plea, setting forth a charter of defendants as a railroad corporation, which gave them no authority to issue circulating notes; and stating the issue by defendants of certain certificates which, as described, might or might not be within the statute against unlawful banking, and then denying that defendants have exercised the franchises charged, "except as aforesaid." Held, that as the plea neither confessed nor denied the exercise of banking powers, the issue tendered by it was immaterial. *Ibid.*

2889. To an information in the nature of a quo warranto, requiring a corporation to answer by what warrant it claimed to have, use and enjoy certain corporate powers, &c., which it was therein alleged to have usurped, a plea setting forth the charter of the corporation, by which the powers claimed were conferred *in presenti*, is a prima facie defense; for the commencement of a legal existence being thus shown, it will be presumed that the corporation continued to exist, and to perform its duties, until the contrary is alleged. *Attorney General v. Michigan State Bank*, 2 Doug., 359.

2890. And where, in addition to this, the plea contained allegations designed to show, either a continued existence of the corporation down to the filing of the information, or that the State was estopped from insisting upon forfeiture of the corporate franchises for causes which arose prior to a certain period, it was held that these allegations were surplusage, and on motion they were ordered to be struck out. *Ibid.*

2891. Conclusion of plea. Information charging respondent with intruding into a public office; averring that an election to fill the office was held; that relator received a certain number of votes, and was thereby elected. A plea to this information, that no election was held for this office, and that no votes were cast for the purpose, should conclude to the country, and not with a verification. *People v. Hartwell*, 12 Mich., 508.

2892. Replication: duplicity. A replication which, to show that defendants usurp the franchise of banking, avers that certificates issued by them are in the similitude of bank bills, and also that they are issued with intent to be put in circulation as money, is double. *People v. River Raisin and Lake Erie R. R. Co.*, 12 Mich., 389.

2893. Judgment on default. Upon the default of defendant, where the information is filed on relation of the claimant to a public office, the Court will render judgment of ouster against the defendant, but cannot adjudge the relator entitled to the office. *People v. Connor*, 13 Mich., 238.

2894. Trial of issues: motion for new trial. Where issues framed in the Supreme Court are sent to one of the Circuit Courts for trial, the Circuit Judge should make report of the trial, embracing sufficient of the proceedings to show the bearing of any legal rulings made by him to which exception was taken, that the parties may have such rulings reviewed on motion for a new trial. The motion cannot be heard on affidavits as to what the proceedings were. *People v. Sackett*, 14 Mich.

2895. If a party moves for a new trial on the ground that the verdict was against evidence, the Judge must report the evidence in full, and also whether the verdict upon the evidence was satisfactory to him. And he should fix a time for settling his report, and cause notice thereof to be given to the parties, that they may be present. *Ibid.*

RAILROAD CORPORATIONS.

2896. Fences. Under the General Railroad Act, the liability of corporations organized under it, and their agents, for damages which may result from the neglect of the corporation to erect and maintain fences on the sides of the line of road, attaches as soon as they have possession of the route for the purpose of constructing the road. *Gardner v. Smith*, 7 Mich., 410.

2897. A contractor for the construction of the road is an *agent* of the corporation within the meaning of this provision. And he is primarily liable to the same extent that the corporation would have been for the same acts or omissions. *Ibid.*

2898. Where, therefore, while a contractor was engaged in constructing a railroad through certain premises, and had taken away fences for the purpose, the sheep of the owner of the land escaped and were lost in consequence, it was *held*, that the contractor was liable for the loss, notwithstanding the owner turned the sheep into the field after the route was taken possession of, and while the contractor was constantly throwing down the fences for his purposes. *Ibid.* As to fencing railroad track, see supra, 1846 to 1849.

2899. Subscription books. Under the General Railroad Act, a railroad company was organized, with articles of association which fixed the amount of capital stock, and named five commissioners to open books for subscriptions to the stock. The commissioners, however, never opened such books, but a subscription paper was circulated by an agent appointed by the directors, and defendant subscribed a sum thereon which he subsequently on several occasions offered to pay. *Held*, that the promise was without consideration, and he was not liable thereon. *Shurtz v. Schoolcraft and Three Rivers Railroad Co.*, 9 Mich., 269.

2900. Assessments. Under said General Railroad Act, no levy of assessments could be made until the whole amount of the capital stock specified in the articles was subscribed. *Ibid.*

2901. Right of way: purchase of undivided interest. A grant by one of several tenants in common to the Detroit and Pontiac Railroad Company, though not effective as a conveyance, as against the others, is effectual as a release of damages by the grantor. *Draper v. Williams*, 2 Mich., 536.

RECOGNIZANCE.

2902. Who may take. Section 6002 of Compiled Laws does not confer authority upon the officers therein named to take recognizance of persons in custody, charged with offences, after indictment found. *People v. Rutan*, 3 Mich., 42.

2903. Execution by sureties alone. Sureties in a recognizance may be bound separately from their principals. *People v. Dennis*, 4 Mich., 609.

2904. Description of offense. A recognizance need not set out the offense with the same particularity as an indictment. If described with such certainty as to show that the case is one in which the officer is empowered to take bail, it is sufficient. *People v. Rutan*, 3 Mich., 42.

2905. The recital of a charge that the principal "did set fire to and wilfully burn a building, situate," &c., "known as the Canal Mills," and stating the ownership, was held sufficient. *Ibid.*

2906. The description of the offense as "the crime of incest" is sufficient; and the facts constituting the offense need not be set out. *Daniels v. People*, 6 Mich., 381.

2907. So also where the description is "the crime of attempt to procure an abortion." *Ibid.*

2908. If the offense has a definite and well understood general name—as larceny—describing it by such name is sufficient. *People v. Dennis*, 4 Mich., 609.

2909. Other recitals. Where a recognizance has a condition to do some act for the doing of which it may properly be taken, and the Court or officer before whom it is taken has authority therefor, the recognizance is valid although it does not recite the special circumstances under which it is taken; and in declaring upon such recognizance, it is not necessary to aver facts showing that the Court or officer had authority to take it. *Ibid.*

2910. Where defendant has been committed for want of bail by the examining magistrate, and subsequently, on his own application, is let to bail by a commissioner, it is not necessary that the recognizance should show upon its face that the offense was committed within the jurisdiction of the magistrate. The entering into such recognizance being a voluntary act of defendant, of which he can only avail himself on his own showing of a legal commitment, the presumptions are in favor of its validity. *Daniels v. People*, 6 Mich., 381.

2911. Loss of indictment. The destruction of an indictment before the term at which the accused is recognized to appear, is no defense to an action upon the recognizance. *People v. Dennis*, 4 Mich., 609.

RECORDING LAWS.

2912. Unauthorized record. The registry of an instrument not required by law to be recorded, is notice to no one. *Wing v. McDowell*, Wal. Ch., 175; *Dutton v. Ives*, 5 Mich., 515; *Galpin v. Abbott*, 6 Mich., 17. This principle applied to a mortgage by one not having the title; to an agreement to pay off a mortgage, and to a deed not sufficiently witnessed, in these cases respectively. See "An act to confirm deeds and instruments intended for the conveyance of real estate in certain cases," Laws of 1861, p. 16, for confirmation of records of defective instruments in certain cases.

2913. Record of mortgage from one having no title. Where a person mortgages lands which he holds under a bond for a deed, he conveys no legal interest in the land, but only an equitable interest, and the registry of such mortgage is notice to no one. *Wing v. McDowell*, Wal. Ch., 175.

2914. The object of registry laws is to protect subsequent bona fide purchasers. An unrecorded deed was good against the grantor, under the Ordinance of 1787. *Godfroy v. Disbrow*, Wal. Ch., 260.

2915. Priority. A party claiming priority under a registry law, must show a compliance with its provisions. *Thompson v. Mack*, Har. Ch., 150.

2916. But where his deed is first duly recorded, the presumption is that he is a bona fide purchaser without notice, until the contrary appears. *Godfroy v. Disbrow*, Wal. Ch., 260.

2917. Although a party may not himself be a bona fide purchaser without notice, yet if his grantor was such purchaser, he is entitled to all the rights of such grantor, and the protection which the law would give him. *Ibid.*

2918. Erroneous record. Where a deed, absolute in form, is in fact a mortgage in its inception, it should be recorded as such; and if recorded as a deed, it will not have priority over a prior unrecorded mortgage. *Thompson v. Mack*, Har. Ch., 150.

2919. The act of 1827 "concerning mortgages," was not controlled in relation to mortgages by the act of the same date "concerning deeds and conveyances." *Weed v. Lyon*, Har. Ch., 363.

2920. Deeds by Governor and Judges. Conveyances of land by the United States, whether directly through the President or by the agency of land boards, like the Governor and Judges, do not come within the purview of recording laws, unless the terms employed specially include them; and there is nothing in the statutes now or heretofore existing in this State, that will render a deed from the Governor and Judges void in favor of a subsequent grantee without notice, whose deed was first recorded. *Moran v. Palmer*, 13 Mich., 367.

2921. Illegible name. It is not a valid objection to the record of a deed, that the name of one of the subscribing witnesses cannot be made out, and that it is apparently a *fac simile* of the original. *Whitwell v. Emory*, 3 Mich., 84.

2922. Mistake in deed. A contract to give a mortgage was put upon record, but by mistake in drafting it, only the starting point in the description of lands was given. A mortgage upon the lands intended to be described was subsequently given and placed upon record. It was *held*, that the record of the contract was not notice to the mortgagee, since no one could say from the contract what was the specific land upon which the mortgage mentioned in it was to be given. *Barrows v. Baughman*, 9 Mich., 213. As to whether the record of a deed containing a mistaken description is notice, see supra, 1005. Also, *Quirk v. Thomas*, 6 Mich., 76.

2923. Where property was described in a mortgage as "lot number one, in section twenty-eight, on the Forsyth or Porter Farm, in the city of Detroit—being on the southwest corner of Fort and Sixth streets," which description was correct, except as to the section, which should have been eighteen, and it did not appear that there was a section twenty-eight on the farm named, it was *held* that the record of such mortgage was notice to subsequent purchasers of the property. *Cooper v. Bigley*, 13 Mich., 463.

2924. Whether, where a description is so framed that it may be intended for one lot as well as another, the record of the instrument is not sufficient to put a purchaser of either upon inquiry, *quere*. *Ibid.* And see supra, 1005.

2925. Indefinite record. A writing was recorded as a separate paper, which referred to the "within mortgage," but did not in any way describe or identify the mortgage. It was held not to be evidence that the writing recorded was indorsed upon any instrument not recorded with it, as that was an extrinsic fact not within the purview of the registry laws. *Bassett v. Hathaway*, 9 Mich., 28.

2926. Collateral writing. Where a chattel mortgage was given to secure the performance of a written agreement, the latter was held to be no part of the mortgage, and therefore not required to be filed with it in order to render the record notice to third persons. *Byram v. Gordon*, 11 Mich., 531.

2927. Deed not executed by all the grantors. Where a deed from several grantors is put upon record, as to only a part of whom it is properly executed and witnessed, the record is evidence of a deed as to those parties only by whom it has been properly executed, and whose execution of it has been duly witnessed so as to entitle it to record had they been the only grantors named. *Hall v. Redson*, 10 Mich., 21.

2928. Notice to prior incumbrancers. The record of a conveyance or incumbrance is not constructive notice to a prior incumbrancer. *Cooper v. Bigley*, 13 Mich., 463; *James v. Brown*, 11 Mich., 25.

RECOUPMENT.

2929. General rule. A defendant can recoup those damages only which spring out of the same contract or transaction upon which the suit is brought. *Ward v. Willson*, 3 Mich., 1.

2930. Where defendant elects to recoup, he can only do so in abatement of the plaintiff's demand. He cannot go beyond that, and have a balance certified in his favor. *Ward v. Fellers*, 3 Mich., 281. See this case for the distinction between set off and recoupment.

2931. By one of two defendants. In an action on a promissory note, given by two, on a contract of purchase by one of the makers only, it is competent to recoup damages growing out of the contract of purchase, to the same extent as if the note had been given by the purchaser alone. *McHardy v. Wadsworth*, 8 Mich., 349.

RELIGIOUS SOCIETIES.

2932. Grant to Bishop for church: control of church. Land was conveyed to L., Bishop of Detroit, and his successors in office, in trust, for the erection of a church thereon to be used as a place of religious worship, and for the spiritual use, benefit and behoof of the German Roman Catholic Congregation, in the city of Detroit, according to the rites and ceremonies of said Roman Catholic Church, and for other trusts therein expressed. The deed also provided that in the event of a vacancy in the office of Bishop happening between the death of Bishop L. and the appointment of his successor, the premises should vest, during such vacancy, in the Archbishop of the Roman Catholic Church, of which the Diocese should be a suffragan. Trustees of the church were afterwards elected under ch. 52 of the Statutes of 1846. In a controversy between the officiating priest and the trustees as to which had the right to rent the slips, it was held:

1. That under the deed of trust, and the constitution, laws and usages for the government of the Roman Catholic Church, by which the administration of the temporalities of the church is vested in the parish priest, the right to rent the slips belonged to the priest, and not to the trustees.

2. That the provisions of said statutes as to the organization of religious societies were not mandatory, but permissive; and that no church could become incorporated under them, where the power the statute would confer upon the corporators was, by the constitution, laws and usages of the church, lodged in another body; but the person or persons in whom such power was vested by the constitution, laws and usages of the church, were entitled to become incorporated under § 23 of said chapter of the statutes. *Smith v. Bonhoof*, 2 Mich., 115.

The statutes as to the organization of religious societies have since been changed. See Comp. L., ch. 68; Laws of 1861, p. 228, and of 1862, p. 48. As to gifts, &c., to religious societies, see WILLS.

REMEDY.

2933. Choice of. That where one holds a chattel mortgage as security for the payment of a note, and afterwards takes a mortgage on real estate conditioned in the usual form for the performance of the condition of the note, he is not obliged to resort to the chattel mortgage before foreclosing that upon real estate, see *Davis v. Rider*, 5 Mich., 423.

2934. Collateral. That the judgment of a Court having jurisdiction of the person and of the subject matter, cannot be assailed collaterally, on the ground that the record does not show the demand sued to have been due, or to have belonged to the plaintiff, see *Van Kleek v. Eggleston*, 7 Mich., 511.

REPLEVIN.

2935. In what cases. A supervisor entitled to the exclusive possession and control of an assessment roll, may bring replevin in his official character therefor. *Phenix v. Clark*, 2 Mich., 327.

2936. One cannot bring replevin for property actually in his own possession at the time, against an officer who has levied upon but has not removed it. *Hickey v. Hinsdale*, 12 Mich., 99.

2937. The rule that a tenant in common of chattels cannot maintain replevin against his co-tenant, for the common property, applies to tenants in common of ships and vessels. *Wetherell v. Spencer*, 3 Mich., 123.

2938. Plaintiff had a contract with a firm engaged in sawing lumber, by which they were to receive certain saw logs belonging to him, manufacture the same into lumber, ship the lumber to parties to whom the same had been contracted, receive the payment therefor, and pay over to him a certain amount per thousand feet, retaining the balance for their services. The contract provided that the logs and lumber were at all times to be the property of the plaintiff until he had received the amount so to be paid to him. The logs having been levied upon in the hands of the firm, as their property, it was held, that plaintiff was entitled to immediate possession, and might maintain replevin therefor. *Bassett v. Armstrong*, 6 Mich., 397.

2939. Defendant being in possession of a quantity of wheat, plaintiff brought replevin for one hundred bushels, which were measured out and taken under the writ from the whole quantity. Held to be no objection to the maintainance of the action, that plaintiff did not demand and take under the writ the whole quantity; the evidence showing the whole to have been the plaintiff's, and that he did not own as tenant in common with others. *Crouse v. Derbyshire*, 10 Mich., 479.

2940. For beasts distrained. The statute—Comp. L., p. 1341—giving a writ of replevin to one whose beasts are distrained or impounded, provides for a special proceeding; and expressly negatives a remedy by replevin in any other manner than is therein provided. *Johnson v. Wing*, 3 Mich., 163.

2941. For exempt property. In replevin for property taken in execution, and claimed by plaintiff as exempt, it is not necessary to specifically set out the character of the property in the declaration, so as to show the exemption. *Elliott v. Whitmore*, 5 Mich., 532.

2942. Demand. Where one's property is disposed of without authority, by the party having it in charge, the owner may bring replevin therefor without a previous demand, notwithstanding the property is in the hands of one who bought in good faith, and without notice of the title of the real owner. *Trudo v. Anderson*, 10 Mich., 357.

2943. One to whom goods have been assigned by way of security, but who has allowed them to remain in possession of the assignor, is not obliged to demand them before bringing replevin against an officer who has seized them under an execution against the assignor. *Jackson v. Dean*, 1 Doug., 519.

2944. Description of property. "A quantity of corn consisting of about two hundred bushels, and a quantity of rye consisting of about one hundred bushels," held an insufficient description. *Stevens v. Osman*, 1 Mich., 92.

2945. Affidavit. Under the Revised Statutes of 1838, it was held, where defendant's christian name was stated incorrectly in the affidavit, that the Court might, after service of the writ and before the execution of the replevin bond, permit the plaintiff to file a new affidavit, and thereupon to amend the writ by inserting the true name. *Parks v. Barkham*, 1 Mich., 95.

2946. The averments in the affidavit—"that the property was not taken for any assessment levied by virtue of any law of the State," and "that it was not seized under any execution against the goods and chattels of the plaintiff liable to execution"—being required by the statute, must be inserted, without regard to the nature of the property replevied. *Phenix v. Clark*, 2 Mich., 327.

2947. Defenses: another suit pending. In replevin by one plaintiff against three defendants, plea in abatement was interposed of a prior action in replevin, by two of the defendants against the plaintiff and another, by virtue of which the other defendant, as sheriff, took and detained the property. Held, that the issues in the two cases were not identical, as the possessory rights of the sheriff under his writ, if valid, could not be impaired or affected, although the plaintiff in the present suit should show a perfect title, as against the other defendants, the plaintiffs in the first suit. *Belden v. Laing*, 8 Mich., 500.

2948. General issue. Under the Revised Statutes of 1838, as amended by Laws of 1839, p. 230, the general issue put in issue every fact stated in the declaration necessary to sustain the plaintiff's action, and not the detention of the property only. *Loomis v. Foster*, 1 Mich., 165.

2949. Under the present statutes, anything going to show that the plaintiff had no right to the possession when he commenced his suit, is a complete bar to the action. As that the defendant lawfully held the property, as against the plaintiff, by virtue of a prior writ of replevin. *Belden v. Laing*, 8 Mich., 500.

2950. The defense that the property was taken under legal proceedings against a third person claimed to be the owner thereof, is admissible under the general issue without notice. *Snook v. Davis*, 6 Mich., 156. See further, *Craig v. Grant*, 6 Mich., 447.

2951. Damages. A judgment for more than nominal damages is erroneous, if no evidence of damages was submitted. *Phenix v. Clark*, 2 Mich., 327.

2952. The plaintiff cannot recover, as a part of his damages, the value of the services of his attorney and counsel in attending the suit. *Hatch v. Hart*, 2 Mich., 289.

2953. Under the statute, *Comp. L.*, § 5033, where either of the parties, at the commencement of the suit, has only a lien upon or a special interest in the goods replevied, he can only recover according to his special interest as against the general owner or one who has taken the goods by his direction; but as against a stranger the full value of the goods may be recovered, although exceeding the lien or special interest, and the plaintiff will be a trustee for the general owner as to the balance. *Davidson v. Gunsolly*, 1 Mich., 388.

2954. Judgment. Where, in replevin against two, the Court finds that each of the defendants has an independent lien to a specified amount, on the property in controversy, it is erroneous to render a joint judgment in their favor for the value of the property. *Sweetzer v. Mead*, 5 Mich., 107.

2955. Where plaintiff recovered judgment before a justice, which was reversed by the Circuit Court on certiorari, and plaintiff in error afterwards moved for an order that a jury be impanelled to assess his damages; it was *held*, that the Circuit Court, under the Statutes of 1838, had no such power; but that under §§ 170 and 135 of the Justices' Act of 1841, it had power to award a restitution of the property. *People v. Judges of Jackson Circuit Court*, 1 Doug., 302.

2956. Executions against the body cannot be issued on judgments in replevin. *Fuller v. Bowker*, 11 Mich., 204.

2957. Bond. Under the Statutes of 1838 the Court could not compel the plaintiff to file a new replevin bond. *Lynch v. Bruce*, 2 Doug., 123. But see Comp. L., §§ 5020 *et seq*, for new provisions.

2958. Suit on bond. Where plaintiff in replevin is nonsuited, the defendant, if he waive a return of the property, is entitled to a judgment for its full value. And in an action upon the replevin bond afterwards, the measure of damages is the amount of the judgment; and the obligors cannot show, in mitigation of damages, that the defendant in replevin was but a part owner of the property. *Williams v. Vail*, 9 Mich., 162.

2959. After judgment for the defendant in replevin, an execution was issued, in form in assumpsit, and purporting to be in favor of a plaintiff. It was not amended, but, after return unsatisfied, the replevin bond was sued. It was *held* that this could not be considered an execution on the judgment, and that consequently no liability upon the replevin bond was created by its return. *Ibid.*

2960. A recovery cannot be had on the bond for a sum exceeding the amount of the penalty and costs of suit. *Fraser v. Little*, 13 Mich., 195.

RES JUDICATA.

2961. A decision once made in a case must continue to govern it, notwithstanding the point then decided is not held to be law in other cases. *Newberry v. Trowbridge*, 13 Mich., 263.

REVISED STATUTES OF 1846.

2962. The whole body of laws designated as the "Revised Statutes" of 1846 was passed as one act, and must be construed together as such. *Perry v. Hepburne*, 4 Mich., 165.

SCHOOLS AND SCHOOL DISTRICTS.

2963. Districts. Under the statute of 1840—Laws 1840, p. 215—empowering the school inspectors of any township "to divide the township into such number of districts, and to regulate and alter the boundaries of said school districts, as may from time to time be necessary," they might dissolve one organized district and annex it to another. *People v. Davidson*, 2 Doug., 121.

2964. The city of Saginaw was incorporated of territory which constituted about one-fourth of School District No. One of the township of Saginaw. The charter provided for a board of city school inspectors, and it was *held*, that it had the effect to sever from the school district the territory included in the city, without in any other respect depriving the district of any of its legal rights. *Township of Saginaw v. School District No. One of the City of Saginaw*, 9 Mich., 541.

2965. The city in such case has no remedy to recover its proper-tion of the school district moneys or other property; there being no statute providing for such recovery. *Ibid.*

2966. Director. The director of a school district is not legally entitled to compensation from the district for his services. *Hinman v. School District No. One*, 4 Mich., 168. The law is since changed, so as to authorize compensation to be voted by the district. *Laws of* 1859, *p.* 1047, § 49.

2967. Consolidation of districts: former debts. Where two districts are united under the statute—Comp. L., § 2335—the new district is alone liable for all the former debts of each; and a judgment afterwards rendered against one of the former districts is a nullity. *Brewer v. Palmer*, 13 Mich., 104.

SET OFF.

2968. Of secured demand. A defendant who holds collateral security for a demand due him, cannot be required to deliver up the securities as a condition to his demand being received as a set off. *Wallace v. Finnegan*, 14 Mich.

2969. Unliquidated damages. Where the plaintiff's demand is for goods which the defendant has agreed to sell and deliver, the damages are unliquidated, and consequently no set off can be allowed under the statute. *Smith v. Warner*, 14 Mich.

2970. Demand assigned after suit brought. Where the assignees of a bank brought suit upon a promissory note, but sold it pending the suit, and the suit was afterwards continued for the benefit of the purchaser, it was held that the note was subject to any offset which could have been made to it in an action by the bank itself. *Newberry v. Trowbridge*, 13 Mich., 263.

2971. Set off by one joint defendant after death of the other. Where one of the defendants dies and the suit is continued against the other, he may set off against the plaintiff's demand a debt due to himself individually. *Ibid.*

2972. Election of remedies. One who has given a mortgage for the purchase price of lands, which were conveyed to him with a covenant against incumbrances, is not confined to his remedy upon the covenant, but may set off the amount of a prior mortgage which he has paid against his own mortgage when suit is brought to foreclose it. *Detroit and Milwaukee Railroad Co. v. Griggs*, 12 Mich., 45. See also, *Disbrow v. Jones*, Har. Ch., 102. As to set off in equity generally, see supra, 1218 to 1226.

SHERIFF.

2973. Deputy. A sheriff cannot constitute a deputy for a particular act except by warrant in writing. *People v. Moore*, 2 Doug., 1.

2974. The under sheriff may act in his own name, and need not sign a return to a writ made by him in the name of the sheriff. *Callendar v. Olcott*, 1 Mich., 344.

2975. Oath and bond. The statute which requires of the person elected to the office of sheriff, that he shall file the oath and bond of office within twenty days after receiving official notice of his election, or within days after the commencement of the term for which he was elected, only applies to the person declared elected by the board of canvassers, and not to one to whom the board refuse a certificate. *People v. Mayworm*, 5 Mich., 146.

2976. Suit on bond. By statute, the party for whose use a sheriff's bond is sued, is to be deemed the plaintiff in the action. Where one of two persons jointly entitled to prosecute the action died, it was *held* that action should be brought in the name of the people for the use of the survivor alone, without joining the administrator of the one deceased. *Jackson v. People*, 6 Mich., 154.

2977. Sale without notice. The sheriff is not liable to the penalty given by the statute, for selling lands on execution without giving the notice required by law, if the sale be void on account of the unconstitutionality of the law under which it is made. *Willard v. Longstreet*, 2 Doug., 172.

2978. Return of process. That, for the purposes of a creditor's bill, an execution cannot be legally returned until the return day, see *Williams v. Hubbard*, 1 Mich., 446; *Smith v. Thompson*, Wal. Ch., 1; *Beach v. White*, Wal. Ch., 495. But that, for obtaining a new execution to another county return may be made at any time, see *Freeman v. Michigan State Bank*, Wal. Ch, 62. If a debtor offers to turn out property upon execution in another county, the creditor must take execution to that county; and if he files creditor's bill without doing so, a plea setting forth the offer will be a bar to the suit. *Ibid.*

SLANDER.

2979. Declaration in slander contained the usual inducement, without the averment of any extrinsic facts or circumstances showing the actionable quality of the words spoken, except that the plaintiff was postmaster at F., and one count charged the defendant with having spoken and published of and concerning the plaintiff as postmaster, &c., that "he did not think Marlatt's resignation or his petition had gone to Washington; he had no doubt they were embezzled at F.;" adding, by innuendo, (" at the post office at F., of which the plaintiff was postmaster, meaning), meaning and intending thereby that the plaintiff had delayed and prevented the transmission of the said resignation and petition to the Postmaster-General at Washington," &c. *Held*, that the count was fatally defective, the words charged to have been spoken and published appearing not to be actionable. *Taylor v. Kneeland*, 1 Doug., 67.

2980. The words would have become actionable had the inducement of the declaration further averred, that the letters or papers referred to were placed in the post office at F., or entrusted to the care of the defendant as postmaster at F., or were passed through said post office to their place of destination; since the embezzlement by defendant of papers which so came into his possession, is made criminal. *Ibid.*

2981. Extrinsic facts or circumstances showing the actionable quality of words, not actionable *per se*, must be directly averred in the inducement of the declaration. *Ibid.*

2982. The office of an innuendo is merely to apply the different parts of the charge contained in the words, to the different facts before averred in the inducement. Its truth must always appear from precedent averments, and it must be supported by the inducement and colloquium. *Ibid.*

2983. The omission of any averment, in a count in slander, that the defendant *maliciously* published the matter alleged, is cured by verdict, though it would be fatal on special demurrer. *Ibid.*

2984. Proof of words as laid. A count in slander alleging that the defendant uttered and published that the plaintiff, who was postmaster at F., embezzled certain papers, is not supported by proof that he said he had no doubt that the papers were embezzled at F., or he thought the papers were embezzled at the post office at F. *Ibid.*

2985. Malice. Words spoken by defendant after the commencement of the suit, are not admissible in evidence to show malice, unless they expressly refer to those which are the subject matter of the action, and do not constitute a distinct calumny for which the plaintiff would have a separate right of action. *Ibid.* But see *Thompson v. Bowers*, 1 Doug., 321.

2986. Notice of defense. To a declaration in slander, alleging that the defendant charged the plaintiff with having sworn falsely, the defendant pleaded the general issue, and gave notice that he would prove on the trial " that the plaintiff was guilty of the facts charged on and imputed to him by the defendant, in the several conversations in the declaration mentioned, and that if the words were uttered and published as charged in the declaration, the defendant had good reason for uttering and publishing, and did it from good motives and for justifiable ends." *Held*, that the notice was fatally defective, especially in omitting any averment that the plaintiff *wilfully and deliberately* swore falsely. *Thompson v. Bowers*, 1 Doug., 321.

2987. Mitigation of damages. Evidence of the truth, or tending to prove the truth of the slanderous words, is inadmissible under the general issue in mitigation of damages. *Ibid.*

2988. So also is evidence that the specific facts in which the slander consisted were communicated to the defendant by third persons. *Ibid.*

2989. But the defendant may show under the general issue in mitigation of damages, that previous to the publication of the slanderous words by himself, reports to the same effect were in common circulation in the vicinity of the plaintiff's residence, and were communicated to the defendant. *Farr v. Rasco*, 9 Mich., 353. See *Moyer v. Pine*, 4 Mich., 409.

2990. Where the words are actionable in themselves, and general damages only are claimed, the defendant is not entitled to show in mitigation of damages under the general issue, that, "during the six years prior to the suit, inveterate feelings of hostility had existed between the plaintiff and the defendant, and that the plaintiff had taken every opportunity to irritate the defendant." *Porter v. Henderson*, 11 Mich., 20.

2991. Where the action is for charging plaintiff with perjury, evidence cannot be given by defendant, that on an occasion not appearing to have any connection with the matter in controversy, the plaintiff called him a liar and a perjured wretch. *Ibid.*

2992. Nor, where general damages only are claimed, is evidence admissible in mitigation of damages, that plaintiff has stated the slander did him no damage. *Ibid.*

2993. The defendant cannot give evidence under the general issue of a threat by plaintiff "that he would ruin him and drive him out of town;" which threat came to the knowledge of the defendant previous to the speaking of the words alleged to be slanderous. *Moyer v. Pine*, 4 Mich., 409.

2994. Common reports in circulation, in regard to the plaintiff's being suspected, previous to the speaking of the slanderous words, of having committed the crime imputed to him, cannot be given for the purpose of contradicting the statement in the declaration that he had not been suspected, until the speaking of the words, of being guilty of the offense charged. *Ibid.*

SPECIFIC PERFORMANCE.

2995. Parol contract partly performed. A Court of equity will enforce the specific performance of a parol contract for the conveyance of lands, where the purchase money or a part thereof has been paid, possession taken under the contract, and valuable improvements made. *Burtch v. Hogge*, Har. Ch., 31 ; *Bomier v. Caldwell*, Har. Ch., 65 ; *Same case on appeal*, 8 Mich., 463 ; *Norris v. Showerman*, 2 Doug., 16. But the part performance must unequivocally refer to and result from the agreement. *McMurtrie v. Bennette*, Har. Ch., 124 ; *Millard v. Ramsdell*, Har. Ch., 373.

2996. Delivery of possession is an act of part performance. *Weed v. Terry*, Wal. Ch., 501 ; *Same case on appeal*, 2 Doug., 344. But the possession cannot avail complainant when it is sufficiently explained by the relation of father and son between the parties. *Jones v. Tyler*, 6 Mich., 364.

2997. Performance discretionary. Courts of equity do not as a matter of course decree specific performance of contracts, but exercise a discretionary power, upon a view of all the facts in the case; and this discretion must not be arbitrary and capricious, but regulated on grounds that will render it judicial. *McMurtrie v. Bennette*, Har. Ch., 124. The ground of interference is not the parol contract, but that there is fraud in refusing the completion of an agreement partly performed. *Ibid.*

2998. Certainty. The parol contract, in order to be enforced, must be certain in all its essential particulars. *McMurtrie v. Bennette*, Har. Ch., 124 ; *Bomier v. Caldwell*, 8 Mich., 463 ; *Millard v. Ramsdell*, Har. Ch., 373.

2999. It must be proved in the clearest manner, and must be substantially the same set forth in the bill. Where husband and wife filed their bill on behalf of the wife, alleging a parol agreement on the part of the devisor of defendant to convey certain lands to the wife, and asking its specific performance, but from the evidence it appeared that the agreement was to convey to the husband, the bill was dismissed, notwithstanding there was evidence in the case that the husband afterwards directed the conveyance to be made to the wife, and the other party assented to its being so made. *Wilson v. Wilson*, 6 Mich., 9.

3000. Mutuality. The contract must also be mutual, and the tie reciprocal. *McMurtrie v. Bennette*, Har. Ch., 124 ; *Hawley v. Sheldon*, Har. Ch., 420.

3001. Part payment of the purchase price is not, of itself, sufficient to warrant a decree for the specific performance of a parol contract for the purchase of lands. *McMurtrie v. Bennette*, Har. Ch., 124.

3002. Inadequacy of price alone, without being so gross and palpable as to prove fraud, is not a good objection to specific performance. *Burtch v. Hogge*, Har. Ch., 31. See *Hunt v. Thorne*, 2 Mich., 213.

3003. But where the price agreed for in the contract greatly differs from the value, it is an ingredient which, associated with others, will contribute to prevent the interference of a Court of equity. *Wallace v. Pidge*, 4 Mich., 570.

3004. What deemed material. Time, place and mode of payment are not considered matters of substance, unless, by express stipulation of the parties, they are declared to be so, or unless from the special nature of the case, and the necessary intention and understanding between the parties, they must be deemed material. Therefore, though the contract varies in these particulars from that set out in the bill, if it corresponds in other respects the Court may enforce it. *Bomier v. Caldwell*, 8 Mich., 463. That time is not material, see also, *Wallace v. Pidge*, 4 Mich., 570; *Morris v. Hoyt*, 11 Mich., 9; *Richmond v. Robinson*, 12 Mich., 193; *Converse v. Blumrick*, 14 Mich.

3005. Waiver of laches. Where the owner permitted another person to occupy and improve lands for a number of years, under a verbal contract of purchase, and under the impression that he might pay for it when demanded, and the purchaser offered to pay when notified to do so, it was held that there was no such laches imputable to the purchaser as should debar him from specific performance. *Ingersoll v. Horton*, 7 Mich., 405.

3006. A notice served by the owner, in such a case, requiring the purchaser to pay for the land in a specified time, and take a deed therefor, estops him from taking advantage of laches of the purchaser prior to such notice. *Ibid.*

3007. The bill must set out the special facts relied upon as showing part performance to take the case out of the statute. *Bomier v. Caldwell*, 8 Mich., 463.

3008. Unauthorized contract. A contract made by a special agent who has exceeded his authority, will not be enforced. *Chamberlain v. Darragh*, Wal. Ch., 149.

3009. And where the agent acted for his trustee in selling the land, and the bill charged that the contract was made by him as agent for the trustee, it was held that he could not be required to convey his equitable interest as *cestui que trust*, notwithstanding the contract did not on its face disclose the agency. *Ibid.*

3010. Compromise agreement. Where the parties claimed the same land under conflicting titles, and made a parol agreement for a division, and each took possession of the part set off to him, a specific performance was decreed. *Weed v. Terry*, Wal. Ch., 501; *Same case on appeal*, 2 Doug., 344. See also, *Hunt v. Thorne*, 2 Mich., 213.

3011. Wife's dower. In decreeing the specific performance by a husband of his contract to convey, the wife will not be compelled to unite in his deed and thereby release her dower. *Weed v. Terry*, 2 Doug., 344. But where the husband causes lands to be conveyed to the wife, which he has agreed to convey to complainant, and she was aware of his contract and paid no consideration, specific performance may be decreed against her, and she is not entitled to dower. *Daily v. Litchfield*, 10 Mich., 29.

3012. Assignees of a contract may have it specifically performed in their favor. *Street v. Dow*, Har. Ch., 427.

3013. Illegal contract. A contract of purchase by a bank in violation of its charter will not be enforced in its favor. *Bank of Michigan v. Niles*, 1 Doug., 401, and Wal. Ch., 99.

3014. Disappointed expectations. A defendant cannot resist the specific performance of a contract, on a plea that his expectation of aid in money &c. from the other party formed the sole inducement and consideration to him of entering into the contract, where it appears that these expectations were merely the operations of his own mind, and not raised by any promise or suggestion of the other party. *Hunt v. Thorne*, 2 Mich., 213.

3015. Laches. A party who has enjoyed the use of the estate, and of the moneys arising from sales which he had covenanted to share jointly with another, cannot object the lapse of time where the complainant filed his bill for specific performance thirteen years after his rights accrued—there being no fraud or unfairness imputed to complainant. *Ibid.*

3016. A contract was made for the sale of lands, the payments to be made to a third person who held a mortgage given by the seller. Payment was not made by the day, and the seller declared the contract forfeited. The purchaser subsequently paid the money to the mortgagee, but without the seller's assent. It appearing that the land contract was designed to provide for the payment of the mortgage, it was held that, when that was done, as it did not concern the seller whether the mortgage was paid one way or another, the contract was to be regarded as substantially complied with. *Richmond v. Robinson*, 12 Mich., 193.

3017. The title contracted to be conveyed is to be presumed good, and the party denying it, or insisting upon incumbrances as an objection to performance, should put the title or incumbrances in issue by his pleadings; and the burden of proof will then be upon him to show defects. *Daily v. Litchfield*, 10 Mich., 29. See also, *Dwight v. Cutler*, 3 Mich., 566.

3018. The vendor will not be allowed to forfeit the contract for non-payment, when, not having the title to convey, he is not in position to perform on his own part. *Converse v. Blumrick*, 14 Mich.

3019. Demand of deed. The failure of the vendee to tender performance and demand a deed before filing his bill only affects the question of costs. *Morris v. Hoyt*, 11 Mich., 9.

3020. Complainants notified the other party to the contract for the exchange of lands, to meet them at the office where the contract was drawn, and exchange deeds—that place having been agreed upon for the purpose at the time the contract was entered into. Complainants went to the office at the time specified, executed a deed of the lands to be conveyed by them, and left it there for delivery—the other party not having appeared. They afterwards notified him of what they had done. *Held* equivalent to a tender of their deed, and a sufficient request for a deed from the other party. It is not necessary in such case for the party claiming specific performance to prepare and tender a deed to be executed by the other party. *Daily v. Litchfield*, 10 Mich., 29.

3021. One of the defendants held the land agreed to be conveyed by him, under a contract of purchase. Instead of taking a deed to himself, he had it made to his wife, who had notice of his agreement to convey to complainants, and paid no consideration. *Held*, that it was not necessary to demand a deed of the wife before filing a bill against both for specific performance. *Ibid.*

3022. Penalty. The fixing by the contract of a penalty for non-performance, is no objection to specific performance. *Ibid.*

3023. Averment of performance. Where a part of the consideration consisted in clearing and fencing, a general allegation that the same had been performed, was held sufficient. *Ibid.*

3024. Stipulation for improvements. A stipulation in the contract that the vendee shall "improve the premises," but specifying neither the kind nor the extent of the improvements, is so indefinite that the intention of the parties cannot be known; and on a bill for specific performance it will be treated as immaterial. *Morris v. Hoyt*, 11 Mich., 9.

3025. Taxes. A failure of the vendee to pay taxes as stipulated in the contract, stands upon the same basis, as respects specific performance, as a default in the payment of instalments of the purchase money. *Ibid.* See also, *Richmond v. Robinson*, 12 Mich., 193.

3026. Stipulation for forfeiture. A provision that on the failure of the vendee to fulfill the agreements on his part at the times specified, the vendor may re-enter and take possession of the land, and all rights of the vendee under the contract shall be null and void, and all payments and improvements made be forfeited, does not make time so far of the essence of the contract as that all rights of the vendee become *ipso facto* forfeited merely by a failure to pay at the times agreed upon, without any act on the part of the vendor indicating an intention to insist upon the forfeiture. *Morris v. Hoyt*, 11 Mich., 9.

3027. Under such a provision, the only mode by which the vendor can forfeit the rights of the vendee, is by re-entering and taking possession of the land, or some act equivalent thereto. *Ibid.*

3028. A contract which empowers the vendor, on default being made in payment, to terminate it, is not forfeited by mere lapse of time until the vendor has signified his election to put an end to it. Until such election, the vendee is liable for the purchase money, and entitled to specific performance on making payment. *Converse v. Blumrick*, 14 Mich.

3029. Interest. Where the vendee seeks specific performance after default in paying instalments of principal and interest, he will be required to pay interest on the instalments of interest from the time they fell due. *Morris v. Hoyt*, 11 Mich., 9.

3030. Parties. Where land contracted to be conveyed is deeded away to a third person, both the party to the contract and the person to whom the land has been conveyed, should be made parties to the bill. *Daily v. Litchfield*, 10 Mich., 29; *Morris v. Hoyt*, 11 Mich., 9.

3031. Where the vendee has deceased, his heir at law, and not his personal representative, is the proper person to file the bill. *House v. Dexter*, 9 Mich., 246.

3032. Decree for account. If specific performance is denied, the Court may retain the bill for the purpose of adjusting the accounts between the parties. *Hawley v. Sheldon*, Har. Ch., 420.

STAMPS.

3033. A person being the holder of a draft drawn in August, 1863, made a gift of it *causa mortis* to her mother, and after her death, her administrator, treating the draft as void for want of a sufficient stamp, brought suit against the drawer upon the original consideration. The drawer, defending in the interest of the donee, produced the draft on the trial, and placed the requisite stamp upon it, in pursuance of the act of Congress of June 30, 1864. It was held that the draft was thereby made valid from its inception, rendering the gift valid, and defeating the plaintiff's right of recovery. *Gibson v. Hibbard*, 13 Mich., 214.

3034. Where the grantee in a deed seeks to recover in ejectment under it, it is competent for the defendant, although no party to the deed, to show that a third person caused it to be made to the grantee without consideration; as in such a case the stamps required would depend upon the value of the land. *Groesbeck v. Seeley*, 13 Mich., 329.

STARE DECISIS.

3035. Where an erroneous principle has been established by the judicial decisions of the State, and individuals acting upon it as settled law have acquired rights under it, the Court should hesitate long before overruling it; it being better and safer to leave the Legislature to correct the error, as in that case all intervening rights would be saved, and injustice done to no one. *Emerson v. Atwater*, 7 Mich., 12.

3036. But the Court will not follow as precedents adjudications outside the State—except the adjudications of the Federal Courts on questions arising under the constitution and laws of the Federal Government—any further than they appear to the Court to be warranted by the fundamental principles of the common law. *Caldwell v. Gale*, 11 Mich., 77.

STATE OF MICHIGAN.

3037. The State of Michigan came into existence, and possessed the power of independent State legislation, on the adoption and ratification, by the people of the territory, of the constitution of the State, and the organization of the State government, notwithstanding the State was not admitted into the Union for some time afterwards. *Scott v. Detroit Young Men's Society*, 1 Doug., 119.

3038. Suits against. A State cannot be sued in its own Courts, [there being at the time no statute providing therefor]. *Michigan State Bank v. Hastings*, Wal. Ch., 9. But this rule only applies where the State itself is a party defendant, and not where it is sought to reach property in the hands of the State officers, in which the State has ceased to have any legal interest. *Michigan State Bank v. Hammond*, 1 Doug., 527.

3039. The Michigan State Bank conveyed to the State certain property on condition subsequent [see CONDITIONS, 561 to 568] that the State should indemnify and save harmless the bank against certain liabilities. By act of the legislature, the Auditor General, State Treasurer and Secretary of State were made trustees, on behalf of the State, to take charge of the property assigned, and dispose of it, and pay the proceeds into the State treasury. Afterwards the State refused to indemnify the bank, and a judgment was recovered on one of the liabilities which the bank was compelled to pay. On bill filed by the bank against the State officers to obtain relief from the property in their hands, against the failure of the State to indemnify, it was held, that the State having failed to perform the condition, the property had reverted to the bank, and that the possession thereof by the deefendants had ceased to be the possession of the State, and that equity had jurisdiction to compel the defendants to account as trustees of the bank, and pay any damages the bank had suffered by reason of the failure to indemnify. *Michigan State Bank v. Hammond*, 1 Doug., 527.

3040. *It seems*, that as to any money actually received as proceeds of the property by the State Treasurer, he could not be compelled to account, since money paid into the State Treasury must be regarded as in possession of the State. *Ibid.*

3041. But the bank would only be entitled to the relief prayed on waiving any forfeiture for breach of the condition, and on delivering over to the State a portion of the property which they had neglected and refused to deliver according to the original agreement. *Ibid.*

3042. Maxims of equity. See this case for a recognition of the maxims, that he who asks equity must do equity; and that equity, while it will lend its aid to relieve against penalties and conditions, cannot be evoked to enforce them.

STATE LANDS.

3043. Sale of School Lands. A certificate of the sale of primary school lands, signed by a clerk in the office of the Superintentent of Public Instruction, was held not well executed under the laws in force in 1841, though he added after his name "for J. D. P., Superintendent of Public Instruction." *Lee v. Payne*, 4 Mich., 106.

3044. Swamp lands. The ninth section of the act for the sale of the State Swamp Lands, (*Laws of* 1858, *p.* 173) made provisions for two distinct classes of purchasers, namely: settlers and occupants of such lands at the time of the passage of such act, who should have been such December 1, 1857, and owners and occupants of adjoining lands who were such December 1, 1857. *People v. State Treasurer*, 7 Mich., 366.

3045. Occupancy of the adjoining lands, under this act, might consist of cultivation and use, without actual residence, or might be by a tenant. *Ibid.*

3046. Though this act might make void any certificate of purchase issued through mistake, fraud, &c., it did not confer upon the Commissioner of the State Land Office power to adjudge void and cancel such certificate; and he could not resell the land unless the certificate was voluntarily returned, or adjudged void by the proper Court. *Ibid.*

STATE PRISON.

3047. The constitution provides that "No mechanical trade shall hereafter be taught to convicts in the State prison, in this State, except the making of those articles of which the chief supply for the consumption of the country is imported from other States or countries." What trades are within the spirit of this provision, it is for the agent of the State prison to determine, and the Supreme Court cannot control him in this regard. *People v. Inspectors of State Prison*, 4 Mich., 187.

STATUTES.

3048. General rules of construction. Where one part of an act is equivocal, other portions may be resorted to as guides. The occasion and the reason of the enactment; the letter of the act, whether words be used in their proper or in a technical sense; the context, the spirit of the act, and whether in its nature remedial or penal, are all to be considered; and the intent is not to be collected from any particular expression, but from a general view of the whole act. *Attorney General v. Bank of Michigan*, Har. Ch., 315; *Sibley v. Smith*, 2 Mich., 486.

3049. The intention is to be taken, or presumed, according to what is consonant to reason and good discretion. *Sibley v. Smith*, 2 Mich., 486.

3050. Effect is to be given, if possible, to every clause and sentence; and it is the duty of Courts, so far as practicable, to reconcile the different provisions of a statute so as to make the whole of it consistent and harmonious; and where this is impossible, to give effect to the manifest intent of the legislature. *Attorney General v. Detroit and Erin Plank Road Company*, 2 Mich., 138; *People v. Burns*, 5 Mich., 114.

3051. The intent of the legislature must be gathered from the language used to express that intent: and where the language is clear and explicit, and susceptible of but one meaning, and there is nothing incongruous in the act, the Court is bound to suppose the legislature intended what the language imports. *Barstow v. Smith*, Wal. Ch., 394; *Bidwell v. Whittaker*, 1 Mich., 469.

3052. The application of particular provisions is not to be extended beyond the general scope and object of the statute, unless such extension was obviously designed. *Matter of the Ticknor Estate*, 13 Mich., 44.

3053. Directory and mandatory. The statute requiring that when a defendant arraigned in the County Court requested to be tried before the Circuit Judge, such Judge should, on the first day of the next term, assign a day for the trial, was, as to time, directory only. *People v. Doe*, 1 Mich., 451.

3054. An order made by the County Judge, under Laws of 1848, p.

237, for summoning a jury to try a cause before the Circuit Judge, more than three days before the day assigned for the trial, was held sufficient. *Ibid.*

3055. The statute requiring non-resident plaintiffs to give security for costs before process shall issue in their favor, was held directory, and security allowed to be given *nunc pro tunc* at any time before a motion to set aside process for want of it was granted. *Parks v. Goodwin*, 1 Doug., 56.

3056. The statute requiring a justice of the peace to keep a docket, and to enter therein the judgments rendered by him, is directory only, and the entry when made is not the judgment itself, but only the evidence of it. *Hickey v. Hinsdale*, 8 Mich., 267.

3057. So is the statute directory (*Comp. L.*, § 3436) which requires the Circuit Judge who tries a case without a jury to give his decision on or before the first day of the term succeeding that in which the cause was submitted. *Rawson v. Parsons*, 6 Mich., 401.

3058. Statutes for the assessment and collection of taxes, as to what they require to be done for the protection of the tax payer, are mandatory, and cannot be regarded as directory merely. *Clark v. Crane*, 5 Mich., 151. See *Sibley v. Smith*, 2 Mich., 486.

3059. Changing common law. Statutes in derogation of the common law are to be construed strictly. *Sibley v. Smith*, 2 Mich., 486. This rule applied to the act authorizing proceedings against garnishees. *Maynards v. Cornwell*, 3 Mich., 309. And to the constitutional provision relative to the property of married women. *Brown v. Fifield*, 4 Mich., 322.

3060. The statute dividing murder into degrees does not change the common law definition of murder; and under an indictment in the common law form, the defendant may be found guilty of murder in the second degree. *People v. Doe*, 1 Mich., 451. See *People v. Potter*, 5 Mich., 1; *People v. Scott*, 6 Mich., 287.

3061. Giving a new right. Where a statute gives a new right, and prescribes a particular remedy, the party is confined to that remedy. *Thurston v. Prentiss*, 1 Mich., 193; *Craig v. Butler*, 9 Mich., 21.

3062. Curing defects. On the change from the territorial to the State government, the legislature of the State abolished the Supreme Court of the territory, and transferred certain causes pending therein to the Supreme Court and Court of Chancery of the State; but owing to a defect in the law, certain other causes were not transferred to any Court. Held, that it was competent for the legislature, in the following year, to pass an act transferring these cases to the Supreme Court of the State. *Scott v. Smart's Executors*, 1 Mich., 295.

3063. Error in printing. Where there is a discrepancy between an original law on file, and the printed copy thereof, the original must prevail. *Hulburt v. Merriam*, 3 Mich., 144.

3064. When to take effect. A law was passed February 4, 1859, providing for an election "at the annual township election to be held in April *next*." The law, under the constitution, did not take effect until May 16, 1859. *Held*, by two of the Justices, that to give the law any force, it must be held to apply to the next annual election after the date last mentioned. *Rice v. Ruddiman*, 10 Mich., 125.

3065. A statute passed to take effect at a future day is to be understood as speaking from the time it goes into operation, and not from the time of its passage. The intervening period is allowed to enable the public to become acquainted with its provisions; but until it becomes operative as a law, they cannot be compelled to govern their actions by it. *Price v. Hopkin*, 13 Mich., 318.

3066. Where, therefore, by the law as it stood on the 31st day of December, 1863, a person had sixteen years in which to bring suit for the recovery of a parcel of land claimed by her, and act No. 227 of 1863, (S. L., p. 388) if applied to the case, would have the effect to cut off all remedy the moment it became operative, it was held not to apply to such case. *Ibid.*

3067. Effect of repeal. Where an act appropriated highway taxes collected in a certain town, among others, to a special purpose, and appointed commissioners to disburse the same, but before the taxes had been paid over, though after legal proceedings had been commenced by the commissioners to compel payment, the act was amended by striking out all that related to such town, and the amendatory act contained no saving clause; it was held, that the right, under the original act, to the moneys collected in such town, was thereby terminated. *Tivey v. People*, 8 Mich., 128.

3068. A penal statute being repealed without a saving clause of penalties which had accrued under it, such penalties cannot afterwards be recovered. *Engle v. Shurtz*, 1 Mich., 150.

3069. Where a statute contains unconstitutional provisions, and then a clause repealing all acts and parts of acts inconsistent therewith, the repealing clause has no effect upon prior statutes inconsistent with the unconstitutional provisions, but leaves them still in force. *Campau v. City of Detroit*, 14 Mich.

3070. The repeal of a law giving a Court power to license administrators to sell real estate, after the license has been granted, but before a sale has been made, is a revocation of the license. *Campau v. Gillett*, 1 Mich., 416.

3071. Saving clause. The Statutes of 1838 (p. 395) authorized the renewal of a justice's execution returned unsatisfied. The Justices'

Act of 1841 did not authorize such renewals, but repealed the former law, with this proviso: "The repeal shall not affect any act done, or any right accruing or accrued, or established, or any suit or proceeding commenced, in any civil case," &c. Held, that an execution issued before the repeal could not be renewed afterwards. *Jackson v. Sheldon*, 2 Doug., 154.

3072. Where a statute giving one remedy is repealed, and a new remedy provided, with a saving of *rights accrued*, the saving clause will not authorize the institution of suits under the repealed statutes where the cause of action accrued before. *Robinson v. Steamboat Red Jacket*, 1 Mich., 171.

3073. Revivor by implication. The Detroit Police Act having provided that, on the appointment by the Police Board of a superintendent of police, or captain of police, the office of city marshal should be abolished, a subsequent legislative act, passed before any such appointment of superintendent or captain of police had been made, changing the number of jurors "to be summoned by the marshal," in proceedings in opening, closing or altering streets, could not have the effect to prevent the office of marshal being abolished by the appointment under the police act. *People v. Mahaney*, 13 Mich., 481.

3074. Special acts affecting general statutes. That an act fixing a shorter time of notice for special township meetings for a particular purpose, supersedes, *quoad hoc*, the general statute on the subject, see *Miller v. Grandy*, 13 Mich., 540.

SUPERINTENDENTS OF THE POOR.

3075. When application is made by a pauper to a county superintendent of the poor, under § 1439 Comp. Laws, the superintendent has full power to provide such temporary relief as he may deem proper, without any of the restrictions or qualifications imposed upon directors of the poor on similar applications, by §§ 1443 and 1444. And in granting temporary relief, and in determining who are proper subjects for temporary and permanent relief, a single member possesses the whole power of the board. *Hewitt v. Superintendents of the Poor*, 5 Mich., 166.

TAXATION AND TAX SALES.

3076. Oath of assessors. The absence of any record in the town books showing that the assessors were sworn, does not furnish prima facie evidence that they were not sworn. *Sibley v. Smith*, 2 Mich., 486.

3077. Signing the roll. An assessment roll not signed by the assessors held void under the Statutes of 1838 as amended in 1839, 1840 and 1841. The defect is not cured by the assessors signing the certificate attached to the roll. *Ibid.* But under the law of 1842 the signatures to the certificate were sufficient. *Lacey v. Davis* 4 Mich., 140.

3078. Certificate to roll. A certificate of the assessors which states that they have estimated the real estate " at a sum which, *for the purposes of assessment*, we believe to be the true value thereof, " instead of " at what we believe to be the true cash value thereof" as required by law, is fatally defective. *Clark v. Crane*, 5 Mich., 151.

3079. Levy of tax. Under the Statutes of 1838 the township board had authority, independent of any vote of the electors, to raise money for the purpose of paying the claims audited and allowed against the township. *Wisner v. Davenport*, 5 Mich., 501. See post, 3161.

3080. Description of lands. The description of lands assessessed, or sold for taxes, by the use of initial letters, abbreviations and figures, is sufficient. *Sibley v. Smith*, 2 Mich., 486; *Comp. L.*, § 804.

3081. Ejectment. The plaintiff gave in evidence tax deeds which described the land as " the west half of the southwest fractional quarter of section twenty-eight," &c., containing fifty acres, more or less. It appeared that the southwest fractional quarter was not subdivided by Government, that it contained one hundred acres, was of an irregular shape, somewhat resembling a triangle, and was patented as one parcel. *Held*, that under the statutes—which requires that where the tract is less or other than a Government subdivision, it shall be described for assessment by a designation of the number of the lot or tract, or of other lands by which it is bounded—the description contained in the deeds was not sufficient for the purposes of assessment. *Amberg v. Rogers*, 9 Mich., 332.

3082. But *held*, also, that the description was sufficient for the purposes of a sale for taxes. As the statutes authorize the payment of the tax on any portion of a description which the tax payer will clearly define, and a sale of the remainder, or a redemption of any such portion after sale, and as it also makes the tax deed evidence of the regularity of all the proceedings, and of title in the grantee, it must be presumed that the whole fractional quarter was assessed together, and the tax paid on the east half before sale, or that after sale the east half was redeemed. *Ibid.*

3083. The description of the land as in " town seven of range seven" instead of town seven north of range seven west, is sufficient where the names of the township and county are given, and there is only one town seven of range seven in that township. *Wright v. Dunham* 13 Mich., 414.

3083a. The following description in a tax roll was held void: "Young Men's Society. Gov. and J. P.

Jeff. Av. N. 45 feet. W. pt. lot 11, sec. 1, and E. pt. lot 10, sec. 1. } B. 2."

Detroit Young Men's Society v. Mayor, &c., of Detroit, 3 Mich., 172.

3084. Exemptions. The exemption from taxation of "the real estate belonging to library, benevolent, charitable and scientific institutions, actually occupied by them for the purposes for which they were incorporated," exempts only such distinct tenements as are actually occupied by such institutions for the purposes of their creation, and not tenements, though under the same roof, which are used for other purposes. *Ibid.*

3085. The proper mode of assessing such property is to exclude that which is exempt in the estimate of the value of the whole estate; and the tax levied thereon will be laid only upon the value of that which is not exempt, though the description of the property embraces the whole. *Ibid.*

3086. Certain real estate was deeded to a church in fee, "to the end that they might, from time to time as they should deem necessary, erect thereon any buildings or improvements, suitable for ecclesiastical, literary or benevolent purposes," and was leased to the Sisters of Charity for thirty years, at a nominal rent, for charitable purposes, and was actually occupied for such purposes. Whether the premises, while held and occupied under this lease, are exempt from taxation under the statute as "real estate belonging" to the Sisters of Charity, *quere;* the Court being divided. *Sisters of Charity v. City of Detroit*, 9 Mich., 94.

3087. The compact under which Michigan was admitted into the Union exempts from taxation certain military bounty lands, while they continue to be held by the patentees and their heirs, "for the term of three years from and after the *date of the patents* therefor." This language being clear and unambiguous, must be applied precisely according to its tenor, and cannot be held to mean three years from the *location* of the land. *People v. Auditor-General*, 9 Mich., 134.

3088. Where lands thus exempt have been taxed, the Auditor-General may reject the taxes on his own motion, and he may be compelled to do so on the application of the owner. *Ibid.*

3089. Record of supervisors. The record of the Board of Supervisors did not show who constituted the board, nor that a quorum was present, and there was no signature or authentication by the clerk or presiding officer. *Held*, that the presence of a quorum must be presumed; and that although it was proper and desirable that the record should be signed, it was not necessary. *Lacey v. Davis*, 4 Mich., 140.

3090. Excessive tax. The supervisor having, without authority of law, added a certain amount to the tax roll for township expenses, and that portion of the tax being void, and, from the nature of the case, not distinguishable from the valid part, a sale of premises made for such taxes was held void. *Ibid.*

3091. The mere allowance of illegal demands by the Board of Supervisors the year preceding the levy of a tax, is not sufficient to show that illegal taxes were levied, when there is no evidence to show that the amounts were included in the tax levy, or that there was not money enough on hand to pay them at the time of their allowance. *Wright v. Dunham*, 13 Mich., 414.

3092. Re-assessment. The Board of Supervisors having authority to re-assess taxes for errors, a re-assessment made by them will be held good until some error therein is shown. *Tweed v. Metcalf*, 4 Mich., 579.

3093. Reducing assessments. It is competent for the Board of Supervisors to reduce the aggregate of the assessments below that of the assessors. *Ibid.*

3094. Erroneous footings. The fact that the assessment of the township was stated at one sum on the roll, and at another in the tabular statement of the supervisors, is not material. *Ibid.*

3095. Tax roll. The certificates of assessors and the chairman of the Board of Supervisors, need not be copied as a part of the tax roll. *Ibid.*

3096. Warrant. The supervisor's warrant attached to the tax roll is not void because not running " in the name of the People of the State of Michigan." *Tweed v. Metcalf*, 4 Mich., 579 ; *Wisner v. Davenport*, 5 Mich., 501.

3097. Collection. Where lands are assessed as non-resident the collector has no power to levy upon any property for the tax. *Tweed v. Metcalf*, 4 Mich., 579.

3098. A penalty of ten per cent, added to taxes remaining unpaid up to a certain period, is not excessive, and may be lawfully imposed by statute. *Lacey v. Davis*, 4 Mich., 140.

3099. The statement of the collector under oath, of the moneys received by him as collector—being required for the purpose of securing an accurate accounting by him, and having no connection with the return of lands for delinquent taxes—the failure to make it will not invalidate a tax sale. *Tweed v. Metcalf*, 4 Mich., 579.

3100. The collector has no right to receive in payment of taxes the draft of his creditor upon himself. *Elliott v. Miller*, 8 Mich., 132.

3101. Notice of sale. Under the Revised Statutes of 1846, it was not necessary that the Auditor-General should specify in his notice of tax sales the particular place at the county seat where the sales would take place. A notice which stated that the sale would take place at such public and convenient place as the county treasurer should select at the county seat, was sufficient. *Clark v. Mowyer*, 5 Mich., 462; *Wisner v. Davenport*, 5 Mich., 501.

3102. And a notice by the county treasurer of the place where the tax sales would be made, posted at the court house, county treasurer's office, and other public places at the county seat, a week before the day of sale, was a reasonable and sufficient notice by him if any was required. *Ibid.*

3103. Sales. Where under the statute the tax sales were to commence on the first Monday of October, and to continue from day to day, &c., and the tax deed recited a sale made on the *eleventh* of October, it was held incumbent on the party disputing the validity of the deed to show a non-compliance with the statute. *Lacey v. Davis*, 4 Mich., 140.

3104. There is no limitation by statute of the amount of land that may be sold from any parcel for the taxes assessed thereon. *Sibley v. Smith*, 2 Mich., 486. And where the whole is sold, no presumption of fraud can arise from that fact. *Tweed v. Metcalf*, 4 Mich., 579.

3105. Lands might be sold for delinquent school taxes under the school law of 1843. *Ibid.*

3106. A tenant in common can acquire no title to the interest of his co-tenant, by bidding in the lands at a sale of the whole for delinquent taxes. *Page v. Webster*, 8 Mich., 263. Even though not in possession. *Butler v. Porter*, 13 Mich., 292.

3107. One who has taken possession of lands claiming title, after taxes have become a lien thereon, can acquire no additional interest by suffering the lands to be sold for such taxes and becoming the purchaser. *Lacey v. Davis*, 4 Mich., 140; *Tweed v. Metcalf*, 4 Mich., 579.

3108. But a tax purchaser, before the time of redemption under his purchase has expired, may bid upon the same lands at a tax sale, and have the benefit of the bid. *Tweed v. Metcalf*, 4 Mich., 579.

3109. Whether a tax sale of a town lot, as such, is valid where the town plat has never been recorded, *quere*. *Johnstone v. Scott*, 11 Mich., 232.

3110. A sale made after the tax has been paid is void. *Rowland v. Doty*, Har. Ch., 3; *Johnstone v. Scott*, 11 Mich., 232.

3111. Sale of undivided interest. In a contest between one claiming an undivided interest in lands by original title, and a purchaser of an undivided interest in the same premises at a tax sale, the burden is upon the latter to show that the interest purchased by him is the same as, or includes, the interest claimed by the former. *Butler v. Porter*, 13 Mich., 292.

3112. Deed. The Auditor-General cannot convey lands sold for taxes, without authority by statute therefor. But by the Laws of 1843, in connection with the preceding statutes in force, such authority was conferred. *Sibley v. Smith*, 2 Mich., 486.

3113. Under the Codes of 1827 and 1833, the county treasurer's deed of lands sold for taxes, was evidence only that the *sale* made by him was regular. The party claiming under the deed must show the regularity of the prior proceedings. *Rowland v. Doty*, Har. Ch., 3; *Scott v. Detroit Young Men's Society*, 1 Doug., 119; *Latimer v. Lovett*, 2 Doug., 204; *Ives v. Kimball*, 1 Mich., 308.

3114. Sec 65 of the act of 1843—Laws, 1843, p. 80—which declares that "the deed shall be *prima facie* evidence of the regularity of all the proceedings to the date of the deed," changes this rule, and throws the burden of proof upon the other party. *Sibley v. Smith*, 2 Mich., 486. See *Amberg v. Rogers*, 9 Mich., 332; *Groesbeck v. Seeley*, 13 Mich., 329; *Wright v. Dunham*, 13 Mich., 414.

3115. To obviate the effect of the statute making the deed prima facie evidence of the regularity of all proceedings, the party objecting should produce such evidence as will exclude reasonable presumption of regularity. It should be such evidence of irregularity, not pertaining to mere directory requirements, as to require explanation. Some specific defect, the insufficiency of some particular act, or the non-performance of some requisite duty, should be shown. *Lacey v. Davis*, 4 Mich., 140.

3116. It is not sufficient to prove facts from which an inference of irregularity might be drawn, if such facts are consistent with the existence of others which would make the proceedings regular. *Wright v. Dunham*, 13 Mich., 414.

3117. Where, to show that a tax was erroneously assessed upon a part instead of the whole of a parcel of land, the collector's return was put in evidence which showed a tax against a part of the land only, but it was consistent with this return that a tax might have been correctly levied upon the whole, and a part of the land then cleared of the tax by payment before the return, it was held that the Court, in support of the deed, must presume such payment. *Ibid.*

3118. The tax deed need not recite the proceedings prior to the sale. The recitals need not show more than the capacity in which the officer acts. *Sibley v. Smith*, 2 Mich., 486.

3119. Auditor-General witholding deed. The act of 1843 (S. L., p. 81) authorizing the Auditor-General in certain cases to forbear to sell, or to withhold a conveyance of lands sold, conferred upon him judicial powers, into the proper exercise of which the Supreme

Court could not inquire on motion for mandamus. *People v. Auditor-General*, 3 Mich., 427.

3120. Right to surplus moneys. One who had bought lands at a tax sale, but had not yet become entitled to a deed when it was sold for another year's tax, was not the owner, within the meaning of the Statutes of 1838, so as to be entitled to a surplus received on the last sale, even though such surplus was deposited in the State treasury, and remained there until he had obtained his deed. *People v. Hammond*, 1 Doug., 276.

3121. Specific taxes. The statute of 1853—*Comp. L.*, § 990—is a standing appropriation of one-half the specific taxes collected from mining companies, to the counties respectively. *People v. Auditor-General*, 9 Mich., 141.

3122. A railroad company incorporated before the Revision of 1846, whose charter was silent on the subject of taxation, was liable to pay the specific tax imposed by R. S., Ch. 21, §5. *People v. Detroit and Pontiac Railroad Co.*, 1 Mich., 458.

3123. Assessments for improvements in cities. An assessment upon a city lot for the expense of paving the street, is not invalid from the paving having been contracted for before the assessment was made. *LeFevre v. Mayor, &c., of Detroit*, 2 Mich., 586.

3124. The exemption from taxation of houses of public worship, &c., does not extend to assessments for the expenses of paving streets, &c., imposed upon the owners or occupants of lots. *Ibid.*

3125. An assessment upon "St. Peters and St. Paul's Cathedral," the roll neither describing the lots nor naming the owners or occupants, was held void under the charter and ordinances of Detroit. *Ibid.*

3126. The several ordinances established by the Common Council of Detroit, prescribing the several steps to be taken to perfect assessments and enforce their collection, are binding upon the Common Council and its officers, as well as upon individuals. When the provisions of those ordinances affecting the substantial rights of individuals are not complied with, the Common Council have no authority to cure the irregularity by resolution. *Williams v. Mayor &c., of Detroit*, 2 Mich., 560.

3127. The determination by the Common Council of Detroit to pave a street with stone, is sufficiently declared by an order directing a contract for the work to be made. *Ibid.*

3128. Under an authority in the charter to provide funds for the construction of pavements, the contracts for pavement may be made to include grading, curb stones, gutters and cross walks. *Ibid.*

3129. The Common Council of Detroit were not required by the act of April 13, 1841 (S. L., p. 192), to permit persons to pave the street in front of the lots owned or occupied by them, but were merely *au-*

thorized so to do when they should deem it for the interest of the city. And the city ordinances contemplated the paving by lot owners or occupants only in case of special permission to do so from the Council. *Ibid.*

3130. Notice of making the assessment was not required to be given personally, but was sufficient if published in a city paper as required by the ordinances. *Ibid.*

3131. Under the Detroit city charter, as in force in 1852, the warrant issued for the collection of a street assessment might lawfully authorize the marshal to collect five per cent. in addition for his fees. *Ibid.*

3132. It was not material that the aseessment roll did not distinguish those who were residents from those who were not; as no rights were thereby affected. *Ibid.*

3133. The authority to pave streets in a city is a continuing power, and does not cease on being once exercised. *Ibid.*

3134. The omission to appoint an officer to superintend the paving of a street in Detroit, as provided by the city ordinances, would not invalidate an assessment for the paving, when the paving was done under a contract which the Common Council had a right to make. *Ibid.*

3135. Action against supervisor. When a supervisor is sued in trespass for the taking of personal property under a warrant for the collection of taxes, issued by him and attached to the tax roll, evidence that he was at the time supervisor, and, as such, signed the warrant, does not make out a prima facie justification. He must also show that the roll had come to his hands from the Board of Supervisors, as provided by law, and that the various taxes had been certified to him for assessment by the competent authorities. When his jurisdiction has been thus shown, his acts will be presumed regular and valid till the contrary appears. *Clark v. Axford*, 5 Mich., 182.

3136. A supervisor is not liable in trespass on account of any errors or defects in the description of real estate in the assessment roll. *Ibid.*

3137. Collector's compensation. Under the statutes in force in 1861 and 1862, the township treasurer had the right to retain, of his own authority, only two per cent. of the taxes of 1861 collected by him, for his fees, where neither the electors of the township, nor the supervisor, had fixed his compensation at a higher rate. *Township of Texas v. Wager*, 12 Mich., 39.

3138. Whether the supervisor has the right to fix the compensation when the electors have neglected to do so, *quere*. *Ibid.*

3139. Where the electors did not determine what percentage should be added to the taxes for the collection expenses, and the supervisor added two and a half per cent., and, in his warrant for their collection, directed the treasurer to retain that amount for his fees, and the treasurer retained four per cent., paying over the remainder ; it was held that he was liable to the township for the amount he had retained over two and a half per cent. *Ibid.*

3140. Redemption of undivided interest in Detroit. That since the charter of 1857 the owner of an undivided interest in lands in Detroit may redeem such interest from a sale made of the whole land, by paying a proportionate amount of the tax, see *People v. Treasurer of Detroit*, 8 Mich., 14.

3141. Taxation and eminent domain. The difference between taking property under the right of taxation and under the power of eminent domain pointed out. *Williams v. Mayor, &c., of Detroit*, 2 Mich., 560 ; *Woodbridge v. City of Detroit*, 8 Mich., 274.

TENANT IN COMMON.

3142. Crops put in on shares. One J. put in wheat on shares on defendant's lands, and was to have possession of the land, and do other farm duties upon shares of other produce. As there was no proof that it was agreed that J.'s rights in the crops should be forfeited by non-fulfillment of any other conditions, and no evidence of damages from any such non-fullfilment, it was held, in a controversy between defendant and plaintiffs, to whom J. had mortgaged the crops while growing, that J. was clearly tenant in common of the crops. *Fiquet v. Allison*, 12 Mich., 328.

3143. When the crops were ripened plaintiffs harvested them, but defendant threshed them, put them in his granary, and refused to recognize any rights of plaintiffs therein. Held that he was liable to plaintiffs for the value of their share in assumpsit. *Ibid.* See *Webb v. Mann*, 3 Mich., 139.

TENDER.

3144. A tender to be valid must be made to the creditor or some one authorized to act for him. It is insufficient if made to a mere servant of the creditor. *Thurber v. Jewett*, 3 Mich., 295.

3145. A tender for the purpose of cancelling a judgment should include both damages and costs. A tender of damages with the clerk's receipt for the costs is not sufficient. *Ibid.*

3146. Where a bill holder presents at one time to a bank for redemption, several bills of the denomination of $5, it is competent for the bank, under the act of Congress of Feb. 23, 1853, entitled " An act amendatory of the existing laws relative to the half dollars," &c., to tender payment of the whole sum so presented in half dollars issued under said act. *Strong v. Farmers and Mechanics' Bank*, 4 Mich., 350.

3147. The Legal Tender Act is constitutional. *Van Husan v. Kanouse*, 13 Mich., 302. And in a suit on a note given since its passage and expressly by its terms made payable in gold, it is not competent for the Court to receive evidence that gold is worth a premium over legal tender notes, and to award to the plaintiff as damages a sum equal to such premium in addition to the amount specified in the note. *Buchegger v. Shultz*, 13 Mich., 420.

3148. That a tender of the amount of a debt for which property is held in mortgage discharges the lien, see *Fuller v. Parish*, 3 Mich., 211; *Moynahan v. Moore*, 9 Mich., 9; *Caruthers v. Humphrey*, 12 Mich., 270; *Van Husan v. Kanouse*, 13 Mich., 303.

TERRITORIAL COUNCIL.

3149. The Legislative Council of the Territory of Michigan had power to pass acts of incorporation, which were valid until disapproved by Congress. *Mercer v. Williams*, Wal. Ch., 85; *Swan v. Williams*, 2 Mich., 427.

TIME.

3150. Conflicting dates. Where a date is given, both as a day of the week and a day of the month, and the two are inconsistent, the day of the month must govern. *Ingersoll v. Kirby*, Wal. Ch., 27. See supra, 678.

3151. Computation of. Where a statute prescribes that a process should be served a certain number of days before the return day, both the day of service and the day of the return must be excluded in the computation. *Dousman v. O'Malley*, 1 Doug., 450; *Sallee v. Ireland*, 9 Mich., 154.

3152. Where by statute an act is required to be done in any number of days less than a week, Sunday is to be excluded. *Drake v. Andrews*, 2 Mich., 203. See supra, 130, 2799.

3153. No time specified. A chattel mortgage may be given to secure the performance of any other act or contract by the mortgagor. or by a third person, besides the payment of money; and where no time of performance is specified, the omission does not vitiate the contract, but the law steps in and requires performance within a reasonable time. *Byram v. Gordon*, 11 Mich., 531. At to reasonable time, see further, supra 386 to 388, 401 to 404.

TOWN PLATS.

3154. Public grounds. Where the proprietors of a village or town plan have dedicated lands for streets, or for a public square, and sold lots with reference to such plan, they cannot resume and exercise acts of ownership over the land thus dedicated which will deprive the grantees of any privileges which they might derive from having such streets or squares open. *Sinclair v. Comstock*, Har. Ch., 404.

3155. The dedication for the purpose claimed must be clearly apparent. *Ibid.* See *Lee v. Lake*, 14 Mich. And see further to the same effect, *People v. Beaubien*, 2 Doug., 256; *Cook v. Village of Hillsdale*, 7 Mich., 115; *People v. Jones*, 6 Mich., 176.

3156. Where a lot was dedicated for the purpose of having a court house and jail erected thereon, and the county erected those buildings on another lot in the same village, it was held that the first mentioned lot reverted to the original owner, and that persons who had purchased adjoining lots had no right to insist that it should be kept open as a public square or common. *Sinclair v. Comstock*, Har. Ch., 404.

3157. A town plat executed and recorded under the statute, vests the fee of the public grounds in the county. *Wanzer v. Blanchard*, 3 Mich., 11.

For a case where the making and recording of a town plat, and the designating ground as public square, were held, in connection with the other facts in the case, not to establish a dedication, see *Lee v. Lake*, 14 Mich.

TOWNSHIPS.

3158. Liabilities. A township was sued on the following instrument: " The commissioners of highways of the township of R. will pay the bearer twenty two dollars, when funds in road district number three and four :" dated, and signed by the commissioners. *Held*, that the action could not be sustained. *Monroe v. Township of Rowland*, 1 Mich., 318.

3159. A township is not liable for interest on damages appraised for laying out a highway. *People v. Township Board of La Grange*, 2 Mich., 187.

3160. Townships are not liable for damages sustained by individuals, in consequence of the non-repair of bridges and highways. And they cannot be subjected to such liability through an action against the commissioners of highways. *Commissioners of Highways of Niles v. Martin*, 4 Mich., 557.

A statute has since been passed — Laws of 1861, p. 407 — designed (perhaps) to give a remedy against the township in such cases.

3161. Taxes. Under the Statutes of 1838, townships had authority to vote to raise money for building bridges upon the report of the highway commissioners. Also to raise money for the destruction of Canada thistles. Also to raise a sum for contingent expenses generally, without specifying for what particular purposes. *Tweed v. Metcalf*, 4 Mich., 579. And the township boards, independent of any vote of the electors, might raise money to pay claims audited and allowed against the townships. *Wisner v. Davenport*, 5 Mich., 501.

3162. Division of townships: indebtedness. Where, after the division of a township, the town boards have met and determined the amount of the township indebtedness to be paid by the new township, such amount is a fixed and liquidated demand against the new township, which it is the duty of its town board to allow and issue order for. If the town board refuse to perform this duty, mandamus is the proper remedy, and not an action against the township. *Marathon Township v. Oregon Township*, 8 Mich., 372.

3163. Board of health. When the board of health of a township necessarily incurs expenses in providing for the protection of its inhabitants against a sickness dangerous to the public health, by the removal of persons infected to a building provided for them, such expenses are a charge against the county which it is the duty of the Board of Supervisors to allow. *People v. Supervisors of Macomb*, 3 Mich., 475.

TREATY.

3164. Identity of beneficiaries. Where a treaty makes no provision for deciding questions of individual identity, they must be decided by the judicial tribunals of the country. *Stockton v. Williams*, Wal. Ch., 120; *same case on appeal*, 1 Doug., 546. See also, *Campau v. Dewey*, 9 Mich., 381. See supra, 1940 to 1943.

3165. Jay's treaty. The stipulations contained in the treaty of London, known as Jay's Treaty, for the protection of private rights of property, imposed no new obligation upon the Government of the United States, but were only in affirmance of the law of nations. *May v. Specht*, 1 Mich., 187.

3166. Force of a treaty. Where a treaty has been made and ratified by the proper Federal authority, it becomes the law of the land; and Courts have not the power to question the powers or rights recognized by it in the nation or tribe with whom it was made. *Maiden v. Ingersoll*, 6 Mich., 373.

3167. Construction. A treaty with Indian tribes, after reciting that they felt a strong consideration for aid rendered by certain of their half breeds, and that, wishing to testify their gratitude, they had assigned certain locations of land to such individuals, and had united in a strong appeal for the allowance of the same in the treaty, but that no such reservations could be permitted in carrying out the instructions of the President, it was agreed that, in addition to the general fund set apart for half breeds in another article, the sum of $48,148 should be paid for the relinquishment of this class of claims, to be divided in the following manner: " To John A. Drew, for a tract of one section and three quarters, to his Indian family, at Cheboygan Rapids, at $4 an acre," &c. *Held*, that the money was given to Drew absolutely, and not in trust for his Indian family. *Cook v. Biddle*, 2 Mich., 269.

3168. The Court cannot, from a construction of the Treaty of Saginaw of Sept. 24, 1819, interpret the words " Indians by descent," as used therein, to mean persons of mixed white and Indian blood only, and not full blooded Indians. *Campau v. Dewey*, 7 Mich., 381.

3169. Nor can the Court say, from the language of the treaty, the policy of the Government as indicated by the Indian treaties, public records and dispatches, and the habits and modes of life of the Chippewa nation, that a presumption arises that all the reservees in said taeaty were persons of mixed white and Indian blood. *Ibid.*

TRESPASS TO LANDS.

3170. A party having title to unoccupied lands is constructively in possession, and may maintain trespass against one who, without his license or authority, having no color of title to the lands, and whose acts evince no intention to retain permanent possession, enters upon them and cuts and carries away timber. *Safford v. Basto*, 4 Mich., 406.

3171. The defendants went upon unoccupied lands under a void tax title, and cut and carried away the timber. The plaintiff, having the title, brought trespass. It was held that he was constructively in possession, and that if the defendants entered upon the lands with the intention to cut and remove the timber as soon as they could, and then abandon it, the act did not constitute a disseizin, and they were liable in this action. *Ibid.*

3172. The statute giving treble damages for trespass on lands in certain cases—Comp. L., p. 1147—was not framed to protect mere possessory rights, but to give the owner of the fee the right to sue, under the form of trespass, for injuries to his inheritance. And it is therefore not a defense to the action that defendant had disseized the plaintiff, though it may prevent treble damages. *Achey v. Hull*, 7 Mich., 423.

TRUSTS AND TRUSTEES.

3173. What constitutes. County commissioners, authorized to take a mortgage to the county, but taking it to themselves, hold it as trustees for the county. *Rood v. Winslow*, 2 Doug., 68.

3174. The act of Congress of March 3, 1807, " regulating the grants of land in the territory of Michigan, " recognized no right in claimants but that of occupancy and possession, as the stock in which the fee was to be engrafted; and where three brothers, on the death of their father, claimed a tract of land under a " substitution," or kind of entailment, by which the land belonged to the eldest son his life time, and after his death to the second son his life time, &c., the eldest son, under the claim set up by the brothers, being entitled to the occupancy or possession in his own right, to the exclusion of his brothers, was also entitled to the fee simple in his own right; and having presented his claim, and procured its allowance, and obtained a patent for the land, there was not a resulting trust in favor of his brothers. *Chene v. Bank of Michigan*, Wal. Ch., 511.

3175. Whether certain facts constitute a trust or an agency, see *Titus v. Minnesota Mining Co.*, 8 Mich., 183. That one good trust inserted in a fraudulent conveyance cannot support it, see *Kirby v. Ingersoll*, Har. Ch., 172. That State officers to whom property has been assigned on condition subsequent that the State shall indemnify the assignors against certain liabilities, may be required, as trustees, to appropriate the property in indemnifying the assignors when the State refuses to perform the condition, see *Michigan State Bank v. Hammond*, 1 Doug., 527.

3176. Declaration. To take the case out of the Statute of Frauds, the terms and conditions of a trust in lands which have been conveyed by absolute deed, must be in writing, under the hand of the grantees. *Wright v. King*, Har. Ch., 12.

3177. Resulting trust. A resulting trust only exists where the actual payment of the purchase money is clearly and distinctly proved. Payment of a part only will not be sufficient. *Bernard v. Bougard's Heirs*, Har. Ch., 130. And see *Wright v. King*, Har. Ch., 12. Resulting trusts in such cases, except in behalf of creditors, have since been abolished by statute. Comp. L., §§ 2637, 2638.

3178. The trust in favor of creditors, where one has purchased land with his own money and caused it to be conveyed to another to keep it beyond their reach, is not executed by the Statutes of 1846, and cannot be enforced by levy and sale on execution. *Trask v. Green*, 9 Mich., 358; *Maynard v. Hoskins*, 9 Mich., 485. But where the debtor has conveyed away lands to which he had title, for the same fraudulent purpose, it remains subject to execution in the hands of the grantee, and the purchaser at the execution sale may recover possession in ejectment. *Cleland v. Taylor*, 3 Mich., 201.

3179. What does not create a trust. A conveyance by husband and wife, with condition that the grantee, during the natural lives of the grantors, should farm the land conveyed, and pay a portion of the products to the grantors, and at their decease, convey to their surviving children, and in default of such, to the right heirs of the grantors;—the deed not being executed by the grantee—does not create an irrevocable trust, and vests no estate in the children. And it was accordingly held, that after reconveyance by the grantee to the grantors, they might dispose of the fee. *Lewis v. Nelson*, 4 Mich., 630.

3180. The clause in the deed directing a conveyance, &c., is a mere power to convey in the event of the grantors dying without making other or further disposition. *Ibid.*

3181. Dealings of trustee with cestui que trust. A trustee is not allowed to deal with his *cestui que trust* as with a third person; and purchases of trust property made by him will not be sustained, unless the Court is satisfied that he has acted throughout with the most perfect fairness, and taken no advantage of his peculiar position. *Schwarz v. Wendell*, Wal. Ch., 267. Under the facts appearing in this case, the Court set aside a purchase made by the *cestui que trust* of the trustee, and ordered the latter to deliver up to be cancelled a note given for the purchase price, or to account for the amount.

3182. The agreements of the husband of a *cestui que trust* with the trustee are not binding upon the wife. *Ibid.*

3183. Set off by trustees. Land was conveyed to a railroad company by deed containing a covenant against incumbrances. The railroad afterwards passed into the hands of trustees. A mortgage which was upon the lands so purchased by the railroad company was foreclosed, and the trustees bid in the land, not as trustees, but in their own right. It was held that this could not be regarded as a *payment*, so as to authorize the trustees to set off the amount of their bid against a mortgage given by the railroad company for the purchase price of the land when they bought. *Griggs v. Detroit and Milwaukee Railway Co.*, 10 Mich., 117.

3184. Subrogation. One whose sole interest in lands is under a trust deed, by virtue of which he is to become entitled to them on paying certain mortgages upon them, and also certain other specified demands, is not entitled, if he repudiates the trust, to make any arrangements with the mortgagees by which he can be subrogated in equity to their rights without paying the other demands. *Smith v. Austin*, 11 Mich., 34.

UNIVERSITY OF MICHIGAN.

3185. The corporation. The "Regents of the University of Michigan" are the legal successors of the "Trustees of the University of Michigan," incorporated by the act of April 30, 1821, (Code of 1827, p. 448). *Regents of the University v. Board of Education of Detroit*, 4 Mich., 213.

3186. Grant of lands in Detroit. The conveyance by the Governor and Judges of Michigan territory of certain lands in Detroit to the Trustees of the University of Michigan, held valid. *Ibid.*

3187. Power of Regents to hold lands. The Regents of the University have power to take, hold and convey real estate, for any purpose tending to promote the interests of the University, to increase its funds, or otherwise to further the great public objects for which the corporation was created. *Regents of the University v. Detroit Young Men's Society*, 12 Mich., 138.

3188. Suit by the Regents to recover the purchase price of lands sold by them. The declaration averred their ownership, but did not show the nature of their title, nor how acquired, and it was demurred to on the ground that the Regents had no power to make sale of lands without special legislative authority. Held that as it was legally possible for the Regents, in some modes and for some purposes, to be vested with the title to lands with power to convey the same, judgment on the demurrer must be for the plaintiff. *Ibid.*

3189. Control of the University. The financial and other interests of the University are entrusted to the judgment and discretion of the Regents. It is a sufficient answer to an application for a mandamus to show cause why they do not fill a professorship established by law, that the appointment being likely to interfere with the harmony of the institution, and being one requiring great care and deliberation in making, they had commenced and were still making the investigations necessary to enable them to make a proper appointment; especially where there appeared to be no unncessary delay or want of good faith in their proceedings. *People v. Regents of the University*, 4 Mich., 68.

USAGE.

3190. Foreign moneys. The relative value of foreign and American currency is a question of commercial usage, and may be proved by any one acquainted with the usage. *Kermott v. Ayer*, 11 Mich., 181.

USES.

3191. If the Statute of Uses was ever in force in Michigan, it was repealed by the act of September 16, 1810, repealing the acts of Parliament, &c.; from which date until March 1, 1847, when the Revised Statutes of 1846 took effect, no statute involving the principle of the Statute of Uses was in force here. *Trask v. Green*, 9 Mich., 358. There was consequently nothing to prevent the creation of any trust which would have been valid at the common law. *Ready v. Kearsley*, 14 Mich.

USURY.

3192. Construction of statute. The effect of usury under our statute is, not to avoid the contract, but to reduce the amount which the usurer is entitled to recover to the money actually loaned, with legal interest. And the borrower has no other remedy but such reduction. *Craig v. Butler*, 9 Mich., 21. See also, *Thurston v. Prentiss*, Wal. Ch., 529, and 1 Mich., 193.

3193. The deduction may be made as well when suit is brought on the usurious contract in a Court of equity, as when it is brought at law. *Coatsworth v. Barr*, 11 Mich., 199.

3194. Usury is a personal defense, to be interposed by the party to the contract, and a subsequent purchaser of land upon which the usurious contract is a lien, cannot avail himself of it. *Farmers and Mechanics' Bank v. Kimmel*, 1 Mich., 84; *Sellers v. Botsford*, 11 Mich., 59.

3195. Evidence. Where a contract with a corporation on its face imports a reservation of interest, in excess of what its charter allows, there is no room left for presumption: the intent is apparent. Where, however, it is fair on its face, the law will not infer an intent, or a corrupt agreement, to take illegal interest, in violation of the charter; but this must be clearly established. *Orr v. Lacey*, 2 Doug., 230. For a case where the facts were held to prove usury, see *Caruthers v. Humphrey*, 12 Mich., 270.

3196. What is usury. On an usurious contract the plaintiff may always recover interest up to the highest legal rate not prohibited by the statute, if such are the express terms of the contract. *Smith v. Stoddard*, 10 Mich., 148.

3197. New security. Where unlawful interest has been paid, and a new security is afterwards taken for the principal, the debtor is not entitled to have the amount of the usury so paid deducted when suit is brought on the new security. *Smith v. Stoddard*, 10 Mich., 148; *Craig v. Butler*, 9 Mich., 21.

3198. But if in the new security a sum is included for unlawful unpaid interest, the security, to the extent of the unlawful interest, is without consideration. *Smith v. Stoddard*, 10 Mich., 148. So if a sum is included for statutory damages when the statute allows none. *Collins Iron Co. v. Burkham*, 10 Mich., 283.

3199. Foreign contract. Where a contract made in another State is usurious, but the law of that State does not avoid it on that ground, but only affects the remedy upon it, the Courts of this State can enforce the contract, but only by those remedies afforded by our own law. *Collins Iron Co. v. Burkham*, 10 Mich., 283.

3200. The provisions of the Ohio statute for the recovery or appropriation of usury paid upon a contract, form no part of the contract, but relate solely to the remedy which will be afforded by the Courts of that State to the party from whom usury is taken. *Ibid.*

VARIANCE.

3201. An allegation that defendants acknowledged themselves held and firmly bound unto "the board of supervisors of the county of St. Joseph," is not sustained by a bond to "the supervisors of the county of St. Joseph;"—the declaration not alleging that the bond was made to the plaintiffs by the name mentioned in the bond. *Board of Supervisors of St. Joseph v. Coffenbury*, 1 Mich., 355.

3202. Ejectment. The plaintiffs, by their declaration, claimed the premises as trustees "to sell the said premises, and apply the moneys which they should obtain to the payment of certain debts" of one B. The declaration of trust put in evidence on the trial, and signed by B., provided for the payment of certain notes signed by another person, and to which B. was not a party. Held, that it was fairly to be inferred that B. was in some way bound for the payment of these notes; and if not, that his providing for their payment rendered them so far his debts as to satisfy the averment in the declaration. *Ives v. Kimball*, 1 Mich., 308.

VENDOR AND PURCHASER.

3203. What is a sale. Where property is taken at a fixed money price, the transaction is a *sale*, whether the price is paid in money or in goods. *Picard v. McCormick*, 11 Mich., 68.

3204. Sale of chattels: delivery. The sale of a chattel, where the consideration is actually paid, is valid without actual delivery, or even if the chattel at the time is lost or withheld from the vendor by a wrong doer. *Davis v. Ransom*, 4 Mich., 238.

3205. A contractor for convict labor, while engaged within the State prison, had a watch worth $125 stolen, which, not being found after diligent search, he offered to sell at $25. The agent of the State prison and one of the guards accepted the offer, and paid the $25. It was held that the purchase was not void for want of delivery, nor as against public policy because made by such officers. *Ibid.*

3206. The defendant sent wheat by railroad from Hudson to Toledo, consigning part of it to H. & Co. and part to F. On its arrival at Toledo, the wheat was mingled with other like grain, in the railroad elevator. The receipts given for the wheat made it deliverable to the consignees or order. Defendant then made sale of the wheat to plaintiff, and received payment for the same, and gave him an order on F. for its delivery. Before plaintiff found F., or obtained delivery of the wheat, it was destroyed by the burning of the elevator. Held:

1. That the legal control of the wheat was in the consignees, through whose co-operation alone the title could be vested in the plaintiff.

2. That the order upon F. was an undertaking on the part of defendant that F. would complete the sale by delivery of the wheat; and that he was liable to the plaintiff for a breach of that undertaking. *Perkins v. Dacon*, 13 Mich., 81.

3207. That where a note is made and indorsed for the purpose of being sold or discounted, it is the delivery of the note to the purchaser which completes the contract as between him and the parties to it, see *Kinzie v. Farmers and Mechanics' Bank*, 1 Doug., 105, and *Vinton v. Peck*, 14 Mich.

3208. Sale of goods: risk of sending. Where a merchant sells goods to a purchaser at a distance, and contracts to ship them at a certain time by a specified route, but, instead of doing so, sends them by some other, it is at his own risk of loss or unseasonable delivery. *Fleming v. Mills*, 5 Mich., 420.

2209. Executory contract. Whether an agreement for a sale of lands, by the usual executory contract—the title to be conveyed when the purchase price is paid—constitutes a *sale* within the meaning of the act of the legislature of February 12, 1853, exempting lands donated for the construction of the Sault Ste. Marie Canal, from taxation for five years, except as to any portion *sold*, *quere*. *People v. Auditor General*, 7 Mich., 84.

3210. Consideration. As to the sufficiency of consideration to support a transfer of property, see *Goff v. Thompson*, Har. Ch., 60; *Cicotte v. Gagnier*, 2 Mich., 381. That third persons have no concern with the consideration for the transfer of property or rights, unless they are creditors of the assignor, see *Morey v. Forsyth*, Wal. Ch., 465.

3211. Notice through deeds. That where a vendee cannot make out a title except through a deed which leads him to a certain fact, he must be presumed to have knowledge of that fact, see *Mason v. Payne*, Wal. Ch., 459; *Norris v. Hill*, 1 Mich., 202; and is chargeable with all reasonable inferences therefrom. *Fitzhugh v. Barnard*, 12 Mich., 104.

3212. Purchase subject to mortgage. One who buys land subject to a mortgage, cannot contest the mortgage on the ground that it is defectively executed. *Disbrow v. Jones*, Har. Ch., 48.

3213. Vendor's lien. The vendor of real estate has an equitable lien upon it for the purchase money, where no security for the payment has been taken by him. *Carroll v. Van Renselaer*, Har. Ch., 225; *Payne v. Atterbury*, Har. Ch., 414; *Palmer et al., appellants*, 1 Doug., 422; *Sears v. Smith*, 2 Mich., 243; *Mowrey v. Vandling*, 9 Mich., 39.

3214. But if the vendor takes a distinct and independent security for the purchase money, other than the personal obligation of the vendee—as the note or other obligation of a third person, or the obligation of the vendee with sureties—the lien is gone. *Palmer et al., appellants*, 1 Doug., 422; *Sears v. Smith*, 2 Mich., 243. An administrator who receives such obligation on a sale of lands belonging to the estate, is personally liable to the estate for the amount if not collected. 1 Doug., 422.

3215. Lien of vendee. A vendee who has paid his purchase money punctually, has a lien as against the vendor analogous to that of a vendor against a vendee who has not paid the purchase money. *Payne v. Atterbury*, Har. Ch., 414.

3216. Vendor becoming purchaser. No one without express authority of law can become purchaser of property which it is his duty to sell for the highest price he can obtain. *Ames v. Port Huron Log Driving and Booming Co.*, 11 Mich., 139. See also, *Moore v. Mandlebaum*, 8 Mich., 433; *Dwight v. Blackmar*, 2 Mich., 330; *Beaubien v. Poupard*, Har. Ch., 206; *Clute v. Barron*, 2 Mich., 192; *People v. Township Board of Overyssel*, 11 Mich., 222.

WAGER.

3217. Recovery of stakeholder. If the loser of money, deposited upon an unlawful wager, claim his money before it has been actually paid over by the holder, even though it be after the wager has been decided, the stake holder is bound to return it to him, and is liable to an action therefor if he refuses. *Whitwell v. Carter*, 4 Mich., 329.

3218. Suit against the winner. Suit under the statute—Comp. L., § 1582—which authorizes the loser of money by betting, "who shall pay and deliver the same" "to the winner," to "sue for and recover such money, in an action for money had and received." The parties had made a wager upon the result of an election, depositing their negotiable notes for the amount, instead of money. When the result was determined, the stakeholder delivered the notes to the winner—the defendant—who afterwards sold plaintiff's note at a discount. Plaintiff then brought assumpsit against defendant, for money had and received, and on the trial, produced his note as evidence that he had paid it. Held, that the production of the note was not sufficient evidence of its payment by plaintiff to authorize him to maintain the statutory action. *Buckley v. Saxe*, 10 Mich., 328.

WAIVER.

3219. A waiver of a legal right is not to be implied from slight circumstances. *Bird v. Hamilton*, Wal. Ch., 361.

3220. A joint promissor has no power to waive the performance of a condition precedent, when the effect would be to create an obligation against the other joint promissor which would not otherwise exist. *Thompson v. Richards*, 14 Mich..

3221. An administrator does not preclude himself from maintaining a suit for a fund, in his representative capacity, by borrowing a part of it in his individual capacity, and executing his bond and mortgage therefor. *Cullen v. O'Hara*, 4 Mich., 132.

3222. Diversion of water. Where complainant had stood by, without objecting, and allowed defendant to go on and expend a considerable amount of money in the erection of a mill, in violation of the terms of a grant made by complainant, in consideration of the erection of the mill, of the right to use the water of a creek in a particular manner, it was held, that by his silence he had waived all right to relief in equity, by injunction, against diverting the water. *Jacox v. Clark*, Wal. Ch., 249.

3223. Account of rents. Where one neglects for several years after the time of redemption expires, to perfect his title under an execution sale, he waives all right to an account of the rents and profits for the intermediate period. The officer's deed relates back to the time of the sale, for the purpose of protecting possession under the title purchased, or for the purpose of supporting a conveyance made by the purchaser or his assignee; but not to give the purchaser or his assignee compensation for the use and occupation of the premises before his own title is perfected. *Whipple v. Farrar*, 3 Mich., 436.

3224. In legal proceedings. By going to trial without objection, a party waives any he might have to the want of proper qualification of jurors. *Owners of Ship Milwaukee v. Hale*, 1 Doug., 306.

3225. A nonsuit was set aside on condition of payment of costs by the plaintiff. Afterwards defendants stipulated in writing, unconditionally, to try the cause on a certain day. Held to be a waiver of the prior payment of costs. *Higley v. Lant*, 3 Mich., 612.

3226. A plea in bar is a waiver of an objection to the jurisdiction of a Court of general jurisdiction. *Webb v. Mann*, 3 Mich., 139.

3227. Where a witness is excluded on objection, but afterwards, the Court doubting the correctness of its ruling, offers to open the question and hear further argument, which the counsel declines, the objection will be considered waived. *McBride v. Cicotte*, 4 Mich., 478.

3228. A defendant in chancery attending and examining witnesses before a master, on complainant's notice, will be regarded as waiving all objections to the service of replication. *Brooks v. Mead*, Wal. Ch., 389.

3229. By appearing and going to trial in an attachment suit, defendant waives all prior irregularities. *Crane v. Hardy*, 1 Mich., 56.

See further, *Vanderhoof v. Dean*, 1 Mich., 163; *Stewart v. Hill*, 1 Mich., 265; *Shaw v. Moser*, 3 Mich., 71; *Durfee v. McClurg*, 5 Mich., 532; *Sallee v. Ireland*, 9 Mich., 154.

WAREHOUSEMEN.

3230. That warehousemen who have received goods from carriers who had no right to the possession of them, and advanced charges for freight, have no lien upon them for such freight, or for any charge of their own for storage, as against the owner, see *Fitch v. Newberry*, 1 Doug., 1.

3231. A railroad company which has entered into a contract to deliver flour on shipboard, continues liable as common carriers until this delivery is made; and if the flour is destroyed in their warehouse, they cannot claim that their liability, while it was there, was that of warehousemen merely. *Moore v. Michigan Central R. R. Co.*, 3 Mich., 23.

WARRANT OF ATTORNEY.

3232. The practice of giving or filing warrants of attorney, authorizing the prosecution of a suit, has never prevailed in this State, and a judgment will not be reversed for the want of one, even where the plaintiff below was a corporation. *Farmers and Mechanics' Bank v. Troy City Bank*, 1 Doug., 457.

WARRANTY.

3233. A fanning mill was sold on the representation that it was good, and would do a good business. The purchaser gave his note for it, to which it was added, that the note was given for the mill, which was warranted to be good and to do a good business, and that if was not good, the purchaser was to have the privilege of returning it within a certain time, and the seller was to furnish a new mill in exchange, which should be good. In an action on the note, it was held, that unless it was shown the seller knew at the time of the sale that the mill was not good, the purchaser was bound to return it according to the condition annexed to the note, before he could avail himself of any defect in the mill in his defense. *Horner v. Fellows*, 1 Doug., 51.

WATER RIGHTS.

3234. License. An unrevoked parol license to flow lands, given by one who at the time had the right to flow, is a good defense to an action for flowing lands. *Millard v. Reeves*, 1 Mich., 107.

3235. Water leased : measurement. Water was leased by the following words: "The right and privilege of drawing from the west side of the race now making by the said party of the first part, in Ypsilanti, and leading to his new saw mill, at any place within sixteen rods of the head gate of said race, as much water as will run through an aperture of two feet square, under a head of four feet from the top of said aperture, for the use of carrying machinery for iron works, provided so much shall be needed by the said party of the second part for such use." And the lease further provided as follows : That "in case the two feet square of water should not be enough for the use of such iron works as the said party of the second part may hereafter erect, near said race, he shall have as much more as shall be necessary for such use, by paying therefor at the same rate as for the two feet square aforesaid;" and also that "in case a sufficient quantity of ore cannot conveniently be procured for carrying on said iron works to advantage, the said two feet square of water may be used for such other machinery as the said party of the second part shall think fit and proper." Held, that construing the words of demise by the other parts of the instrument, the lessee was entitled to as much water as would run from the race into a flume conducting it to the iron works, through an aperture two feet square, made in the side of the race, not lower down than four feet below the surface of the water in the race ; and not to as much water as would flow through an aperture of the size and under the head mentioned, into open space, or directly upon the wheel where it was applied. *Norris v. Showerman*, 2 Doug., 16, affirming *same case*, Wal. Ch., 206.

WAYS.

3236. Classification. All ways are either public or private; there is no intermediate species of way for any purpose of passage. *Tillman v. People*, 12 Mich., 401.

3237. Private. A canal through a marsh in which a stream is lost, cut by private individuals through the land of one of them, for the purpose of affording floatage for timber and lumber through the same in connection with the stream—there being no evidence that the waters of the stream ever ran along its line, or that it was the improvement of an existing water channel—is a *private* way, and the public are not entitled to use it, unless it be dedicated to their use. *Ward v. Warner*, 8 Mich., 508.

3238. City streets; obstructions. The Common Council of Detroit had no right, though acting under a resolution of a public meeting of the freemen, to lease a portion of a public street to the Commissioners of Internal Improvement for the use of the State, for the purposes of a railroad depot, and tracks connected therewith. *Cooper v. Alden*, Har. Ch., 72.

3239. Neither the Governor and Judges nor the Common Council, had or have any power or authority to grant the exclusive use of any of the streets or alleys of the city to individuals. *People v. Carpenter*, 1 Mich., 273.

3240. Rights of adjacent owners. Purchasers of lots on the Governor and Judges' plan of Detroit have no other or greater rights in the streets and alleys, than if the plan had been laid out by an individual, who had legally dedicated the streets and alleys. *Cooper v. Alden*, Har. Ch., 72.

3241. On the application of purchasers who are interested in the preservation or appropriation of a street or square to the purposes to which it was dedicated, equity will restrain the public authorities from putting it to other uses destructive of the ends for which the dedication was made. *Ibid.*

3242. When obstruction a nuisance. Every obstruction in a street or highway is not a nuisance. Whether it is such, or not, is a question of fact, and not of law. A flight of stairs, described in the case, within the limits of Woodwood avenue, was held to be an obstruction not authorized by the Governor and Judges, or by the Common Council. *People v. Carpenter*, 1 Mich., 273.

3243. Dedication. If the owner of land do such acts as show, unequivocally, an intent to dedicate his land to the public for a highway, such dedication, if properly accepted, will make the land dedicated a public highway, without reference to any particular period of time. *People v. Jones*, 6 Mich., 176.

3244. In determining whether there has been a dedication, all the acts of the owner bearing upon the question are to be considered together. One act may be explained or qualified by another. *Ibid.* And see *Cook v. Village of Hillsdale*, 7 Mich., 115; *People v. Beaubien*, 2 Doug., 256; *Lee v. Lake*, 14 Mich.

3245. A dedication cannot be made out without an intent to dedicate, clearly manifested. *Ibid.*

3246. It is essential to a dedication that it be accepted by the public. In the case of city streets, the acceptance should be manifested by some act of the authorities, either formally confirming the dedication, and ordering their opening, or exercising authority over them in some of the ordinary modes of improvement or regulation. *People v. Jones*, 6 Mich., 176; *Tillman v. People*, 12 Mich., 401; *People v. Beaubien*, 2 Doug., 256. An indictment against the proprietor for obstructing a street is not of itself a sufficient acceptance. 2 *Doug.*, 256,

3247. Governor and Judges' plan of Detroit. The adoption by the Governor and Judges of the plan of the city of Detroit, in 1807, did not, of itself, make public highway of that portion of the projected streets which was covered by private claims, and occupied as private property. *People v. Jones*, 6 Mich., 176.

3248. That portion of Shelby street, between Jefferson avenue and Woodbridge street, as projected on the plan, being, at the time of its adoption, claimed and occupied as private property, and so continuing to be claimed and occupied thereafter, and the corporate authorities of Detroit having, many years after the adoption of the plan, under their authority to lay out streets through private property, caused a street to be laid out along it, but of less width than the street as originally projected, paying the occupants of the land for the strip so taken; it was held that this was a waiver of any right of the authorities, if they had any under the plan, to that portion of the projected street outside of the lines of the street so opened. *People v. Jones*, 6 Mich., 176. See also, *Tillman v. People*, 12 Mich., 401.

3249. Imperfect town plat. Where a proprietor caused a plat to be recorded, of land which he had had surveyed into lots, blocks and streets, but the plat was not acknowledged, this was held no dedication, under Code of 1833, p. 531, of the streets to the public. *People v. Beaubien*, 2 Doug., 256.

3250. Conveyances by deeds duly acknowledged and recorded, of lots laid down on the plan; the deeds describing the lots according to the plat, and refering to it as of record, will not supply the want of acknowledgment of the plat. *Ibid.*

3251. But the making and recording of the plat, and the conveyances, are acts *in pais*, tending to establish a dedication, though subject to explanation. *Ibid.*

3252. Where a public way was claimed as dedicated by certain plats, and also by acts *in pais*, and it appeared that the owners of the premises had always occupied the *locus* as private property, and excluded the public therefrom, it was held that the right of way must depend upon the plats alone, and could not be claimed unless the plats showed an intention to give it. *Cook v. Village of Hillsdale*, 7 Mich., 115.

3253. Constitutional protection. The constitutional provision respecting the taking of private property for public purposes, has no application to the case of a dedication of a highway by the owner, or where, from his long acquiescence in the public use of it, a dedication is presumed by law. *Bumpus v. Miller*, 4 Mich., 159.

3254. Roads by user. The Statute—R. S. of 1846, Ch. 25, § 29—providing, among other things, that all roads not recorded, which have been used as public highways twenty years or more, shall be deemed public highways, applies not only to cases where the twenty years had elapsed at the taking effect of the law, but also to cases where a portion of that time had elapsed, and it was completed afterwards. *Ibid.*

3255. A variation of two or three rods in the travelled track at one end of a highway, made such by twenty years user—the variation having existed only twelve years—will not take away the right of the public to use the road. *Ibid.*

3256. The statute providing that public highways shall be four rods wide, a dedication, when not expressly or impliedly restricted by the owner, will not be confined to the beaten track, but will include four rods in width. *Ibid.*

3257. Cul de sac; obstruction; indictment. To make the obstruction of a way an indictable offense, it must injuriously affect some right in which the public, in their aggregate capacity, have a common interest, as distinguished from a mere individual or private right. If it affect only the rights of an individual, or of a definite number of persons, less than the whole, in their individual capacity, no indictment lies. *People v. Jackson*, 7 Mich., 432. See *Tillman v. People*, 12 Mich., 401.

3258. To constitute a highway, the way must be one over which all the people of the State have a common and an equal right to travel; or, at least, a general interest to keep unobstructed. *People v. Jackson*, 7 Mich., 432.

3259. When the obstruction of a way can prejudice only the rights of owners or occupants of adjoining lots, they have their remedy by private action ; if it affect only the rights of the inhabitants of a city, or the rights of a city in its corporate capacity, it may be a proper subject for the local police of the city, to be regulated by ordinances and by laws; but in neither case would it be the proper subject of an indictment. *Ibid.*

3260. A cul de sac, fifty feet in length, in the interior of a city block, opening into other alleys which extend to public streets, but having itself no communication with streets except through those alleys; not being capable of forming a passage way from one street to another, but furnishing access only to the rear of lots in the block; and never opened, worked or used as a highway, and not shown to have dwellings upon or adjoining it, to which it gives access, is not a way for the obstruction of which an indictment will lie. *Ibid.*

3261. The parties interested in the adjacent lots would have a right to close such a *cul de sac*, or to regulate its use as to them should seem proper, so far, at least, as respects its use as a way for passage or travel, where it appears that there has never been any act of the public authorities accepting it, and the owners have been allowed to keep a large portion of it closed, and to erect valuable buildings upon it. *Tillman v. People*, 12 Mich., 401.

3262. It makes no difference in this respect, that buildings erected along it, but since removed, were for a time used as dwellings. Any right of way dependent upon such use would cease when the buildings were removed. *Ibid.*

3263. Regulation by city by-laws. Until an alley in the city of Detroit has been actually open to the uses for which it was designed, the occupation or obstruction of it cannot properly be punished under city by-laws. In giving the power to regulate the use of alleys, and remove obstructions from them, the city charter contemplates the preservation of actual, and not theoretical easements, and the protection of the community against actual nuisances, which interfere with the accustomed use of the passages. *Jackson v. People*, 9 Mich., 111.

3264. Laying out highway. Under the Statutes of 1846, it was requisite to the valid laying out of a highway, that application should be made therefor in writing by ten or more freeholders, and notice of the application given to the persons interested in the lands ; and that a survey of the road should be made and incorporated in an order to be made by the commissioners, and filed in the office of the township clerk. And where none of these facts were shown, and the road had never been opened or used, or regarded by the commissioners as a highway, a mandamus to the township board, to show cause why they should not pay the damages to a party though whose land a road was claimed to have been laid, was refused. *People v. Township Board of Scio*, 3 Mich., 121.

3265. Under said statutes, a township board had no power to review the proceedings of the commissioners in laying out and establishing a road, except on appeal; nor to review the proceedings of the appraisers, except to see that they were not void for want of jurisdiction. *People v. Township Board of La Grange*, 2 Mich., 187.

3266. Section two of Ch. 25 of said Statutes, made it the duty of the township clerk, on receiving an order from the commissioners of highways laying out a road, forthwith to post a copy of such order on the outer door of the house or building where the township meeting was usually held, or, if there was no such house or building, then in one of the most public places in the township. Where it appeared that a copy of the order was posted up on an inside door of a tavern, which was one of the two places in the township at which the township meeting was held alternately, it was held, *first*, that there was no house, or building, within the contemplation of the statute, where the township meeting was usually held; *second*, that the Court would presume, in the absence of any showing to the contrary, that the tavern where the notice was posted was one of the most public places in the township. *Ibid.*

3267. Commissioners must lay out whole road. Where application is made for laying out a highway, under the statute of 1861, the commissioners must lay out the whole road applied for, or no part of it. *People v. Township Board of Springwells*, 12 Mich., 434.

3268. Who may complain of their action. Where a road is regularly applied for, and the commissioners decide to lay out a part of it only, any person through whose lands the road runs as laid, is entitled to take proceedings to test the validity of their action. *Ibid.*

3269. New application. Under the statute of 1861, p. 256, the commissioners of highways have no power to entertain a second application for laying out the same road within one year from the first. *People v. Township Board of Springwells*, 13 Mich., 462.

3270. Compensation for land taken. A township is not liable for interest on damages appraised for laying out a highway. *People v. Township Board of La Grange*, 2 Mich., 187.

3271. A jury was summoned in 1859, on the warrant of a justice, to determine the necessity of taking the relator's lands for a highway, and to assess his damages. The jury found the taking necessary, and assessed the damages; and their finding was filed in the town clerk's office, but not certified by the justice as required by law. The amount of the damages was levied and collected by tax, and the road opened. It was held that the town could not resist the payment of the damages to the relator, on the ground that the justice had failed to certify the finding. *People v. Township Board of Lowell*, 9 Mich., 144.

3272. There was no law in Michigan in 1857 under which a highway could be legally laid out through condemnation of the land to be taken therefor. And therefore township authorities cannot refuse to make payment for lands taken for a highway in 1859, on the ground that a road was laid out over the same line in 1857. *Ibid.* See *People v. Kimball*, 4 Mich., 95.

3273. Where a highway was laid out through the lands of an individual in 1860, and his damages were appraised, and an order on the township treasurer tendered for the amount, which order was payable "to the owner or occupant, or to the person entitled thereto, for the land so taken," it was held that the order was insufficient, and its tender did not authorize the highway commissioners to take possession of the land. It should have designated the payee, so as to show on its face the person to whom it was payable. *Lull v. Curry*, 10 Mich., 397.

3274. Legislative control. The Legislature may authorize a plank road company to take possession of a highway for the purposes of their road. *Detroit and Howell Plank Road Co. v. Fisher*, 4 Mich., 37.

3275. Highway funds. The highway commissioners of a township drew orders upon the township treasurer, payable out of any moneys in the treasury belonging to one of the road districts. These orders were not paid, and a mandamus was applied for to compel the township board to levy a tax on the township for their payment. But there being nothing in the case to show that the township had had the benefit of the district fund, by misappropriation or otherwise, the mandamus was denied. *People v. Township Board of Zilwaukie*, 10 Mich., 274.

WILL.

3276. What essential to validity. A will is not valid unless the testator not only intends, of his own free will, to make such disposition, but is capable of knowing what he is doing, of understanding to whom he gives his property, and in what proportions, and whom he is depriving of it as heirs, or as devisees under the will he revokes. *Beaubien v. Cicotte*, 12 Mich., 459.

3277. Form. It is not necessary that any particular form of words should be used to make a will. An instrument in the form of a letter probated in this case. *Rue High, appellant*, 2 Doug., 515.

3278. By what law governed. A will of personal property, regularly made according to the forms and solemnities required by the law of the testator's domicil, is sufficient to pass such property in every other country in which the same is situate. *Ibid.*

3279. Under Statutes of 1838. R. S. of 1838, p. 270, § 4, was merely declaratory of the right which every person had, at the common law, to dispose of his personal property by will. *Ibid.*

3280. Section five, same page, as to the mode of execution, as amended by S. L., 1839, p. 220, § 14, which required wills to be attested by three or more witnesses, applied only to wills executed within the State. As to wills executed abroad by persons domiciled here, the common law prevailed. *Ibid.*

3281. By the common law, it was not essential to the validity of a will that it should be attested by witnesses. Accordingly, it was held, that a will of personal property, executed abroad, by a person who died there, but whose domicil was, at the time, in Michigan, was valid though not attested by three witnesses. *Ibid.*

3282. Construction. The general words in a will may be restrained in their meaning, or rejected entirely, to carry out the intention of the testator. So general words may be construed by the particular words which follow. *Jameson et. al., appellants*, 1 Mich., 99.

3283. A will, after devising the real estate of the testator, contained the following clause: "It is my will that all my furniture and property be in common to my beloved wife, Elizabeth, and daughter Jane, so long as they live and keep house together, and that whenever they separate or break up house keeping, that the furniture be divided between them, at their own discretion, and the stock of cattle to be given up to my beloved wife Elizabeth, for her sole use and behoof." *Held*, that a claim which the testator had against the Chippewa Indians, and which was allowed and paid over to the executor under a treaty concluded after the testator's death, did not pass under the will to the widow and daughter. *Ibid.*

3284. Rule in Shelly's case. A will contained the following clause: I give and bequeath to my beloved son, G. C., the farm I now reside on, for and during his life time, with all the appurtenances thereon; and after his decease, then the right, title and appurtenances of the aforesaid farm is to become the property of the said G. C.'s male heirs. Held, that G. C. took an estate tail, which, by statute—Code of 1827, p. 261; see Comp. L., § 2587—was changed into a fee simple. *Fraser v. Chene*, 2 Mich., 81. The rule in Shelly's case is now abolished in this State by statute. *Comp. L.*, § 2612.

3285. Restraints upon alienation. Provisions in restraint of alienation are not to be favored. *Walton v. Torrey*, Har. Ch., 259.

3286. The provision in a will that the estate shall remain undivided until the youngest of the devisees becomes of the age of twenty one years, is not such a limitation as will inhibit any one of the devisees from conveying his interest in the premises. *Ibid.*

3287. Where a will provided that each disposal of real estate made by it should only be for the use and benefit of the persons in whose favor it was made, his or her life lasting; that no parcel of the real estate should be sold or alienated in any manner, but after the decease of those several to whom shares or parcels of the estate were assigned, said shares should remain for the use and benefit of the descendants of him or her to whom a share had been assigned, their lives lasting, and so on; and in case of demise without posterity, the said share should accrue to the use and benefit of the owners being of the testator's relations or descendants, their lives lasting, of the next share or shares, and so on, as long as any posterity should exist, and in case of extinction, to the next heirs;—it was held that the will, inasmuch as it sought to create an indefinite succession of life estates, and to render the property inalienable, was void as being against the policy of the law. *St. Armour v. Rivard*, 2 Mich., 294.

3288. Such devise cannot be sustained as an executory devise. An executory devise directing limitations beyond the period allowed by law, is void for the whole, and not merely for the excess beyond the legal period. *Ibid.*

3289. Cy pres. The *cy pres* doctrine cannot be applied in support of a will of this description, there being no general intention of the testator, not conflicting with the law, which the Court could sustain by sacrificing the testator's particular intention. *Ibid.*

3290. Section 5, title 1, part 2, R. S. 1838, provided that "When lands are given by deed or will to any person for life, and after his death to his heirs in fee, or by words to that effect, the conveyance shall be construed to vest an estate for life only in such first taker, and a remainder in fee simple in his heirs." See *Comp. L.*, § 2612. It is not competent under this section so to construe the above devise (*supra* 3287) as to give a life estate to the first takers, remainder over in fee to the second takers. *Ibid.*

3291. Power in trust. A testator by his will directed his executors or administrators to sell his real estate to the best advantage, and invest the proceeds. Held that this was a general power in trust, and that the executors or administrators were authorized to sell and convey such real estate without a license from the Probate Court. *Battelle v. Parks*, 2 Mich., 531.

3292. Probate. The averments on the part of the propounder of a will should include everything necessary to constitute it a valid will under the statute, so that a verdict finding the truth of those averments, without more, would bring the will within all the express requirements of the statute. He must therefore aver the soundness of mind of the testator at the time the will was executed. *Beaubien v. Cicotte*, 8 Mich., 9.

3293. Who may contest. Where the will of a father appoints a testamentary guardian for his minor child, (whose mother is deceased) the grandfather, or other next of kin, is entitled to appear and contest its validity, and to appeal from an order admitting it to probate. *Taff v. Hosmer*, 14 Mich.

3294. Practice in probate cases. Where the validity of a will is contested, the proponents open and close the case, both with the evidence and on the argument. And where the issue is as to the competency of the decedent, they are not required to do more at the outset than to make a prima facie showing on that point, and the case will be fully open to affirmative proofs on their part after the contestants have put in their evidence. *Taff v. Hosmer*, 14 Mich., (second case).

3295. Evidence on probate. The burden of proof is on the propounder of a will to show the soundness of mind of the testator at the time of its execution. But upon questions of evidence, growing out of any presumption of sanity affecting the burden of proof, the Court express no opinion. *Beaubien v. Cicotte*, 8 Mich., 9.

3296. Where a subscribing witness to a will was called to prove it upwards of thirty years after its date, and testified that he signed it as a witness, but that he had no distinct recollection of seeing the testatrix sign it; *Held*, that questions to him whether, looking at the attestation clause, he had any doubt she signed it in his presence, and whether he ever witnessed an instrument in that form without knowing what it was, and whether he had any doubt that the persons whose names were to it were present at the time of its execution, were not incompetent, and it was for the jury to give such weight to his evidence in answer thereto as they might think it entitled to under all the circumstances of the case. *Lawyer v. Smith*, 8 Mich., 411.

3297. After the death of a testatrix, a will twenty-five years old was discovered in a barrel, among waste papers, and either worn or torn into several pieces, which were scattered loose among the papers in the barrel. Whether the injury to the instrument was done by the testatrix, or by some other person, and if by her, whether accidentally, or intentionally and for the purpose of revoking the will, are questions of fact for the jury; and to aid them in determining these questions, and not as separate and independent evidence of a revocation, the declarations of the testatrix, made after the date of the will, that she had destroyed it, are competent evidence. *Ibid.*

3298. Bequests to religious societies. The last clause of § 25 of the Act concerning Churches and Religious Societies—Comp. L., § 2033—which makes void certain bequests to the amount of $100 or more, made to religious societies by last will, unless the will is proved in open Court by three subscribing witnesses, does not apply to wills executed before the act took effect; and consequently bequests to religious societies to the amount of $100 or more, made by a last will executed before that time, having two subscribing witnesses only, may be valid, notwithstanding the death of the testator occurred after the act took effect. *American Baptist Missionary Union v. Peck*, 10 Mich., 341.

3299. The sections in said act relating to gifts, bequests, &c., to religious societies, refer to such societies and organizations as exercise their functions in this State, and are therefore within legislative control so far as their temporal affairs are concerned; and do not embrace foreign corporations or associations. *Matter of the Ticknor Estate*, 13 Mich., 44.

3300. The receipt of money under the will, or the institution of legal proceedings to recover it, are not the exercise of such corporate franchises as are forbidden by said act to any but domestic corporations. *Ibid.*

3301. Bequest to unincorporated association. A bequest of money generally, and not upon permanent uses, to an unincorporated association capable of clear identity, is valid. *Ibid.*

WITNESS.

3302. A verdict of guilty on a charge of perjury, did not, at the common law, without judgment, render the defendant infamous, so as preclude his being a competent witness. *Smith v. Brown*, 2 Mich., 161.

3303. Defendant, after filing a sworn answer in chancery, was indicted and tried for perjury contained in it, and verdict of guilty rendered. He then moved an arrest of judgment and for a new trial; but before these motions were disposed of, died. It was held that the verdict could not be used for the purpose of discrediting his answer in the chancery suit. *Ibid.*

3304. That where one is on trial for continuing an alleged nuisance, witnesses for the prosecution may be questioned as to their interest in procuring a conviction, with a view to its effect upon their evidence, see *Crippen v. People*, 8 Mich., 117.

MAXIMS OF THE LAW.

Following are a few familiar legal maxims, with a reference to decisions illustrative of them, reported in the Michigan Reports.

3305. Res inter alios. A transaction between two parties ought not to operate to the disadvantage of a third.

Stockton v. Williams, 1 Doug., 546.
Campau v. Dewey, 9 Mich., 381.
(Adjudications to which the claimant was not a party.)
Dawson v. Hall, 2 Mich., 390.
Glover v. Alcott, 11 Mich., 470.
Benedict v. Denton, Wal. Ch., 336.
Horner v. Fellows, 1 Doug., 51.
Converse v. Blumrick, 14 Mich.
Lockwood v. Beckwith, 6 Mich., 168.
(Admissions or declarations by third parties.)
Russell v. Waite, Wal. Ch., 31.
Dutton v. Ives, 5 Mich., 515.
Nichols v. Lee, 10 Mich., 526.
Millerd v. Reeves, 1 Mich., 107.
Converse v. Blumrick, 14 Mich.
(Assignment by one party not to affect rights of another.)

3306. Argumentum ab inconvenienti. An argument drawn from inconvenience is forcible in law.

Emerson v. Atwater, 7 Mich., 12.
Clark v. Mowyer, 5 Mich., 462.

3307. Conclusiveness of adjudication. No man ought to be twice vexed for one and the same cause.

Delavan v. Bates, 1 Mich., 97.
Prentiss v. Holbrook, 2 Mich., 372.
Van Kleek v. Eggleston, 7 Mich., 511.
McGraw v. Pettibone, 10 Mich., 530.
Tucker v. Rohrback, 13 Mich., 73.

3308. Jurisdiction. Consent cannot confer jurisdiction.

Beach v. Botsford, 1 Doug., 199.
Clark v. Holmes, 1 Doug., 390.
Spear v. Carter, 1 Mich., 19.
Wilson v. Davis, 1 Mich., 156.
Shadbolt v. Bronson, 1 Mich., 85.
Farrand v. Bentley, 6 Mich., 281.
Bennett v. Nichols, 12 Mich., 22.
People v. Smith, 9 Mich., 193.

3309. Omnia rite acta. All acts are presumed to have been rightly and regularly done.

Comstock v. Hollon, 2 Mich., 355.
Burnham v. People, 3 Mich., 195.

Rash v. Whitney, 4 Mich., 495.
Sweetzer v. Mead, 5 Mich., 33 and 107.
Achey v. Hull, 7 Mich., 423.
Maynard v. Penniman, 10 Mich., 153.
Kermott v. Ayer, 11 Mich., 181.
Morrissey v. People, 11 Mich., 327.
Dann v. Cudney, 13 Mich., 329.
Farmers and Mechanics' Bank v. Troy City Bank, 1 Doug., 457.
Gaines v. Betts, 2 Doug., 98.
Snow v. Perkins, 2 Mich., 238.
(Correctness of judicial proceedings.)
Newberry v. Trowbridge, 13 Mich., 263.
(Res judicata.)
Savier v. Chipman, 1 Mich. 116.
(Obedience to law.)
Buck v. Sherman, 2 Doug., 176.
Orr v. Lacey, 2 Doug., 230.
Hollister v. Loud, 2 Mich., 309.
Baldwin v. Buckland, 11 Mich., 389.
Booth v. McNair, 14 Mich.
Nye v. Van Husan, 6 Mich., 329.
Leavitt v. Leavitt, 13 Mich., 452.
(Honesty rather than fraud.)
Benedict v. Denton, Wal. Ch., 336.
(Seal of corporation presumed properly affixed.)
Lacey v. Davis, 4 Mich., 140.
(Quorum of supervisors presumed present.)

3310. Equity. He who seeks equity must do equity.
Michigan State Bank v. Hammond, 1 Doug., 527.
Morris v. Hoyt, 11 Mich., 9.

3311. Consensus tollit errorem. The acquiescence of a party who might take advantage of an error obviates its effect.
Falkner v. Beers, 2 Doug., 117.
Stewart v. Hill, 1 Mich., 265.
Crane v. Hardy, 1 Mich., 56.
Vanderhoof v. Dean, 1 Mich., 463.
Webb v. Mann, 3 Mich., 139.
Shaw v. Moser, 3 Mich., 71.
Wells v. Scott, 4 Mich., 347.
McBride v. Cicotte, 4 Mich., 478.
Durfee v. McClurg, 5 Mich., 532.
Tower v. Lamb, 6 Mich., 362.

Johnstone v. Scott, 11 Mich., 232.
Brown v. Bissell, 1 Doug., 273.
Owners of Ship Milwaukee v. Hale, 1 Doug., 306.
Higley v. Lant, 3 Mich., 612.
Higgins v. Carpenter, Har. Ch., 256.
Brooks v. Mead, Wal. Ch., 389.
(Waiver in judicial proceedings.)
Newberry v. Trowbridge, 13 Mich., 263.
(Payment by indorser after defective notice.)
People v. Oakland County Bank, 1 Doug., 282.
(Waiver of forfeiture of corporate rights.)

3312. Dwelling house. Every man's house is his castle.
Pond v. People, 8 Mich., 150.
People v. Horton, 4 Mich., 67.

3313. Nemo est hæres viventis. No one can be heir during the life of his ancestor.
Ready v. Kearsley, 14 Mich.
(Deed to one named, "or his heirs," held good.)

3314. Actions based on illegal transactions. A right of action cannot arise from the party's own wrong.
Adams v. Hamel, 2 Doug., 73.
Byrne v. Beeson, 1 Doug., 179.
Bank of Michigan v. Niles, 1 Mich., 401, and Wal. Ch., 99.
Orr v. Lacey, 2 Doug., 230.
Wells v. River Raisin and Grand River R. R. Co., Wal. Ch., 35.
(Illegal contracts.)
Bagg v. Jerome, 7 Mich., 145.
(Illegal contract performed.)

3315. Nudum pactum. No action arises from a bare promise.
Hall v. Soule, 11 Mich., 494.
Rood v. Jones, 1 Doug., 188.
Austin v. Grant, 1 Mich., 490.
Bishop v. Felch, 7 Mich., 371.
Colman v. Post, 10 Mich., 422
Davis v. Rider, 5 Mich., 423.

3316. Agency. The act which one does through another he is considered as doing himself.
Peoria Marine and Fire Insurance Co. v. Hall, 12 Mich., 202.
Niagara Fire Insurance Co. v. De Graff, 12 Mich., 124.

3317. Respondeat superior. Let the principal be held responsible.

De Forest v. Wright, 2 Mich., 368.
Moore v. Sanborne, 2 Mich., 519.
City of Detroit v. Corey, 9 Mich., 165.
Michigan Central R. R. Co. v. Leahey, 10 Mich., 199.

3318. Ratification. A subsequent ratification is equivalent to a prior command.

Newsom v. Hart, 14 Mich.
Peninsular Bank v. Hanmer, 14 Mich.
Scott v. Detroit Young Men's Society's Lessee, 1 Doug., 119.

3319. Land ownership. He who possesses the soil, possesses also that which is above it.

Lorman v. Benson, 8 Mich., 18.
Rice v. Ruddiman, 10 Mich., 125.

3320. Fictions of law. A legal fiction is always consistent with equity.

Whipple v. Farrar, 3 Mich., 436.
(Sheriff's deed relating back to sale).
Newsam v. Hart, 14 Mich.
(Ratification cannot avail when judgment of the principal was required).
Bacon v. Kimmel, 14 Mich.
(Title by judicial proceedings cannot relate back so as to make innocent acts trespasses.)
Quirk v. Thomas, 6 Mich., 76.
(Whether mistake in fraudulent deed can be corrected on behalf of purchasers.)

3321. Idem sonans. The name is the same where the pronunciation is the same.

People v. Mayworm, 5 Mich., 146.
People v. Tisdale, 1 Doug., 59.

3322. Construction of instruments. The words of an instrument shall be taken most strongly against the party employing them.

Cicotte v. Gagnier, 2 Mich., 381.

3323. Latent ambiguity, being raised by extrinsic evidence, may be removed in like manner.

Ives v. Kimball, 1 Mich., 308.

3324. In the absence of ambiguity, no exposition shall be made which is opposed to the express words of the instrument.

Sutherland v. Crane, Wal. Ch., 523.
Jones v. Phelps, 5 Mich., 218.
Adair v. Adair, 5 Mich., 204.

Harvey v. Cady, 3 Mich., 439.

Holmes v. Hall, 8 Mich., 66.

Erwin v. Clark, 13 Mich., 10.

Schwarz v. Wendell, Wal. Ch., 267.

Barstow v. Smith, Wal. Ch., 394.

Bidwell v. Whittaker, 1 Mich., 469.

3325. That is certain which is capable of being made certain.

Daily v. Litchfield, 10 Mich., 29.

3326. Surplusage does not vitiate that which in other respects is good and valid.

Anderson v. Baughman, 7 Mich., 69.

Regents of University v. Detroit Young Men's Society, 12 Mich., 138.

Sweetzer v. Mead, 5 Mich., 107.

3327. Mere false description does not make an instrument inoperative.

Johnstone v. Scott, 11 Mich., 232.

Anderson v. Baughman, 7 Mich., 69.

Cooper v. Bigley, 13 Mich., 463.

3328. The best and surest way of expounding an instrument, is by referring to the time when, and the circumstances under which it was made.

Paddack v. Pardee, 1 Mich., 421.

Norris v. Showerman, Wal. Ch., 206, and 2 Doug., 16.

Ives v. Kimball, 1 Mich., 308.

Facey v. Otis, 11 Mich., 213.

Bronson v. Green, Wal. Ch., 56.

Norris v. Hill, Wal. Ch., 302.

3329. Mortgages. Once a mortgage always a mortgage.

Batty v. Snook, 5 Mich., 231.

Thompson v. Mack, Har. Ch., 150.

Comstock v. Howard, Wal. Ch., 110.

Thurston v. Prentiss, 1 Mich., 193.

3330. Vigilance. The laws assist those who are vigilant, not those who sleep over their rights.

Whipple v. Farrar, 3 Mich., 436.

Graydon v. Church, 7 Mich., 36.

(Account of profits refused to one who had been remiss in perfecting or asserting his right.)

Benedict v. Thompson, Wal. Ch., 446.

(Re-hearing refused where right to appeal lost by delay.)

Wright v. King., Har. Ch., 12.

Roberts v. Miles, 12 Mich., 267.
Wixom v. Davis, Wal. Ch., 15.
(Relief refused after judgment.)
Carne v. Hall, 7 Mich., 159.
Lathrop v. Hicks, 2 Doug., 223.
Matter of Lantis, 9 Mich., 324.
Johnson v. Johnson, Wal. Ch., 309.
Thayer v. Swift, Wal. Ch., 384.
Spafford v. Beach, 2 Doug., 150.
People v. Judges of Calhoun Circuit Court, 1 Doug., 417.
(Relief refused on ground of laches.)

3331. Innocence. Every man is presumed innocent until proved guilty.
Maher v. People, 10 Mich., 212.
People v. Getchell, 6 Mich., 496.
Durant v. People, 13 Mich., 351.

3332. Evidence. No man is to be compelled to criminate himself.
People v. Thomas, 9 Mich., 314.
Carne v. Litchfield, 2 Mich., 340.

3333. The best evidence of which the nature of the case admits must be produced.
Jones v. Phelps, 5 Mich., 218.
(Suit brought before subscribing witness.)
Higgins v. Watson, 1 Mich., 428.
Rash v. Whitney, 4 Mich., 495.
(As to sufficiency of search for lost papers.)
People v. Dennis, 4 Mich., 609.
Lacey v. Davis, 4 Mich., 140.
Norvell v. McHenry, 1 Mich., 227.
Van Kleek v. Eggleston, 7 Mich., 511.
(Proof of lost papers or records.)
Jackson v. Evans, 8 Mich., 476.
(Party's own books as evidence.)
Schwarz v. Wendell, Wal. Ch., 267.
Hunt v. Thorn, 2 Mich., 213.
(Admissions not to vary written instruments.)
Stockton v. Williams, 1 Doug., 546.
Campau v. Dewey, 9 Mich., 381.
(Hearsay and reputation on questions of identity.)
Scott v. Detroit Young Men's Society's Lessee, 1 Doug., 119.
Ready v. Kearsley, 14 Mich.

Thompson v. Richards, 14 Mich.

(Proof of conveyance by parol evidence.)

Moore v. People, 2 Doug., 420.

Platt v. Stewart, 10 Mich., 260.

Angell v. Rosenbury, 12 Mich., 241.

(Records must be proved as a whole.)

Kermott v. Ayer, 11 Mich., 181.

People v. Lambert, 5 Mich., 346.

(Proof of foreign statutes must be by copies.)

3334. Judicial immunity. A wrongful intent is not to be presumed in one who acts under judicial authority.

Ward v. Cozzens, 3 Mich., 252.

Ortman v. Greenman, 4 Mich., 291.

People v. Rix, 6 Mich., 144.

3335. Audi alteram partem. No man should be condemned unheard.

Buck v. Sherman, 2 Doug. 176.

Ames v. Port Huron Log Driving and Booming Co., 11 Mich., 139.

Palmer v. Oakley, 2 Doug., 433.

Montgomery v. Henry, 10 Mich., 19.

Freeman v. Freeman, 1 Mich., 480.

Outwite v. Porter, 13 Mich., 533.

3336. Judge interested. No man can be Judge in his own cause.

Ames v. Port Huron Log Driving and Booming Co., 11 Mich., 139.

Walton v. Torrey, Har. Ch., 259.

3337. De minimis, &c. The law does not concern itself about trifles.

Hickey v. Baird, 9 Mich., 32.

(Erroneous judgment affirmed where only nominal damages involved.)

A TABLE

OF THE

REPORTED CASES

CONTAINED IN THIS DIGEST.

The following table contains all the cases reported in the several volumes of Michigan decisions hitherto issued, together with some of the most important now decided and to be reported in 14th Michigan Reports.

Under the proper title of each case will be found a reference to the sections of this work where the points decided therein are stated, with the title of the subdivision in which the section occurs.

Each case is given twice; *first*, by the proper title, and *second*, with the parties reversed; but it has not been deemed important to repeat the references. There will also be found under each case which has been subsequently cited in the Reports, a reference to the book and page when the citation occurs. If the case has subsequently been overruled or modified, that fact is also stated.

Beach v. Botsford, 1 Doug., 199.
Jurisdiction, 2136; Justices' Courts, 2160, 2174; Officer, 2433, 2434.
Cited, 1 Mich., 22, 160, 491, 13 Mich., 509.
Beach v. People, 11 Mich., 106.
Criminal Law, 881, 882.
Beach, Spafford v.
Beach v. White, Wal. Ch., 495.
Equity, 1190, 1191, 1194, 1200, 1259; Fraud, &c., 1880; Husband and Wife, 2027, 2028.
Cited, 6 Mich., 466.
Beard v. Port Huron Log Driving and Booming Co., 11 Mich., 155.
Note to Ames v. Same Def't.
Beard v. Spalding, 12 Mich., 309.
Practice in Circuit Courts, 2697.
Beardslee v. Horton, 3 Mich., 560.
Action, 54, 57; Bills and Notes, 376; Interest, 2073; Payment, 2501.
Cited, 8 Mich., 449; 13 Mich., 112.
Beaubien v. Cicotte, 8 Mich., 9.
Evidence, 1838; Wills, 3292, 3295.
Cited, 8 Mich., 318.
Beaubien v. Cicotte, 12 Mich., 459.
Error, 1542; Evidence, 1635, 1676, 1684, 1690, 1691, 1697, 1728, 1730 to 1734, 1741 to 1745; Wills, 3276.
Beaubien, People v.
Beaubien v. Poupard, Har. Ch., 206.
Estates of Deceased Persons, 1601, 1603.
Cited, 2 Mich., 333; 11 Mich., 226.
Beckwith, Lockwood v.
Beecher v. Baldy, 7 Mich., 488.
Homestead, 1988 to 1992, 1999.
Cited, 8 Mich., 55; 9 Mich., 528; 10 Mich., 297, 540.
Beebee v. Young, 13 Mich., 221.
Appeal from Chancery, 129, 136.
Beers, Falkner v.
Beeson, Byrne v.
Beeson v. Hollister, 11 Mich., 193.
Practice in Circuit Courts, 2703, 2733.
Belden v. Laing, 8 Mich., 500.
Pleadings, 2566, 2567; Replevin, 2947, 2949.
Benedict v. Denton, Wal. Ch., 336.
Corporations, 724; Evidence, 1718.
Benedict v. Thompson, Wal. Ch., 446.
Equity, 1514.
Benedict v. Thompson, 2 Doug., 299.
Appeal from Chancery, 105, 106, 141, 143.
Benhard v. Darrow, Wal. Ch., 519.
Equity, 1526.
Bennett, Heald v.
Bennett, Jewett v.
Bennett v. Nichols, 12 Mich., 22.
Appeal from Chancery, 119, 142; Equity, 1108, 1109, 1113, 1230.
Cited, 13 Mich., 31.
Bennette, McMurtrie v.
Benson, Lorman v.
Bentley, Farrand v.
Bergh v. Poupard, Wal. Ch., 5.
Equity, 1369.

Freeman v. Michigan State Bank, Har. Ch., 311.
Equity, 1401, 1402.
Freeman v. Michigan State Bank, Wal. Ch., 62.
Sheriff, 2978.
Cited, Wal. Ch., 325.
French v. Highway Commissioners of Springwells, 12 Mich., 267.
Certiorari, 522.
Frost, Welch v.
Fry, Coon v.
Fuller v. Bowker, 11 Mich., 204.
Action, 36; Constitutional Law, 662; Damages, 988, 989; Replevin, 2956.
Fuller v. Parish, 3 Mich., 211.
Evidence, 1766; Mortgage of Chattels, 2301; Tender, 3148.
Cited, 3 Mich., 205; 7 Mich., 23, 25; 9 Mich., 44; 10 Mich., 268.
Fuller, Tillman v.
Gagnier, Cicotte v.
Gaines v. Betts, 2 Doug., 98.
Certiorari, 535, 537; Justices' Courts, 2150.
Cited, 2 Mich., 241; 7 Mich., 317; 10 Mich., 12, 15.
Gale, Caldwell v.
Gallagher, People v.
Galloway v. Holmes, 1 Doug., 330.
Action, 37, 38; Conflict of Laws, 573; Contracts, 688, 690; Fraud, &c., 1862; Payment, 2494.
Cited, 2 Mich., 420; 3 Mich., 535; 4 Mich., 512.
Galpin v. Abbott, 6 Mich., 17.
Deed, 1018, 1019; Recording Laws, 2912.
Cited, 10 Mich., 23.
Gamber v. Holben, 5 Mich., 331.
Equity, 1253.
Gard v. Stevens, 12 Mich., 9.
Practice in Circuit Courts, 2736.
Gard v. Stevens, 12 Mich., 292.
Guaranty, 1946, 1947; Payment, 2504; Practice in Circuit Courts, 2741.
Gardner, Brown v.
Gardner v. Gorham, 1 Doug., 507.
Payment, 2489, 2490; Pleadings, 2536.
Cited, 7 Mich., 365.
Gardner v. Smith, 7 Mich., 410.
Railroad Corporations, 2896 to 2898.
Cited, 9 Mich., 192.
Garlinghouse v. Dixon, Wal. Ch., 440.
Equity, 1158.
Garlock, People v.
Garratt v. Litchfield, 10 Mich., 451.
Appeal from Chancery, 135, 137.
Cited, 13 Mich., 221.
Garratt, Litchfield v.
Garrison, Bates v.
Gates v. Shutts, 7 Mich., 127.
Compromise of Claims, 554, 555.
Gay v. Bidwell, 7 Mich., 519.
Fraud, &c., 1882, 1884, 1886, 1887; Mortgage of Chattels, 2306.
Gay, People v.
Gay, Scribner v.
Geddes, People v.
George, Herschfeldt v.
Getchell, People v.

31

www.ingramcontent.com/pod-product-compliance
Lightning Source LLC
LaVergne TN
LVHW021303110826
845150LV00003B/469